RESEARCH READINGS

IN

CHILD PSYCHOLOGY

RESEARCH
READINGS
IN
CHILD
PSYCHOLOGY

Edited by David S. Palermo
UNIVERSITY OF MINNESOTA
and Lewis P. Lipsitt
BROWN UNIVERSITY

HOLT, RINEHART AND WINSTON, INC.
NEW YORK · CHICAGO · SAN FRANCISCO·
TORONTO · LONDON

PREFACE

THIS COLLECTION of research readings is intended to (1) exemplify various research approaches to the study of child behavior, and (2) provide an orderly grouping of studies dealing with a variety of behavior phenomena (such as discrimination, generalization, transposition, and motivation) that have been studied extensively in children.

This is not a handbook of methods. It is nevertheless organized around methods for studying child behavior and around the historical and theoretical influences that have made these methods appear appropriate or desirable. Each methodological section is prefaced by the authors, attempting to place that section into its context. Generally, we have followed chronologically the historical development of methods for behavioral studies of children. It should be clear, however, that the methods exemplified toward the beginning of the book are not now outmoded, nor are those exemplified toward the end of the book entirely new. An attempt has been made to present within each section those readings which seem best to illustrate the approach under discussion from historical, theoretical, and methodological vantage points.

A word needs to be said about the subject matter of child psychology. Child psychology deals principally in statements of fact about child behavior, not in methods as such. Methods are tools that the scientist employs in adducing evidence for statements of fact. Methods are not the substance of the science. It is the intent of this collection of readings to make readily available certain facts or empirical statements about child behavior, and to highlight the *nature* of the evidence that seems to support these facts. As child psychologists we are primarily concerned, first, with the credibility of factual propositions about child behavior, and second, with the procedures used to examine the credibility of these propositions. We hope that the student will easily recognize that the kinds of hypotheses investigated by the scientific psychologist and the procedures he uses to investigate them are interdependent.

The following three objectives, then, have guided our organization of this book and the selection of readings: (1) to demonstrate that there are facts about child behavior that can be discovered through empirical investigation and demonstration; (2) to argue that empirical demonstration may take various forms, depending upon the kind of fact or relationship investigated; and (3) to show that the scientific value of any research endeavor is determined by the degree to which it accomplishes the substantiation or verification of the particular facts sought or found.

The authors wish to remark here that the programmatic contributions of two men to child psychology are underrepresented in this book, relative to their personal and historical contributions to the field. These men are Kurt Lewin and Robert R. Sears. Both of these researchers have provided historical landmarks in the progress of child psychology to its present state: Lewin by rebelling against the rather strictly age-oriented work in the developmental psychology of the 1930s, by introducing a crusade for experimental manipulative studies of child behavior, by seeking to determine other important antecedents for child behavior than age, and by introducing theoretical constructs and the deductive method of hypothesis-construction; Sears, by insisting on the learned character of much of child and adult behavior, by seeking the parental correlates (and, he hoped, causes) of children's personality attributes, and by pursuing a *rapprochement* of dynamic psychoanalytic theory with American learning theory. Our apparent neglect, however, is not real, for their respective contributions have helped make such a book of readings as this possible, and certainly the majority of studies from our fourth section onward came about as a partial result of their influences. We decided to forego the pleasure of their more extensive inclusion here for two major reasons: the limited amount of space within which to construct a book of readings with continuity, and the easy availability of Lewin's and Sears' work in other volumes, including books of readings. With respect to these points, it may be noted that the works of both Lewin and Sears are extensive and diversified, and most do not bear condensation or selection very well. It is our hope that students of child development and child psychology will avail themselves of their works, many of which are referred to throughout this book.

It may also be noted in reviewing the selections that some authors have been included several times. Our goal has been to exemplify research approaches dealing with a variety of behavior phenomena, and it happens that certain experimenters have made substantial contributions in a number of areas. It was our desire, in order to achieve our goals, to take advantage of these contributions rather than to exclude some merely because the author had been included in another area.

A book such as this is not completed by the editors alone, but involves numerous persons whose dedicated assistance, encouragement, and support transform an idea about a book into reality. The editors could not have achieved this without the understanding and support of their respective departments and their chairmen. Harold W. Stevenson, Director of the Institute of Child Development, University of Minnesota, and Harold Schlosberg, Chairman of the Department of Psychology at Brown University, both provided encouragement and advice about various problems related to the book as it was formulated. In addition, others gave freely of their time to read and make suggestions about the content. Included among these were Alfred Castaneda, Gordon N. Cantor, Ronald K. Penney, Charles C. Spiker, and John C. Wright. Their suggestions were invaluable. In addition, a number of students in our departments have helped in many ways from the inception of the book to its final page proofs. In particular, we would like to mention Sara Allen, George Flamer, Kay Goodman, Herbert Kaye, Nancy Nikkel, Elizabeth Reinicke, and David Wicklund. The typing skills and time of Annie Eggen, who did most of the secretarial work, and Phyllis Beckendorf, who pitched in when needed, are gratefully appreciated. Credit should also be given to our wives for the cheerful way in which both accepted many impositions throughout this endeavor. Finally, we are, of course, most grateful to those many authors and publishers whose permissions we received to include each of the papers which make up the main body of this volume.

Minneapolis, Minnesota   D. S. P.
Providence, Rhode Island   L. P. L.
1963

CONTENTS

CONTENTS

RESEARCH READINGS

IN

CHILD PSYCHOLOGY

APPROACHES TO RESEARCH: 1
METHODOLOGICAL PROBLEMS

THE FIRST SECTION of this book is devoted to papers that attempt analyses of how child psychology, as a science, may most successfully be approached. As indicated by the title of the first paper, the problems associated with the most fruitful scientific approach to any area are not new ones to science, although perhaps new to child psychology. Certainly the question of how we may assess the factors that determine the behavior of the child has broad implications for the future of the field. The papers in this section might be conceived as parts of a debate on the question: *Resolved,* That child psychology shall be conceived as an endeavor consisting of the collection of *empirical, descriptive* facts related to the child and tied together by the thread of age, as opposed to being conceived as an area within the broader field of psychology, distinguished by the *experimental manipulative* evidence which it can contribute to a *behavior theory,* which is the goal of that broader field of psychology.

Insofar as child psychology is concerned, this debate may be said to have started with the paper by Lewin that is the first one in this section. The resolution of the debate for child psychology is, however, still in process (and indeed may always be), until through their research child psychologists demonstrate that one approach or the other will in the long run prove to be more fruitful. Since the question is one of fact, it is only through research that the resolution will occur. The papers in this section, however, attempt to provide historical and logical arguments for each approach. As with any hotly contested debate, the points made by the various authors focus upon the strengths of one point of view and the weaknesses of the other, but the attainment of the goal of explanation and prediction of behavior will be reached through the use of the strengths of both approaches.

It is necessary for any science to begin with description. Descriptive facts about a phenomenon are a prerequisite to a determination of the factors that govern the occurrence of the phenomenon. If, however, we assume that the establishment of lawful relationships is the goal of scientific child psychology, then description is not enough. Experimental manipulation must become a part of the method if we are to be able to establish laws which will predict, explain, and allow us to control behavior. Progress in child psychology must therefore involve both the descriptive and the experimental approaches to its subject matter. Traditionally, child psychology has been predominantly de-

1

scriptive in its research. Recently many scientists in the field have felt that a shift must be made to include a strong focus upon research which is experimental in nature. The authors of this book feel that the experimental method should take its place as a prominent part of child psychology, but it may be seen from the selections in this book that one can not do one kind of research to the exclusion of the other. Description and experimentation are inextricably entwined.

In the first selection, Lewin clearly delineates the differences between the descriptive, inductive methods of Aristotle and the experimental, deductive methods of Galileo. He suggests that psychologists have limited themselves to Aristotelian science and ignored Galilean science. He argues for a strong affiliation with the latter approach. Although Lewin was a child psychologist, his immediate effect upon the research methods of the rest of child psychology was small. It was not until some twenty years after the first appearance of the Lewin paper that child psychology became seriously concerned with the problems he was discussing. In 1951, Barker, an associate of Lewin, complained in the *Annual Review of Psychology* that child psychology lacked vigor, well-executed research, and well-trained personnel. He chided his fellow child psychologists with the observation that their field was dying as measured by research productivity and quality. Barker's position was endorsed the following year in the same *Review* by Nowlis and Nowlis, who added the observation that research in the area lacked reference to systematic theory, a point made by Keller in 1950.

Harris, spokesman for the more traditional developmental point of view, attempted in 1953 to rebut the arguments that the field lacked vigor and argued for a return to the interdisciplinary research which characterized the more productive years of child study. In 1955, Bijou renewed the quest for a more systematic approach to the study of child behavior with suggestions for an experimental program including descriptions of laboratory equipment and procedures. (See the fourth paper in this section.) The question was brought clearly in focus in the successive presidential addresses presented by McCandless in 1955 and Harris (see the second paper) in 1956 before the Division of Developmental Psychology of the American Psychological Association. Most of the points made by McCandless are presented by McCandless and Spiker in the third paper of this section. In these two speeches the major points of the two sides of the controversy were presented to this national organization by two of their leading exponents, the elected presidents. The question has not been resolved by the papers presented here and the interested student will wish to read other papers that continue to appear in the literature (for example, Gollin, 1960; and Martin, 1960).

The last two papers in this section deal with two problems that have long concerned child psychologists: heredity versus environment, and intelligence. A review of the literature in the field would indicate that more research effort has been devoted to these two areas than to all others combined.

From the time of Binet and Simon, child psychologists have attempted to discover the variables that determine man's intelligent behavior. Today, perhaps more than any other time, this would seem to be a problem of extreme importance both practically and theoretically. Equally intriguing has been the question of the role heredity and environment play in the determination of the behaviors exhibited by children. In each case, however, research has been plagued by ambiguous definitions and philosophical pitfalls that have confused the issues involved. The papers here represent, in part, the impact of the philosophy of science on these old problems. Neither paper suggests a retreat from experimental attacks upon the questions related to heredity, environment, and intelligence; rather they indicate how research may contribute in a more significant manner. These papers help to clarify the definitional and methodological difficulties and thus suggest research that will avoid previous errors.

REFERENCES

BARKER, R. G.   Child psychology. Chapter I in *Annu. Rev. of Psychol.*, 1951.

GOLLIN, E. S.   Observations on method in child psychology. *Merrill-Palmer Quart.*, 1960, *6*, 250–260.

HARRIS, D. B.   Why an interdisciplinary society for research in child development. *Child Develpm.*, 1953, *24*, 249–255.

KELLER, F. S.   Animals and children. *Child Develpm.*, 1950, *21*, 7–12.

MARTIN, W. E.   Rediscovering the mind of the child: a significant trend in research in child development. *Merrill-Palmer Quart.*, 1960, *6*, 67–76.

NOWLIS, V., and NOWLIS, H. H.   Child psychology. Chapter I in *Annu. Rev. of Psychol.*, 1952.

The Conflict Between Aristotelian and Galileian Modes of Thought in Contemporary Psychology

KURT LEWIN

IN THE DISCUSSION of several urgent problems of current experimental and theoretical psychology I propose to review the development of the concepts of physics, and particularly the transition from the Aristotelian to the Galileian mode of thought. My purpose is not historical, rather do I believe that certain questions, of considerable importance in the reconstruction of concepts in present-day psychology, may be clarified and more precisely stated through such a comparison, which provides a view beyond the difficulties of the day.

I do *not* intend to infer by deduction from the history of physics what psychology "ought" to do. I am not of the opinion that there is only one empirical science, namely, physics; and the question whether psychology, as part of biology, is reducible to physics or is an independent science may here be left open.

Since we are starting from the point of view of the researcher, we shall, in our contrast of Aristotelian and Galileian concept formation, be less concerned with personal nuances of theory in Galileo and Aristotle than with certain rather ponderable differences in the modes of thought which determined the actual research of the mediaeval Aristotelians and of the post-Galileian physicists. Whether some particular investigator had previously shown the later sort of thinking in respect of some special point, or if some very modern speculations of the relativity theory should accord in some way with Aristotle's, is without relevance in the present connection.

In order to provide a setting especially for the theoretical treatment of the dynamic problems, I shall consider first the *general* characteristics of Aristotelian and Galileian physics and of modern psychology.

I. GENERAL CHARACTER OF THE TWO MODES OF THOUGHT

A. IN PHYSICS

If one asks what is the most characteristic difference between "modern" post-Galileian physics and Aristotelian, one receives, as a rule, the following reply, which has had an important influence upon the scientific ideals of the psychologist: The concepts of Aristotelian physics were *anthropomorphic* and *inexact*. Modern physics, on the contrary, is quantitatively exact, and pure mathematical, functional relations now occupy the place of the former anthropomorphic explanations. These have given to physics that abstract appearance in which modern physicists are accustomed to take special pride.

This view of the development of physics is, to be sure, pertinent. But if

Reprinted, by permission, from *Journal of General Psychology*, 1931, 5, 141–162.

one fixes one's attention less upon the "style" of the concepts employed, and more upon their actual functions as instruments for understanding the world, these differences appear to be more of a secondary nature, consequences of a deeper lying difference in the conception of the relationship between the world and the task of research.

1. *Aristotelian Concepts*

a. Their valuative character. As in all sciences, the detachment of physics from the universal matrix of philosophy and practice was only gradually achieved. Aristotelian physics is full of concepts which today we consider not only as specifically biological, but preeminently as *valuative* concepts. It abounds in specifically normative concepts taken from ethics, which occupy a place between valuative and non-valuative concepts: The "highest" forms of motions are circular and rectilinear, and they occur only in "heavenly" movements, those of the stars. The "earthly" sublunar world is endowed with motion of inferior types. There are similar valuative differences between causes: On one side there are the good or, so to speak, authorized forces of a body which come from its tendency toward perfection (τέλος), and on the other side the "disturbances" due to chance and to the opposing forces (Βία) of other bodies.

This kind of classification in terms of values plays an extraordinarily important part in mediaeval physics. It classes many things with very slight or unimportant relationships together and separates things that objectively are closely and importantly related.

It seems obvious to me that this extremely "anthropomorphic" mode of thought plays a large rôle in psychology,

even to the present day. Like the distinction between earthly and heavenly, the no less valuative distinction between "normal" and "pathological" has for a long time sharply differentiated two fields of psychological fact, and thus separated phenomena which are fundamentally most nearly related.

No less important is the fact that value concepts completely dominate the conceptual setting of the special problems, or have until very recently done so. Thus, not till lately has psychology begun to investigate the structural (Gestalt) relations concerned in perception, thus replacing the concept of optical *illusion,* a concept derived not from psychological but from epistemological categories, which unwarrantedly lumps all these "illusions" together and sets them apart from the other phenomena of psychological optics. Psychology speaks of the "errors" of children, of "practice," of "forgetting," thus classifying whole groups of processes according to the value of their products, instead of according to the nature of the psychological processes involved. Psychology is, to be sure, beyond classifying events *only* on the basis of value when it speaks of "disturbances," of inferiority and superiority in development, or of the quality of performance on a test. On all sides there are tendencies to attack actual psychological processes. But there can hardly be any doubt that we stand now only at the beginning of this stage, that the same transitional concepts that we have seen in the Aristotelian physics to lie between the valuative and the non-valuative are characteristic of such antitheses as those of intelligence and feeblemindedness, or of drive and will. The detachment of the conceptual structure of psychology from the utilitarian concepts of pedagogy, medicine, and ethics is only partly achieved.

It is quite possible, indeed I hold it to be probable, that the utility or performance concepts such as, for example, a "true" cognition versus an "error," may later acquire a legitimate sense. If that is the case, however, an "illusion" will have to be characterized not epistemologically but biologically.

b. Abstract classification. When the Galileian and post-Galileian physics disposed of the distinction between heavenly and earthly, and thereby extended the field of natural law enormously, it was not due solely to the exclusion of value concepts, but also to a changed interpretation of *classification.* For Aristotelian physics the membership of an object in a given class was of critical importance, because for Aristotle the class defined the essence or essential nature of the object, and thus determined its behavior in both positive and negative respects.

This classification often took the form of paired opposites, such as cold and warm, dry and moist, and compared with present-day classification had a rigid, "absolute" character. In modern quantitative physics dichotomous classifications have been entirely replaced by *continuous gradations.* Substantial concepts have been replaced by functional concepts *(1).*

Here also it is not difficult to point out the analogous stage of development in contemporary psychology. The separation of intelligence, memory, and impulse bears throughout the characteristic stamp of Aristotelian classification; and in some fields, for example, in the analysis of feelings (pleasantness and unpleasantness), or of temperaments *(10),* or of drives *(8),* such dichotomous classifica-

tions as Aristotle's are even today of great significance. Only gradually do these classifications lose their importance and yield to a conception which seeks to derive the same laws for all these fields, and to classify the *whole* field on the basis of other, essentially *functional,* differences.

c. The concept of law. Aristotle's classes are *abstractly* defined as the sum total of those characteristics which a group of objects have in common. This circumstance is not merely a characteristic of Aristotle's logic, but largely determines his conception of *lawfulness* and *chance,* which seems to me so important to the problems of contemporary psychology as to require closer examination.

For Aristotle those things are lawful, conceptually intelligible, which occur *without exception.* Also, and this he emphasizes particularly, those are lawful which occur *frequently.* Excluded from the class of the conceptually intelligible as "mere chance" are those things which occur only *once,* individual events as such. Actually since the behavior of a thing is determined by its essential nature, and this essential nature is exactly the abstractly defined class (that is, the sum total of the common characteristics of a whole group of objects), it follows that each event, as a particular event, is chance, undetermined. For in these Aristotelian classes individual differences disappear.

The real source of this conception may lie in the fact that for Aristotelian physics *not all* physical processes possess the lawful character ascribed to them by post-Galileian physics. To the young science of physics the universe it investigated appeared to contain as much that was chaotic as that which was lawful. The lawfulness, the intelligibility of physical processes was still narrowly limited. It was really present only in *some* processes, as, for example, the courses of the stars, but by no means in all the fleeting and transitory events of the earth. Just as for other young sciences, it was still a *question* for physics, whether and how far physical processes were subject to law. And this circumstance exercised its full effect on the formation of physical concepts, even though in philosophical "principle" the idea of general lawfulness already existed. In post-Galileian physics, with the elimination of the distinction between lawful and chance events, the necessity also disappeared of proving that the process under consideration was lawful. For Aristotelian physics, on the contrary, it was necessary to have criteria to decide *whether* or not a given event was of the lawful variety. Indeed the regularity with which similar events occurred in nature was used essentially as such a criterion. Only such events, as the celestial, which the course of history proves to be regular, or at least frequent, are subject to law; and only insofar as they are frequent, and hence "more" than individual events, are they conceptually intelligible. In other words, the ambition of science to understand the complex, chaotic, and unintelligible world, its faith in the ultimate decipherability of this world, was limited to such events as were *certified* by repetition in the course of history to possess a certain persistence and stability.

In this connection it must not be forgotten that Aristotle's emphasis on frequency (as a further basis for lawfulness, besides absolute regularity) represents, relative to his predecessors, a tendency toward the extension and concrete application of the principle of lawfulness.

The "empiricist" Aristotle insists that not only the regular but the frequent is lawful. Of course, this only makes clearer his antithesis of individuality and law, for the individual event as such still lies outside the pale of the lawful and hence, in a certain sense, outside the task of science. Lawfulness remains limited to cases in which similar events recur, and classes (in Aristotle's abstract sense) reveal the essential nature of the events.

This attitude toward the problem of lawfulness in nature, which dominated mediaeval physics and from which even the opponents of Aristotelian physics, such as Bruno and Bacon, escaped only gradually, by small steps, had important consequences in several respects.

As will be clear from the preceding text, this concept of lawfulness had throughout a quasi-statistical character. Lawfulness was considered as equivalent to the highest degree of generality, as that which occurs very often in the same way, as the extreme case of regularity, and hence as the perfect antithesis of the infrequent or of the particular event. The statistical determination of the concept of lawfulness is still clearly marked in Bacon, as when he tries to decide through his *"tabula praesentia"* whether a given association of properties is real (essential) or fortuitous. Thus he ascertains, for example, the numerical frequency of the cases in which the properties "warm" and "dry" are associated in everyday life. Less mathematically exact, indeed, but no less clear is this statistical way of thinking in the whole body of Aristotelian physics.

At the same time—and this is one of the most important consequences of the Aristotelian conception—regularity or particularity was understood entirely in *historical* terms.

The complete freedom from exceptions, the "always" which is found also in the later conceptions of physical lawfulness, still has here its original connections with the frequency with which similar cases have occurred in the *actual, historical* course of events in the everyday world. A crude example will make this clearer: light objects, under the conditions of everyday life, relatively frequently go up; heavy objects usually go down. The flame of the fire, at any rate under the conditions known to Aristotle, almost always goes upward. It is these frequency rules, within the limits of the climate, mode of life, etc., familiar to Aristotle, that determine the nature and tendency to be ascribed to each class of objects, and lead in the present instance to the conclusion that flames and light bodies have a tendency upward.

Aristotelian concept formation has yet another immediate relation to the geographically-historically given, in which it resembles, as do the valuative concepts mentioned above, the thinking of primitive man and of children.

When primitive man uses different words for "walking," depending upon its direction, north or south, or upon the sex of the walker, or upon whether the latter is going into or out of a house (5), he is employing a reference to the historical situation that is quite similar to the putatively "absolute" descriptions ("upward" or "downward") of Aristotle, the real significance of which is a sort of *geographic* characterization, a place definition relative to the earth's surface.[1]

The original connection of the concepts with the "actuality," in the special sense of the given historic-geographic circumstances, is perhaps the most important feature of Aristotelian physics. It is from this almost more even than from its teleology that his physics gets its general anthropomorphic character. Even in the minute particulars of theorizing and in the actual conduct of research it is always evident, not only that physical and normative concepts are still undifferentiated, but that the formulation of problems and the concepts that we would today distinguish, on the one hand, as "historic"[2] and, on the other, as non-historic or "systematic" are inextricably interwoven. (Incidentally, an analogous confusion exists in the early stages of other sciences, for example in economics.)

From these conceptions also the attitude of Aristotelian physics toward lawfulness takes a new direction. So long as lawfulness remained limited to such processes as occurred repeatedly in the same way, it is evident, not only that the young physics still lacked the courage to extend the principle to all physical phenomena, but also that the concept of lawfulness still had a fundamentally historic, a

---

[1] In the following pages we shall frequently have to use the term "historic-geographic." This is not in common usage, but it seems to me in-

accurate to contrast historic and systematic questions. The real opposition is between "type" (of object, process, situation) and "occurrence." And for concepts that deal with "occurrence," the reference to "absolute" geographic space-coordinates is just as characteristic as that to "absolute" time-coordinates by means of dates. At the same time, the concept of the "geographic" should be understood in such a general sense as to refer to juxtaposition, correlative to historical *succession*, that the concept is applicable, for example, to psychical events.

[2] There is no term at present in general use to designate non-historic problem formulations. I here employ the term "systematic," meaning thereby, not "ordered," but collectively non-historic problems and laws such as those which form the bulk of present-day physics. (Cf. infra.)

temporally particular, significance. Stress was laid not upon the "general validity" which modern physics understands by lawfulness, but upon the events in the historically given world which displayed the required stability. The highest degree of lawfulness, beyond mere frequency (ἐπὶ τὸ πολύ), was characterized by the idea of always eternal (ἀεί). That is, the stretch of historic time for which constancy was assumed was extended to eternity. General validity of *law* was not yet clearly distinguished from eternity of *process*. Only permanence, or at least frequent repetition, was proof of more than momentary validity. Even here in the idea of eternity, which seems to transcend the historical, the connection with immediate historic actuality is still obvious, and this close connection was characteristic of the "empiricist" Aristotle's method and concepts.

Not only in physics but in other sciences, for example, in economics and biology, it can be clearly seen how in certain early stages the tendency to empiricism, to the collection and ordering of "facts," carries with it at the same time a tendency to historical concept formation, to excessive valuation of the historical.

2. Galileian Physics. From the point of view of this sort of empiricism the concept formation of Galileian and post-Galileian physics must seem curious and even paradoxical.

As remarked above, the use of mathematical tools and the tendency to exactness, important as they are, cannot be considered the real substance of the difference between Aristotelian and Galileian physics. It is indeed quite possible to recast in mathematical form the essential

content of, for example, the dynamic ideas of Aristotelian physics. (Cf. *infra.*) It is conceivable that the development of physics could have taken the form of a mathematical rendition of Aristotelian concepts such as is actually taking place in psychology today. In reality, however, there were only traces of such a tendency, such as Bacon's quasi-statistical methods mentioned above. The main development took another direction and proved to be a change of content rather than a mere change of form.

The same considerations apply to the "exactness" of the new physics. It must not be forgotten that in Galileo's time there were no clocks of the sort we have today, that these first became possible through the knowledge of dynamics founded upon Galileo's work (9). Even the methods of measurement used by Faraday in the early investigations of electricity show how little exactness, in the current sense of *precision* to such and such a decimal place, had to do with these critical stages in the development of physics.

The real sources of the tendency to quantification lie somewhat deeper, namely in a new conception by the physicist of the nature of the physical world, in an extension of the demands of physics upon itself in the task of understanding the world, and in an increased faith in the possibility of their fulfillment. These are radical and far-reaching changes in the fundamental ideas of physics, and the tendency to quantification is simply one of their expressions.

a. Homogenization. The outlook of a Bruno, a Kepler, or a Galileo is determined by the idea of a comprehensive, all-embracing unity of the physical world. The same law governs the courses of the stars, the falling of stones, and the flight of birds. This "homogenization" of the physical world with respect to the validity of law deprives the division of physical objects into rigid abstractly defined classes of the critical significance it had for Aristotelian physics, in which membership in a certain conceptual class was considered to determine the physical nature of an object.

Closely related to this is the loss in importance of logical dichotomies and conceptual antitheses. Their places are taken by more and more fluid transitions, by gradations which deprived the dichotomies of their antithetical character and represent in logical form a transition stage between the class concept and the serial concept (1).

b. Genetic concepts. This dissolution of the sharp antitheses of rigid classes was greatly accelerated by the coeval transition to an essentially functional way of thinking, to the use of *conditional-genetic* concepts. For Aristotle the immediate perceptible appearance, that which present-day biology terms the *phenotype*, was hardly distinguished from the properties that determine the object's dynamic relations. The fact, for example, that light objects relatively frequently go upward sufficed for him to ascribe to them an upward tendency. With the differentiation of phenotype from *genotype* or, more generally, of "descriptive" from "conditional-genetic" (7) concepts, and the shifting of emphasis to the latter, many old class distinctions lost their significance. The orbits of the planets, the free falling of a stone, the movement of a body on an inclined plane, the oscillation of a pendulum, which if classified according to their phenotypes would fall into quite different, indeed into antithetical classes, prove to be simply various expressions of the same law.

c. Concreteness. The increased emphasis upon the quantitative which seems to lend to modern physics a formal and abstract character is not derived from any tendency to logical formality. At the same time as the development of the problem of classification, or rather, much earlier, the tendency to a full description of the concrete actuality, even that of the particular case, was influential, a circumstance which should be especially emphasized in connection with present-day psychology. The particular object in all departments of science is determined not only in kind and thereby qualitatively, but it possesses each of its properties in a special intensity or to a definite degree. So long as one rewards as important conceptually intelligible only such properties of an object as are common to a whole group of objects, the individual differences of degree remain without scientific relevance, for in the abstractly defined classes these differences more or less disappear. With the mounting aspirations of research toward an understanding of actual events and particular cases, the task of describing the differences of degree that characterized individual cases had necessarily to increase in importance, and finally required actual quantitative determination.

It is the increased desire, and also the increased ability, to comprehend *concrete particular cases,* and to comprehend them fully, which, together with the idea of the *homogeneity* of the physical world and that of the *continuity* of the properties of its objects, constituted the main impulse to the increasing quantification of physics.

d. Paradoxes of the new empiricism. This tendency toward the closest possible contact with actuality, which today is usually regarded as characteristic and ascribed to an "anti-speculative" tendency, led to a mode of concept formation diametrically opposed to that of Aristotle, and, surprisingly enough, involved also the direct antithesis of his "empiricism."

The Aristotelian concepts show, as we have seen above, an immediate reference to the historically given reality and to the actual course of events. This reference, or at any rate this *immediate* reference to the historically given, is lacking in modern physics. The fact, so decisively important for Aristotelian concepts, that a certain process was only once, or very frequently, or invariably repeated in the course of history, is practically irrelevant to the most essential questions of modern physics.[3] This circumstance is considered fortuitous or "merely historical."

The law of falling bodies, for example, does *not* assert that bodies very frequently fall downward. It does *not* assert that the event to which the formula, $s = \frac{1}{2} gt^2$, applies, the "free and unimpeded fall" of a body, occurs regularly or even frequently in the actual history of the world. Whether the event described by the law occurs rarely or often has nothing to do with the law. Indeed, in a certain sense, the law refers only to cases that are *never* realized, or only approximately realized, in the actual course of events. Only in experiment, that is, under artificially constructed conditions, do cases occur which approximate the event with which the law is concerned. The propositions of modern physics, which

are often considered to be "anti-speculative" and "empirical," unquestionably have in comparison with Aristotelian empiricism a much less empirical, a much more constructive character than the Aristotelian concepts based immediately upon historical actuality.

B. PSYCHOLOGY

Here we are confronted by questions which, as real problems of actual research and of theory, have strongly influenced the development of psychology and which constitute the most fundamental grounds of its present crisis.

The concepts of psychology, at least in certain decisive respects, are thoroughly Aristotelian in their actual content, even though in many respects their form of presentation has been somewhat "civilized," so to speak. The present struggles and theoretical difficulties of psychology resemble in many ways, even in their particulars, the difficulties which culminated in the conquest over Aristotelian ways of thinking in physics.

1. Aristotelian Concepts

a. Fortuitousness of the individual case. The concept formation of psychology is dominated, just as was that of Aristotelian physics, by the question of regularity and indeed of regularity in the sense of frequency. This is obvious in its immediate attitude toward particular phenomena as well as in its attitude toward lawfulness. If, for example, one show a film of a concrete incident in the behavior of a certain child, the first question of the psychologist usually is: "Do all children do that, or is it at least common?" And if one must answer this question in the negative the behavior involved loses

---

[3] So far as it is not immediately concerned with an actual "History of the Heavens and the Earth" or a geography. (Cf. *infra.*)

for that psychologist all or almost all claim to scientific interest. To pay attention to such an "exceptional case" seems to him a scientifically unimportant bit of folly.

The real attitude of the investigator toward particular events and the problem of individuality is perhaps more clearly expressed in this actual behavior than in many theories. The individual event seems to him fortuitous, unimportant, scientifically indifferent. It may, however, be some extraordinary event, some tremendous experience, something that has critically determined the destiny of the person involved, or the appearance of an historically significant personality. In such a case it is customary to emphasize the "mystical" character of all individuality and "originality," comprehensible only to "intuition," or at least not to science.

Both of these attitudes toward the particular event lead to the same conclusion: that that which does not occur repeatedly lies outside the realm of the comprehensible.

b. Lawfulness as frequency. The esteem in which frequency is held in present-day psychology is due to the fact that it is still considered a *question* whether and how far the psychical world is lawful, just as in Aristotelian physics it was due to a similar uncertainty about lawfulness in the physical world. It is not necessary here to describe at length the vicissitudes of the thesis of the lawfulness of the psychic in philosophical discussion. It is sufficient to recall that even at present there are many tendencies to limit the operation of law to certain "lower" spheres of psychical events. For us it is more important to note that the field which is considered lawful, not in prin-

ciple, but in the actual research of psychology—even of experimental psychology—has only been extended very gradually. If psychology has only very gradually and hesitantly pushed beyond the bounds of sensory psychology into the fields of will and affect, it is certainly not due only to technical difficulties, but mainly to the fact that in this field actual repetition, a recurrence of the same event, is not to be expected. And this repetition remains, as it did for Aristotle, to a large extent the basis for the assumption of the lawfuless or intelligibility of an event.

As a matter of fact, any psychology that does not recognize lawfulness as inherent in the nature of the psychic, and hence in *all* psychical processes, even those occurring only once, *must* have criteria to decide, like Aristotelian physics, whether or not it has in any given case to deal with lawful phenomena. And, again, just as in Aristotelian physics, frequency of recurrence is taken as such a criterion. It is evidence of the depth and momentum of this connection (between repetition and lawfulness) that it is even used to define experiment, a scientific instrument which, if not directly opposed to the concepts of Aristotelian physics, is as least significant only in relatively modern times.[4] Even for Wundt repetition inhered in the concept of experiment. Only in recent years is psychology beginning to give up this requirement, which withholds a large field of the psychic from experimental investigation.

But even more important perhaps than the restriction of experimental investigation is the fact that this extravagant valuation of repetition (i.e., considering

---

[4] The Greeks, of course, *knew* of experiment.

frequency as the criterion and expression of lawfulness) dominates the formation of the concepts of psychology, particularly in its younger branches.

Just as in Aristotelian physics, contemporary child psychology regards as characteristic of a given age, and the psychology of emotion as characteristic of a given expression, that which a group of individual cases have in common. This abstract Aristotelian conception of the class determines the kind and dominates the procedure of classification.

c. Class and essence. Present-day child psychology and affect psychology also exemplify clearly the Aristotelian habit of considering the abstractly defined classes as the essential nature of the particular object and hence as an "explanation" of its behavior. Whatever is common to children of a given age is set up as the fundamental character of that age. The fact that three-year-old children are quite often negative is considered evidence that negativism is inherent in the nature of three-year-olds, and the concept of a negativistic age or stage is then regarded as an explanation (though perhaps not a complete one) for the appearance of negativism in a given particular case!

Quite analogously, the concept of drives, for example, the hunger drive or the maternal instinct, is nothing more than the abstract selection of the features common to a group of acts that are of relatively frequent occurrence. This abstraction is set up as the essential reality of the behavior and is then in turn used to explain the frequent occurrence of the instinctive behavior, for example, of the care of infant progeny. Most of the explanations of expression, of character, and of temperament are in a similar state.

Here, as in a great many other fundamental concepts, such as that of ability, talent, and similar concepts employed by the intelligence testers, present-day psychology is really reduced to explanation in terms of Aristotelian "essences," a sort of explanation which has long been attacked as faculty psychology and as circular explanation, but for which no other way of thinking has been substituted.

d. Statistics. The classificatory character of its concepts and the emphasis on frequency are indicated methodologically by the commanding significance of statistics in contemporary psychology. The statistical procedure, at least in its commonest application in psychology, is the most striking expression of this Aristotelian mode of thinking. In order to exhibit the common features of a given group of facts, the *average* is calculated. This average acquires a representative value, and is used to characterize (as "mental age") the properties of "the" two-year-old child. Outwardly, there is a difference between contemporary psychology, which works so much with numbers and curves, and the Aristotelian physics. But this difference, characteristically enough, is much more a difference in the technique of execution than in the actual content of the concepts involved. Essentially, the statistical way of thinking, which is a necessary consequence of Aristotelian concepts, is also evident in Aristotelian physics, as we have already seen. The difference is that, owing to the extraordinary development of mathematics and of general scientific method, the statistical procedure of psychology is clearer and more articulate.

All the efforts of psychology in recent years toward exactness and precision have been in the direction of refinement and extension of its statistical methods. These efforts are quite justified insofar as they indicate a determination to achieve an adequate comprehension of the full reality of mental life. But they are really founded, at least in part, on the ambition to demonstrate the scientific status of psychology by using as much mathematics as possible and by pushing all calculations to the last possible decimal place.

This formal extension of the method has not changed the underlying concepts in the slightest: they are still thoroughly Aristotelian. Indeed, the mathematical formulation of the method only consolidates and extends the domination of the underlying concepts. It unquestionably makes it more difficult to see their real character and hence to supplant them with others; and this is a difficulty with which Galileian physics did not have to contend, inasmuch as the Aristotelian mode of thought was not then so entrenched and obscured in mathematics. (*Cf. supra.*)

e. Limits of knowledge. Exceptions. Lawfulness is believed to be related to regularity, and considered the antithesis of the individual case. (In terms of the current formula, lawfulness is conceived as a correlation approaching $r = \pm 1$.) So far as the psychologist agrees at all to the validity of psychological propositions, he regards them as only *regularly* valid, and his acceptance of them takes such a form that one remains aware of a certain distinction between mere regularity and full lawfulness; and he ascribes to biological, and above all to psychological propositions (in contrast to physical), only regularity. Or else lawfulness is believed to be only the *extreme* case of regularity,[5] in which case all differ-

ences (between lawfulness and regularity) disappear in principle while the necessity of determining the degree of regularity still remains.

The fact that lawfulness and individuality are considered antitheses has two sorts of effect on actual research. It signifies in the first place a limitation of research. It makes it appear hopeless to try to understand the real, unique, course of an emotion or the actual structure of a particular individual's personality. It thus reduces one to a treatment of these problems in terms of mere averages, as exemplified by tests and questionnaires. Any one to whom these methods appear inadequate usually encounters a weary scepticism or else a maudlin appreciation of individuality and the doctrine that this field, from which the recurrence of similar cases in sufficient numbers is excluded, is inaccessible to scientific comprehension and requires instead sympathetic intuition. In both cases the field is withdrawn from experimental investigation, for qualitative properties are considered as the direct opposite of lawfulness. The manner in which this view is continually and repeatedly advanced in the discussion of experimental psychology resembles, even to its particulars, the arguments against which Galileian physics had to struggle. How, it was urged at that time, can one try to embrace in a single law of motion such qualitatively different phenomena as the movements

---

[5] As is well known, the concept of possible exceptions and the merely statistical validity of laws has very recently been revived in physical discussion. Even if this view should finally be adopted, it would not in any way mean a return to Aristotelian concepts. It suffices here to point out that even in that event, it would not involve setting apart within the physical world a class of events on the basis of its "degree" of lawfulness, but the whole physical universe would be subject only to a statistical lawfulness. On the relation of this statistical view to the problem of precision of measurement, see Lewin (7).

of the stars, the flying of leaves in the wind, the flight of the birds, and the rolling of a stone downhill. But the opposition of law and individual corresponded so well with the Aristotelian conception and with the primitive mode of thinking which constituted the philosophy of everyday life, that it appears often enough in the writings of the physicists themselves, *not*, however, in their physics but in their philosophy.[6]

The conviction that it is impossible wholly to comprehend the individual case as such implies, in addition to this limitation, a certain laxity of research: it is satisfied with setting forth mere regularities. The demands of psychology upon the *stringency* of its propositions go no farther than to require a validity "in general," or "on the average," or "as a rule." The "complexity" and "transitory nature" of life processes make it unreasonable, it is said, to require complete, exceptionless, validity. According to the old saw that "the exception proves the rule," *psychology does not regard exceptions as counter-arguments so long as their frequency is not too great.*

The attitude of psychology toward the concept of lawfulness also shows clearly and strikingly the Aristotelian character of its mode of thought. It is founded on a very meager confidence in the lawfulness of psychological events, and has for the investigator the added charm of not requiring too high a standard of validity in his propositions or in his proofs of them.

f. Historic-geographic concepts. For

the view of the nature of lawfulness and for the emphasis upon repetition which we have seen to be characteristic of Aristotelian physics, in addition to the motives which we have just mentioned, the *immediate reference* to the concerned "actuality" in the historic-geographic sense was fundamental. Likewise, and this is evidence of the intimacy with which these modes of thought are related, present-day psychology is largely dominated by the same immediate reference to the historic-geographic datum. The historical bent of psychological concepts is again not always immediately obvious as such, but is bound up with nonhistoric, systematic concepts and undifferentiated from them. This quasi-historical set forms, in my opinion, the central point for the understanding and criticism of this mode of concept formation.

Although we have criticized the "statistical" mode of thought, the particular formulae used are not ultimately important to the questions under discussion. It is not the fact that an arithmetic mean is taken, that one adds and divides, that is the object of the present critique. These operations will certainly continue to be used extensively in the future of psychology. The critical point is, not that statistical methods are applied, but *how* they are applied, and especially, that cases are combined into groups.

In contemporary psychology the reference to the historic-geographic datum and the dependence of the conclusions upon frequency of actual occurrence are striking. Indeed, so far as immediate reference to the historic datum is concerned, the way in which the nature of the one-, two-, or three-year-old child is arrived at through the calculation of statistical averages corresponds exactly to Bacon's col-

---

[6] To avoid misunderstanding, the following should be emphasized: when we criticize the opposition of individual and law, as is customary in psychology, it does not mean that we are unaware of the complex problems of the concept of individuality.

lection of the given cases of dryness in his *tabluae praesentiae*. To be sure, there is a certain very crude concession made in such averages, to the requirements of non-historic concepts: patently pathological cases, and sometimes even cases in which an "unusual" environment is concerned, are usually excluded. Apart from this consideration, the exclusion of the most extreme abnormalities, the determination of the cases to be placed in a statistical group is essentially on historic-geographic grounds. For a group defined in historic-geographic terms, perhaps the one-year-old children of Vienna or New York in the year 1928, averages are calculated which are doubtless of the greatest significance to the historian or to the practical school man, but which do not lose their dependence upon the "accidents" of the historic-geographic given even though one go on to an average of the children of Germany, of Europe, or of the whole world, or of a decade instead of a year. *Such an extension of the geographic and historic basis does not do away with the specific dependence of this concept upon the frequency with which the individual cases occur within historically-geographically defined fields.*

Mention should have been made earlier of that refinement of statistics which is founded upon a *restriction* of the historic-geographic basis, as, for example, a consideration of the one-year-old children of a proletarian quarter of Berlin in the first years after the War. For such groupings usually are based on the qualitative individuality of the concrete cases as well as upon historic-geographic definitions. But even such limitations really contradict the spirit of statistics founded on frequency. Even they signify methodologically a certain shift

to the concrete particulars. Incidentally, one must not forget that even in the extreme case of such refinement, perhaps in the statistical investigation of the "only child," the actual definition is in terms of historic-geographic or at best of sociological categories; that is, according to criteria which combine into a single group cases that psychologically are very different or even antithetical. Such statistical investigations are consequently unable as a rule to give an explanation of the dynamics of the processes involved.

The immediate reference to the historically given actuality which is characteristic of Aristotelian concept formation is evident also in the discussion of experiment and nearness to life conditions. Certainly one may justly criticize the simple reaction experiments, the beginnings of the experimental psychology of the will or the experiments of reflexology on the ground of their wide divergence from the conditions of life. But this divergence is based in large part upon the tendency to investigate such processes as do not present the individual peculiarities of the particular case but which, as "simple elements" (perhaps the simplest movements), are common to all behavior, or which occur, so to speak, in everything. In contrast, approximation of life conditions is required, say of the psychology of will. By this is usually meant that it should investigate those cases, impossible to produce experimentally, in which the most important decisions of life are made. And here also we are confronted by an orientation toward the historically significant. It is a requirement which, if transferred to physics, would mean that it would be incorrect to study hydrodynamics in the laboratory; one must rather investigate the largest rivers in the world.

Two points then stand out in the field of theory and law: the high valuation of the historically important and disdain of the "ordinary;" in the field of experiment, the choice of processes which occur frequently (or are common to many events). Both are indicative in like measure of that Aristotelian mixing of historical and systematic questions which carries with it for the systematic the connection with the abstract classes and the neglect of the full reality of the concrete case.

2. Galileian Concept Formation. Opposed to Aristotelian concept formation which I have sought briefly to characterize, there is now evident in psychology a development which appears occasionally in radical or apparently radical tendencies, more usually in little half-steps, sometimes falling into error (especially when it tries most exactly to follow the example of physics), but which on the whole seems clearly and irresistibly to be pushing on to modifications which may ultimately mean nothing less than a transition from Aristotelian to Galileian concept formation.

a. No value concepts. No dichotomies. Unification of fields. The most important general circumstances which paved the way for Galileian concepts in physics are clearly and distinctly to be seen in present-day psychology.

The conquest over *"valuative,"* "anthropomorphic" classifications of phenomena on bases other than the nature of the mental process itself is not by any means complete, but in many fields, especially in sensory psychology, at least the chief difficulties are past.

As in physics, the grouping of events and objects into paired opposites and similar logical dichotomies is being replaced by groupings with the aid of *serial* concepts which permit of continuous variation, partly owing simply to wider experience and the recognition that transition stages are always present.

This has gone farthest in sensory psychology, especially in psychological optics and acoustics, and lately also in the domain of smell. But the tendency toward this change is also evident in other fields, for example, in that of feeling.

Freud's doctrine especially—and this is one of its greatest services—has contributed largely to the abolition of the boundary between the normal and the pathological, the ordinary and the unusual, and hereby furthered the *"homogenization"* of all the fields of psychology. This process is certainly still far from complete, but it is entirely comparable to that introduced in modern physics by which "heavenly" and "earthly" processes were united.

Also in child and animal psychology the necessity is gradually disappearing of choosing between the two alternatives of regarding the child as a little adult, the animal as an undeveloped inferior human, or else trying to establish an unbridgeable gap between the child and adult, animal and man. This homogenization is becoming continually clearer in all fields, and it is not a purely "philosophical" insistence upon some sort of abstract fundamental unity but influences concrete research in which differences are fully preserved.

b. Unconditional general validity of psychological laws. The clearest and most important expression of increasing homogeneity, beside the transition from class to serial concepts, is the fact that the validity of particular psychological laws is no longer limited to particular fields, as it was once limited to the "normal human adult" on the ground that anything might be expected of psychopathics or of geniuses, or that in such cases "the same laws do not hold." It is coming to be realized that every psychological law must hold without exception.

In actual content, this transition to the concept of strict exceptionless lawfulness signifies at once the same final and all-embracing homogenization and harmonization of the whole field that gave to Galilean physics its intoxicating feeling of infinite breadth, because it does not, like the abstract class concepts, level out the rich variety of the world and because a single law embraces the whole field.

Tendencies toward a homogeneity based upon the exceptionless validity of its laws have become evident in psychology only very recently, but they open up an extraordinarily wide perspective.[7]

The investigation of the laws of structure—particularly the experimental investigation of wholes—has shown that the same laws hold not only within different fields of psychological optics but also in audition, and in sensory psychology in general. This in itself constitutes a large step in the progress toward homogeneity.

Further, the laws of optical figures and of intellectual insight have turned out to be closely related. Important and similar laws have been discovered in the experimental investigation of behavioral wholes, of will processes, and of psychological needs. In the fields of memory and expression, psychological development appears to be analogous. In short, the thesis of the general validity of psychological laws has very recently become so much more concrete, particular laws have shown such capacity for fruitful application to fields that at first were qualitatively completely separated, that the thesis of the homogeneity of psychic life in respect to its laws gains tremendously in vigor and is destroying the boundaries of the old separated fields.[8]

c. Mounting ambitions. Methodologically also the thesis of the exceptionless validity of psychological laws has a far-reaching significance. It leads to an extraordinary increase in the demands made upon *proof*. It is no longer possible to take exceptions lightly. They do not in any way "prove the rule," but on the contrary are completely valid disproofs, even though they are rare, indeed, so long as one single exception is demonstrable. The thesis of general validity permits of no exceptions in the entire realm of the psychic, whether of child or adult, whether in normal or pathological psychology.

On the other hand, the thesis of ex-

---

[7] The association psychology contains an attempt at this sort of homogeneity, and it has really been of essential service in this direction. Similarly, in our time reflexology and behaviorism have contributed to the homogenization of "man and animal" and of "bodily and mental." But the Aristotelian view of lawfulness as regularity (without which it would have been impossible to support the law of association) brought this attempt to nothing. Consequently, the experimental association psychology, in its attempt at the end of the nineteenth century to derive the whole mental life from a single law, displayed the circular and at the same time abstract character that is typical of the speculative early stages of a science, and of Aristotelian class concepts.

Indeed, it seems almost as if, because of the great importance of frequency and repetition for Aristotelian methodological concepts, the law of association had been designed to make use of these as the actual *content* of psychological principles, inasmuch as frequent repetition is regarded as the most important cause of mental phenomena.

[8] For this section compare especially Wertheimer (*11*), Köhler (*4*), Koffka (*2*), and Lewin (*6*). A review of the special researches is found in Köhler (*3*).

ceptionless validity in psychological laws makes available to investigation, especially to experiment, such processes as do *not* frequently recur in the same form, as, for example, certain affective processes.

d. From the average to the "pure" case. A clear appreciation of this circumstance is still by no means habitual in psychology. Indeed, from the earlier, Aristotelian point of view the new procedure may even seem to conceal the fundamental contradiction we have mentioned above. One declares that one wants to comprehend the full concrete reality in a higher degree than is possible with Aristotelian concepts, and yet considers this reality in its actual historical course and its given geographical setting as really "accidental." The general validity, for example, of the law of movement on an inclined plane is not established by taking the average of as many cases as possible of real stones actually rolling down hills, and then considering this average as the most probable case.[9] It is based rather upon the "frictionless" rolling of an "ideal" sphere down an "absolutely straight" and hard plane, that is, upon a process that even the laboratory can only approximate, and which is most extremely improbable in daily life. One declares that one is striving for general validity and concreteness, yet uses a method which, from the point of view of the preceding epoch, disregards the historically given facts and depends entirely

upon individual accidents, indeed upon the most pronounced "exceptions."

How physics arrives at this procedure, which strikes the Aristotelian views of contemporary psychology as doubly paradoxical, begins to become intelligible when one envisages the necessary methodological consequences of the change in the ideas of the extent of lawfulness. When lawfulness is no longer limited to cases which occur regularly or frequently but is characteristic of *every* physical event, the necessity disappears of demonstrating the lawfulness of an event by some special criterion, such as its frequency of occurrence. Even a "particular case" is then *assumed*, without more ado, to be lawful. Historical rarity is no disproof, historical regularity no proof of lawfulness. For the concept of lawfulness has been quite detached from that of regularity; the concept of the complete absence of exceptions to laws is strictly separated from that of historical constancy (the "forever" of Aristotle).[10]

Further, the content of a law cannot then be determined by the calculation of averages of historically given cases. For

---

[9] In psychology it is asserted, often with special emphasis, that one obtains, perhaps from the construction of baby tests, a representation of the "general human," through the fact that those processes are selected which occur most frequently in the child's *daily life.* Then one may expect with sufficient probability that the child will spontaneously display similar behavior in the test.

[10] The contrast between Aristotelian and Galileian views of lawfulness and the difference in their methods may be briefly tabulated as follows:

	For Aristotle	For Galileo
1. The regular is	lawful	lawful
The frequent is	lawful	lawful
The individual case is	chance	lawful
2. Criteria of lawfulness are	regularity frequency	not required
3. That which is common to the historically occurring cases is	an expression of the nature of the thing	an accident, only "historically" conditioned

Aristotle the nature of a thing was expressed by the characteristics common to the historically given cases. Galileian concepts, on the contrary, which regard historical frequency as "accident," must also consider it a matter of chance which properties one arrives at by taking averages of historical cases. If the concrete event is to be comprehended and the thesis of lawfulness without exception is to be not merely a philosophical maxim but determinative of the mode of actual research, there must be another possibility of penetrating the nature of an event, some other way than that of ignoring all individual peculiarities of concrete cases. The solution of this problem may only be obtained by the elucidation of the paradoxical procedures of Galileian method through a consideration of the problems of dynamics.

REFERENCES

1. CASSIRER, E. *Substanzbegriff und Funktionsbegriff, Untersuchungen uber die Grundfragen der Erkenntniskritik.* Berlin: B. Cassirer, 1910. Pp. xv + 459.

2. KOFFKA, K. *The growth of the mind: an introduction to child psychology.* (Trans. by R. M. OGDEN.) New York: Harcourt, Brace; London: Kegan, Paul, 1924. Pp. xvi + 383. (2nd ed., 1928.)

3. KÖHLER, W. *Gestaltprobleme und Angange einer Gestalttheorie.* Berlin, 1924.

4. KÖHLER, W. *Gestalt psychology.* New York: Liveright, 1929. Pp. x + 403.

5. LEVY-BRUHL, L. *La méntalite primitive.* Paris: Alcan, 1922, Pp. 537. (5th ed., 1927.)

6. LEWIN, K. *Vorsatz, Wille and Bedürfnis, mit Vorbemerkungen über die psychischen Kräfte und Energien und die Strikture der Seele.* Berlin: Springer, 1926. Pp. 92.

7. LEWIN, K. *Gesetz und Experiment in der Psychologie. Berlin-Schlachtensee:* Benary, 1927. Pp. 49.

8. LEWIN, K. *Die Entwicklung der experimentellen Willinspsychologie und die Psychotherapie.* Liepzig: S. Hirzel, 1929. Pp. 28.

9. MACH, E. *Die Mechanik in ihrer Entwicklung.* Leipzig, 1921.

10. SOMMER, R. *Über Persönlichkeitstypen. Ber. Kong. f. exper. Psychol.,* 1925.

11. WERTHEIMER, M. Untersuchungen zur Lehre von der Gestalt. II. *Psychol. Forsch.,* 1923, 4, 301–350.

CHILD PSYCHOLOGY AND THE CONCEPT
OF DEVELOPMENT

DALE B. HARRIS

THE BEHAVIOR THEORIST working in child psychology affirms the value of unitary concepts, the prime importance of theory, and the power of the hypothetico-deductive method in child psychology. He sees the behavior of all living things as subject to one set of laws; one set of general behavior principles suffices for rats and men. Children become convenient, not necessarily essential, subjects for the study of behavior. Within this framework of thinking, child psychology truly is anomalous, and it is difficult to discern any definitive meaning for the term "development." One able presentation of this viewpoint (McCandless and Spiker, 1956) accuses many child psychologists of being too much concerned with application, too little with conceptual formulation and experimentation, for the health of their science.

CHILD VS. DEVELOPMENTAL
PSYCHOLOGY

There are others who hold that the developmental point of view in psychology contributes something unique which general behavior theory as presently conceived does not supply. Not only may it be necessary to phrase somewhat different principles for the explanation of behavior when we move from rats to men; it may

Presidential address read before the Division on Developmental Psychology of the American Psychological Association, September 3, 1956. Reprinted by permission of the author.

also be necessary to redefine the principles according to which behavior becomes organized as we move from lesser to greater maturity of subjects. Thus, children become *essential* subjects for the understanding of human behavior. The study of animal behavior, on a *comparative* basis, is also essential in a truly developmental psychology, but cannot substitute for the study of children, of adults, and of older people. The child psychologist with a *developmental* point of view has a somewhat different approach in theory, method and application than the child psychologist who is more strictly oriented in behavior or learning theory. Furthermore, he affirms that a developmental interpretation of behavior will contribute effectively to psychology by conceptualizing certain problems and phenomena which the behavior theorist tends to overlook or to bypass.

At the present time, a developmental conceptualization of behavior differs somewhat from behavior or learning theory with respect to the use of components of formal theory, though ultimately both the behavior or learning theorist and the developmental theorist would hope to phrase their formulations in terms of basic axioms. The behavior theorist presently goes beyond the developmentalist in his use of analytical terms; in so doing he achieves the appearance of a more elegant and formal structure, but whether he actually has attained greater flexibility in manipulating formal concepts is perhaps debatable.[1]

In this contrast of viewpoints there is also implied a distinction which has troubled life sciences for many years. It was rife in the mechanistic-vitalistic arguments of the last century. The implication that this difference is real and significant is found again in many contemporary discussions, though it takes a different form from the earlier controversy. The behavior theorist primarily seeks to discuss phenomena in terms of cause. He hopes ultimately to derive the behavior phenomena commonly subsumed by "purpose" from a set of constructs not themselves purposive. But at the present he concentrates on the experimental manipulation of antecedents. The developmentalist more frankly thinks in terms of "ends" or "purposes," albeit uneasily, because of his intellectual traditions which rule out teleology. The developmentalist, like the biologist, cannot escape the fact that predictable end states result from origins in which these states, though not discernible, are somewhat implicit; that function is circumscribed by structure, yet serves to maintain that structure. It should be clear that the modern biologist in speaking of "purpose" invokes nothing outside the material universe. Rather, his "purpose" is in the configurations themselves. It is seen in the intrinsic forces which operate to give characteristic form and function to the growing organism. "As to just how this structure is developed and main-

tained," says Sinnott, "biology is almost without a clue" (1955, p. 22).

For the behavior theorist, useful constructs are inferred states or processes such as perception or motivation. The constructs offered by the developmentalist cut across such processes, taking the form of motor behavior, social development, and intellectual growth—classes of behavior described phenomenally, and more readily susceptible to the language of the "purpose" or functions ultimately served.

The methodology of the behavior theorist is primarily theoretical formulation, the conceptual isolation of variables, and the crucial experiment; the developmentalist leans much more heavily upon directed observation and upon the use of the experiment empirically to define and isolate variables as well as to test the significant relationship of variables.[2] The ideal of behavior theory is systematic design and the laboratory experiment; the developmental viewpoint perhaps comes closer to Egon Brunswik's concept of the representative design and insists that in many instances we may be forced to rely upon experiments of nature. When phenomena have remote historical antecedents, as those revealed in the psychotherapeutic session for example, it may not be possible fully to replicate them, or to formulate suitable principles to understand them in the phenomena available in the laboratory surrogate for the life history. Behavior theory focuses its attention relatively more on the specific stimulus conditions which elicit behavior and on the effect of variability in the stimulus condition on a given behavior response. The developmental viewpoint,

---

[1] In discussion of this point, Professor Paul E. Meehl has pointed out that possibly the more we learn the more must sentences constitute our theoretical framework; this position suggests a limit to the expression in one set of terms of a complete behavior theory adequate to incorporate all necessary concepts of behavior processes. This problem has been discussed with clarity and insight by Mandler and Kessen (1959).

[2] For a skillful discussion of this issue which seeks to resolve the difference, see Russell (1957).

while recognizing the importance of the environment and paying considerable attention to variability in stimulus conditions, studies both constancy and variability in responses of the organism in relation to the complexity of the environing situation, especially as this complexity alters over time.

Because the developmentalist is interested in global phenomena and tends to use a phenomenistic terminology, he inevitably becomes more concerned with practical applications than does the behavior theorist, who usually wishes to avoid them. In the field of child psychology this problem is especially acute. Children are socially significant, and the developmentalist tends to take his cues from the attention given the problems of growth and adjustment which practical workers from many professions continually face. These problems, they insist, have their most definite meaning in the context of the child's experience, and, at any rate, for the developmental psychologist who works with human behavior, the problems must be phrased in a language which treats of the phenomenon of "purpose" or "goal-seeking." Hence, these problems are scientifically meritorius as they occur. The behavior theorist wishes to restate the problems in conceptual terms which are not themselves intrinsically purposive. The developmentalist has no fundamental quarrel with this position except that he believes that at the present stage of knowledge, it is not possible to work at such a reduced level of analysis and still deal with certain pressing scientific issues.

In drawing these opposing positions, we are, of course, not affirming an all or none position. We see each of these distinctions as a matter of relative emphasis.

Perhaps this relative emphasis bespeaks differences in habits of thinking in two groups. Lest it seem that this statement merely charges off to "personality differences" some rather vague distinctions which one cannot otherwise assign, it may be well to recognize that a similar division in viewpoint appears in the biological literature. At least three eminent biological writers, Arber (1954), Sommerhoff (1950), and Tinbergen (1955) have been quite willing to ascribe this distinction in emphasis to differences in temperament and habits of thought of the proponents. Perhaps we are saying the difference is due merely to differences in the sets of constructs which the proponents have been trained to use. However, this may be, in biology as in most science, there is no disposition at the moment to put all eggs into one theoretical basket, although this is what some behavior theorists apparently wish to do.

THEORY IN CONTEMPORARY CHILD PSYCHOLOGY

Of today's child psychologists who are most concerned with theory, Sears and his colleagues come closer than most to bridging the gap between a formal behavior theory and the phenomena of development and change in child behavior. By giving descriptive terms quite carefully delimited definitions, Sears (1957) constructs a systematic theory of behavioral or action change which goes far to account for molar phenomena. His recent contributions are taking form as a carefully wrought scientific contribution to developmental theory. His identification of the dimensions of action permits study of the person-as-a-whole, one primary omission of most behavior theories, and his accounting for both dependency and aggression in terms of learning theory goes a long way toward handling two particularly complex phenomena.

Baldwin's recent contribution to developmental theory (1955) is frankly based on intuitive or common sense understanding of child behavior. Theory grows out of such understanding by the scientist concerning himself with *observable* phenomena and by developing ever broader principles which will embrace more phenomena. Baldwin's approach, thus, attempts to take account of the phenomena of behavior as it occurs; he tries to translate the child in his phenomenal world into general and abstract principles; he does not develop a system of theorems which are then tested by crucial experiments. Baldwin, then stays closer to the developmental tradition.

Werner's idea of differentiation from primitive wholistic or global responses into more specific responses calls attention to the progressive emergency of more complex forms from simpler antecedents (1948). Piaget's work (1954), calling attention to the significance of early sensory experience in the infant's exploratory contacts with his world, shows how these more complex forms may be shaped by the circumstances under which the simpler antecedents have occurred.

John E. Anderson's description of principles of a developmental theory (1957) go far toward stating the problems of child behavior study in terms of biological principles and models. Of particular value is his treatment of development as *process,* involving the environing conditions. In this, he comes close to the concept advanced by the ecologist which embraces the totality of living and non-living things in the natural world in one vast, complexly interwoven web of relationships (Storer, 1953). Ecological principles have been very useful to at least one current program of research on child behavior (Barker and Wright, 1954).

LIMITATIONS OF DEVELOPMENTAL THEORY

What is the developmental concept in psychology? Does it offer something different, something valuable in the study of human behavior? Two general limitations must be noted—that concepts often depend upon instruments, and that concepts may limit our observations and information.

We have affirmed that the developmental study of behavior processes finds its models in biological studies of growth, and we claim that developmental concepts are useful in organizing many of the ideas and observations of psychology. But often our concepts depend upon our instrumentation. Early concepts of prenatal growth, for instance, based on work with very crude microscopes offered the notion of development as merely increase in size. With the improvement of instruments the process of development was seen to be far more complex, changing in form and organization as well as size. Early attempts in psychology to study mental differences sought energetically for intelligence within the individual differences which could be observed by the simple brass instruments which were psychology's tools of that day. The introduction of problem-solving tests, and the recognition that these too could be useful psychological tools made possible a totally new concept of intelligence. Likewise, Barker and Wright's work (1954) gives us new tools to describe the child's psychological habitat, and promises to re-shape our understanding of the reiterative character of much of the young child's experience. It may be that developmental concepts depend upon a particular meth-odology—the observation of molar behav-ior units with or without the aid of specialized instruments. It is yet too soon to know whether either psychological science or human welfare will profit more from the consideration of behavior in de-scriptive molar units or its conceptualiza-tion in more abstract, derived units. And it may be instructive to observe that the tremendous advances permitted by the atomic theory in physics have not dis-placed or made less useful the principles of so-called classical mechanics.

Furthermore, there is a distinct danger in borrowing concepts, however useful in one field, for application in a quite different area. While it is true that our concepts must wait upon our instru-ments, it is also true that our concepts predetermine the kind of information we will obtain—the order, range, and scope and even the significance of our data. Psy-chological concepts are usually formu-lated in terms or words. Words are used to transfer information. Sometimes they transfer too much or the wrong informa-tion. In using simile and metaphor and in formulating analogies we should rec-ognize that we are doing at best a partial or approximate job of conveying informa-tion. The figurative use of language across phenomenological levels is seductive. The developmentalist is prone to fall into a deep pit, dug by the language of common-sense observations. It is this danger which so deeply impresses those who emphasize the priority of hypothetico-deductive the-ory in scientific work. Yet physicists, who have used the hypothetico-deductive

method with great success, have cautioned (e.g., Oppenheimer, 1956), that for the study of behavior, scientists should not eschew the use of description, induction, and analogy.

But behavior theorists also are sub-ject to this semantic hazard. Terms trans-ferred from one area of experience to another must be reconfirmed empirically in the new area. The proponents of con-ceptual theory in psychology should sub-ject their symbols to an empirical verification, whenever such terms risk carrying extra meanings from the contexts in which the terms are more commonly used. Mathematics and symbolic logic, being purely formal systems, are free from this semantic error, but few behavior or learning theorists have consistently tried to reduce their concepts to such formal symbols, when they have used human subjects.

THE CONCEPT OF DEVELOPMENT IN PSYCHOLOGY

With these general precautions let us take a closer look at concepts of de-velopment as applied to the study of human behavior. Several of these concepts have their origin in biological science.

Modern biology tends to be organis-mic—that is, it regards the living capable of maintaining its existence as a unitary system and of reproducing itself. Like-wise, the developmental concept in psy-chology deals with the human individual as a living system and within an environ-ing system. Although the developmen-talist in psychology pays attention to the complexly patterned character of the stimulus situation, his primary emphasis is on the tendency of the organism to organize its responses in a self-maintaining fashion over major divisions of the life span. He is concerned with continuities in behavior as well as variability among responses. In the case of the human being, he is particularly interested that the individual develops a highly complex symbolic representation of its self.

DEVELOPMENT AND THE OPEN SYSTEM

In studying the living system, the developmentalist regards it as "open." Physical or "closed" systems tend toward an equilibrium which is attained from reversible reactions, usually chemical in nature. Living systems, on the contrary, are said to be never truly in equilibrium, but rather in a steady state (Bertalanffy, 1950) attained by irreversible reactions. By importing complex organic molecules, using their energy and turning back simpler end products to the environment, the living system builds irreversible changes into itself. It is this feature which possibly makes the mechanical model unsuitable for the living organism and accounts for the complexity which so impresses the developmentalist. Once changes are built into the organism, they modify permanently the relationship of the organism to the environment, changing the probabilities that other sorts of changes will or will not occur. Over time, these changes become cumulative and modify the character of the organism's behavior. But this modification occurs slowly; the very complexity of the system gives it behavioral durability without complete rigidity.

Thus, the organism itself becomes a factor in its own development. To say that the organism acts in part as an agent in shaping its developmental course may merely group a number of antecedents and relegate them to the background, un-analyzed. Yet the concept of organism, which by the character of its organization up to a given point of the developmental process serves as an agent to shape the further course of that process, can be an important corrective for the notion that behavior is simply reactive, and situationally determined, the product of forces acting at the moment. The developmentalist tends to see determinism as much more complex. Furthermore, with his emphasis on history, the developmentalist sees deterministic sequences reaching far back in time. To enable himself to move forward in his thinking, the developmentalist, it must be admitted, sometimes invokes concepts which have been called "mentalistic." Biologists and philosophers of science also struggle with such concepts as "determinism" and "purpose." Some such term as "purpose" is difficult to avoid in discussing motivated human behavior.

ORGANIZATION IN THE SYSTEM

The concept of organization is the second major contribution of the developmental point of view in psychology. Behavior is seen as having a complex, diversified structure made up of many parts; that is, any one behavior response is made up of many part movements woven together in complex fashion. Behavior development consists in the modification, the elaboration of this structure. It is not merely additive. The fundamental question is, how do these units combine and change their combination over time? Can this best be described by such terms as differentiation or integration or both? For the developmental view stresses the fact that over long reaches of time the simple paradigms of learning theory seem not to describe adequately the patterned responses which increase in complexity, yet show greater specificity of parts, as an infant and youthful organism matures. This is not the occasion to rehearse the familiar difficulties with the concepts of differentiation and integration. Here the developmentalist's use of figurative language and analogy undoubtedly have created part of the trouble. And although we use these expressions less often now than formerly, the phenomena they were coined to express still perplex us.

Werner has phrased the idea of differentiation as the orthogenetic principle of development (1957), that development "proceeds from a state of relative globality and lack of differentiation to a state of increasing differentiation, articulation, and hierarchic integration." Through development the individual becomes less bound to the particulate stimulus properties. In man, particularly, the language function permits those stimulus properties to extend over time and yet be effective. The developmentalist insists that part of this process of modification is due to neurological and hormonal changes which occur with growth, modifying the sensitiveness of the organism to the immediate context through incorporating the experience traces which general psychology calls learning.

Some biologists insist that function, itself, becomes a factor in differentiation after the organ or part begins to take on its adult use, and that this process continues throughout the life of the individual. Embryologists tend to dispute this position, but for the moment let us affirm it as a principle. If oft repeated experience may be necessary to establish species-characteristic behaviors sometimes thought to be "instinctive," then the organism must have the requisite experience to develop such patterns. In the normal course of growth, the organism does come into contact with the requisite experience. Therefore, deprivation sufficient to disrupt the normal sequence of experience becomes an important constraint on development. We have already noted Piaget's contribution to the importance of the environing stimulation in supporting development. At this juncture, also, Hebb's work and that of Harlow and his colleagues take on particular significance for the developmentalist.

The possibility that complexity itself may become a limited factor in further differentiation and organization must be recognized. John E. Anderson has pointed out (1957) that through learning the organism becomes progressively less multi-potential, more efficient, but also more rigid. The child who spends his hours after school playing baseball rather than practicing music is not as likely to gain skill with an instrument in adult life. Whether or not the baseball skill becomes "significant," in Anderson's sense, depends on still other events which have their own probabilistic character. The changing probabilities occasioned by these irreversible sequences in development thus exercise a cumulative, constraining character on development. No current learning theory adequately considers these "built in" limitations on behavior organization which the developmentalist recognizes.

Another important limitation on development is found in the competition among growth processes within the individual. We see this illustrated functionally in the arrest sometimes occurring in language development at the onset of rapid motor development. Certain phenomena in adolescence studied so thoroughly by Jones and his associates suggest that a similar process may occur in social and attitudinal development during these years. Still another limitation on development is found in the demands made on the individual by his social context. Here the formulations of sex and class role investigated by Havighurst and his associates and students, have a particularly meaningful connotation. Such concepts represent a different order of phenomena than those which relate only to the limits imposed on the subject by a piece of candy, the discrimination box, and the exhortation of the experimenter.

THE PROBLEM OF STAGES OR STATES

In the third place, the developmental point of view deals with the accumulation and organization of experiences into recognizable stages or phases over time. This emphasis on stages, continuous with each other, yet separable and recognizable as delineating phases of development, is distinctive. Applied to ontogeny, measurement of increments of behavioral change in the smallest discriminable units may fail to reveal boundaries or zones between stages or phases. Continuity is the rule. It is chiefly in the description of *characteristics* of behavior that we note the discontinuities in the relationship of the organism to its context which we describe as stages or phases. We use the word characteristics deliberately, rather than properties, because we wish to emphasize that behavior has the quality of organization; it has a character. And many areas of contemporary natural, as well as of social science, are grappling with qualitative features of phenomena which quantitative analysis seems unable to capture.

In the fourth place, the developmental viewpoint places considerable emphasis on the organism as living in a field of forces which has a complex, reticulate character. We have characterized the organism as an open system, one which tends to extract energy from its environment. It also develops energy in its relationship to its environment; it does things *to* the environment. The developmentalist reminds general psychology that this capacity to take from and to do things to the environment is not adequately described by concepts of reaction to or interaction with stimuli, but is best described as *transactional* in character. Such a term perhaps more adequately describes the transfer of energy relationships between the environment and the organism and the fact that both the organism and the environment are modified as they mutually interrelate through time. The field of child *development* has, perhaps, been more ready than child *psychology* to incorporate social and sociological principles and concepts. Child development has emphasized the interpersonal relationship as central to human development, the development of man as a cultural and social being.

CONVERGENCE VS. DIVERGENCE

The developmentalist's interest in the complexity of the context may be of value to psychology at still another point. Irving Langmuir (1943) some years ago classified phenomena into two categories: convergent and divergent. While science in the past has been preoccupied with the convergent, he notes that science in the near future may give considerably more attention to the divergent. Convergent phenomena deal with those events which can be determined if we know the component causes; divergent phenomena are indeterminate—they follow from a single event. They are chain reactions in which the ultimate outcome seems to be all out of proportion to the precipitating or "trigger" factor.

The developmentalist frequently uses the principle of multiple causation in his delineation of the complexity of behavior and of the organism's environing context. In citing this principle he clearly refers to convergent events. But the developmentalist, particularly as he views his longitudinal records, also notes that some behavior events have sequelae which accumulate to significance as these sequelae become incorporated into the experience of the organism; other behavioral events phenomenally similar appear to have no such cumulative significance. The developmentalist speaks of the principle of cumulation of effect to treat a phenomenon with which the experimental psychologist is little concerned, since he seldom follows for any length of time the results of his laboratory experimentation. The developmentalist has an opportunity through the application of the longitudinal method to accumulate the observations that will permit the identification of such "divergent" events in the experience of persons and follow them out in the course of time. This is at the outset more an observational task than an experimental one, except as it takes advantage of experiments of nature.

THE IMPORTANCE OF SYMBOLIC PROCESSES IN DEVELOPMENT

Finally, the developmentalist calls particular attention to the symbolic processes of which the human organism alone is capable. While the symbolic function of signs as a language of expression or of command is found in lower animals, the reference of symbols to content or things is found only in man. This symbolic function is essentially the function of "mind," with which the psychologist has traditionally been concerned. Even when we consider such "mental" activities only as a form of behavior, we must admit that symbolizing behavior constitutes a great share of human behavior.

The developmentalist emphasizes for general psychology the fact that the aspects of the internal environment which we call psychological to distinguish them conveniently from the physiological or biochemical, owe much of their constancy to this symbolizing process. This symbolizing capacity of man enables him to develop a concept of himself and to elaborate this self-concept as he grows more complex over time. Child development has always stressed the significance of language in conceptual processes and in the development of the self-image. The psychoanalytically inclined student of the self-image emphasizes the non-verbal aspects of the body image, such as organic sensations, id drives, and the like. While recognizing the importance of these, the developmental psychologist stresses the significance of the so-called higher mental processes which are implemented and carried forward by this symbolic function. The clinician notes that conflicts between biologic drives and emotionalized social controls lead to adjustmental difficulties, and the developmentalist points out that social controls are mediated by symbol systems, that conflicts between symbol systems can themselves cause trouble and that various performance skills acquired and evaluated within the framework of a complex symbolic system, have distinct adjustive functions.

The capacity to represent experience by symbols and to deal with it apart from its context permits man to some extent to manipulate the future through goal-setting activities. Thus symbols become controlling devices and, in man, are clearly the basis of "purpose" or of the end-serving activities which are so important to social psychologists, clinical psychologists, and educational psychologists. The developmentalist thus inevitably becomes concerned with the "phenomenal world."

The biological capacity of the organism to resist damage and to heal itself from environmental insults appears to have its psychological counterpart. The symbol system, being the basis of the self-image, permits man a good deal of psychological maintenance and self-repair. The developmentalist, along with the phenomenologist, remarks on the capacity of the personality to perceive experience in such a way as to support its organization or integration. Modifications are resisted, particularly if those modifications threaten the unitary character of the personality or its capacity to maintain its integrity over time. We see this behavioral characteristic vividly in young children, denoting it as resistance or negativism when it comes athwart our purpose. It is this concept of behavioral durability which the developmentalist recommends to the clinical worker, or to any one prone to analyze behavior in terms of a simple situational determinism.

We have noted how the organism's history becomes an important determiner of its future development. In man, the symbolic capacity gives his personal history a particular significance. To experimental psychology's concern with present states and functions the developmental viewpoint adds a concern with process, how the organism came to its present state. The developmentalist has a point to make to the educator, the clinician, the social worker when he discusses behavior change or therapy as fundamentally a process of reorganization brought about either by change of external forces or by change of the internal organization or by both.

General psychology has tended to neglect if not actually to deny the possibility that the symbol system can exert a controlling effect on behavior through the representation of goals and their anticipation. The emphasis on drive satisfaction as fundamental to motivation tends to neglect the significance of the symbol system. Reduction of behavior to a system of motives which are controlled solely by manipulation of drives has led us to recognition of possibilities of manipulating man in the mass which have the frightening implications of Orwell's *1984* or Huxley's *Brave New World*.

Increasingly we are coming to see that the scientist cannot pursue the truth with indifference to its application. Vivas (1950) has arrestingly called to our attention the problem of ethics in science and Redfield (1953) unashamedly states that he proposes, as anthropologist, to carry on his scientific work as a valuing human being. The child development worker need, then, scarcely apologize for his applied bent. Children matter very much to a vast multitude of parents, teachers, and others. What the parent or teacher believes about the contribution by the child himself to his learnings as compared with the contribution by the stimulus situations matters very much to what the adult does with the child and eventually to what the child acquires.

Developmental psychology, being concerned with the complex character of the organism conceived as system, with its intricate interrelationships with environing systems, is not likely to yield a tightly knit theory such as the behavior theorist attempts. But developmental psychology, with its sensitivity to phenomena of growth and change, can continue to call attention to phenomena which behavior theorists need to recognize and which they often ignore, can offer concepts which help order some of the complex aspects of psychology at a molar level, and can help keep a psychology of human behavior in perspective with human life.

REFERENCES

ANDERSON, J. E. "Dynamics of Development: Systems in Process" in *The Concept of Development*, D. B. Harris, editor. Minneapolis: University of Minnesota Press, 1957.

ARBER, AGNES. *The Mind and the Eye.* Cambridge: Cambridge Univ. Press, 1954.

BALDWIN, A. L. *Behavior and Development in Childhood.* New York; Dryden Press, 1955.

BARKER, R. G. & WRIGHT, H. F. *Midwest and Its Children.* Evanston: Row, Peterson & Co., 1954.

BERTALANFFY, L. VON. "The theory of open systems in physics and biology." *Science,* 1950, III: 23–29.

LANGMUIR, IRVING. "Science, common sense, and decency." *Science,* 1943, 97: 1–7.

MANDLER, G. and KESSEN, W. *The Language of Psychology.* N. Y., Wiley, 1959.

McCANDLESS, B. R. & SPIKER, C. C. "Experimental research in child psychology." *Child Developm.,* 1956, 27: 75–80.

OPPENHEIMER, R. "Analogy in Science." *Amer. Psychologist,* 1956, 11: 127–35.

PIAGET, J. *The Construction of Reality in the Child.* New York: Basic Books, 1954.

REDFIELD, ROBERT. *The Primitive World and Its Transformations.* Ithaca: Cornell University Press, 1953.

RUSSELL, W. A. "An Experimental Psychology of Development: Pipe Dream or Possibility?" in *The Concept of Development*, D. B. Harris, editor, Minneapolis: University of Minnesota Press, 1957.

SEARS, R. R. "Identification as a Form of Behavioral Development" in *The Concept of Development*, D. B. Harris, editor, Minneapolis: University of Minnesota Press, 1957.

SINNOTT, E. W. *The Biology of the Spirit.* New York: Viking Press, 1955.

SOMMERHOFF, G. *Analytical Biology.* New York: Oxford University Press, 1950.

STORER, J. H. *The Web of Life.* New York: Devin-Adair, 1953.

TINBERGEN, N. "Psychology and Ethology as Supplementary Parts of a Science of Behavior" in B. Schaffner, editor, *Group Process,* pp. 75–167. New York: Josiah Macy Foundation, 1955.

VIVAS, ELISEO. *The Moral Life and the Ethical Life.* Chicago: University of Chicago Press, 1950.

WERNER, H. *Comparative Psychology of Mental Development.* (Rev.) Chicago: Follett, 1948.

WERNER, H. "The Organismic Concept of Development" in *The Concept of Development*, D. H. Harris, editor, Minneapolis: University of Minnesota Press, 1957.

EXPERIMENTAL RESEARCH
IN CHILD PSYCHOLOGY

BOYD R. MC CANDLESS
CHARLES C. SPIKER

FROM THE LITERATURE of child psychology, and from discussions with child psychologists throughout the country, the writers have obtained the definite impression that child psychologists are concerned and somewhat troubled about the present and future status of their field. In particular, two deficiencies in the area appear to be arousing consternation. The first concern has to do with an alleged deficiency in the quality and quantity of research conducted by child psychologists, and the second with an alleged lack of interest in theory on the part of child psychologists. The writers agree that these two deficiencies exist. Rarely, however, have they observed the two discussed in relation to each other. It seems to them that there is actually a close connection between the type of research that has predominated in the field and the failure of theory to develop. It is the purpose of this paper to attempt to show what this connection is.

First, perhaps, a few comments should be made concerning the essential characteristics of scientific theories. A scientific theory consists of (*a*) a set of clearly defined terms that refer to empirical phenomena; (*b*) a set of basic principles (axioms) that relate many of the concepts to each other; and (*c*) a further set of empirical laws that may be deduced, according to the rules of mathe-

matics and/or formal logic, from the basic principles. For the scientist, explanation consists in the deduction of the phenomenon to be explained from the set of basic principles. In this strict interpretation of scientific theory, it is clear that neither child psychology nor general psychology has thus far met with more than moderate success in theory construction.

There are no logical rules to specify what characteristics the axioms of a theory must have, other than that additional laws must be deducible from them. There are, however, some empirical considerations that are suggested by examining the histories of other, more mature sciences. For one thing, the axioms of mature scientific theories have contained concepts that refer to basic variables. The discovery of which variables are basic demands that the scientist isolate, in some manner, the independent variable in such a way that he can discover if and how it affects the dependent variable. The usual method of isolating the independent variables is by means of the scientific experiment. The scientist sets up an experiment in which the independent variable is under his control and manipulation. He then systematically varies the independent variable and determines whether or not, and how, it affects the dependent system. It is, of course, not always possible or necessary to manipulate the independent variable experimentally. The most extensive use of a non-manipulative method of isolating

Reprinted by permission from *Child Development*, 1956, *27*, 78–80.

the independent variables can be found in classical astronomy, where none of the variables is subject to the scientist's manipulations. It is interesting to note, however, that Newton's theoretical integration of terrestrial and celestial mechanics made extensive use of Galileo's experimental data on falling bodies, and it is improbable that he would have invented his concept of mass if he had not had the Galileo data available.

While a relevant variable can be isolated without the experimenter's having control over it, the difficulty of this procedure is vastly increased as the number of relevant variables affecting the dependent system is increased. That a very large number of variables affects the behavior of the living organism is a fact that has long been recognized. And if several variables, each of which is a potentially relevant variable, are simultaneously present, the experimenter cannot possibly say which has affected his dependent variable, nor to what degree.

Examination of a list of "independent" variables in child psychology leads one to the conclusions that (a) it is often difficult to say which are the dependent and which are the independent variables (e.g., correlations among various tests or other response measures); (b) where it is possible to make a distinction, it is often clear that the "independent" variables cannot possibly be either manipulated or isolated from other possibly relevant variables (e.g., chronological age, level of parent education, racial or nationality background, intelligence, socio-economic status, etc.); and (c) in many cases, the so-called independent variables were never meant to be anything more than a name for a whole host of potentially relevant variables (e.g., chronological

age, sex, school grade, delinquency, etc.). It was undoubtedly in reaction to the selection of such independent variables that Lewin made his persistent pleas for the study of genotypic rather than phenotypic variables in child behavior. For Lewin, genotypic variables were worthy candidates for inclusion in the axioms of theory; phenotypic variables were those that had to be accounted for in terms of the theory.

Another useful consideration in the construction of a theory arises from the recognition that somewhere among the axioms of the theory there must be some that instruct the scientist about the analysis of more complex phenomena than he has yet encountered experimentally. The scope of a theory—that is, the number and variety of phenomena that it can explain—is closely dependent on the existence of these composition laws among its axioms. Some of the best, and simplest, examples of such laws in psychology can be found in current conditioning theories of learning, where there are laws that specify how conditioning principles can be made to apply in situations in which conditioning and extinction occur at the same time, in which two or more stimuli conditioned to the same response are presented simultaneously, in which two or more stimuli evoking incompatible responses are given together, and so on. Such laws are almost always discovered through series of experiments designed to discover the limits of previous generalizations and to isolate the conditions under which previous generalizations actually hold.

It is indeed rare that one finds empirical laws in child psychology that show any promise of successful use as composition laws in the construction of theory. It seems doubtful, for example, that any-one expects the concept of chronological age to be among the basic concepts in any theory of behavior. Rather, we recognize that changes in behavior associated with chronological age are to be explained in terms of amount of previous learning experiences; of physiological and anatom-ical changes; of changes in the nature of social rewards, punishments, and sta-tus; and of other variables that are also more or less incidentally related to time since birth. In spite of this, the research literature reports more relationships of behavior to age than to any other vari-able except, possibly, intelligence.

It seems to the writers that the fun-damental need of child psychology—the development of promising theories—has been greatly handicapped by child psy-chologists' tendencies to avoid experi-mental research. In stating this, there is no implication that laws discovered in nonexperimental research are useless; no responsible scientist scoffs at well-estab-lished laws. Rather, the objection is to the imbalance. Child psychologists may well look to general psychology for an object lesson. As limited as the theories in gen-eral psychology are, compared to what they will undoubtedly be some day, it is not difficult to see the tremendous strides that the field has made in theory construc-tion during the last 25 years. Examination of the empirical bases of these theories shows that they have been obtained from experimentation in which relevant vari-ables have been isolated and controlled.

The writers were trained and have worked as child psychologists, and believe they understand the factors that have led child psychologists away from experi-mental research. Carefully planned re-search requires time—time which many child psychologists do not have because the tendency of their employers is to re-quire heavy teaching and service loads of them. Experimental research worthy of publication often requires numerous unpublishable preliminary experiments, which require still more time. On the other hand, it has been the experience of the writers that it is a relatively simple matter for an ordinary insightful research worker to take several tests, administer them to a group of subjects, obtain the intercorrelations, and produce some cor-relation coefficients that are statistically significant. In this same connection, it is usually easier to arrange with school ad-ministrators to obtain subjects for two or three hours of time from total classes than it is to arrange to have the subjects on an individual basis for a half-an-hour or so, even more so when a frequently illusory appearance of immediate applica-tion of results exists.

Another important factor is prece-dent. We have in mind not only a social or professional reluctance to stray from a trodden path, but also the additional work that is required to do so. Only a few fruitful experimental apparatus and pro-cedures have been worked out for use with children and many of these have been used so rarely that little useful normative information is available. Thus, the child psychologist who is inclined to be experi-mental must first invent appropriate ap-paratus and develop workable procedures and instructions. A similar difficulty arises when the potential experimenter attempts to select a problem to investigate. Few of the textbooks and articles in child psy-chology can be said to be rich sources for experimental hypotheses. On the con-trary, most of them are preoccupied with the application of available knowledge.

The problems that suggest themselves to the research worker tend to be concerned with immediate, practical situations. This tendency is reinforced by the nature of the duties of the typical child psychologist. He has usually been hired primarily to teach and to perform service. The types of problems that lend themselves to experimental investigation, under such employment and service exigencies, do not seem "big" enough to him, i.e., he can see no immediate prospect of their helping practically to serve society.

All the reasons for our failure to have produced a wealth of experimental research, unfortunately, are not as socially acceptable as those just mentioned. The fact is that child psychologists as a group, not unlike clinical psychologists as a group, have not been trained to do experimental research. The literature testifies to our naivete with respect to statistical techniques, the philosophy of science, research methods, and understanding of theory construction. Our statistical analyses are often outmoded and otherwise inadequate; our reasoning is sometimes confused and our concepts are often vaguely defined; our control groups are all too frequently poorly conceived; our notions of what constitutes scientific theory are most unsophisticated.

In order to improve our scientific status, there are several concrete steps that we may take. First, we should stop marking time, waiting for a brilliant theorist to appear who will organize our data into a satisfactory theory. Only a mind sufficiently clairvoyant to intuit the missing basic laws could possibly integrate the data we have available. Second, we can well look to the relatively more sophisticated field of general psychology for suggestions concerning apparatus, procedures, and hypotheses. There are many techniques that have been used successfully with adults and infrahuman organisms that can be relatively easily modified for use with younger children. It is the writers' belief, too, that current theories in general psychology are replete with hypotheses for the test of which children are not only satisfactory subjects, but *ideal* subjects. Those of us who have dealt with both children and adults know, for example, that the purpose of an experiment is more easily disguised from children than from college sophomores; that learning problems for children can be much simpler (and perhaps the laws discovered more basic) than corresponding problems for adults; that the learning and functions of language can be more fruitfully studied with children than with adults; that children are the ideal subjects for the study of imitation learning; that children can be more easily excited, frustrated, and angered in an experimental situation than can adults; and so on. Several recent experiments with children as subjects have been among the most widely quoted in psychological literature. It is not to the credit of our profession that many of these have been conducted by persons not formally trained in child psychology.

Third, while some of us can, and should, deliberately shirk our applied, clinical responsibilities, there is probably little that most of us can do about the applied and teaching demands that our positions place upon our time. But those of us who are in a position to do so can spend some of our energies in placing well-trained students in positions that both require and allow time for research. Evidence indicates that there is a supply of relatively well-paid positions of this type at the present time. Furthermore, there is likely to be an increase in the number of such positions, since many institutions have become aware that they are not producing psychological research with children and that a fruitful research field may be opened up if they can find properly trained personnel.

Fourth, the availability of good research positions will not help our field if we do not have properly trained personnel to fill them. While there are limits to the extent to which those of us who are several years out of graduate school can improve our personal research competence, there is much that we can do for our students. We can provide them with graduate curricula that include adequate training in statistics, considerable work in the philosophy of science, and thorough familiarity with current theories and with both current and past research in general psychology.

The writers also think that there are more economical ways of achieving familiarity with the conventional content of child psychology and development than have been employed by training centers traditionally. Lectures can be pointed toward organizing and evaluating, rather than endlessly summarizing factual material. Theoretical hunches and fractional ordering concepts about the material can serve as both an interesting and an integrating framework for students, who can then read what portion of the vast accumulation of normative and developmental material they or their instructors believe to be essential. From such an instructional approach, research ideas may even germinate. The writers suspect that less emphasis on applied duties may profitably (or at least without harm) be given to graduates in training, and that instead of being drilled and practicumed for every imaginable future professional contingency, they may be trained to *think* and to react flexibly and adaptively instead of as well drilled automatons. We feel it is vital to the field that we instill in our students the *fundamental* importance of doing experimental research with children.

Given properly trained personnel who conduct sound experimental research on problems oriented toward theory construction, our contemporary concern for the deficiency in theoretical integration within our field can be constructively put to use and eventually allayed.

A SYSTEMATIC APPROACH TO AN EXPERIMENTAL ANALYSIS OF YOUNG CHILDREN [1]

SIDNEY W. BIJOU

FROM TIME TO TIME someone makes a persuasive appeal for a systematic laboratory approach to child behavior and development (4, 8, 11). Such pleas invariably evoke sympathetic comments, yet little has been done in initiating programs of this nature. The current situation is such that a re-emphasis of this need and a proposed approach would not be inappropriate.

At present, research interest in genetic psychology is rapidly moving away from correlating objective descriptions of behavior with age, and toward searching for relevant, antecedent conditions of social behavior. This much-to-be-desired shift in interest is, unfortunately being accompanied by the belief that such studies, to be adequate and meaningful, must be made in the natural setting. And, when it is impractical to make the required observations, methods are employed which are believed "to estimate" the variables and their relationships. Hence, most approaches involve controlled or uncontrolled field observations, modified clinical techniques and procedures, psychometric devices, or some combination of the three. These research procedures will undoubtedly produce information suggestive of pertinent functional relationships. However, it is regrettable that those involved in the movement devaluate the contributions that may be made by a systematic laboratory approach.

A case can be made for a systematic laboratory approach if on no other basis than what it has accomplished in other fields of science and in other branches of psychology. As a matter of fact, the method has already proven its worth in child psychology. It was widely employed during the normative-topographic era that is passing. Perhaps we should repeat many of the "normative laboratory experiments", but this time observe not only the behavior "as it unfolds", but also the independent, manipulatable conditions.

The purpose of this paper is to describe and briefly discuss a promising laboratory method for the systematic study of the behavior of pre-school children. A number of considerations influenced the development of the technique. First it was believed the method should involve a relatively simple situation, one allowing for considerable control of the experimental variables. Second, it should require the child to make a relatively uncomplicated voluntary response, the frequency of which could be automatically and objectively recorded. Third, it should be adequate to explore problems sug-

[1] This research has been supported in part by a grant from the Agnes Anderson Foundation. The author wishes to express his appreciation to Mrs. Deborah Leukel and Mrs. Joanne Tobin for serving as experimenters.

Reprinted by permission from *Child Development*, 1955, *26*, 161–168.

gested by laboratory studies with animals as well as those growing out of "field" studies with children.[2] Perhaps the procedures developed do not incorporate to the fullest degree all of these requirements; nevertheless, they have served as excellent guideposts.

The operant or instrumental conditioning situation of the type described by Skinner (13) suggested a promising beginning point. There are a handful of instrumental conditioning studies with children (1, 3, 5, 6, 7, 12, 14), which, though encouraging, are not particularly helpful in establishing a versatile technique. For the most part, the investigators were interested only in demonstrating that selected hypotheses from animal studies hold for young children. Furthermore, these studies, while employing similar learning concepts, were not intended to be systematic in the sense of working out and standardizing the relationships among experimental conditions and procedures. For example, the kinds of reinforcers varied widely. One experimenter used party mints, another chocolate bits, and another plastic balls. No one has yet attempted to determine the relative effectiveness of classes of reinforcers for children at the various developmental stages.

Our preliminary work, therefore, was concerned with evaluating types of reinforcements (appearance of a toy dog, candy, balls, pleasant sounding tones, trinkets, etc.), various kinds of responses (push buttons and lights, peg boards and lights, pump handles, dropping a ball in a hole, etc.), and ways of setting up experimental procedures. From these efforts emerged the apparatus and the procedures described below.

APPARATUS [3]

The apparatus, shown schematically in Figures 1 and 2, is the core of a standard experimental situation. Like most operant conditioning devices, it consists of three parts—a response mechanism, a reinforcer dispenser, and a recording device.

To make a response, the child simply takes a ball from a receptacle and drops it into a hole. The ball, a Spaulding handball, is always presented in the lower tube, and the situation is such that it can be dropped only into the upper hole. Findings from exploratory investigations indicated that this type of response would be practical with children. The task was simple and so obvious that the child could almost instruct himself. The device also provided for control over the frequency of responding, since a response could not be made until the ball appeared. The appearance of the ball thus served as a discriminative stimulus. Finally, such a mode of responding could readily be adopted to study a variety of problems, (a) by merely varying the number of receiving holes, and (b) by changing the time between presentations of the ball. The former can be accomplished by interchanging the panel with one hole, as shown in the diagram, with others containing two or more receiving holes; the latter by adjusting the timing mechanism which detains the ball inside of the box.

[2] Relationships based on animal studies need to be tested with human subjects before reasonable generalizations may be made; likewise, relationships suggested by field studies with children require evaluation under laboratory conditions to permit greater control of the relevant antecedent variables.

[3] The apparatus was constructed in the Psychology Department Shop by Mr. George E. Price. The author wishes to express his appreciation to Mr. Price for his many valuable and ingenious suggestions.

Thus with two modifications in the response mechanism the apparatus may be adapted for problems of learning, discrimination, response maintenance, and problem solving. It should be emphasized that we have developed a controlled operant rather than a free operant situation.

The device controlling time between trials also starts and stops the machine which delivers reinforcers. Essentially the dispenser is a motor-driven bicycle-type chain on which are attached hooks five-eighths of an inch apart. "Loading" consists of hanging plastic trinkets [4] on the hooks. Each time the ball strikes the delaying mechanism the chain is moved forward one unit, and the trinket on the hook under the front bearing falls into the chute below. The final destination of the incentive is a covered, clear plastic box placed at the front edge of the table to the left of the child. The delivery of a trinket is accompanied by two distinct auditory stimuli—a brief hum of the motor, and the sound of the trinket sliding down the metal chute and striking the side of the receiving box.

The type of dispenser employed proved to be eminently suitable for studying reinforcement and extinction under a diversity of conditions. For instance, by using two dispensers in series it is possible to set up an almost infinite number of intermittent schedules. It is also possible to study the amount of reinforcement per trial by varying the number of trinkets delivered, and the quality of reinforcement by using candy or other edibles in place of trinkets.

A word about the trinkets. Nowlis and Nowlis (8), have stated that the

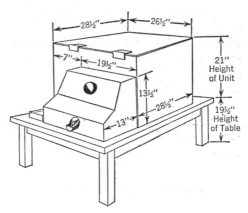

Figure 1. Exterior view of the apparatus.

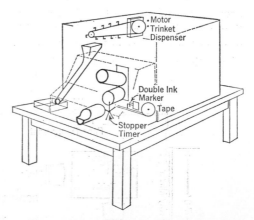

Figure 2. Cutaway view of the apparatus showing the timing device, dispenser, and marker system.

multi-color and form plastic trinkets (the kind seen in the omnipresent gum-ball machines) serve admirably as reinforcers for preschool children. Our experience confirms this. These "toys" or "charms" have an almost universal appeal for boys and girls between the ages of two and seven, and when "mixtures" are used interest remains high during an experiment and between experimental periods. They have the additional obvious advantage of

[4] These trinkets may be obtained from the Viking Company, 530 Golden Gate Avenue, San Francisco 2, California.

avoiding problems associated with edible incentives. The use of these trinkets as they relate to age, sex, socio-economic status, and to other types of incentives, comprises a block of studies that need to be worked out.

Responses are recorded on a polygraph. Paper tape, three-eighths of an inch wide, moves under two ink-writing pens at the rate of one millimeter per second. One marker indicates the number of responses and intervals between responses; the other records the reinforcements. A switch controlling the polygraph motor is on a 15-foot extension cord so as to be readily available to the experimenter.

EXPERIMENTAL PROCEDURE

As in experimental work with animals (2), it is highly desirable, and even necessary, to have a standard preparation procedure for child subjects. This preparation serves to reduce the influence of emotional reaction to a new situation on the behavior to be observed, and to minimize marked differences in rapport that may be established between the child and the experimenter. (Further systematic, objective evidence on this interrelationship would be of tremendous value.) Preliminary operations consist of the experimenter's becoming acquainted with all children in the nursery school, "playing" with the subject immediately preceding the experimental "run", and orienting the child to the experimental task and conditions prior to allowing the first response.

In preparing for a study, the experimenter, a young woman, first makes herself known to the children by watching them at play in the yard and in the school rooms. Soon she is regarded as a member of the staff or as a teacher-in-training. When a child is selected to be a subject, the experimenter approaches him and invites him to come and "play with some toys". On entering the laboratory, she suggests that the child sit at a table upon

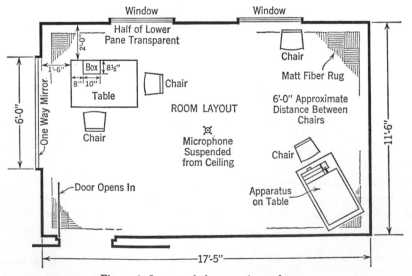

Figure 3. Layout of the experimental room.

which is a plastic dog and a tin dog house.[5] After a few introductory remarks, the experimenter puts the dog in the house and shows the child that tapping on the table will make the dog shoot out. She next demonstrates that the dog will also pop out if called by his name, "Sparky". The subject is then encouraged "to make the dog come out". Once the child takes charge of the toy, play is permitted until he has made the dog come out at least four times. A delay of 15 seconds or more between insertion and pop-out is the criterion for termination of warm-up activity.

The next step consists of inviting the subject to the table with the apparatus. After he is settled in the juvenile chair in front of the apparatus, a plywood screen is removed and the experimenter proceeds with the orientation and instructions. She shows a handful of trinkets and says: "You can get some of these to keep, to take home with you." She hands the child the ball and says: "When you put the ball in there (pointing to the upper opening) some of these toys will come down here (pointing to the covered plastic box). The ball will come out here again. You can put it back into the top hole as many times as you like. We will leave all the toys that come down in the box until we are finished, and are ready to go." The experimenter takes a seat six feet to the rear of the subject and offers no further suggestions or instructions.

Comments and questions addressed to her are reacted to in a pleasant non-directive fashion, e.g., "You think the thing is broken." "You think no more will

come out." When the experiment has been completed the receiving box is opened, the trinkets are given to the child, and the child is returned to his group.

Required variations in manipulatable conditions during an experiment, such as running extinction trials without the sound of the motor hum, are accomplished by flipping silently operating switches on a small control panel concealed under the experimenter's chair.

In addition to measures of frequency of responding, a second measure of behavior has been attempted (9, 10). To record emotional behavior, an observer behind a one-way screen made judgements every ten seconds, describing activity level. Each judgement is subdivided into verbal-motor components and direction of behavior.

To date, two groups of studies have been conducted. The first series has been designed to explicate some of the aspects of the situation, e.g., the reinforcing value of putting the ball in the hole, the relationship of age and sex to performance and extinction, and the effects of different lengths of extinction periods. The other group of studies has been concerned with exploring some functional relationship suggested by animal experiments, e.g., the relationships between number of responses and resistance to extinction; percentages of intermittent reinforcement and resistance to extinction; and the effect of a secondary reinforcing stimulus on extinction.

To summarize. The position is taken that a systematic laboratory approach can offer significant contributions to a scientific analysis of child behavior and development. On the basis of this conviction, a laboratory methodology has been developed involving a simple man-

[5] The toy is made by Byron Products, Western Distributors, Pacific Trading Company, Los Angeles, California.

ual operant, trinkets for reinforcers, and a device for recording response frequencies. The experimental procedures are such that findings and "hunches" from experiments with animals and studies with human subjects may be evaluated in a laboratory setting. Although systematic exploration could profitably begin with any of a number of interesting problems, the present program is concerned with conditioned reinforcement since most of the current viewpoints on child behavior and development rest heavily on this concept. Initial efforts have been devoted to analyzing the consequences of different schedules of reinforcement and the influence of two auditory stimuli that accompany reinforcement during training.

REFERENCES

1. Caditz, S. B.   A study of partial reinforcement of a lever pressing response in young children. Unpublished master's dissertation, Univer. of Washington, 1953.
2. Ferster, C. B.   The use of the free operant in the analysis of behavior. *Psychol. Bull.* 1953, *50*, 263–274.
3. Grosslight, J. H. & Child, I. L.   Persistence as a function of previous experience of failure followed by success. *Amer. J. Psychol.* 1947, *60*, 378–387.
4. Keller, F. S.   Animals and children. *Child Developm.* 1950, *21*, 7–12.
5. Lambert, W. W., Lambert, E. C., & Watson, P. D.   Acquisition and extinction of an instrumental response in the token-reward situation. *J. exp. Psychol.*, 1953, *45*, 321–326.
6. Lasko, A. A.   A theoretical study of partial reinforcement within the framework of Rotter's social learning theory of personality. Unpublished master's thesis, Ohio State Univer., 1950.
7. Mitrano, A. J.   Principles of conditioning in human goal behavior. *Psychol. Monogr.*, 1939, *51*, No. 4 (Whole No. 230).
8. Nowlis, V., & Nowlis, Helen H.   Child psychology. *Annu. Rev. Psychol.*, 1952, *3*, 1–28.
9. Pumroy, D. K.   The effects of intermittent reinforcement on resistance to extinction and emotional behavior in preschool children. Unpublished doctor's dissertation, Univer. of Washington, 1954.
10. Pumroy, Shirley S.   The effects of amount of reinforcement on resistance to extinction and emotional behavior with preschool children. Unpublished doctor's dissertation, Univer. of Washington, 1954.
11. Sears, R. R.   Child psychology. In W. Denis (Ed.), *Current trends in psychology*. Pittsburgh: Univer. of Pittsburgh Press, 1947.
12. Siegel, P. S. & Foshee, J. G.   The law of primary reinforcement in children. *J. exp. Psychol.*, 1953, *45*, 12–14.
13. Skinner, B. F.   *The behavior of organisms*. New York: Appleton-Century-Crofts, 1938.
14. Warren, A. B., & Brown, R. H.   Conditioned operant response phenomenon in children. *J. gen. Psychol.*, 1943, *28*, 184–207.

THE CONCEPT OF INTELLIGENCE
AND THE PHILOSOPHY OF SCIENCE

CHARLES C. SPIKER
BOYD R. MC CANDLESS

A CAREFUL APPLICATION of the principles of the philosophy of science to controversial issues within an area of an empirical science has often proved clarifying. These methodological (logical) analyses have occasionally demonstrated that some of the questions which scientists considered appropriate for experimental attack could actually be resolved only after linguistic analysis. The major contribution of any such analysis is the reformulation of some of the traditional questions. The present paper attempts such an analysis of the psychological concept, "intelligence."

The paper is presented in two parts. The first contains a summary of the important points, relevant to this analysis, of the frame of reference within which the writers evaluate the methodological problems of their science. Writers of the philosophical school of "logical positivism," or "scientific empiricism," have written explicitly on the methodology of psychology, formulating principles that may be regarded as the fundamental principles of neo-behaviorism (2, 3, 5, 8). The second part deals with the application of these philosophical principles to problems associated with the investigation of human intelligence.

Reprinted by permission from *Psychological Review*, 1954, *61*, 255–266.

THE METHODOLOGICAL FRAME OF REFERENCE

The principles that scientists have followed in the formulation of their concepts have been made explicit by philosophers as a result of their analyses of the language of science, of which the language of the physical sciences is the prototype. The language of science is a physicalistic language; that is, the referents of the descriptive terms occurring in scientific discourse are physical objects or events, their properties, and their relationships. There is, therefore, implicit in the philosophy of scientists a basic assumption regarding a "real world." The scientist assumes that there is a blueness "out there" when he has a sensation of blue. This "naive realism" of the scientist is not to be confused with any metaphysical viewpoints with reference to the nature of "reality." The scientist's position in this respect may be regarded as a convenient working assumption. It is simply another way of stating his belief that the data with which he deals have sufficient generality and significance to warrant further study.

Concepts that have been accepted in science and have proved useful for theoretical reasons, and for more pragmatic reasons as well, can be defined so that they are reducible to very simple

43

terms, which have been designated by Carnap as *primitive predicates* (6). This class of terms is distinguished in part by the fact that they cannot be further reduced, in the sense that they cannot be given *linguistic* definitions; understanding of such terms can be obtained only through acquaintance with their referents. While philosophers have not troubled to delimit this class of terms categorically, its important characteristics may be given by a few examples. There are the property or quality terms such as "blue," "green," "bright," "hard," etc.; the relational terms such as "to the left of," "above," "between," "brighter than," etc.; and, of course, a subclass of terms naming physical objects and events.

We may point out, parenthetically, that in scientific practice, concepts are not ordinarily reduced to (defined in terms of) such simple concepts. This would be laborious and, except for certain formal purposes, unprofitable. Words that may be reduced relatively easily to such a level are used without explicit definitions. Let us use the term "abstract" to refer to words whose definitional chains are long in the sense that numerous statements are required for defining them solely in terms of the primitive predicates. We may then describe scientific *practice* in this regard as that which utilizes explicit definitions only for the more abstract concepts; (even in these cases, the reduction process is carried down only so far as is necessary to avoid serious ambiguity). Such a statement, and rightly so, does not specify a crucial or necessary length of the definitional chain in order that the concept thereby defined be an abstract one.

If each acceptable term in a scientific language can be defined with reference to such terms as "blue," "above," "hard," etc., then the concepts in science refer in the last analysis to things that are *immediately observable* in a very simple sense of this italicized phrase. It is just this characteristic of scientific language which is intended when it is said that the language of science is a physicalistic language or that it has physicalistic verification basis.

The formation of scientific concepts may be best understood through an exposition of the grammatical (logical) form of definitions in general, technically known as "definitions in use." Conventionally, one finds on the left side of an equation-like arrangement of two sentences a sentence in which the term to be defined occurs. This sentence ordinarily states one of the simplest things that can be said about the term to be defined. For example, we may wish to define the concept "length." On the left side we may write the simple statement, "the length of this table is five feet." In the more important definitions, there is on the right-hand side of the definition a statement (or set of statements) that presents a relatively complex set of interrelationships among other terms, typically of the form: "If . . . then - - - ." The two statements, the one on the right and the one on the left, are then connected by a symbol which carries the meaning, "means by verbal agreement the same as." If we fill in the right-hand side of the definition, the above statement about length means the same as: "*If* one takes a foot rule and repeatedly places it so that there is no gap and no overlapping of one placement and another, and if each placement is parallel to the edge of the table, *then* five such placements may be made between the edges perpendicular to the direction of the placements." The meaning of length is not explicitly carried, of course, unless the right-hand statement contains only terms which are already meaningful.

The groundwork has now been laid for an exposition of the phrase that has become so popular among psychologists—"operational definition." Bergmann (2) has pointed out that this term refers to nothing more complex than that science requires all terms occurring on the right-hand side of a definition to be, or to be reducible to, the primitive concepts we have already discussed. This requirement may be designated the *empiricist meaning criterion*, thereby avoiding some of the confusions which have become associated with "operationism." In order for a word to be meaningful by this criterion, it must be reducible, in the sense discussed above, to primitive predicates.

Obviously, this discussion describes an ideal procedure. One may look vainly through some introductory physics textbooks for an *explicit* definition of the concept of "mass." What one ordinarily finds are several statements about mass, any one of which might according to our discussion of meaning, be construed as a definition. This fact points up the need for considering the second methodological principle concerning scientific concepts. Analyses of scientifically acceptable concepts show that these concepts not only meet the empiricist's meaning criterion, but in addition are lawfully related to other meaningful concepts—such relationships being exemplified by statements of the form: "If A, then B," where A and B are both meaningful concepts. In general, the more relationships a given concept has to other concepts, the more fruitful or useful it is said to be. Thus, in physics, the concepts of time, force, energy, mass,

distance, etc. are extremely useful since they enter in some form into all laws of mechanics.

Many discussions of operationism have been found objectionable by some scientists—particularly by some psychologists—because they have not emphasized this second aspect of scientific concepts. The scientist may insist that his term "means" more than just what is contained on the right-hand side of any definition of it. To anticipate later discussions, he may insist that intelligence means more than just an IQ from a given test: a high "amount" for a given individual means that this individual will probably do well in school, is probably good at arithmetic, is not likely to be found in an institution for the feebleminded, probably has parents with high average school achievement, and the like. The present formulation does not rob the scientist of the richness of his "meaning." This *additional* meaning is carried by the statements of relationships between the unambiguously defined concept and the other concepts (i.e., school achievement, institutionalization, level of parental education, etc.). Conveniently, Bergmann (2) distinguishes between meaning I (formal, operational meaning) and meaning II (significance, usefulness, fruitfulness). A concept that does not meet the first criterion cannot meet the second. A concept that meets only the first criterion will eventually be discarded as useless.

Since scientists are usually not so formal and explicit as are philosophers about such matters, one frequently finds in a scientific discipline useful concepts for which formal definitions have not been given. In some such cases, it is possible to formulate two or more equally correct and equally simple definitions.

The question of which definition to select for a given purpose is therefore a matter of convenience. It is not consistent, *in a formal sense*, to speak of alternative definitions for a concept, since an unambiguous term can have only a single definition within the same context; but one may speak loosely of a number of concepts in science for which, in practice, several definitions are possible. This fact merely points out that it often happens in science that two or more grammatically different definitions may define concepts which are so highly interrelated that it is convenient to give each set of referents the same name. In other words, the relationships between each of these formally different concepts on the one hand, and other concepts on the other, are, within acceptable limits of error, identical. It makes little difference for most purposes which concept is used. A case in point is the concept of electric current, which may be quantitatively defined in terms of the deflection of a magnetic needle, the amount of heat generated, or the amount of silver deposited in a solution of nitrate of silver. When such clearly invariant relationships are found, it is often tempting (and, perhaps, of heuristic value) to speak and think of the concept involved as if it referred to a "thing" ontologically independent of all the sets of operations, the description of any one of which could serve as the definition of the concept. It is usually implied in such discussions that the "thing" itself cannot be directly sensed, but that we "infer" its existence from the observable evidence (i.e., from the pattern of invariant relationships among the operationally defined concepts). Hence, it would be said, we may *measure* electricity, even though we cannot directly sense it, in much the same way that we might assemble evidence concerning the existence and size of a hidden room in a house by comparing external measurements of the building with measurements of the observable rooms in it. It should be apparent from what has been said previously that this is merely a manner of speaking, and like many metaphorical expressions, generates little confusion unless one begins to accept its literal meaning. In the latter event, scientifically sterile arguments arise as to what the "thing" would look like if we *could* directly sense it, or as to what the "correct" way is to measure (define) it.

It frequently happens in the development of a science that a word appearing in the everyday, common-sense language is taken into the language of that discipline and is given a new definition. In most such cases, the new meaning is in some sense similar to the meaning of the word in the ordinary language. The words "force" and "mass," for example, occurred in the English language before they were utilized in Newtonian physics. Most high school students of introductory physics learn to distinguish between the two meanings such words have, and little confusion seems to result. In the newer sciences, however, attempts are often made to convey factual information through the use of words from the ordinary language without explicit redefinition of such concepts. In extreme cases, it appears that some scientists, particularly those in the social sciences, conceive of science as a technique for "measuring" the things to which many of the words in the ordinary language presumably refer. While it is not the writers' intention to depreciate the usefulness of common-sense knowledge, they wish to point out that if it had no limitations, scientific knowledge would not be necessary. Also, if the language of common sense were sufficiently precise, it would be unnecessary to study mathematics and logic. In many cases it appears that attempts to quantify (redefine) words from the natural language are uneconomical. Many such concepts refer in a vague way to highly complex sets of interrelations among distinguishable phenomena. It appears that the most economical way to study such patterns would be to define several concepts referring to these phenomena, with subsequent attempts to make explicit by empirical investigations the interrelationships holding among them. An all too frequent substitute for such a procedure consists of an attempt to "capture" all the phenomena and relationships in the definition of a single concept.

The complaint is not infrequently heard that if one subscribes to operationism, he places severe and perhaps crippling limitations upon the extent of the generalizations he can make. The argument proceeds along the following lines: Suppose a psychologist does a series of experiments on the learning of a task under certain conditions, using adult human subjects, and concomitantly defines a concept that he calls "habit$_1$." Operationally, the definition of this term includes references to the specific task, the conditions of learning, and the human subjects. Now, if he changes the task and the conditions, he must, according to the principles of operationism, define a new concept, "habit$_2$." If he keeps the same task and conditions, but uses chimpanzees, he must again define a new concept, "habit$_3$." Obviously—the argument continues—such a procedure requires an inconvenient number of terms. Thus, operationism is too stringent and

places too many restrictions upon scientific generalization. Since the business of science is the discovery of general laws, operationism defeats the purpose of science.

There are two distinct issues involved in the preceding argument. First, no one would argue that the subscripts to the above concepts do not have discriminable referents, and phenomena which *can* be reliably discriminated *may*, if one's purpose requires it, be given different names. Scientific practice may not typically be so formal as to apply subscripts to the terms, but it does differentiate among habits as studied in T mazes, in Skinner boxes, or in classical conditioning situations. Therefore, second, the question actually is whether a differentiation among such referents, either by name or by description, is a convenience or a hindrance. Concept analysis may be useful in pointing to the gaps in factual information where more careless terminological usage has obscured this lack. While it may point out logical differences among several concepts, it cannot indicate when there is sufficient empirical evidence to collapse these several concepts into a single one, or, more precisely, when it is possible and useful to define a more general concept which incorporates subsidiary concepts previously defined. Much of what is called theory in present-day psychology represents attempts to formulate more and more general concepts, whether they be called "habit," "drive," "aggression," "sign-gestalt-expectations," or what. In this last respect, scientists, without aid from the methodologist, are generally on guard against what Bergmann calls "that spurious comprehensiveness which is paid for by vagueness and triviality" (*3*, p. 438).

A similar objection to operationism probably arises from a failure to understand the formal (analytic) approach utilized by many writers in the exposition of this principle. The logician instructs us that a definition is arbitrary in the sense that it is the designation of a symbol (word) as a representation of an idea or complex set of ideas; which particular symbol is selected is of no formal importance; what is important is that the relationship between the word and its meaning be made clear and explicit. There is no empirical connection between a word and its referent. Objections to this formulation often take a form that suggests some type of word fixation or "concretism." It seems doubtful that such a mode of thought actually underlies many of these objections. What such people probably intend to emphasize—and logicians would be the first to agree—is that, in science, concepts are defined for some purpose. The scientist always wishes to define his concept in such a way that it will have a factual exemplification; that is, the referent of the term must exist in the same way that the referent of "chair" exists. Moreover, the scientist wants his concept to enter into statements of laws—in many cases, to enter only into certain laws. These two requirements depend upon factual matters for their realization. Thus, when the logician says that definitions are purely arbitrary, he speaks from a formal point of view and does not intend anything so nonsensical as that empirical considerations do not enter into the scientist's selection of a particular definition. It should be apparent that the answers to this objection, as well as to the one just previously stated, constitute re-

statements of the Meaning I—Meaning II distinction in slightly different guises.

The reader may note in this section of the paper an omission of any discussion of measurement and quantification. Since intelligence testing has been traditionally associated with such matters ("mental measurement"), this omission may be regarded by some as serious. The writers offer three reasons for their decision: First, the over-all logic of measurement, especially in psychology, has been clearly set forth by Bergmann and Spence (*4*). Second, the internal logic of test construction, together with its most widely accepted methods and techniques, has been comprehensively covered in such articles as that by Bechtoldt (*1*) and others. Finally, the writers consider this problem unessential to the understanding of the broader logic of the concept of intelligence, the primary concern of this paper. Misconceptions concerning the additivity of IQ points, the equality of units, the normal distribution of intelligence, etc., probably do not frequently occur among workers who are well grounded in the logic of statistics and measurement, and much of the confusion may be expected to disappear with improvement in such training.

THE ANALYSIS OF INTELLIGENCE

The term "intelligence" is one of a number of words that psychologists have taken from the natural language. Its common-sense meaning, like that of many similar concepts, is complex and indefinite. An unequivocal characterization of the common-sense notion is probably both impossible and unprofitable. Reflection on the common-sense meaning of intelligence, however, leads to the discovery of two important points: First, the meaning leads to logical contradiction since, on the one hand, an individual may be regarded as generally bright, and on the other, an individual may be considered intelligent with respect to one thing and unintelligent with respect to others. The second point is that the common-sense meaning of intelligence always refers to behavioral consistency. There is the implication that the behavior of the individual is in some way trans-situational. Intelligence, in the common-sense usuage, is not a momentary state of the individual, but transcends to some degree the specific situations in which the individual behaves.

In reading the nonexperimental ("theoretical") literature concerning intelligence, one must conclude that much time and energy have been devoted to attempts to capture and make explicit the several connotations of the natural language concept. Such attempts have probably stimulated much research. It is the writers' opinion, however, that numerous sterile controversies and confusions have arisen from an inadequate analysis of the goals and purposes of work on intelligence.

The Organization of Intelligence. There is one important assumption common to all the frames of reference in which intelligence tests have been constructed, from Binet to the present day. This is the assumption of trans-situational consistency of behavior. However, the different emphases of different test constructors have drawn attention to the inconsistencies of the original common-sense notion of intelligence. Some have argued that there is a general intelligence, that the trans-situational consistency in the level of behavior extends to all situations requiring "intellectual" problem solving. The term "intellectual" has actually been defined by the items selected for the tests rather than by attempts to circumscribe the "population" of intellectual behavior. But others, utilizing factor analysis as a tool, see no a priori limitations to the number of factors required to account for the variability of "intellectual behavior" (e.g., Thurstone [10]). For them, the empirical data determine the number of factors. Still another group of investigators has consistently distinguished between "verbal" and "performance" intelligence, or between "abstract" and "concrete" intelligence.

It seems correct to state that no one, in any of these groups, has unambiguously circumscribed the population of "intellectual behavior" or has provided explicit sampling criteria for the selection of items for his tests. While this seriously limits the significance and objectivity of the frames of reference ("theories") in which the tests were said to be constructed, it does not detract in any way from any success in prediction that has been achieved by means of the tests; that is, the descriptions of the finished tests, and the accompanying instructions for administering and scoring them, constitute formally satisfactory definitions of the several concepts of intelligence, despite the lack of independent objective criteria for the initial selection of the items that constitute the tests.

The mathematical apparatus of factor analysis tends to obscure for some the fundamental logic of factor analytic investigations. The apparatus has been developed to handle simultaneously great quantities of interrelated data representing responses of individuals to test items. The completed analysis, if successful, indicates classes of test items that have elicited, within classes, similar responses from each individual in the sample, but on which similar responses have differed from individual to individual. The several empirically identified classes of items (stimuli) are then given names (e.g., "perceptual speed test," "number test," "test Y," etc.), and individuals receiving high scores on these classes are said to be high in "perceptual speed ability," in "number ability," etc. The prediction can be made that individuals from the appropriate population will tend to behave with intra-individual consistency on items within a class and will differ from each other in the consistent mode of behavior within classes of items, and that relatively little consistency in behavior will be manifested from class to class. One of the presumed goals of this procedure is that tasks other than those used previously will yield to an objective analysis which will permit one to specify the combination of scores on the isolated factors that will be appropriate for successful performance on the task. Explicit rules for such analyses are not yet available. If such rules are ever specified, the utility of this approach will have been demonstrated.

Experimentation using factor analysis has attempted to study simultaneously groups of items toward which individuals behave with intra-individual consistency and with individual differences in the manner of responding to these classes of items. Except for the latter problem, the procedure does not differ in fundamental logic from the procedures that have been used to scale the psychological similarity of stimulus items. The meaning of the term "number test" or any other test can be given by stating the

criteria for classifying the items into the test; this includes the entire factor analytic procedure. The meaning of the term "numerical ability" is given when the test is specified, the rules for administering it are given, and the scoring criteria stated. The term "factor" has often been used to refer to these different, though related, concepts. More "operational" definitions of psychological concepts could scarcely be given. It should be clear, however, that no "primary" factors, in the sense of physiologically or phenomenologically fundamental variables, can be said to have been isolated by the procedure utilized by the factor analyst any more than this could be said of other definitional procedures in psychology.

There is little sense to the question: "Which of these definitions of intelligence is correct (or most nearly correct)?" *Formally* correct definitions of all these concepts may be given. Which of the several concepts of intelligence proves to be the most useful, in the sense of entering into laws which lead ultimately to more accurate predictions of human behavior, remains to be seen. There is little use in speculating unduly on this point, considering our current state of ignorance concerning the variables associated with these concepts. Only empirical research can provide an unequivocal answer.

A similar analysis clarifies arguments concerning whether or not intelligence tests *need* to contain "nonintellective" items. We may recognize, first, that the occurrence of the terms "intellective" and "nonintellective" in everyday language does not guarantee that they refer to any features or phenomena that may be either consistently or usefully distinguished. If it is assumed for the moment that the terms are both useful and unambiguous, the proper question to ask is whether or not such items in a test will facilitate the achievement of the purpose for which the test was constructed. Test constructors are (understandably) rarely explicit about *all* the predictions they wish to make with their tests, and it is impossible to determine, a priori, whether or not any particular class of items will prove generally useful. Many of the controversial points concerning "the nature of intelligence" stem from an assumption that all investigators constructing or working with "intelligence tests" have a single common goal.

In this connection, Wechsler (*11*) asks if "the capacity for social adaptation" is not also a "sign of intelligence." He states that intelligence tests involve more than "mere learning ability or reasoning ability or even general intellectual ability." They also contain other "capacities which cannot be defined as either purely cognitive or intellective." He goes on to state that this is desirable, and that such factors should be included with greater premeditation. One might well ask how one is to arrive at a sensible decision on this proposal until the goals of intelligence testing have been relatively clearly set forth. The issue, it would seem, is not one of a definition of an "absolute" intelligence that will be used generally; rather, it is necessary to state explicitly the criterion (or criteria) to be predicted, and then to discover the tasks that will predict it.

Heredity-environment. One of the most intense controversies in psychology in recent years was the heredity-environment issue. On the one side was a group of individuals insisting that "intelligence" is something not directly influenced by

the environment, i.e., not directly influenced by learning. On the other side, it was maintained that intelligence could be affected by learning experiences. This issue was closely related to the argument over the constancy of IQ, the insistence that IQ's obtained from certain tests (viz., the Stanford-Binet) did or did not fluctuate markedly from time to time for a given individual. Reverberations of these controversies are still heard in current discussions of culture-free intelligence tests.

The salient points in this controversy were rarely, if ever, clearly and explicitly delineated. The polemical papers written on the subject indicate that much of the difficulty centered around careless use of terminology on both sides, and they suggest that a methodological analysis should prove clarifying. For example, the terms "environment" and "heredity" were never clearly defined, thus sharing the same ambiguity as "intelligence"—the concept they were intended to clarify. In the biological sciences, the term "heredity" is used precisely only in relation to the genotypically traced characteristics of the ancestors of the individual whose heredity is under discussion. Any attempts to define "intelligence" by referring to "heredity" would presuppose application of the procedures of the geneticist to the "intelligence" of the ancestry—and the circularity of this is apparent.

When one turns to research on the relationships between "heredity" and "environment" on the one hand and "intelligence" on the other, and construes these concepts operationally in terms of the research reports, one finds numerous definitions. A typical pattern of research was to provide an experimental group of children with specified experiences, to give pre- and posttraining intelligence tests, and then to compare the IQ gains with those of a control group not having the same intervening training. If greater gains occurred for the experimental group than for the control, it was held that the "environment" had influenced "intelligence." Few, if any, of these studies were devoid of serious experimental errors, the most damaging of which, in the writers' opinion, was the typical failure to assign subjects at random to the experimental and control groups. The foster home studies provide another pattern of research used by the "environmentalists," and were similarly limited by experimental errors.

The "hereditarians" had their own crucial experimental designs. If the IQ's for pairs of siblings reared separately correlated positively and significantly, it was the result of common heredity. If the IQ's for pairs of monozygotic twins correlated significantly higher than the IQ's for pairs of bizygotic twins, it was the result of more similar heredity for the former. Questions arise as to the importance of common uterine experiences, of the physical similarity of identical twins in leading to more similar environmental experiences, of the reliability in identifying identical twins except at birth, and so on. Jones (9) includes critical analyses of many papers in this area.

Much of the argument on the heredity-environment issue was not confined to such empirical questions as the foregoing paragraphs describe. Many workers in the area desired and expected a concept of intelligence which would provide a quantitative index that would not change with time for the individual except under the most unusual conditions, e.g., brain damage, psychosis, paralysis, etc. An intelligence test which suggested that intelligence fluctuated from day to day was therefore unsatisfactory; it was not a "real measure" of intelligence. The first empirical studies reporting systematic changes in IQ for groups were looked upon with considerable suspicion by many investigators. These studies and their supporters were answered with suggestions about uncontrolled variables that might have produced changes in IQ scores without affecting the fundamental intelligence. It now appears that this objection referred to the plausible possibility that IQ scores may be changed without materially affecting performances on tasks for which there was either a presumed or an experimentally established relationship with IQ scores. The literature shows an interesting neglect of this possibility by those who insisted on the effectiveness of environmental factors in changing the level of intelligence. An obvious example of such a factor is coaching.

A terminological analysis helps to bring the conflicting conclusions into agreement. If intelligence is understood to refer to the performance on a given scale (Meaning I only), then without question, some environmental influences (e.g., coaching, repetition of tests, etc.) can produce changes in intelligence. On the other hand, if intelligence is understood to refer to some complex set of interrelated behaviors (Meaning I *and* Meaning II), and if we have neither a complete list of the behaviors nor explicit statements of the relations holding among them, then we do not know and cannot determine whether or not learning experiences can produce changes in intelligence. As a matter of fact, if intelligence is understood in this sense, we can never know fully what intelligence "means," since subsequent investigations may uncover new relationships between the behavior and other concepts. One of the more important results of a methodological analysis of a scientific concept is the distinction made between the formal meaning of the concept and the empirical knowledge about the concept.

Analysis of the heredity-environment issue cannot be considered complete until mention has been made of the scientifically irrelevant values that have still further clouded the issues involved. The common-sense meaning of "intelligence" has a high value connotation for most of us, a characteristic it shares with many other psychological concepts (e.g., "rigidity," "neurosis," "prejudice," etc.). Intelligence tests have thus been evaluated by some, not only in terms of their predictive power, but also in terms of the "desirability" of the content. The evaluations seem to state: "Intelligence is 'good,' and if the test does not predict 'good' behavior, then it is not an intelligence test." This attitude often results in either a high evaluation of the IQ, per se, without adequate consideration for what can be predicted from it, or in bitter denunciation of test constructors who include questions in the test which handicap certain groups.

To ask whether it is good or bad for an individual to have high intelligence is about as scientifically relevant as to ask whether it is good or bad to have an object weigh a lot. After scientists have defined their terms and have stated the interrelations among them, societies may decide whether or not a given term refers to something desirable. To reverse the procedure places on the scientist "pious" restrictions that are irrelevant to his purposes.

A survey of current literature on culture-free intelligence tests demonstrates the confusion of value and factual matters. For example, Eells et al. (7), with the most articulate of frames of reference, criticize the modern educational system and, therefore, the intelligence tests that predict success in it. They point out that middle-class teachers, with their particular middle-class version of what is the "best" and "true" culture, inflict their values upon school curricula, judgments of their pupils, and intelligence test items. Thus, they fail to develop the "full mental capacities" of their pupils particularly of those pupils from lower classes. Present intelligence tests seek to predict behavior closely related to the school culture. They are, therefore, inadequate "to measure the general problem-solving activities of human beings." What is needed is an intelligence test that reflects or measures the "genetic mental equipment," "the general problem-solving activities," "the real talents," etc. Such an index would permit us to show that class differences in intelligence do not exist and thus help to prevent social class prejudice and untoward discrimination.

Without arguing for or against the educational goals of Eells and his coworkers, we make the following comments. Most psychologists would now agree that the predictive power of intelligence tests has been grossly overestimated, in both scope and accuracy, by many professional and nonprofessional people. But to criticize a test because it predicts one thing and not another seems pointless. Whether or not a test can be constructed to predict important behavior, and yet not discriminate among social classes, is entirely a question of fact. Apparently Eells et al. (7) are attempting to construct such a test, and their attempts to make explicit the behavior they consider it important to predict should aid them. That part of their program concerned with a reformulation of educational goals can find no direct support from scientific knowledge since science cannot tell us what the "better life" is.

The validity of intelligence tests. Attemps to use technically the ambiguous term "validity" have generated much confusion in literature on intelligence. Consider the basic question, "Is this intelligence test valid?" One possible clear meaning of this vague question has to do with the usefulness of the test for predictive purposes. The answer to the question, by this interpretation, requires only a summary of the empirical research with the test. There is, of course, not much point in asking the question about a new test since little empirical knowledge will be available. If a new test is demonstrated to predict the scores on an older, well-established test, then the evaluation of the predictive power of the older test may be used for the new one. In this sense, the "validity" of a new test may be established relatively easily. Usually, however, the publication of a new test should be regarded as an invitation for other investigators to help to discover the predictive power of the test. If a given investigator judges that claims are made for the test that are not warranted by the empirical data, then it is his duty to register his objections. But a bland statement that the test is not valid contributes nothing but confusion and polemics to psychological knowledge. It amounts to nothing more than a forecast of future uselessness of the test.

The previous interpretation of the basic question has the virtue of permitting an eventual empirical answer. Another frequent interpretation is not so fortunate, having to do with whether or not the test is a *true* measure of intelligence. It presupposes a meaningful concept of *true intelligence.* It seems that such a question, unanalyzed, has led many workers to attempt to discover the "underlying nature of intelligence." It is rarely clear from their writings what is the "nature" of the "nature" they expect to find. It appears to have something to do either with the physiology or with the mental data of their subjects. The comments that follow are devoted to the issues that seem to be involved.

If one defines "intelligence" (or any other psychological concept) in terms of the individual's responses to items on a standardized test, one may still ask, "What are the physiological correlates of this type of behavior?" That every bit of behavior has physiological correlates is something of which psychologists are, as Bergmann puts it, "as certain of as we are of anything in science" (*3*, p. 422). Unfortunately, the more complex (molar) the behavior, the more likely it is that our present best attempts to specify which physiological variables underlie the behavior will be pure speculation and probably will be neither good psychology nor good physiology.

The problem is not greatly different in practice if one asks, "What are the mental correlates of this type of behavior?" No psychologist claims direct observation of his subject's mental data. If he is to do more than speculate, he must settle for observation of the subject's behavior (including verbal behavior) and the situations in which it occurs. He must assume that no mental states occur which are not *in some way* reflected in observable behavior.

The only important point that needs to be made is that both the mental and the physiological correlates remain forever distinct from the behaviorally defined (psychological) concepts. Even if one finds an invariant relationship between a psychological and a physiological variable, they remain two things. One has found a law relating them. The failure to recognize this point has apparently led some writers to think of the physiological or mental variables as the "true" ones, which are only approximately "measured" by behavioral variables. What some psychologists seem to ask is whether or not the test reflects accurately the appropriate mental variables. The hopelessness of any immediate attempt to answer such a question is obvious. The most convincing answer one could give is the same answer one would give to the question, "How adequately does the test predict certain areas of behavior?"

To avoid misunderstanding, it should be made explicit that this formulation does not suggest that the study of the relationship between psychological and physiological variables is either an illegitimate or an unprofitable area for psychologists. Nor does it suggest that the study of subjects' verbal responses, under special instructional sets and conditions, as they relate to other situational or behavioral variables, is either a logical or factual error. The argument is merely that there are no a priori reasons why these variables are more fundamental ("real") than those at the behavioral level.

This is a matter to be determined only by empirical trial and error.

SUMMARY

This paper is an attempt to examine some of the controversial issues in the field of intelligence by an application of some basic principles in the philosophy of science. A summary of the most relevant of these principles was given, and the principles were then applied to such problems as the organization of intelligence, the heredity-environment issue, and the validity of intelligence tests. The aim of the analysis in each case was to separate terminological and other logical issues from the factual issues with which they have become confused. It was seen that there is little left that can be considered controversial, except in the sense that any question of fact may be a controversial point until adequate evidence is provided for its resolution. The confusions that arise as a result of trying to formulate single answers to multibarrelled questions can be eliminated.

REFERENCES

1. BECHTOLDT, H. P. Selection. In S. S. Stevens (Ed.), *Handbook of experimental psychology.* New York: Wiley, 1951. Pp. 1237–1266.

2. BERGMANN, G. The logic of psychological concepts. *Phil. Sci.,* 1951, *18,* 93–110.

3. BERGMANN, G. Theoretical psychology. *Annu. Rev. Psychol.,* 1953, *4,* 435–458.

4. BERGMANN, G. & SPENCE, K. W. The logic of psychophysical measure-

ment. *Psychol. Rev.*, 1944, *51*, 1–24.

5. BRUNSWIK, E.   The conceptual framework of psychology. Chicago: Univer. of Chicago Press, 1952. (*Int. Encycl. unified Sci.*, v. 1, no. 10.)

6. CARNAP, R.   Testability and meaning. *Phil. Sci.*, 1936, *3*, 418–471; 1937, *4*, 1–40.

7. EELLS, K., DAVIS, A., HAVIGHURST, R., HERRICK, V. E., & TYLER, R. *Intelligence and cultural differences.* Chicago: Univer. of Chicago Press, 1951.

8. FEIGL, H.   Operationism and scientific method. *Psychol. Rev.*, 1945, *52*, 250–259.

9. JONES, H. E.   Environmental influences on mental development. In L. Carmichael (Ed.), *Manual of child psychology.* New York: Wiley, 1946. Pp. 582–632.

10. THURSTONE, L. L.   *Multiple factor analysis.* Chicago: Univer. of Chicago Press, 1947.

11. WECHSLER, D.   *The measurement of adult intelligence.* Baltimore: Williams & Wilkins, 1944.

HEREDITY, ENVIRONMENT,
AND THE QUESTION "HOW?" [1]

ANNE ANASTASI

TWO OR THREE DECADES AGO, the so-called heredity-environment question was the center of lively controversy. Today, on the other hand, many psychologists look upon it as a dead issue. It is now generally conceded that both hereditary and environmental factors enter into all behavior. The reacting organism is a product of its genes and its past environment, while present environment provides the immediate stimulus for current behavior. To be sure, it can be argued that, although a given trait may result from the combined influence of hereditary and environmental factors, a specific difference in this trait between individuals or between groups may be traceable to either hereditary or environmental factors alone. The design of most traditional investigations undertaken to identify such factors, however, has been such as to yield inconclusive answers. The same set of data has frequently led to opposite conclusions in the hands of psychologists with different orientations.

[1] Address of the President, Division of General Psychology, American Psychological Association, September 4, 1957.

Reprinted by permission from *Psychological Review*, 1958, *65*, 197–208.

Nor have efforts to determine the proportional contribution of hereditary and environmental factors to observed individual differences in given traits met with any greater success. Apart from difficulties in controlling conditions, such investigations have usually been based upon the implicit assumption that hereditary and environmental factors combine in an additive fashion. Both geneticists and psychologists have repeatedly demonstrated, however, that a more tenable hypothesis is that of interaction (15, 22, 28, 40). In other words, the nature and extent of the influence of each type of factor depend upon the contribution of the other. Thus the proportional contribution of heredity to the variance of a given trait, rather than being a constant, will vary under different environmental conditions. Similarly, under different hereditary conditions, the relative contribution of environment will differ. Studies designed to estimate the proportional contribution of heredity and environment, however, have rarely included measures of such interaction. The only possible conclusion from such research would thus seem to be that both heredity and environment contribute to all behavior traits and that the extent of their respective contributions cannot be specified for any trait. Small wonder that some psychologists regard the heredity-environment question as unworthy of further consideration!

But is this really all we can find out about the operation of heredity and environment in the etiology of behavior? Perhaps we have simply been asking the wrong questions. The traditional questions about heredity and environment may be intrinsically unanswerable. Psychologists began by asking *which* type of factor, hereditary or environmental, is respon-sible for individual differences in a given trait. Later, they tried to discover *how much* of the variance was attributable to heredity and how much to environment. It is the primary contention of this paper that a more fruitful approach is to be found in the question *"How?"* There is still much to be learned about the specific *modus operandi* of hereditary and environmental factors in the development of behavioral differences. And there are several current lines of research which offer promising techniques for answering the question "How?"

VARIETY OF INTERACTION MECHANISMS

HEREDITARY FACTORS

If we examine some of the specific ways in which hereditary factors may influence behavior, we cannot fail but be impressed by their wide diversity. At one extreme, we find such conditions as phenylpyruvic amentia and amaurotic idiocy. In these cases, certain essential physical prerequisites for normal intellectual development are lacking as a result of hereditary metabolic disorders. In our present state of knowledge, there is no environmental factor which can completely counteract this hereditary deficit. The individual will be mentally defective, regardless of the type of environmental conditions under which he is reared.

A somewhat different situation is illustrated by hereditary deafness, which may lead to intellectual retardation through interference with normal social interaction, language development, and schooling. In such a case, however, the hereditary handicap can be offset by appropriate adaptations of training procedures. It has been said, in fact, that the degree of intellectual backwardness of the deaf is an index of the state of development of special instructional facilities. As the latter improve, the intellectual retardation associated with deafness is correspondingly reduced.

A third example is provided by inherited suspectibility to certain physical diseases, with consequent protracted ill health. If environmental conditions are such that illness does in fact develop, a number of different behavioral effects may follow. Intellectually, the individual may be handicapped by his inability to attend school regularly. On the other hand, depending upon age of onset, home conditions, parental status, and similar factors, poor health may have the effect of concentrating the individual's energies upon intellectual pursuits. The curtailment of participation in athletics and social functions may serve to strengthen interest in reading and other sedentary activities. Concomitant circumstances would also determine the influence of such illness upon personality development. And it is well known that the latter effects could run the gamut from a deepening of human sympathy to psychiatric breakdown.

Finally, heredity may influence behavior through the mechanism of social stereotypes. A wide variety of inherited physical characteristics have served as the visible cues for identifying such stereotypes. These cues thus lead to behavioral restrictions or opportunities and—at a more subtle level—to social attitudes and expectancies. The individual's own self concept tends gradually to reflect such expectancies. All of these influences eventually leave their mark upon his abilities and inabilities, his emotional reactions, goals, ambitions, and outlook on life.

The geneticist Dobzhansky illustrates this type of mechanism by means of a dramatic hypothetical situation. He points out that, if there were a culture in which the carriers of blood group AB were considered aristocrats and those of blood group O laborers, then the blood-group genes would become important hereditary determiners of behavior (12, p. 147). Obviously the association between blood group and behavior would be specific to that culture. But such specificity is an essential property of the causal mechanism under consideration.

More realistic examples are not hard to find. The most familiar instances occur in connection with constitutional types, sex, and race. Sex and skin pigmentation obviously depend upon heredity. General body build is strongly influenced by hereditary components, although also susceptible to environmental modification. That all these physical characteristics may exert a pronounced effect upon behavior within a given culture is well known. It is equally apparent, of course, that in different cultures the behavioral correlates of such hereditary physical traits may be quite unlike. A specific physical cue may be completely unrelated to individual differences in psychological traits in one culture, while closely correlated with them in another. Or it may be associated with totally dissimilar behavior characteristics in two different cultures.

It might be objected that some of the illustrations which have been cited do not properly exemplify the operation of hereditary mechanisms in behavior development, since hereditary factors enter only indirectly into the behavior in question. Closer examination, however, shows this distinction to be untenable. First it may be noted that the influence of heredity upon behavior is always indirect. No psychological trait is ever inherited as such. All we can ever say directly from behavioral observations is that a given trait shows evidence of being influenced by certain "inheritable unknowns." This merely defines a problem for genetic research; it does not provide a causal explanation. Unlike the blood groups, which are close to the level of primary gene products, psychological traits are related to genes by highly indirect and devious routes. Even the mental deficiency associated with phenylketonuria is several steps removed from the chemically defective genes that represent its hereditary basis. Moreover, hereditary influences cannot be dichotomized into the more direct and the less direct. Rather do they represent a whole "continuum of indirectness," along which are found all degrees of remoteness of causal links. The examples already cited illustrate a few of the points on this continuum.

It should be noted that as we proceed along the continuum of indirectness, the range of variation of possible outcomes of hereditary factors expands rapidly. At each step in the causal chain, there is fresh opportunity for interaction with other hereditary factors as well as with environmental factors. And since each interaction in turn determines the direction of subsequent interactions, there is an ever-widening network of possible outcomes. If we visualize a simple sequential grid with only two alternatives at each point, it is obvious that there are two possible outcomes in the one-stage situation, four outcomes at the second stage, eight at the third, and so on in geometric progression. The actual situation is undoubtedly much more complex, since there will usually be more than two alternatives at any one point.

In the case of the blood groups, the relation to specific genes is so close that no other concomitant hereditary or environmental conditions can alter the outcome. If the organism survives at all, it will have the blood group determined by its genes. Among psychological traits, on the other hand, some variation in outcome is always possible as a result of concurrent circumstances. Even in cases of phenylketonuria, intellectual development will exhibit some relationship with the type of care and training available to the individual. That behavioral outcomes show progressive diversification as we proceed along the continuum of indirectness is brought out by the other examples which were cited. Chronic illness *can* lead to scholarly renown or to intellectual immaturity; a mesomorphic physique *can* be a contributing factor in juvenile delinquency or in the attainment of a college presidency! Published data on Sheldon somatotypes provide some support for both of the latter outcomes.

Parenthetically, it may be noted that geneticists have sometimes used the term "norm of reaction" to designate the range of variation of possible outcomes of gene properties (cf. *13*, p. 161). Thus heredity sets the "norm" or limits within which environmental differences determine the eventual outcome. In the case of some traits, such as blood groups or eye color, this norm is much narrower than in the case of other traits. Owing to the rather different psychological connotations of both the words "norm" and "reaction," however, it seems less confusing to speak of the "range of variation" in this context.

A large portion of the continuum of

hereditary influences which we have described coincides with the domain of somatopsychological relations, as defined by Barker et al. (6). Under this heading, Barker includes "variations in physique that affect the psychological situation of a person by influencing the effectiveness of his body as a tool for actions or by serving as a stimulus to himself or others" (6, p. 1). Relatively direct neurological influences on behavior, which have been the traditional concern of physiological psychology, are excluded from this definition, Barker being primarily concerned with what he calls the "social psychology of physique." Of the examples cited in the present paper, deafness, severe illness, and the physical characteristics associated with social stereotypes would meet the specifications of somatopsychological factors.

The somatic factors to which Barker refers, however, are not limited to those of hereditary origin. Bodily conditions attributable to environmental causes operate in the same sorts of somatopsychological relations as those traceable to heredity. In fact, heredity-environment distinctions play a minor part in Barker's approach.

ENVIRONMENTAL FACTORS: ORGANIC

Turning now to an analysis of the role of environmental factors in behavior, we find the same etiological mechanisms which were observed in the case of hereditary factors. First, however, we must differentiate between two classes of environmental influences: (a) those producing organic effects which may in turn influence behavior and (b) those serving as direct stimuli for psychological reactions. The former may be illustrated by food intake or by exposure to bacterial infection; the latter, by tribal initiation ceremonies or by a course in algebra. There are no completely satisfactory names by which to designate these two classes of influences. In an earlier paper by Anastasi and Foley (4), the terms "structural" and "functional" were employed. However, "organic" and "behavioral" have the advantage of greater familiarity in this context and may be less open to misinterpretation. Accordingly, these terms will be used in the present paper.

Like hereditary factors, environmental influences of an organic nature can also be ordered along a continuum of indirectness with regard to their relation to behavior. This continuum closely parallels that of hereditary factors. One end is typified by such conditions as mental deficiency resulting from cerebral birth injury or from prenatal nutritional inadequacies. A more indirect etiological mechanism is illustrated by severe motor disorder—as in certain cases of cerebral palsy—*without* accompanying injury to higher neurological centers. In such instances, intellectual retardation may occur as an indirect result of the motor handicap, through the curtailment of educational and social activities. Obviously this causal mechanism corresponds closely to that of hereditary deafness cited earlier in the paper.

Finally, we may consider an environmental parallel to the previously discussed social stereotypes which were mediated by hereditary physical cues. Let us suppose that a young woman with mousy brown hair becomes transformed into a dazzling golden blonde through environmental techniques currently available in our culture. It is highly probable that this metamorphosis will alter, not only the reactions of her associates toward her, but also her own self concept and subsequent behavior. The effects could range all the way from a rise in social poise to a drop in clerical accuracy!

Among the examples of environmentally determined organic influences which have been described, all but the first two fit Barker's definition of somatopsychological factors. With the exception of birth injuries and nutritional deficiencies, all fall within the social psychology of physique. Nevertheless, the individual factors exhibit wide diversity in their specific *modus operandi*—a diversity which has important practical as well as theoretical implications.

ENVIRONMENTAL FACTORS: BEHAVIORAL

The second major class of environmental factors—the behavioral as contrasted to the organic—are by definition direct influences. The immediate effect of such environmental factors is always a behavioral change. To be sure, some of the initial behavioral effects may themselves indirectly affect the individual's later behavior. But this relationship can perhaps be best conceptualized in terms of breadth and permanence of effects. Thus it could be said that we are now dealing, not with a continuum of indirectness, as in the case of hereditary and organic-environmental factors, but rather with a continuum of breadth.

Social class membership may serve as an illustration of a relatively broad, pervasive, and enduring environmental factor. Its influence upon behavior development may operate through many channels. Thus social level may determine the range and nature of intellectual stimulation provided by home and community

through books, music, art, play activities, and the like. Even more far-reaching may be the effects upon interests and motivation, as illustrated by the desire to perform abstract intellectual tasks, to surpass others in competitive situations, to succeed in school, or to gain social approval. Emotional and social traits may likewise be influenced by the nature of interpersonal relations characterizing homes at different socioeconomic levels. Somewhat more restricted in scope than social class, although still exerting a relatively broad influence, is amount of formal schooling which the individual is able to obtain.

A factor which may be wide or narrow in its effects, depending upon concomitant circumstances, is language handicap. Thus the bilingualism of an adult who moves to a foreign country with inadequate mastery of the new language represents a relatively limited handicap which can be readily overcome in most cases. At most, the difficulty is one of communication. On the other hand, some kinds of bilingualism in childhood may exert a retarding influence upon intellectual development and may under certain conditions affect personality development adversely (2, 5, 10). A common pattern in the homes of immigrants is that the child speaks one language at home and another in school, so that his knowledge of each language is limited to certain types of situations. Inadequate facility with the language of the school interferes with the acquisition of basic concepts, intellectual skills, and information. The frustration engendered by scholastic difficulties may in turn lead to discouragement and general dislike of school. Such reactions can be found, for example, among a number of Puerto

Rican children in New York City schools (3). In the case of certain groups, moreover, the child's foreign language background may be perceived by himself and his associates as a symbol of minority group status and may thereby augment any emotional maladjustment arising from such status (34).

A highly restricted environmental influence is to be found in the opportunity to acquire specific items of information occurring in a particular intelligence test. The fact that such opportunities may vary with culture, social class, or individual experiential background is at the basis of the test user's concern with the problem of coaching and with "culture-free" or "culture-fair" tests (cf. 1, 2). If the advantage or disadvantage which such experiential differences confer upon certain individuals is strictly confined to performance on the given test, it will obviously reduce the validity of the test and should be eliminated.

In this connection, however, it is essential to know the breadth of the environmental influence in question. A fallacy inherent in many attemps to develop culture-fair tests is that the breadth of cultural differentials is not taken into account. Failure to consider breadth of effect likewise characterizes certain discussions of coaching. If, in coaching a student for a college admission test, we can improve his knowledge of verbal concepts and his reading comprehension, he will be better equipped to succeed in college courses. His performance level will thus be raised, not only on the test, but also on the criterion which the test is intended to predict. To try to devise a test which is not susceptible to such coaching would merely reduce the effectiveness of the test. Similarly, efforts to rule out cultural differentials from test items so as to make them equally "fair" to subjects in different social classes or in different cultures may merely limit the usefulness of the test, since the same cultural differentials may operate within the broader area of behavior which the test is designed to sample.

METHODOLOGICAL APPROACHES

The examples considered so far should suffice to highlight the wide variety of ways in which hereditary and environmental factors may interact in the course of behavior development. There is clearly a need for identifying explicitly the etiological mechanism whereby any given hereditary or environmental condition ultimately leads to a behavioral characteristic—in other words, the "how" of heredity and environment. Accordingly, we may now take a quick look at some promising methodological approaches to the question "how."

Within the past decade, an increasing number of studies have been designed to trace the connection between specific factors in the hereditary backgrounds or in the reactional biographies of individuals and their observed behavioral characteristics. There has been a definite shift away from the predominantly descriptive and correlational approach of the earlier decades toward more deliberate attempts to verify explanatory hypotheses. Similarly, the cataloguing of group differences in psychological traits has been giving way gradually to research on *changes* in group characteristics following altered conditions.

Among recent methodological developments, we have chosen seven as being particularly relevant to the analysis of etiological mechanisms. The first represents an extension of selective breeding investigations to permit the identification of specific hereditary conditions underlying the observed behavioral differences. When early selective breeding investigations such as those of Tryon (36) on rats indicated that "maze learning ability" was inherited, we were still a long way from knowing what was actually being transmitted by the genes. It was obviously not "maze learning ability" as such. Twenty—or even ten—years ago, some psychologists would have suggested that it was probably general intelligence. And a few might even have drawn a parallel with the inheritance of human intelligence.

But today investigators have been asking: Just what makes one group of rats learn mazes more quickly than the other? Is it differences in motivation, emotionality, speed of running, general activity level? If so, are these behavioral characteristics in turn dependent upon group differences in glandular development, body weight, brain size, biochemical factors, or some other organic conditions? A number of recent and ongoing investigations indicate that attempts are being made to trace, at least part of the way, the steps whereby certain chemical properties of the genes may ultimately lead to specified behavior characteristics.

An example of such a study is provided by Searle's (31) follow-up of Tryon's research. Working with the strains of maze-bright and maze-dull rats developed by Tryon, Searle demonstrated that the two strains differed in a number of emotional and motivational factors, rather than in ability. Thus the strain differences were traced one step further, although many links still remain to be found between maze learning and genes. A promising methodological development within the same general area is to be found in the recent research of Hirsch and Tryon (18). Utilizing a specially devised technique for measuring individual differences in behavior among lower organisms, these investigators launched a series of studies on selective breeding for behavioral characteristics in the fruit fly, *Drosophila*. Such research can capitalize on the mass of available genetic knowledge regarding the morphology of *Drosophila*, as well as on other advantages of using such an organism in genetic studies.

Further evidence of current interest in the specific hereditary factors which influence behavior is to be found in an extensive research program in progress at the Jackson Memorial Laboratory, under the direction of Scott and Fuller (30). In general, the project is concerned with the behavioral characteristics of various breeds and cross-breeds of dogs. Analyses of some of the data gathered to date again suggest that "differences in performance are produced by differences in emotional, motivational, and peripheral processes, and that genetically caused differences in central processes may be either slight or non-existent" (29, p. 225). In other parts of the same project, breed differences in physiological characteristics, which may in turn be related to behavioral differences, have been established.

A second line of attack is the exploration of possible relationships between behavioral characteristics and physiological variables which may in turn be traceable to hereditary factors. Research on EEG, autonomic balance, metabolic processes, and biochemical factors illustrates this approach. A lucid demonstration of the process of tracing a psychological condition to genetic factors is provided by the identification and subsequent investigation of phenylpyruvic amentia. In this case, the causal chain from defective gene, through metabolic disorder and consequent cerebral malfunctioning, to feeblemindedness and other overt symptoms can be described step by step (cf. *32; 33*, pp. 389–391). Also relevant are the recent researches on neurological and biochemical correlates of schizophrenia (*9*). Owing to inadequate methodological controls, however, most of the findings of the latter studies must be regarded as tentative (*19*).

Prenatal environmental factors provide a third avenue of fruitful investigation. Especially noteworthy is the recent work of Pasamanick and his associates (*27*), which demonstrated a tie-up between socioeconomic level, complications of pregnancy and parturition, and psychological disorders of the offspring. In a series of studies on large samples of whites and Negroes in Baltimore, these investigators showed that various prenatal and paranatal disorders are significantly related to the occurrence of mental defect and psychiatric disorders in the child. An important source of such irregularities in the process of childbearing and birth is to be found in deficiencies of maternal diet and in other conditions associated with low socioeconomic status. An analysis of the data did in fact reveal a much higher frequency of all such medical complications in lower than in higher socioeconomic levels, and a higher frequency among Negroes than among whites.

Direct evidence of the influence of prenatal nutritional factors upon subsequent intellectual development is to be found in a recent, well controlled experiment by Harrell et al. (*16*). The subjects were pregnant women in low-income groups, whose normal diets were generally quite deficient. A dietary supplement was administered to some of these women during pregnancy and lactation, while an equated control group received placebos. When tested at the ages of three and four years, the offspring of the experimental group obtained a significantly higher mean IQ than did the offspring of the controls.

Mention should also be made of animal experiments on the effects of such factors as prenatal radiation and neonatal asphyxia upon cerebral anomalies as well as upon subsequent behavior development. These experimental studies merge imperceptibly into the fourth approach to be considered, namely, the investigation of the influence of early experience upon the eventual behavioral characteristics of animals. Research in this area has been accumulating at a rapid rate. In 1954, Beach and Jaynes (*8*) surveyed this literature for the *Psychological Bulletin*, listing over 130 references. Several new studies have appeared since that date (e.g., *14, 21, 24, 25, 35*). The variety of factors covered ranges from the type and quantity of available food to the extent of contact with human culture. A large number of experiments have been concerned with various forms of sensory deprivation and with diminished opportunities for motor exercise. Effects have been observed in many kinds of animals and in almost all aspects of behavior, including perceptual responses, motor activity, learning, emotionality, and social reactions.

In their review, Beach and Jaynes

pointed out that research in this area has been stimulated by at least four distinct theoretical interests. Some studies were motivated by the traditional concern with the relative contribution of maturation and learning to behavior development. Others were designed in an effort to test certain psychoanalytic theories regarding infantile experiences, as illustrated by studies which limited the feeding responses of young animals. A third relevant influence is to be found in the work of the European biologist Lorenz (23) on early social stimulation of birds, and in particular on the special type of learning for which the term "imprinting" has been coined. A relatively large number of recent studies have centered around Hebb's (17) theory regarding the importance of early perceptual experiences upon subsequent performance in learning situations. All this research represents a rapidly growing and promising attack on the *modus operandi* of specific environmental factors.

The human counterpart of these animal studies may be found in the comparative investigation of child-rearing practices in different cultures and subcultures. This represents the fifth approach in our list. An outstanding example of such a study is that by Whiting and Child (38), published in 1953. Utilizing data on 75 primitive societies from the Cross-Cultural Files of the Yale Institute of Human Relations, these investigators set out to test a number of hypotheses regarding the relationships between child-rearing practices and personality development. This analysis was followed up by field observations in five cultures, the results of which have not yet been reported (cf. 37).

Within our own culture, similar surveys have been concerned with the diverse psychological environments provided by different social classes (11). Of particular interest are the study of Williams and Scott (39) on the association between socioeconomic level, permissiveness, and motor development among Negro children, and the exploratory research by Milner (26) on the relationship between reading readiness in first-grade children and patterns of parent-child interaction. Milner found that upon school entrance the lower-class child seems to lack chiefly two advantages enjoyed by the middle-class child. The first is described as "a warm positive family atmosphere or adult-relationship pattern which is more and more being recognized as a motivational prerequisite of any kind of adult-controlled learning." The lower class children in Milner's study perceived adults as predominantly hostile. The second advantage is an extensive opportunity to interact verbally with adults in the family. The latter point is illustrated by parental attitudes toward mealtime conversation, lower-class parents tending to inhibit and discourage such conversation, while middle-class parents encourage it.

Most traditional studies on child-rearing practices have been designed in terms of a psychoanalytic orientation. There is need for more data pertaining to other types of hypotheses. Findings such as those of Milner on opportunities for verbalization and the resulting effects upon reading readiness represent a step in this direction. Another possible source of future data is the application of the intensive observational techniques of psychological ecology developed by Barker and Wright (7) to widely diverse socioeconomic groups.

A sixth major approach involves research on the previously cited somato-psychological relationships (6). To date, little direct information is available on the precise operation of this class of factors in psychological development. The multiplicity of ways in which physical traits—whether hereditary or environmental in origin—may influence behavior thus offers a relatively unexplored field for future study.

The seventh and final approach to be considered represents an adaptation of traditional twin studies. From the standpoint of the question "How?" there is need for closer coordination between the usual data on twin resemblance and observations of the family interactions of twins. Available data already suggest, for example, that closeness of contact and extent of environmental similarity are greater in the case of monozygotic than in the case of dizygotic twins (cf. 2). Information on the social reactions of twins toward each other and the specialization of roles is likewise of interest (2). Especially useful would be longitudinal studies of twins, beginning in early infancy and following the subjects through school age. The operation of differential environmental pressures, the development of specialized roles, and other environmental influences could thus be more clearly identified and correlated with intellectual and personality changes in the growing twins.

Parenthetically, I should like to add a remark about the traditional applications of the twin method, in which persons in different degrees of hereditary and environmental relationships to each other are simply compared for behavioral similarity. In these studies, attention has been focused principally upon the amount of resemblance of monozygotic as contrasted to dizygotic twins. Yet such a comparison is particularly difficult to interpret because of the many subtle differences in the environmental situations of the two types of twins. A more fruitful comparison would seem to be that between dizygotic twins and siblings, for whom the hereditary similarity is known to be the same. In Kallmann's monumental research on psychiatric disorders among twins (20), for example, one of the most convincing bits of evidence for the operation of hereditary factors in schizophrenia is the fact that the degrees of concordance for dizygotic twins and for siblings were practically identical. In contrast, it will be recalled that in intelligence test scores dizygotic twins resemble each other much more closely than do siblings—a finding which reveals the influence of environmental factors in intellectual development.

SUMMARY

The heredity-environment problem is still very much alive. Its viability is assured by the gradual replacement of the questions, "Which one?" and "How much?" by the more basic and appropriate question, "How?" Hereditary influences—as well as environmental factors of an organic nature—vary along a "continuum of indirectness." The more indirect their connection with behavior, the wider will be the range of variation of possible outcomes. One extreme of the continuum of indirectness may be illustrated by brain damage leading to mental deficiency; the other extreme, by physical characteristics associated with social stereotypes. Examples of factors falling at intermediate points include deafness, physical diseases, and motor disorders.

Those environmental factors which act directly upon behavior can be ordered along a continuum of breadth or permanence of effect, as exemplified by social class membership, amount of formal schooling, language handicap, and familiarity with specific test items.

Several current lines of research offer promising techniques for exploring the *modus operandi* of hereditary and environmental factors. Outstanding among them are investigations of: (*a*) hereditary conditions which underlie behavioral differences between selectively bred groups of animals; (*b*) relations between physiological variables and individual differences in behavior, especially in the case of pathological deviations; (*c*) role of prenatal physiological factors in behavior development; (*d*) influence of early experience upon eventual behavioral characteristics; (*e*) cultural differences in child-rearing practices in relation to intellectual and emotional development; (*f*) mechanisms of somatopsychological relationships; and (*g*) psychological development of twins from infancy to maturity, together with observations of their social environment. Such approaches are extremely varied with regard to subjects employed, nature of psychological functions studied, and specific experimental procedures followed. But it is just such heterogeneity of methodology that is demanded by the wide diversity of ways in which hereditary and environmental factors interact in behavior development.

REFERENCES

1. ANASTASI, ANNE. *Psychological testing.* New York: Macmillan, 1954.
2. ANASTASI, ANNE. *Differential psychology.* (3rd ed.) New York: Macmillan, 1958.
3. ANASTASI, ANNE, & CORDOVA, F. A. Some effects of bilingualism upon the intelligence test performance of Puerto Rican children in New York City. *J. educ. Psychol.*, 1953, *44*, 1–19.
4. ANASTASI, ANNE, & FOLEY, J. P., JR. A proposed reorientation in the heredity-environment controversy. *Psychol. Rev.*, 1948, *55*, 239–249.
5. ARSENIAN, S. Bilingualism in the postwar world. *Psychol. Bull.*, 1945, *42*, 65–86.
6. BARKER, R. G., WRIGHT, BEATRICE A., MYERSON, L., & GONICK, MOLLIE R. Adjustment to physical handicap and illness: A survey of the social psychology of physique and disability. *Soc. Sci. Res. Coun. Bull.*, 1953, No. 55 (Rev.).
7. BARKER, R. G., & WRIGHT, H. F. *Midwest and its children: The psychological ecology of an American town.* Evanston, Ill.: Row, Peterson, 1955.
8. BEACH, F. A., & JAYNES, J. Effects of early experience upon the behavior of animals. *Psychol. Bull.*, 1954, *51*, 239–263.
9. BRACKBILL, G. A. Studies of brain dysfunction in schizophrenia. *Psychol. Bull.*, 1956, *53*, 210–226.
10. DARCY, NATALIE T. A review of the literature of the effects of bilingualism upon the measurement of intelligence. *J. genet. Psychol.*, 1953, *82*, 21–57.
11. DAVIS, A., & HAVIGHURST, R. J. Social class and color differences in child rearing. *Amer. sociol. Rev.*, 1946, *11*, 698–710.
12. DOBZHANSKY, T. The genetic nature

of differences among men. In S. Persons (Ed.), *Evolutionary thought in America.* New Haven: Yale Univer. Press, 1950. Pp. 86–155.

13. DOBZHANSKY, T. Heredity, environment, and evolution. *Science,* 1950, *111,* 161–166.

14. FORGUS, R. H. The effect of early perceptual learning on the behavioral organization of adult rats. *J. comp. physiol. Psychol.,* 1954, *47,* 331–336.

15. HALDANE, J. B. S. *Heredity and politics.* New York: Norton, 1938.

16. HARRELL, RUTH F., WOODYARD, ELLA, & GATES, A. I. *The effect of mothers' diets on the intelligence of the offspring.* New York: Bur. Publ., Teach. Coll., Columbia Univer., 1955.

17. HEBB, D. O. *The organization of behavior.* New York: Wiley, 1949.

18. HIRSCH, J., & TRYON, R. C. Mass screening and reliable individual measurement in the experimental behavior genetics of lower organisms. *Psychol. Bull.,* 1956, *53,* 402–410.

19. HORWITT, M. K. Fact and artifact in the biology of schizophrenia. *Science,* 1956, *124,* 429–430.

20. KALLMANN, F. J. *Heredity in health and mental disorder; Principles of psychiatric genetics in the light of comparative twin studies.* New York: Norton, 1953.

21. KING, J. A., & GURNEY, NANCY L. Effect of early social experience on adult aggressive behavior in C57BL10 mice. *J. comp. physiol. Psychol.,* 1954, *47,* 326–330.

22. LOEVINGER, JANE. On the proportional contributions of differences in nature and in nurture to differences in intelligence. *Psychol. Bull.,* 1943, *40,* 725–756.

23. LORENZ, K. Der Kumpan in der Umwelt des Vogels. Der Artgenosse als auslösendes Moment sozialer Verhaltungsweisen. *J. Orn., Lpz.,* 1935, *83,* 137–213; 289–413.

24. LUCHINS, A. S., & FORGUS, R. H. The effect of differential postweaning environment on the rigidity of an animal's behavior. *J. genet. Psychol.,* 1955, *86,* 51–58.

25. MELZACK, R. The genesis of emotional behavior: An experimental study of the dog. *J. comp. physiol. Psychol.,* 1954, *47,* 166–168.

26. MILNER, ESTHER A. A study of the relationships between reading readiness in grade one school children and patterns of parent-child interaction. *Child Develpm.,* 1951, *22,* 95–112.

27. PASAMANICK, B., KNOBLOCH, HILDA, & LILIENFELD, A. M. Socioeconomic status and some precursors of neuropsychiatric disorder. *Amer. J. Orthopsychiat.,* 1956, *26,* 594–601.

28. SCHWESINGER, GLADYS C. *Heredity and environment.* New York: Macmillan, 1933.

29. SCOTT, J. P., & CHARLES, MARGARET S. Some problems of heredity and social behavior. *J. gen. Psychol.,* 1953, *48,* 209–230.

30. SCOTT, J. P., & FULLER, J. L. Research on genetics and social behavior at the Roscoe B. Jackson Memorial Laboratory, 1946–1951 —A progress report. *J. Hered.,* 1951, *42,* 191–197.

31. SEARLE, L. V. The organization of

hereditary maze-brightness and maze-dullness. *Genet. Psychol. Monogr.*, 1949, *39*, 279–325.

32. SNYDER, L. H.   The genetic approach to human individuality. *Sci. Mon., N. Y.*, 1949, *68*, 165–171.

33. SNYDER, L. H. & DAVID, P. R.   *The principles of heredity.* (5th ed.) Boston: Heath, 1957.

34. SPOERL, DOROTHY T.   Bilinguality and emotional adjustment. *J. abnorm. soc. Psychol.*, 1943, *38*, 37–57.

35. THOMPSON, W. R. & MELZACK, R.   Early environment. *Sci. Amer.*, 1956, *194* (1), 38–42.

36. TRYON, R. C.   Genetic differences in maze-learning ability in rats. *Yearb. nat. Soc. Stud. Educ.*, 1940, *39*, Part I, 111–119.

37. WHITING, J. W. M., et al. *Field guide for a study of socialization in five societies.* Cambridge, Mass.: Harvard Univer., 1954 (mimeo.).

38. WHITING, J. W. M., & CHILD, I. L. *Child training and personality: A cross-cultural study.* New Haven: Yale Univer. Press, 1953.

39. WILLIAMS, JUDITH R., & SCOTT, R. B. Growth and development of Negro infants: IV. Motor development and its relationship to child rearing practices in two groups of Negro infants. *Child Develpm.*, 1953, *24*, 103–121.

40. WOODWORTH, R. S.   Heredity and environment: A critical survey of recently published material on twins and foster children. *Soc. Sci. Res. Coun. Bull.*, 1941, No. 47.

DEVELOPMENTAL STUDIES | 2

THE DEVELOPMENTAL METHOD of investigation is characterized by the continuous or extended observation of behavior as a function of time. Developmental psychology (formerly termed "genetic psychology") sought to record the changing characteristics of the child with age. Many of its observational techniques, and certainly the underlying constructs that were utilized to "explain" the child's changing behavior, were drawn from the fields of biology and comparative psychology. The interest was mainly in the inborn characteristics of the species that determined the manner in which the child's new behaviors would emerge with increasing age. Thus, Gesell (1954) employed such principles as *developmental direction, reciprocal interweaving, and functional asymmetry* (all morphological terms) to account for the variability of, and the trial-and-error behaviors of, the growing child.

The developmental orientation manifested itself in two major types of investigation. One of these was the *longitudinal* study, in which the same children were studied at periodic intervals and their physical growth and changing behavioral characteristics were plotted as a function of age. The Shirley study exemplifies this approach. The major interest here is in the serial order in which certain specified new behaviors occur.

The second type of developmental study is the *cross-sectional* investigation, wherein the major interest is not so much what changes take place in a specific child's behavior over time, but rather the physical and behavioral characteristics of age groups. Thus, Smith (1925) investigated in this manner the vocabulary sizes of groups of children of various age levels from one year to five years.

The developmental approach in its simplest form was exemplified by the well-known anecdotal reports of Preyer and Hall (in Dennis, 1948, pp. 251–276) on the growth and development of individual children. The biographical observation technique sought to record bits of data that, if completely enough recorded, would constitute a natural history of the development of a child. Standardized situations for the observation and recording of such behaviors were, of course, not used. The reliability of these observations can often be questioned, for the observer is often the perhaps-biased parent of the child under investigation. It is likely that observational distortion and selectivity occurs under such conditions. Furthermore, the generality of findings from such observation of individual cases can be questioned: there is no easy way of knowing how typical for his age group the child being observed may be, and in all likelihood such a child (being the progeny of a gifted person) would be atypical in many respects.

As investigators became more adept in making behavioral observations, however, they developed standardized techniques for such observations and eventually became much concerned with the reliability of the observations and the generality of their "norms." Test items were gradually constructed, and infants of varying ages were subjected to the observation and stimulation demanded by these items. Many infant developmental scales and children's intelligence tests (for example, Bayley [1943]; Cattell [1940]) grew out of this standardized observational procedure.

Many detailed data on the development of behavior in infants and children exist in the literature today. Many researchers (Pratt, Nelson, and Sun [1930]; Irwin [1943], and others) have developed exceedingly well controlled observational techniques for the pursuit of these laws about behavior as a function of age. One of the criticisms of the approach is that it has tended to produce many unrelated facts. Some sort of theoretical integration or explication of processes must be achieved to truly account for or "explain" changing behavior as a function of age. Some critics argue that developmental psychology has been primarily "descriptive" in its account of behavior rather than "explanatory." The developmentalists' reply to such criticism has been that all science is decriptive in its early stages, and theorizing is premature when it occurs in the absence of a sizable number of *facts*.

Critics of the developmental approach have on occasion suggested also that the approach does not yield psychological *laws* from which predictions about behavior may be made. The developmentalists' reply has been that this approach does yield a kind of scientific law, one relating age or time as the independent variable to behavior as the dependent variable. It is true that laws have been obtained and predictions may be made from the data of developmental studies. Perhaps, however, the most serious drawback of the approach is that it has tended to remain oriented toward the assessment of age-determined differences and has tended to neglect the specific stimulating factors or antecedant conditions that might account for other portions of the variance of children's behavior. Normative data do provide us with an indication of the probability of occurrence of particular kinds of behaviors (say walking) at each age level. At two months, no child walks; at twenty-four months, almost all children walk; and in between percentages can be determined. Normative data do *not* tell us about the processes or mechanisms underlying these age changes. They do not tell us, for example, whether the child who walks at eight months of age has been subjected to a special kind of learning experience making this behavior possible, or whether the child's genetic predisposition has instigated the behavior.

Piaget has been included as a reading in this section because his orientation is a developmental one. The procedures that he typically employs involve the enumeration of certain classes of behaviors over time or as a function of age. Indeed, his theoretical approach to these developmental data bears the stamp of his biological training and interest in children's development. Piaget's work is distinguished for his attempt to employ developmental and natural-history modes of investigation in the study of the higher thought processes and intelligence of children.

The Kagan and Moss selection indicates that longitudinal investigations can be carried on over long periods of time, and that certain kinds of data obtained from children may serve as modest predictive indices of adult characteristics. Furthermore, this selection exemplifies the possibility of utilizing long-range longitudinal data in accounting for complex personality attributes in adulthood.

Finally, it must be stated that developmental and naturalistic observations of children (as well as lower animals) may often provide the idea and impetus for carefully controlled experimental studies. A recent paper by Salk (1961) is remarkable for its integration of at least three modes of attack on a simple and well-known developmental phenomenon, namely the characteristic loss of weight in the first few days of an infants life. Salk noted that maternal monkeys in a zoo seemed to carry their young in a characteristic fashion—with the infant's head oriented toward the left side of her body. He wondered if this characteristic served some "purpose" and whether humans tended to do the same. He conducted a normative investigation of the manner in which mothers in a maternity ward tended to hold their infants and found that human mothers also characteristically place their infants' heads toward the left sides of their bodies, "close to their heart." The finding led to the formulation of an hypothesis which the author then sought to test experimentally in the newborn nursery: that the sound of the maternal heartbeat was in some sense rewarding, comforting, and beneficial to the welfare of the newborn child. His experiment supported the proposition that the amplified sound of an adult heartbeat in the nursery results in a reversal of the usual weight loss during the lying-in period. Infants not systematically subjected to this sound characteristically lost weight and tended to be more fussy. While the "meaning" of the heartbeat sound to the child may be debated and systematically investigated further for greater clarification, the study exemplifies the usefulness of naturalistic observations, even of infrahuman organisms, in the formulation of experimentally testable propositions about developmental characteristics of children.

REFERENCES

BAYLEY, NANCY.   Mental growth during the first three years. In R. G. Barker, J. S. Kounin, and H. F. Wright (Eds.), *Child behavior and development.* New York: McGraw-Hill, 1943. Pp. 87–105.

CATTELL, PSYCHE.   *The measurement of intelligence of infants and young children.* New York: The Psychological Corporation, 1940. Pp. 274.

DENNIS, W.(Ed).   *Readings in the history of psychology.* New York: Appleton, 1948.

GESELL, A.   The ontogenesis of infant behavior. In L. Carmichael (Ed.), *Manual of child psychology.* (2nd ed.) New York: Wiley, 1954. Pp. 335–373.

IRWIN, O. C.   The activities of newborn infants. In R. G. Barker, J. S. Kounin, and H. F. Wright (Eds.), *Child behavior and development.* New York: McGraw-Hill, 1943. Pp. 29–47.

PRATT, K. C., NELSON, A. K., and SUN, K. H.   The behavior of the newborn infant. *Ohio State Univ. Stud., Contrib. Psychol.,* 1930, No. 10.

SALK, L.   The importance of the heartbeat rhythm to human nature: Theoretical, clinical, and experimental observations. Paper presented at Session on Personality Development, Third World Congress of Psychiatry, Montreal, Canada, June 8, 1961.

SMITH, M. E.   An investigation of the development of the sentence and the extent of vocabulary in young children. *Univ. Iowa Stud. Child Welf.,* 1925, 3, No. 5.

THE FIRST TWO YEARS:

THE MOTOR SEQUENCE

MARY M. SHIRLEY

THE METHOD

WHATEVER CONTRIBUTIONS this study may make to our knowledge of infancy will be largely attributable to the method used. Certain fundamental problems of development have only one avenue of approach, that of long continued, or frequently repeated, observations of the same individual. A view of the child as a whole and an understanding of the detailed course of child development, its continuity and its rate, are the rewards of pursuing this route.

Thus far the longitudinal road has been sparingly traveled by students of child development, the reason being, of course, that one can progress much faster and much farther toward an understanding of many fundamental principles by taking a short cut that crosses the lives of many children at the same time than by following a few babies down the long lanes of the months and years. For many years interested parents and relatives were the only ones to undertake such long journeys, the obvious reason being that they were perhaps the only persons who had continuous and easy access to the child over long periods. With all their obvious faults and defects, the contributions of these biographies of children kept by parents and relatives are of inestimable value to the modern student of child development. From them one not only gets an impression of the continuous onsweep of developmental processes, but he also feels intimately acquainted with the child as a person.

The growth of the intelligence-testing movement and the theoretical problem of the constancy of the *IQ* that it has raised has resulted in the practice of making "follow-up" studies, whereby individuals tested or measured at an early age are examined again at a later age. Perhaps the largest and most completely organized follow-up work has been done by Terman and his co-authors (8) in their *Genetic Studies of Genius*. Indeed, so comprehensive is the study and so continuous is the contact that it might be called the first of the "follow-through" studies, if we may designate as follow-through studies those in which the contact is maintained over a long period and observations are made at repeated intervals. These are in contrast to the "follow-up" studies, in which the contact may be broken and reestablished once or oftener during the individual's childhood. In the field of follow-up work Gesell has retested enough children to enable him to draw up developmental curves.

The present study is, so far as the author is aware, the first of the follow-through studies of babyhood. A few months after it was begun, a similar study was initiated at the University of Califor-

Reprinted by permission from: *The first two years: A study of twenty-five babies*, Vol. 2 by Mary M. Shirley (Child Welfare Monograph No. 7), University of Minnesota Press, Minneapolis, Copyright 1933 by The University of Minnesota.

nia, where Bayley and Wolff made repeated monthly examinations of a group of sixty babies. The Minnesota study does not include so many subjects, but the deficiency in that respect is perhaps offset by the greater frequency of the examinations and by the fact that the study was conducted in the homes instead of being confined to the laboratory.

In brief, the general procedure consisted of observations of a sizable group of babies in the hospital and in the homes from the day of birth. Examinations were made daily during the first week of the hospital period and every two days during the second week. During the remainder of the first year the babies were observed at weekly intervals in their homes and at biweekly intervals during the second year. At the age of two years two of the children became regular attendants at the Institute nursery school and entered into the regular program of observations and tests carried out by Institute workers. The remaining seventeen children, whose parents still live in the Twin Cities, are visited four times a year for the collection of anthropometric data and twice for psychological data, and once a year they are brought to the Institute for a mental test. The weekly examinations of the first year were supplemented by the mothers' daily records of food intake and habits of sleep and by their summaries of elimination, developmental items, and general behavior. A more complete description of the observational program and a schedule of examinations for the first two years are given in Volume I, pages 8–31. The complete list of babies is given in Volume I, pages 210–211.[1]

_____

[1] Volume I, which deals with *Postural and Locomotor Development*, was published by the University of Minnesota Press in 1931.

By virtue of its follow-through character this study for the most part treats the order of development without respect to age. Conducting the observations in the home introduced considerable informality into the examining situation, and the systematic record that was kept of incidental reactions in addition to responses to the tests greatly increases the value of the data as an index to the ordinary course of behavior development. In view of the similarity of this approach to that of the biographical studies, it is not surprising that there are similarities in the results. The course of development, as will appear later, is so consistent from baby to baby that it may be studied more effectively by the careful, continuous observation of one baby than by a cross-section survey of many babies at widely spaced age intervals.

Similarity of the two methods may account likewise for the high consistency of this study with that of Bühler (1). Her method was to observe constantly for an entire day and night the activities of a small group of babies on each monthly birthday. The observations were made without aritficial stimulation; the observer merely sat near the infant, watching and recording his spontaneous behavior in his usual daily environment. The present study differs from Bühler's in that simple tests were planned in the hope of tapping the baby's entire repertoire of acts in a brief half hour of examination each week. However, the examining situation soon became a usual part of the baby's routine, and the mother's presence and the familiar home environment completely robbed the examination of all strangeness. The tests themselves closely duplicated the parents' play stimulation and were appropriate for calling forth the babies' abilities and interests. Responses to the tests were recorded in descriptive terms rather than in terms of arbitrary standards of behavior, and the records of incidental behavior and the mothers' records adequately supplemented the test data. For all these reasons it is likely that this material is almost as free from the unfavorable influences of artificial stimulation as is that of Bühler. It presents the additional advantages, moreover, of being somewhat more controlled and of including a larger number of babies of each age than Bühler's. The qualitative descriptions of infant behavior obtained by the two methods are strikingly similar. . . .

Before we attempt to say just what the present study has added to our knowledge of motor development let us consider briefly the things it has not added. Only with a clear understanding of the scope of a piece of scientific work may its contributions be evaluated and allocated among the existing body of facts.

There are four or more courses that a student of motor development in infancy might follow. He might set up age norms of development by means of a study of large numbers of babies; he might measure the degree of motor skill possessed by the individual baby; he might devote his attention to the modification of given motor items after they were established and determine the conditions that led to modification; or he might interest himself in the sequence of motor development. In this study the fourth course was followed; a few minor facts relating to the other three were gathered, but they were only incidental to the main objective.

The reason for rejecting the first three methods may be briefly stated. In the first place, age standards of development derived from so small and so selected a group of babies as entered into this study would be valueless for future comparisons. It cannot be stressed too often that the age figures given in this work apply to this group alone and are not to be used as criteria for other groups. Far better norms have already been established by Gesell (3), Jones (5), and others, and therefore there is no great need for a normative study at the present time.

A study of the degree of motor skill possessed by each baby could be conducted only if accurate ways of measuring the skill could be devised. This is not beyond the limits of possibility, but it is not an easy task. The difficulty of even estimating degrees of head control and the skill involved in sitting alone and other motor accomplishments is baffling. Although the investigator is able to judge the degree of skill in an older child by putting him through a strict set of performance tests, it is likely that he would have to limit the items in his tests of babies to the things they do spontaneously in order to insure their whole-hearted cooperation. Such a study would entail the establishment of standards of degree of skill. Worthwhile as the investigation would be, it could be carried out only with the aid of better controlled experimental conditions and more refined examining techniques than were possible in this investigation.

Likewise, a study of the nature and degree of modification that motor skills undergo from their earliest manifestation to their perfection would require more time and more elaborate treatment than was possible in this study. One phase of motor development, walking, has been fairly adequately studied in this way, but techniques for similar studies of other aspects of motor development were not available, so they were not attempted.

There remains the developmental order, or motor sequence, the only aspect of motor development on which this study offers new and reasonably complete data. Before entering upon a description of the sequence and a discussion of its importance it is necessary to make clear two distinctions: first, the difference between motor activity and motor control and, secondly, the difference between ability and proficiency in the performance of motor acts.

MOTOR ACTIVITY VERSUS MOTOR CONTROL

In centering attention on the order of motor development the observer did not fail to take cognizance of the profuse and varied activity present in the babies at birth. It is difficult to define this activity in such a way that the differences between it and the controlled acts that developed later may be readily apparent. The early activities of kicking, waving, and squirming were not uncoordinated, nor were they altogether random and spontaneous. Perhaps the most characteristic earmark of the activity of this period was that it "didn't get the baby anywhere"; it apparently was directed toward no goal, or if it was it did not effect an adjustment to the environment. Controlled motor acts, on the other hand, were successful responses to definite stimuli, and with the development of motor control the baby began to manipulate and manage his environment to a considerable degree. Through the work of Coghill (2), Minkowski, and others knowledge of the motor sequence has been pushed back to the prenatal period, and their work furnishes good evidence that generalized mass activity develops first and that out of it specific reflexes are differentiated. Neonatal activity well repays a quantitative study, as Irwin (4) has amply demonstrated. The motor sequence, however, represents only the development of motor control and not the manifestation of undirected motor activity.

ABILITY VERSUS PROFICIENCY

The reader must also remember that there is a great difference between ability to do and excellency in the doing of motor acts. The motor sequence takes into account only the former. It represents the order in which the babies were first able to watch, to reach, to sit alone, and so forth; it is not concerned with the proficiency with which they performed each act. It goes without saying that the babies differed in proficiency at the onset of each new phase of motor development even though the degree of difference could not be measured, and that proficiency increased in individual babies at different rates and to different degrees. But the transition from the inability to reach, creep, or walk to the ability, however feeble, to perform these acts was well marked. The order of these transitions from uncontrolled generalized activity to successfully controlled motor acts comprises the motor sequence.

SEQUENCE NOT A BY-PRODUCT
OF THE MOTOR TESTS

The reader may question whether the motor sequence is not merely a product of the motor tests. That possibility was safeguarded against in two ways; first, by the recording method, by which the observer wrote down in consistent descriptive terms exactly what the baby did in response to each motor test instead of marking them passed or failed; and, secondly, by including in the sequence items that were not tested for but that occurred spontaneously. The consistency with which the items of motor play fit into the sequence is a strong argument against its artificiality.

SEQUENCE OF MOTOR DEVELOPMENT

Much has been made of the point that motor development in the first two years follows a definite sequence, at least when its various phases—postural control, locomotion, and manipulation—are considered separately. It remains to be seen whether the sequence holds when these different aspects of development are thrown together into one series. Under such treatment the sequence might conceivably break down; granting that the sequence comes about by virtue of the fact that coordinations acquired through the perfection of one motor item are essential components of the item next developed, then the sequence of these items would be a logical necessity. Undoubtedly this is true in such a sequence as that of reaching, touching, grasping, and retaining; it is mechanically impossible for the baby to grasp a toy without having first reached and touched it, although it is not quite clear why the ability to do these three acts does not appear simultaneously instead of at intervals of one or two weeks. It is a little less obvious but still well within reason that chest up succeeds chin up, rolling succeeds swimming movements, and creeping succeeds scooting backward, because coordinations acquired in preceding acts are used in the ones following. If this explanation fully accounts for the sequence within any given

phase of development, such as manipulation or assumption of an upright posture, one might expect to find no sequence from one type of motor performance to another where the coordinations acquired in the first motor act seemingly play no part, or an obscure and minor one, in the second. One would not expect that head control would precede reaching in the lying posture, or that reaching, grasping, and holding would precede sitting alone, nor would the sequence of the play reactions of scratching, playing with the toes, bouncing, and rocking, be an obvious inference.

When all the motor items are thrown together, however, the sequence is just as well defined as when each motor phase is considered separately. To be sure, some items of the manipulatory phase develop simultaneously with items of the locomotor and postural phases, but simultaneity of items does not impair the fundamental sequence. For the most part, the items of one phase dovetail with those of the others. The extent of simultaneity and of dovetailing in the sequence may be seen in Table 1. In Figure 1 the items have been made to appear equally spaced for the sake of a more diagrammatic effect, but since the order of the items rather than the expansion or contraction of their spacing is of most interest, the equality of the spacing does not distort the facts.

CONSISTENCY OF THE SEQUENCE

The tables and charts depict only the order of the medians. To show that the sequence does not break down when it is applied to the progress of an individual baby the data on individual comparisons will be given. There were 42

TABLE 1 · MEDIAN AGES AND PARTS OF THE BODY CONTROLLED IN VARIOUS REACTIONS IN THE MOTOR SEQUENCE

Median age in weeks	Eye coordination	Locomotion	Fine motor reactions	Motor play	Parts of body controlled
6 da.	Follow light				
2.0	Watch person				
3.0		Chin up			Eyes, head, and neck
5.0	Follow tape H				
9.0	Follow tape V	Chest up		Smile at person	
10.0	Follow tape C				
14.0		Adjust for lifting	Reach and touch		
15.0			Grasp object	Play with hands	Arm and upper trunk
18.0		Sit on lap	Retain object (thumb opposition)		
21.0			Grasp dangling object	Object to mouth	
25.0		Sit alone momentarily	Transfer object from hand to hand	Play with toes	Hands and lower trunk
28.5		Roll		Pat toy	
30.5		Sit alone 1 minute		Rock, shake head	
31.5		Stand with help			
38.0		Some progress on stomach		Suspension bridge	
41.0		Scoot backward		Pat-a-cake Peek-a-boo	
42.0		Stand holding to furniture	Point with index finger		Pelvic region, legs, and fingers
45.0		Creep			
45.0		Walk when led			
47.0		Pull to stand by furniture	Open simple boxes		
56.0–62.0				Put fingers in holes	
62.0		Stand alone			
66.0		Walk alone		Run, climb	

motor items developed between the median ages of 4 days and 47 weeks;[2] during this period the items were naturally spaced at frequent intervals, and there were only three intervals of three weeks or more during which no new motor item was developed.

In order to obtain a measure of the extent to which individual babies adhered to the sequence, each item was paired with another having a different median, and the number of babies in which the order of the medians was reversed was obtained. With 42 items it would have been possible to compare 861 pairs of items, but items at the extremes would have been separated by an age range so great that there would have been no overlapping. Consequently a range of 6 weeks was arbitrarily chosen as the limit for

[2] The reason for discontinuing the comparisons at a median of 47 weeks was that after this age the motor items were spaced at less frequent intervals. All but two of the locomotor items, standing and walking alone, had been developed at this age. The manipulatory items excluded by this age limit consist chiefly of specific reactions to specific boxes that are hard to analyze into their motor components.

THE MOTOR SEQUENCE

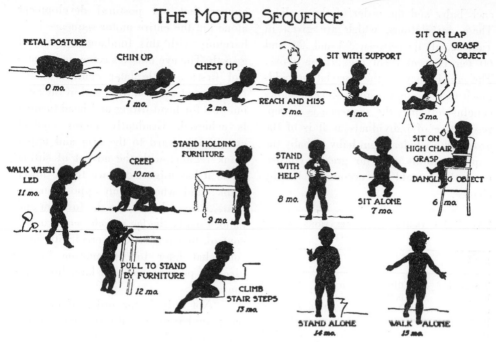

Figure 1.

comparisons. In all there were 224 pairs of items separated by a median range of 6 weeks or less; items with identical medians were not compared. The average separation of the medians of these items was 3.66 weeks. These 224 pairs embraced a total of 5,019 case comparisons, of which 4,294 were consistent with the order of the median. Thus the number of reversals was 725, or 14.45 per cent.

Generally speaking, the reversals were more frequent on those items that were difficult to define and for which the criteria was somewhat vague, such as tensing to be lifted, early stepping, and straightening the knees in the standing posture, and on those items that were not tested for but were noted when they spontaneously occurred, such as scratching, transferring the object from hand to hand, playing with the toes, ringing the

bell, and pointing with the index finger. A partial explanation is that there is less likelihood that spontaneous items occurred in the examiners' presence during the same week the babies were first capable of performing them than that the items tested for were called forth and observed as soon as the capacity developed. Moreover, examinations were occasionally missed; if several new motor items appeared simultaneously at the next examination the observer might fail to note all of them, and thus the possibility of reversals would be increased. Considering all these possibilities for error, the wonder is not that reversals in the sequence are so many but that they are so few.

The sequence was further tested for consistency by running rank order correlations between the order of items for each baby and the order of the median. These correlations, which are given in Table 2, all lie between .93 and .98, and 60 per cent of them are .97 or above. The consistency of the correlations adds much to their significance, since it shows conclusively that the sequence is as representative of individuals as it is of the group as a whole. From baby to baby the sequence holds with far greater consistency than could be accounted for by chance.

TABLE 2 · INDIVIDUAL CORRELATIONS ON THE MOTOR SEQUENCE

Baby		Baby	
Winifred	.95±.010	Martin	.93±.012
Fred	.98±.009	Quentin	.97±.009
Carol	.96±.010	Virginia Ruth	.96±.010
Doris	.94±.010	Sibyl	.93±.012
David	.95±.010	Maurice	.95±.010
Donovan	.97±.009	Torey	.98±.009
Harvey	.97±.009	Judy	.97±.009
James D.	.97±.009	Peter	.98±.009
Irene May	.97±.009	Patricia	.97±.009
Larry	.97±.009	Walley	.97±.009

HARMONY WITH ANATOMICAL LAWS

The well-known anatomical law of developmental direction [3]—which may be stated briefly as the law that the growth wave which sweeps over the body begins at the head and travels toward the feet— has already been mentioned as being exemplified by the assumption of postural control. From a study of Table 1 it would

_____

[3] This law has been stated by Jackson and Scammon (7, page 267) as follows: "While each part passes through its own cycle of changes these changes as a whole tend to follow what is known as the *law of developmental direction*; for it is generally found that development (including growth and differentiation) in the long axis of the body appears first in the head region of the body and progresses toward the tail region, and similarly development in the transverse plane begins in the mid-dorsal region and progresses lateroventrally (in the limbs proximodistally)."

appear that not postural development alone but the entire motor sequence is in harmony with this fundamental law of growth. The eye muscles come under control first; a little later control of the facial muscles for smiling and of the neck muscles for head-lifting and head-turning is achieved. Gradually motor control creeps downward to the arm and upper trunk region; with the advent of sitting alone it has migrated down to the lower trunk; and when thumb opposition appears, it has advanced to the forearm and hand. Finally the leg muscles come under control, first for standing erect with help, somewhat later for locomotion in the creeping posture, and still later for walking alone.

Not only is the order of development in harmony with the law of developmental direction, but the speed of development also seems to be graduated from the head downward. Control of eyes, head, neck, upper trunk, and arms follow each other in rapid succession. About the time the ability to sit alone is achieved, however, the rate becomes noticeably slower. Whereas the attainment of a new motor item was a matter of days at the outset, it now becomes a matter of months. These differences in the rate of assuming motor control suggest that the growth gradient that makes for different rates of growth in different parts of the body is also operative, or at least has a counterpart in the development of functional control.

A second interesting feature of the sequence is that postural control of a given part always precedes controlled movements of that part. The baby holds his head erect before he turns it; he sits alone before he sways and rocks in this posture; and he stands before he climbs or walks. This is probably just a matter of body mechanics; it would be impossible to execute coordinated movements in a given posture before the posture itself could be maintained. The progress from flexion to extension in babyhood is, however, worthy of note. In the newborn baby the dominance of the flexor muscles over the extensors is so great that arms, hands, and legs can hardly be stretched out for measuring. Gradually the extensors begin to oppose this state of flexion, and the early flexed lying posture gives way to more extended postures. It is largely the extensor muscles that are involved in the maintenance of upright postures. Investigators are still pretty much in the dark as to the nervous mechanism of postural control, but whatever the mechanism, it is logical for extensor muscles to come under control for posture before they work together with the flexors to execute directed acts involving a rapid losing and regaining of postural equilibrium.

MATURATION AS AN EXPLANATION OF THE MOTOR SEQUENCE

In order to prevent misunderstandings that might lead to controversy, the term "maturation" must be rigidly defined. In this study it is used to connote the sum total of the growth processes. It is not used in the more restricted sense of the development or maturing of the nervous system alone. The writer favors the definition of Marquis (6), who designates as maturation all development carried out by the interaction of the organism upon its inner environment.

Maturation, defined in this way, appears to be the most satisfactory way of accounting for the motor sequence. To review briefly, the number of items included in the sequence and the closeness of their spacing certainly precludes the possibility of a consistent order being established by chance; the consistency of the sequence from baby to baby, not only in the motor functions tested but also in spontaneous play reactions, casts doubt upon the learning hypothesis as an explanatory principle. Finally, the harmony of the sequence with the fundamental law of anatomical growth is a strong argument for the acceptance of the maturation hypothesis.

HOW MATURATION FUNCTIONS

In accepting the maturation hypothesis it is not necessary to settle the question as to whether the motor sequence is a function of growth or whether it is merely a manifestation of growth. It may be that the relationship between body growth and motor development is one of cause and effect, or it may be that the two are merely parallels, the one being the manifestation of growth in body structure and the other the manifestation of growth in body function. But in either case maturation is at work.

The present study does not enable us to say what matures or how maturation operates in bringing about the motor sequence. No doubt the fact that motor control begins at the head and moves toward the feet is partly a matter of body mechanics; to a certain extent it is true that outlying muscles are incapable of making adequate adjustment to peripheral stimuli until the larger, proximal muscles work to bring them directly in contact with the stimuli. It is also true that motor development consists largely of the differentiation of specific movements from generalized mass activity. Neither of these possibilities, however, weakens the sequence itself nor precludes the interpretation of it by the maturation hyphothesis, since neither of them is adequate to completely account for a sequence of such remarkable length and detail. The consistency of the sequence from baby to baby speaks well for it reliability, and its harmony with the accepted laws of growth attests to its validity as a maturing process.

SUMMARY

Progress in motor control follows an orderly sequence beginning at the head and traveling toward the feet. The sequence as determined from the medians of the group holds for individual babies, and it includes, in addition to items specifically tested for, items of motor play that occurred spontaneously. Hence it is unlikely that the sequence is merely the by-product of the tests. The sequence of development strongly supports the maturation theory of motor development. It appears that maturation gives ability to do motor acts and that subsequent practice gives proficiency in doing them.

REFERENCES

1. BÜHLER, CHARLOTTE. *The first year of life.* New York: The John Day Co. 1930.

2. COGHILL, G. E. "Correlated anatomical and physiological studies of the growth of the nervous system in amphibia." *J. Comp. Neurol., 41:* 95–152. 1926.

3. GESELL, ARNOLD. *Mental growth of the preschool child.* New York: The Macmillan Co. 1926.

4. IRWIN, O. C. "The amount and nature of activities of newborn infants." *Genet. Psychol. Monog., 8:* 1–192. 1930.

5. JONES, MARY COVER. "The development of early behavior patterns in young children." *Ped. Sem. and J. Genet. Psychol., 33:* 537–585. 1926.

6. MARQUIS, D. G. "The criterion of innate behavior." *Psychol. Rev., 37:* 334–349. 1930.

7. SCAMMON, RICHARD E., AND CALKINS, LEROY A. *The development and growth of the external dimensions of the human body in the fetal period.* Minneapolis: The University of Minnesota Press. 1929.

8. TERMAN, L. M., ET AL. *Genetic studies of genius.* Vol. I. Stanford University: Stanford University Press. 1926.

THE USE OF REFLEXES

JEAN PIAGET

IF, IN ORDER TO ANALYZE the first mental acts, we refer to hereditary organic reactions, we must study them not for their own sake but merely so that we may describe *in toto* the way in which they affect the individual's behavior. We should begin, therefore, by trying to differentiate between the psychological problem of the reflexes and the strictly biological problem.

Behavior observable during the first weeks of life is very complicated, biologically speaking. At first there are very different types of reflexes involving the medulla, the bulb, the optic commissures, the ectoderm itself; moreover, from reflex to instinct is only a difference of degree. Next to the reflexes of the central nervous system are those of the autonomic nervous system and all the reactions due to "protopathic" sensibility. There is, above all, the whole group of postural reflexes whose importance for the beginnings of the evolution of the mind has been demonstrated by H. Wallon. It is hard to envisage the organization of the foregoing mechanisms without giving the endocrine processes their just due as indicated by so many learned or spontaneous reactions. Physiological psychology is confronted at the present time by a host of problems which consist of determining the effects on the individual's behavior of each of these separate mechanisms. H. Wallon analyzes one of the most important of

these questions in his excellent book on the disturbed child (*l'Enfant turbulent*): "Is there an emotional stage, or a stage of postural and extrapyramidal reactions prior to the sensorimotor or cortical stage?" Nothing better reveals the complexity of elementary behavior and the need to differentiate between the successive stages of concurrent physiological systems than Wallon's scholarly study of their genesis in which a wealth of pathologic material always substantiates his analysis.

Notwithstanding the fascinating conclusions thus reached, it seems to us difficult at the present time to go beyond a general description when it comes to grasping the continuity between the earliest behavior of the nursling and the future intellectual behavior. That is why, although in complete sympathy with Wallon's attempt to identify psychic mechanisms with those of life itself, we believe we should limit ourselves to emphasizing functional identity, from the point of view of simple external behavior.

In this respect the problem which arises in connection with reactions in the first weeks is only this: How do the sensorimotor, postural, and other reactions, inherent in the hereditary equipment of the newborn child, prepare him to adapt himself to his external environment and to acquire subsequent behavior distinguished by the progressive use of experience?

The psychological problem begins to pose itself as soon as the reflexes,

From J. Piaget, *Origins of intelligence in children,* copyright 1952 by International Universities Press, Inc.

postures, etc., are considered no longer in connection with the internal mechanism of the living organism, but rather in their relationships to the external environment as it is subjected to the individual's activity. Let us examine, from this point of view, the various fundamental reactions in the first weeks: sucking and grasping reflexes, crying and vocalization, movements and positions of the arms, the head or the trunk, etc.

What is striking about this is that such activities from the start of their most primitive functioning, each in itself and some in relation to others, give rise to a systematization which exceeds their automatization. Almost since birth, therefore, there is "behavior" in the sense of the individual's total reaction and not only a setting in motion of particular or local automatizations only interrelated from within. In other words, the sequential manifestations of a reflex such as sucking are not comparable to the periodic starting up of a motor used intermittently, but constitute an historical development so that each episode depends on preceding episodes and conditions those that follow in a truly organic evolution. In fact, whatever the intensive mechanism of this historical process may be, one can follow the changes from the outside and describe things as though each particular reaction determined the others without intermediates. This comprises total reaction, that is to say, the beginning of psychology.

1. SUCKING REFLEXES

Let us take as an example the sucking reflexes or the instinctive act of sucking; these reflexes are complicated, involving a large number of afferent fibers of the trigeminal and the glossopharyngeal nerves as well as the efferent fibers of the facial, the hypoglossal and the masseteric nerves, all of which have as a center the bulb of the spinal cord. First here are some facts:

OBSERVATION 1

From birth sucking-like movements may be observed: impulsive movement and protrusion of the lips accompanied by displacements of the tongue, while the arms engage in unruly and more or less rhythmical gestures and the head moves laterally, etc.

As soon as the hands rub the lips the sucking reflex is released. The child sucks his fingers for a moment but of course does not know either how to keep them in his mouth or pursue them with his lips. Lucienne and Laurent, a quarter of an hour and a half hour after birth, respectively, had already sucked their hand like this: Lucienne, whose hand had been immobilized due to its position, sucked her fingers for more than ten minutes.

A few hours after birth, first nippleful of collostrum. It is known how greatly children differ from each other with respect to adaptation to this first meal. For some children like Lucienne and Laurent, contact of the lips and probably the tongue with the nipple suffices to produce sucking and swallowing. Other children, such as Jacqueline, have slower coordination: the child lets go of the breast every moment without taking it back again by himself or applying himself to it as vigorously when the nipple is replaced in his mouth. There are some children, finally, who need real forcing: holding their head, forcibly putting the nipple between the lips and in contact with the tongue, etc.

OBSERVATION 2

The day after birth Laurent seized the nipple with his lips without having to have it held in his mouth. He immediately seeks the breast when it escapes him as the result of some movement.

During the second day also Laurent again begins to make sucking-like movements between meals while thus repeating the impulsive movements of the first day: his lips open and close as if to receive a real nippleful, but without having an object. This behavior subsequently became more frequent and we shall not take it up again.

The same day the beginning of a sort of reflex searching may be observed in Laurent, which will develop on the following days and which probably constitutes the functional equivalent of the gropings characteristics of the later stages (acquisition of habits and empirical intelligence). Laurent is lying on his back with his mouth open, his lips and tongue moving slightly in imitation of the mechanism of sucking, and his head moving from left to right and back again, as though seeking an object. These gestures are either silent or interrupted by grunts with an expression of impatience and of hunger.

OBSERVATION 3

The third day Laurent makes new progress in his adjustment to the breast. All he needs in order to grope with open mouth toward final success is to have touched the breast or the surrounding teguments with his lips. But he hunts on the wrong side as well as on the right side, that is to say, the side where contact has been made.

OBSERVATION 4

Laurent at 0;0 (9) is lying in bed and seeks to suck, moving his head to the left and to the right. Several times he rubs his lips with his hand which he immediately sucks. He knocks against a quilt and a wool coverlet; each time he sucks the object only to relinquish it after a moment and begins to cry again. When he sucks his hand he does not turn away from it as he seems to do with the woolens, but the hand itself escapes him through lack of coordination; he then immediately begins to hunt again.

OBSERVATION 5

As soon as his cheek comes in contact with the breast, Laurent at 0;0 (12) applies himself to seeking until he finds drink. His search takes its bearings: immediately from the correct side, that is to say, the side where he experienced contact.

At 0;0 (20) he bites the breast which is given him, 5 cm. from the nipple. For a moment he sucks the skin which he then lets go in order to move his mouth about 2 cm. As soon as he begins sucking again he stops. In one of his attempts he touches the nipple with the outside of his lips and he does not recognize it. But, when his search subsequently leads him accidentally to touch the nipple with the mucosa of the upper lip (his mouth being wide open), he at once adjusts his lips and begins to suck.

The same day, same experiment: after having sucked the skin for several seconds, he withdraws and begins to cry. Then he begins again, withdraws again, but without crying, and takes it again 1 cm. away; he keeps this up until he discovers the nipple.

OBSERVATION 6

The same day I hold out my crooked index finger to Laurent, who is crying from hunger (but intermittently and without violence). He immediately sucks it but rejects it after a few seconds and begins to cry. Second attempt: same reaction. Third attempt: he sucks it, this time for a long time and thoroughly, and it is I who retract it after a few minutes.

OBSERVATION 7

Laurent at 0;0 (21) is lying on his right side, his arms tight against his body, his hands clasped, and he sucks his right thumb at length while remaining completely immobile. The nurse made the same observation on the previous day. I take his right hand away and he at once begins to search for it, turning his head from left to right. As his hands remained immobile due to his position, Laurent found his thumb after three attempts: prolonged sucking begins each time. But, once he has been placed on his back, he does not know how to coordinate the movement of the arms with that of the mouth and his hands draw back even when his lips are seeking them.

At 0;0 (24) when Laurent sucks his thumb, he remains completely immobile (as though having a nippleful: complete sucking, pantings, etc.). When his hand alone grazes his mouth, no coordination.

OBSERVATION 8

At 0;0 (21): Several times I place the back of my index finger against his cheeks. Each time he turns to the correct side while opening his mouth. Same reactions with the nipple.

Then I repeat the same experiments as those in observation 5. At 0;0 (21) Laurent begins by sucking the teguments with which he comes in contact. He relinquishes them after a moment but searches with open mouth, while almost rubbing the skin with his lips. He seizes the nipple as soon as he brushes against it with the mucosa of his lower lip.

That evening, the same experiment, but made during a nursing which has been interrupted for this purpose. Laurent is already half asleep; his arms hang down and his hands are open (at the beginning of the meal his arms are folded against his chest and his hands are clasped). His mouth is placed against the skin of the breast about 5 cm. from the nipple. He immediately sucks without reopening his eyes but, after a few moments, failure awakens him. His eyes are wide open, his arms flexed again and he sucks with rapidity. Then he gives up, in order to search a little further away, on the left side which happens by chance to be the correct side. Again finding nothing, he continues to change places on the left side, but the rotatory movement which he thus gives his head results in making him let go the breast and go off on a tangent. In the course of this tangential movement he knocks against the nipple with the left commissure of his lips and everything that happens would

seem to indicate that he recognizes it at once. Instead of groping at random, he only searches in the immediate neighborhood of the nipple. But as the lateral movements of his head made him describe a tangential curve opposite and not parallel to the curve of the breast, he oscillates in space guided only by light, haphazard contacts with the breast. It takes a short time for these increasingly localized attempts to be successful. This last phase of groping has been noteworthy for the speed with which each approach to it has been followed by an attempt at insertion of the nipple, while the lips open and close with maximum vigor; and noteworthy also for the progressive adjusting of the tangential movements around the points of contact.

At 0;0 (23) a new experiment. Laurent is 10 cm. from the breast, searching for it on the left and on the right. While he searches on the left the nipple touches his right cheek. He immediately turns and searches on the right. He is then moved 5 cm. away. He continues to search on the correct side. He is brought nearer as soon as he grasps the skin; he gropes and finds the nipple.

Same experiment and same result that evening. But, after several swallows, he is removed. He remains oriented to the correct side.

At 0;0 (24) Laurent, during the same experiments, seems much faster. To localize his search it suffices for the nipple to be brushed by the outside of his lips and no longer only by the mucosa. Besides, as soon as he has noticed the nipple, his head's lateral movements become more rapid and precise (less extensive). Finally, it seems that he is henceforth capable not only of lateral movements but also of raising his head when his upper lip touches the nipple.

OBSERVATION 9

At 0;0 (22) Laurent is awakened an hour after his meal, and only cries faintly and intermittently. I place his right hand against his mouth but remove it before he begins to suck. Then, seven times in succession he does a complete imitation of sucking, opening and closing his mouth, moving his tongue, etc.

OBSERVATION 10

Here are two facts revealing the differences in adaptation according to whether the need for nourishment is strong or weak. At 0;0 (25) Laurent is lying on his back, not very hungry (he has not cried since his last meal) and his right cheek is touched by the nipple. He turns to the correct side but the breast is removed to a distance of 5 to 10 cm. For a few seconds he reaches in the right direction and then gives up. He is still lying on his back, facing the ceiling; after a moment his mouth begins to move slightly, then his head moves from side to side, finally settling on the wrong side. A brief search in this direction, then crying (with commissures of the lip lowered, etc.), and another pause. After a moment, another search in the wrong direction. No reaction when the middle of his right cheek is touched. Only when the nipple touches his skin about 1 cm. from his lips does he turn and grasp it.

On reading this description it would seem as though all the practice of the last weeks were in vain. It would seem, above all, that the excitation zone of the reflex stops about 1 cm. from the lips, and that the cheek itself is insensitive. But on the next day the same experiment yields opposite results, as we shall see.

At 0;0 (26) Laurent is lying on his back, very hungry. I touch the middle of his cheek with my index finger bent first to the right, then to the left; each time he immediately turns to the correct side. Then he feels the nipple in the middle of his right cheek. But, as he tries to grasp it, it is withdrawn 10 cm. He then turns his head in the right direction and searches. He rests a moment, facing the ceiling, then his mouth begins to search again and his head immediately turns to the right side. This time he goes on to touch the nipple, first with his nose and then with the region between his nostrils and lips. Then he twice very distinctly repeats the movement observed at

0;0 (24) (see Obs. 8) : He raises his head in order to grasp the nipple. The first time he just catches the nipple with the corner of his lips and lets it go. A second or two later, he vigorously lifts his head and achieves his purpose.

The way in which he discerns the nipple should be noted; at 0;0 (29) he explores its circumference with open and motionless lips before grasping it.

The theoretical importance of such observations seems to us to be as great as their triteness.[2] They make it possible for us to understand how a system of pure reflexes can comprise psychological behavior, as early as the systematization of their functioning. Let us try to analyze this process in its progressive adaptational and organization aspects.

2. THE USE OF REFLEXES

Concerning its *adaptation*, it is interesting to note that the reflex, no matter how well endowed with hereditary physiological mechanism, and no matter how stable its automatization, nevertheless needs to be used in order truly to adapt itself, and that it is capable of gradual accommodation to external reality.

Let us first stress this element of *accommodation*. The sucking reflex is hereditary and functions from birth, influenced either by diffuse impulsive movements or by an external excitant (Obs. 1) ; this is the point of departure. In order that a useful function may result, that is to say, swallowing, it often suffices to put the nipple in the mouth of the new-

[2] We are particularly happy to mention their agreement with those of R. Ripin and H. Hetzer: Frühestes Lernen des Säuglings in der Ernährungs-situation, *Zeitschr. f. Psychol.*, 118, 1930, pp. 82–127. Observations of our children, made several years ago, were independent of the latter which makes their convergence a real one.

born child, but, as we know (Obs. 1), it sometimes happens that the child does not adapt at the first attempt. Only practice will lead to normal functioning. That is the first aspect of accommodation: contact with the object modifies, in a way, the activity of the reflex, and, even if this activity were oriented hereditarily to such contact, the latter is no less necessary to the consolidation of the former. This is how certain instincts are lost or certain reflexes cease to function normally, due to the lack of a suitable environment.[3] Moreover, contact with the environment not only results in developing the reflexes, but also in coordinating them in some way. Observations 2, 3, 5 and 8 show how the child, who first does not know how to suck the nipple when it is put in his mouth, grows increasingly able to grasp and even to find it, first after direct touch, then after contact with any neighboring region.[4]

---

[3] Thus Larguier des Brancels (*Introduction à la Psychologie*, 1921, p. 178), after recalling Spalding's famous experiments concerning the decline of instincts in newly hatched chickens, adds: "The sucking instinct is transitory. A calf which has been separated from its mother and fed by hand for a day or two and then is taken to another cow, more often than not refuses to nurse. The child behaves somewhat similarly. If he is first spoon-fed, he subsequently has great difficulty in taking the breast again."

[4] See Preyer (*L'Ame de l'Enfant*, translated by Variguy, 1887, pp. 213–217), in particular the following lines: "To be sure, sucking is not as fruitful the first as the second day and I have often observed in normal newborn children (1869) that attempts at sucking were completely vain in the first hours of life: when I made the experiment of putting an ivory pencil in their mouth, they were still uncoordinated" (p. 215). Also: "It is well known that newborn children, when put to the breast do not find the nipple without help; they only find it by themselves a few days later (in one case only on the eighth day), that is to say, later than animals" (pp. 215–216). And: "When the child is put to the breast the nipple often does not enter his mouth and he sucks the neighboring skin; this is still evident in the third week . . ." (p. 216).

How can such accommodations be explained? It seems to us difficult to invoke from birth the mechanism of acquired associations, in the limited sense of the term, or of "conditioned reflexes," both of which imply systematic training. On the contrary, the examining of these behavior patterns reveals at once the respects in which they differ from acquired associations: Whereas with regard to the latter, including conditioned reflexes, association is established between a certain perception, foreign to the realm of the reflex, and the reflex itself (for example, between a sound, a visual perception, etc., and the salivary reflex), according to our observations, it is simply the reflex's own sensibility (contact of the lips with a foreign body) which is generalized, that is to say, brings with it the action of the reflex in increasingly numerous situations. In the case of Observations 2, 3, 5 and 8, for example, accommodation consists essentially of progress in the continuity of the searching. In the beginning (Obs. 2 and 3) contact with any part of the breast whatever sets in motion momentary sucking of this region, immediately followed by crying or a desultory search, whereas after several days (Obs. 5), the same contact sets in motion a groping during which the child is headed toward success. It is very interesting, in the second case, to see how the reflex, excited by each contact with the breast, stops functioning as soon as the child perceives that sucking is not followed by any satisfaction, as is the taking of nourishment (see Obs. 5 and 8), and to see how the search goes on until swallowing begins. In this regard, Observations 2 to 8 confirm that there is a great variety of kinds of accommodation. Sucking of the eider down quilt, of the coverlet, etc., leads to rejection, that of the breast to acceptance: sucking of the skin (the child's hand, etc.) leads to acceptance if it is only a matter of sucking for the sake of sucking, but it leads to rejection (for example when it involves an area of the breast other than the nipple) if there is great hunger; the paternal index finger (Obs. 6) is rejected when the child is held against the breast, but is accepted as a pacifier, etc. In all behavior patterns it seems evident to us that learning is a function of the environment.

Surely all these facts admit of a physiological explanation which does not at all take us out of the realm of the reflex. The "irradiations," the "prolonged shocks," the "summations" of excitations and the intercoordination of reflexes probably explains why the child's searching becomes increasingly systematic, why contact which does not suffice to set the next operation in motion, does suffice in doing so a few days later, etc. Those are not necessarily mechanisms which are superposed on the reflex such as habit or intelligent understanding will be, later. But it remains no less true that the environment is indispensable to this operation, in other words, that reflex adaptation is partly accommodation. Without previous contact with the nipple and the experience of imbibing milk, it is very likely that the eider down quilt, the wool coverlet, or the paternal index finger, after setting in motion the sucking reflex, would not have been so briskly rejected by Laurent.[5]

But if, in reflex adaptation, allowances must be made for accommodation,

accommodation cannot be dissociated from progressive *assimilation,* inherent in the very use of the reflex. In a general way, one can say that the reflex is consolidated and strengthened by virtue of its own functioning. Such a fact is the most direct expression of the mechanism of assimilation. Assimilation is revealed, in the first place, by a growing need for repetition which characterizes the use of the reflex (functional assimilation) and, in the second place, by this sort of entirely practical or sensorimotor recognition which enables the child to adapt himself to the different objects with which his lips come in contact (recognitory and generalizing assimilations).

The need for repetition is in itself alone very significant; in effect, it is a question of a behavior pattern which shows a history and which proceeds to complicate the simple stimuli connected with the state of the organism considered at a given moment in time. A first stimulus capable of bringing the reflex into play is contact with an external object. Preyer thus set in motion the sucking movements of a newborn child by touching his lips, and Observation 1 shows us that children suck their hand a quarter of an hour or half an hour after birth. In the second place, there are internal stimuli, connected with the somato-affective states: diffuse impulsive movements (Obs. 1) or excitations due to hunger. But to these definite excitations, connected with particular moments in the life of the organism, there is added, it seems to us, the essential circumstance that the very repetition of the reflex movements constitutes a cynamogeny for them. Why, for instance, does Lucienne suck her fingers soon after birth for ten minutes in succession? This could not be because of

[5] In animals every slightly complicated reflex mechanism occasions reactions of the same kind. The beginnings of copulation in the mollusks, for example, give way to very strange gropings before the act is adapted.

hunger, since the umbilical cord had just been cut. There certainly is an external excitant from the moment the lips touch the hand. But why does the excitation last, in such a case, since it does not lead to any result except, precisely, to the use of the reflex? It therefore seems that, from the start of this primitive mechanism, a sort of circular process accompanies the function, the activity of the reflex having augmented due to its own use. If this interpretation remains doubtful, insofar as the point of departure is concerned, it obtains increasingly, on the other hand, with regard to subsequent behavior patterns. After the first feedings one observes, in Laurent (Obs. 2), sucking-like movements, in which it is difficult not to see a sort of autoexcitation. Besides, the progress in the search for the breast in Observations 2–5 and 8 seems also to show how much the function itself strengthened the tendency to suck. The counterproof of this is, as we have seen, the progressive decay of reflex mechanisms which are not used. How to interpret these facts? It is self-evident that "circular reaction," in Baldwin's sense of the term, could not yet be involved, that is to say, the repetition of a behavior pattern acquired or in the process of being acquired, and of behavior directed by the object to which it tends. Here it is only a matter of reflex and not acquired movements, and of sensibility connected with the reflex itself and not with the external objective. Nevertheless the mechanism is comparable to it from the purely functional point of view. It is thus very clear, in Observation 9, that the slightest excitation can set in motion not only a reflex reaction but a succession of seven reactions. Without forming any hypothesis on the way of conserving this excita-

tion, or *a fortiori,* without wanting to transform this repetition into intentional or mnemonic behavior, one is compelled to state that, in such a case, there is a tendency toward repetition, or, in objective terms, cumulative repetition.

This need for repetition is only one aspect of a more general process which we can qualify as assimilation. The tendency of the reflex being to reproduce itself, it incorporates into itself every object capable of fulfilling the function of excitant. Two distinct phenomena must be mentioned here, both equally significant from this particular point of view.

The first is what we may call "generalizing assimilation," that is to say, the incorporation of increasingly varied objects into the reflex schema. When, for example, the child is hungry but not sufficiently so to give way to rage and to crying, and his lips have been excited by some accidental contact, we witness the formation of this kind of behavior pattern, so important due to its own future developments and the innumerable analogous cases which we shall observe in connection with other schemata. Thus, according to chance contacts, the child, from the first two weeks of life, sucks his fingers, the fingers extended to him, his pillow, quilt, bedclothes, etc.; consequently he assimilates these objects to the activity of the reflex.

To be sure, we do not claim, when speaking of "generalizing" assimilation, that the newborn child begins by distinguishing a particular object (the mother's breast) and subsequently applies to other objects the discoveries he has made about this first one. In other words, we do not ascribe to the nursling conscious and intentional generalization with regard to transition from the particular to the general, especially as generalization, in itself intelligent, never begins by such a transition but always proceeds from the undifferentiated schema to the individual and to the general, combined and complementary. We simply maintain that, without any awareness of individual objects or of general laws, the newborn child at once incorporates into the global schema of sucking a number of increasingly varied objects, whence the generalizing aspect of this process of assimilation. But is it not playing on words to translate a fact so simple into the language of assimilation? Would it not suffice to say "the setting in motion of a reflex by a class of analogous excitants?" And, if one sticks to the term assimilation, must the conclusion then be reached that the nonhabitual excitants of any reflex (for example the aggregate of objects capable of setting in motion the palpebral reflex when they approach the eye) give rise to an identical phenomenon of generalizing assimilation? There is nothing to it. What does present a particular and truly psychological problem, in the case of the sucking reflex, is that the assimilation of objects to its activity will gradually be generalized until, at the stage of acquired circular reactions and even at the stage of intentional movements, it gives birth to a very complex and strong schema. From the end of the second month the child will suck his thumb systematically (with acquired coordination and not by chance), then at nearly five months his hands will carry all objects to his mouth and he will end by using these behavior patterns to recognize bodies and even to compose the first form of space (Stern's "buccal space"). It is thus certain that the first assimilations relating to sucking, even if they reveal a lack of differentiation between contact with the breast and contact with other objects, are not simple confusion destined to disappear with progress in nutrition, but constitute the point of departure for increasingly complex assimilations.

How to interpret this generalizing assimilation? The sucking reflex can be conceived as a global schema of coordinated movements which, if it is accompanied by awareness, certainly does not give rise to perception of objects or even of definite sensorial pictures but simply to an awareness of attitudes with at most some sensorimotor integration connected with the sensibility of the lips and mouth. Now this schema, due to the fact that it lends itself to repetitions and to cumulative use, is not limited to functioning under compulsion by a fixed excitant, external or internal, but functions in a way for itself. In other words, the child does not only suck in order to eat but also to elude hunger, to prolong the excitation of the meal, etc., and lastly, he sucks for the sake of sucking. It is in this sense that the object incorporated into the sucking schema is actually assimilated to the activity of this schema. The object sucked is to be conceived, not as nourishment for the organism in general, but, so to speak, as aliment for the very activity of sucking, according to its various forms. From the point of view of awareness, if there is awareness, such assimilation is at first lack of differentiation and not at first true generalization, but from the point of view of action, it is a generalizing extension of the schema which foretells (as has just been seen) later and much more important generalizations.

But, apart from this generalizing assimilation, another assimilation must be noted from the two first weeks of life, which we can call "recognitory assimilation." This second form seems inconsistent with the preceding one; actually it only reveals progress over the other, however slight. What we have just said regarding the lack of differentiation which characterizes generalizing assimilation is, in effect, true only with respect to states of slight hunger or of satiety. But it is enough that the child be very hungry for him to try to eat and thus to distinguish the nipple from the rest. This search and this selectivity seem to us to imply the beginning of differentiation in the global schema of sucking, and consequently a beginning of recognition, a completely practical and motor recognition, needless to say, but sufficient to be called recognitory assimilation. Let us examine, from this point of view, the way in which the child rediscovers the nipple. Ever since the third day (Obs. 3), Laurent seems to distinguish the nipple from the surrounding teguments; he tries to nurse and not merely to suck. From the tenth day (Obs. 4), we observe the alacrity with which he rejects the eider down quilt or the coverlet which he began to suck, in order to search for something more substantial. Furthermore, his reaction to his father's index finger (Obs. 6) could not be more definite: disappointment and crying. Lastly, the gropings on the breast itself (Obs. 5 and 8) also reveal selectivity. How is this kind of recognition to be explained?

Of course there could be no question, either here or in connection with generalizing assimilation, of the recognition of an "object" for the obvious reason that there is nothing in the states of consciousness of a newborn child which could enable him to contrast an external universe with an internal universe. Suppos-

ing that there are given simultaneously visual sensations (simple vision of lights without forms or depth), acoustic sensations and a tactile-gustatory and kinesthetic sensibility connected with the sucking reflex, it is evident that such a complexus would in no way be sufficient to constitute awareness of objects: the latter implies, as we shall see,[6] characteristically intellectual operations, necessary to secure the permanence of form and substance. Neither could there be a question of purely perceptive recognition or recognition of sensorial images presented by the external world, although such recognition considerably precedes the elaboration of objects (recognizing a person, a toy or a linen cloth simply on "presentation" and before having a permanent concept of it). If, to the observer, the breast which the nursling is about to take is external to the child and constitutes an image separate from him, to the newborn child, on the contrary, there can only exist awareness of attitudes, of emotions, or sensations of hunger and of satisfaction. Neither sight nor hearing yet gives rise to perceptions independent of these general reactions. As H. Wallon has effectively demonstrated, external influences only have meaning in connection with the attitudes they arouse. When the nursling differentiates between the nipple and the rest of the breast, fingers, or other objects, he does not recognize either an object or a sensorial picture but simply rediscovers a sensorimotor and particular postural complex (sucking and swallowing combined) among several analogous complexes which constitute his universe and reveal a total lack of differentiation between subject and object. In other

_____
[6] Volume II, *La Construction du Réel chez l'Enfant.*

words, this elementary recognition consists, in the strictest sense of the word, of "assimilation" of the whole of the data present in a definite organization which has already functioned and only gives rise to real discrimination due to its past functioning. But this suffices to explain in which respect repetition of the reflex leads by itself to recognitory assimilation which, albeit entirely practical, constitutes the beginning of knowledge.[7] More precisely, repetition of the reflex leads to a general and generalizing assimilation of objects to its activity, but, due to the varieties which gradually enter this activity (sucking for its own sake, to stave off hunger, to eat, etc.), the schema of assimilation becomes differentiated and, in the most important differentiated cases, assimilation becomes recognitory.

In conclusion, assimilation belonging to the adaptation reflex appears in three forms: cumulative repetition, generalization of the activity with incorporation of new objects to it, and finally, motor recognition. But, in the last analysis, these three forms are but one: The reflex must be conceived as an organized totality whose nature it is to preserve itself by functioning and consequently to function sooner or later for its own sake (repetition) while incorporating into itself objects propitious to this functioning (generalized assimilation) and dis-

cerning situations necessary to certain special modes of its activity (motor recognition). We shall see—and this is the sole purpose of this analysis—that these processes are again found, with the unwedging accounted for by the progressive complexity of the structures, in the stages of acquired circular reactions, of the first voluntary schemata and of truly intelligent behavior patterns.

The progressive adaptation of the reflex schemata, therefore, presupposes their *organization*. In physiology this truth is trite. Not only does the reflex arc as such presuppose an organization but, in the animal not undergoing laboratory experimentation, every reflex system constitutes in itself an organized totality. According to Graham Brown's theories, the simple reflex is, in effect, to be considered as a product of differentiation. From the psychological point of view, on the other hand, there is too great a tendency to consider a reflex, or even a complex instinctive act such as sucking, to be a summation of movements with, eventually, a succession of conscious states juxtaposed, and not as a real totality. But two essential circumstances induce us to consider the sucking act as already constituting psychic organization: The fact that sooner or later this act reveals a meaning, and the fact that it is accompanied by directed searching.

Concerning the meanings, we have seen how much sucking acts vary according to whether the newborn child is hungry and tries to nurse, or sucks in order to calm himself, or whether in a way he plays at sucking. It seems as though they have a meaning for the nursling himself. The increasing calm which succeeds a storm of crying and weeping as soon as the child is in position

[7] Let us repeat that we do not claim to specify the states of consciousness which accompany this assimilation. Whether these states are purely emotional or affective, connected with the postures accompanying sucking, or whether there exists at first conscious sensorial and kinesthetic discrimination, we could not decide by studying behavior of the first two or three weeks. What this behavior simply reveals is the groping and the discernment which characterizes the use of the reflex, and these are the two fundamental facts which authorize us to speak of psychological assimilation at this primitive stage.

to take nourishment and to seek the nipple is sufficient evidence that, if awareness exists at all, such awareness is from the beginning awareness of meaning. But one meaning is necessarily relative to other meanings, even on the elementary plane of simple motor recognitions.

Furthermore, that organization exists is substantiated by the fact that there is directed search. The precocious searching of the child in contact with the breast, in spite of being commonplace, is a remarkable thing. Such searching, which is the beginning of accommodation and assimilation, must be conceived, from the point of view of organization, as the first manifestation of a duality of desire and satisfaction, consequently of value and reality, of complete totality and incomplete totality, a duality which is to reappear on all planes of future activity and which the entire evolution of the mind will try to abate, even though it is destined to be emphasized unceasingly.

Such are, from the dual point of view of adaptation and organization, the first expressions of psychological life connected with hereditary physiological mechanisms. This survey, though schematic, we believe suffices to show how the psyche prolongs purely reflex organization while depending on it. The physiology of the organism furnishes a hereditary mechanism which is already completely organized and virtually adapted but has never functioned. Psychology begins with the use of this mechanism. This use does not in any way change the mechanism itself, contrary to what may be observed in the later stages (acquisition of habits, of understanding, etc.). It is limited to strengthening it and to making it function without integrating it to new organizations which go beyond it. But within

the limits of this functioning there is room for a historical development which marks precisely the beginning of psychological life. This development undoubtedly admits of a physiological explanation: if the reflex mechanism is strengthened by use or decays through lack of use, this is surely because coordinations are made or unmade by virtue of the laws of reflex activity. But a physiological explanation of this kind does not exclude the psychological point of view which we have taken. In effect, if, as is probable, states of awareness accompany a reflex mechanism as complicated as that of the sucking instinct, these states of awareness have an internal history. The same state of awareness could not twice reproduce itself indenticaly. If it reproduces itself it is by acquiring in addition some new quality of what has already been seen, etc., consequently some meaning. But if, by chance, no state of awareness yet occurred, one could nevertheless speak of behavior or of behavior patterns, given, on the one hand, the *sui generis* character of their development and, on the other, their continuity with those of subsequent stages. We shall state this in precise terms in our conclusion.

The true character of these behavior patterns involves the individual utilization of experience. Insofar as the reflex is a hereditary mechanism it perhaps constitutes a racial utilization of experience. That is a biological problem of which we have already spoken (Introduction, §3) and which, while of highest interest to the psychologist, cannot be solved by his particular methods. But, inasmuch as it is a mechanism giving rise to use, and consequently a sort of experimental trial, the sucking reflex presupposes, in addition to heredity, an individual utilization of experience. This is the crucial fact which permits the incorporation of such a behavior pattern into the realm of psychology, whereas a simple reflex, unsubordinated to the need for use or experimental trial as a function of the environment (sneezing for example) is of no interest to us. Of what does this experimental trial consist? An attempt can be made to define it without subordinating this analysis to any hypothesis concerning the kinds of states of consciousness which eventually accompany such a process. Learning connected with the reflex or instinctive mechanism is distinguished from the attainments due to habits or intelligence by the fact that it retains nothing external to the mechanism itself. A habit, such as that of a 2- or 3-month old baby who opens his mouth on seeing an object, presupposes a mnemonic fixation related to this object. A tactile-motor schema is formed according to the variations of the object and this schema alone explains the uniformity of the reaction. In the same way the acquisition of an intellectual operation (counting, for instance) implies memory of the objects themselves or of experiments made with the objects. In both cases, therefore, something external to the initial mechanism of the act in question is retained. On the other hand, the baby who learns to suck retains nothing external to the act of sucking; he undoubtedly bears no trace either of the objects or the sensorial pictures on which later attempts have supervened. He merely records the series of attempts as simple acts which condition each other. When he recognizes the nipple, this does not involve recognition of a thing or of an image but rather the assimilation of one sensorimotor and postural complex to another. If the ex-

perimental trial involved in sucking presupposes environment and experience, since no functional use is possible without contact with the environment, this is a matter of a very special kind of experimental trial, of an autoapprenticeship to some extent and not of an actual acquisition. This is why, if these first psychological behavior patterns transcend pure physiology—just as the individual use of a hereditary mechanism transcends heredity—they still depend on them to the highest degree.

But the great psychological lesson of these beginnings of behavior is that, within the limits we have just defined, the experimental trial of a reflex mechanism already entails the most complicated accommodations, assimilations and individual organizations. Accommodation exists because, even without retaining anything from the environment as such, the reflex mechanism needs the environment. Assimilation exists because, through its very use, it incorporates to itself every object capable of supplying it with what it needs and discriminates even these objects thanks to the identity of the differential attitudes they elicit. Finally, organization exists, inasmuch as organization is the internal aspect of this progressive adaptation. The sequential uses of the reflex mechanism constitute organized totalities and the gropings and searchings apparent from the beginnings of this period of experimental trial are oriented by the very structure of these totalities.

But if these behavior patterns transcend pure physiology only to the very slight extent in which individual use has a history independent of the machine predetermined by heredity (to the point where it could seem almost metaphorical to characterize them as "behavior patterns" as we have done here), they nevertheless seem to us to be of essential importance to the rest of mental development. In effect, the functions of accommodation, of assimilation and of organization which we have just described in connection with the use of a reflex mechanism will be found once more in the course of subsequent stages and will acquire increasing importance. In a certain sense, we shall even see that the more complicated and refined intellectual structures become, the more this functional nucleus will constitute the essence of these very structures.

THE STABILITY OF PASSIVE

AND DEPENDENT BEHAVIOR

FROM CHILDHOOD THROUGH ADULTHOOD [1]

JEROME KAGAN
HOWARD A. MOSS

A BASIC ASSUMPTION of developmental theory is that adult behaviors are often established in early childhood. Although retrospective reports obtained from the verbal protocols of adults support this assumption, it has been difficult to produce a more objective demonstration of the long term stability of childhood behavior patterns. This unhappy state of affairs is a consequence of the expense and difficulty associated with collecting long term longitudinal information on a large sample of children. Only extensive, longitudinal research programs, as exemplified by the Berkeley Growth Study or the Fels Research Institute, can furnish the answers to this developmental problem.

This paper presents one set of results which have emerged from a recent study of a group of "normal" adults from the Fels longitudinal research population for whom extensive information was available from birth through adolescence. The findings deal specifically with the long term stability of passive and dependent behavior in the face of situations which are frustrating and/or demand problem solving activity. This particular behav-

[1] This research was supported, in part, by research grant M–1260 from the National Institute of Mental Health, United States Public Health Service. Parts of this paper were presented at the annual meeting of the Midwestern Psychological Association in Chicago, May 1959.

Reprinted by permission from *Child Development*, 1960, *31*, 577–591.

ioral variable was chosen for initial analysis because theoretical essays on personality development emphasize that the early dependence of the child on the parent is of the utmost importance in shaping his future personality. That is, the development of a variety of adult motives and behaviors are based on the quality and intensity of the dependent relationship with the mother and mother-substitute figures. Further, psychological symptoms are theoretically attributed to inconsistency in the gratification of the child's dependent overtures and/or to denial or inhibition of dependent motives or behavior.

In addition to the longitudinal material, each subject was recently assessed during early adulthood by means of both interview and test procedures. The adult assessment was focused on the behavioral variables of dependency, aggression, achievement, and sexuality and on the degree of conflict and type of defensive responses associated with behavioral strivings in these areas. It was anticipated that there might be important sex differences with respect to occurrence of these behaviors, and the assessment procedures were designed to detect these potential sex differences.

METHOD

THE SAMPLE

The subjects (Ss) in this analysis were 27 male and 27 female Caucasian adults born between 1930 and 1939 who had recently been through a comprehensive assessment program which included an average of five hours of tape recorded interview and a variety of test procedures. The Ss were between 20 and 29 years of age at the time of the assessment. In addi-

tion, these Ss had fairly complete longitudinal records from 3 to 10 years of age. The Ss were predominantly middle class but came from a variety of vocational backgrounds including agricultural, skilled labor, tradesmen, and professional groups. The religious affiliations of the group included 43 Protestants, 10 Catholics and 1 Jewish subject. The mean Wechsler-Bellevue IQ of the group was 120 with an IQ range of 97 to 142.

INTERVIEW VARIABLES:
ADULT ASSESSMENT

Each S was interviewed by the senior author for approximately five hours over two to three sessions. *The interviewer had absolutely no knowledge of any of the longitudinal information on the Ss.* Since these Ss had been studied by psychologists for over 20 years, rapport was usually excellent, and defensive and evasive answers were infrequent. Following the interviews, each S was rated (7-point scale) on 59 variables. Six of these adult interview variables dealt specifically with passive and dependent behavior; abridged definitions of these variables follow:

Degree to which dependent gratifications were sought in choice of vocation. This variable assessed the degree to which security was an important aspect of job choice, the degree to which the subject looked to his employer for gratification of his dependent needs, reluctance to shift jobs because of temporary loss of security. For nonworking women, emphasis was placed on her attitudes about the importance of security in her husband's job.

Degree of dependent behavior toward a love object. This variable assessed the degree to which the subject sought advice and emotional support from a love object (sweetheart, husband, wife), degree to which the subject looked for stability and wisdom in a love object, degree to which responsibility for decision making was given to love object.

Degree of dependent behavior with parents. This variable assessed the degree to which the subject looked for advice, support, emotional encouragement, and nurturance from one or both parents.

Degree of dependent behavior toward nonparental figures. This variable assessed the degree to which the subject sought advice, emotional support, and nurturance from nonparental figures who were not love objects, e.g., friends, relatives, and teachers.

Tendency to display behavioral withdrawal in the face of anticipated failure. This variable assessed the frequency and consistency with which S tended to withdraw from tasks and situations which he thought were difficult to master and in which failure was anticipated.

Degree of conflict over dependent behavior. This variable assessed the degree to which the subject avoided placing himself in dependent positions, his derogation of dependent behavior in self and others, and his emphasis on the value and importance of independent behavior.

A random sample of 32 taped interviews were independently studied and rated. The interrater reliabilities for the six dependency variables ranged from .63 to .82 with an average coefficient of .74.

PROCEDURE FOR EVALUATION
OF CHILDHOOD BEHAVIOR

The junior author, who had no knowledge of the adult psychological status of the Ss, evaluated narrative reports based on direct observation of the child in a variety of situations. Summaries of interviews with the child and the mothers were also available. The observation reports were based on (a) semiannual visits to the home in which a staff member observed the child interact with mother and siblings for a two to four hour period, (b) semiannual or annual observations of the child in the Fels experimental nursery school and day camp settings, (c) interviews with the child, and (d) observations of the child in the classroom. After studying this material, the psychologist rated each child for a comprehensive set of variables (7-point scale). The rater studied the material for each S for ages 3 to 6 and made his ratings. Following a period of interpolated work, he then studied all the material for each S for ages 6 to 10 and again made the ratings. A period of approximately six months intervened between the evaluation of the material for any one child for ages 3 to 6 and 6 to 10. The rater felt that retroactive inhibition was sufficiently intense to mask any halo effect of the preschool ratings upon the later ratings made for 6 to 10 years of age. That is, the amount of material studied and the large number of variables rated militated against the recall of specific ratings over such a long period of time. In addition, the high degree of interrater reliability for these ratings supports the above statement. Independent ratings of the four childhood dependency variables by a second psychologist produced satisfactory interrater reliabilities. The product-moment correlations for each variable were all in the .80's with an average reliability of .86. The four childhood variables which involved passive and dependent behavior were defined as follows:

Tendency to behave in a passive manner when faced with environmental obstacles or stress (rated for ages 3 to 6 and 6 to 10). This variable assessed the degree to which the child was behaviorally passive in the face of external frustrations and failed to make any active mastery attempts to obtain desired goal objects following frustration. The rating of a passive behavioral reaction emphasized withdrawal from the frustration but included whining, crying, and soliciting help.

Tendency to seek support, nurturance, and assistance from female adults when under stress: general dependence (rated for age 3 to 6). This variable assessed the S's behavioral tendency to obtain assistance, nurturance, or affection from mother and other female adults when confronted with a threat to his well-being, a problem, or loss of a desired goal object. Dependent behavior included seeking out adults when faced with a problem or personal injury, reluctance to start a task without help or encouragement, seeking assistance of others, seeking affection from and close contact with female adults.

Tendency to seek affection and emotional support from female adults (rated for ages 6 to 10). This variable assessed the degree to which the child sought affection or emotional encouragement from mother or mother substitute figures. Evidence included kissing, holding hands, clinging, seeking encouragement or proximity to female adults.

Tendency to seek instrumental assistance from female adults (rated for ages 6 to 10). This variable assessed the degree to which the child sought instrumental help with specific problems from mother, teachers, or other female authority figures. Instrumental dependent acts included seeking help with tasks, seeking help when physically threatened.

As mentioned above the average interrater reliability for these four variables was +.86.

The distributions for both the childhood and interview variables were normal. Product-moment correlations were computed between each of the childhood variables and the six interview based dependency variables obtained in adulthood with separate analyses for males and females.

TACHISTOSCOPIC PERCEPTION

After the interviews and interview ratings were completed, each adult S was seen for a variety of test procedures, one of which was a tachistoscopic perception task. A series of 14 scenes were drawn to suggest action in the areas of dependency, aggression, sexuality, and physical danger. Three motivationally neutral, control pictures were also included.[2] For nine of the 14 pictures, separate pairs of illustrations were made for males and females so that the sex of the central figure was the same as the sex of the subject. The pictures were black and white line drawings with minimal background details. A brief description of the three dependency pictures follows:

1. A young adult in the foreground (male for male Ss and female for female Ss) is on his knees clutching to the waist of a figure of the same age but of opposite sex who is standing and looking forward. The figure on the floor is looking up at the face of the standing figure.

2. A young adult in the foreground (male for male Ss and female for female Ss) has his arms extended in an imploring gesture toward an adult of the same sex who is standing in the background with his back to the figure in the foreground.

3. A young adult (male for male Ss and female for female Ss) is seated on a chair with head buried in the abdomen of an adult of the opposite sex who is standing and comforting the seated figure.

The 14 pictures were presented seven times at seven different exposure speeds and in six different orders. The seven speeds ranged from .01 to 1.0 seconds. The pictures were shown initially at the fastest exposure (.01 second), and each succeeding series was presented at a slower exposure speed. All exposures were above threshold and all Ss reported seeing something at each exposure. The S sat in a light proof room, 22 in. from a flash-opal milk glass screen. The image was projected from the back of the screen, and the field was constantly illuminated

_____

[2] Photostats of the 14 stimuli are available upon request.

51707

by a 35 mm. projector (30 ft.-candles at the screen). The subject was told to state for each picture (a) the sex of each figure, (b) the approximate ages of each figure, and (c) what each figure on the picture was doing. The S was given three practice pictures to adapt him to the task and its requirements, and the entire protocol was electrically recorded and transcribed verbatim.

The protocols were scored for recognition threshold for each picture. Recognition threshold was defined as the first series at which the picture was described accurately and all succeeding trials were accurately described. The distribution of recognition thresholds differed among the 14 pictures and were markedly skewed either to the low or high end of the scale. Thus, the distribution of recognition thresholds for each picture was divided at the median into early and late recognition groups for statistical operations.

RESULTS

STABILITY OF DEPENDENT BEHAVIOR

Table 1 presents the product-moment correlations between the childhood and adult ratings of passive and dependent behavior.

The major result is that passive and dependent behaviors were fairly stable for females but not for males. For girls the ratings of passivity during ages 6 to 10 correlated significantly with the adult ratings of a dependent orientation in vocational choice, dependency on love object, dependency on parents, and withdrawal to failure. Childhood passivity was inversely correlated with adult conflict over dependent behavior. That is, females who were passive as children were apt to accept their dependent behavior in adulthood and show minimal anxiety over their dependent motives. Only dependent behavior toward nonparental figures failed

TABLE 1 · CORRELATIONS BETWEEN PASSIVE-DEPENDENT BEHAVIOR IN CHILDHOOD AND ADULTHOOD

| | ADULT DEPENDENCY VARIABLES | | | | | | | | | | | |
| | Dependency in vocation | | Dependency on love object | | Dependency on parents | | Dependency on others | | Withdrawal to failure | | Dependency conflict | |
Childhood variables	M	F	M	F	M	F	M	F	M	F	M	F
Passivity (ages 3 to 6)	−.07	.24	.10	.23	−.28	.25	.04	.19	.06	.26	.03	.01
Passivity (ages 6 to 10)	.11	.73**	.25	.36*	−.20	.54**	.04	.06	.21	.52**	−.26	−.63**
General dependence (ages 3 to 6)	−.06	.21	.13	.20	−.07	.07	.11	−.06	.12	.00	.05	.26
Emotional dependence (ages 6 to 10)	.21	.08	.18	.37*	.02	.51**	−.02	.06	.35*	.37*	−.12	−.31
Instrumental dependence (ages 6 to 10)	.19	.39*	.06	.58**	.14	.32	.37*	.01	.09	.39*	−.04	−.17

  * p < .05, one tail.
 ** p < .01, one tail.

to show a significant, positive correlation with the childhood ratings of passivity. Similarly, the childhood ratings of both instrumental and emotional dependency on female adults, for girls aged 6 to 10, predicted adult ratings of dependency on love object, dependency on parents, and withdrawal to anticipated failure situations.

For the men there were only two significant correlations between the childhood dependency ratings and those based on the adult interview. Boys who were high on instrumental dependency for ages 6 to 10 were high on dependent behavior towards nonparental figures in adulthood. Second, emotional dependence during ages 6 to 10 was positively correlated with adult withdrawal to failure.

Of the 18 correlations between each of the three childhood variables for ages 6 to 10 and the six adult variables, 60 per cent were significant in the expected direction for females, while only 9 per cent were significant for the men.

Tables 2 and 3 present the intercorrelations among the childhood and adult interview variables respectively.

The correlations among the passive and dependency variables between ages 3 to 6 and 6 to 10 were generally more consistent for girls than for boys. That is,

for girls the correlations among passivity and general dependence for ages 3 to 6 and the three variables for ages 6 to 10 were all consistently high. For boys the stability of the passivity rating for ages 3 to 6 and 6 to 10 was quite high. However, the relationships between passivity for 3 to 6 and the two dependency behaviors for 6 to 10 were not as high as they were for girls. This finding suggests that overt seeking of affection and/or instrumental aid in school age boys begins to be dissociated from a passive withdrawal reaction to problem situations.

The intercorrelations among the adult dependency variables were generally positive for both sexes. Dependency on parents and dependency on love objects were each associated with withdrawal to failure and negatively related to conflict over dependency. It is interesting to note that women who are dependent on their parents tended to be dependent on their love object but not on friends or authority figures. Men, on the other hand, who were dependent on their parents tended to be dependent on friends and authority figures rather than on a love object. Dependency on parents and friends usually involves instrumental aid with problems, while dependency on a love object more often included the solic-

TABLE 2 · Intercorrelations among Childhood Dependency Variables

	Passivity (6 to 10)		Gen. dep. (3 to 6)		Emot. dep. (6 to 10)		Instr. dep. (6 to 10)	
	M	F	M	F	M	F	M	F
Passivity (3 to 6)	.82**	.76**	.74**	.83**	.26	.80**	.38	.79**
Passivity (6 to 10)	..	..	.40*	.63**	.43*	.65**	.53**	.61**
General dependence (3 to 6)	..	..	..	..	.37	.61**	.38*	.63**
Emotional dependence (6 to 10)	..	..	..	..	..	..	.60**	.79**
Instrumental dependence (6 to 10)	..	..	..	..	..	..	..	..

* $p < .05$, two tails.
** $p < .01$, two tails.

TABLE 3 · INTERCORRELATIONS AMONG ADULT DEPENDENCY VARIABLES

	Dependence love object		Dependence parents		Dependence others		Withdrawal		Dependence conflict	
	M	F	M	F	M	F	M	F	M	F
Dep. vocation	.61**	.42*	.53**	.49**	.12	−.10	.41*	.50**	−.61**	−.56**
Dep. love object	..	..	.24	.54**	.48**	.16	.49**	.54**	−.66**	−.50**
Dep. parents	..	..	..	..	.39*	.03	.44**	.57**	−.59**	−.71**
Dep. others	..	..	..	..	..	..	.38*	−.15	−.46**	.15
Withdrawal	..	..	..	..	..	..	..	..	−.57**	−.70**
Dep. conflict	..	..	..	..	..	..	..	..	..	..

* $p < .05$, two tails.
** $p < .01$, two tails.

iting of emotional support and affection. It will be recalled that one of the two significant correlations for males between childhood and adult dependency involved instrumental dependency for ages 6 to 10 with adult dependency on nonparental authority figures. Emotional dependency for boys age 6 to 10 showed no correlations with the adult dependency variables. Thus, male dependent behavior is apt to emphasize the seeking of instrumental assistance with problems, while females are likely to seek affection and emotional support in addition to instrumental aid.

It is important to note that passive and dependent behavior for ages 6 to 10 showed a better relation to adult dependent behavior than the ratings for 3 to 6 years of age. This finding indicates that important age changes occur between ages 3 and 10 and that behavior displayed during the first few years of school is a better index of adult functioning than the earlier preschool behavior patterns.

TACHISTOSCOPIC PERCEPTION
OF DEPENDENT PICTURES

There were significant sex differences in recognition threshold for the three dependency pictures with the females recognizing all three pictures earlier than the males. The scene that depicted a person imploring a same sexed adult (picture 2) yielded the most significant sex difference ($p < .001$, two tails). The picture of the adult on his knees clutching on to an opposite sexed adult (picture 1) and that of the seated adult holding on to an opposite sexed adult (picture 3) yielded sex differences significant at the .005 and .08 levels, respectively, for two tails. The aggressive pictures, on the other hand, produced opposite results, for the females recognized two of the four aggression pictures significantly later than the men ($p < .01$, two tails). There were no significant sex differences for the sex, physical danger, or three neutral scenes.

There was not a highly consistent relationship between recognition threshold for the dependent scenes and the interview ratings of dependency conflict. Only recognition of the scene that illustrated a man on his knees in front of a woman (picture 1) showed a relation to dependency conflict, and this held only for males. The males who were above the median in recognition threshold for this scene (late recognition) were rated as more conflicted over dependent behavior than males who recognized this picture early

($p = .07$, two tails). For the females, recognition threshold for the dependency pictures showed no significant relation to ratings of dependency conflict.

DISCUSSION

The results support a basic hypothesis of developmental theory which states that the acquisition of certain adult response patterns begins in early childhood. The differential stability of passive-dependent behavior for men and women is probably the result of several factors. However, one set of processes which may contribute to this phenomenon is derived from the commonly accepted hypothesis that passive and dependent behavior is less punished in females than in males. Further, females are often encouraged to be passive while men are expected to be independent and autonomous in the face of frustration. Parental and peer group punishment for passive and dependent behavior should result in some inhibition of this behavior in males. Thus, we would not expect this class of behavior to be as stable for men as for women. Studies of both overt behavior and fantasy (2, 3, 4, 6, 7) all indicate that dependent responses are more frequent for girls than for boys. Further, the sex stereotypes presented by communication media fit this description. The analysis of children's books by Child, Potter, and Levine (1) indicated that girls are portrayed as passive while boys are presented as independent and heroic. Finally, a study of the likes and dislikes of 10-year-old children (5) confirms the belief that girls accept passive behavior as more appropriate for their sex role than do boys.

The present tachistoscopic threshold data support the notion that men are more conflicted over dependent behavior than women. It will be recalled that the women recognized all three scenes depicting dependent behavior much earlier than the men. This finding suggests that the tendency to perceive dependent behavior in adults is much weaker in men than it is in women. One possible cause of this "weaker perceptual hypothesis" is that dependent action is less acceptable to men, i.e., that men are more conflicted over dependent behavior. This conclusion finds support in the correlation, for men, between late recognition of dependency and the interview rating of dependency conflict.

Detailed analysis of the 54 cases indicates that there was a greater proportion of men, than women, who shifted from high dependency during childhood to independent behavior as adults. The women tended to be either dependent or independent for both childhood and adulthood. For example, in comparing emotional dependence for ages 6 to 10 with adult dependency on parents, not one female showed a major shift from high dependency in childhood to low dependency in adulthood. For the men, however, 20 per cent were rated very dependent during the ages 6 to 10 and very independent in adulthood.

The authors do not suggest that passive and dependent behavior in girls is rigidly fixed at school age and that change is a rare or unusual phenomenon. It must be kept in mind that the social milieu of these particular subjects remained rather constant throughout their lives. Their familial and extrafamilial environments were not disrupted to any marked degree. The parents and peers of these Ss retained their same values, their reference groups remained constant, and, in most cases, their geographical travel was limited. Thus, the degree of behavioral stability obtained for these females might not hold for populations that are more mobile or transient, for different ethnic or class samples, or for people subjected to major traumata during adolescence and early adulthood.

Implicit in these results is a strategy for certain research problems in developmental psychology. It would appear that a select group of theoretically relevant behaviors become clearly established as preferential response tendencies as early as 6 to 10 years of age. This means that one can study the child longitudinally without having to wait 15 to 20 years before asking important questions of the data. Since the current philosophy of financial support for research allows an investigator to chart a 5 to 10 year program, it is now feasible for one investigator to see the products of a longitudinally oriented project in a reasonable length of time.

Although case history material can never prove an hypothesis, it often facilitates scientific communication by placing some flesh on the skeleton of a correlation matrix. The following case material is presented to give the reader a clearer picture of the material upon which our childhood evaluations were based and to illustrate dramatically the degree of constancy of behavioral passivity for two specific individuals.

Case A. Miss A is a 21-year-old, unmarried woman, who was in her senior year in an Eastern college. She was one of the most independent women in our sample and one who showed a strong reaction against dependent behavior in a wide variety of situations. As an adult she was described as a woman with a very strong need for recognition by others combined with a striving for achievement related goals. She had a strong desire to nurture others and often sought out situations in which she could give advice, support, and encouragement to peers. Miss A stated during the interview that she liked to keep her personal problems to herself. She did not like to discuss her personal problems because she felt that this behavior made her appear "helpless and weak." Statements like this indicate very strong conflict and anxiety over being in a passive-dependent position with other people. She was trying to sever any semblance of a dependent relation with her mother and derogated the latter because the mother seemed to be dependent upon her for companionship. Miss A sometimes felt lonely but said that she fights these feelings and tries to be able to live with them, for she does not like to admit that she needs friends or companionship. Her relationship with men seems to be consistent with the above pattern, for she tends to withdraw from heterosexual relationships that become too intense. Miss A said that she does not like men that make demands upon her, and she avoids men who attempt to place her in a passive role or position.

The following material represents selected verbatim excerpts from the longitudinal material on this subject.

Age 3 years, 4 months: Summary of Fels Nursery School Observations. S seems to be able to control and channel her behavior so that she got done just what she wanted to get done. In this activity she was very independent and capable. She was very social but also had a streak of aloof self-sufficiency, and she always made her individuality felt. She was what might be called a strong personality, often very intense, quite stubborn.

. . . Her most outstanding characteristic was her consistent independence and integrity. In spite of the fact that she imitated and followed certain boys, she seemed to do this very much from her own choice, and she never lost the flavor of her individuality. She was capable of being social and seemed to enjoy contacts but at all times she was her own master. She would often withdraw from play and go on in her own direction at any time that she wished. . . . She was independent with adults and at times negativistic just to be devilish. She seemed somewhat self-conscious and had some cute little tricks. . . . In all, she could be characterized best by being called "tough minded." She shows determination and will, originality and spark, curiosity and interest in factual detail. She likes to quibble and argue, to verbalize, to construct, to accomplish. She is an individualist, independent and stubborn.

Age 5 years, 4 months: Fels Nursery School Observation. S seems to be vigorous, ruthless, competitive, highly sensual young woman, but one felt quite often that antagonism toward others was simply a direct response to their behavior. . . . She has grown far more social and also popular with an increasingly large crowd of special friends in a gang. She could be, when she chose, quite a successful leader, forging ahead and organizing a group on a hike, directing them and arranging things, and particularly keeping order in a fair sharing of the tools in the carpentry shop. . . . Many of S's conflicts with the adult world seemed a direct imitation of a certain boy. She needed a chance to grumble, would scornfully refuse any adult suggestions or orders, would usually go officially ahead to carry them out. She was quite demanding, often shouting an order to an assistant. . . . With her other work the same drive for strong achievement was also evident, sticking to anything until it was finished, whatever the group stimuli. S still had real trouble in fine motor coordination, would growl as she worked, "I'm doing this as well as I can steer my pencil." For all her teeth gritted effort, the final results would still be relatively crude. She was very skilled in the use of puzzles and interested in the problems of designs and the way things fit together. She scorned any of the ready-made designs for the Christmas tree decorations.

Age 7 years: Observation in Fels Day Camp. S came accompanied by one friend. S did not seem overwhelmed by the large proportion of adults around, but in her sturdy self-sufficient manner went ahead with her own activities. Her friend was at first rather shy and withdrawn and S, with her usual confident bullying and bossing of the adults, tended to take the girl under her wing and make sure she had a good time. S remains an exceptionally eager, imperturbable young woman. On a number of small issues she did insist on her own way, on just how long she would stay in the gym and play before lunch, but was quite reasonable about making compromises. She chose a rather difficult necklace to make and got quite mad 'when it didn't work out well. She kept doggedly with it, very self-sufficient, and continuing all on her own after getting some initial advice. . . . Her major effort was put on self-appointed tasks, to be able to master jumping over the horse at the gym where she took numerous tumbles until she succeeded. In spite of her distractability and preference for the apparatus she did set herself to learning the new skills required there.

Age 9 years: Report from Teacher. S is one of the most responsible children in the group. . . . She is self-reliant, independent, and knows how to plan her time well. She enters all games with enthusiasm, is very well coordinated, is full of personality and "joie de vivre."

Case B. Miss B is a 23-year-old, unmarried woman, who is working and living with her parents. She was one of the most overtly dependent women in the sample. During the interview she was very dependent on the interviewer for structure and was rather mild and meek. Her most typical reaction to failure or stressful situations is to deny or withdraw and she says quite blithely, "I'm not a worrier." She is very sensitive to the opinions of other people and usually conforms with their expectations for her. She accepts her passive-dependent role with authority people and with love objects. S tends to be very dependent on peers for advice, likes being close to the family, and tends to see herself as inadequate in the face of problem situations.

Following are selected excerpts from her longitudinal records:

Age 2 years, 6 months: Fels Nursery School Observation. At the first day of nursery school, S seemed rather frightened and very reluctant to leave her mother this morning. The mother had to carry her and hold her in the car until the door was shut. For the first few miles she cried and then suddenly stopped and began to take an interest in the various animals and objects. She cried when she reached the nursery school but stopped as soon as she left the other children. On the second day of nursery school she cried again but seemed much less frightened and more angry. During the nursery school she stood watching the other children and at one point ran to another girl and stood beside her. The other little girl paid no attention, and S trailed after her. S wandered around and, when the teacher went to the house, S rushed to follow her and stood around the teacher. S tagged after another little girl all morning. During the nursery school two-week period she was timid and tense.

Age 3 years: Fels Nursery School Summary. At first, S was timid and tense and was gathered under the wing of another peer and her cohorts. From then on she was "at home" with the group. She followed another girl's lead and joined in the activities the other girl organized. On days when this girl was absent she was at loose-ends and tended to return to her original dependence on an adult. Several weeks after her nursery school stay she visited the school one morning for several hours. She was a little apprehensive at first but made no real protest. She stood around not joining in the play until an adult suggested an activity.

Age 4 years: Fels Nursery School Summary. S cried the first day of nursery school after she saw another girl cry. She stayed close to the teacher the first few days and watched the other children with a worried expression on her face. Indoors she chose small blocks or color cubes to play with. In the yard S was very cautious about trying out the apparatus, particularly when there was any balancing involved. She has a high, whining nasal voice, and several letter substitutions made her speech rather difficult to understand. She was quite complying with adult requests. Frequently, she appealed to adults for help in conflicts, such as getting a turn to slide, which is a situation she could have handled for herself.

Age 6 years: Visit to the School. S is retiring, quiet, and shy. She doesn't show the enthusiasm that most of the children in the class do. She seems content.... She goes to the teacher for suggestions and skips to her seat jubilantly with a word of approval from the teacher. S recites a bit timidly in front of the whole class but accepts the teacher's support and gets through successfully. Her voice is a little soft and her enunciation is not clear. S volunteers information a bit tentatively and without enthusiasm. The teacher reports that S is about the brightest of the average group. S is not a leader but she is very sweet and cooperative and is never any trouble.

Age 6 years, 6 months: Summary of Fels Day Camp Observations. S was outclassed in almost every respect in this group but fluttered happily about after the others doing the best she could. She occasionally withdrew or grew silent but, when encouraged by an adult, she soon recovered. She was not insensitive and did not seem to have her security disturbed more than momentarily. She seems to feel a great confidence and trust in adults and could always be bought off or led along. She lacked initiative in almost every way. She could not go ahead on any craft project nor could she assert herself socially. She needed help and encouragement, hung about the adults, not exposing herself to the center of the group. She is essentially a conformist and wanted only to do what was right. She got into no mischief and had little sense of fun. She was happiest when settled into a situation that was approved and guided by an adult, and at these times she would proddle along very happily.

Her main interests lay in conforming to any plans laid by adults and working on simple handcrafts. She was rather unsure in her accomplishments. She was often physically apprehensive.

Age 7 years, 6 months: Summary of Fels Day Camp Observations. The most characteristic aspect of S's day camp behavior was her ability, high conformity, and social reticence. She did not participate in social activities to any extent and was generally ignored by the other children. She clung to adults, wanted to assist them when possible, and wanted their approval and comforting in all her activities. She seemed to be somewhat apprehensive of physical contacts, especially if they became at all rough. She was apprehensive about almost any physical danger. Her actual physical ability was not particularly poor, and, when she was put into athletic situations, she did suprisingly well. Her general lack of physical participation seems not to be due to poor ability as much as to lack of motivation and apprehension.

Age 8 years: Visit to the School. S is always anxious to do what is right all of the time. She is not a discipline problem. S shows no interest in physical activities. Initially, she is lost at school work and takes some time to adjust to new work. S was pretty tentative in her first attempt to get the teacher's attention and held up her paper hesitantly. She was very pleased when the teacher came to her. She was uncertain about the problems although they had similar ones before.

Age 8 years, 8 months: Fels Day Camp Summary. S is a small, dark looking girl, bent over, with thick dark hair and a tired face. Her voice is high but with no force; her hands hanging limp at the wrists. Much of this lack of force seemed related to her personality, and at the races she surprised us by doing remarkably well. S obeyed adults implicitly and wanted to have their sanction for even small acts which the group had already been given permission for. She has a rather cringing, servile manner. This clinging around adults was particularly marked the first day when she ate her lunch with them.

Age 9 years, 8 months: Fels Day Camp Summary. S is a rather pathetic looking little girl. Rather thin, droopy eyed, clammy handed, somehow reminiscent of an orphan in an old melodrama. She seems nearer to seven or eight than her actual age and with a kind of naivete and unsureness about all she did. She was an exceedingly compliant child in taking the tests, even the reading tests which she obviously disliked, without a murmur.

SUMMARY

This paper summarized some results from a larger investigation of the stability of behavior in a group of subjects who were part of the Fels Research Institute's longitudinal population. This report dealt specifically with the long term stability of passive and dependent behavior from childhood through adulthood.

The Ss were 27 males and 27 females for whom extensive longitudinal information was available from birth through adolescence. One psychologist studied narrative reports based on observations of the child in various settings and rated each child on four variables describing types of passive and dependent behavior for ages 3 to 6 and ages 6 to 10. A second psychologist, who had no knowledge of the childhood data, interviewed each S in adulthood and rated each S on six variables related to aspects of adult passive and dependent behavior. In addition, each adult S was administered a tachistoscopic perception task in which scenes illustrating dependent activity were presented at seven different exposure speeds.

The results revealed that passive and dependent behaviors were quite stable for women, but minimally stable for men. Over 60 per cent of the correlations between the childhood (ages 6 to 10) and adult ratings of dependency were statistically significant for females, while only 9 per cent were significant for men. For example, the correlation between passive withdrawal from problem situations for ages 6 to 10 and adulthood was .52 ($p < .01$) for women and .21 for men. Similarly, the correlation between emotional dependence for ages 6 to 10 and adult dependency on parents was .51 ($p < .01$ for women and .02 for men. The correlations between the ratings for ages 3 to 6 and adulthood were considerably lower and not statistically significant.

It was suggested that environmental disapproval and punishment of dependent behavior in young males led to inhibition of and conflict over dependency in the growing boy. The social acceptance of passive and dependent behavior in females would be expected to result in greater stability for this class of responses for women than for men. The fact that females recognized the tachistoscopically presented dependency scenes earlier than the men was interpreted as support for this explanation.

Case history material for two female subjects was presented to illustrate the type of information utilized in this study.

REFERENCES

1. CHILD, I. L., POTTER, E. H., & LEVINE, ESTELLE M. Children's textbooks and personality development: an exploration in the social psychology of education. *Psychol. Monogr.*, 1946, *60*, No. 279.
2. HATTWICK, BERTHA. Sex differences in behavior of nursery school children. *Child Develpm.*, 1937, *8*, 323–355.
3. KAGAN, J. The stability of TAT fantasy and stimulus ambiguity. *J. consult. Psychol.*, 1959, *23*, 266–271.
4. SANFORD, R. N., ADKINS, M. M., MILLER, R. B., & COBB, E. N. Physique, personality and scholarship: a comprehensive study of school children. *Monogr. Soc. Res. Child Develpm.*, 1943, *8*, No. 1.
5. TYLER, LEONA E. The development of vocational interests. I. The organization of likes and dislikes in ten-year-old children. *J. genet. Psychol.*, 1955, *86*, 33–44.
6. WATSON, R. I. *Psychology of the child.* New York: Wiley, 1959.
7. WHITEHOUSE, ELIZABETH. Norms for certain aspects of the Thematic Apperception Test on a group of nine and ten-year-old children. *J. Pers.*, 1949, *1*, 12–15.

COMPARATIVE
AND CROSS-CULTURAL 3
APPROACHES

Two TYPES of approach have been incorporated in one section here since the procedures employed are quite similar. In both comparative and cross-cultural studies the intent is to examine behavior as a function of species, class, group, regional, or other "membership" designation. In comparative studies the groups are constituted through species differences, while in cross-cultural studies the species is the same but the ethnic origin may differ. In both cases, it may be said that the interest is a comparative one.

In a sense, the design of comparative and cross-cultural studies is very similar to that of developmental investigations in which designation of subjects through group membership is an age classification. Species membership and ethnic or regional designations constitute independent variables in the same sense in which age is an independent variable. Like developmental investigations, comparative and cross-cultural studies tend to provide essentially descriptive laws or relationships rather than truly explanatory functional relationships, for in all these cases the mechanisms underlying the species or cultural differences are not clearly revealed by the descriptive relationships obtained. Whiting and Child (1953), however, point out that cross-cultural comparisons can and do provide information about the generality of psychological laws and the opportunity to assess the behavioral correlates of variables whose limits in any one culture preclude their study in the extreme. The first selection in this series, that by Hunter, suggests as well that cross-species comparisons with respect to behavioral attributes serve to illuminate or suggest evolutionary processes, a point implied also by Harlow (1958).

In comparative and cross-cultural studies the experimenter sets up observational procedures that are roughly comparable from one species to another or from one culture to another. Margaret Mead's well-known chapter (1954) describes some of the methodological problems involved in utilizing a study technique developed in one culture on another quite different culture. Marcelle Geber and her associates (1957, 1958) have utilized the Gesell developmental scales to report on the developmental accomplishments of African children; her data and photos indicate considerable precocity in these children's performance levels at different ages within the first year of life. An interesting question raised by these studies is whether the precocity is real (the children seem to return to the norm levels of American and North

European children in the second year of life) or attributable to an artifact of scoring within the tests themselves.

In Hunter's study of the delayed reaction in animals and children, the investigator was interested in the delayed-reaction time limits of several species. He therefore constructed similar test-situations for the different organisms studied, adapting the size of the apparatus in each case to the size of the subject under investigation. Hunter was thus able to rank the subjects in terms of their capacities to tolerate delay intervals between the presentation of the stimuli and the permitting of a discriminative response. It is noteworthy, also, that Hunter goes beyond a mere descriptive reporting of the various subjects' behavior, and attempts an analysis of the complexities of the mediational processes with increased phylogenetic levels.

The second selection, by the Harlows, presents an analysis of thought processes derived from the study of animals' and children's behavior in relatively simple learning situations. Their thesis is that much complex behavior, particularly in the higher organisms, is accounted for parsimoniously by reference to the basic discrimination learning process, particularly as revealed in studies of "learning to learn" and "learning set."

The third study in this series, by Carson and Rabin, is a well-controlled cross-cultural study of vocabulary attainment and ability in verbal communication. They matched as carefully as possible three groups of children designated as North White, North Negro, and South Negro. The white children proved superior to the Negro children in these skills, and the North Negro group proved superior to South Negro. Thus these investigators were able to infer that the superiority of the white children over the Negroes seemed largely a matter of regional rather than racial differences. Again, this study is noteworthy in that it has attempted to build into the research design the possibility of assessing the mechanisms or processes underlying the group-membership differences obtained. Sometimes these process-differences in different cultures are not so easily inferred from the data. For example, a study by Kluckhohn (1947) of Navaho infants depends very heavily on the investigator's prior knowledge of other cultures for its conclusions concerning the differences between the Navaho infant's early history and the consequences thereof, on the one hand, and other infants' histories and their consequences, on the other.

REFERENCES

GEBER, MARCELLE.   The psycho-motor development of African children in the first year, and the influence of maternal behavior. *J. soc. Psychol.*, 1958, 47, 185–195.
GEBER, MARCELLE and DEAN, R. F. A.   Gesell tests on African children. *Pediatrics*, 1957, 20, 1055–1065.

HARLOW, H. F.   The evolution of learning. In Anne Roe, and G. G. Simpson (Eds.), *Behavior and evolution*. New Haven: Yale Univer. Press, 1958.

KLUCKHOHN, C.   Some aspects of Navaho infancy and early childhood. In *Psychoanalysis and the social sciences*. New York: International Universities Press, 1947, *1*, 37–86.

MEAD, MARGARET.   Research on primitive children. In L. Carmichael (Ed.), *Manual of child psychology*. New York: Wiley, 1954.

WHITING, J. W. M. and CHILD, I. L.   *Child training and personality: a cross-cultural study*. New Haven: Yale Univer. Press, 1953.

THE DELAYED REACTION IN ANIMALS

AND CHILDREN

WALTER S. HUNTER

I. INTRODUCTION

THE EXPERIMENTS in this monograph [1] aim at an analysis of typical mammalian behavior under conditions where the determining stimulus is absent at the moment of response. Associations were first set up between movements that

[1] Experimentation on the present problem was first begun in the University of Chicago laboratory by a graduate student, W. R. Hough. The following year the work was taken up and carried somewhat further by another student, H. B. Reed. Both students worked with white rats. Although in each case the results obtained were in strict harmony with those presented in this paper, in neither case were they conclusive. The chief value of the work lay in its suggestiveness. The apparatus used by Reed—Prob. Box D—is described below. The present investigation was carried on in the same laboratory from October, 1910 to April, 1912.

Reprinted by permission from W. S. Hunter: *The delayed reaction in animals and children*, copyright 1914, The Williams and Wilkin Co.

led to food and a light which might be in any one of three boxes. Controls were used to make sure that the position of the light alone determined the reactions of the subject. Tests were then instituted in which the light was turned off before the reaction was made. The subject thus had to respond in the absence of the stimulus that hitherto had guided his reactions.

The nature of the present experiment may be further set forth by contrasting it with the following type of adjustment: A cat watches for a mouse and sees it appear at an open hole. The mouse vanishes before the cat can react, yet the cat goes over to the hole. There can be no question here but that the determining stimulus is absent at the moment of response, provided possible olfactory stimuli be neglected. Our experiment differs from this in complexity. If there were three holes that differed only in their several directions from the cat, and if in the past the mouse had appeared an equal number of times in all three holes, the conditions would be the same as in our tests. A selection between the three holes would need to be made on the basis of the immediately previous presence of the rat, if a correct reaction were to occur. If an animal *can* manifest behavior that does not lend itself to a "stimulus and response" explanation, this is one type of situation in which that behavior should appear. That, in fact, it is the situation *par excellence* for the eliciting of this behavior will, I believe, appear as this monograph progresses.

In the present experiments, two main factual questions arise: (1) How long after the determining stimulus has disappeared can an animal wait and still react correctly? (2) Does the animal give any behavior cues as to its method of solving the problem? If so, what are they? With these data given, there remains the task of interpretation. If a selective response has been initiated and controlled by a certain stimulus, and if the response can still be made successfully in the absence of that stimulus, then the subject must be using something that functions for the stimulus in initiating and guiding the correct response. Our investigation thus forces us to the consideration of the functional presence of a representative factor in the behavior of animals and children. Not only this, but the problem of the nature of this representative factor confronts us. Is it an overt motor attitude, or not? If not, is it sensory or imaginal, i.e., ideational?

In the interpretative study, I shall

proceed on the assumption that animals are conscious. What the nature of this consciousness is, it will be the task of this paper to help determine. (If the reader does not choose to follow this line of interpretation, he may state everything in neurological terms without marring the significance of this discussion.) But *a propos* of the term "image" or "idea," let it be said once for all that wherever these terms are used by the present writer with reference to animal consciousness, they should be supplemented by the phrase "or functionally equivalent process." I use the structural term chiefly for the sake of its brevity. . . .

III. NOTES ON THE ANIMALS AND CHILDREN TESTED

Four classes of reagents were used in the experiments whose description is to follow: white rats, dogs, raccoons (Procyon lotor) and children. A few words descriptive of these subjects will not be amiss.

1. RATS

Twenty-two rats were used during the entire course of the experiments. Five of these were normal adults and were used only in preliminary tests in which the purpose was the perfection of a method. The remaining seventeen (normal) were all started in the experiments when approximately four weeks old. All were vigorous, healthy animals whose records may stand as typical.

2. DOGS

The two dogs tested were mongrels in whom the rat terrier strain was dominant. They were very bright and intelligent looking, very active, playful and affectionate,—indeed they seemed to possess all the qualities that are attributed to intelligent dogs in countless anecdotes. This was the unanimous testimony of many observers. The two dogs, Blackie and Brownie, both females of the same litter, were secured from an animal dealer when they were small puppies and were started on the preliminary tests at about the age of five months. They were usually kept in a kennel out of doors and remained in excellent condition during the experiments. Of the two, Brownie was the more aggressive and, to the ordinary observer, appeared possibly the more intelligent.

3. RACCOONS

Four raccoons, two males—Bob and Jack—and two females—Betty and Jill, were tested. Bob and Betty had been pets and were secured from their owner when about five or six months old. Jack and Jill were caught in the woods when about two and a half months old. Preliminary experiments were started almost immediately with all four. The raccoons were and remained in perfect health throughout the experiments. The only physical defects possessed by any of them were the cataracts which developed in Bob's eyes about a month after his purchase. Although this interfered with his accurate vision of objects and resulted in his colliding frequently with them, he was able to distinguish such changes in brightness as were necessary in the experiments. This fact was demonstrated conclusively by many control tests which will be described later. Of the four, Betty was the quietest and most timid. She was the least promis-

ing subject among them. Further facts about these animals are given in the appendix.

4. CHILDREN

Five children were used in the course of the present tests: two boys, Hd and L, and three girls, F, M, and H. H, Hd and L were each approximately six years old. M was about eight years old; and F, about two and a half. Hd and L were in kindergarten work, and M and H were in the graded schools. The indications were that they were children both of normal ability and of normal intellectual advancement for their ages. F was a bright little girl and made an excellent subject. All of the children were more or less timid at first; but this was overcome, in all save possibly H's case, before tests were begun. Particular pains were taken with F. The experimenter was in her company a great deal, and by the beginning of the tests was a gladly accepted play-fellow. . . .

VII. SUMMARY AND CONCLUSIONS

The following is a statement of the results and conclusions that have been reached as a result of the foregoing experiments and analyses:

1. The rats (one excepted), dogs, raccoons and children made successful reactions in situations where the customary determining stimulus was absent at the moment of response. The stimulus might appear in any one of three boxes. These boxes were qualitatively alike, but situated in different directions from the release box. At every trial, three possibilities of reaction confronted the subject. A selection had to be made and that box

chosen in which the stimulus had appeared most recently.

2. The conditions under which the maximal delay was tested and the results obtained are indicated as follows:

(a) Different classes of subjects were used. Table 14 gives the maximum and minimum delays that were obtained from the different classes.

TABLE 14

Subjects	Min. delay	Max. delay
Rats	either no learning or 3rd stage of delay	10 secs.
Dogs	2 secs.	5 mins.
Raccoons	3 secs.	25 secs.
Children	50 secs.	25 mins.

(b) Backgrounds of widely different grades of brightness did not affect the intervals of delay.

(c) The use of a large release which gave the animals the freedom of the interior of the box lengthened the intervals of delay in the case of some subjects.

(d) The use of two boxes as opposed to three lengthened the intervals of delay by increasing the accuracy of response.

(e) Neither punishment nor the particular number of trials per day appear to have affected the interval of delay.

3. An analysis of the possible cues that may have been used by the subjects in the solution of the present problem gave the following results: (a) Overt orienting attitudes were the probable cues for many reactions of the raccoons. These attitudes must be assumed as cues for the rats and dogs in order to explain their reactions. (b) Some intra-organic (non-orientation) factor not visible to the experimenter must be assumed in order to

explain a significant number of the correct reactions of the raccoons and all of the successful reactions of the children. These cues fulfilled an ideational function. (c) All of the reagents were influenced by external stimuli that were constantly present from trial to trial, e.g., those given by the box itself. However, these could not be used as a basis for selective responses inasmuch as they were constant from trial to trial and hence could not furnish varying, or alternating, cues.

4. No animal that had used overt motor attitudes in solving the problem when the small release and similar backgrounds were used adopted another type of cue either when a large release or when backgrounds of different brightnesses were used.

5. The method used in the present tests for attacking the question of the functional presence of a representative factor in animal behavior is superior to that of imitation, use of tools and others that have been used in the past, because here it is possible to determine what stimulus controls the behavior. It is therefore possible to insure the absence of the stimulus at the moment of response.

6. The representative factor for which search as been instituted in this monograph stands primarily for "objects" and not movements. A technique that would make certain a control of the latter factor so as to insure its presence or absence at the will of the experimenter has not as yet been perfected.

7. From a consideration of the theoretical advantages to be derived from interpreting this representative factor as sensory rather than as imaginal, a decision was reached in favor of the former alternative for all reagents save possibly

the older children, H, Hd, M and L. Illustrations were given from human consciousness where a sensation performed a memory function or served as a link in a train of thought. Such cases have been termed "conscious attitudes" or "imageless thought." This function, as considered in this paper, was designated *sensory thought*.

8. The theory was advanced that such a function as sensory thought represents the highest grade of behavior in raccoons and probably also in children of some two and one-half years of age. This theory is supported by the hardly-to-be-doubted presence of sensations in animal consciousness and by the assumption that these sensations can function as the illustrations indicate that such processes do in human behavior. Such a theory seems more in accordance with the law of parsimony than would a theory which made images perform the representative function found in the raccoons and the child F.

9. From this theory, it follows that subjects may be put into at least four classes on the basis of the highest type of learning present in their behavior: (a) Absence of learning; (b) trial and error; (c) sensory thought, and (d) imaginal thought.

LEARNING TO THINK

HARRY F. AND MARGARET KUENNE HARLOW

HOW DOES AN INFANT, born with only a few simple reactions, develop into an adult capable of rapid learning and the almost incredibly complex mental processes known as thinking? This is one of psychology's unsolved problems. Most modern explanations are not much more enlightening than those offered by 18th-century French and English philosophers, who suggested that the mind developed merely by the process of associating ideas or experiences with one another. Even the early philosophers realized that this was not a completely adequate explanation.

The speed and complexity of a human being's mental processes, and the intricacy of the nerve mechanisms that presumably underlie them, suggest that the brain is not simply a passive network of communications but develops some kind of organization that facilitates learning and thinking. Whether such organizing principles exist has been a matter of considerable dispute. At one extreme, some modern psychologists deny that they do and describe learning as a mere trial-and-error process—a blind fumbling about until a solution accidentally appears. At the other extreme, there are psychologists who hold that people learn through an innate insight that reveals relationships to them.

To investigate, and to reconcile if possible, these seemingly antagonistic positions, a series of studies of the learning process has been carried out at the University of Wisconsin. Some of these have been made with young children, but most of the research has been on monkeys.

For two basic reasons animals are particularly good subjects for the investigation of learning at a fundamental level. One is that it is possible to control their entire learning history: the psychologist knows the problems to which they have been exposed, the amount of training they have had on each, and the record of their performance. The other reason is that the animals' adaptive processes are more simple than those of human beings, especially during the first stages of the attack on a problem. Often the animal's reactions throw into clear relief certain mechanisms that operate more obscurely in man. Of course this is only a relative simplicity. All the higher mammals possess intricate nervous systems and can solve complex problems. Indeed, it is doubtful that man possesses any fundamental intellectual process, except true language, that is not also present in his more lowly biological brethren.

Tests of animal learning of the trial-and-error type have been made in innumerable laboratories. In the special tests devised for our experiments, we set out to determine whether monkeys could progress from trial-and-error learning to the ability to solve a problem immediately by insight.

One of the first experiments was a simple discrimination test. The monkeys were confronted with a small board on which lay two objects different in color, size and shape. If a monkey picked up the correct object, it was rewarded by finding raisins or peanuts underneath. The position of the objects was shifted on the board in an irregular manner from trial to trial, and the trials were continued until the monkey learned to choose the correct object. The unusual feature of the experiment was that the test was repeated many times, with several hundred different pairs of objects. In other words, instead of training a monkey to solve a single problem, as had been done in most previous psychological work of this kind, we trained the animal on many problems, all of the same general type, but with varying kinds of objects.

When the monkeys first faced this test, they learned by the slow, laborious, fumble-and-find process. But as a monkey solved problem after problem of the same basic kind, its behavior changed in a most dramatic way. It learned each new problem with progressively greater efficiency, until eventually the monkey showed perfect insight when faced with this particular kind of situation—it solved the problem in one trial. If it chose the correct object on the first trial, it rarely made an error on subsequent trials. If it chose the incorrect object on the first trial, it immediately shifted to the correct object, and subsequently responded almost perfectly.

Thus the test appeared to demonstrate that trial-and-error and insight are but two different phases of one long continuous process. They are not different capacities, but merely represent the orderly development of a learning and thinking process.

Figure 1. Monkey experiments at the University of Wisconsin illustrate the process of learning. In the drawing at the upper right a monkey is confronted with two different objects. Under one of them is always a raisin or a peanut. In the drawing at the right the monkey has learned consistently to pick the same object. In the drawing above the monkey has learned consistently to choose one object which differs from two others. In the two drawings below the monkey has learned a much more complicated process. In the drawing at the lower left it has learned that when the board is of a certain color it must choose the object that is odd in shape. In the drawing at the lower right it has learned that when the board is of another color it must choose the object that is odd in color. In all these problems the monkey first learned to solve the problem by trial and error. Later it solved them immediately by understanding.

Figure 2. More complicated test involves teaching a monkey to choose certain objects not by matching but by response to a symbol. In the pair of drawings at the top of this page the monkey is shown a triangular object and pushes forward all the red objects. In drawings at bottom the monkey, shown a round object, pushes forward blue objects, here indicated by gray tone.

A long series of these discrimination problems was also run on a group of nursery-school children two to five years of age. Young children were chosen because they have a minimum of previous experience. The conditions in the children's tests were only slightly different from those for the monkeys: they were rewarded by finding brightly colored macaroni beads instead of raisins and peanuts. Most of the children, like the monkeys, made many errors in the early stages of the tests and only gradually learned to solve a problem in one trial. As a group the children learned more rapidly than the monkeys, but they made the same types of errors. And the "smartest" monkeys learned faster than the "dullest" children.

We have called this process of progressive learning the formation of a "learning set." The subject learns an organized set of habits that enables him to meet effectively each new problem of this particular kind. A single set would provide only limited aid in enabling an animal to adapt to an ever-changing environment. But a host of different learning sets may supply the raw material for human thinking.

We have trained monkeys and children to solve problems much more complex than the ones thus far described. For instance, a deliberate attempt is made to confuse the subjects by reversing the conditions of the discrimination test. The previously correct object is no longer rewarded, and the previously incorrect object is always rewarded. When monkeys and children face this switch-over for the first time, they make many errors, persistently choosing the objects they had previously been trained to choose. Gradually, from problem to problem, the number of such errors decreases until finally the first reversal trial is followed by perfect performance. A single failure becomes the cue to the subject to shift his choice from the object which has been rewarded many times to the object which has never been rewarded before. In this type of test children learn much more rapidly than monkeys.

A group of monkeys that had formed the discrimination-reversal learning set was later trained on a further refinement of the problem. This time the reward value of the object was reversed for only one trial, and was then shifted back to the original relationship. After many problems, the monkeys learned to ignore the single reversal and treated it as if the experimenter had made an error!

The problem was made more complicated, in another test, by offering the subjects a choice among three objects instead of two. There is a tray containing three food wells. Two are covered by one kind of object, and the third is covered by another kind. The animal must choose the odd object. Suppose the objects are building blocks and funnels. In half the trials, there are two blocks and a funnel, and the correct object is the funnel. Then a switch is made to two funnels and one block. Now the correct object is the block. The animal must learn a subtle distinction here: it is not the shape of the object that is important, but its relation to the other two. The meaning of a specific object may change from trial to trial. This problem is something like the one a child faces in trying to learn to use the words "I," "you," and "he" properly. The meaning of the words changes according to the speaker. When the child is speaking, "I" refers to himself, "you" to the person addressed, and "he" to some third person. When the child is addressed, the child is no longer "I" but "you." And when others speak of him, the terms shift again.

Monkeys and children were trained on a series of these oddity problems, 24 trials being allowed for the solution of each problem. At first they floundered, but they improved from problem to problem until they learned to respond to each new problem with perfect or nearly perfect scores. And on this complex type of problem the monkeys did better than most of the children!

One of the most striking findings from these tests was that once the monkeys have formed these learning sets, they retain them for long periods and can use them appropriately as the occasion demands. After a lapse of a year or more, a monkey regains top efficiency, in a few minutes or hours of practice, on a problem that it may have taken many weeks to master originally.

All our studies indicate that the ability to solve problems without fumbling is not inborn but is acquired gradually. So we must re-examine the evidence offered in support of the theory that animals possess some innate insight that has nothing to do with learning.

The cornerstone of this theory is the work of the famous Gestalt psychologist Wolfgang Köhler on the behavior of chimpanzees. In a series of brilliant studies he clearly showed that these apes can use sticks to help them obtain bananas beyond their reach. They employed the sticks to knock the bananas down, to rake them in, to climb and to vault. The animals sometimes assembled short sticks to make a pole long enough to reach the food, and even used sticks in combination with stacked boxes to knock down high-dangling bait. That the chimpanzees frequently solved these problems suddenly, as if by a flash of insight, impressed Köhler as evidence of an ability to reason independently of learning. He even suggested that this ability might differentiate apes and men from other animals.

Unfortunately, since Köhler's animals had been captured in the jungle, he had no record of their previous learning. Recent studies on chimpanzees born in captivity at the Yerkes Laboratory of Primate Biology at Orange Park, Fla., throw doubt on the validity of Köhler's interpretations. Herbert Birch of the Yerkes Laboratory reported that when he gave sticks to four-year-old chimps in their cages, they showed little sign at first of ability to use them as tools. Gradually, in the course of three days, they learned to use the sticks to touch objects beyond their reach. Later the animals solved very simple stick problems fairly well, but they had difficulty with more complex problems.

Extending Birch's investigations, the late Paul Schiller presented a series of stick tasks to a group of chimpanzees from two to over eight years of age. The younger the animal, the more slowly it mastered the problems. Some young subjects took hundreds of trials to perform efficiently on even the simplest problems, while old, experienced animals solved them with little practice. None of the apes solved the tasks initially with sudden insight.

Even at the human level there is no evidence that children possess any innate endowment that enables them to solve tool problems with insight. Augusta Alpert of Columbia University tried some of Köhler's simple chimpanzee tests on bright nursery-school children. The younger children typically went through a trial-and-error process before solving the problems. Some of them failed to solve the easiest problem in the series in five experimental sessions.

Eunice Mathieson presented more difficult Köhler-type tasks to a group of University of Minnesota nursery-school children. The results were even more overwhelmingly against the notion that tool problems are solved by flashes of natural insight. The children rarely solved a problem without making many mistakes.

This research, then, supports our findings. In all clear-cut tests—that is, whenever the animals' entire learning history is known—monkeys, apes and children at first solve problems by trial-and-error. Only gradually does such behavior give way to immediate solutions.

We began by pointing out that psychologists have sought to find in the higher mental processes some organizing mechanism or principle that would explain learning and thinking. We can now suggest such a mechanism: the learning set. Suppose we picture mental activity as a continuous structure built up, step by step, by the solution of increasingly difficult problems, from the simplest problem in learning to the most complex one in thinking. At each level the individual tries out various responses to solve each given task. At the lowest level he selects from unlearned responses or previously learned habits. As his experience increases, habits that do not help in the solution drop out and useful habits become established. After solving many problems of a certain kind, he develops organized patterns of responses that meet the demands of this type of situation. These patterns, or learning sets, can also be applied to the solution of still more complex problems. Eventually the individual may organize simple learning sets into more complex patterns of learning sets, which in turn are available for transfer as units to new situations.

Thus the individual learns to cope with more and more difficult problems. At the highest stage in this progression, the intelligent human adult selects from innumerable, previously acquired learning sets the raw material for thinking. His many years of education in school and outside have been devoted to building up these complex learning sets, and he comes to manipulate them with such ease that he and his observers may easily lose sight of their origin and development.

The fundamental role that language plays in the thinking process may be deduced easily from our experiments. They suggest that words are stimuli or signs that call forth the particular learning sets most appropriate for solving a given problem. If you listen to yourself "talk" while you are thinking, you will find that this is exactly what is happening. You review the different ways of solving a problem, and decide which is the best. When you ask a friend for advice, you are asking him to give you a word stimulus which will tell you the appropriate learning set or sets for the solution of your problem.

This principle is particularly well illustrated by some of our monkey experiments. Though monkeys do not talk, they can learn to identify symbols with appropriate learning sets. We have trained our monkeys to respond to signs in the form of differently colored trays on which the test objects appear. In one test the monkeys were presented with three different objects—a red U-shaped block, a green U-shaped block and a red cross-shaped block. Thus two of the objects were alike in form and two alike in color. When the objects were shown on an orange tray, the monkeys had to choose the green block, that is, the object that was odd in color. When they were shown on a cream-colored tray, the animals had to choose the cross-shaped block, that is, the object odd in form. After the monkeys had formed these two learning sets, the color cue of the tray enabled them to make the proper choice, trial after trial, without error. In a sense, the animals responded to a simple sign language. The difficulty of this test may be judged by the fact that the German neurologist Kurt Goldstein, using similar tests for human beings, found that people with organic brain disorders could not solve such tasks efficiently.

At the Wisconsin laboratories, Benjamin Winsten devised an even more difficult test for the monkeys. This problem tested the animals' ability to recognize similarities and differences, a kind of task frequently used on children's intelligence tests. Nine objects were placed on a tray and the monkey was handed one of them as a sample. The animal's problem was to pick out all identical objects, leaving all the rest on the tray. In the most complicated form of this test the monkey was given a sample which was not identical with the objects to be selected but was only a symbol for them. The animal was handed an unpainted triangle as a sign to pick out all red objects, and an unpainted circle as a sign to select all blue objects. One monkey learned to respond almost perfectly. Given a triangle, he would pick every object with any red on it; given a circle, he selected only the objects with blue on them.

All these data indicate that animals,

human and subhuman, must learn to think. Thinking does not develop spontaneously as an expression of innate abilities; it is the end result of a long learning process. Years ago the British biologist, Thomas Henry Huxley, suggested that "the brain secretes thought as the liver secretes bile." Nothing could be further from the truth. The brain is essential to thought, but the untutored brain is not enough, no matter how good a brain it may be. An untrained brain is sufficient for trial-and-error, fumble-through behavior, but only training enables an individual to think in terms of ideas and concepts.

VERBAL COMPREHENSION AND COMMUNICATION IN NEGRO AND WHITE CHILDREN [1]

ARNOLD S. CARSON
A. I. RABIN [2]

COMPARISONS of intellectual functioning in Negroes and whites have been of concern to research workers for some time. The classical review and summary by Klineberg (1935) is not yet outdated. For the most part, the superiority of the whites, especially on verbal tasks, has been demonstrated. However, the improvement in intelligence test scores of Negro children who migrated to the North from Southern states has also been shown. Moreover, the degree of improvement tends to be related to duration of residence in the North.

Performance tasks which correlate highly with "general intelligence," such as the Goodenough Draw-A-Man IQ Test, have not yielded significant differences between Negro and white children (Anastasi & D'Angelo, 1952). It would appear that tasks requiring verbal comprehension and verbal expression are the ones that are to a large extent responsible for the significant differences between the groups.

The present study is concerned with the investigation of these two functions, comprehension and expression or communication, in Negro and white children.

[1] Based on master's thesis (Carson, 1959) submitted to the Department of Psychology, Michigan State University by A. S. Carson and supervised by A. I. Rabin.

[2] The authors are grateful to G. F. King and C. F. Wrighley for their valuable assistance and suggestions.

Reprinted by permission of *Journal of Educational Psychology*, 1960, *51*, 47–51.

We propose to study these functions separately, and in relation to each other, in Southern and Northern Negro, and in Northern white, children. Our prediction was, in consonance with previous related findings, that when groups are matched for age, grade placement, sex, and level of verbal comprehension, the white children will be superior to the Southern and Northern Negroes in verbal communication; also, that the Northern Negro children will be superior to the Southern Negro children on measures of verbal communication.

METHOD

The Full Range Picture Vocabulary Test (Ammons & Ammons, 1949) was selected as the method of determining the level of verbal comprehension. This test requires no verbal response from the subjects (S). It consists of a series of cards with several pictures on each card. The S is merely required to point to the specific picture each time the examiner reads a word from the vocabulary test.

Two measures of verbal communication were employed for comparative purposes. First, the WISC Vocabulary (Weschsler, 1949) was presented in the standard manner and the responses scored as provided in the manual. Second, the words of the Full-Range Picture Vocabulary Test (FRPVT) which were "defined" by gesticulation were presented as a conventional vocabulary test, requiring oral definition.

The conventional scoring of vocabulary tests is an "all or none" affair. No provisions are made for qualitative differences in definitions or in levels of abstraction, precision and communication. This lack of sensitivity in the conventional

scoring of vocabulary tests has been pointed out long ago by Yacorzynski (1940).

In order to provide for scoring of levels of communication with the vocabulary of the FRPVT an adaptation of a method reported in the literature (Rabin, King, & Ehrmann, 1955) was utilized. A description of this Qualitative Vocabulary Scale, of the categories of responses and definitions of the word "wagon" as illustrative of the levels of communication appear below.

Class 1. Categorization and Synonym

a. Categorization. The categorization responses classified by some definite scheme in terms of its universal characteristics.

Response—"a vehicle"

b. Synonym. The synonym response may essentially be used to replace the object or idea with no or little change in the denotative aspects of the stimulus word.

Response—"a cart"

Class 2. Essential Description. An essential description response must give the characterizing features of the stimulus word. If the stimulus word is abstract, the response must create mental imagery of the relevant situation. If the stimulus word is concrete (physically tangible), the response must differentiate between the stimulus word and members in its class.

Response—"It's a wooden thing with four wheels, and it looks like a box."

Class 3. Essential Function. An essential function response must describe primary rather than peripheral usage or purpose of an object or an idea.

Response—"You ride in it out West."

Class 4. Example. An example response defines an object or idea in terms of its aspects or members.

Response—"There's a red wagon kids play with."

Class 5. Vague Description and Vague Function

a. Vague Description. A vague description is a response that is not totally irrelevant but does not give the characterizing features of the object or idea.

Response—"Something that has four wheels."

b. Vague Function. A vague function response describes the peripheral rather than primary usage or purpose of the object or the idea.

Response—"It bumps into people."

Class 6. Error. The error response is totally irrelevant to the stimulus word.

Response—"The dog 'wagons' his tail."

Class 7. Don't Know. A "don't know" response is a statement or a lack of statement designating that the S is unable to verbally define a word *which he had previously designated recognition* for by a gesticulation response.

Response—"Don't know."

SUBJECTS

The Ss were Southern Negro (SN), Northern Negro (NN), and Northern white (NW) children in the fourth, fifth, and sixth grades. None of the Ss were advanced or behind in their age-grade placement. The SN group comprised all of the Negro children within the age range from 9.5 to 11.5 years who were born and reared in the South and had migrated to Lansing, Michigan within 28 months of the date tested. All of the NW and NN children were born and reared in Ingham County, Michigan. Data was collected on the occupational levels of the NW and NN children in accordance with the *Dictionary of Occupational Titles* (United States Government Printing Office, 1944) classification. Two of the main wage earners in the NW children's families were professional, technical or managerial workers, 4 were clerical or sales workers, 3 were service employees, 9 were mechanical workers, and 12 were manual laborers; respectively, there were 0, 5, 2, 5, and 18 NN main wage earners. It may be noted that the occupational levels of main wage earners from the two samples are similar. Due to the recent relocation of the SN families, the main wage earners' vocations were unsettled and therefore unavailable as data.

Children were tested with the FRPVT at random from the NW and NN groups in order to acquire Ss whose scores could be individually matched with the scores of children in the SN group. Table 1 summarizes relevant data for the three groups of children.

PROCEDURE

The FRPVT and the two oral vocabulary devices were administered individually to the Ss by the same examiner in single testing sessions. The SN children were tested first followed by random testing of NN and NW children who would qualify for the respective samples. When each SN child was matched with a NW

TABLE 1 · GRADE, SEX, AGE, AND MEAN PICTURE VOCABULARY TEST SCORES OF THE THREE GROUPS

Group	N	Grade			Sex		Ages (months)		Raw score of FRPVT	
		4th	5th	6th	Male	Female	Mean	SD	Mean	SD
NW	30	16	8	6	16	14	128	10.9	43.67	4.95
NN	30	16	8	6	15	15	125	10.9	43.57	5.74
SN	30	16	8	6	14	16	128	13.5	43.53	5.21

and NN child in terms of the FRPVT scores, the testing was discontinued.

Two independent scorers tallied verbal responses to the FRPVT. These responses were scored according to the classification system described above. The total percentage of interscorer agreement was .79. Complete agreement between the two scorers was obtained after the debatable responses were discussed.

RESULTS AND DISCUSSION

As a preliminary step in the treatment of the data, all Ss were classified into "high" and "low" responders. The Ss whose majority of responses were tallied in categories 1, 2 and 3 were placed in the former classification; the predominance of the remaining four categories characterized the second group. Table 2 reports the incidence of members of each sample in the "high" and "low" categories. The differences in the distribution are statistically significant.

As predicted, the white children assume the top position. It is also interesting to note that the NN group place in an intermediate position between the white and SN children.

The responses of the three groups were also compared on each of the seven categories comprising our qualitative (levels of communication) scoring system. Table 3 summarizes the levels of significance of the differences between the groups computed by means of the Wilcoxon matched-pairs signed-rank test (Siegel, 1956). Thirteen of the 21 comparisons were significant in the predicted direction. The table indicates that the general prediction is supported to a considerable degree. This is especially true with the extremes of the qualitative categories.

The results of the study demonstrated that NW children, of comparable nonverbal word recognition (or comprehension) abilities, manifest higher levels of verbal communication than NN children, and, in turn, the NN children manifest higher levels of verbal communication than SN children.

All comparisons by means of the WISC vocabulary subtest yield significant differences in the predicted direction (using Wilcoxon's test mentioned above).

TABLE 2 · A COMPARISON OF THE INCIDENCE OF HIGH AND LOW RESPONDERS ON THE QUALITATIVE VOCABULARY SCALE IN THE THREE GROUPS

Group	High	Low	x^2	p[1]
NW	25	5		
NN	18	12		
SN	7	23	22.54	<.001

[1] One-tailed test.

Again, global vocabulary scores, as in the case of the more refined treatment of the FRPVT, indicate the superiority of the white children compared with the two Negro samples. Also, the NN group is inferior to the NW but superior to the SN children. This finding is consistent with the results in the previous two tables.

The children's pattern of responding is interesting in that it was unique for each of the groups and may therefore be a clue to differences in characteristic thinking among the three groups. The NW children favor the higher levels of verbal communication (Classes 1, 2, 3). Their percentage of responses decreases sharply in the Example classification and after a slight increase in the Vague classification, their percentage of responses continues to decrease lower than that of the two Negro groups in the Error and Don't Know classifications. NN children favor

the Vague type response and manifest a greater percentage of Error type responses than the white children. The SN children's pattern is the only one which manifests a high peak in the Don't Know classification.

The differences among the groups cannot be consistently explained according to one theoretical viewpoint. Differences between the NW and NN children could lend support to the contention that constitutional racial differences in intelligence exist or to the viewpoint that a difference of cultural opportunities accounts for the variance between racial groups. However, there are sufficient possibilities of differences in the cultural milieu of the two samples to question their equivalence of social opportunities. The two groups remain segregated from

TABLE 3 · Summary of Levels of Significance Obtained from Comparisons of Ranks on the Qualitative Vocabulary Scale

| Class | GROUPS | | | | | | | | | | | |
| | NW vs. SN (T) (T') | | | | NW vs. NN (T) (T') | | | | NN vs. SN (T) (T') | | | |
	T	T'	z	p	T	T'	z	p	T	T'	z	p
1	271.0	29.0	3.44	<.0005	289.0	62.0	2.87	<.0025	181.0	72.0	1.76	<.05
2	327.5	107.5	2.36	<.01	283.5	122.5	1.82	<.05	206.5	171.5	.41	ns
3	350.0	85.0	2.85	<.0005	233.0	118.0	1.45	ns	326.0	139.0	1.91	<.05
4	274.5	160.5	1.22	ns	126.5	198.5	.82	ns	301.0	105.0	2.22	<.025[1]
5	154.5	223.5	.82	ns	147.0	231.0	1.00	ns	202.5	203.5	.00	ns
6	34.5	316.5	3.57	<.0005	57.5	218.5	2.43	<.01	55.5	295.5	3.04	<.0025
7	3.0	432.0	4.63	<.0001	95.5	229.5	1.79	<.05	40.5	394.5	3.82	<.0005

[1] If a two-tailed test were employed, the difference would have been significant in a direction contrary to the current hypothesis.

TABLE 4 · Summary of Comparisons of Ranks on the WISC Vocabulary Subtest

| Comparisons | Total ranks | | | Theoretical | | | Significance |
	NW	NN	SN	Mean	SD	z	
NW vs. SN	432.0	. .	3.0	217.5	46.25	4.62	<.0001
NN vs. SN	. .	345.5	60.6	203.0	43.92	3.24	<.001
NW vs. NN	334.0	101.0	. .	217.5	46.25	2.51	<.01

each other in activities other than those which revolve around school. The NN sample, for the most part, lives in a section of town which is a homogeneous Negro settlement. Their cultural milieu is definitely not characteristic of white middle-class modes of living.

The comparisons of the NN and SN children lend themselves to a more clear-cut interpretation since the cultural variable of geographical residence was considered in the experimental design. It is contended that the superior educational environment and the greater opportunity for cultural advancement of the NN child over the SN child accounts for the significant differences between the two groups.

The present study supports Klineberg's (1947) research findings that geographical residency of the Negro child is an important determinant of vocabulary performance. Coppinger and Ammons' (1952) contention that different norms should be utilized when making intergroup comparisons involving Negroes where the members of the groups have different cultural backgrounds is also supported.

Finally, it should be pointed out that verbal comprehension and verbal communication seem to be two different functions. Although the groups were equated on comprehension, they showed marked differences with respect to communication. The former task requires recognition within a certain context, which is quite different from verbal communication and definition of a word in isolation, and not in context. It would appear that differences between Negroes and whites on conventional intelligence tests, and especially on vocabulary subtests, may be primarily due to failure in verbal communication rather than in comprehension.

SUMMARY

Three groups (30 in each group) of NW, NN, and SN school children, matched for age, sex, grade placement, and level of verbal comprehension, were compared on two vocabulary tests requiring verbal communication. In accord with the original prediction, the white children were superior to the Negro children, and the NN children were superior to the SN children on these two measures. The results were discussed in relation to the possible racial and cultural geographic factors involved.

REFERENCES

AMMONS, R. B., & AMMONS, H. S. The Full-Range Picture Vocabulary Test. *Amer. Psychologist*, 1949, *4*, 267–268.

ANASTASI, ANN, & D'ANGELO, RITA Y. A comparison of Negro and white preschool children in language development and Goodenough Draw-A-Man IQ. *J. genet. Psychol.*, 1952, *81*, 147–165.

CARSON, A. S. Verbal comprehension and verbal communication in Negro and white children. Unpublished master's thesis, Mich. State Univer., 1959.

COPPINGER, N. W., & AMMONS, R. B. The Full-Range Picture Vocabulary Test: VIII. A normative study of Negro children. *J. clin. Psychol.*, 1952, *8*, 136–140.

KLINEBERG, O. *Race differences.* New York: Harper, 1935.

KLINEBERG, O. Negro intelligence and urban residence. In T. M. Newcomb & E. L. Hartley (Eds.), *Readings in social psychology.* New York: Holt, 1947. Pp. 24–32.

RABIN, A. J., KING, G. F., & EHRMANN, J. C. Vocabulary performance of short-term and long-term schizophrenics. *J. abnorm. soc. Psychol.*, 1955, *50*, 255–258.

SIEGEL, S. *Nonparametric statistics for the behavioral sciences.* New York: McGraw-Hill, 1956.

UNITED STATES GOVERNMENT PRINTING OFFICE, Division of Occupational Analysis. *Dictionary of occupational titles.* Part IV. Washington, D.C.: Author, 1944.

WECHSLER, D. *Wechsler Intelligence Scale for Children.* New York: Psychological Corp., 1949.

YACORZYNSKI, G. K.   An evaluation of the postulates underlying the Babcock deterioration test. *Psychol. Bull.*, 1940, *37*, 425–426. (Abstract.)

PSYCHODYNAMIC HYPOTHESES | 4

ONE OF THE TASKS of the psychologist as a scientist is to establish laws of behavior, that is, to determine stable relationships between sets of events. Spence (1948, 1956) has discussed the various kinds of laws that are of interest within this field. One of these that has been of primary concern to those interested in psychopathology has been labeled by Spence as $R = f(R)$ or R–R laws. Laws of this kind specify the relationships, usually of the correlational variety, between responses made in one situation and responses made in another. Such relations may be between scores on one test and scores on another, or scores on a test and responses in an experimental task, or responses in an experimental task and diagnostic category.

In contrast, the experimental psychologist has been primarily interested in $R = f(S)$, or S–R laws. In this case, the attention is focused upon determining how responses vary as a function of manipulations of the stimulus conditions. The stimuli may be those presented in the immediate present, as in a psychophysical experiment attempting to determine a threshold, or in the relatively recent or distant past, as in the case of learning experiments and studies of the effects of pervious experience on current behavior.

While a great deal of research directed toward the examination of psychodynamic hypotheses has attempted to discover R–R relationships, the selections in this section focus primarily on the determination of how behaviorally different groups respond to different stimulus conditions. These studies are therefore aimed at establishing, in addition to R–R laws, laws of the S–R type. Each of the studies demonstrates differences in the responses of the different groups of children selected for observation, the groups being defined in terms of common responses. In addition, however, most of the studies also attempt to provide data relative to the variation in responses of the different groups of children as a function of the type of antecedent stimulation provided.

The discovery of the determinants of personality or behavioral characteristics of children is a complex problem deserving of considerably more attention than this section provides. The writings of Freud and others have focused a great deal of attention upon childhood and the factors that occur during this period to determine personality characteristics both in childhood and later in life. As a result, a great deal of effort has been devoted to the study of the variables that determine children's personality attributes. Much research has been directed to the discovery of the influences of parental treatment upon the behaviors of children. Sears and his colleagues, for example, have worked extensively in this area to test some of the psychoanalytic hypotheses and extend some of the principles of learning to parent-child relationships. Their work has taken the form of relating responses of parents in an interview about child-rearing practices to the observed behaviors of the children in nursery school and home behavior as reported by the parents (Nowlis, 1953; Sears, Maccoby and Levin, 1957).

Others have attempted to relate the personality characteristics of adults to childhood experiences through retrospective reports and analyses. R. G. Harlow (1951), for instance, has attempted to reconstruct, through a Freudian theoretical framework, certain relationships between childhood experiences, on the one hand, and adult behavior patterns and response to projective techniques, on the other. He found different sets of response characteristics in a group of weight-lifters and a group of otherwise matched non-weight-lifters with respect to such variables as heterosexual responsiveness and amount of hostility to mother figures. The study, while of an R–R variety (relating weight-lifting to other kinds of response), provides suggestions about some of the underlying dynamics or antecedent conditions leading to weight-lifting.

Such research efforts are extremely useful in developing hypotheses about the factors that determine the personality characteristics of children and form one of the few approaches available for the study of these complex behaviors. They are, however, always subject to criticism, for they take the behavior as it exists and attempt to show correlates of that behavior. Since we are well aware that correlation does not mean causation, it is always necessary to interpret the results cautiously. If the research is conceived within a theoretical system, as in both of the cases cited, one can feel greater confidence in the results of such studies when the data and other evidence both support the theory.

Ideally, one might wish to select a sample of children and their parents, assign them at random to different treatment groups, and examine the differences in behavioral reactions of the children in response to their particular treatment. For example, one group of parents might be instructed to behave in a rejecting fashion toward their children and another group to indulge their children. Such a procedure is, of course, impossible. Parents obviously would not cooperate in such a venture and most researchers, sensing the potency of some of these variables, would not be interested in trying it. Researchers, therefore, have attempted to find parents who tend to behave in these ways anyway, contrasting the behavior of children reared by parents adhering to different child-rearing practices.

It is possible, however, to study experimentally the effects of some variables on parents' behaviors, as Merrill (1946), for example, has done. She indicated to mothers that their children were not performing adequately in an experimental situation and observed the effects such instructions had on the ways in which the mothers subsequently handled their children in the same task.

Most of the studies in the present section have been designed to manipulate experimentally some variables in a small-scale study to determine the effects upon the behaviors of deviant groups of children. This research approach may take considerable time but may provide useful information in the long run if a systematic effort is made to integrate the results of several studies. In fact, each of the studies included here forms a part of a group of studies which have been done by the authors of the studies and their colleagues.

The first study, by Ruebush, is one of a series being directed by Sarason (1960) dealing with test anxiety and conceived within a psychoanalytic theoretical framework. This study is designed to formulate laws of an R–R sort by relating scores on tests of anxiety and cautiousness to responses in an experimental task. The results suggest that cautiousness is one of the defense mechanisms used by anxious children to avoid the deleterious effects which anxiety can have on their test performance.

The second study is designed, as are the last two studies in this section, to determine the effects of experimental manipulations of the environment upon the behavior of children. This experiment uses normal children, while the next two involve comparisons of deviant and normal groups under different experimental treatments. Taking advantage of the well-established finding that frustration leads to aggression, Bandura, Ross, and Ross demonstrate that aggression resulting from frustration may be manifest in specific ways if the child is provided with models demonstrating methods of expressing aggression. Simulating a TV set for presentation of some of the models assured the attention of the children and maximal experimental control.

The third study is one of a series to determine some of the variables that differentially affect the behavior of emotionally disturbed and normal children. In an earlier study it had been shown that success increased level of aspiration less while failure decreased level of aspiration more in emotionally disturbed than in normal boys. The findings in this study, that the disturbed boys showed inferior performance on the verbal task and superior performance on the motor task, are attributed to differences in anxiety levels and are related to the results of other research done with test-measured anxiety reported in the section on Motivational factors in learning (Section XIV).

Recently, an increasing amount of research attention has been focused upon mentally retarded children and the factors that affect their learning, perception, and performance. The last study in this section is one that contributes to this area. Working with an old problem derived from Lewinian theory, the results suggest some modifications in the interpretation of Kounin's older study and demonstrate the marked effects that adult approval and disapproval may have upon the performance of retarded children in contrast to normal children.

REFERENCES

HARLOW, R. G. Masculine inadequacy and compensatory development of physique. *J. Pers.*, 1951, *19*, 312–333.

MERRILL, BARBARA. A measurement of mother-child interaction. *J. abnorm. soc. Psychol.*, 1946, *41*, 37–49.

NOWLIS, V. The development and modification of motivational systems in personality. In M. R. Jones (Ed.), *Nebraska symposium on motivation*. Lincoln, Neb., University of Nebraska Press, 1953.

SARASON, S. B., DAVIDSON, K. S., LIGHTHALL, F. F., WAITE, R. R., and RUEBUSH, B. K. *Anxiety in elementary school children*. New York: Wiley, 1960.

SEARS, R. R., MACCOBY, E. E., and LEVIN, H. *Patterns of child rearing*. Evanston, Ill.: Row, 1957.

SPENCE, K. W. The postulates and methods of behaviorism. *Psychol. Rev.*, 1948, *55*, 67–78.

SPENCE, K. W. *Behavior theory and conditioning*. New Haven: Yale University Press, 1956.

INTERFERING AND FACILITATING EFFECTS
OF TEST ANXIETY [1]

BRITTON K. RUEBUSH

INTERFERING EFFECTS of test anxiety in children were observed in an experimental learning study reported by Waite, Sarason, Lighthall, & Davidson (1958). In another study, Lighthall, Ruebush, Sarason, & Zweibelson (1959) found that while low test anxious (LA) children improved more than high test anxious (HA) children over a two-year time span on the "test-like" Otis Beta Intelligence Test, the HA improved more over the same period on the "game-like" Davis-Eells Test of Problem-solving Ability. These findings suggest that although test anxiety has interfering effects upon intellectual performance under some conditions, it may have *facilitating* effects under other conditions.

The present study was designed as a test of several predictions derived from a simple theoretical model, formulated to account for the fact that test anxiety may have both interfering and facilitating effects upon intellectual performance. In general, the model holds that the effect of anxiety upon performance is mediated primarily by defensive reactions to the anxiety. This hypothesis is supported by the results of a study in which it was found that the Rorschach performance of HA children was significantly affected by their cautious and dependent behavior in the test situation (Sarason, Davidson, Lighthall, & Waite, 1958b). In particular, the model states that (a) defensive reactions such as cautiousness have been strongly overlearned and thus are stable "automatic" responses to the anxiety triggered off by such situations such as tests, (b) the effects of anxiety upon performance are mediated by these defensive reactions to the anxiety, (c) in problem solving situations where such defensive reactions are an asset, anxiety has a facilitating effect upon performance, and (d) in problem solving situations where such defensive reactions are a liability, anxiety has an interfering effect upon performance.

The criterion task selected for the present study provided a problem solving situation in which cautious behavior was expected to facilitate performance. Therefore, three specific predictions were made: (a) Highly cautious Ss do better than law cautious Ss on the criterion task; (b) HA Ss obtain higher cautiousness scores than LA Ss; and (c) HA Ss perform more effectively on the criterion task than LA Ss.

[1] This study is part of a project of which Seymour B. Sarason is the principal investigator and which is being supported by a grant from the United States Public Health Service (M-712). The author wishes to express his deep appreciation to Seymour Sarason, Kenneth Davidson, Frederick Lighthall, and Richard Waite for their interest and helpful suggestions in the design and execution of this investigation.

Reprinted by permission from *Journal of Abnormal and Social Psychology*, 1960, *60*, 205–212.

METHOD

SUBJECTS AND RESEARCH DESIGN

The population from which the children in this study were selected was composed of 280 sixth-grade boys from the 11 elementary schools in the predominantly middle-class community of Hamden, Connecticut. Within a period of approximately two months preceding the selection of the final sample, the entire sampling population received the Yale Test Anxiety and Yale General Anxiety Scales, as well as the Beta Test Form Em of the Otis Mental Ability Tests.[2] Previous reports have described the Yale anxiety scales and given evidence pertaining to their validity (Sarason, Davidson, Lighthall, & Waite, 1958a; Sarason et al., 1958b; Sarnoff, Lighthall, Waite, Davidson, & Sarason, 1958; Waite et al., 1958; Zweilbelson, 1956). As the first step in selecting the final sample, Ss whose test anxiety scores were ≤5 designated as LA, and those whose test anxiety scores were ≥15 were termed HA. These cutoff points included approximately the lower and upper quartiles of the total sampling population. Second, each of these LA and HA Ss whose Otis Beta IQ score fell within the interval 89–122 was then assigned to one of three levels of intelligence: 89–100, 101–110, or 111–122, designated as low, medium, and high levels, respectively. Third, eight Ss were selected by a table of random numbers from each of the six anxiety-IQ groups. Fourth, each of the groups of eight Ss was randomly split into two groups of four, one of which was to receive the easy criterion task items first, the other to receive the difficult items first. To sum up, the research design of the present study was a 2 (anxiety levels) × 3 (intelligence levels) × 2 (order of administration of easy and difficult items) mixed factorial arrangement, with four Ss in each cell. The within-Ss effect consisted of a main effect of trials (item difficulty) plus the interaction of trials with the between-Ss effects (anxiety, intelligence, and order).

2 The author wishes to thank Kenneth Davidson and Jane Maltby for their help in collecting these data.

CRITERION TASK

The criterion task used in this study consisted of the 12-item short form of the Witkin Embedded Figures Test developed by Jackson (1956). Diagrams and detailed information about the figures are given by Witkin (1950). Previous studies have demonstrated that the criterion task is well within the intellectual grasp of the population used in the present study (Witkin, Lewis, Hertzman, Machover, Meissner, & Wafner, 1954). The task items were ranked in order of difficulty according to the mean solution time achieved on each item by an independent sample of 26 13-year-old-boys.[3] Ranked from easiest to most difficult and using Witkin's (1950) numbering system, the rank order of difficulty of the items was as follows (mean solution times in parentheses): D-2 (19 sec.); G-1 (23); A-3 (25); C-2 (36); E-3 (58); E-5 (60); C-3 (67); H-1 (72); D-1 (79); C-1 (102); A-2 (104); and E-1 (105).

PROCEDURE

E, who did not know the anxiety or IQ level of the Ss, worked with them individually in the public schools. After bringing each S from the classroom to the testing room, a brief conversation took place during which the establishment of good rapport was attempted. Then the following instructions were given.

This is like the game in the Sunday papers where you have to find a hidden animal in a picture. Only this time you won't be looking for an animal. This is a test to see how fast you can find a design.

E then gave S the practice complex figure for 15 sec., during which he asked S whether it reminded him of anything. The complex figure was then removed, and S was given the simple practice figure for 10 sec., during which E advised S to "learn this one carefully" because he would have to locate it in the complicated figure he had just seen. Finally, E removed the simple

3 The author is grateful to H. A. Witkin for making these data available.

figure and presented the complex figure again, at the same time telling S to find the simple figure in the complicated one. After S had located the practice embedded figure, he was asked to trace its outline with a blunt instrument so that E could see that S understood the task. Then the instructions continued as follows.

This is the way the test will be done. You will be shown the complicated design and then the little simple figure. Finally, you will have to locate the simple figure in the complicated one just as you did. The simple design will always be present in the complicated one, and it will always be right side up. Also, if you forget the simple figure, you may ask to see it again as many times as you wish and it won't count against you since I stop the watch while you're looking at the simple figure. And remember, there may be some more lines crossing the simple figure when it is in the complicated figure. Find the simple figure as fast as you can, since I will be timing you and your grade depends on your time, but be sure that the figure you find has exactly the same size and shape as the one you're supposed to be looking for. As soon as you think you have found the figure, tell me at once so that I can note your time and then show me where it is by tracing its outline. If you are right, I will give you the time when you said you saw it. If you are wrong, you will just go on looking and your guess won't count against you. So remember, tell me as soon as you have found the figure, and then show me where it is. Any questions?

E then presented the items in one of two orders, depending upon the order group to which S had been randomly assigned. If S had been assigned to order Easy-Difficult (ED), he was given the figures in the order, 1–12. If he had been assigned to order Difficult-Easy (DE), the order of administration was reversed—S got the figures in order 12–1.

Each time S requested to see the simple figure again, E stopped the watch and recorded the time and a figure "S." The watch was not stopped during a guess, although when S made a guess the time was recorded, and if the guess was incorrect a "G" was also recorded after the time. If S had not located the embedded figure within five minutes, this was noted on the recording sheet, and S was then shown the correct location of the embedded figure.

SCORING

Latency. The time in seconds taken by each S to solve each figure was recorded and then transformed to logarithms in order to achieve normally distributed item distributions and homogeneity of the variances of the 12 groups. The rationale for this use of logarithmic transformations has been presented by Quenouille (1950). Normality of the item distributions was ascertained by observation and the group variances were found to be homogeneous according to the F_{max} test (Walker & Lev, 1953). The logarithms of each S's latency scores on figures D-2 and G-1, A-3 and C-2, E-3 and E-5, C-3 and H-1, D-1 and C-1, A-2 and E-1, respectively, were summed so that, for purposes of the analysis, each S had 6 log-latency scores. In addition, a total log-latency score was obtained for each S by summing his 12 log-latency scores.

Number of figures solved. Each S was also given a score consisting of the total number of figures solved without regard for the time taken to solve them. Observation of the distribution and homogeneity of variances of these scores revealed no consequential deviation from normality, and thus no need for a transformation of scores.

Cautiousness Index. The instructions preceding administration of the criterion task included statements that S could request to see the original (simple) figure as often as he liked and without penalty (he was told the watch would be stopped while he looked). In addition, he was told that guessing was permitted and wouldn't count against him, although he was *not* told that the watch would be stopped during a guess. He was also told that if he made a "wrong" guess, he would be so informed and could then continue his search for the embedded figure. Thus, the task was structured so that a cautious approach in which S made sure that he knew the correct response before he made a guess would be rewarded by success (since the watch continued running during guesses). A ratio consisting of the number of requests to see the simple figure divided by the number of "wrong" guesses was computed for each S. This ratio is relatively independent of latency because it was possible for S to obtain high or low ratios regardless of the amount of time he took to solve the figures. The S who obtains a high ratio score is one who asks to see the simple figure many time before he ventures a guess, and although there are elements of both dependency and cautiousness involved in this sort of behavior, the ratio score has been labeled the *Cautiousness Index*, because this term seems to provide the most accurate description of the variable under study. Since these ratio scores were not normally distributed, the logarithmic transformation was again utilized successfully to normalize the distribution so that t ratios could be computed.

RESULTS

ANALYSIS OF LATENCY SCORES [4]

The results of the analysis of variance of the log-latency scores are given in Table 1. Although the main effects of both Anxiety and linear IQ only approached statistical significance, the Anxiety × linear IQ interaction was found to be statistically significant ($p < .05$). This interaction resulted from the fact that, in comparison with the LA Ss, the performance of the HA Ss was superior at the low and middle levels of IQ and inferior at the high IQ level. As a statistical check on this observation, separate t tests were computed for the differences between the mean log-latency scores of the HA and LA groups at each level of IQ. The results revealed that the HA per-

[4] The author wishes to express his thanks to Norman Anderson for his helpful advice on the statistical analysis.

formed significantly better than the LA at the low IQ level ($p < .01$) and at the middle IQ level ($p < .03$), whereas the superior performance of the LA at the high IQ level only approached statistical significance ($.10 < p < .20$). The mean log-latency scores for the HA and LA groups at each level of IQ, as well as the results of the t tests of the differences between these means, are given in Table 2.

TABLE 1 · ANALYSIS OF VARIANCE OF LOG-LATENCY SCORES

	SS	df	MS	F	P
Anxiety	3.146	1	3.15	2.23	$p<.15$
IQ	4.781	2	2.39		
Linear	4.624	1	4.624	3.28	$p<.10$
Resid.	0.157	1	0.157		
Order	0.005	1	0.005		
A × IQ	6.843	2	3.42	2.43	$p<.10$
Linear	6.388	1	6.39	4.53	$p<.05$
Resid.	0.455	1	0.455		
A × O	2.024	1	2.024		
O × IQ	2.005	2	1.002		
A × O × IQ	1.767	2	0.884		
Error	50.791	36	1.41		
Within trials (task difficulty)	51.096	5	10.219	14.45	$p<.001$
T × A	0.765	5	0.153		
T × O	15.847	5	3.169	4.48	$p<.001$
T × IQ	2.542	10	0.254		
T × A × O	2.876	5	0.575		
T × A × IQ	3.279	10	0.328		
T × O × IQ	3.858	10	0.386		
T × A × O × IQ	2.635	10	0.264		
Error	127.242	180	0.707		

TABLE 2 · MEAN LOG-LATENCY SCORES FOR ANXIETY—IQ GROUPS

	HA	LA	SE_{Dm}	t	df	p*
L IQ	22.29	25.39	0.79	3.92	14	<.01
M IQ	21.65	23.58	0.75	2.57	14	<.03
H IQ	22.61	21.34	0.88	1.44	14	$.10 < p <.20$

* All significance tests two-tailed.

With respect to the within-Ss effects listed in Table 1, the main effect of Trials and the Trials × Order interaction were both found to be statistically significant ($p < .001$) and to account for the major portion of the within-Ss variance. The Trials × Order interaction resulted from the fact that both the LA and the HA Ss did better on the items which came last in sequence. The Trials effect showed that the criterion task items did differ in level of difficulty. Duncan's Test (Snedecor, 1956) was carried out on the six over-all mean log-latency scores for Trials in order to determine more precisely the extent of the difference in task difficulty level of the criterion task items. Since there was no Anxiety × Trials interaction, the overall MS within was used in computing SE_m for Duncan's Test. The results of the 14 simultaneous comparisons indicated that, with the exception of the comparison of the first pair (D-2 and G-1) with the second pair (A-3 and C-2), each of the six pairs of figures differed significantly in task difficulty from every other pair according to Duncan's Test with the 99% protection level.

TABLE 3 · MEAN NUMBERS OF FIGURES SOLVED FOR ANXIETY—IQ GROUPS

	HA	LA	SE_{Dm}	t	df	p*
L IQ	8.88	6.38	0.71	3.52	14	<.01
M IQ	9.50	7.88	0.63	2.57	14	<.05
H IQ	8.62	8.75	0.77	0.17	14	NS
Total	9.00	7.67	0.43	3.09	46	<.01

* All significance tests two-tailed.

ANALYSIS OF NUMBER SOLVED

The t testing technique was utilized for testing the difference between the mean number of figures solved by the two anxiety groups, as well as for testing the differences between the means of these groups at each IQ level. The results of the t tests are given in Table 3. They show that the HA solved significantly more figures than the LA ($p < .01$), although, as in the analysis of the latency scores, the tests of the differences between the means at each IQ level show that the superior performance of the HA was limited to the low and middle levels of IQ. In addition, and in contrast with the results of the analysis of the log-latency scores, the superiority of the LA Ss at the high IQ level in the present analysis was not found to approach statistical significance.

MULTIVARIATE ANALYSIS OF LOG-LATENCY AND NUMBER SOLVED

A statistical procedure given by Rao (1952) was used in carrying out a simultaneous multivariate analysis of both log-latency and number of figures solved. The only significant effects to result from this analysis were the main effect of Anxiety ($p < .05$) and the Order × IQ interaction ($p < .05$). That is, when both variables are allowed to operate simultaneously in the same analysis, the Anxiety × IQ interaction drops out, and the main effect of Anxiety becomes significant, with the HA showing superior over-all performance. It is apparent that when these two variables are combined in an analysis of this type, the marked superiority of the HA Ss at the low and middle IQ levels overrides the Anxiety × IQ interaction found in the analysis of variance of the log-latency scores. The Order × IQ interaction resulted from the fact that the high and low IQ groups performed more efficiently when they were given the easy figures first, whereas the middle IQ groups performed more efficiently when given the more difficult figures first.

ANALYSIS OF CAUTIOUSNESS INDEX (CI)

After collapsing the groups on IQ, the mean log CI score for the 24 HA Ss was .174, whereas the mean log CI score for the 24 LA Ss was .056. The SE of the difference between these means was .054, and the t ratio was 2.19 with 46 degrees of freedom. This ratio is significant at the $p < .02$ level of significance (one-tail). The LA mean log CI score was raised considerably by the fact that one LA S obtained a log CI score of 1.061. If the highly deviant score of this LA S had been excluded, the mean log CI score for the LA group would have dropped to .011. In any event, it remains clear that the HA group was significantly more cautious than the LA group.

The groups were also collapsed on Anxiety in order to determine whether the three IQ groups also differed in degree of cautiousness. The mean log CI score for the 16 high IQ Ss was .101; for the 16 middle IQ Ss, .123; and for the 16 low IQ Ss, .121. Since the differences between these means were not found even to approach statistical significance, it was concluded that the three IQ groups did not differ in degree of cautiousness.

For purposes of further analysis and comparison, it was decided to define the highly cautious S (whether HA or LA) as one with a raw S-over-G ratio [5] $\geqslant 2$ (log S-over-G ratio $\geqslant .301$) because there was a break in the total distribution of cautiousness scores between the 17 Ss with raw S-over-G ratios $\geqslant 2$ and the 31 Ss with S-over-G ratios < 2. According to this criterion of high and low cautiousness, there were 11 HA Ss and 6 LA Ss who were defined as being highly cautious.

[5] This ratio is defined in the section describing the scoring procedure.

tious. The mean log-latency scores, the mean number of figures solved, and the mean log CI scores of the high and low cautious Ss—both within and across Anxiety groups—are given in Table 4. It is apparent that the HA highly cautious Ss solved more figures ($p < .001$) in less time ($p < .001$) than the HA low cautious Ss. Similarly, the LA highly cautious Ss also solved more figures ($p < .001$), in less time ($p < .001$) than the LA low cautious Ss. Furthermore, inspection of the data in Table 4 reveals that the performance of the 11 HA highly cautious Ss did not differ appreciably from the performance of the 6 LA highly cautious Ss, nor did the performance of the 13 HA low cautious Ss differ appreciably from that of the 18 LA low cautious Ss. Finally, when the groups were collapsed on Anxiety and IQ, the highly cautious Ss were found to solve more figures ($p < .001$) in less time ($p < .001$) than the low cautious Ss.

TABLE 4

	Log-latency	No. solved	CI
HA			
Cautious	20.928	10.27	0.493
Not cautious	23.244	7.92	—0.095
Mean diff.	2.316*	2.35*	0.588*
LA			
Cautious	21.156	9.67	0.512
Not cautious	24.197	7.00	—0.097
Mean diff.	3.041*	2.67*	0.609*
Total			
Cautious	21.042	10.06	0.502
Not cautious	23.721	7.39	—0.096
Mean diff.	2.679*	2.67*	0.598*

* Significant at the $p < .001$ level (two-tailed).

Since General Anxiety (GA) scores from the Yale General Anxiety Scale for Children were also available for all of

TABLE 5 · MEAN GA AND TA SCORES OF HIGH AND LOW TA, CAUTIOUS AND NONCAUTIOUS Ss

	HA		
	Cautious	Noncautious	Diff.
TA	18.2	19.8	1.6
GA	15.7	16.5	0.8
	LA		
TA	3.0	2.6	0.4
GA	10.0	6.3	3.7*

* Significant p at $< .01$ level (22 df).

these Ss, the mean GA scores as well as the mean TA scores for the highly cautious and low cautious Ss within TA groups were computed in an attempt to shed some light upon the fact that, contrary to expectations, six of the low TA Ss were also highly cautious. T tests revealed that the mean GA score for the six highly cautious low TA Ss was significantly higher than the mean GA score for the 18 low cautious low TA Ss ($p < .01$), even though their TA scores were not significantly different. On the other hand, the mean GA and TA scores of the highly cautious and low cautious high TA Ss were not significantly different. These means are listed in Table 5.

DISCUSSION

The prediction that highly cautious Ss do better than low cautious Ss on the criterion task is confirmed by the findings. This supports the original analysis of the embedded figures task as one in which cautious behavior is an asset in problem solving.

The prediction that HA Ss obtain significantly higher cautiousness scores than LA Ss is also confirmed, consistent with the thesis that (a) in the case of the test anxious S, the evaluative characteristic of tests has become connected with certain unconscious material involving his early interpersonal relationships and conflicts with important authority figures; (b) as a consequence, tests have become equated with danger and thus trigger his anxiety; (c) the test anxious child gradually has learned certain methods of defending against the anxiety engendered in him by evaluative situations; (d) these defenses include the type of behavior here labeled "cautiousness"; and (e) because these defenses have been strongly overlearned, they have become "automatic" responses to the anxiety triggered off by tests.

The prediction that the performance of HA Ss on the criterion task would be significantly better than that of the LA Ss is confirmed by the results of the multivariate analysis. However, despite the fact that this analysis accounted for both the control and criterion variables simultaneously, more detailed analysis revealed that the superiority of the HA Ss was limited to the low and medium level of IQ. For these IQ groups, then, wherever the tasks in a test situation are defined or structured so that cautiousness, as here defined, is a positive asset in solving the tasks; the test anxious child will do well. It is in this sense that the results show that anxiety is not always disorganizing, but that under certain conditions it may be facilitating. It is important to emphasize, however, that the superior performance expected of the HA child in some situations is a "fortuitous" result of defensive reactions to his anxiety over which he has little conscious control, and thus does not at all imply that he will do well in all problem solving areas. That is, in problem solving areas where his stable defensive reactions conflict with the type of behavior required for solution of the problem, they are expected to function as a liability rather than as an asset.

The results of the analysis of the cautiousness scores suggest that cautiousness was indeed the defensive reaction to anxiety which served as a mediating variable between anxiety and performance on the criterion task. It is relevant that the 6 Ss who were low on TA and highly cautious had significantly higher GA scores than the 18 Ss who were low on TA and less cautious. This seems to constitute further support for the hypothesized strong relationship between anxiety and cautiousness, since in view of their higher GA scores, it is more likely than not that the six low TA, highly cautious Ss may also be anxious about tests, although they did not admit it on the TA questionnaire. Sarason et al. (1958b) discussed the problem of differentiating among Ss who are really not anxious about tests and those who are test anxious, but who cannot or refuse to admit their anxiety. It is also relevant to the present discussion that in a Rorschach study (Sarason et al., 1958b), it was found that the HA asked more questions of the examiner and rejected more cards than did the LA. In other words, their response to the test situation was to become dependent or cautious. However, this kind of behavior was not rewarded in the Rorschach situation. S got no help from the examiner and no reward for cautious behavior in terms of success and failure. In the Embedded Figures situation used in the present study, on the other hand, cautious behavior was rewarding because the cautious S could ask to see the simple figure again without incurring the disapproval of the examiner (and stop the watch in so doing) and could easily tell when his behavior re-

sulted in success. Thus, with these particular instructions and this type of task, the cautious behavior of HA Ss facilitates their performance. In summary, the findings of the present study agree with certain past findings which support the generalization that the effect of anxiety on performance, whether facilitating or interfering, is mediated primarily by defensive reactions to the anxiety. It follows that two research problems of major importance are (a) the detection and detailed theoretical and experimental analysis of common defensive reactions to anxiety and (b) the detection and detailed theoretical and experimental analysis of the type of response requisite to success in a wide variety of task-instruction situations. Such research would improve our ability to predict the problem-solving behavior of children with different personality structures in various types of problem-solving situations.

The significant interaction between Anxiety and IQ yielded by the analysis of variance of the log-latency scores was not predicted in advance. The interaction resulted from the fact that the performance of the HA was superior to that of the LA at the low and middle levels of IQ and inferior at the high IQ level. One tentative explanation is that the LA Ss who were highly intelligent were able to perceive that this situation called for a specific type of approach and performed accordingly, whereas the less intelligent LA Ss were not this analytic. To the extent that this is valid, the low and medium IQ HA Ss, in contrast to their LA counterparts in intelligence, have an initial advantage in a situation in which cautious behavior is an asset because they characteristically tend to react with caution in *all* evaluative situations in order to defend against their anxiety.

It is well known that the behavior of two *S*s may appear to be the same in a specific situation although the behavior is a neurotic symptom in one case and not in the other. Just as close observation of such cases over time enables us to differentiate the neurotic behavior from that which is more flexible, it is possible that the type of cautiousness utilized by the LA highly intelligent group may be qualitatively different from that which characterizes the behavior of the HA group. That is, whereas cautiousness *as an anxiety reaction* may dominate all aspects of the response to the anxiety-arousing situation, regardless of appropriateness, the LA child may be able to limit this type of behavior to those situations which he can recognize as requiring this type of response; and, in contrast with HA *S*s at all levels of IQ, he may also be able to combine speed of response with his cautious approach. In any event, this particular aspect of the findings suggests that the differential effects of anxiety upon performance—as mediated by defensive reactions—may vary systematically depending upon both intelligence level and type of task and instructions.

The statistically significant Trials × Order interaction found in the analysis of variance of the log-latency scores is a reflection of the fact that both the HA and LA performed much better on whatever came last in sequence, regardless of order of task difficulty. This result is interpreted to mean that there was a large learning effect operating within trials, with both the HA and LA learning with about equal facility.

The fact that no Anxiety × Difficulty interaction was found in the present study is relevant in at least two respects. First, it is interpreted as supporting the hypothesis that with respect to the effect of anxiety upon performance, qualitative differences in type of task, task instructions, and stable defensive reactions to the anxiety are more important than quantitative differences in the level of difficulty of the tasks. Second, the absence of such an interaction—despite the fact that the analysis also showed clearly that the variation in task difficulty was extremely large—may be of theoretical significance in view of the fact that those who conceive of anxiety as a simple "motivational drive" rely upon the presence of an interaction between anxiety and task difficulty for support of their theory (Castaneda, Palermo, & McCandless, 1956).

Finally, in view of the success of the Yale Test Anxiety Scale for Children in differentiating between efficient and inefficient performers at several levels of intelligence and between high and low cautious *S*s, the results contribute to the validity of the scale for predicting the problem solving behavior of groups. However, it remains clear that the size of the group differences is not so great that one may confidently predict the behavior of individual *S*s.

SUMMARY

Two anxiety scales and an intelligence test were administered to 280 sixth-grade boys. Forty-eight *S*s, divided into 12 groups in a 2 (high and low anxious) × 3 (high, medium, and low IQ) × 2 (order of administration of easy and difficult items) design, were individually administered an embedded figures task. The task items ranged from extremely easy to extremely difficult. Three scores were derived from the criterion task for each S: a latency score, number of figures solved, and a cautiousness index. Three predictions were made: (a) Highly cautious Ss do better than low cautious Ss on the criterion task; (b) HA Ss obtain higher cautiousness scores than LA Ss; (c) The performance of HA Ss on the criterion task is superior to that of the LA Ss. The first two predictions were confirmed. The third prediction was confirmed for Ss at the low and medium IQ levels. The analysis of variance of the latency scores yielded a significant Anxiety $\times$ linear IQ interaction which resulted from the fact that the performance of the HA was superior to that of the LA at the low and middle levels of IQ and inferior at the high IQ level. The results of the analysis of the cautiousness scores were interpreted as supporting the thesis that the effect of anxiety on performance, whether facilitating or interfering, is mediated primarily by defensive reactions to the anxiety. It was also concluded that the differential effects of anxiety upon performance may vary systematically depending upon both intelligence level and type of task and instructions.

REFERENCES

Castaneda, A., Palermo, D. S., & Mc-Candless, B. R. Complex learning and performance as a function of anxiety in children and task difficulty. *Child Develpm.*, 1956, 27, 327–332.

Jackson, D. N. A short form of Witkin's embedded figures test. *J. abnorm. soc. Psychol.*, 1956, 53, 254–255.

Lighthall, F. F., Ruebush, B., Sarason, S. B., & Zweibelson, I. Change in mental ability as a function of test anxiety and type of mental test. *J. consult. Psychol.*, 1959, 23, 34–38.

Quenouille, M. H. *Introductory statistics.* London: Butterworth, 1950.

Rao, C. R. *Advanced statistical methods in biometric research.* New York: Wiley, 1952.

Sarason, S. B., Davidson, K. S., Lighthall, F. F., & Waite, R. R. A Test Anxiety Scale for children. *Child Develpm.*, 1958, 29, 105–113. (a)

Sarason, S. B., Davidson, K. S., Lighthall, F. F., & Waite, R. R. Rorschach behavior and performance of high and low anxious children. *Child Develpm.*, 1958, 29, 277–285. (b)

Sarnoff, I., Lighthall, F. F., Waite, R. R., Davidson, K. S., & Sarason, S. B. A cross-cultural study of anxiety among American and English school children. *J. educ. Psychol.*, 1958, 49, 129–136.

Snedecor, G. W. *Statistical methods.* Ames, Iowa: Iowa State Coll. Press, 1956.

Waite, R. R., Sarason, S. B., Lighthall, F. F., & Davidson, K. S. A study of anxiety and learning in children. *J. abnorm. soc. Psychol.*, 1958, 57, 267–270.

Walker, H. M., & Lev, J. *Statistical inference.* New York: Holt & Co., 1953.

Witkin, H. A. Individual differences in ease of perception of embedded figures. *J. Pers.*, 1950, 19, 1–15.

Witkin, H. A., Lewis, H. B., Hertzman, M., Machover, Karen, Meissner, P. B., & Wafner, S. *Personality through perception.* New York: Harper, 1954.

Zweibelson, I. Test anxiety and intelligence test performance. *J. consult. Psychol.*, 1956, 20, 479–481.

IMITATION OF FILM-MEDIATED

AGGRESSIVE MODELS [1]

ALBERT BANDURA
DOROTHEA ROSS [2]
SHEILA A. ROSS

MOST of the research on the possible effects of film-mediated stimulation upon subsequent aggressive behavior has focused primarily on the drive reducing function of fantasy. While the experimental evidence for the catharsis or drive reduction theory is equivocal (Albert, 1957; Berkowitz, 1962; Emery, 1959; Feshbach, 1955, 1958; Kenny, 1952; Lövaas, 1961; Siegel, 1956), the modeling influence of pictorial stimuli has received little research attention.

A recent incident (San Francisco Chronicle, 1961) in which a boy was seriously knifed during a reenactment of a switchblade knife fight the boys had seen the previous evening on a televised rerun of the James Dean movie, *Rebel Without a Cause*, is a dramatic illustration of the possible imitative influence of film stimulation. Indeed, anecdotal data

suggest that portrayal of aggression through pictorial media may be more influential in shaping the form aggression will take when a person is instigated on later occasions, than in altering the level of instigation to aggression.

In an earlier experiment (Bandura & Huston, 1961), it was shown that children readily imitated aggressive behavior exhibited by a model in the presence of the model. A succeeding investigation (Bandura, Ross, & Ross, 1961), demonstrated that children exposed to aggressive models generalized aggressive responses to a new setting in which the model was absent. The present study sought to determine the extent to which film-mediated aggressive models may serve as an important source of imitative behavior.

Aggressive models can be ordered on a reality-fictional stimulus dimension with real-life models located at the reality end of the continuum, nonhuman cartoon characters at the fictional end, and films portraying human models occupying an intermediate position. It was predicted, on the basis of saliency and similarity of cues, that the more remote the model was from reality, the weaker would be the tendency for subjects to imitate the behavior of the model.

Of the various interpretations of

[1] This investigation was supported in part by Research Grants M-4398 and M-5162 from the National Institute of Health, United States Public Health Service, and the Lewis S. Haas Child Development Research Fund, Stanford University.

The authors are indebted to David J. Hicks for his generous assistance with the photography and to John Steinbruner who assisted with various phases of this study.

[2] This research was carried out while the junior author was the recipient of an American Association of University Women International Fellowship for postdoctoral research.

Reprinted by permission from *Journal of Abnormal and Social Psychology*, 1963, 66, 3–11.

imitative learning, the sensory feedback theory of imitation recently proposed by Mowrer (1960) is elaborated in greatest detail. According to this theory, if certain responses have been repeatedly positively reinforced, proprioceptive stimuli associated with these responses acquire secondary reinforcing properties and thus the individual is predisposed to perform the behavior for the positive feedback. Similarly, if responses have been negatively reinforced, response correlated stimuli acquire the capacity to arouse anxiety which, in turn, inhibits the occurrence of the negatively valenced behavior. On the basis of these considerations, it was predicted subjects who manifest high aggression anxiety would perform significantly less imitative and nonimitative aggression than subjects who display little anxiety over aggression. Since aggression is generally considered female inappropriate behavior, and therefore likely to be negatively reinforced in girls (Sears, Maccoby, & Levin, 1957), it was also predicted that male subjects would be more imitative of aggression than females.

To the extent that observation of adults displaying aggression conveys a certain degree of permissiveness for aggressive behavior, it may be assumed that such exposure not only facilitates the learning of new aggressive responses but also weakens competing inhibitory responses in subjects and thereby increases the probability of occurrence of previously learned patterns of aggression. It was predicted, therefore, that subjects who observed aggressive models would display significantly more aggression when subsequently frustrated than subjects who were equally frustrated but who had no prior exposure to models exhibiting aggression.

METHOD

SUBJECTS

The subjects were 48 boys and 48 girls enrolled in the Stanford University Nursery School. They ranged in age from 35 to 69 months, with a mean age of 52 months. Two adults, a male and a female, served in the role of models both in the real-life and the human film-aggression condition, and one female experimenter conducted the study for all 96 children.

GENERAL PROCEDURE

Subjects were divided into three experimental groups and one control group of twenty-four subjects each. One group of experimental subjects observed real-life aggressive models, a second group observed these same models portraying aggression on film, while a third group viewed a film depicting an aggressive cartoon character. The experimental groups were further subdivided into male and female subjects so that half the subjects in the two conditions involving human models were exposed to same-sex models, while the remaining subjects viewed models of the opposite sex.

Following the exposure experience, subjects were tested for the amount of imitative and nonimitative aggression in a different experimental setting in the absence of the models.

The control group subjects had no exposure to the aggressive models and were tested only in the generalization situation.

Subjects in the experimental and control groups were matched individually on the basis of ratings of their aggressive behavior in social interactions in the nursery school. The experimenter and a nursery school teacher rated the subjects on four five-point rating scales which measured the extent to which subjects displayed physical aggression, verbal aggression, aggression toward inanimate objects, and aggression inhibition. The latter scale, which dealt with the subjects' tendency to inhibit aggressive reactions in the face of high instigation, provided the measure of aggression anxiety. Seventy-one percent of the subjects were rated independently by both judges so as to permit an assessment of interrater agreement. The reliability of the composite aggression score, estimated by means of the Pearson product-moment correlation, was .80.

Data for subjects in the real-life aggression condition and in the control group were collected as part of a previous experiment (Bandura et al., 1961). Since the procedure is described in detail in the earlier report, only a brief description of it will be presented here.

EXPERIMENTAL CONDITIONS

Subjects in the Real-Life Aggressive condition were brought individually by the experimenter to the experimental room and the model, who was in the hallway outside the room, was invited by the experimenter to come and join in the game. The subject was then escorted to one corner of the room and seated at a small table which contained potato prints, multicolor picture stickers, and colored paper. After demonstrating how the subject could design pictures with the materials provided, the experimenter escorted the model to the opposite corner of the room which contained a small table and chair, a tinker toy set, a mallet, and a 5-foot inflated Bobo doll. The experimenter explained that this was the model's play area and after the model was seated, the experimenter left the experimental room.

The model began the session by assembling the tinker toys but after approximately a minute had elapsed, the model turned to the Bobo doll and spent the remainder of the period aggressing toward it with highly novel responses which are unlikely to be performed by children independently of the observation of the model's behavior. Thus, in addition to punching the Bobo doll, the model exhibited the following distinctive aggressive acts which were to be scored as imitative responses:

The model sat on the Bobo doll and punched it repeatedly in the nose.

The model then raised the Bobo doll and pommeled it on the head with a mallet.

Following the mallet aggression, the model tossed the doll up in the air aggres-sively and kicked it about the room. This sequence of physically aggressive acts was repeated approximately three times, interspersed with verbally aggressive responses such as, "Sock him in the nose . . . ," "Hit him down . . . ," "Throw him in the air . . . ," "Kick him . . . ," and "Pow."

Subjects in the Human Film-Aggression condition were brought by the experimenter to the semi-darkened experimental room, introduced to the picture materials, and informed that while the subjects worked on potato prints, a movie would be shown on a screen, positioned approximately 6 feet from the subject's table. The movie projector was located in a distant corner of the room and was screened from the subject's view by large wooden panels.

The color movie and a tape recording of the sound track was begun by a male projectionist as soon as the experimenter left the experimental room and was shown for a duration of 10 minutes. The models in the film presentations were the same adult males and females who participated in the Real-Life condition of the experiment. Similarly, the aggressive behavior they portrayed in the film was identical with their real-life performances.

For subjects in the Cartoon Film-Aggression condition, after seating the subject at the table with the picture construction material, the experimenter walked over to a television console approximately three feet in front of the subject's table, remarked, "I guess I'll turn on the color TV," and ostensibly tuned in a cartoon program. The experimenter then left the experimental room. The cartoon was shown on a glass lens screen in the television set by means of a rear projection arrangement screened from the subject's view by large panels.

The sequence of aggressive acts in the cartoon was performed by the female model costumed as a black cat similar to the many cartoon cats. In order to heighten the level of irreality of the cartoon, the floor area was covered with artificial grass and the walls forming the backdrop were adorned with brightly colored trees, birds, and butterflies creating a fantasyland setting. The cartoon began with a close-up of a stage on which the curtains were slowly drawn revealing a picture of a cartoon cat along with the title, *Herman the Cat*. The remainder of the film showed the cat pommeling the Bobo doll on the head with a mallet, sitting on the doll and punching it in the nose, tossing the doll in the air, and kicking it about the room in a manner identical with the performance in the other experimental conditions except that the cat's movements were characteristically feline. To induce further a cartoon set, the program was introduced and concluded with appropriate cartoon music, and the cat's verbal aggression was repeated in a high-pitched, animated voice.

In both film conditions, at the conclusion of the movie the experimenter entered the room and then escorted the subject to the test room.

AGGRESSION INSTIGATION

In order to differentiate clearly the exposure and test situations subjects were tested for the amount of imitative learning in a different experimental room which was set off from the main nursery school building.

The degree to which a child has learned aggressive patterns of behavior through imitation becomes most evident when the child is instigated to aggression on later occasions. Thus, for example, the effects of viewing the movie, *Rebel Without a Cause*, were not evident until the boys were instigated to aggression the following day, at which time they re-enacted the televised switchblade knife fight in considerable detail. For this reason, the children in the experiment, both those in the control group, and those who were exposed to the aggressive models, were mildly frustrated before they were brought to the test room.

Following the exposure experience, the experimenter brought the subject to an anteroom which contained a varied array of highly attractive toys. The experimenter explained that the toys were for the subject to play with, but, as soon as the subject became sufficiently involved with the play material, the experimenter remarked that these were her very best toys, that she did not just let anyone play with them, and that she had decided to reserve these toys for

some other children. However, the subject could play with any of the toys in the next room. The experimenter and the subject then entered the adjoining experimental room.

It was necessary for the experimenter to remain in the room during the experimental session; otherwise, a number of the children would either refuse to remain alone or would leave before the termination of the session. In order to minimize any influence her presence might have on the subject's behavior, the experimenter remained as inconspicuous as possible by busying herself with paper work at a desk in the far corner of the room and avoiding any interaction with the child.

TEST FOR DELAYED IMITATION

The experimental room contained a variety of toys, some of which could be used in imitative or nonimitative aggression, and others which tended to elicit predominantly nonaggressive forms of behavior. The aggressive toys included a 3-foot Bobo doll, a mallet and peg board, two dart guns, and a tether ball with a face painted on it which hung from the ceiling. The nonaggresive toys, on the other hand, included a tea set, crayons and coloring paper, a ball, two dolls, three bears, cars and trucks, and plastic farm animals.

In order to eliminate any variation in behavior due to mere placement of the toys in the room, the play material was arranged in a fixed order for each of the sessions.

The subject spent 20 minutes in the experimental room during which time his behavior was rated in terms of predetermined response categories by judges who observed the session through a one-way mirror in an adjoining observation room. The 20-minute session was divided in 5-second intervals by means of an electric interval timer, thus yielding a total number of 240 response units for each subject.

The male model scored the experimental sessions for all subjects. In order to provide an estimate of interjudge agreement, the performances of 40% of the subjects were scored independently by a second observer. The responses scored involved highly specific concrete classes of behavior, and yielded high interscorer reliabilities, the product-moment coefficients being in the .90s.

RESPONSE MEASURES

The following response measures were obtained:

Imitative aggression. This category included acts of striking the Bobo doll with the mallet, sitting on the doll and punching it in the nose, kicking the doll, tossing it in the air, and the verbally aggressive responses, "Sock him," "Hit him down," "Kick him," "Throw him in the air," and "Pow."

Partially imitative responses. A number of subjects imitated the essential components of the model's behavior but did not perform the complete act, or they directed the imitative aggressive response to some object other than the Bobo doll. Two responses of this type were scored and were interpreted as partially imitative behavior:

Mallet aggression. The subject strikes objects other than the Bobo doll aggressively with the mallet.

Sits on Bobo doll. The subject lays the Bobo doll on its side and sits on it, but does not aggress toward it.

Nonimitative aggression. This category included acts of punching, slapping, or pushing the doll, physically aggressive acts directed toward objects other than the Bobo doll, and any hostile remarks except for those in the verbal imitation category; for example, "Shoot the Bobo," "Cut him," "Stupid ball," "Knock over people," "Horses fighting, biting."

Aggressive gun play. The subject shoots darts or aims the guns and fires imaginary shots at objects in the room.

Ratings were also made of the number of behavior units in which subjects played nonaggressively or sat quietly and did not play with any of the material at all.

RESULTS

The mean imitative and nonimitative aggression scores for subjects in the various experimental and control groups are presented in Table 1.

TABLE 1 · MEAN AGGRESSION SCORES FOR SUBGROUPS OF EXPERIMENTAL AND CONTROL SUBJECTS

Response category	EXPERIMENTAL GROUPS					Control group
	Real-life aggressive		Human film-aggressive		Cartoon film-aggressive	
	F Model	M Model	F Model	M Model		
Total aggression						
Girls	65.8	57.3	87.0	79.5	80.9	36.4
Boys	76.8	131.8	114.5	85.0	117.2	72.2
Imitative aggression						
Girls	19.2	9.2	10.0	8.0	7.8	1.8
Boys	18.4	38.4	34.3	13.3	16.2	3.9
Mallet aggression						
Girls	17.2	18.7	49.2	19.5	36.8	13.1
Boys	15.5	28.8	20.5	16.3	12.5	13.5
Sits on Bobo doll [a]						
Girls	10.4	5.6	10.3	4.5	15.3	3.3
Boys	1.3	0.7	7.7	0.0	5.6	0.6
Nonimitative aggression						
Girls	27.6	24.9	24.0	34.3	27.5	17.8
Boys	35.5	48.6	46.8	31.8	71.8	40.4
Aggressive gun play						
Girls	1.8	4.5	3.8	17.6	8.8	3.7
Boys	7.3	15.9	12.8	23.7	16.6	14.3

a This response category was not included in the total aggression score.

Since the distributions of scores departed from normality and the assumption of homogeneity of variance could not be made for most of the measures, the Freidman two-way analysis of variance by ranks was employed for testing the significance of the obtained differences.

TOTAL AGGRESSION

The mean total aggression scores for subjects in the real-life, human film, cartoon film, and the control groups are 83, 92, 99, and 54, respectively. The results of the analysis of variance performed on these scores reveal that the main effect of treatment conditions is significant ($\chi_r^2 = 9.06, p < .05$), confirming the prediction that exposure of subjects to aggressive models increases the probability that subjects will respond aggressively when instigated on later occasions. Further analyses of pairs of scores by means of the Wilcoxon matched-pairs signed-ranks test show that subjects who viewed the real-life models and the film-mediated

models do not differ from each other in total aggressiveness but all three experimental groups expressed significantly more aggressive behavior than the control subjects (Table 2).

IMITATIVE AGGRESSIVE RESPONSES

The Freidman analysis reveals that exposure of subjects to aggressive models is also a highly effective method for shaping subjects' aggressive responses ($\chi_r^2 = 23.88, p < .001$). Comparisons of treatment conditions by the Wilcoxon test reveal that subjects who observed the real-life models and the film-mediated models, relative to subjects in the control group, performed considerably more imitative physical and verbal aggression (Table 2).

Illustrations of the extent to which some of the subjects became virtually "carbon copies" of their models in aggressive behavior are presented in Figure 1. The top frame shows the female model performing the four novel aggressive responses; the lower frames depict a male

TABLE 2 · Significance of the Differences between Experimental and Control Groups in the Expression of Aggression

Response category	χ_r^2	p	COMPARISON OF TREATMENT CONDITIONS [a]					
			Live vs. film p	Live vs. cartoon p	Film vs. cartoon p	Live vs. control p	Film vs. control p	Cartoon vs. control p
Total agression	9.06	<.05	ns	ns	ns	<.01	<.01	<.005
Imitative aggression	23.88	<.001	ns	<.05	ns	<.001	<.001	<.005
Partial imitation								
Mallet aggression	7.36	.10>p>.05						
Sits on Bobo doll	8.05	<.05	ns	ns	ns	ns	<.05	<.005
Nonimitative aggression	7.28	.10>p>.05						
Aggressive gun play	8.06	<.05	<.01[b]	ns	ns	ns	<.05	ns

a The probability values are based on the Wilcoxon test.
b This probability value is based on a two-tailed test of significance.

and a female subject reproducing the behavior of the female model they had observed earlier on film.

The prediction that imitation is positively related to the reality cues of the model was only partially supported. While subjects who observed the real-life aggressive models exhibited significantly more imitative aggression than subjects who viewed the cartoon model, no significant differences were found between the live and film, and the film and cartoon conditions, nor did the three experimental groups differ significantly in total aggression or in the performances of partially imitative behavior (Table 2). Indeed, the available data suggest that, of the three experimental conditions, exposure to humans on film portraying aggression was the most influential in eliciting and shaping aggressive behavior. Subjects in this condition, in relation to the control subjects, exhibited more total aggression, more imitative aggression, more partially imitative behavior, such as sitting on the Bobo doll and mallet aggression, and they engaged in significantly more aggressive gun play. In addition, they performed significantly more aggressive gun play than did subjects who were exposed to the real-life aggressive models (Table 2).

INFLUENCE OF SEX OF MODEL
AND SEX OF CHILD

In order to determine the influence of sex of model and sex of child on the expression of imitative and nonimitative aggression, the data from the experimental groups were combined and the significance of the differences between groups was assessed by t tests for uncorrelated means. In statistical comparisons involving relatively skewed distributions of scores the Mann-Whitney U test was employed.

Sex of subjects had a highly significant effect on both the learning and the performance of aggression. Boys, in relation to girls, exhibited significantly more total aggression ($t = 2.69$, $p < .01$), more imitative agression ($t = 2.82$, $p < .005$), more aggressive gun play ($z = 3.38$, $p < .001$), and more nonimitative aggressive behavior ($t = 2.98$, $p < .005$). Girls, on the other hand, were more inclined than boys to sit on the Bobo doll but refrained from punching it ($z = 3.47$, $p < .001$).

The analyses also disclosed some influences of the sex of the model. Subjects exposed to the male model, as compared to the female model, expressed significantly more aggressive gun play ($z = 2.83$, $p < .005$). The most marked differences in aggressive gun play ($U = 9.5$, $p < .001$), however, were found between girls exposed to the female model ($M = 2.9$) and males who observed the male model ($M = 19.8$). Although the overall model difference in partially imitative behavior, Sits on Bobo, was not significant, Sex $\times$ Model subgroup comparisons yielded some interesting results. Boys who observed the aggressive female model, for example, were more likely to sit on the Bobo doll without punching it than boys who viewed the male model ($U = 33$, $p < .05$). Girls reproduced the nonaggressive component of the male model's aggressive pattern of behavior (i.e., sat on the doll without punching it) with considerably higher frequency than did boys who observed the same model ($U = 21.5$, $p < .02$). The highest incidence of partially imitative responses was yielded by the group of girls who viewed

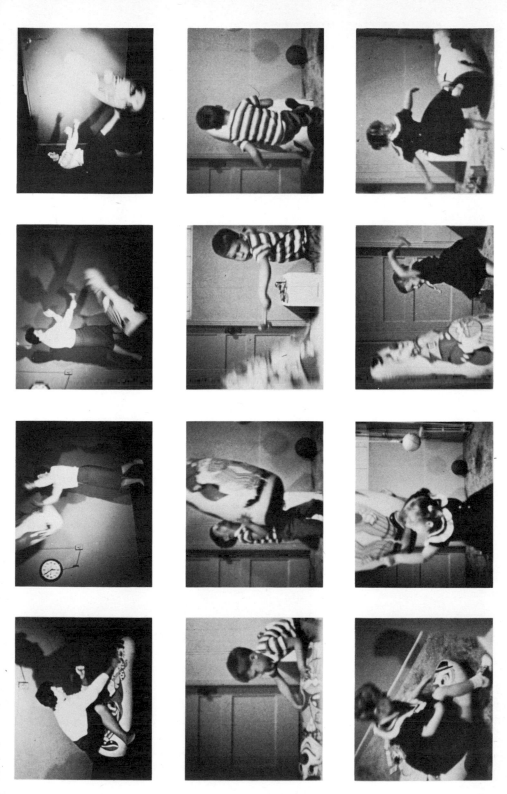

Figure 1. Photographs from the film, *Social learning of aggression through imitation of aggressive models.*

the aggressive female model ($M = 10.4$), and the lowest values by the boys who were exposed to the male model ($M = 0.3$). This difference was significant beyond the .05 significance level. These findings, along with the sex of child and sex of model differences reported in the preceding sections, provide further support for the view that the influence of models in promoting social learning is determined, in part, by the sex appropriateness of the model's behavior (Bandura et al., 1961).

AGGRESSIVE PREDISPOSITION AND IMITATION

Since the correlations between ratings of aggression and the measures of imitative and total aggressive behavior, calculated separately for boys and girls in each of the experimental conditions, did not differ significantly, the data were combined. The correlational analyses performed on these pooled data failed to yield any significant relationships between ratings of aggression anxiety, frequency of aggressive behavior, and the experimental aggression measures. In fact, the array means suggested nonlinear regressions although the departures from linearity were not of sufficient magnitude to be statistically significant.

DISCUSSION

The results of the present study provide strong evidence that exposure to filmed aggression heightens aggressive reactions in children. Subjects who viewed the aggressive human and cartoon models on film exhibited nearly twice as much aggression than did subjects in the control group who were not exposed to the aggressive film content.

In the experimental design typically employed for testing the possible cathartic function of vicarious aggression, subjects are first frustrated, then provided with an opportunity to view an aggressive film following which their overt or fantasy aggression is measured. While this procedure yields some information on the immediate influence of film-mediated aggression, the full effects of such exposure may not be revealed until subjects are instigated to aggression on a later occasion. Thus, the present study, and one recently reported by Lövaas (1961), both utilizing a design in which subjects first observed filmed aggression and then were frustrated, clearly reveal that observation of models portraying aggression on film substantially increases rather than decreases the probability of aggressive reactions to subsequent frustrations.

Filmed aggression, not only facilitated the expression of aggression, but also effectively shaped the form of the subjects' aggressive behavior. The finding that children modeled their behavior to some extent after the film characters suggests that pictorial mass media, particularly television, may serve as an important source of social behavior. In fact, a possible generalization of responses originally learned in the television situation to the experimental film may account for the significantly greater amount of aggressive gun play displayed by subjects in the film condition as compared to subjects in the real-life and control groups. It is unfortunate that the qualitative features of the gun behavior were not scored since subjects in the film condition, unlike those in the other two groups, developed interesting elaborations in gun play (for example, stalking the imaginary opponent, quick drawing, and rapid firing), characteristic of the Western gun fighter.

The view that the social learning of aggression through exposure to aggressive film content is confined to deviant children (Schramm, Lyle, & Parker, 1961), finds little support in our data. The children who participated in the experiment are by no means a deviant sample, nevertheless, 88% of the subjects in the Real-Life and in the Human Film condition, and 79% of the subjects in the Cartoon Film condition, exhibited varying degrees of imitative aggression. In assessing the possible influence of televised stimulation on viewers' behavior, however, it is important to distinguish between learning and overt performance. Although the results of the present experiment demonstrate that the vast majority of children *learn* patterns of social behavior through pictorial stimulation, nevertheless, informal observation suggests that children do not, as a rule, *perform* indiscriminately the behavior of televised characters, even those they regard as highly attractive models. The replies of parents whose children participated in the present study to an open-end questionnaire item concerning their handling of imitative behavior suggest that this may be in part a function of negative reinforcement, as most parents were quick to discourage their children's overt imitation of television characters by prohibiting certain programs or by labeling the imitative behavior in a disapproving manner. From our knowledge of the effects of punishment on behavior, the responses in question would be expected to retain their original strength and could reappear on later occasions in the presence of appropriate eliciting stimuli, particularly if instigation is high, the instruments for

aggression are available, and the threat of noxious consequences is reduced.

The absence of any relationships between ratings of the children's predisposition to aggression and their aggressive behavior in the experimental setting may simply reflect the inadequacy of the predictor measures. It may be pointed out, however, that the reliability of the ratings was relatively high. While this does not assure validity of the measures, it does at least indicate there was consistency in the raters' estimates of the children's aggressive tendencies.

A second, and perhaps more probable, explanation is that proprioceptive feedback alone is not sufficient to account for response inhibition or facilitation. For example, the proprioceptive cues arising from hitting responses directed toward parents and toward peers may differ little, if any; nevertheless, tendencies to aggress toward parents are apt to be strongly inhibited while peer aggression may be readily expressed (Bandura, 1960; Bandura & Walters, 1959). In most social interaction sequences, proprioceptive cues make up only a small part of the total stimulus complex and, therefore, it is necessary to take into consideration additional stimulus components, for the most part external, which probably serve as important discriminative cues for the expression of aggression. Consequently, prediction of the occurrence or inhibition of specific classes of responses would be expected to depend upon the presence of a certain pattern of proprioceptive or introceptive stimulation together with relevant discriminative external stimuli.

According to this line of reasoning, failure to obtain the expected positive relationships between the measures of aggression may be due primarily to the fact that permissiveness for aggression, conveyed by situational cues in the form of aggressive film content and play material, was sufficient to override the influence of internal stimuli generated by the commission of aggressive responses. If, in fact, the behavior of young children, as compared to that of adults, is less likely to be under internal stimulus control, one might expect environmental cues to play a relatively important role in eliciting or inhibiting aggressive behavior.

A question may be raised as to whether the aggressive acts studied in the present experiment constitute "genuine" aggressive responses. Aggression is typically defined as behavior, the goal or intent of which is injury to a person, or destruction of an object (Bandura & Walters, 1959; Dollard, Doob, Miller, Mowrer, & Sears, 1939; Sears, Maccoby, & Levin, 1957). Since intentionality is not a property of behavior but primarily an inference concerning antecedent events, the categorization of an act as "aggressive" involves a consideration of both stimulus and mediating or terminal response events.

According to a social learning theory of aggression recently proposed by Bandura and Walters (in press), most of the responses utilized to hurt or to injure others (for example, striking, kicking, and other responses of high magnitude), are probably learned for prosocial purposes under nonfrustration conditions. Since frustration generally elicits responses of high magnitude, the latter classes of responses, once acquired, may be called out in social interactions for the purpose of injuring others. On the basis of this theory it would be predicted that the aggressive responses acquired imita-tively, while not necessarily mediating aggressive goals in the experimental situation, would be utilized to serve such purposes in other social settings with higher frequency by children in the experimental conditions than by children in the control group.

The present study involved primarily vicarious or empathic learning (Mowrer, 1960) in that subjects acquired a relatively complex repertoire of aggressive responses by the mere sight of a model's behavior. It has been generally assumed that the necessary conditions for the occurrence of such learning is that the model perform certain responses followed by positive reinforcement to the model (Hill, 1960; Mowrer, 1960). According to this theory, to the extent that the observer experiences the model's reinforcement vicariously, the observer will be prone to reproduce the model's behavior. While there is some evidence from experiments involving both human (Lewis & Duncan, 1958; McBrearty, Marston, & Kanfer, 1961; Sechrest, 1961) and animal subjects (Darby & Riopelle, 1959; Warden, Fjeld, & Koch, 1940), that vicarious reinforcement may in fact increase the probability of the behavior in question, it is apparent from the results of the experiment reported in this paper that a good deal of human imitative learning can occur without any reinforcers delivered either to the model or to the observer. In order to test systematically the influence of vicarious reinforcement on imitation, however, a study is planned in which the degree of imitative learning will be compared in situations in which the model's behavior is paired with reinforcement with those in which the model's responses go unrewarded.

SUMMARY

The present investigation was designed to test the hypothesis that exposure of children to film-mediated aggressive models would increase the probability of subjects' aggression to subsequent frustration and would shape their aggressive responses through imitative learning.

One group of experimental subjects observed real-life aggressive models, a second observed these same models portraying aggression on film, while a third group viewed a film depicting an aggressive cartoon character. Following the exposure treatment, subjects were mildly frustrated and tested for the amount of imitative and nonimitative aggression in a different experimental setting. A control group of subjects who had no prior exposure to the models was also studied.

The overall results provide evidence for both the disinhibitory and the modeling influence of film-mediated aggressive stimulation. Subjects who observed the aggressive human and cartoon models on film patterned their aggressive behavior to some extent after the models, and performed approximately twice as much aggression relative to the subjects in the control group. Subjects were less likely, however, to imitate the aggressive responses exhibited by the cartoon model than those performed by actual persons in the children's presence. In addition, the findings reveal that boys in relation to girls emit significantly more imitative and nonimitative aggression as a function of exposure to aggressive models, and that the male model was more influential in eliciting some forms of aggressive behavior than was true for the female model. Contrary to prediction, the data failed to yield any relationship between children's predisposition to aggression and their imitative learning of aggressive behavior.

REFERENCES

ALBERT, R. S.   The role of mass media and the effect of aggressive film content upon children's aggressive responses and identification choices. *Genet. psychol. Monogr.*, 1957, *55*, 221–285.

BANDURA, A.   Relationship of family patterns to child behavior disorders. Progress Report, 1960, Stanford University, Project No. M-1734, United States Public Health Service.

BANDURA, A., & HUSTON, ALETHA C. Identification as a process of incidental learning. *J. abnorm. soc. Psychol.*, 1961, *63*, 311–318.

BANDURA, A., ROSS, DOROTHEA, & ROSS, SHEILA A.   Transmission of aggression through imitation of aggressive models. *J. abnorm. soc. Psychol.*, 1961, *63*, 575–582.

BANDURA, A., & WALTERS, R. H.   *Adolescent aggression.* New York: Ronald, 1959.

BANDURA, A., & WALTERS, R. H.   *The social learning of deviant behavior: a behavioristic approach to socialization.* New York: Holt, Rinehart, & Winston, in press.

BERKOWITZ, L.   *Aggression: A social psychological analysis.* New York: McGraw-Hill, 1962.

DARBY, C. L., & RIOPELLE, A. J.   Observational learning in the Rhesus monkey. *J. comp. psysiol. Psychol.*, 1959, *52*, 94–98.

DOLLARD, J., DOOB, L. W., MILLER, N. E., MOWRER, O. H., & SEARS, R. R.   *Frustration and aggression.* New Haven: Yale Univer. Press, 1939.

EMERY, F. E. Psychological effects of the Western film: A study in television viewing: II. The experimental study. *Hum. Relat.*, 1959, *12*, 215–232.

FESHBACH, S. The drive-reducing function of fantasy behavior. *J. abnorm. soc. Psychol.*, 1955, *50*, 3–11.

FESHBACH, S. The stimulating versus cathartic effects of a vicarious aggressive activity. Paper read at the Eastern Psychological Association, 1958.

HILL, W. F. Learning theory and the acquisition of values. *Psychol. Rev.*, 1960, *67*, 317–331.

KENNY, D. T. An experimental test of the catharsis theory of aggression. Unpublished doctoral dissertation, University of Washington, 1952.

LEWIS, D. J., & DUNCAN, C. P. Vicarious experience and partial reinforcement. *J. abnorm. soc. Psychol.*, 1958, *57*, 321–326.

LÖVAAS, O. J. Effect of exposure to symbolic aggression on aggressive behavior. *Child Develpm.*, 1961, *32*, 37–44.

McBREARTY, J. F., MARSTON, A. R., & KANFER, F. H. Conditioning a verbal operant in a group setting: Direct vs. vicarious reinforcement. *Amer. Psychologist*, 1961, *16*, 425. (Abstract)

MOWRER, O. H. *Learning theory and the symbolic processes.* New York: Wiley, 1960.

SAN FRANCISCO CHRONICLE. "James Dean" knifing in South City. *San Francisco Chron.*, March 1, 1961, 6.

SCHRAMM, W., LYLE, J., & PARKER, E. B. *Television in the lives of our children.* Stanford: Stanford Univer. Press, 1961.

SEARS, R. R., MACCOBY, ELEANOR E., & LEVIN, H. *Patterns of child rearing.* Evanston: Row, Peterson, 1957.

SECHREST, L. Vicarious reinforcement of responses. *Amer. Psychologist*, 1961, *16*, 356. (Abstract)

SIEGEL, ALBERTA E. Film mediated fantasy aggression and strength of aggressive drive. *Child Develpm.*, 1956, *27*, 365–378.

WARDEN, C. J., FJELD, H. A., & KOCH, A. M. Imitative behavior in cebus and Rhesus monkeys. *J. genet. Psychol.*, 1940, *56*, 311–322.

Learning, Performance, and Retention Under Stress in Emotionally Disturbed and Normal Children [1]

ANTHONY DAVIDS
GERALDINE R. OLIVER

EXPERIMENTAL FINDINGS in regard to the influence of anxiety on learning have been far from unequivocal. In general, it has been found that in simple learning situations anxiety has a facilitative effect as evidenced by more rapid learning by Ss who are high on anxiety (Taylor, 1956). However, when the experiment involves a complex learning situation, high-anxiety Ss have been found to learn less well than do low-anxiety Ss (Taylor, 1956). In most of the recent studies that are relevant to this problem, anxiety has been defined in terms of responses to an objective questionnaire (Taylor, 1953), and in most cases the Ss have been psychologically normal.

Related to this problem is the issue of performance under conditions of stress. Here again, the literature contains contradictory findings. A major source of difficulty in this regard is the inconsistent definition of "stress" in the various independent studies (Lazarus, Deese, & Osler, 1952). In some instances stress is defined in terms of the Ss employed, in others in terms of the nature of the stimuli utilized, in some it is induced by physically painful experiences such as electric shock, and in others it is believed to result from verbal manipulations on the part of the E such as informing the Ss that they have failed. Moreover, to date, the majority of experimental investigations of anxiety, stress, and performance have been conducted with adult Ss.

The present study, which was aimed at obtaining further understanding of these perplexing psychological phenomena, utilized children as Ss. The influence of anxiety was investigated by comparing the performances of emotionally disturbed children, who were known to be high on anxiety, and normal children from the public school system. The psychological stress to be employed was of two kinds. One was in the form of "emotionally loaded" stimuli, and the other was obtained through failure stress induced by E's comments. Performance was assessed in experimental situations involving the learning and retention of both verbal material and motor behavior.

METHOD

SUBJECTS

Two groups of Ss were employed in this study. One group consisted of 30 boys from the public school system, ranging in age

[1] We wish to express our appreciation to the administration and staff of the Bradley Hospital, in Riverside, Rhode Island, for facilitating the study of the emotionally disturbed children. Also, we wish to acknowledge our gratitude to Mr. Edward L. Martin, superintendent of public schools in East Providence, Rhode Island, and Mrs. Louise Favorite, school psychologist, for their cooperation in providing normal children for this study.

Reprinted by permission from *Journal of Personality*, 1960, *28*, 368–381.

from 9 to 12 years, with a mean age of 10 years, 8 months. The second group consisted of 26 boys who were undergoing residential psychiatric treatment for emotional disturbances. The majority of these patients were diagnosed psychiatrically as passive-aggressive personalities, aggressive type. There were no schizophrenic children in this group. Rather, they represented a homogeneous sample of impulsive, hyperaggressive, "acting out" children. Morever, most of these children had experienced considerable difficulty in coping with the demands of school work, and, in this regard, could be categorized as children with "learning difficulties." The patients in this disturbed group ranged in age from 9 to 12 years, with a mean age of 10 years, 7 months. The mean IQ in the normal group was 100, and the mean IQ in the disturbed group was 96. Thus, the groups were well matched for both age and IQ. However, it seems warranted to conclude that the emotionally disturbed boys were considerably higher on anxiety and aggressive psychopathology.

TEST MATERIALS AND APPARATUS

Verbal learning. Learning of verbal material was studied by means of the paired-associates method. Six flash cards were employed, each containing a printed word on one side and a number on the reverse side. The words were all verbs, selected from the Thorndike-Lorge (1944) word list, and from the AA category—100 or more occurrences per million words. The following three words were judged to be "aggressive" in connotation: kill, fight, hurt. The following three words were judged to be "neutral": rise, hear, begin. A sample card was used to acquaint S with the experimental task.

Motor learning. The apparatus used was an 18″ by 15″ board, upon which was mounted an 11 choice-point finger maze. A manually operated stopwatch was used to record time per trial. A smaller sample maze, similar to the test maze and containing 2 choice points, was used to acquaint S with the nature of this procedure. A blindfold was used to prevent the use of visual cues.

PROCEDURE

Verbal learning and retention. The first day, each S was seen individually and assured that the tests he was going to take would not go on his record—either school record for the normal Ss or hospital record for the disturbed Ss. S was then given the following instructions. "First, I want to see how many words you can learn. Each of these cards is like this one. It has a word on one side and a number on the other side. I want you to learn which words go with which numbers. The first time through I will just show you the number (E shows number and repeats it) and then show you the word on the other side (E shows word and repeats it). After that, I will just show you the number and see if you can remember the word that goes with it." Each time through the series, the number and words were repeated by E in order to cancel out any reading differences that may have existed among the Ss. The cards were shuffled after each trial and presented in random order, and there was no time limit on the length of time the numbers were exposed. S was encouraged to guess on those pairs he did not know. The pairs were preselected so that they would not be learned by the end of 10 trials, but some Ss succeeded in attaining a criterion of two consecutive trials without error. Number and content of errors were recorded. Twenty-four hours later, S was retested on the same paired-associates task, with errors and content again being recorded.

Motor learning and retention. The second day, upon completion of the verbal relearning procedure, S was shown the sample maze and was given the following instructions.

We are going to play a little game. This is called a finger maze. The object of this game is to get from this end of the maze [E points to starting point] to the other end without going off the path. Each time you come to one of these 'choice points' you can turn either right or left. If you turn this way [E demonstrates], you go off the maze and that's wrong. If you make the correct turn you get closer to the end of the path. If you do make a mistake, do not go back to the beginning, but just retrace your path to the choice point and go the other way. After I put this blindfold on you, we will try this little one that you have seen, and then go on to this bigger one that you haven't seen.

It should be noted that E attempted to get S interested in the task under as neutral conditions as possible. No mention was made of the fact that the trials would be timed, but no attempt was made to conceal the stopwatch. Pilot research indicated that 10 trials were sufficient to measure individual differences in learning, but did not permit perfect mastery of the task. Number of errors and time per trial were recorded as indices of motor learning.

Although all Ss commenced the motor learning task under conditions designed to be neutral, in the course of the experimental procedure half of the Ss in the normal group and half the Ss in the disturbed group were administered 'failure stress'. For these stressed Ss, after the third, sixth, and ninth trials E made the statement "That wasn't very good that time," or "That wasn't a good trial either." On the neutral trials, Ss received no verbal report from E. At the completion of 10 trials, the board was turned face down, S's blindfold was removed, and he was told that the testing was completed. However, 24 hours later, S was returned for a relearning task employing the same maze. Again, errors and time per trial were recorded for the 10 trials, all of which were under neutral conditions.

PREDICTIONS

On the basis of previous experimental findings and clinical experience, the following predictions were formulated. Since the disturbed boys are higher on anxiety, in comparison with the normal boys, they will perform more poorly on the complex verbal-learning task and will perform better on the motor-learning task. Also, since the disturbed boys are more susceptible to the disrupting effects of stress, in comparison with the normal boys, they will experience greater difficulty in learning and retention under conditions of stress.

RESULTS

VERBAL LEARNING

The measure of verbal learning used in this study was the number of errors on neutral and on aggressive words. As shown in Table 1, the two groups did not differ significantly on mean number of errors on the neutral words, but the disturbed group did make significantly more errors than the normal group on the aggressive words. When the means for the two kinds of words were compared within each of the groups of Ss, it was found that the difference within the disturbed group was not significant ($t = 1.54$), but within the normal group the mean number of errors on the aggressive words was significantly lower than the mean errors on the neutral words ($t = 2.43, p = .05$).

In addition to differences in the number of errors made, a marked qualitative difference was noted in the type of errors that were made in the two groups. It was found that whereas the normal Ss made errors of confusing word-number pairs in the series, the disturbed Ss often substituted irrelevant and seemingly unrelated words for those they missed. The total number of unrelated words intruded was 6 in the normal group and 76 in the disturbed group, a difference that is significant beyond the .05 level.

In an attempt to obtain further understanding of the dynamics that were operating in this verbal-learning situation, the data were analyzed for errors that could be classified as "aggressive"— either those words that were actually in the test series or unrelated aggressive words. The mean percentage of aggressive words evidenced in the error scores was 62 in the normal group and 52 in the disturbed group. This difference in proportions is significant beyond the .05 level. Thus, these findings indicate that not only did the disturbed Ss learn the aggressive words less well than did the normal Ss, but they were less able (probably due to some mechanism such as repression, inhibition, or denial) to use aggressively toned words in their attempts to master this verbal-learning task.

TABLE 1 · COMPARISON OF ERRORS IN VERBAL LEARNING

Variable	NORMAL GROUP		DISTURBED GROUP		F	t
	Mean errors	Vari-ance	Mean errors	Vari-ance		
Aggressive words	8.00	19.26	10.85	30.42	1.58	2.08*
Neutral words	11.42	40.71	13.58	47.15	1.16	1.20

* Significant beyond the .05 level.

VERBAL RELEARNING AND RETENTION

As shown in Table 2, the two groups did not differ significantly on the mean number of errors in relearning the neutral words, but the mean number of errors in relearning the aggressive words was significantly lower in the normal group than in the disturbed group. In comparing the within-group means for the two kinds of words, it was found that within the disturbed group the mean error score on the aggressive words was very slightly, and nonsignificantly ($t = .15$), higher than the mean error score on the neutral words. Within the normal group, the difference was also nonsignificant, but there was a tendency ($t = 1.23$, $p = .22$) in the direction indicating more errors on the neutral words than on the aggressive words.

MOTOR LEARNING

The two measures of learning the finger maze were (a) average time per trial, and (b) average errors for the 10 trials. In Tables 3 and 4, the scores have been presented separately for motor learning under neutral conditions and under conditions of failure stress. The results presented in these tables show that under both experimental conditions, the disturbed group performed significantly faster and made significantly fewer errors than did the normal group. Analyses of learning curves showed a steady decrease in both times and errors throughout the 10 trials for both groups of Ss, and on every trial the scores indicated faster performance and fewer errors in the disturbed group. Moreover, this trial by trial analysis revealed no noticeable effect of the mild failure stress on either time or error scores.

TABLE 2 · COMPARISON OF ERRORS IN VERBAL RELEARNING

Variable	NORMAL GROUP		DISTURBED GROUP		F	t
	Mean errors	Vari-ance	Mean errors	Vari-ance		
Aggressive words	1.58	9.10	3.62	12.08	1.33	2.32*
Neutral words	2.87	23.97	3.46	16.15	1.48	.49

* Significant beyond the .05 level.

MOTOR RELEARNING AND RETENTION

Relearning of the finger maze took place under neutral experimental conditions for all Ss. In considering the time and error scores, however, account was taken of whether the original learning had been under entirely neutral conditions or under conditions in which the Ss received failure stress. The findings in regard to speed in relearning, presented in Table 5, show faster performance in the disturbed group than in the normal group. However, whereas the disturbed Ss who originally learned under conditions of failure stress did not perform significantly faster than their normal controls who had also originally learned under conditions of failure stress, the disturbed Ss who were not subjected to failure stress in original learning did perform significantly faster than the normal Ss in the relearning situation. Within-group comparisons showed absolutely no difference in speed of relearning within the normal group between the subgroups that had originally learned under neutral or failure conditions. However, within the disturbed group, speed of performance in relearning was significantly faster ($t = 2.19$, $p = .05$) in the subgroup that had not been experimentally stressed in the original learning session.

TABLE 3 · COMPARISON OF TIME PER TRIAL (IN SECONDS) IN MOTOR LEARNING

	NORMAL GROUP		DISTURBED GROUP			
Condition	Mean time	Variance	Mean time	Variance	F	t
Failure	59.72	372.03	38.60	147.13	2.53	3.26**
Neutral	59.59	625.07	32.28	144.45	4.34**	3.78**

** Significant beyond the .01 level.

TABLE 4 · COMPARISON OF ERRORS IN MOTOR LEARNING

	NORMAL GROUP		DISTURBED GROUP			
Condition	Mean errors	Variance	Mean errors	Variance	F	t
Failure	42.07	62.93	27.58	91.08	1.45	2.95**
Neutral	36.86	144.57	25.75	48.50	2.98*	2.82**

* Significant beyond the .05 level.
** Significant beyond the .01 level.

TABLE 5 · COMPARISON OF TIME PER TRIAL (IN SECONDS) IN MOTOR RELEARNING

Condition of original learning	NORMAL GROUP		DISTURBED GROUP			
	Mean time	Variance	Mean time	Variance	F	t
Failure	31.51	103.14	25.63	47.28	2.18	1.68
Neutral	31.63	105.38	19.38	42.55	2.48	3.54**

** Significant beyond the .01 level.

Analyses of the error scores, presented in Table 6, show exactly the same results. The disturbed Ss made fewer errors in relearning the finger maze, but whereas the disturbed Ss who originally learned under failure conditions did not make significantly fewer errors than their normal control Ss, the difference in relearning errors between disturbed Ss and normal Ss who had originally learned under neutral conditions was highly significant. Within groups comparisons show no significant differences in relearning errors within the normal group as a function of the original learning conditions, but within the disturbed group the mean relearning errors was significantly lower ($t = 2.42$, $p = .05$) in the subgroup that had not been administered failure stress in original learning of this motor task.

In order to obtain measures of relative retention, for both time and error scores, each S's times and errors on the relearning trials were compared with

TABLE 6 · COMPARISON OF ERRORS IN MOTOR RELEARNING

Condition of original learning	NORMAL GROUP		DISTURBED GROUP			
	Mean errors	Variance	Mean errors	Variance	F	t
Failure	26.86	108.00	21.17	72.92	1.48	1.60
Neutral	25.07	36.64	14.50	71.75	1.96	2.67**

** Significant beyond the .01 level.

his performance in the original learning situation, and mean improvement scores were obtained for the four subgroups. The greatest improvement (decrease in both time and errors) was found in the group of normal Ss who had originally learned under conditions of mild failure stress and the smallest improvement, which was significantly less ($p = .01$ for time and .05 for errors) than that evidenced by normal Ss, was found in the group of disturbed Ss who had been administered mild failure stress in original learning. Thus it appears that the disturbed Ss relearned the motor task faster and more efficiently than did the normal Ss, but that whereas mild failure stress in original learning led to considerable improvement in the normal Ss' retention, as evidenced by improved relearning performance, the original failure stress had a relatively detrimental influence on retention in the disturbed Ss.

DISCUSSION

In the verbal-learning experiment, it was found that the disturbed Ss made significantly more errors than the normal Ss on the aggressive words, but there was no significant difference between the two groups in learning the neutral words. This finding is consistent with the prediction that high-anxiety Ss would perform less well in a complex verbal-learning situation involving emotionally loaded stimuli which should place them under conditions of psychological stress. This sort of impaired performance of high-anxiety Ss under conditions of stress has been reported by several previous investigators (Child, 1954; Lucas, 1952; Saltz & Hoehn, 1957; Taylor, 1956). Taylor (1956) has suggested that under condi-

tions of psychological stress, internal responses of the type that Child (1954) has referred to as "task-irrelevant" are more easily or more intensely aroused in Ss who are high on anxiety. According to Taylor (1956 & 1958), in experimental situations in which extra-task responses interfere with efficient performance (e.g., verbal learning), high-anxiety Ss under stress conditions should show inferior performance to normal control Ss. The finding in the present experiment, of significantly more irrelevant insertions in the responses of the disturbed Ss, lends empirical confirmation to this theoretical expectation. In this regard, the fact that the disturbed Ss evidenced significantly fewer aggressive "guesses" in their incorrect responses is also noteworthy. This result may well be attributable to the operation of defense mechanisms such as repression, inhibition, or denial, which have a detrimental effect on the disturbed Ss' attempt to cope with this emotionally loaded verbal material.

These findings from the original verbal-learning situation were confirmed in the relearning experiment, where again it was found that the disturbed Ss made significantly more errors than the normal Ss on the aggressive words but did not differ significantly on relearning of the neutral verbal material.

The results obtained from the motor-learning experiment are also in keeping with both drive theory and previous empirical findings. It was predicted that the high-anxiety Ss would perform better than the normal Ss in this motor-learning situation under neutral conditions, and this prediction was confirmed. It seems that the high drive level (Taylor, 1956) leads to relatively good performance in a situation that requires rather simple motor learning which does not suffer from the intrusion of the kind of irrelevant responses that operate in the verbal-learning situation. In a previous study of disturbed children (Davids & White, 1958) we also found that disturbed Ss performed better than normal control Ss on a simple motor task (i.e., turning blocks on the Minnesota Rate of Manipulation Test). In that study, however, the disturbed Ss were relatively less affected in a more complex task involving verbal material. In the present study, under both neutral and failure stress conditions, the disturbed Ss performed faster and made fewer errors than the normal Ss. It was not until the relearning experiment, 24 hours later, that the negative effect of the failure stress was evident. In this retention and relearning phase of the investigation, it was only the disturbed Ss who had originally learned under neutral conditions who were able to perform significantly faster than their normal controls. Moreover, within the disturbed group, those Ss who had originally learned under neutral conditions performed significantly faster in the relearning study than did the other disturbed Ss who had been subjected to failure stress in original learning. These findings based on time scores are identical with findings based on error scores. Again, the disturbed Ss who had not been stressed in original learning made significantly fewer relearning errors than did either their normal controls or the other disturbed Ss who had been stressed 24 hours previously. Thus, it is evident that failure stress, of even such a mild degree as that employed in this study, had a pronounced detrimental influence on retention and relearning of high-anxiety Ss. In comparing relative improvement from original to later learning, it is partic-

ularly noteworthy that with low-anxiety Ss (normals) the mild failure stress in original learning had a positive effect, as evidenced by decrease in both time and errors in relearning the motor performance. It is evident, therefore, that the same experimental manipulation in a learning situation may well have completely opposite effects depending upon the type of S that is being studied. Much of the conflict and ambiguity in the research literature on effects of stress (Lazarus, Deese, & Osler, 1952) may well be attributable to this fact. Thus, the present experimental findings may serve to clarify theoretical understanding of these matters as well as making some practical contribution to the field of special education of emotionally disturbed children.

The present finding of differential effects of failure stress on disturbed and normal children is in keeping with results reported by Hutt (1947). In his well-known experiment, he employed two types of Stanford-Binet administration: one called an "adaptive procedure" in which each failed item was followed by an item on which the child would succeed, and the other according to standard methods in which the child met with increasing failure as he progressed through the examination. Hutt found that the adaptive (nonstressful) procedure led to significantly higher IQ performance in a group of maladjusted children, but no difference between the two procedures was found with normal children. Our study confirms this finding that failure stress is particularly disturbing to maladjusted (high-anxiety) Ss, but also suggests that some experience with not too severe stress in the course of learning may well have beneficial effects on normal children.

Results reported by Taylor and Farber (1948) are in accord with this latter suggestion about differences between disturbed and normal Ss. They found that submissive children showed a decrement in performance following failure stress, while ascendent children showed improvement under the same experimental conditions.

Several studies by Sarason (1956; 1957; 1958) are also directly relevant to the present investigation. He reports that high-anxiety Ss emit interfering responses under stressful learning conditions, and found that both relevant and irrelevant failure (in terms of the experimental task) were capable of raising drive level in high-anxiety Ss with consequent adverse effects on performance. He also found that high- and low-anxiety Ss did not differ under neutral conditions, but differed only under stressful conditions. Sarason concludes that high-anxiety Ss bring with them into experimental situations certain response tendencies, and a sensitivity to failure stimuli, that interfere with performance under conditions of stress.

Thus, findings from the present investigation fit very harmoniously with results from previous studies conducted both with children and adults. Moreover, this unified experiment, which employed two kinds of Ss, two kinds of learning, and two kinds of psychological stress, may help to clarify and extend theoretical notions concerned with each of these variables. The fact that we utilized meaningful verbal material and mild failure stress that is similar to that used in everyday relations between teacher and pupil should make the findings of some value to educators as well as to theoreticians and laboratory investigators.

As Lazarus, Deese, and Osler (1952) concluded after their review of the field, there is relatively little information available about personality measures and reaction to stress. According to these reviewers, this is a most heterogeneous field of research activity, and although pronounced individual differences have been found in studies of behavior under stress, few fruitful attempts have been made to study their nature. Since the phenomena of anxiety, stress, and learning are of such paramount importance in our contemporary society, it would seem of crucial significance to continue systematic research in this perplexing area of psychological investigation.

SUMMARY

Utilizing a group of emotionally disturbed boys and a group of normal boys, verbal and motor learning and retention were studied under neutral and stressful conditions. In the verbal-learning situation, stress was introduced in the form of aggressive stimulus words to be learned by the paired-associates method. In the motor-learning situation, failure stress was administered in the form of negative comments about the Ss' performance on an elevated finger maze.

The major findings may be summarized as follows:

1. The two groups did not differ significantly in learning neutral words, but the disturbed Ss made significantly more errors than the normal Ss on the aggressive words.

2. In the normal group, there were significantly fewer errors on the aggressive words than on the neutral words.

3. There were significantly more irrelevant insertions in the verbal learning

responses of the disturbed Ss, and also significantly fewer aggressive words evidenced in their incorrect guesses.

4. Following a 24-hour interval, the two groups did not differ significantly in relearning the neutral words, but the disturbed Ss made significantly more relearning errors on the aggressive words than did the normal Ss.

5. In motor learning, the disturbed Ss performed significantly faster and made significantly fewer errors than did the normal Ss under both neutral and failure conditions.

6. Following a 24-hour interval, under neutral relearning conditions for all Ss, the disturbed Ss performed faster in relearning the motor task, but the difference in speed of performance was significant only in the disturbed subgroup that had originally learned under neutral conditions.

7. Within the disturbed group, there was significantly faster relearning in the subgroup that had originally learned the motor performance under neutral conditions.

8. The disturbed Ss made fewer relearning errors under both conditions of original motor learning, but the difference was significant only in the disturbed subgroup that had originally learned under neutral conditions.

9. Within the disturbed group, there were significantly fewer relearning errors in the subgroup that had originally learned the motor performance under neutral conditions.

10. There was significantly greater improvement, evidenced in relearning by decrease in both time and errors, in the normal group that had originally learned the motor performance under failure conditions than in the disturbed group that had originally learned under failure conditions.

These findings are in keeping with predictions based on drive theory and previous research on performance under stress. It was concluded that in addition to having practical implications, these findings may provide some further clarification in understanding of effects of anxiety on various kinds of learning and the differential effects of psychological stress on the performance of normal and disturbed Ss. In view of the crucial importance of phenomena such as anxiety, stress, and learning, from the viewpoint of both psychological theory and educational practice, it would seem essential to continue systematic research in this complex area of investigation.

REFERENCES

CHILD, I. L. Personality. *Annu. Rev. Psychol.*, 1954, *5*, 149–170.

DAVIDS, A., & WHITE, A. A. Effects of success, failure, and social facilitation on level of aspiration in emotionally disturbed and normal children. *J. Pers.*, 1958, *26*, 77–93.

HUTT, M. L. A clinical study of "consecutive" and "adaptive" testing with the revised Stanford-Binet. *J. consult. Psychol.*, 1947, *11*, 93–103.

LAZARUS, R. S., DEESE, J., & OSLER, SONIA F. The effects of psychological stress upon performance. *Psychol. Bull.*, 1952, *49*, 293–317.

LUCAS, J. D. The interactive effects of anxiety, failure, and interserial duplication. *Amer. J. Psychol.*, 1952, *65*, 59–66.

SALTZ, E., & HOEHN, A. J. A test of the Taylor-Spence theory of anxiety. *J.*

abnorm. soc. Psychol., 1957, *54*, 114–117.

SARASON, I. G. Effect of anxiety, motivational instructions, and failure on serial learning. *J. exp. Psychol.*, 1956, *51*, 253–260.

SARASON, I. G. The effects of anxiety and two kinds of failure on serial learning. *J. Pers.*, 1957, *25*, 383–392.

SARASON, I. G. Effects on verbal learning of anxiety, reassurance, and meaningfulness of material. *J. exp. Psychol.*, 1958, *56*, 472–477.

TAYLOR, JANET A. A personality scale of manifest anxiety. *J. abnorm. soc. Psychol.*, 1953, *48*, 285–290.

TAYLOR, JANET A. Drive theory and manifest anxiety. *Psychol. Bull.*, 1956, *53*, 303–320.

TAYLOR, JANET A. The effects of anxiety level and psychological stress on verbal learning. *J. abnorm. soc. Psychol.*, 1958, *57*, 55–60.

TAYLOR, JANET A., & FARBER, I. E. The effect of failure and success as a function of ascendancy and submission. *Amer. Psychologist*, 1948, *3*, 361. (Abstract)

THORNDIKE, E. L., & LORGE, I. *The teacher's word book of 30,000 words.* New York: Columbia Univer., 1944.

RIGIDITY, NEGATIVE REACTION TENDENCIES, AND COSATIATION EFFECTS IN NORMAL AND FEEBLEMINDED CHILDREN [1]

PATRICIA SHALLENBERGER
EDWARD ZIGLER

THREE THEORETICAL POSITIONS have been advanced to explain the differences in the amount of rigidity manifested by familial feebleminded subjects and normal children of the same MA. A view that has had considerable influence on the training and treatment of feebleminded individuals is that of Lewin (1936) and Kou-

[1] This paper is based upon a Master of Arts thesis done by the first author (1959) under the direction of the second. We wish to thank George A. Johns, Superintendent of the Missouri State School, and Virginia Fisher, Ruth Ragsdale, and the staff and directors of the Home Economics Child Development Laboratory of the University of Missouri for their aid in making subjects available. Preparation of this paper was facilitated by Research Grant M-3945, National Institute of Mental Health, United States Public Health Service.

Reprinted by permission from the *Journal of Abnormal and Social Psychology*, 1961, Vol. 63, No. 1, 20–26.

nin (1941, 1948), who attributed the greater rigidity of the feebleminded to the lessened permeability of the boundaries separating intrapersonal regions. Other investigators (O'Connor & Hermelin, 1959) have explained the differences by the hypothesis that feebleminded subjects employ verbal cues to a lesser degree than do normal subjects of the same MA.

Although in certain cases these two positions generate contradictory predictions, they share a common underlying assumption. Both views assume that although a normal and a feebleminded person may have the same MA, the defective possesses characteristics that somehow inhere in his feeblemindedness. Thus, both emphasize an immutable difference between normal and feebleminded individuals, even when matched on MA.

A third group of investigators have taken exception to the view that rigidity is an inherent characteristic of the feebleminded. Stevenson and Zigler (1957) have advanced the alternative that such differences are related to motivational discrepancies between the groups. This hypothesis assumes that institutionalized defectives tend to be relatively deprived of adult contact and approval and, hence, to have a higher motivation to secure such contact and approval through compliance with the experimenter's instructions than do normal children. Supporting this line of reasoning is the finding that the differential reinforcing effects of attention and support are positively related to the amount of social deprivation experienced (Zigler, 1958).

A cosatiation type of task has often been employed as a measure of rigidity. The subject is instructed to perform a response and is allowed to continue until he wishes to stop. He is then instructed to perform a highly similar response until again satiated. The cosatiation score is a measure of the degree to which performance on the first task influences performance on the second. Both the theoretical positions of Lewin (1936) and Kounin (1941, 1948) and of Stevenson and Zigler (1957) predict that feebleminded subjects should continue the second task longer than normal subjects. However, none of the positions outlined here appears capable of explaining the recurring finding (Kounin, 1941; Zigler, 1958; Zigler, Hodgden, & Stevenson, 1958) that feebleminded subjects under certain conditions perform longer on the second than the first task.

In an effort to explain this finding Zigler (1958) advanced the following hypothesis:

Institutionalized feebleminded subjects begin Task One with a positive reaction tendency higher than that of normal subjects. This higher positive reaction tendency is due to the higher motivation of feebleminded subjects to interact with an approving adult. At the same time, feebleminded subjects begin Task One with a negative reaction tendency higher than that of normal subjects. This higher negative reaction tendency is due to a wariness of adults which stems from the more frequent negative encounters that feebleminded subects experience at the hands of adults. If Task One is given under a support condition, subject's negative reaction tendency is reduced more during Task One than is his positive reaction tendency.

The institutionalized child learns during Task 1 that the experimenter is not like the adults he encounters in the institution who often initiate painful experiences (physical examinations, shots, etc.) with supportive comments. This reappraisal of the experimental situation results in a reduction of the negative reaction tendency. When the deprived child is then switched to Task 2, he meets it with a positive reaction tendency that has been reduced less than has been his negative tendency. The result is a longer performance on Task 2.

The finding (Zigler et al., 1958) that normal children exhibit a decrease in length of performance during Task 2 as compared to Task 1 follows if one assumes that normal children have a relatively low negative reaction tendency when they begin Task 1. When normal subjects are switched to Task 2, their positive reaction tendency has been reduced more through fatigue and satiation effects than any negative reaction tendency they may have had. The result is a briefer performance on Task 2. The hypothesis concerning the operation of a negative reaction tendency in the institutionalized feebleminded gains some support from the clinical impression advanced by Sarason and Gladwin (1958) that one of the major effects of institutionalization is an "avoidance and fear of new problem solving situations."

Thus, the cosatiation score may be a measure of motivational determinants rather than of "inherent" rigidity. The purpose of the present study was to provide an experimental test of this position. The two-part experimental task employed in this study to obtain cosatiation scores was similar to one employed earlier (Zigler, 1958; Zigler et al., 1958). The present study differs from earlier ones in that three pre-experimental games—under two conditions of reinforcements—preceded the experimental task. In a positive reinforcement condition, all of the subject's responses met with success, and he was further rewarded with verbal and nonverbal support from the experimenter. This condition was assumed to reduce the subject's negative reaction tendency. In a negative reinforcement condition that presumably increased negative reaction tendency, all of the subject's responses met with failure, and the experimenter further punished the subject by noting his lack of success. Both normal and feebleminded subjects were used.

TABLE 1 · MEAN MA, CA, AND IQ FOR ALL GROUPS

Group	Mean MA	Mean CA	Mean IQ
Normal, positive	6.1	5.1	119
Normal, negative	6.0	5.2	115
Feebleminded, positive	6.3	11.9	53
Feebleminded, negative	6.3	12.6	50

The two conditions were introduced to provide a test of the following predictions, derived from the hypothesis that feebleminded subjects have both higher positive and negative reaction tendencies than do normal subjects:

1. Subjects who play the pre-experimental games under the negative reinforcement condition evidence a greater increase in time spent on Task 2 over that spent on Task 1 than do subjects who play the pre-experimental games under the positive reinforcement condition.

2. Feebleminded subjects who play the pre-experimental games under the negative reinforcement condition evidence a greater increase in time spent on Task 2 over Task 1 than do normal subjects who play the pre-experimental games under this condition.

3. Subjects who play the pre-experimental games under the positive reinforcement condition spend more time on Task 1 than do those subjects who play the pre-experimental games under the negative reinforcement condition.

4. Of the subjects who play the pre-experimental games under the positive reinforcement condition, the feebleminded spend more time on Task 1 than the normals.

METHOD

SUBJECTS

The subjects consisted of a group of 20 feebleminded and a group of 20 normal children, matched on the basis of MA and sex. There were 10 boys and 10 girls in each group. The normal subjects were obtained from the Missouri University Nursery School and the feebleminded subjects from the Missouri State School at Marshall, Missouri. The feebleminded subjects were all of the familial type, and no individuals with gross motor or sensory disturbances were used. The 1937 revision of the Stanford-Binet, Form L, was used to obtain MA ratings. Two reinforcement conditions were employed. Half of the normal and half of the feebleminded subects were assigned to one condition. The other half of the subjects was assigned to the other. Assignment was made so that all groups would have comparable MAs and so that there would be an equal number of boys and girls in each group. The mean MA, CA, and IQ of each group are presented in Table 1.

APPARATUS

Three pre-experimental games were employed, the Card Game, the Nursery School Game, and the Nail Board Game. The experimental task used was Marble-in-the-Hole.

The Card Game apparatus consisted of two sets of cards. The cards were constructed of cardboard, 2×3 inches, with small rectangles of red or black paper mounted on them. There were 12 cards in each deck, one set containing only red rectangles, the other only black rectangles.

The Nursery School Game apparatus entailed two green panels, each 17 inches square and each having six hooks. Twelve pictures of young children mounted in plastic covers with a hole at the top of each were also provided. A small red light was placed above each panel.

The Nail Board Game apparatus consisted of a red board 18 inches square, inclined at a 50-degree angle with two small boxes at the bottom of the board, one painted yellow and the other green. Nails placed on the surface of the board formed several paths, all of which led to the yellow box. A round glass container was used to hold 12 marbles.

The Marble-in-the-Hole apparatus consisted of a yellow box, $9 \times 8 \times 7$ inches, with two small round holes in the lid 2 inches apart, 300 blue and 300 orange marbles, and a red open container, $5 \times 6 \times 7$ inches, to hold the 600 marbles.

PROCEDURE

All subjects were given the three pre-experimental games in a random order, followed by the experimental task. Half the normal and feebleminded subjects were given the pre-experimental games under a positive reinforcement condition and the other half of the subjects under a negative reinforcement condition. The type of subject, normal (N) and feebleminded (F), and the reinforcement condition, positive (p) and negative (n) were used to designate the four experimental groups: N-p, N-n, F-p, and F-n. The responses of the subjects in the N-p and F-p groups always met with success on the pre-experimental games, i.e., the games were prearranged so that the positive groups could make only correct responses. The N-n and F-n groups could make only incorrect responses due to the prearranged nature of the games.

Additional reinforcement was given to the N-p and F-p groups in the form of verbal and nonverbal support. The nonverbal support consisted of smiling and nods of approval. The verbal support consisted of four statements made in random order at predetermined times during the subject's performance. The four support statements used were, "You really know how to play this game," "That's fine," "Very good," and

"You really know how to play (name of the game), don't you?" One of these statements was given after every ninth response the subject made.

The N-n and F-n groups received four statements of disapproval: "You're not doing very well," "That's not very good," "You aren't getting any right," and "You really don't play (name of the game) very well, do you?" These comments were also made in random order after every ninth response. Care was taken to avoid nodding, smiling, or giving other types of nonverbal support to the subjects in these groups.

All groups received nonverbal and verbal support from the experimenter on both parts of the experimental task, the Marble-in-the-Hole game. The four statements used in the positive reinforcement condition were employed in a random order, one after every tenth marble was inserted. Following the completion of the experimental task, all subjects were told how well they had played the games. After completing the experimental task, each subject in the negative groups was allowed to play the pre-experimental games again. This time he received positive reinforcement for his efforts, to overcome any remaining negative feelings he might have about his performance.

Subjects were tested individually. Upon meeting the subject, the experimenter said, "We're going to play some games today. These are all fun games, and I think that you will like them." The experimenter then explained the instructions for the first pre-experimental game.

The instructions and procedure for the three pre-experimental games are described below:

In the Card Game one of the decks of cards was placed in front of the subject. He was instructed to draw one card at a time from the top of the deck. He was told that red cards were right and black cards were wrong. The decks were prearranged so that for the N-p and F-p groups all the cards were red, and for the N-n and F-n groups all the cards were black. After each red card was exposed, the experimenter said "right," and after each black card, the experimenter said "wrong."

In the Nail Board Game, the subject was shown the apparatus and told that he was to start a marble at the top of the board. If it rolled into the right box he "won." As the marble always went into the yellow box, the subjects in the N-p and F-p groups were told that the yellow box was correct. The subjects in the N-n and F-n groups were told that the green box was correct.

In the Nursery School Game, the subject was told that the panels represented nursery schools and that half of the children in the pictures went to one nursery school and half to the other. If he placed the picture of the child in the correct nursery school panel, the red light would go on. Since there was no principle by which the pictures could be separated, reinforcement was given arbitrarily, depending upon the group to which the subject belonged. All of the responses of the subjects in the N-p and F-p groups were reinforced, whereas none of those in the N-n and F-n groups were.

After completing the three pre-experimental games, the subject was introduced to Part I of the experimental task, Marble-in-the-Hole. With the container filled with 600 marbles and the yellow box placed in front of the subject, the experimenter said:

This is a game we call Marble-in-the-Hole. I'll tell you how to play it. You see these marbles. Some of them are blue and some of them are orange. They go in these holes. The blue ones go in the front hole and the orange ones go in the back hole. (The experimenter points to the appropriate holes.) Now show me a blue marble. Put it in the hole it goes in. Now show me an orange marble. Put it in the hole it goes in. You can put as many marbles in the holes as you want to. You tell me when you want to stop.

The subject then played the game until he indicated that he wished to stop, either by telling the experimenter he wanted to stop, or by not inserting a marble for 30 seconds.

In Part II, after the subject indicated that he wished to stop, the experimenter emptied the marbles from the box back into the container and then said:

Now I'll tell you how to play *this* game. This time we put the orange marbles in the front hole and the blue marbles in the back hole. Put an orange marble where it goes. Now put a blue marble where it goes. You can put as many marbles in the hole as you want to. You tell me when you want to stop.

The subject was allowed to continue until he told the experimenter that he wanted to stop or did not insert a marble for 30 seconds.

RESULTS

The experimental task, Marble-in-the-Hole, provided satisfactory measures of performance. No subject in any group mentioned that Part II was similar to Part I. Each subject responded to Part II as if it were a new game. The maximum number of responses permitted by the task was large enough so that only four subjects inserted all 600 marbles, two in the F-n Group and two in the F-p Group.

ANALYSIS OF PREDICTIONS

The results were analyzed initially in terms of the predictions made at the beginning of the study. One-tailed tests of significance were employed. Because of the nonhomogeneity of variance found for the groups, all estimates of standard

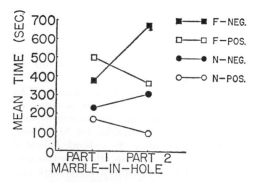

Figure 1. Mean time in seconds spent on Part 1 and Part 2 of the experimental task by each group of subjects.

errors were computed from the sums of the separate variances, and the table of t was entered with half the usual number of degrees of freedom. The performance of the four groups on the experimental task is presented in Figure 1. The cosatiation score for each subject was obtained by subtracting the time he spent on Part I from the time he spent on Part II.

The first prediction was that both feebleminded and normal subjects who received negative reinforcement on the pre-experimental games would evidence higher cosatiation scores than those who received positive reinforcement. The results were analyzed separately for each type of subject. The difference in the average cosatiation scores of Groups F-n (295.7 seconds) and F-p (-136.4 seconds) was 432.1 seconds, which is significant ($t = 3.34$; $p < .005$). The difference in the average cosatiation scores of Groups N-n (77.4 seconds) and N-p (-72.4 seconds) was 149.8 seconds, which is also significant ($t = 3.66$; $p < .005$). The prediction was fulfilled.

The second prediction, that feebleminded subjects who received negative reinforcement on the pre-experimental games would evidence higher cosatiation scores than normal subjects who received such negative reinforcement was also confirmed. The difference in the average cosatiation scores of Groups F-n (295.7 seconds) in N-n (77.4 seconds) was significant at exactly the .05 level ($t = 1.83$).

The third prediction was that subjects who received positive reinforcement on the pre-experimental games would spend more time on Part I of the experimental task than subjects who received negative reinforcement. Again the results were analyzed separately for each type of subject. The difference in the average time spent on Part I by Groups F-p (500.3 seconds) and F-n (376.2 seconds) was 124.1 seconds. While this difference was in the predicted direction, it was not significant ($t < 1.00$). The difference in the average time spent on Part I by Groups N-p (170.0 seconds) and N-n (231.9 seconds) was 61.9 seconds. This difference was significant in the direction opposite to that predicted ($t = 2.42$; $p < .05$, two-tailed test).

The fourth prediction was that feebleminded subjects who received positive reinforcement on the pre-experimental games would spend more time on Part I of the experimental task than normal subjects who had received such positive reinforcement. The difference in the average time spent on Part I by Groups F-p (500.3 seconds) and N-p (170.0 seconds) was 330.3 seconds, which is a significant difference ($t = 2.64$; $p < .02$).

OTHER MEASURES OF PERFORMANCE

In earlier studies (Zigler, 1958; Zigler et al., 1958), the total time spent on the experimental task was used as the measure of the subject's motivation to secure contact and approval, i.e., his positive reaction tendency. Therefore, the total time scores—time spent on Part I plus time spent on Part II—of the four groups of subjects were analyzed for differences. Again the heterogeneity of the variances necessitated the use of individual t tests. The average total times spent on the experimental task by Groups F-n, F-p, N-n, and N-p were 1048.1, 864.2, 541.2, and 267.6 seconds, respectively. Across reinforcement conditions, the difference of 551.8 seconds in the average total time spent on the task by feebleminded (956.2 seconds) and normal subjects (404.4 seconds) was found to be a significant one ($t = 3.90$; $p < .001$). The difference in the average total times of Groups F-n and F-p was 183.9 seconds, which is not significant ($t < 1.00$). The difference in the average total times of Groups N-n and N-p was 273.6 seconds, which is significant ($t = 5.54$; $p < .001$). Feebleminded subjects, thus, played the game longer than the normal subjects, and following the pre-experimental negative reinforcement condition, normal subjects played the game longer than they did when the game was preceded by the positive reinforcement condition. No evidence was found to indicate that the pre-experimental reinforcement conditions affected the amount of total time the feebleminded subjects spent on the game.

In order to assess the comparability of the cosatiation scores obtained in this study—difference in amount of time spent on Parts I and II—with Kounin's type of cosatiation scores—difference in amount of time spent on Parts I and II divided by time spent on Part I—Kounin's formula was employed to compute a second cosatiation score for each subject. A product-moment correlation was then run between the two types of cosatiation scores. The resulting correlation ($r = .904$) indicated that the two measures are highly related.

DISCUSSION

The findings of the present study indicate that cosatiation effects do not mirror the person's inherent rigidity. Instead, cosatiation scores appear to be measures of the relative strength of certain motivational variables or positive and negative reaction tendencies. These tendencies and their relative strengths seem to be the product of particular environmental events that the person has experienced and apparently are open to manipulation and modification. Thus, the present study presents further evidence that differences in the performance of feebleminded and normal subjects of the same MA can be attributed most parsimoniously to the different environmental histories and motivations of the two groups.

Although the findings of the present study offer further validation for the motivational hypothesis advanced in earlier studies (Stevenson & Zigler, 1957; Zigler, 1958; Zigler et al., 1958), they also represent evidence favoring an extension of this hypothesis. Whereas the earlier studies emphasized an increased desire to interact with and receive the support of an adult, the present study demonstrates the role of another motivational variable, negative reaction tendency. The experiencing of events of the sort that has been described as socially depriving gives rise to both an increased desire to interact as well as a wariness to do so. It remains for future research to isolate the specific events that give rise to each of these opposing motivational factors.

The findings of an earlier study, in conjunction with the results of the present one, allow for a tentative suggestion as to the chronology of the growth of positive and negative tendencies. Degree of pre-institutional social deprivation (Zigler, 1958) was found to be directly related to positive motivation to perform on the two-part experimental task, but it was not found to be related to the cosatiation score. Cosatiation scores, however, were found to be related to length of institutionalization. Since the present study indicates that the cosatiation score is sensitive to the amount of negative reaction

present, it may be that the negative reaction tendency is a product of institutional rather than preinstitutional events.

There is a distinct possibility that preinstitutional and institutional experiences differ in kind. This follows if one conceptualizes preinstitutional social deprivation as characterized by the relative absence of positive social reinforcers, whereas institutional social deprivation not only lacks such reinforcers but includes punishing events as well. This attempt at a discrete division between such events raises certain questions. One may wonder if severe deprivation or extreme absence of social reinforcers does not itself constitute a punishment condition. Furthermore, one may wonder whether if, when punishing events are present, positive social reinforcers are necessarily absent.

One of the findings of the present study offers evidence that conceptualizing a particular set of environmental events as producing *only* a negative reaction tendency results in an inaccurate prediction. Whereas three of the four predictions made at the outset of the study were confirmed, the prediction that subjects who received positive reinforcement would spend more time on Part I of the experimental task than subjects who received negative reinforcement was not confirmed. In fact, normal subjects receiving negative pre-experimental reinforcement played Part I of the task significantly longer than did normal subjects who received positive reinforcement.

The unconfirmed prediction was derived from the view that the negative condition builds up the negative tendency which would result in decreased performance on Part I. How then can one explain the lengthier performance by the negative normal group over that of the positive? Conceivably, the condition built up the positive reaction tendency as well as the negative tendency. This heightening of both reaction tendencies occurred because the negative condition not only consisted of mildly punishing events that promoted wariness and reluctance in the subjects, but it also represented an absence of positive social reinforcers. Thus, following the deprivation of positive reinforcement on the pre-experimental games, the subjects had an increased desire to secure such reinforcement. It then becomes understandable why the support experienced on Part I of the experimental task retains reinforcing value longer for the normal subjects who played the pre-experimental games under the negative condition than for those who received prior positive reinforcement.

Evidence that the negative reaction tendency also was built up during the negative pre-experimental condition can be found in the confirmation of the prediction that negative normal subjects show an increase in time spent on Part II over that spent on Part I. Further evidence that the negative condition builds up the positive reaction tendency is demonstrated in the finding that the total time spent on the experimental task is significantly greater for negative normal than for positive normal subjects. Coincidentally, the finding that the total time normal subjects spent on the experimental task is significantly related to the pre-experimental reinforcement condition contradicts Kounin's (1939) view that lengthy performance on this type of task is attributable to the "rigid state" of the individual and adds support to the notion that length of performance may be explained more parsimoniously in terms of motivational factors.

In light of the suggestion that the negative condition builds up the positive as well as the negative reaction tendency, one may ask why negative feebleminded subjects did not spend more total time on the experimental task or on Part I of it than did the positive feebleminded subjects. The simplest explanation would seem to be that the institutionalized feebleminded person has such a high motivation to interact with and gain the support of an adult that it is relatively difficult to increase his positive tendency above this already existing high level.

One further suggestion is in order. Further investigation of such positive and negative reaction tendencies, their interactions, and the specific events which give rise to them, may clarify issues much broader than the troublesome finding that under certain conditions feebleminded individuals play a second part of a two-part cosatiation task longer than the first part. The current controversy over whether social deprivation leads to an increase in the interaction of the socially deprived individual or whether such social deprivation leads to apathy and withdrawal (Cox, 1953; Goldfarb, 1953; Irvine, 1952; Wittenborn & Myers, 1957) is a case in point.

SUMMARY

Feebleminded and normal children played three pre-experimental games under two conditions of reinforcement, followed by a two-part experimental task given under a support condition. Half the subjects in each group received positive and half negative reinforcement during the games. Following satiation on Part I of the experimental task, subjects were switched to Part II and again allowed to play until satiated. Four predictions were advanced, derived from the hypothesis that the cosatiation score is a measure of motivational determinants rather than a measure of the inherent rigidity of individuals. The results in general supported this hypothesis.

REFERENCES

Cox, F. The origins of the dependency drive. *Aust. J. Psychol.*, 1953, 5, 64–73.

Goldfarb, W. The effects of early institutional care on adolescent personality. *J. exp. Educ.*, 1953, *12*, 106–129.

Irvine, E. Observations on the aims and methods of child rearing in communal settlements in Israel. *Hum. Relat.*, 1952, 5, 247–275.

Kounin, J. Experimental studies of rigidity as a function of age and feeblemindedness. Unpublished doctoral dissertation, State University of Iowa, 1939.

Kounin, J. Experimental studies of rigidity: I. The measurement of rigidity in normal and feebleminded persons. *Charact. Pers.*, 1941, *9*, 251–273.

Kounin, J. The meaning of rigidity: A reply to Heinz Werner. *Psychol. Rev.*, 1948, *55*, 157–166.

Lewin, K. *A dynamic theory of personality.* New York: McGraw-Hill, 1936.

O'Connor, N., & Hermelin, B. Discrimination and reversal learning in imbeciles. *J. abnorm. soc. Psychol.*, 1959, *59*, 409–413.

Sarason, S., & Gladwin, T. Psychological and cultural problems in mental subnormality: A review of research. *Genet. psychol. Monogr.*, 1958, 57, 7–269.

Stevenson, H., & Zigler, E. Discrimination learning and rigidity in normal and feebleminded individuals. *J. Pers.*, 1957, *25*, 699–711.

Wittenborn, J., & Myers, B. *The placement of adoptive children.* Springfield, Ill.: Charles C. Thomas, 1957.

Zigler, E. The effect of pre-institutional social deprivation on the performance of feebleminded children. Unpublished doctoral dissertation, University of Texas, 1958.

Zigler, E., Hodgden, L., & Stevenson, H. The effect of support on the performance of normal and feebleminded children. *J. Pers.*, 1958, *26*, 106–122.

SENSATION AND PERCEPTION | 5

THERE ARE relatively few definitive studies of sensation and perception in children, considering the wealth of data potentially available to the researcher with parametric interests in these areas. Sensory processes, strictly speaking, refer to those mechanisms by which the organism receives and responds to stimulation in the various modalities—vision, hearing, smell, taste, and touch. The classical psychophysical methods are usually used to assess the sensory attributes of an organism, including the child subject. Studies of perceptual processes, which are usually considered elaborations of more basic sensory processes, seek to investigate the effects of various kinds of experiential factors (such as attitudinal and emotional attributes) upon sensory reception. As one would expect, it is most difficult to separate the two kinds of process, if indeed there are two, for the assessment of one almost invariably involves the simultaneous measurement of the other. For a review of the many techniques for the determination of sensory thresholds and perceptual attributes of the child, the reader is referred to Riesen (1960) and Gibson and Olum (1960).

If one wants to know if a child "can tell" the difference between two physically different stimuli, such as two hues on the color continuum, he must in some way ask the child if he can distinguish them. In the articulate older human, this does not present too much of an assessment problem, for the subject can be asked: "Is there a difference between these two colors, or are they the same?" Even with such a subject, however, one must take cognizance of the fact that the subject's reply may well be influenced by such factors as his understanding of the question, his previous experience in discriminating hues, and his attitude toward the experimenter. Thus, even with the articulate subject, our knowledge as experimenters about the sensory processes of the subject will always be response-based. That is to say, we cannot know about the subject's perceptual attributes exclusive of his responses to the stimuli we present to him. The very fact that there are various ways in which to elicit responses from subjects and different kinds of responses that may be selected as indicants of the subject's perceptions should make clear that sensation and perception are always, for the psychologist, a matter of stimulus-response relations. Thus it may be seen that whether we consider a child "able" to discriminate certain stimuli depends upon the manner in which we elicit differential responses from him.

The study of sensory and perceptual processes in the very young, in-articulate child presents still other problems. In dealing with nonverbal or-ganisms who do not understand our instructions and cannot tell us whether the stimuli presented are the "same" or "different" it becomes necessary to devise other techniques for the assessment of sensory or perceptual attributes. For instance, if one wants to discover whether the newborn child "senses" different odors in his environment and whether his "perception" of them changes within the first few days of life, he may place the infant in a stabil-imeter (a movement-detection device) and attach a pneumograph around the child's abdomen to detect breathing changes. Then various odorants may be administered to the infant, along with control trials of no odorant, while the experimenter notes whether a movement or breathing reaction takes place in response to the odorant that does not also occur to the control stimulus. In this way, the infant's reaction to various odorants may be studied, as well as any changes that occur to those odorants over trials or days (Lipsitt, Engen, and Kaye, 1962). Whether the infant can "smell" depends upon the nature and adequacy of our response-measurement or response-detection procedure. Con-ceivably, one kind of response might suggest the infant cannot smell a certain odor, while another response-assessment procedure might indicate that the infant does smell that odor.

The first selection in this section is a study of the capacity of the new-born child to react to chemical stimuli placed before his nostrils. In addition to determining whether or not the newborn reacts to a given odorant, the experimenters were interested also in the changing characteristics of the baby's response to the same stimulus presented several times in succession. As the data reveal, newborns not only react to such stimuli, but their tendency to re-spond diminishes with successive presentations of the stimulus, a process known as adaptation or habituation. This adaptation process, while interesting in and of itself, presents a problem for the psychophysicist interested in dis-covering the maximum sensory discriminative capacity of the newborn, for he must try to assess this capacity before adaptation has changed the organism.

The second selection, by Murray, is a now widely quoted study that capitalized on a real-life fear-inducing circumstance to determine whether emotional factors affect children's judgments of the maliciousness of other persons. Five children rated on a nine-point scale a series of stimuli consist-ing of photographs of people. Ratings were obtained from the children under a neutral condition and also under a condition presumed to arouse fear, namely, a game of "murder." It was found that, in general, the children called the people in the pictures bad, cruel, or wicked more after the fear-arousing situation than when they were not fearful. Thus Murray obtained objective evidence for the proposition that people tend to "project" psychological at-tributes onto others in accordance with their anxieties. That is, beyond the actual physical determinants of response to stimuli individual differences in the perceiver also determine the nature of the response. This assumption, of course, is basic to the use of projective techniques for the assessment of psychological disturbances, one of which techniques (the Thematic Apperception Test) was devised by Murray and his colleagues.

The third selection, by Lambert, Solomon, and Watson, is an experimental extension of a previous study which had demonstrated that economically poor children tend to overestimate coin sizes more than do their solvent peers. The conclusion was made that a "need" for money may influence one's perceptions of coin sizes. The Lambert, Solomon, and Watson study demonstrated that this perceptual overestimation of size can be attributed to the reinforcement history of the subject. Children first estimated the size of a poker chip to determine a base-level judgment, following which the children were entered into a reinforcement situation involving the receipt of poker chips that could be traded for candy. After this reward experience, judgments of the size of the poker chips became significantly higher. When the children were then subjected to an extinction condition in which no candy was received for chips earned, size estimations of the chips returned to their base level. Thus, the last two studies, considered together, demonstrate that psychophysical and psychological judgments are influenced considerably by the context in which the judgments are made and by the attributes or histories of the judges.

REFERENCES

GIBSON, ELEANOR J. and OLUM, VIVIAN.   Experimental methods of studying perception in children. In P. H. Mussen (Ed.), *Handbook of research methods in child development*. New York: Wiley, 1960. Pp. 311–373.

LIPSITT, L. P., ENGEN, T. and KAYE, H.   The changing olfactory threshold in the neonate. *Child Develpm.*, 1962, in press.

RIESEN, A. H.   Receptor functions. In P. H. Mussen (Ed.), *Handbook of research methods in child development*. New York: Wiley, 1960. Pp. 284–307.

Olfactory Responses and Adaptation in the Human Neonate [1]

TRYGG ENGEN
LEWIS P. LIPSITT
HERBERT KAYE

THIS PAPER REPORTS the results of research in olfaction related to a general study program of sensory and learning processes of infants currently carried out at Brown University in cooperation with the Providence Lying In Hospital. The purpose of this study was to observe human neonates' responses to olfactory stimulation during the first few days of life and the change in such responses with repeated stimulation.

There is a lack of data concerning the newborn's capacity to smell, for virtually no research on this topic has been done in the past three decades. Until about 30 yr. ago, there had been a few such studies but with ambiguous findings (see Disher, 1934; Pratt, 1954 for reviews). Definite responses were obtained only to such stimuli as acetic acid and ammonia, but it was believed these responses were largely the result of pain or irritation (i.e., through stimulation of the trigeminal nerve) rather than smell. Some investigators believed they observed responses to so-called pure odor stimuli,

e.g., valerian, mint, and essence of lavender, but others could not verify the observation. Some suggested that newborn infants are able to discriminate between pleasant and unpleasant odors, but others held that olfactory sensitivity is not present or is poorly developed at birth.

Perhaps the chief reason for the lack of clear-cut conclusions is that many of these studies relied on E's rapid judgment rather than automatically recorded responses which could be viewed repeatedly, and most failed to establish interobserver reliability of the observations made. Recent developments in apparatus make possible a study of this sensory process under more objective experimental conditions, especially with respect to measures of the infant's responses (Lipsitt & DeLucia, 1960).

The present paper reports the results of two related experiments, the first designed to compare the responses made to acetic acid and phenylethyl alcohol, and the second to compare responses made to anise oil and asafoetida. On the basis of adults' reports, acetic acid would be classified as irritating or painful but phenylethyl alcohol would probably be described as a pure odor. Anise oil is typically called a "pleasant" and asafoetida an "unpleasant" odor. However, few describe asafoetida as "irritating" or "annoying" as in the case of acetic acid.

[1] This research was made possible by the Institute for Health Sciences at Brown University, under a Research Grant B-2356 from the National Institute of Neurological Diseases and Blindness. The writers wish to thank Glidden L. Brooks, Director of the Institute for Health Sciences at Brown, and the staff of the Providence Lying In Hospital for facilitating this research.

Reprinted by permission from *Journal of Comparative and Physiological Psychology*, 1963, 3, 56, 77–81.

Moreover, Allen (1937) obtained conditioned responses in the dog for asafoetida and anise only through the olfactory nerve and not through the trigeminal nerve. On the other hand, recent dual channel electro-physiological recordings from animal preparations have indicated that a so-called odor stimulus (e.g., phenylethyl alcohol) in relatively high concentration might elicit a response in *both* the trigeminal and olfactory nerves, while a lower concentration of the same stimulus might produce a response in only the olfactory nerve (Tucker, 1961). There is reason, therefore, to question the present classification of chemical agents into irritants vs. olfactory stimuli, for the neutral mechanisms mediating the response are not yet clearly understood. The present concern is to determine (*a*) to what extent the neonate responds to these stimuli and (*b*) how the response changes with repetitive stimulation.

METHOD

SUBJECTS

Twenty apparently normal infants, 10 for each experiment, were Ss. There were 4 boys and 6 girls in each experiment. The average age of the infants was 50 hr. with a range from 32 to 68 hr.

RESPONSE MEASURES

Portions of the apparatus used to measure the infant's responses have been described earlier (Lipsitt & DeLucia, 1960), and only the essential details will be discussed here. The major device sensitively measures leg-withdrawal and general bodily activity. Respiration was recorded by attaching a Phipps and Bird infant pneumograph around the abdomen. Heart rate was measured in the second experiment in connection with the possibility of differen-

tial activity resulting from anise oil and asafoetida, and was recorded from the wrists with EEG electrodes being prepared with Bentonite paste. All recordings were made on a four-channel Grass polygraph, Model 5.

STIMULI

The experiments employed full-strength acetic acid, phenylethyl alcohol, anise oil (Anethol, U.S.P.), and tincture asafoetida.[2] One cc. of each odorant was kept in a 10×75 mm. pyrex test tube stopped with a cork wrapped in aluminum foil. The stimulus was presented to S on a commercial Q-Tip, one end of which was attached to the cork, the other end containing cotton saturated with and positioned just above the liquid odor.

PROCEDURE

The experiments were performed in a ventilated laboratory with the temperature at about 80°F. The Ss were tested individually between 10 and 11 A.M., 15 to 90 min. after feeding. Noise and illumination were kept at a minimum. After S had been placed in the apparatus, Es waited until S appeared to be asleep (i.e., eyes were closed), respiration was steady and regular, and activity was at a minimum. This state was required before the presentation of all stimulus and control trials.

Each S was presented two odors, either acetic acid and phenylethyl alcohol (first experiment), or anise oil and asafoetida (second experiment). Half of the Ss received, for example, 10 trials with acetic acid first and then 10 trials with phenylethyl alcohol, while for the other half this order was reversed. A stimulus presentation consisted of E removing the cork with the attached Q-Tip and placing it between and about 5 mm. away from the S's nostrils. The control trial involved the presentation of a clean (dry) Q-Tip in exactly the same man-

---

[2] We are indebted to Fritzsche Brothers, Incorporated, of New York for supplying the odorants for the second experiment.

ner. Presentation of stimulus and control trials was alternated. The duration of trials was recorded on the polygraph and was, with one exception, 10 sec. Responses to acetic acid were of such amplitude that the Q-Tip was maintained in the prescribed position for no more than 2.5 sec. The time between trials was approximately 1 min.; a longer period was required occasionally before S's behavior returned to pretrial standards.

With one minor exception, the procedure was the same in both experiments. In the second experiment, 4 posttest trials were added to obtain further data on order effects in the presentation of different odors. Two

trials of the odor presented first in the session were reintroduced and again alternated with two control trials at the end of the session. There were thus a total of 40 trials per S in the first and 44 in the second experiment.

RESULTS

The raw data consist of simultaneous tracings of leg-withdrawal, general activity, respiration, and heart rate on the polygraph with paper speed at 5 mm. per sec. A sample record is shown in Figure 1.

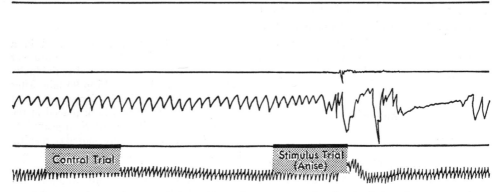

Figure 1. A sample record showing simultaneous records of stimulus and response events. (Reading from top to bottom, the lines shown are leg-withdrawal, an event marker not used in this study, stabilimeter movement, breathing, stimulus and control marker, and heart rate.)

For each odor two methods were used to evaluate individual records. Both methods yielded essentially the same results, and in both cases the frequency of response was evaluated with the Wilcoxon matched-pairs signed-ranks test. All p values reported are two-tailed. The three judges evaluating the records independently agreed on 86% of the total number of individual trials. Whether a response was ultimately judged to have occurred or not

depended on the majority rule, i.e., the judgment of the two agreeing judges was taken as correct in the 14% of the trials where unanimity did not prevail.

The Es first judged whether or not any or all of the polygraph tracings during stimulus and control trials were larger than those observed for the 10-sec. interval immediately preceding the trial. The response measures tend to be correlated, although respiration appeared to be most sensitive with this particular stimulus material. The first analysis revealed a significantly higher frequency of differences for stimulus trials than for control trials $(p < .01)$. However, the information of basic interest from this analysis was that about 15% of the controls gave a larger response than that obtained during the 10-sec. period immediately preceding it. This difference is not significant, nor are the differences among the control trials for the four odors. The responses observed on control trials appear to reflect the infants' "baseline activity"; the fact that they sometimes do occur emphasizes the necessity for including such control trials in any study of olfactory responses in infants.

The control trial was used as baseline and a response on a stimulus trial was judged positive only when it was *greater* than that observed on the accompanying control trial. The average results of this analysis are presented below. Figure 2 presents the results obtained with the 10 Ss in the first experiment with acetic acid and phenylethyl alcohol. The points plotted indicate the percentage of Ss giving a larger response on a stimulus trial than on the control trial. Averages of two successive trials produce a smoothed but undistorted picture of the trend of individual trials. It is evident that responses were obtained to both stimuli, but significantly more to acetic acid than to phenylethyl alcohol $(p < .001)$. In the case of neither stimulus was there a reliable diminution of response from early to later trials, as determined by a t test for related proportions. Nor was there a reliable effect of presentation order of the two odors. In the second experiment heart rate was recorded along with leg-withdrawal, stabilimeter activity, and respiration, but the former measure seemed to show no differential effects of anise oil and asafoetida, nor did it prove feasible to count accurately changes in heart rate resulting from the olfactory stimuli. (This difficulty was probable due to the relatively slow speed at which the polygraph had to be run to record the other three measures accurately. The heart rate record was often buffered by movement artifacts.)

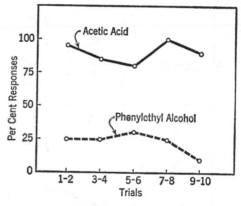

Figure 2. Percentage responses as a function of trials.

Figure 3 presents the percentage of responses as a function of trials for anise oil and asafoetida when each of them is presented first and second in the session to subgroups of five Ss. A greater percentage of responses was obtained with asafoetida than anise oil $(p < .001)$, and for both there is a decrement in response from the first to the last block of trials $(p < .001$ for asafoetida, and $p < .02$ for anise oil, all 10 Ss combined). The effect of order of presentation (i.e., first or second) on the frequency of response can also be observed. There is evidence of an interaction effect, for the order of presentation seems to affect response to anise oil significantly, $(p < .001)$ but not to asafoetida ($p > .05$). Finally, it can be seen in Figure 3 that in the posttest trials, the percentage of responses returns to nearly the level observed for the first several trials with each odor ($p < .08$ for anise, and $p < .05$ for asafoetida,

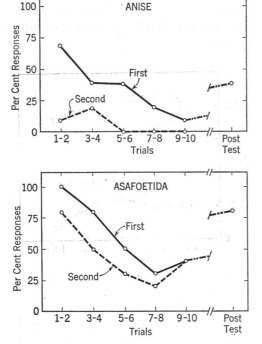

Figure 3. Percentage responses as a function of trials.

based on five Ss, two-tailed t test for proportions between last block of trials and posttest trials). There occurred, then, both a decrement in response as a function of repeated stimulus presentations and recovery following stimulation with another odor.

DISCUSSION

The present experiments yielded clear-cut evidence that the neonate responds to olfactory stimulation. As might be expected on the basis of past findings,

the largest number of responses was elicited by acetic acid, with asafoetida next and followed by phenylethyl alcohol and anise oil. The reason for this rank order is not clear. It could reflect differences in intensity of the odors, for intensity was not controlled in the present experiments. Another possibility is that magnitude of response is inversely related to pleasantness of the stimuli. However, an attempt to judge the obtained records as well as the behavior of the infant, e.g., facial expression and posture, provided no support for such speculation. In brief, infants can smell soon after birth, but the quantitative and reinforcing properties of various chemical agents are problems for future research.

The observed decrement in response as a function of trials (see also Bridger, 1961; Bartoshuk, 1962) presents an interesting problem of interpretation, because it is difficult to distinguish operationally between *sensory* adaptation (i.e., changes in receptor organs produced by repeated stimulation) and *response* habituation or adaptation (i.e., extinction of a response to an originally novel or effective stimulus) in the present experiment. The recovery from the adaptation observed in the posttrials and the cross-adaptation indicated by the effect of order of presentation of the stimuli seem consistent with a phenomenon of sensory adaptation, as does the relative absence of adaptation to a noxious stimulus, acetic acid. Only further study can illuminate the distinction between these two types of adaptation phenomena, and determine which of the two is occurring here.

A related experiment has been reported by Bronstein, Antonova, Kamenstskaya, Luppova, & Sytova (1958) who used suppression of sucking as an indicator of smelling and hearing in newborns. The pacifier was placed in the infant's mouth and, during sucking, an odor or a tone was presented. If the infant stopped sucking, this was taken as a response to the stimulus. The suppression of sucking in response to the stimulus decreased over 10 trials, and eventually the stimulus failed to produce any change in sucking. Data showing suppression of sucking are presented, in order of effectiveness, for iodoform, peppermint, and anise oil. These investigators found that the weaker the stimulus, the more rapid and complete the adaptation.

One final observation may be made concerning qualitative aspects of the infants' responses to the odor stimuli. It was often observed that with successive presentations of some stimuli, mostly acetic acid, but often asafoetida, S's response changed progressively from a diffuse, seemingly disorganized response (similar to a mild startle) to a smooth, efficient response in escaping the odor stimulus. In early trials the baby's entire body seemed to respond, while in later trials, a simple retraction or turn of the head from the locus of the odorant was executed. It is quite likely that this *response differentiation*, similar to that obtained by Marinesco and Kreindler in older infants (Munn, 1955, pp. 201–204), is a rudimentary form of learning resulting from differential reinforcement of different response components. Further studies should attempt to document either photographically or mechanically these changing characteristics of the infants' head-movement responses.

REFERENCES

ALLEN, W. F. Olfactory and trigeminal conditioned reflexes in dogs. *Amer. J. Physiol.*, 1937, *118*, 532–540.

BARTOSHUK, A. K. Response decrement with repeated elicitation of human neonatal cardiac acceleration to sound. *J. comp. physiol. Psychol.*, 1962, *55*, 9–13.

BRIDGER, W. H. Sensory habituation and discrimination in the human neonate. *Amer. J. Psychiatr.*, 1961, *117*, 991–996.

BRONSTEIN, A. I., ANTONOVA, T. G., KAMENSTSKAYA, A. G., LUPPOVA, N. N., & SYTOVA, V. A. [On the development of the functions of analyzers in infants and some animals at the early stage of ontogenesis.] In, *Problemy evolyutaii fisiologicheskikh funktsii.* [Problems of evolution of physiological functions.] (Office of Technical Services Report No. 60–61066, 1960, pp. 106–116. Translation obtainable from the United States Department of Commerce, Office of Technical Services.) Moscow-Leningrad: Akademiya Nauk SSSR, 1958.

DISHER, D. R. The reactions of newborn infants to chemical stimuli administered nasally. In F. C. Dockeray (Ed.), *Studies of infant behavior.* Columbus: Ohio State Univer. Press, 1934. Pp. 1–52.

LIPSITT, L. P., & DELUCIA, C. A. An apparatus for the measurement of specific response and general activity of the human neonate. *Amer. J. Psychol.*, 1960, *73*, 630–632.

MUNN, N. L. *The evolution and growth of human behavior.* New York: Houghton Mifflin, 1955.

PRATT, K. C. The neonate. In L. Carmichael (Ed.), *Manual of child psychology.* New York: Wiley, 1954. Pp. 215–291.

TUCKER, D. Physiology of olfaction. *Amer. Perfumer,* 1961, *76*, 48–53.

THE EFFECT OF FEAR UPON ESTIMATES
OF THE MALICIOUSNESS
OF OTHER PERSONALITIES

HENRY A. MURRAY, JR.

THE PRESENT PAPER describes an attempt to demonstrate in quantitative terms the generally recognized fact that the emotional state of a subject may affect his judgments of other personalities. It is one of several experiments now in progress in this laboratory which have been designed to expose some of the internal—physical and psychical—factors which influence a subject's perceptions, interpretations, and appraisals of the objects and situations in the world about him.

The diagnosis of traits of character from the face depends, it is often said in common language, upon (1) the observation of the features (physical signs) and (2) the interpretation of them on the basis of associations—associations which in the past have been found by the observer to exist between somewhat similar physical signs and particular types of behavior. Psychologically, we speak here of two processes which may for convenience be differentiated, namely, perception and apperception. Such is the nomenclature, at least, which we have provisionally adopted for the purposes of this discussion. The term *perception* is confined to the *conscious* recognition of configurated sense impressions or segregated sensory wholes; whereas *apperception* is used to designate the process—whatever its an-

tecedents—whereby meaning, in other than sensory terms, is assigned to the physical stimulus. This use of the term apperception is at least within the definition given by Stout. For, according to this authority, it is by the process of apperception that "a presentation acquires a certain significance for thought by connecting itself with some mental preformation as this has been organized in the course of previous experience" (3, p. 110). The term is used to include understanding, interpreting, classifying, subsuming, and so forth.

The distinction we make between perception and apperception is, of course, somewhat arbitrary. For, under most conditions, the two processes are inseparably fused. For instance, as Köhler has so succinctly remarked: "If in a friendly-looking face we try to separate the mere bodily configuration and the friendliness, we find the task rather difficult, as long as we look at the whole face and do not analyze the face itself as a mosaic of colored spots" (1, p. 239). . . .

This is not the place to discuss in detail all the processes which contribute to a knowledge of our fellows. We merely wish to suggest how it may come about that apperceptions of the personality (feelings, motives, and probable behavior) of others are commonly influenced—as experience seems to teach—by the total bodily state of the perceiving subject. Our

Reprinted by permission from *Journal of Social Psychology*, 1933, 4, 310–329.

hypothesis would be, then, that certain meanings, or categories we might call them, such as "friendly" and "unfriendly," become integrated with certain muscular sets and emotions, and when the latter are aroused the former will be mobilized and come to mind. These intermediary physical processes would seem on superficial glance to be entirely irrelevant to the task at hand, but when we consider that they are conspicuously present—at least in an imaginatively representative form—in persons, such as novelists, whose insight into character is generally regarded as most acute, we have cause for reflection.

Now, when such processes can be accounted for by reference to the presented stimulus and its similarity to past stimuli, and hence to *traces* (a fictional concept) in the mind of the subject, we should consider them—at least for that subject—legitimate, normal, and objectively valid. If they happen to be inappropriate and unadaptive, well, it is a matter of ignorance, insufficient experience, and so forth. When, however, the internal processes which are determining apperception have recently been aroused by some other essentially dissimilar and irrelevant stimulus, or may be shown to be more or less inveterate in the subject, then we must refer to another process—a process which distorts the external world or adds something to it which is not there.

According to the terminology of some psychologists the process whereby psychic elements—needs, feelings and emotions, or images and contexts of images activated by such affective states—are referred by the experiencing subject to the external world without sufficient objective evidence is called *projection*. When this process is active, what is in truth mental and within the personality comes to appear as if it were outside the personality. We may speak of *perceptive projection* when sensory elements are projected, i.e., when an image takes on the vividness, substantiality, and outthereness of a real object—as in a dream and in an hallucination—or when an image transforms or makes additions to the actual physical features of an inadeqately perceived real object so that the latter is taken for the object of which the image is a representation—as in an illusion. And we may speak of *apperceptive projection* when non-sensory elements are projected. This occurs (1) when imaginal contexts, or the categories under which the activated images are subsumed, are believed, with insufficient objective evidence, to be descriptive of or to pertain to objects in the environment—as in delusions; or (2) when the needs, feelings, and emotions themselves, rather than the images or imaginal meanings activated by them, are believed by the subject to be existent in other personalities—also as in delusions. The former might be termed *complementary apperceptive projection* and the latter *supplementary apperceptive projection*. . . .

The reader may have noticed that in defining projection we spoke rather nonchalantly of images; we said that hallucinations were projected images and so forth. How can they be projected images, when for the experiencing subject there are no images; there are only external objects? The answer is that they are projected *unconscious* images—a purely fictional concept. In dreams and in hallucinations we know that they are not external objects which the subject perceives; nor is he conscious of imagery in the usual sense. Common experience, however, bears witness to the inseparable gradations between dreams and phantasies —the latter being admittedly composed of images—as well as to the similarity between memory images and some of the objects which appear in dreams; and consequently some psychologists have been led to speak of projected unconscious images, since *qua* images the subject is unaware of them. It will be remembered, furthermore, that Prince (2) performed experiments upon an hallucinating dissociated subject, and by means of automatic writing demonstrated to his own satisfaction that the hallucinated objects were similar to the imagery of a contemporary unconscious (or co-conscious) mental process. . . .

Projections, then, by distorting a subject's recognition and interpretation of external reality prevent a detached and disinterested objectivity. They may, nevertheless, serve the cause of truth. For instance, a young man who has suffered undeservedly through the treacherous and malicious behavior of others—he has a fixed feeling of inferiority, let us say— may thenceforth suppose that strangers and acquaintances whom he meets are prompted solely by selfish motives, and at least towards him are critical and scornful. He may, indeed, like Timon of Athens, generalize his particular experiences and become a misanthrope. In so far as such a man overemphasizes the selfishness of human beings to the exclusion of their other more engaging traits he is the victim of a complementary apperceptive projection. We might say that he is mistaken in his proportions, since he attributes so much evil and so little good to others. But we must not lose sight of the fact that in some respects he may be a better observer than the average citizen, since as a result of his particular sensitiveness

to malice he may very well discover and precisely analyze subtle and hidden forms of it which others have neglected, and so make a valuable contribution to psychological knowledge.

We have discussed the probable influence of bodily changes upon apperception, and how, when the former are relatively unconnected with the immediate stimulus, misapperceptions or delusions may occur. These we agreed to call apperceptive projections. Finally, we proposed the hypothesis of unconscious images to explain both perceptive projections and complementary apperceptive projections.

Such were the speculations which led us to the present enterprise: an attempt to prove by experiment that a functional relationship between emotional and apperceptive processes exists normally, and, by changing the former, a qualitative or quantitative alteration of the latter will occur. More specifically, we might characterize this experiment as an attempt to produce measurable variations in the apperception of benevolence or malice in other people by the excitation of fear in the apperceiving subject, the variation or exceptionality of the apperception in each case being estimated by comparing it with the subject's habitual apperception of the same object.

The particular form of our hypothesis and the technique devised to test it were based upon such a common phenomenon as that of a person who in a fear-invoking situation—for instance while walking through a "tough" neighborhood at night—apperceives some of the strangers whom he encounters as "dangerous characters." It was supposed that, if, for purposes of standardization, photographs of people, rather than living personalities, were used as material to be judged, the subjects—especially children —after a fear-invoking situation would estimate the faces in the photographs to be more malicious than they would estimate them to be when they were free from fear. Such at least was our hypothesis, and when the daughter of the author planned a week-end country house-party of five girls, eleven years of age, it seemed that this might provide an opportunity to test it. It was supposed that during this party there would be many chances for control tests after relatively normal pleasure-invoking circumstances, and, since the children wanted to play the game of *murder* in the evening, it seemed that a fear-invoking situation would occur in the natural course of events.

We judged that the game of *murder* alone would not be sufficiently exciting, so we planned to tell the first half of a ghost story after the end of the game, on the supposition that the combination of the two situations would give rise to a state of anxiety which would perseverate long enough to affect the results on a test given immediately afterwards. At the last minute, however, circumstances interfered with the telling of the ghost story, and so we were forced to depend upon the efficacy of two games of *murder* for the evocation of fear.

TECHNIQUE

Thirty photographs approximately 5.5 x 7.5 cm. in size—most of which were taken from the magazine *Time*—were mounted upon white cards and divided into two roughly comparable series; each of which was composed of eleven photographs of men and four photographs of women, all of them unknown to the sub-

jects of the experiments. The first series of fifteen faces was called Test A, the second series was called Test B.

Tests were given on three occasions as follows:

FIRST OCCASION

Test A after pleasure-invoking situation (control). This experiment was performed at 12:30 P.M., Saturday, after the children had returned from motoring about the country.

SECOND OCCASION

Test A and Test B after fear-invoking situation. This experiment was performed at 7:30 P.M., Saturday, after the children had played two games of *murder*. The thirty photographs were arranged in one series so that the even numbers belonged to Test A and the odd numbers to Test B.

THIRD OCCASION

Test B after pleasure-invoking situation (control). This experiment was performed at 12:30 P.M., Sunday, after the children had returned from hitching behind a sleigh. In this way each test (A and B) was performed twice—after a fear-invoking situation and after a pleasure-invoking situation (control). We shall speak of the two trials of Test A together as Experiment A, and the two trials of Test B together as Experiment B.

On all three occasions each of the subjects—five girls, eleven years of age (designated as Mary, Jane, Lou, Jill, and Nan)—was seated at the same place, separate from the others, in a well-lighted room. The experiments were conducted as group tests, the photographs being passed around from subject to subject in order.

For the first experiment instructions were as follows:

"I shall show you a series of fifteen photographs of persons whom you do not know. Some are nice, some are bad, and some are just average. I want you to guess from the photographs how good or how bad they are."

At this point each S was given a sheet of paper on which were ruled fifteen lines divided into three columns. The instructions were continued as follows:

"On the sheet of paper which I have given you there are three columns. In the first column each line is numbered from one to fifteen. These stand for the numbers of the photographs. When you are presented with a photograph—each photograph is numbered from one to fifteen—please look at the face and immediately decide how good or how bad is the character of the person. It has been found that you are more likely to be right if you are guided by your first impression than if you try to reason it out. The mark or rating for goodness or badness which you give the person should be placed in the second column opposite the number of the photograph. The scale for marking runs from one to nine as follows: 1 = extremely good, i.e., generous, kind, loving and tender; 2 = very good; 3 = good; 4 = fairly good; 5 = average; 6 = fairly bad; 7 = bad; 8 = very bad; 9 = extremely bad, i.e., cruel, malicious, and wicked. Remember now: 5 is average, 9 is extremely bad and 1 is extremely good.

"In the third column there is space for you to write down what you think the person in the photograph is thinking or saying. You should spend about thirty seconds on each photograph, but I shall allow you more time if necessary."

After these directions were read and explained, two sample photographs not belonging to the series—one of a man smiling and one of a man scowling—were shown to the children and they were asked to announce their ratings so that all could hear. This, so that the experimenter could be certain that the directions were understood.

On the second occasion, that is, after the fear-invoking situation, the instructions did not have to be repeated. It was pointed out, however, that there were now thirty instead of fifteen faces to be diagnosed.

For those who are not acquainted with the game of *murder* it may be said that it is played after dark throughout a house with all lights extinguished. The players commence by drawing lots from a hat; one of the players, unknown to the others, drawing the lot of murderer. After the draw, the players, with the exception of the one amongst them who has drawn the lot of detective, sneak about the house in the dark until the murderer "kills"—by touching—any one of the players whom he chooses. The victim, after counting ten, yells aloud, and then all the players join the detective, who proceeds by cross-questionings to discover the culprit. Everyone must tell the truth except the murderer, and he may lie as much as he likes.

Among children there are individual differences in sentiment towards this game. Some children love it and play it without disquietude; others wish to play but experience an unpleasant apprehension throughout; still others are afraid to play and avoid it if possible.

RESULTS

At the cross-examination after the "murder" one of the subjects, Mary, said that she was "frightened to death" and again: "I was so scared I hid under the table the whole time." Lou also admitted that she was afraid. No other remarks of a like nature were volunteered, and it was our general impression that the amount of occasioned excitement was less than usual.

That the two games of *murder*, however, were effective in arousing some degree of fear was attested not only by the results of the experiments, but also by an event which occurred in the early morning of the next day—that is, on Sunday. This event bears reporting since it helps to confirm the validity of the tests. It happened in this way. Jane, who had been sleeping in one of the spare rooms with Lou, woke the household at six-thirty in the morning to inform us that for more than an hour two burglars had been prowling about her room. She was in tears and shaking with fright while she explained that it was not a dream but a fact. She had seen the two men clearly with her eyes open; they had taken things from the closet and from the bureaus and had escaped finally by way of the window. She had heard the dogs chase them down the lane, and if we came to the window, she assured us, we would see their tracks in the snow. A careful examination of the premises, however, proved that no one had been about and that nothing had been stolen. Evidently Jane had had a vision, a hypnapompic vision—because, as she explained, it was real and nothing like a dream—due to a perceptive projection. Never before had she had such a vision, so it is probable that the *murder* game was the exciting agent which aroused the imagery. This was more of an effect than we had anticipated. Jane insisted despite the protestations of her companions that the event had really occurred; in fact, it seemed very important to her—as if, let

us say, her sanity depended upon it—that she should be believed. None of her friends, however, gave credence to her story during the day. It was not until nightfall that Mary and Lou—but not Jill and Nan—were inclined to believe her. Belief for Mary and Lou seemed to depend upon the uneasiness aroused by darkness. The outcome of the matter was that Jane, Mary, and Lou announced that they would not sleep in the ill-fated room "for anything" and, even when given another room, they insisted that we should look for burglars in the closet and under the bed, draw the shades down to the sill, speak in a low voice so that the burglars —supposedly sneaking about the house— should not hear, put a night-light in the room and visit them at intervals throughout the night to make sure that everything was all right. Jill and Nan, however, consented to occupy the spare room where the burglars had been seen and without any ado dropped off to sleep. This difference in attitude between Mary, Jane, and Lou, on the one hand, and Jill and Nan, on the other, should be borne in mind when the test results are examined.

Now let us turn our attention to the experiments. To discover whether fear affected the subjects' judgments of personality we should compare the results obtained after *murder* in each of the two tests (A and B) with those obtained after normal conditions. In making this comparison we should bear in mind that, according to the adopted method of scoring, an increase in the rating of a photograph signified an increase in the apparent badness (maliciousness) of a face, and a decrease in the rating signified an increase in the apparent goodness (benevolence) of a face.

The results were as follows: In Test

TABLE 1

S's	EXPERIMENT A			EXPERIMENT B			BOTH EXPERIMENTS
	Average rating per photograph		Difference in rating	Average rating per photograph		Difference in rating	Difference in rating
	Control	After fear		After fear	Control		
			b—a			d—e	$\frac{c+f}{2}$
	a	b	c	d	e	f	g
Mary	4.53	5.73	+1.20	6.47	5.40	+1.07	+1.15
Jane	6.53	7.47	+0.94	7.80	7.00	+0.80	+0.87
Lou	5.67	6.07	+0.40	6.07	5.13	+0.94	+0.67
Jill	5.60	5.93	+0.33	5.33	5.53	—0.20	+0.06
Nan	6.33	6.13	—0.20	6.67	7.27	—0.60	—0.40
Average	5.73	6.26	+0.53	6.47	6.07	+0.40	+0.47

A, as compared with the scores obtained after ordinary conditions, the average ratings after the fear-invoking situation remained the same in 1 photograph, were lower (indicating more "goodness") in 2 photographs, and were higher (indicating more "badness") in 12 photographs. In Test B, as compared with the results obtained after ordinary conditions, the average ratings after the fear-invoking event remained the same in 2 photographs, were lower (indicating more "goodness") in 3 photographs, and were higher (indicating more "badness") in 10 photographs. The slightly less significant results in Test B, as compared with Test A, might be explained by supposing that Jane's recital of her burglar vision aroused in her friends (by suggestion) subjective states which were somewhat similar to those which followed *murder*, and so nullified to some extent the significance as a control of the Sunday test trial. If the results of the two experiments (A and B) are taken together, it appears that out of a total of 30 photographs 22 (73%) were scored higher—that is, the character of

the faces in these photographs were judged to be more malicious—after the fear-invoking event than after normal pleasure-invoking events; or, to state it otherwise, it appears that out of 27 photographs, the average ratings of which were different under the two conditions, 22 (81%) were scored higher after fear.

The results might have been more striking if the experimenter had not made the mistake of including several photographs of persons whose faces were so distinctly forbidding that some subjects assigned to them the maximum mark of 9 on the control test, thereby making a further increase of rating after fear impossible. Out of a total of 150 [15 (photographs) × 5 (subjects) × 2 (tests)] ratings assigned after ordinary conditions, there were 19 ratings of 9 which did not change when conditions changed. Of the 131 remaining ratings, 96 (73%) were different after the fear-invoking situation; and of the 96 ratings which were different, 67 (70%) were higher (indicating more badness).

An examination of the tabulated results reveals the fact that for the five subjects there was an average change per photograph of $+0.53$ in Experiment A, and of $+0.40$ in Experiment B; the average of the two tests being $+0.465$, or approximately one-half a point towards badness per photograph. In other words, after the fear-invoking situation one-half the faces were judged, on an average, to be one point less good (more wicked) than they were judged after ordinary conditions. There are, of course, other methods of scoring the subjects, but, since intercorrelations between the results obtained by a variety of methods indicated that the present system of scoring was the best, the other methods have not been included in this report.

These results seem to show that complementary apperceptive projection did occur in the subjects, or, to state the matter more specifically, that fear tended to increase the apparent maliciousness of other personalities.

Examining Table 1 from the point of view of individual differences it may be observed that of the five subjects, one (Nan) in Experiment A and two (Nan and Jill) in Experiment B had lower scores after the fear-invoking event; whereas four subjects in Experiment A and three in Experiment B had higher scores after this exent. If the two experiments are taken together it appears that one subject (Jill) showed relatively little change in her ratings, whereas the four other subjects did change. Of the four who did change, three, or 75% of them (Mary, Jane, and Lou) judged faces as more malicious after *murder* than after ordinary conditions.

As a part of the test the children had been asked to write down what they thought the person in each photograph was saying or thinking. We guessed that fear might make the supposed thoughts more frightening and melodramatic, but there were few differences between the thoughts written under ordinary conditions and those written under exceptional conditions. What changes did occur, however, were for the most part in the positive direction. For instance, in Jane's paper after ordinary conditions a woman said: "What shall I do next?" and after *murder* she said: "So all your children are sick. Well I hope they die"; and after ordinary conditions a man said: "I'll do it if I like," and after *murder* he said: "You brute, you fool, you hypocrite!"; and after ordinary conditions a man said: "Yeah, I understand" and after *murder* he said: "So you *got* them, did you?" ...

THEORETICAL CONSIDERATIONS

To explain the positive results obtained in these experiments it seems that we should take account of at least three processes: (1) the activation of fear by the game of *murder*; (2) the perseveration of this emotion; and (3) the projection of integrated elements into the material to be diagnosed.

All of these processes must have occurred, it seems, in the three subjects who gave consistently positive results (Mary, Jane, and Lou). The two who gave negative results (Jill and Nan) may not have been aroused to anxiety by the game; or, if they were so activated, the emotion may have dissipated itself before the test was given; or, finally, they may have been experiencing some anxiety during the test but the emotion did not affect their judgments of personality.

That the positive results depended to a large extent upon the evocation of fear is suggested by the fact that the only subjects (Mary and Lou) who spoke of being afraid during the *murder* game were both in the positive group. The third member of the positive group (Jane) happened to be the "victim" in the first game of *murder* and the "murderer" in the second, circumstances which militate against the admission of fear even if the subject is experiencing it.

We must suppose that perseveration and projection were both present to account for Jane's vision of burglars ten hours later. That Mary and Lou were subjects who gave credence—but only after nightfall—to the substantiality of Jane's vision is a fact which fits in with the other positive responses given by these two children. It demonstrates, moreover, the determining effect of emotion and of projection in the genesis of belief.

It is difficult to give a satisfactory account of the psychological processes revealed by our findings without reference to a theory of motivation. But since the theory which we believe best describes the functional aspect of human nature has not yet found its way into the literature, and hence cannot be referred to by name, and since space does not allow for an outline of it at this time, we shall omit mention of the particular need (instinct) or combination of reflexes aroused in our subjects. In lieu of this, we shall refer all the bodily affections which occurred in our subjects to the emotion of fear, since its existence in children after playing *murder* is easy to establish by means of subjective reports as well as by the observation of its usual objective correlates.

In accordance with our introductory speculations and hypotheses we should attempt to explain the results of this investigation by saying that the bodily processes operative in the subjective experience

known as fear were aroused by the game of *murder;* that these in turn mobilized the integrated images and categories (the more general imaginal meanings). We have in mind such categories as "dangerous situations," "criminals and burglars," "malicious characters," and so forth. Then, when the test was presented to the children, the photographs which fulfilled the requirements of sufficient similitude functioned as foci for the projection of these images and categories, a photograph, for instance, being assimilated to the category "very bad" instead of to the category "bad" in which it seemed to fit best when the subject was without emotion.

It was as if the subjects, experiencing an emotion without adequate stimulus, sought something in the external world to justify it—as if the idea had come to mind: "there must be malicious people about." The result of this was that the photographs appeared to change in the direction of adequacy as stimuli. It is clear that we have here a typical complementary apperceptive projection....

Now, from the standpoint of an interest in the individual differences of personality, we should like to know whether the two groups distinguished by this test —namely, the susceptible class (Mary, Jane, and Lou) with an average change per photograph of +.90 points, and the non-susceptible class (Jill and Nan) with an average change per photograph of —.17 points—are characterized by personality differences which are more or less permanent. In other words, would these two groups show approximately the same difference in their responses to other comparable tests or to the same test at a later time or to somewhat similar circumstances in everyday life? We cannot, of course, give a positive answer to this question, but the following facts suggest that the tests did reveal some more or less consistent personality traits:

1. The coefficient of correlation (product-moment method) between Experiment A and Experiment B was $+.84$.

2. The hostess of the week-end party who knew the children intimately, when the nature of the experiment was explained to her, guessed that Mary and Jane would score the highest. This prophecy was correct.

3. Jane's hypnapompic vision was a manifestation of the same process which was responsible for her high score on the test. Jane had never before experienced such a vision, but in the past few months had had several nightmares in which burglars figured prominently.

4. Mary and Lou came to believe in the truth of Jane's story about the burglars but Jill and Nan did not.

Thus the behavior of the children during the week-end, the estimations of their temperaments by the hostess, and the results on both tests showed a considerable degree of correlation.

There is no generally accepted concept of type or trait to describe the response of the positive group as differentiated from the negative group. Psychologists have written of emotionality and of subjectivity, but, since these words have been used without precision, it is impossible to say whether our group of projectors should be subsumed under one or both of these headings. By definition there is no projection without affection or emotion, but there is no evidence to show that projection invariably parallels intensity of emotion. Other factors—such as conglomeration and the partial dissociation of the personality itself—seem to be important. *Conglomeration* is a name given to the psychical condition—as found in children —in which little or no differentiation is made between images and objects, between what is internal and psychical and what is external and substantial.

SUMMARY

Five girls, eleven years of age, estimated from photographs the degree of goodness (benevolence) or badness (maliciousness) of other personalities. These estimates were made under two different conditions: (*a*) after ordinary pleasurable activity in the sunshine, and (*b*) after two games of *murder* in the dark. A comparison of the ratings assigned under these two conditions revealed the following:

1. Seventy-three per cent of the faces were estimated by a majority of the group as more malicious when judged after the fear-invoking situation than when judged after ordinary conditions.

2. Of the four subjects whose ratings differed under the two conditions, three (75%) estimated the series of faces as more malicious after the fear-invoking situation than after ordinary conditions.

These results may be attributed to complementary apperceptive projection subsequent to the activation of an emotional state. The conclusion which may be drawn from this experiment is that under some conditions the emotion of fear will cause some experiencing subjects to increase their estimates of the maliciousness of other personalities.

REFERENCES

1. KÖHLER, W.   Gestalt psychology. New York: Liveright, 1929. Pp. x+ 403. London: Bell, 1930. Pp. 312.

2. PRINCE, M.   An experimental study

of the mechanism of hallucinations. *Brit. J. Med. Psychol.*, 1922,
2, 165–208.
3. STOUT, G. F. Analytic psychology.
London: Swann, Sonnenschein;

New York: Macmillan, 1896. Pp.
314. (5th ed., 1928).
4. WHITEHEAD, A. N. Symbolism: its
meaning and effect. New York:
Macmillan, 1927. Pp. x+88.

REINFORCEMENT AND EXTINCTION AS FACTORS IN SIZE ESTIMATION [1]

WILLIAM W. LAMBERT
RICHARD L. SOLOMON
PETER D. WATSON

I. INTRODUCTION

IN RECENT EXPERIMENTS on the psychology of perceiving, there has been a
noticeable tendency to emphasize determinants which might be classed as motivational in character. The work of
Sanford (6, 7) involving the relationship
between drive states and 'autistic perceiving,' and the extension of this work by
Murphy and his collaborators (3, 5, 8),
and by McClelland and Atkinson (4),
illustrate this trend. More closely related
to the present problem is the work of

[1] This research was facilitated by the Labora-
tory of Social Relations, Harvard University.
The authors wish to thank Miss Winifred Lydon,
Director of the Harvard Veteran's Nursery
School, and Major Gertrude Atkinson, of the
Salvation Army Nursery School, Boston, for
their indispensable help and cooperation in car-
rying out this study.

Reprinted by permission from *Journal of Experimental Psychology*, 1949, 39, 637–641.

Bruner, Postman, and their collaborators
(1, 2) dealing with the 'selection' and
'accentuation' of perceived objects relative to the 'value systems' of an individual.
Two of their experiments in particular illustrate the operation of the conceptualized value dimension. Bruner and Postman (2) found that circles of the same
diameter, embossed with (1) a high-val-
ued social symbol, and (2) a low-valued
social symbol, were judged to be larger
than circles embossed with (3) a neutral
symbol. This might indicate that 'perceptual accentuation' is a U-shaped function of a value dimension varying from
—1 to + 1, with a minimum of accentuation at 'neutrality.' Bruner and Goodman
(1) have shown that poor children tend to
overestimate the size of coins more than
rich children do. These experimenters
stated: "The reasonable assumption was
made that poor children have a greater

subjective need for money than rich ones."
(1, p. 39) They further asserted that "the greater the value of the coin, the greater is the deviation of *apparent* size from *actual* size." (1, p. 38)

The multitude of influences correlated with being rich or poor makes it difficult to analyze the specific determinants of size overestimation. It was thought that some light could be shed on this problem by experimentally controlling the life history of children with respect to an initially neutral object. Specifically, we wished to associate a relatively neutral poker chip [2] with candy reward and later extinguish this association by removal of reward and to measure the effects of such procedures on the estimated size of the poker chip. Our hypothesis was that 'value,' as defined by changes in apparent size, is a function of both reinforcement and extinction procedures.

II. SUBJECTS AND PROCEDURE

In the first study, 32 children from the Harvard Nursery School (ages three to five) were divided into 22 experimental subjects and 10 control subjects. In the second study, 22 children of comparable age from a Salvation Army Nursery School provided 15 experimental subjects and 7 control subjects.

The experimental subjects were individually introduced to a token-reward situation where they turned a crank 18 turns in order to receive a white poker chip which, when put into a slot, led to the automatic delivery of a piece of candy. The control subjects were introduced into the same situation, but candy came directly after work, *without* the mediation of a poker chip. In the first study, both groups worked (and were rewarded) once a day for 10 days; in the second study, the subjects worked (and

[2] Only one of our children knew what a poker chip was. It was called a circle in our experiment.

were rewarded) *five* times a day for 10 days.

Size estimates of the white poker chip token were made by the subjects (1) prior to the experiment; (2) after 10 days of reward; (3) after extinction had occurred (11th day); and (4) after reward had been reinstated (12th day).

Measurements were taken with the equipment designed and used by Bruner and Goodman (1). This equipment was composed of a rectangular wooden box (9 $\times$ 9 $\times$ 18 in.) with a 5-in. square ground-glass screen in the center of the front panel, and a control knob at the lower right-hand corner. At the center of the ground-glass screen the subject was presented with a circular patch of light (16.2 app. ft. cdls.) the diameter of which was under the control of the knob. The light source was a 60-watt incandescent light shining through an iris diaphragm which could be varied (in terms of the visible light patch) from ⅛ to 2 in. As Bruner and Goodman reported: "The circle was not truly round, containing the familiar nine-elliptoid sides found in the Bausch and Lomb iris diaphragm. It was so close, however, that subjects had no difficulty making the subjective equations required of them." (1, p. 37)

The subjects stood in front of the apparatus with the light patch at or slightly below eye level, and about 12 to 18 in. away. The token, pasted on a 5-in. square gray cardboard, was held by the experimenters so that it was parallel to the circular patch. About 7 in. separated the centers of the two objects to be compared.

The judgment problem was presented to the children of both groups as a game. Each child made his estimates alone. Two judgments starting from the open and two starting from the closed position of the iris were obtained from each child at each measurement session; these judgments were made in an order which was counter-balanced for direction of turning of the control knob. The children were not informed of their success in approximating the actual size of the poker chip.

On the 11th day—after 10 days of rewarded trials—extinction was instituted. The children of both groups worked, but no candy was forthcoming. They worked until they met the arbitrary criterion of extinction: three min. during which they did not turn the handle of the work machine. The size estimates were made immediately after the subject had met the extinction criterion.

On the 12th day the subjects were reintroduced to the reward sequence, and the work brought candy to the control group and token plus candy to the experimental group. Size estimates were made immediately after this 12th session.

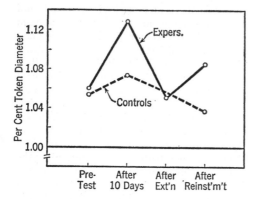

Figure 1. Effects of the experimental conditions upon children's estimates of the diameter of a token when these estimates are taken as percents of the true diameter.

III. RESULTS

The results for both nursery schools were combined and they are shown graphically in Fig 1. The four size estimation sessions are distributed on the x-axis; the mean estimate of the token size in terms of percent of actual size is shown on the y-axis. The actual size is indicated by the horizontal line parallel to the x-axis. The means for the experimental group are connected by the solid lines, and the means for the control group are connected by the dotted lines. The connecting lines are meant to increase legibility; they do not imply a continuous function of any sort.

It would appear that the control group showed no significant changes with experience. The experimental group, however, showed a rise in the apparent size of the token after ten days of using the token to obtain reward. The estimates dropped to the level of the beginning estimates following the extinction procedure in which the token no longer led to candy reward. The estimates went back in the direction of over-estimation when reward was reinstated on the 12th day.

The mean size estimates in arbitrary units of the comparison-stimulus diameter are given in Table 1, together with the corresponding percent of the actual token diameter, for each of the four points in our experiment. The results for our two studies are combined, since there were no appreciable differences between the 10-reinforcement and the 50-reinforcement experiments.

Analyses of variance [3] were per-

TABLE 1 · THE ALTERATION OF SIZE ESTIMATION WITH EXPERIENCE IN THE EXPERIMENTAL SITUATION

EXPERIMENTAL GROUP		
Mean estimated size *	σ_m	Percent actual size
Pretest	66.8	1.2	1.06
After 10 days	70.9	1.1	1.13
After extinction	66.3	1.3	1.05
After reinstatement	68.5	1.8	1.09
CONTROL GROUP		
Mean estimated size *	σ_m	Percent actual size
Pretest	66.4	1.5	1.05
After 10 days	67.7	1.2	1.07
After extinction	66.6	1.2	1.06
After reinstatement	65.4	1.4	1.04

* Actual size of poker chip is 63.0 in arbitrary units of diameter. The error of measurement of diameter by experimenter is ±0.2 units.

[3] These analyses are uncorrected for the correlation between successive sets of estimates. They are thus conservative.

formed on the data which are summarized in Table 1. The following differences are of interest: (1) In the experimental group, the estimated size of the token after 10 days of reinforcement was significantly greater than at the pretest. This difference is reliable at the one percent level of confidence. (2) In the experimental group, the size estimates after extinction were significantly smaller than they were after the 10 days of reinforcement. This difference is reliable at the one percent level of confidence. (3) In the experimental group the rise in estimated size following reinstatement of reward is significant at the one percent level of confidence. (4) In the control group, none of the four mean estimates is significantly different from any other. (5) The mean estimates for the experimental and control groups after ten days of reinforcement are significantly different from one another with a reliability between the one and five percent levels of confidence. (6) The mean estimates for the experimental and control groups after reinstatement of reward are not significantly different from one another even though a marked trend seems evident.

IV. DISCUSSION

Several alternative theoretical interpretations for our results could be made. Since experiments are in progress to study further the factors involved, these possibilities will merely be listed at this time. These views are not mutually exclusive, but overlap, as do so many formulations in this field.

1. The estimation changes in the experimental group may be compatible with a generalized pattern of behavior which we could call the 'cookie effect.' That is, the effect may be peculiar to our culture where, for example, a 'bigger cookie is *better* than a little one.' 'Bigness' and 'value,' or 'bigness' and 'goodness,' may be acquired equivalencies for our children, particularly at the ages of the subjects used here. Experiments have been planned which may provide evidence on whether this phenomenon is 'culture bound' or not.

2. These results may provide a measure reflecting some of the secondary reinforcing characteristics taken on by the token during the reinforced trials. These characteristics become lost when reinforcement is not maintained, as during extinction, but are restored when reward is reinstated. This formulation, if further bulwarked with evidence, could serve to integrate perceptual distortion phenomena with learning theory and possibly provide a valuable indirect measure of secondary reinforcement.

3. It is possible that the size enhancement phenomenon can provide us with inferences about perceptual processes as envisioned by Bruner and his collaborators (1, 2). They hypothesize: "The greater the social value of an object, the more will it be susceptible to organization by behavioral determinants." (1, p. 36) In its learning aspects, however, overestimation of size may reflect either 'expectancy' or 'hypothesis' formation (and decay) or it may, as stated above, reflect learned 'needs' which operate in the workings of this conceptualized perceptual process. The actual mechanism which produces overestimation following reinforcement is, however, entirely obscure at the present stage of our research.

In view of the fact that relatively

'neutral' poker chips were used in the experiment, our data cannot be legitimately compared with the coin size data of Bruner and Goodman (*1*). In addition, our two nursery school groups do not fulfill the criteria of distinct economic class differences. In no sense can we call one group 'rich children,' and the other group 'poor children.'

It is interesting to note the possibility that effects such as those discussed here depend on a 'difficult' or 'ambiguous' judgment situation. Probably, the more ambiguous the stimulus situation, the more strongly can reinforcement and motivational factors operate in determining size judgments.

4. It is interesting to note that, following extinction procedures, the estimates of the experimental group do not increase above the original level, when the chip was 'neutral.' This could mean that the U-shaped function postulated to relate accentuation and value does not apply here. Or it could mean that extinction removes positive value without producing negative value. Perhaps extinction by punishment is necessary for producing negativity and an increase in size estimates at the negative end of the U-shaped function.

V. SUMMARY

We have described the results of an experiment which was designed to investigate the effects of reinforcement and extinction on size estimation. It was found that the establishment of a token reward sequence results in relative overestimation of the token size. Extinction of the sequence removes this overestimation tendency to a great extent. The results are thought to have relevance for both learning and perception theory.

REFERENCES

1. BRUNER, J. S., & GOODMAN, C. C. Value and need as organizing factors in perception. *J. abnorm. soc. Psychol.*, 1947, *42*, 33–44.
2. BRUNER, J. S., & POSTMAN, L. Symbolic value as an organizing factor in perception. *J. soc. Psychol.*, 1948, *27*, 203–208.
3. LEVINE, R., CHEIN, I., & MURPHY, G. The relation of the intensity of a need to the amount of perceptual distortion: a preliminary report. *J. Psychol.*, 1942, *13*, 283–293.
4. McCLELLAND, D. C., & ATKINSON, J. W. The projective expression of needs: I. The effect of different intensities of hunger drive on perception. *J. Psychol.*, 1948, *25*, 205–222.
5. PROSHANSKY, H., & MURPHY, G. The effects of reward and punishment on perception. *J. Psychol.*, 1942, *13*, 295–305.
6. SANFORD, R. N. The effect of abstinence from food upon imaginal processes; a preliminary experiment. *J. Psychol.*, 1936, *2*, 129–236.
7. SANFORD, R. N. The effect of abstinence from food upon imaginal processes; a further experiment. *J. Psychol.*, 1937, *3*, 145–159.
8. SHAFER, R., & MURPHY, G. The role of autism in a visual figure-ground relationship. *J. exp. Psychol.*, 1943, *32*, 335–343.

CLASSICAL, RESPONDENT CONDITIONING | 6

PERHAPS THE MOST RUDIMENTARY FORM of associative learning, the classical conditioning process was made famous by Pavlov. Some of the earliest studies utilizing classical conditioning techniques were, in fact, conducted by Russian investigators. The procedure is quite simple, involving the paired presentation of two stimuli for a number of trials. One of these stimuli is called the conditioning stimulus (CS), since it is to this stimulus that a response is to be learned. The other stimulus is called the unconditioned stimulus (UCS), for it is effective at the outset (that is, without training) in eliciting a response. The neutral stimulus, CS, is presented just before the UCS, the two stimuli usually overlapping temporally. For example, a tone (CS) immediately precedes the presentation of an airpuff (UCS) directed to the eyelid. In the beginning, the tone can be demonstrated to result in no eyeblink responses, and the blink occurs to the UCS only. After several paired presentations of the tone and puff, the tone itself can be demonstrated to elicit the eyeblink even in the absence of the airpuff. When this can be demonstrated, classical conditioning is said to have occurred, for the subject is presumed to have acquired a new response to the previously neutral tone CS. One might say that the subject behaves, after conditioning, as if the CS *were* the UCS, or as though the CS were a signal for the imminent onset of the UCS.

Pavlov observed in his dogs salivation to the sight of food-trays prior to the presentation of the food itself. Many examples of analogous conditioning in children could be cited. Infants can be noted, for example, to wince at the sight of a closing refrigerator door just before it slams. Young children can often be seen to become active in their cribs upon hearing footsteps in the hallway, presumably in anticipation of impending greetings and possibly dinner. Children (and some adults) flee from large dogs even before the dog has jumped on them.

There are two major types of classical conditioning, appetitional and aversive. They differ principally in the nature of the UCS on the basis of which the learning takes place. Classical appetitional conditioning is based on a UCS that is in some way "satisfying" while classical aversive conditioning is based on a USC that is in some way "aggravating." Conditioning to food, as reported in the Marquis selection and in the Kantrow (1937) study, is an example of the former, while conditioning to a fear stimulus (the Watson and Rayner

197

selection) or a shock (the Wickens and Wickens selection) are examples of the latter.

Interest in the conditioning of children has come largely from curiosity about the earliest age at which this form of learning is possible in the human species. For the Russian investigators (see Kasatkin and Levikova, 1935), interest centered on conditioning in children through their concern with the morphology of the brain and its developing functions. It was their presumption that the physiological immaturity of the central nervous system in the newborn was such as to preclude the evidencing of conditioning behavior. The influences of Freud and of Watson have also been remarkable, as both of these writers suggested the great importance of early experience in the determination of adult behavior. Thus, most of the studies of children's classical conditioning have been done within the first year or so of life, and relatively little has been done with older children. The three selections included here pertain to the conditioning of infants.

It is regrettable that more research has not been done on the classical conditioning process of children. One reason for this is the aforementioned concern of most investigators with the earliest age at which learning may take place. These studies, then, have tended to concentrate on the developmental aspects of infant conditioning rather than the parameters (such as CS–UCS interval, intertrial interval, intensity of the stimuli, or motivational level of the subject) of which classical conditioning seems to be a function. This has led to the unfortunate consequence, for instance, in a study by Morgan and Morgan (1944), of concluding, on the basis of one relatively crude procedure, that conditioning is impossible before a certain age. These authors concluded that infants could not develop a conditioned eyeblink response much before fifty-four days of age without attempting to develop more refined techniques for control of stimuli and measurement of response. It is likely that the development of a conditioned response, and the speed of its development, is dependent upon a number of interacting properties of the response and the stimulus situation, and only parametric work at various ages will reveal the intricacies of the process.

The Watson and Rayner selection was a successful attempt to produce in an eleven-month-old child a conditioned fear or aversive response to previously neutral stimuli. They were able to demonstrate acquisition of fear, generalization of fear to other stimuli similar to the conditioning stimulus, and finally extinction of the aversive reaction. The Marquis study, on the other hand, constitutes one of the earliest investigations of classical appetitional learning in demonstrating the manner in which neutral stimuli paired with reinforcing stimulation, such as the act of eating (and sucking), may come themselves to produce behavior similar to that involved in eating (and sucking).

Most of the earlier studies of conditioning in the child have involved some ambiguity due to the lack of adequate controls for other processes that could possibly produce increases in response to a neutral stimulus. It is essential in all such studies to guard against the possibility that the increased responding to the CS is a maturational phenomenon whereby the CS may itself become a more and more effective stimulus with increasing age. Similarly, it is possible that the mere administration of effective stimuli (such as an aversive UCS) tends to lower the organism's theshold to any other stimulation presented; such a sensitization process would be quite different from the associative-learning process presumed to underlie the classical conditioning phenomenon. The Wickens and Wickens study is a well-developed set of procedures designed to guard against the erroneous conclusion of classical conditioning in its actual absence.

REFERENCES

MORGAN, J. J. B. and MORGAN, S. S.   Infant learning as a developmental index. *J. genet. Psychol.*, 1944, *65*, 281–289.

KANTROW, R. W.   An investigation of conditioned feeding responses and concomitant adaptive behavior in young infants. *Univ. Iowa Stud. Child Welf.*, 1937, *13*, No. 3.

KASATKIN, N. I. and LEVIKOVA, A. M.   On the development of early conditioned reflexes and differentiations of auditory stimuli in infants. *J. exp. Psychol.*, 1935, *18*, 1–19.

CONDITIONED EMOTIONAL REACTIONS

JOHN B. WATSON
ROSALIE RAYNER

IN RECENT LITERATURE various speculations have been entered into concerning the possibility of conditioning various types of emotional response, but direct experimental evidence in support of such a view has been lacking. If the theory advanced by Watson and Morgan [1] to the effect that in infancy the orginal emotional reaction patterns are few, consisting so far as observed of fear, rage and love, then there must be some simple method by means of which the range of stimuli which can call out these emotions

[1] Emotional Reactions and Psychological Experimentation, *American Journal of Psychology*, April, 1917, Vol. 28, pp. 163–174.

and their compounds is greatly increased. Otherwise, complexity in adult response could not be accounted for. These authors without adequate experimental evidence advanced the view that this range was increased by means of conditioned reflex factors. It was suggested there that the early home life of the child furnishes a laboratory situation for establishing conditioned emotional responses. The present authors have recently put the whole matter to an experimental test.

Experimental work has been done so far on only one child, Albert B. This infant was reared almost from birth in a hospital environment; his mother was a wet nurse in the Harriet Lane Home for Invalid Children. Albert's life was normal: he was healthy from birth and one of the best developed youngsters ever brought to the hospital, weighing twenty-one pounds at nine months of age. He was on the whole stolid and unemotional. His stability was one of the principal reasons for using him as a subject in this test. We felt that we could do him relatively little harm by carrying out such experiments as those outlined below.

At approximately nine months of age we ran him through the emotional tests that have become a part of our regular routine in determining whether fear reactions can be called out by other stimuli than sharp noises and the sudden removal of support. Tests of this type have been described by the senior author in another place [2] in brief, the infant was confronted suddenly and for the first time successively with a white rat, a rabbit, a dog, a monkey, with masks with and without hair, cotton wool, burning newspapers, etc. A permanent record of Albert's reactions to these objects and situations has been preserved in a motion picture study. Manipulation was the most usual reaction called out. *At no time did this infant ever show fear in any situation.* These experimental records were confirmed by the casual observations of the mother and hospital attendants. No one had ever seen him in a state of fear and rage. The infant practically never cried.

Up to approximately nine months of age we had not tested him with loud sounds. The test to determine whether a fear reaction could be called out by a loud sound was made when he was eight months, twenty-six days of age. The sound was that made by striking a hammer upon a suspended steel bar four feet in length and three-fourths of an inch in diameter. The laboratory notes are as follows:

One of the two experimenters caused the child to turn its head and fixate her moving hand; the other, stationed back of the child, struck the steel bar a sharp blow. The child started violently, his breathing was checked and the arms were raised in a characteristic manner. On the second stimulation the same thing occurred, and in addition the lips began to pucker and tremble. On the third stimulation the child broke into a sudden crying fit. This is the first time an emotional situation in the laboratory has produced any fear or even crying in Albert.

We had expected just these results on account of our work with other infants brought up under similar conditions. It is worth while to call attention to the fact that removal of support (dropping and jerking the blanket upon which the infant was lying) was tried exhaustively upon this infant on the same occasion. It

_____
2 *Psychology from the Standpoint of a Behaviorist*, p. 202.

was not effective in producing the fear response. This stimulus is effective in younger children. At what age such stimuli lose their potency in producing fear is not known. Nor is it known whether less placid children ever lose their fear of them. This probably depends upon the training the child gets. It is well known that children eagerly run to be tossed into the air and caught. On the other hand it is equally well known that in the adult fear responses are called out quite clearly by the sudden removal of support, if the individual is walking across a bridge, walking out upon a beam, etc. There is a wide field of study here which is aside from our present point.

The sound stimulus, thus, at nine months of age, gives us the means of testing several important factors. I. Can we condition fear of an animal, e.g., a white rat, by visually presenting it and simultaneously striking a steel bar? II. If such a conditioned emotional response can be established, will there be a transfer to other animals or other objects? III. What is the effect of time upon such conditioned emotional responses? IV. If after a reasonable period such emotional responses have not died out, what laboratory methods can be devised for their removal?

I. The establishment of conditioned emotional responses. At first there was considerable hesitation upon our part in making the attempt to set up fear reactions experimentally. A certain responsibility attaches to such a procedure. We decided finally to make the attempt, comforting ourselves by the reflection that such attachments would arise anyway as soon as the child left the sheltered environment of the nursery for the rough and tumble of the home. We did not begin

this work until Albert was eleven months, three days of age. Before attempting to set up a conditioned response we, as before, put him through all of the regular emotional tests. *Not the slightest sign of a fear response was obtained in any situation.*

The steps taken to condition emotional responses are shown in our laboratory notes.

11 MONTHS 3 DAYS

1. White rat suddenly taken from the basket and presented to Albert. He began to reach for rat with left hand. Just as his hand touched the animal the bar was struck immediately behind his head. The infant jumped violently and fell forward, burying his face in the mattress. He did not cry, however.

2. Just as the right hand touched the rat the bar was again struck. Again the infant jumped violently, fell forward and began to whimper.

In order not to disturb the child too seriously no further tests were given for one week.

11 MONTH 10 DAYS

1. Rat presented suddenly without sound. There was steady fixation but no tendency at first to reach for it. The rat was then placed nearer, whereupon tentative reaching movements began with the right hand. When the rat nosed the infant's left hand, the hand was immediately withdrawn. He started to reach for the head of the animal with the forefinger of the left hand, but withdrew it suddenly before contact. It is thus seen that the two joint stimulations given the previous week

were not without effect. He was tested with his blocks immediately afterwards to see if they shared in the process of conditioning. He began immediately to pick them up, dropping them, pounding them, etc. In the remainder of the tests the blocks were given frequently to quiet him and to test his general emotional state. They were always removed from sight when the process of conditioning was under way.

2. Joint stimulation with rat and sound. Started, then fell over immediately to right side. No crying.

3. Joint stimulation. Fell to right side and rested upon hands, with head turned away from rat. No crying.

4. Joint stimulation. Same reaction.

5. Rat suddenly presented alone. Puckered face, whimpered and withdrew body sharply to the left.

6. Joint stimulation. Fell over immediately to right side and began to whimper.

7. Joint stimulation. Started violently and cried, but did not fall over.

8. Rat alone. *The instant the rat was shown the baby began to cry. Almost instantly he turned sharply to the left, fell over on left side, raised himself on all fours and began to crawl away so rapidly that he was caught with difficulty before reaching the edge of the table.*

This was as convincing a case of a completely conditioned fear response as could have been theoretically pictured. In all seven joint stimulations were given to bring about the complete reaction. It is not unlikely had the sound been of greater intensity or of a more complex clang character that the number of joint stimulations might have been materially reduced. Experiments designed to define the nature of the sounds that will serve best as emotional stimuli are under way.

II. When a conditioned emotional response has been established for one object, is there a transfer? Five days later Albert was again brought back into the laboratory and tested as follows:

11 MONTHS 15 DAYS

1. Tested first with blocks. He reached readily for them, playing with them as usual. This shows that there has been no general transfer to the room, table, blocks, etc.

2. Rat alone. Whimpered immediately, withdrew right hand and turned head and trunk away.

3. Blocks again offered. Played readily with them, smiling and gurgling.

4. Rat alone. Leaned over to the left side as far away from the rat as possible, then fell over, getting up on all fours and scurrying away as rapidly as possible.

5. Blocks again offered. Reached immediately for them, smiling and laughing as before.

The above preliminary test shows that the conditioned response to the rat had carried over completely for the five days in which no tests were given. The question as to whether or not there is a transfer was next taken up.

6. Rabbit alone. The rabbit was suddenly placed on the mattress in front of him. The reaction was pronounced. Negative responses began at once. He leaned as far away from the animal as possible, whimpered, then burst into tears. When the rabbit was placed in contact with him he buried his face in the mattress, then got up on all fours and crawled away, crying as he went. This was a most convincing test.

7. The blocks were next given him,

after an interval. He played with them as before. It was observed by four people that he played far more energetically with them than ever before. The blocks were raised high over his head and slammed down with a great deal of force.

8. Dog alone. The dog did not produce as violent a reaction as the rabbit. The moment fixation occurred the child shrank back and as the animal came nearer he attempted to get on all fours but did not cry at first. As soon as the dog passed out of his range of vision he became quiet. The dog was then made to approach the infant's head (he was lying down at the moment). Albert straightened up immediately, fell over to the opposite side and turned his head away. He then began to cry.

9. The blocks were again presented. He began immediately to play with them.

10. Fur coat (seal). Withdrew immediately to the left side and began to fret. Coat put close to him on the left side, he turned immediately, began to cry and tried to crawl away on all fours.

11. Cotton wool. The wool was presented in a paper package. At the end the cotton was not covered by the paper. It was placed first on his feet. He kicked it away but did not touch it with his hands. When his hand was laid on the wool he immediately withdrew it but did not show the shock that the animals or fur coat produced in him. He then began to play with the paper, avoiding contact with the wool itself. He finally, under the impulse of the manipulative instinct, lost some of his negativism to the wool.

12. Just in play W. put his head down to see if Albert would play with his hair. Albert was completely negative. Two other observers did the same thing. He began immediately to play with their hair. W. then brought the Santa Claus mask and presented it to Albert. He was again pronouncedly negative.

11 MONTHS 20 DAYS

1. Blocks alone. Played with them as usual.

2. Rat alone. Withdrawal of the whole body, bending over to left side, no crying. Fixation and following with eyes. The response was much less marked than on first presentation the previous week. It was thought best to freshen up the reaction by another joint stimulation.

3. Just as the rat was placed on his hand the rod was struck. Reaction violent.

4. Rat alone. Fell over at once to left side. Reaction practically as strong as on former occasion but no crying.

5. Rat alone. Fell over to left side, got up on all fours and started to crawl away. On this occasion there was no crying, but strange to say, as he started away he began to gurgle and coo, even while leaning far over to the left side to avoid the rat.

6. Rabbit alone. Leaned over to left side as far as possible. Did not fall over. Began to whimper but reaction not so violent as on former occasions.

7. Blocks again offered. He reached for them immediately and began to play.

All of the tests so far discussed were carried out upon a table supplied with a mattress, located in a small, well-lighted dark-room. We wished to test next whether conditioned fear responses so set up would appear if the situation were markedly altered. We thought it best before making this test to freshen the reaction both to the rabbit and to the dog by showing them at the moment the steel bar was struck. It will be recalled that this was the first time any effort had been made to directly condition response to the dog and rabbit. The experimental notes are as follows:

8. The rabbit at first was given alone. The reaction was exactly as given in test (6) above. When the rabbit was left on Albert's knees for a long time he began tentatively to reach out and manipulate its fur with forefingers. While doing this the steel rod was struck. A violent fear reaction resulted.

9. Rabbit alone. Reaction wholly similar to that on trial (6) above.

10. Rabbit alone. Started immediately to whimper, holding hands far up, but did not cry. Conflicting tendency to manipulate very evident.

11. Dog alone. Began to whimper, shaking head from side to side, holding hands as far away from the animal as possible.

12. Dog and sound. The rod was struck just as the animal touched him. A violent negative reaction appeared. He began to whimper, turned to one side, fell over and started to get up on all fours.

13. Blocks. Played with them immediately and readily.

On this same day and immediately after the above experiment Albert was taken into the large well-lighted lecture room belonging to the laboratory. He was placed on a table in the center of the room immediately under the skylight. Four people were present. The situation was thus very different from that which obtained in the small dark room.

1. Rat alone. No sudden fear reaction appeared at first. The hands, however, were held up and away from the animal. No positive manipulatory reactions appeared.

2. Rabbit alone. Fear reaction

slight. Turned to left and kept face away from the animal but the reaction was never pronounced.

3. Dog alone. Turned away but did not fall over. Cried. Hands moved as far away from the animal as possible. Whimpered as long as the dog was present.

4. Rat alone. Slight negative reaction.

5. Rat and sound. It was thought best to freshen the reaction to the rat. The sound was given just as the rat was presented. Albert jumped violently but did not cry.

6. Rat alone. At first he did not show any negative reaction. When rat was placed nearer he began to show negative reaction by drawing back his body, raising his hands, whimpering, etc.

7. Blocks. Played with them immediately.

8. Rat alone. Pronounced withdrawal of body and whimpering.

9. Blocks. Placed with them as before.

10. Rabbit alone. Pronounced reaction. Whimpered with arms held high, fell over backward and had to be caught.

11. Dog alone. At first the dog did not produce the pronounced reaction. The hands were held high over the head, breathing was checked, but there was no crying. Just at this moment the dog, which had not barked before, barked three times loudly when only about six inches from the baby's face. Albert immediately fell over and broke into a wail that continued until the dog was removed. The sudden barking of the hitherto quiet dog produced a marked fear response in the adult observers!

From the above results it would seem that emotional transfers do take place. Furthermore it would seem that the number of transfers resulting from an experimentally produced conditioned emotional reaction may be very large. In our observations we had no means of testing the complete number of transfers which may have resulted.

III. The effect of time upon conditioned emotional responses. We have already shown that the conditioned emotional response will continue for a period of one week. It was desired to make the time test longer. In view of the imminence of Albert's departure from the hospital we could not make the interval longer than one month. Accordingly no further emotional experimentation was entered into for thirty-one days after the above test. During the month, however, Albert was brought weekly to the laboratory for tests upon right and left-handedness, imitation, general development, etc. No emotional tests whatever were given and during the whole month his regular nursery routine was maintained in the Harriet Lane Home. The notes on the test given at the end of this period are as follows:

1 YEAR 21 DAYS

1. Santa Claus mask. Withdrawal, gurgling, then slapped at it without touching. When his hand was forced to touch it, he whimpered and cried. His hand was forced to touch it two more times. He whimpered and cried on both tests. He finally cried at the mere visual stimulus of the mask.

2. Fur coat. Wrinkled his nose and withdrew both hands, drew back his whole body and began to whimper as the coat was put nearer. Again there was the strife between withdrawal and the tendency to manipulate. Reached tentatively with left hand but drew back before contact had been made. In moving his body to one side his hand accidentally touched the coat. He began to cry at once, nodding his head in a very peculiar manner (this reaction was an entirely new one). Both hands were withdrawn as far as possible from the coat. The coat was then laid on his lap and he continued nodding his head and whimpering, withdrawing his body as far as possible, pushing the while at the coat with his feet but never touching it with his hands.

3. Fur coat. The coat was taken out of his sight and presented again at the end of a minute. He began immediately to fret, withdrawing his body and nodding his head as before.

4. Blocks. He began to play with them as usual.

5. The rat. He allowed the rat to crawl towards him without withdrawing. He sat very still and fixated it intently. Rat then touched his hand. Albert withdrew it immediately, then leaned back as far as possible but did not cry. When the rat was placed on his arm he withdrew his body and began to fret, nodding his head. The rat was then allowed to crawl against his chest. He first began to fret and then covered his eyes with both hands.

6. Blocks. Reaction normal.

7. The rabbit. The animal was placed directly in front of him. It was very quiet. Albert showed no avoiding reactions at first. After a few seconds he puckered up his face, began to nod his head and to look intently at the experimenter. He next began to push the rabbit away with his feet, withdrawing his body at the same time. Then as the rabbit came nearer he began pulling his feet away, nodding his head, and wailing "da da." After about a minute he reached out

tentatively and slowly and touched the rabbit's ear with his right hand, finally manipulating it. The rabbit was again placed in his lap. Again he began to fret and withdrew his hands. He reached out tentatively with his left hand and touched the animal, shuddered and withdrew the whole body. The experimenter then took hold of his left hand and laid it on the rabbit's back. Albert immediately withdrew his hand and began to suck his thumb. Again the rabbit was laid in his lap. He began to cry, covering his face with both hands.

8. Dog. The dog was very active. Albert fixated it intensely for a few seconds, sitting very still. He began to cry but did not fall over backwards as on his last contact with the dog. When the dog was pushed closer to him he at first sat motionless, then began to cry, putting both hands over his face.

These experiments would seem to show conclusively that directly conditioned emotional responses as well as those conditioned by transfer persist, although with a certain loss in the intensity of the reaction, for a longer period than one month. Our view is that they persist and modify personality throughout life. It should be recalled again that Albert was of an extremely phlegmatic type. Had he been emotionally unstable probably both the directly conditioned response and those transferred would have persisted throughout the month unchanged in form.

IV. "Detachment" or removal of conditioned emotional responses. Unfortunately Albert was taken from the hospital the day the above tests were made. Hence the opportunity of building up an experimental technique by means of which we could remove the conditioned emo-

tional responses was denied us. Our own view, expressed above, which is possibly not very well grounded, is that these responses in the home environment are likely to persist indefinitely, unless an accidental method for removing them is hit upon. The importance of establishing some method must be apparent to all. Had the opportunity been at hand we should have tried out several methods, some of which we may mention. (1) Constantly confronting the child with those stimuli which called out the responses in the hopes that habituation would come in corresponding to "fatigue" of reflex when differential reactions are to be set up. (2) By trying to "recondition" by showing objects calling out fear responses (visual) and simultaneously stimulating the erogenous zones (tactual). We should try first the lips, then the nipples and as a final resort the sex organs. (3) By trying to "recondition" by feeding the subject candy or other food just as the animal is shown. This method calls for the food control of the subject. (4) By building up "constructive" activities around the object by imitation and by putting the hand through the motions of manipulation. At this age imitation of overt motor activity is strong, as our present but unpublished experimentation has shown.

INCIDENTAL OBSERVATIONS

(a) Thumb sucking as a compensatory device for blocking fear and noxious stimuli. During the course of these experiments, especially in the final test, it was noticed that whenever Albert was on the verge of tears or emotionally upset generally he would continually thrust his thumb into his mouth. The moment the hand reached the mouth he became impervious to the stimuli producing fear. Again and again while the motion pictures were being made at the end of the thirty-day rest period, we had to remove the thumb from his mouth before the conditioned response could be obtained. This method of blocking noxious and emotional stimuli (fear and rage) through erogenous stimulation seems to presist from birth onward. Very often in our experiments upon the work adders with infants under ten days of age the same reaction appeared. When at work upon the adders both of the infants arms are under slight restraint. Often rage appears. They begin to cry, thrashing their arms and legs about. If the finger gets into the mouth crying ceases at once. The organism thus apparently from birth, when under the influence of love stimuli is blocked to all others.[3] This resort to sex stimulation when under the influence of noxious and emotional situations, or when the individual is restless and idle, persists throughout adolescent and adult life. Albert, at any rate, did not resort to thumb sucking except in the presence of such stimuli. Thumb sucking could immediately be checked by offering him his blocks. These invariably called out active manipulation instincts. It is worth while here to call attention to the fact that Freud's conception of the stimulation of erogenous zones as being the expression of an original "pleasure" seeking principle may be turned about and possibly better described

as a compensatory (and often conditioned) device for the blockage of noxious and fear and rage producing stimuli.

(b) Equal primacy of fear, love and possibly rage. While in general the results of our experiment offer no particular points of conflict with Freudian concepts, one fact out of harmony with them should be emphasized. According to proper Freudians sex (or in our terminology, love) is the principal emotion in which conditioned responses arise which later limit and distort personality. We wish to take sharp issue with this view on the basis of the experimental evidence we have gathered. Fear is as primal a factor as love in influencing personality. Fear does not gather its potency in any derived manner from love. It belongs to the original and inherited nature of man. Probably the same may be true of rage although at present we are not so sure of this.

The Freudians twenty years from now, unless their hypotheses change, when they come to analyze Albert's fear of a seal skin coat—assuming that he comes to analysis at that age—will probably tease from him the recital of a dream which upon their analysis will show that Albert at three years of age attempted to play with the pubic hair of the mother and was scolded violently for it. (We are by no means denying that this might in some other case condition it.) If the analyst has sufficiently prepared Albert to accept such a dream when found as an explanation of his avoiding tendencies, and if the analyst has the authority and personality to put it over, Albert may be fully convinced that the dream was a true revealer of the factors which brought about the fear.

It is probable that many of the

---

[3] The stimulus to love in infants according to our view is stroking of the skin, lips, nipples and sex organs, patting and rocking, picking up, etc. Patting and rocking (when not conditioned) are probably equivalent to actual stimulation of the sex organs. In adults of course, as every lover knows, vision, audition and olfaction soon become conditioned by joint stimulation with contact and kinæsthetic stimuli.

phobias in psychopathology are true conditioned emotional reactions either of the direct or the transferred type. One may possibly have to believe that such persistence of early conditioned responses will be found only in persons who are constitutionally inferior. Our argument is meant to be constructive. Emotional disturbances in adults cannot be traced back to sex alone. They must be retraced along at least three collateral lines—to conditioned and transferred responses set up in infancy and early youth in all three of the fundamental human emotions.

CAN CONDITIONED RESPONSES

BE ESTABLISHED

IN THE NEWBORN INFANT? [1]

DOROTHY POSTLE MARQUIS

THE PROBLEM

THE PRESENT PROBLEM was undertaken to investigate the contention made by the Pavlovian school of Russian psychologists and physiologists that the formation of conditioned responses in newborn infants is impossible because the cerebral cortex of the human infant functions only very incompletely the first few months after birth.

Most neurologists agree that the cerebral cortex of the newborn infant functions very imperfectly, if at all. Various investigators (Pavlov, Krasnogorski, Bechterew, and Lang and Olmsted) have failed to establish conditioned responses in infants under five months of age and in decerebrate animals, and have attributed their failure to the incomplete functioning of the cortex of their subjects. Pavlov (8) asserts that no new nervous connections can be formed except in the cerebral hemispheres.

One very important issue, however, seems to have been overlooked by these investigators. It is evident that when the cerebral cortex has reached functional maturity, it is the "dominant part" or the "pace setter" of the central nervous system (Child, 3). On the other hand, is it not logical to assume that before the cortex has reached its full development, the lower centers (thalamus, midbrain, medulla, etc.) serve even more important

[1] The present paper is a brief summary of a dissertation for the doctor's degree, "Habit Formation in the Newborn Infant," a detailed account of which is available at the Graduate School of Ohio State University. The experiment was performed under the direction of Dr. A. P. Weiss.

Reprinted by permission from *Journal of Genetic Psychology*, 1931, *39*, 479–492.

functions than they do at a later time when the inhibitory action of the cortex dominates them? It is a well-established neurological fact that in the human infant at birth, the midbrain, which in the adult is a highly important correlation center for the reflexes of sight, hearing, and touch, is completely myelinated and apparently fully functional. Tracts to and from the red nucleus of the midbrain are also completely developed at birth. In the medulla oblongata there are present at birth important relay centers which regulate sucking, respiration, digestion, and secretion. Moreover, the thalamus, which in adults acts as a relatively complex correlation center for all impulses coming into the cortex, has at the time of birth reached a fairly high degree of functional maturity. Can we assume that the cortex possesses some mysterious function or power qualitatively different from any other part of the nervous system, so that it is only by means of *its* function that a response to one stimulus is replaced by a surrogate response? This seems improbable, since it is largely in the *amount* of its correlating tissue that the cortex differs from the other parts of the nervous system.

If the last conclusion is sound, then it should be possible to set up conditioned responses in the newborn human infant by means of the subcortical correlation centers, whose functions are the more complete before the inhibitory influence of the cortex has developed, *provided* we select reactions which are relatively well integrated at this stage of biological development. For our experimental work, in accordance with the principles above, as the unconditioned response the feeding reactions of the infant (sucking, mouth-opening, and quieting, etc.) to a food

stimulus (milk from the nursing bottle) were chosen. The conditioned stimulus was the sound of a buzzer. In these stimuli there are represented an auditory and a tactual-and-gustatory stimulus, and probably secretory and kinaesthetic stimuli, all of whose impulses possess subcortical correlation centers. The specific experimental problem was to ascertain whether, after a sufficient number of pairings of buzzer and bottle, the buzzer alone would lead to feeding reactions.

METHOD

Ten subjects were used in this experiment, all newborn children of clinical maternity patients at the Ohio State University Hospital. Three Negro infants were used, two girls and one boy, and seven white infants, four girls and three boys. The plan of the experiment was never to permit the infants, from the first time they were fed, to feed without the bottle being immediately preceded or accompanied by the sound of the buzzer. The infants are fed six times each day. Instead of being taken to the mothers for nursing, the subjects of this experiment were brought one at a time into the experimental room and were fed from the bottle, milk which had been pumped from their own mothers' breasts. The period of experimentation extended from the first time the infants were fed (24 hours after birth) to the tenth day of life.

The specific experimental procedure after the infants were brought into the experimental room was as follows:

1. The infant was placed on a stabilimeter [2] in a small compartment, the temperature and lighting of which were

---

[2] For details of the experimental cabinet refer to (*10*).

kept fairly constant, and remained there with no experimental stimulation for a period varying from one to five minutes (control period).

2. At the end of this time the experimenter stepped inside the curtain of the compartment, carefully noted and recorded the infant's reactions for a few seconds, then rang the buzzer for five seconds.

3. As soon as possible after the end of the buzzer, the bottle was inserted in the infant's mouth and the buzzer rung for five seconds more after the infant started sucking.

4. At various times while the infant was sucking, the buzzer was sounded for periods of five seconds.

5. During each experimental period the bottle was removed from the infant's mouth from two to five times, to prevent too quick consumption of milk. Each time the bottle was replaced in the infant's mouth, it was preceded by the buzzer in the manner described above.

Record of the infant's reactions during the experiment was kept in two ways —through the experimenter's recorded observations, and through the polygraph record. The polygraph record furnished (a) a continuous record of the infant's movements by means of registration of the stabilimeter movements; (b) a record of sucking movements by means of pneumatic recording through a balloon-type capsule fastened under the infant's chin and a Marey tambour; (c) a time record including time of stimulation and other events during the experiment; and (d) the protocols of the infant's reactions during the control period. The experimenter's protocols included a detailed record of the specific reactions made by the infant for a few seconds before each

buzzer, and the reactions after the buzzer began to sound, as well as the reactions at other times during the experimental period.

Two experiments served as control for the results. The first was a test in the control periods of the last day or last two days of each infant's experiment to see whether other stimuli would elicit reactions similar to those after the buzzer. As a visual stimulus, a flashlight was projected into the infant's eyes. As an auditory stimulus, a fall hammer striking the end of a tin can was used. As a second control experiment, four subjects of the same age as the experimental group were stimulated by the buzzer at feeding times without being permitted to feed immediately afterwards. The latter experiment was carried out throughout a nine-day period for each infant.

RESULTS

General. The following are the results of this experiment for eight infants. The results of the first two subjects of the experiment are omitted since the method of recording was not uniform with that of the others. Their reactions, in general, however, are not essentially different from those of other infants.

1. Seven of the eight infants, after a period of three to six days, began to show significant changes of reaction following the buzzer. Certain reactions began to increase, others to decrease.

2. The reactions following the buzzer on the first few days with all infants were predominantly an increase in general activity or crying, no change in general activity or crying, or an occasional decrease of general activity.

3. The reactions following the buzzer

which increased were sucking, mouth-opening, and cessation of general activity and crying. All of these reactions are directly related to foodtaking.

4. The reactions following the buzzer which decreased were general activity and crying—reactions which are not usually concomitants of the foodtaking response.

5. Reactions preceding the buzzer showed few significant changes throughout the experiment. In four instances mouth-opening preceding the buzzer increased on the seventh and eighth days of the experiments. This was interpreted as a possible indication that the whole experimental situation might be taking on the properties of conditioned stimuli.

6. Sucking without an object in the mouth very rarely occurred before the buzzer sounded.

7. The infants showed great individual differences in the onset of the change of reaction after the buzzer, in the degree of the change, and in the suddenness with which the change occurred.

8. Increase in mouth-opening and decrease in crying after the buzzer, in most infants, started on the fourth day, while increase in sucking and general activity began, in most instances, on the fifth day.

9. With one exception, the seven infants who showed an increased number of foodtaking reactions *after* the buzzer, showed least increase when they were quiet and asleep *before* the buzzer sounded.

10. One infant failed to show increase in foodtaking reactions following the buzzer. This infant's physiological condition was poor, he never seemed hungry, and was not as responsive generally to stimuli as the other infants. This infant, all through the experiment, showed either no significant change of activity when the buzzer sounded, or increase in general activity and crying.

11. In the first control experiment where the infants were stimulated during the control periods on the last or the last two days of the experiment by the flashlight and by the hammer striking the can, they never responded by any foodtaking reactions. Usually there was no change in general activity and crying or there was increased general activity and crying.

12. In the second control experiment, in which four additional infants were stimulated by the buzzer at feeding times without ever feeding immediately afterward, the infants in the majority of cases showed increase in general activity and crying after the buzzer throughout the nine day period.

RESULTS OF INDIVIDUAL INFANTS

1. *Infant Rn (white, female).* Infant Rn was the "brightest" of all the subjects. She was unusually alert to all stimuli and reached the highest percentage in number of feeding reactions after the buzzer. The changes in her reactions after the buzzer were as follows: *Sucking* reactions increased from zero on the first two days to an average of 74% frequency [3] on the seventh, eighth, and ninth days. *Mouth-opening* increased from zero on the first day to 75% on the last day. *Cessation of crying* increased from zero on the first two days to 100% on the sixth, seventh, eighth, and ninth days; and *cessation of general bodily activity* from zero on the first four days to 100% on the seventh and eighth days. *General activity* after the buzzer decreased

[3] As compared with frequency of the buzzer stimulations.

from 92% on the first day to zero on the last day, and *crying* from 46% on the first day to zero on the last four days. Instances when Rn remained *quiet and awake* after the buzzer decreased from an average of 26% on the first two days to zero on the last two days. There were no significant differences in the number of conditioned responses, whether the infant was quiet and awake, quiet and asleep, or active and awake before the buzzer sounded. In the control experiment she never responded to the light or sound by any feeding reaction.

2. *Infant Cb (white, female).* The change in the Cb infant's reactions to the buzzer proceeded in the following manner. *Sucking* increased from zero on the first four days to an average of 42% on the last two days. *Mouth-opening* after the buzzer showed a significant predominance over mouth-opening before the buzzer from the second day, and a predominance over mouth-closing after the buzzer from the fourth day on. *Cessation of crying* increased from zero on the first three days to 100% on the sixth, seventh, and eighth days. *Cessation or significant decrease of general activity* showed an increase from zero on the first three days to 100% on the last two days. *General activity* after the buzzer decreased from 62% on the first day to zero on the last two days, and crying from an average of 17% on the first three days to zero on the last three days. General activity and crying before the buzzer remained about the same throughout the experiment. When the infant was quiet and asleep before the buzzer, she seldom made "feeding responses" to the buzzer.

3. *Infant Cla (white, female).* Food-taking responses at the sound of the buzzer began in the Cla infant on the fourth day, after approximately 140 to 150 pairings of buzzer and bottle. *Sucking* after the buzzer increased from zero on the first four days to an average of 30% on the last three days. *Mouth-opening* increased from zero on the first day to 62% on the last day. *Cessation of general bodily activity* increased from zero on the first day to 100% on the last day; and *crying*, from zero on the first day to 100% from the fourth day on. *General bodily activity* decreased from 67% on the first day to zero on the last day, and *crying* from 17% on the first day to zero on the last five days. General activity before the buzzer showed no significant change throughout the experiment. Crying before the buzzer varied, but showed no consistent tendency to increase or decrease in the course of the experiment. Fewer "feeding reactions" after the buzzer occurred when the infant was quiet and asleep before the buzzer sounded. No feeding reactions occurred to the stimuli in the control experiment.

4. *Infant Car (Negro, female).* Change of reaction following the buzzer began with the Car infant on the fourth day of the experiment after 125 to 130 pairings of buzzer and bottle. *Sucking* increased from zero on first day to 53% on the last day. *Mouth-opening* increased from 20% on the first day to 35% on the sixth day, then decreased as sucking increased. *Cessation of crying* increased from an average of 17% on the second and third days to an average of 95% on the last two days; *cessation of general activity* from zero on the first four days to 100% on the last two days. Crying before the buzzer increased from zero on the first day to 53% on the last day, while general bodily activity before the buzzer increased from zero on the first day to

47% on the last day. The infant showed more feeding reactions after the buzzer when she was active and awake than when she was quiet and awake or quiet and asleep. No feeding reactions occurred to the control stimuli on the last two days of the experiment.

5. *Infant Mar (Negro, female)*. The change in the reactions to the buzzer was less pronounced in the Mar infant than in most others. The increase in reactions after the buzzer was as follows: *Sucking* increased from zero on the first four days to 41%, 24%, and 23%, respectively, on the seventh, eighth, and ninth days; *cessation of general activity* from zero on the first two days to an average of 56% on the last two days. *Mouth-opening* after the buzzer showed an increase over mouth-opening before the buzzer from the fifth day, with one exception on the seventh day. *General activity* after the buzzer showed a slight decrease from an average of 26% on the first three days to 19% for the last three days, while general activity before the buzzer increased on the last three days. *Crying* after the buzzer decreased from 17% on the first day to zero on the last three days. The instances when the infant remained quiet and awake after the buzzer decreased significantly from the fifth day. Highest frequency of feeding reactions after the buzzer occurred when the infant was active and awake before the buzzer. No feeding reactions occurred to the control stimuli on the last day of the experiment.

6. *Infant Lld (Negro, male)*. With the Lld infant the change of reactions following the buzzer occurred in the following fashion: *Sucking* increased irregularly from zero on the first three days to 32% on the fourth day, 73% on the sixth day, and an average of 40% on the last

three days. *Mouth-opening* increased irregularly from 11% on the first day to 46% on the last day. *Cessation of general activity* increased from zero on the first two days to 50% on the third and fourth days and 100% on the next three days. On the last two days it decreased to an average of 76%. General activity before the buzzer increased from an average of 35% on the first three days to 63% on the last three days, while general activity after the buzzer showed a corresponding decrease from 34% to 14%. *Crying* before the buzzer remained about the same throughout the experiment; crying after the buzzer decreased from 22% on the first day to zero on the second day, never increasing to more than 6% on any day thereafter. The percentage of feeding reactions after the buzzer was highest when the infant was active and awake before the buzzer. In the control experiment the Lld infant responded three times (once to the light and once to the sound) in 24 stimulations, by slight quieting of general activity and crying.

7. *Infant Mont (white, male)*. The changes in the Mont infant's responses to the buzzer occurred in the following manner. Sucking never attained a very high percentage of frequency. However, it increased from zero on the first two days to 6% on the third day, and 33% on the seventh and ninth days. *Mouth-opening* after the buzzer was less than mouth-opening before the buzzer on the first day, equal to it on the second day, and exceeded it from the third day on. A very great increase in mouth-opening after the buzzer occurred on the fourth day when the percentage rose from 6% on the third day to 65% on the fourth. *Crying* after the buzzer exceeded crying before the buzzer on the second day. On

the third day cessation of crying reached 100%, and in almost every case after this crying stopped as soon as the buzzer sounded. *Cessation of general activity* after the buzzer showed a steady increase from 12% on the first day to 100% on the sixth day and 89%, 90%, and 82%, respectively, on the last three days. Although general activity before the buzzer showed no significant change throughout the experiment, general activity after the buzzer decreased from an average of 67% on the first two days to an average of 14% on the last two days. There was little difference in the percentage of feeding reactions after the buzzer whether the infant before the buzzer was quiet, active, or asleep. In the control experiment, the infant reacted to the sound twice out of 24 stimulations by cessation of crying.

8. *Infant Zim (white, male).* The Zim infant was an infant whose physiological condition was very poor. He showed no conditioned reactions to the buzzer. *General activity and crying* after the buzzer exceeded general activity and crying before the buzzer throughout the experiment. In only one instance did *sucking* ever occur after the buzzer. *Mouth-opening* after the buzzer slightly exceeded mouth-opening before the buzzer after the third day, but its highest frequency was only 20%, on the seventh day.

The curves of Figure 1 present graphically the composite results of the seven infants who showed conditioned foodtaking response to the buzzer.

Since the combined average of all infants, such as those shown in Figure 1, obscure individual differences, the following graphs of the results of Infants Rn and Mar are presented to show an instance of a high percentage of conditioning and an instance of a much lower percentage of conditioning.

RESULTS OF SECOND CONTROL EXPERIMENT

In the second control experiment, in which four infants were stimulated by the buzzer at feeding times without ever being permitted to feed immediately afterward, practically no "feeding reactions" ever occurred after the buzzer. Their occurrence after the buzzer was not more frequent than their occurrence before the buzzer. For every infant the most frequent reactions to the buzzer were increased general activity and increased head-movement. No significant change in the infants' reactions after the buzzer was evident on any day of the experiment. The results of this check experiment were therefore negative.

CONCLUSIONS

1. A conditioned response of food-taking reactions to the sound of a buzzer was established in seven out of eight newborn infants during the first ten days of life.

2. Since present neurological evidence indicates that the cerebral cortex of the newborn infant functions only very incompletely the first few months after birth, we may infer that *conditioned responses can be formed in newborn infants, at least, by subcortical correlation.* The type of responses included in the conditioned foodtaking reactions to the buzzer indicates that the midbrain and especially the red nucleus was important as a controlling mechanism.

3. The foodtaking response in the newborn infant includes a wide variety of reactions.

4. The results of this experiment bear out, in general, Pavlov's contention that an alert state of the subject is favorable to the formation of conditioned re-

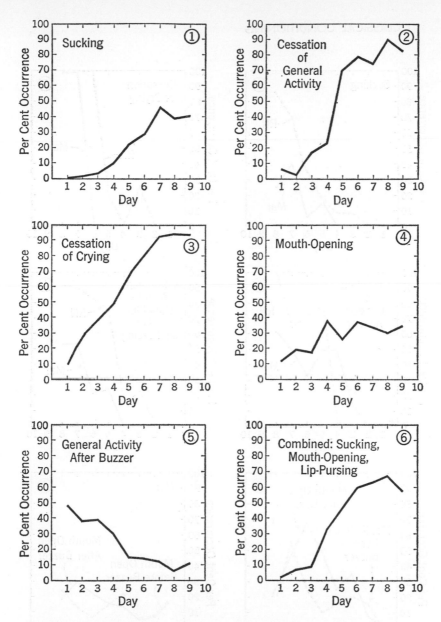

Figure 1. REACTIONS AFTER BUZZER. Composite curves of seven infants (Zim excluded). Percentage of the different conditioning indices. *Sucking* is differentiated from mouth-opening and closing by including more lip-pursing and more tongue movement. *Cessation of general activity* means a sudden cessation of kicking, squirming, etc., as soon as the buzzer sounds. *Cessation of crying* means sudden stopping of crying at the sound of the buzzer. *Mouth-Opening* (4) *and Combined: Sucking, Mouth-Opening, and Lip-Pursing* (5) include only those respective mouth-movement components which were not occurring before the buzzer sounded. Sucking, mouth-opening, and lip-pursing combined includes the percentage of times when one or any combination of these occurred at the sound of the buzzer. *Percentage Occurrence* is derived by dividing the number of times each specific reaction occurred at the sound of the buzzer by the number of pairings of bottle and buzzer on each day.

215

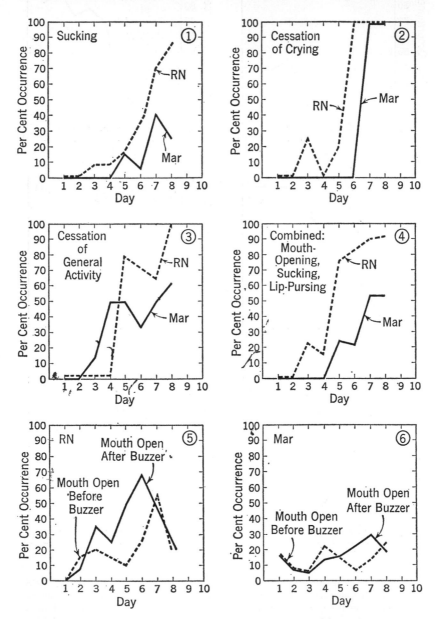

Figure 2. REACTIONS AFTER BUZZER OF INFANT'S RN AND MAR. A comparison of an instance of high percentage and one of low percentage of conditioning.

sponses, since in most cases a higher frequency of feeding reactions after the buzzer occurred when the infants were active and awake.

5. The contention that a good physiological condition of the subject is necessary to the development of conditioned responses finds support in the case of the

Zim infant, who showed no conditioning to the buzzer.

6. Individual differences in learning ability are present even at this early age.

7. Systematic training of human infants along social and hygienic lines can be started at birth.

8. Since habit formation may begin so early, the sharp lines drawn by some writers in their classifications of some acts as instinctive and some acts as learned must be viewed with some hesitation.

REFERENCES

BECHTEREW, W.   Über die Erregbarkeit der Grosshirnrinde neugeborener Thiere. *Neur. Zentralbl.*, 1895, *17*, 148 150.

BECHTEREW, W.   Objektive Psychologie oder Psychoreflexologie. Die Lehre von den Assoziationsreflexen. Leipzig: Teubner, 1913. Pp. viii + 468.

CHILD, C. M.   Physiological foundations of behavior. New York: Holt, 1924. Pp. xii + 330.

KRASNOGORSKI, N.   Über die Bedingungs-reflexe im Kindesalter. *Jahrb. f. Kinderhk.*, 1909, *69*, 1–24.

KRASNOGORSKI, N. Über die Grundmechanismen der Arbeit in der Grosshirnrinde bei Kindern. *Jahrb. f. Kinderhk.*, 1913, *78*, 373–398.

KRASNOGORSKI, N.   Die letzten Fortschritte in der Methodik der Erforschung der bedingten Reflexe an Kindern. *Jahrb. f. Kinderhk.*, 1926, *114*, 255–268.

LANG, J. M., & OLMSTED, J. M. D.   Conditioned reflexes and pathways in the spinal cord. *Amer. J. Physiol.*, 1923, *65*, 603–611.

PAVLOV, I. P. Conditioned reflexes: an investigation of the physiological activity of the cerebral cortex. (Trans. by G. V. Anrep.) London: Oxford Univ. Press, 1927. Pp. xv + 430.

PAVLOV, I. P.   Certain problems in the physiology of the cerebral hemispheres. *Proc. Roy. Soc. Lond.* (B), 1928, *103*, 97–108.

PRATT, K. C., NELSON, A. K., & SUN, K. H. The behavior of the newborn infant. *Ohio State Univ. Stud., Contrib. Psychol.*, 1930, No. 10. Pp. xiii + 237.

A STUDY OF CONDITIONING IN THE NEONATE [1]

DELOS D. WICKENS
CAROL WICKENS

PROBLEM

THE PURPOSE of the present experiment was to investigate the problem of the conditionability of a withdrawal movement in the newborn infant, and, if positive results were obtained, to study other conditioning phenomena such as experimental extinction and spontaneous recovery in these subjects. This general problem has already been attacked in similar subjects by Marquis (4), who used sucking as her unconditioned response, and by Wenger (8), who employed lid closure and the withdrawal of the leg to shock in addition to sucking as a response. Although both of these studies obtained results which the writers interpreted as positive, neither of them is entirely conclusive and both have been subjected to criticism. Pratt (5) and others (8) have suggested that Marquis has not clearly shown that the response to the conditioned stimulus which she obtained after her training series might not have occurred without this training. Further, Wenger, using a procedure similar to that of Marquis, obtained negative results for this particular response. Wenger's own study, although careful and approaching objectivity, must be criticized because of the limited number

[1] This work was done in the Infant Research Laboratory of the Ohio State University.

Reprinted by permission from *Journal of Experimental Psychology*, 1940, *26*, 94–102.

of subjects used; in many groups only two or three infants were used and one important control group consisted of but four subjects. Since there is a considerable overlapping between the results of his control and his experimental group, this limitation in the number of subjects becomes a serious criticism. A further consideration of this point will be given in discussion of our results.

Because of these objections, it was felt that an additional experiment might clarify the question as to whether or not the newborn infant can become conditioned.

SUBJECTS

Subjects were under-ten-day infants born in the Ohio State University Hospital. Throughout this experiment we are indebted to Dr. Floyd C. Dockeray, Department of Psychology, who made available to us the subjects and facilities of the Ohio State Infant Research Laboratory, and to Dr. Andrew Rogers, Head of the Obstetrics Division of the Ohio State University Hospital. Thirty-six infants in all were used in the actual experiment. These were full term babies about equally divided as to sex. Approximately one third of the subjects were of at least partial negro parentage and the remainder were of white parentage. The infants were from three to five days when they were brought in for the first experimental session, and, the study continuing for four days, the subjects were from seven to nine days of age at the last experimental period.

Apparatus and Procedure. All experimentation was done with the infants inclosed in the sound proof, thermostatic isolation cabinet, described by Dockeray and Valentine (2).

Before the formal experimentation on the 36 final subjects was begun, various sorts of stimuli were administrered to a number of other infants with a view to determining the optimal unconditioned stimulus. From these investigations it was concluded that the best type of simulus for the study of conditioning of a withdrawal movement was a shock to the sole of the foot. To this stimulus the infant usually responds bilaterally with flexor movements of legs, feet, and toes, often followed by extensor movements. This response is usually more marked in the member receiving the shock than it is in the other member. Shock then was the unconditioned stimulus. This was delivered from a Harvard inductorium, the current being derived from a 6 volt storage battery. The electrode consisted of two 4×36 bolt heads attached to the surface of a flexible rubber disc about the size of a penny. This was attached to the sole of the right foot by a strip of Sealtex tape. The conditioned stimulus was the sound of a muffled buzzer, placed in the cabinet about two feet from the infant's head. The buzzer and shock were administered by hand, with the buzzer (in the paired stimulation) preceding the shock by about a fourth of a second and continuing about a fourth of a second more, along with the shock. This hand method of giving stimulations was, of course, necessarily subject to some variability. Stimulations were spaced one, two, three, or four minutes apart according to a varied and irregular pattern. An attempt was made to stimulate the infant only when his activity level corresponded with stages three to five of Wagner's criteria of sleep (7), *i.e.*, when it was neither crying nor highly active and yet not in an extremely deep sleep. Since the babies did not always cooperate, the time intervals between the presentations of the paired stimuli occasionally ran over the

one to four minute figures mentioned above. The same infant was always run at the same time on succeeding days, the times being directly following either the two or four o'clock feeding periods. The two experimenters observed and recorded the responses of the infants, one noting the movements of one limb and one the movements of the other. The responses were recorded upon form sheets in terms of flexor and extensor movements of the leg, foot, and toes.

Three separate groups, consisting of 12 infants each, were used—an experimental group and two controls. For all three groups items of initial procedure were the same. The infant was placed in the isolation cabinet, the electrode having been attached to the sole of the right foot. It was allowed about five minutes to become adjusted to the situation; then tests for responses to the buzzer alone were administered. Three different stimulations of the sound of the buzzer were given, and, if the infant responded by any movement of leg, foot, or toe, he was discarded and not used in any of the three groups. From this point on, the procedure for the different groups varied.

The experimental group received 36 paired stimulations of buzzer and shock, 12 each day for three consecutive days. At the end of the third day, the buzzer alone was sounded to test for the presence of conditioning, and these stimulations of the buzzer were administered until there were three consecutive failures to respond—the criterion of extinction in this experiment. On the fourth day, the buzzer alone was administered until the response was extinguished. This was done, of course, to test for the spontaneous recovery of the previously extinguished conditioned response.

In view of the possibility that positive results in the above group, if present, might be due to the effect of repeated presentations of shock, the unconditioned stimulus, rather than to the pairing of the buzzer and shock, the following control group was set up, which we shall call Control Group 1. Following the usual tests to the buzzer alone, the 12 infants of this group were given 36 shocks alone, 12 each day, for three consecutive days. Thus, they never received a paired stimulation of shock and buzzer. At the end of this period, on the third and fourth days, the buzzer alone was sounded, tests for extinction and spontaneous recovery of the response, if any, being administered just as in the experimental group.

Control Group 2 was run to check the possibility that any responses to the buzzer on the third day might be due solely to the factor of maturation rather than to training. The procedure for this group consisted in testing for responses to the buzzer alone on day 1; then, on day 3, after two days delay, during which time no stimulations were given by the experimenters, administering a second test for responses to the buzzer alone.

RESULTS

The results for the experimental group are presented in Table 1. Each baby is listed separately. Day 3 is, of course, the time of the test for presence of the conditioned response, following the training series of 36 paired stimulations; day 4 was the day of tests for spontaneous recovery of the response which had been extinguished on the previous day. By number of responses is meant the number of times the infant responded to the buzzer alone by some movement of both limbs,[2] i.e., gave a conditioned response. For example, subject He gave two conditioned responses on the 3rd day and eight responses on the 4th day. It will be seen that nine of the

[2] Movement of both limbs was demanded as a criterion of the conditioned response since this bilateral movement was typical of the response to the unconditioned stimulus.

twelve infants in the experimental group gave conditioned responses to the buzzer alone on the third day. Only 11 of the 12 subjects were tested for spontaneous recovery. Of those who showed conditioning on the previous day, nine showed spontaneous recovery, and one infant, who gave no conditioned responses on the previous day, gave several such responses on the spontaneous-recovery day. In general, then, the results of the experimental group indicate that conditioning of the withdrawal response, its extinction, and the spontaneous recovery of the response on the following day, are obtainable in the under-ten-day-old infant.

The clearness of this picture is, however, clouded by the findings of the first control group, for the behavior of these subjects was practically identical with that of the experimental group, in spite of the fact that the subjects of Control Group 1 had never had a paired presentation of buzzer and shock. The results for Control Group 1 will be found in Table 2, and may be read in the same manner as Table 1. Ten out of the 12 infants responded to the buzzer, after the 36 shocks alone; all of these showed extinction, and of the ten babies who were tested on the fourth day, 8 showed spontaneous recovery. Needless to say, the slight differences between this control group and the experimental are not statistically significant. Conditioning, if you will, extinction, and spontaneous re-

TABLE 1 · Showing the Number of Responses to the Buzzer Alone for the Experimental Group on the Third and Fourth Days of the Experiment, Day 3 Being the Original Test for the Presence of Conditioning, and Day 4 Being a Test for Spontaneous Recovery

Number of responses	SUBJECTS											
	He	Ca	De	Ch	Re	Mc	Bo	Jo	Ot	Fo	Gr	Ma
Day 3	2	2	4	0	3	1	5	2	0	1	0	3
Day 4	8	9	–	0	4	10	7	1	8	1	0	0

TABLE 2 · SHOWING THE NUMBER OF RESPONSES TO THE BUZZER ALONE FOR CONTROL GROUP I ON THE THIRD AND FOURTH DAYS OF THE EXPERIMENT

Number of responses	SUBJECTS											
	Hi	Al	Ad	Pa	Ja	Th	En	Sm	Am	Kl	Fj	Wi
Day 3	2	1	0	2	3	2	5	2	3	2	2	1
Day 4	2	10	0	9	3	2	3	–	5	–	2	1

covery are just as clearly demonstrated in this group as in the previous one.

It immediately occurred to the experimenters that these results might be due to faulty mechanics in the experimental set-up. It might be possible that, although the infant was enclosed in a supposedly sound proof cabinet, he was able to react to the sound of the vibrator on the inductorium itself, and this might become a conditioned stimulus which could be easily generalized to the buzzer. That this was not true was proved by including checks brought about by activating the inductorium alone without the application of shock. In no cases were any responses made to these checks.

There still remained the possibility that the responses to the buzzer alone given on the third and fourth days were due simply to maturational factors (i.e., increase in auditory acuity) rather than to any effects of the experimental routine. As will be recalled, Control Group 2 was designed to investigate this possibility. This group simply received two tests for responses to the buzzer, separated by two days. Of course, as in the other groups, no subject was included who responded to the buzzer on the first day. Only one out of the 12 subjects used gave any response to the buzzer on the second test. Applying the Chi Square formula we find that there is a statistically significant difference between this group and the experimental group and between this group and Control Group 1.

At this point it would perhaps be in order to consider the only other study we have found which investigated conditioning of the withdrawal movement in the under-ten-day-old infant, at the same time employing a control group similar to our Control Group 1. Wenger (8), using five infants in his experimental group, concluded that the movement of withdrawal from shock in the infant could be conditioned to a tone. He ran a control of four subjects in which shock alone was given, followed by tests for responses to the tone (without any pairing of conditioned and unconditioned stimulus). This control group did give a number of responses to the buzzer alone. However, because the experimental group gave a few more such responses, Wenger concludes that there were essential differences between the two groups. An examination of his tables, however, indicates that this is not necessarily true, that there is no statistically significant difference between his experimental and control groups, and that his results are actually in accord with ours. Whatever differences there exist between the two groups may be attributed to sampling errors.

DISCUSSION

There seems, then, to be an essential similarity between our experimental group and our first control group, both of them showing evidences of 'conditioning,' extinction of the conditioned response, and spontaneous recovery, even though the situation for the control group was not a conventional conditioning situation. This similarity seems not to be due to artifacts of the experimental set-up, or to any maturational effects. There remains the problem of accounting for it. Two possible interpretations present themselves. These are highly speculative, neither proved nor disproved by the extant experimental evidence. However, they are perhaps worthy of consideration with a view to further investigation.

(1) Perhaps the continued stimulation which results in the leg movement characteristic of response to shock serves to sensitize and make this response prepotent. The muscles involved in the response are, then, in a state of readiness, and may be tripped off at almost any stimulation. Highly analogous to this in the field of infant behavior are the findings of Pratt, Nelson, and Sun (6), Jensen (3), and others, which indicate that nearly any stimulus will set off the sucking response, supposedly a prepotent response in the neonate. Possibly analogous in the field of adult conditioning is the phenomenon of sensitization (Bernstein, 1). If this interpretation of sensitization is accepted, it would seem that our infants are not showing conditioning in the ordinary meaning of the term. However, before sensitization can become a complete explanation, we must know more concerning the nature of this phenomenon. The fact that spontaneous recovery existed— that these withdrawal responses to the buzzer appeared as late as twenty-four hours after the last shock, sometimes indeed with greater frequency than in the tests immediately following shock—certainly implies that sensitization is a relatively long-lasting thing.

(2) Perhaps conditioning in the ordinary sense is operating after all, but we, as experimenters, are not clearly recognizing the nature of the conditioned stimulus. Perhaps the infant, in responding to the conditioned stimulus, is not responding to the sound of the buzzer as such, but merely to the buzzer's characteristic of being a sudden change in the environment. If we analyze the nature of the shock, we may see how the infant has become so conditioned, i.e., conditioned to respond to a sudden change in the environment. The shock has two characteristics; it is not alone a pain-giving and response-producing stimulus, but it also possesses the character of being a sudden, sharp change in the environment. That is, first there is no shock; then, suddenly, there is shock. This sudden change in the environment is the conditioned stimulus, and it is always followed by pain, the unconditioned stimulus. Thus, the organism becomes conditioned to a change in the environment, and the buzzer, which is also a change in the environment, may now act as a conditioned stimulus. If this were true, we would expect many other stimuli which are effective to the infant also to set off the conditioned response, and this, of course, could easily be attacked experimentally. The interpretation implies that the infant does not easily make discriminations between specific stimuli, and reacts instead to major changes and characteristics—a view which is also supported by the findings of Pratt, Nelson, and Sun (6).

These theoretical interpretations may be of some value in suggesting problems for future attack. In any case, our data seem to have reopened the question of conditionability of the newborn infant. The results would indicate that, without further experimentation, it cannot be stated that the withdrawal movement in the neonate can be conditioned, in the ordinary sense of that term. Modifiability, however, is clearly shown, and conditioning of some sort may be operating. The investigation points incidentally to the need for adequate controls in conditioning experiments, especially in those which use lower organisms as subjects.

SUMMARY

To investigate the problem of conditionability of the neonate, three groups, consisting of 12 under-ten-day-old infants, were studied, the conditioned stimulus being the sound of a buzzer, the unconditioned stimulus a shock to the sole of the foot.

Members of the experimental group received 12 paired stimulations a day for three consecutive days. They were then tested for conditioned responses to the buzzer alone, the responses were extinguished, and on the following day tests for spontaneous recovery were made. Members of Control Group 1 received 12 shocks alone per day for three consecutive days. Like members of the experimental group, they were tested for responses to the buzzer alone at the end of the third day and on the fourth day. Members of Control Group 2 were tested for responses to the buzzer alone on the first day; then, two days later, during which time no stimulations were given, they were again tested for responses to the buzzer alone.

Results showed that the experimental group gave evidence of conditioning, extinction, and spontaneous recovery. Control Group 1 gave almost identical results, although members of this group had never had a paired presentation of conditioned and unconditioned stimulus. Only one subject in Control Group 2 responded to the buzzer alone on the third day.

Conditionability (in the ordinary sense of the term) of the neonate, and incidentally also of the foetus, is thus not unequivocally supported. Two possible theoretical interpretations are advanced.

REFERENCES

1. BERNSTEIN, A. L., Temporal factors in the formation of conditioned eyelid reactions in human subjects, *J. gen. Psychol.*, 1934, *10*, 173–197.
2. DOCKERAY, F. C., and VALENTINE, W. L. A new isolation cabinet for infant research, *J. exper. Psychol.*, 1939, *24*, 211–214.
3. JENSEN, K., Differential reactions to taste and temperature stimuli in newborn infants, *Genet. Psychol. Monog.*, 1932, *12*, Nos. 5–6.
4. MARQUIS, D. P., Can conditioned response be established in the newborn infant? *J. genet. Psychol.*, 1931, *39*, 479–492.
5. PRATT, K. C., The neonate, (In) Murchison, Carl (editor), *A handbook of child psychology*, Second ed. rev., Worcester, Mass.: Clark Univ. Press, 1930, pp. xiii + 956 (pp. 163–208).
6. PRATT, K. C., Nelson, A. K., and Sun, K. H., *The behavior of the newborn infant*, Columbus, Ohio: Ohio State University Press, 1930, pp. xiii + 237.
7. WAGNER, I. F., The establishment of a criterion of depth of sleep in the newborn infant, *J. genet. Psychol.*, 1937, *51*, 17–59.
8. WENGER, M. A., *An investigation of conditioned responses in human infants*, University of Iowa Studies in Child Welfare. Studies in Infant Behavior III, *12*, No. 1, 9–90.

INSTRUMENTAL, OPERANT CONDITIONING | 7

IN THE PRECEDING SECTION, examples were given of classical conditioning in which a response is to be learned to the conditioning stimulus by appropriate pairing with an unconditioned stimulus. Instrumental or operant conditioning, in contrast, involves no unconditioned stimulus that automatically elicits the to-be-learned response. Instead, the experimenter attempts to arrange the stimulus conditions in such a way that the correct response will occur, along with others perhaps, and provide an opportunity for the experimenter to dispense a reward or reinforcement which will increase the probability of occurrence of that response when the subject is returned to the same stimulus situation.

Viewed in another way, instrumental conditioning is usually a simplified trial-and-error task in which the experimenter frequently tries to minimize the errors made, to reduce the complexities of the learning process under study. For example, in studies using the Skinner box and rat subjects, the experimenter is usually interested in the variables which may affect the rate or amplitude of bar-press responding or the number of trials to extinguish that response. Since the experimenter is little interested in the time it takes the animal to make the first bar-press or the alternative responses which the animal might exhibit, he makes the Skinner box relatively small, places the lever in a position convenient to the animal, and baits the lever with a tasty morsel of food to produce the initial response as quickly as possible and reduce the likelihood that other responses will occur.

Care is taken in the selection of the response to be studied, for it would be difficult to modify a response that is extremely likely to occur and wasteful of time to work with a response that is very unlikely to occur. Thus, experimenters working with pigeons put the key to be pecked on the wall rather than on the floor, since the response of pecking on the wall can be obtained under the proper stimulus circumstances while the response of pecking on the floor occurs too frequently to be easily manipulated. On the other hand, the key is placed on the wall and not on the ceiling because it would take a great deal longer to train the animal to peck the latter. Similar considerations about the response required are necessary when human subjects are used, but the problem may be facilitated by verbal instructions. In the experiments included in this section, the response recorded is either specified in the instructions given by the experimenter or will occur rapidly because the stimulus conditions are arranged to elicit that response even in the absence of instructions.

It is necessary also to clarify what is meant by "stimulus" in instrumental conditioning situations. At least two, and sometimes three, distinctions among possible meanings of the word stimulus have been made (Spence, 1956). There are the stimuli the experimenter arranges to have present such as, in the case of the Skinner box, the walls of a particular color, the floor, the lever, the food tray and delivery mechanism, lights, and sounds. All of these are what might be called potential stimuli, for they are present and responses could be made to any of them. When the animal actually makes the response that the experimenter will record, however, only a limited number of the potential stimuli available will be impinging upon the receptors of the organism. Those stimuli impinging upon the receptors at the time of the response are the actual or effective stimuli. Whether potential stimuli become effective stimuli depends upon the receptor capacities of the organism and the orienting responses made by the subject. Thus, for a human the extremely high pitched dog whistle and a visual stimulus behind the subject's back, while potential stimuli, are not effective stimuli. In the first case the human does not have the necessary receptor capacities and in the second case the proper orienting responses are not being made.

A third meaning of stimulus that is sometimes a concern of the experimenter refers to the stimuli produced by the subject himself and not always visible to the experimenter. These are intraorganic stimuli that may, for example, be associated with drive states or produced by responses of the subject. Some stimuli of this sort may be measured by recording techniques while others can only be presumed present and are hypothetical in nature. We know, for example, that rats can learn to make one response when hungry and another response when thirsty although the external stimuli are exactly the same (Hull, 1933). The animals are apparently responding to internal stimuli associated with the two different states of the organism. Later in this book a great deal of emphasis is placed upon response-produced stimuli in accounting for some kinds of verbal behaviors.

The instrumental or operant conditioning paradigm establishes a relationship between some actual or effective stimuli and an instrumental response. Not, however, until the response is made and can be shown to vary with changes in the stimulus conditions, can it be assumed that the response is occurring as a function of any particular stimulus or set of stimuli. The response is labeled "instrumental" or "operant" because it brings about or sets the occasion for the reinforcement or reward.

Nearly all of the studies reported in subsequent sections of this book are experiments using instrumental procedures. The papers in this section were selected as examples of situations that have been used to demonstrate instrumental learning. They range from the simple lever-pressing task taken directly from studies of rat behavior to more complex tasks involving a variety of responses and stimuli.

The first two studies use the lever-pressing response and demonstrate the influence of reinforcement on maintaining a response during extinction. In the Siegel and Foshee experiment an increase in the number of reinforcements leads to an increase in the number of trials to extinguish the response. Bijou's study indicates that not only the number of reinforcements but also the distribution of reinforcements is important. If the ratio of reinforcement to response is less than one-to-one, it takes longer to extinguish the response. The schedules may be ratio, variable ratio, interval, or variable interval (Skinner, 1938), but in each case the number of trials to extinction tends to be greater than if the same number of reinforcements is given on a 100 per cent schedule.

The third study indicates that the operant procedure is feasible with very young children. The social responsiveness or vocalizations of three-month-old infants is shown to be modifiable by appropriate reinforcement. By making reinforcement contingent upon vocalization of the infant and subsequently withholding the reinforcement, the infant's social behaviors are shown to increase and decrease respectively. In the fourth study social behavior of a cooperative nature in older children is increased and decreased by similar reinforcement procedures. In this case, the children learn to work together to obtain a reinforcement that in turn is divided between them. It is of interest to note that when the two children cooperate in obtaining the reinforcement, continued cooperation is dependent upon continued reinforcement of both children in the form of an equal division of the candy obtained.

The last study involves an extension of the operant conditioning situation to an even more complex task using three response alternatives, each of which has a different reinforcement schedule. The choice of response among three alternative responses available to the subjects tended to be distributed in the same proportion as the pay off or reinforcement ratio.

REFERENCES

HULL, C. L.   Differential habituation to internal stimuli in the albino rat. *J. eomp. Psychol.*, 1933, *16*, 255–273.

SKINNER, B. F.   *The behavior of organisms.* New York: Appleton, 1938

SPENCE, K. W.   *Behavior theory and conditioning.* New Haven: Yale University Press, 1956.

THE LAW OF PRIMARY REINFORCEMENT

IN CHILDREN [1]

PAUL S. SIEGEL
JAMES G. FOSHEE

IN PROTEST of strict "rat psychology," Hilgard has advanced a serious argument for more naturalistic observation and the utilization of the human subject in learning research (1). He feels that principles coming from the animal laboratory should be validated at a human level. Similar considerations have inspired several recent experiments. For example, Hubbard (2) has investigated secondary reinforcement in the human subject and Saltzman (5) has studied the effect of delayed reward. The findings of of both are in accord with the results of infrahuman studies.

The present experiment was designed to examine the principle of primary reinforcement utilizing the human subject. Stated briefly, this principle maintains that the strength of a habit is positively related to the number of times it has been rewarded or accompanied by need or drive reduction. It was elected because of its central role in reinforcement-type learning theories. The experimental findings of Perin (4) and of Williams (8) are usually adduced in its support (3). Employing the rat in a bar-pressing situation, they varied the number of reinforcements and measured subsequent resistance to extinction. The relationship was found to be a positive one. Our methodology parallels theirs with one significant variation. We employed the child as a subject.

METHOD

Apparatus. The apparatus consisted of a Masonite box, painted green, of outside dimensions, height, 20 in., depth, 10 in., and width, 6½ in. In front, at the base, was a wooden tray, 3¼ × 3¼ in. Four inches above the tray, a ¼-in. steel rod projected ¾ in. A pressure of 30 gm. resulted in an excursion of the rod through approximately 1¼ in. This served to close a mercury switch, energizing an electromagnetic release mechanism. A single pellet of candy was released from a magazine and fed by chute to the tray. An impulse counter and a remote switch were wired in series with the release mechanism. Following the fall of each pellet, *E* opened the circuit to prevent "jiggling" and thus ensure a discrete response for each reinforcement. During the extinction series, this switch remained closed. The pellets were fashioned by splitting party mints and trimming to a cylindrical shape. Each weighed approximately .2 gm. The box was either placed upon the floor or on a nursery school table. The *S* was always free to sit or stand as he chose. The *E* was seated to one side at a distance of 3 to 6 ft. depending upon the size of the experimental room.

Subjects. The ages of *S*s ranged from 2 yr., 11 mo. to 5 yr., 8 mo. The *S*s were divided into four groups, matched for age within a range of 3 mo., and balanced for sex. There were ten males and ten females in each of four groups (total = 80). The four groups received 2, 4, 8, or 16 reinforcements. In addition to the 80 *S*s constituting the experiment, 24 others were tried and

[1] This research was supported in part by a grant from the Research Committee of the University of Alabama.

Reprinted by permission from *Journal of Experimental Psychology*, 1953, *45*, 12–14.

discarded for various reasons. Nine failed to follow instructions. In 11 instances, the apparatus jammed. In 4 cases, E could not match for age.

Procedure. Experimental sessions were conducted from 9:30 A.M. to 10:30 A.M. Most of the children were reported as eating breakfast at approximately 7:30 A.M., making for a food-privation interval of 2 to 3 hr. The junior author served as E throughout the entire experiment, making for a uniform social environment. To establish rapport, E devoted a minimum of 4-hr. social interaction with each nursery school or kindergarten group from which Ss were recruited.

TABLE 1 · The Relationship between Resistance to Extinction and Number of Prior Reinforcements

No. prior reinforcements	NUMBER OF RESPONSES DURING EXTINCTION				
	Mean	SD	Median	Mean logs	SD logs
2	32.9	49.8	10.0	1.12	.59
4	41.0	34.0	29.0	1.49	.84
8	51.6	33.7	49.5	1.64	.82
16	94.9	48.9	99.5	1.91	.89

The experimental procedure was conducted as follows. The E entered the school yard and inquired of a child if he cared to see a new game. If he responded negatively, no effort was made to coax him. If he indicated acceptance, he was led to a nearby experimental room and told that he could sit or stand before the apparatus. The E then pointed to a single pellet in the tray and asked, "What is it?" If S indicated recognition, he was told that he could eat it. If no recognition was apparent, E told the child that it was candy and that he was free to eat it. Next, E pointed to the lever and inquired, "What do you think would happen if you pushed this?" If S pressed the lever, ate the candy, and pressed again, E said nothing further. If S pressed the lever and then failed to eat the candy, E said, "You may have as much as you like." No further comment was offered. The S was given a predetermined number of reinforcements, the magazine having been loaded with 2, 4, 8,

or 16 candy pellets. The extinction series was ushered in by the first failure to secure a pellet. The number of unreinforced responses made by the child in the 3 min. immediately following the last reinforced response was recorded. This is our measure of resistance to extinction.[2]

During extinction, E made no response to questions addressed him by the child. He simply maintained a "poker face."

RESULTS AND DISCUSSION

Table 1 summarizes our findings. The means, standard deviations, and medians for the four distributions of raw scores are found there. The relationship between the mean and the median suggested positive skewness, particularly in the instance of the two groups receiving few reinforcements (also true of the Perin-Williams rat data). Snedecor's g_1 test for skewness (6) was applied and significance at the .01 level was indicated. A logarithmic transformation of the data was made and found to be essentially normal. The means and SD's of the log values are also presented in Table 1.

The data of Table 1 strongly suggest a positive relationship between resistance to extinction and number of prior reinforcements. As the number of reinforcements increases, the average number of extinction responses (both means and medians) increases. The statistical significance of this trend may be evaluated in several ways. Basically, we must assess the significance of the differences obtained among groups. We have applied two tests, one to the nonnormal raw score distributions and one to the normal or logarith-

---

[2] A simple enumeration of the number of unreinforced responses occurring during a brief interval of time has been reported by Walker (7) as a reliable index of resistance to extinction in the bar pressing of the rat.

mic transformations. The first, a chi-square analysis, is found in Table 2. The median of the total distribution (combining all groups, $n = 80$) was determined and a simple count of subjects yielding scores above and below this value was noted for each group. If resistance to extinction is independent of number of reinforcements, then with only chance exception, ten cases should fall above this median and ten below within each group. The chi-square value of 14.8, corresponding to a probability value of less than .01, indicates that the hypothesis of independence is scarcely tenable. We conclude that significant differences obtain among our four groups or that resistance to extinction is genuinely dependent upon number of reinforcements. The second test, applied to the transformed distributions, consisted of calculating the regression coefficient for extinction upon reinforcement. This was found to be .0504 with a standard deviation of .00845. The t of 5.96 indicates a probability value of less than .01. Again, we conclude that the relationship is statistically significant.

TABLE 2 · CHI-SQUARE ANALYSIS FOR DIFFERENCES AMONG GROUPS

Number of rein- force- ments	Above median of total group	Below median of total group	N
2	5(10)	15(10)	20
4	7(10)	13(10)	20
8	12(10)	8(10)	20
16	16(10)	4(10)	20
	40	40	80

$x^2 = 14.8$
$p < .01$

In the Perin-Williams study, resistance to extinction was defined as the number of unreinforced responses yielded by the rat to a criterion of no responses within a 5-min. interval. Perin (4) has imposed an exponential function upon the median values with reasonably good agreement. This function could be fitted to our data. Unfortunately, with but four empirical points, many other general functions could be equally well fitted. Nothing seems to be gained by this procedure. We are satisfied to state that our results are in good general agreement with the Perin-Williams findings. It may be fairly said that with the child, we have confirmed the positive relationship between resistance to extinction and number of prior reinforcements. And, viewing our measure of extinction resistance as an index of habit strength, our results constitute a validation of the principle of primary reinforcement at the human level.

SUMMARY

Employing the child as subject in a bar-pressing situation, the principle of primary reinforcement was examined. Number of reinforcements (candy) was varied for each of four groups. The number of unreinforced responses occurring within a 3-min. interval immediately following the last reinforced response was recorded. In good agreement with infrahuman studies, it was found that resistance to extinction or habit strength is positively related to number of prior reinforcements.

REFERENCES

1. HILGARD, E. R. *Theories of learning.* New York: Appleton-Century-Crofts, 1948.

2. Hubbard, W. R. Secondary reinforcement of a simple discrimination in human beings. *J. exp. Psychol.*, 1951, *41*, 233–241.

3. Hull, C. L. *Principles of behavior.* New York: D. Appleton-Century, 1943.

4. Perin, C. T. Behavior potentiality as a joint function of the amount of training and the degree of hunger at the time of extinction. *J. exp. Psychol.*, 1942, *30*, 93–113.

5. Saltzman, I. J. Delay of reward and human verbal learning. *J. exp. Psychol.*, 1951, *41*, 437–439.

6. Snedecor, G. W. *Statistical methods.* Ames, Iowa: Collegiate Press, 1946.

7. Walker, E. L. Variability in extinction scores in Skinner-box problems. *J. comp. physiol. Psychol.*, 1948, *41*, 432–437.

8. Williams, S. B. Resistance to extinction as a function of the number of reinforcements. *J. exp. Psychol.*, 1938, *23*, 506–522.

Patterns of Reinforcement

and Resistance to Extinction

in Young Children [1]

SIDNEY W. BIJOU

Intermittant reinforcement, varying patterns of reinforcement during training, has been the concern of many experimental studies with animals since the results are said to have bearing on significant theoretical issues in behavior theory (*14*). Aside from theoretical considerations, cumulated data indicate that within limits, types of training schedule is one of the conditions covarying with resistance to extinction, i.e., the number of responses emitted during a period of nonreinforcement. More specifically, results have established, for the most part, that intermittent reinforcement (whether fixed or irregular in pattern) markedly increases resistance to extinction as compared to continuous reinforcement (*2, 10, 11*). Our interest, at this stage of laboratory research on child behavior, is to study this relationship in young children.

In discussing this and related stud-

[1] The author wishes to express deep appreciation to the Agnes Anderson Foundation and the Graduate School of the University of Washington for financial support, and to Mrs. Ruth R. Crayne for her services as research assistant.

Reprinted by permission from *Child Development*, 1957, *28*, 47–55.

ies, it may be helpful to offer at the outset some clarification of the terms most frequently employed in investigations of this sort. Our definitions are similar to Skinner's (17, 18).

1. By *continuous reinforcement* we mean that in the experimentally defined situation a response has been reinforced on each occasion of its occurrence.

2. By *intermittent reinforcement* we mean that a reinforced occurrence of a response has been preceded or succeeded on at least one occasion by an unreinforced occurrence of the response. No differentiation is made among the terms descriptive of this procedure; namely, intermittent reinforcement, partial reinforcement and periodic reconditioning.

3. By *interval intermittent reinforcement* we mean that the pattern of a reinforcement is controlled by temporal events in the external environment; and by *ratio intermittent reinforcement,* we mean that it is dependent on the subject's behavior.

4. By *fixed* and *variable patterns* of *intermittent reinforcement* we refer to the relationship between the reinforced and nonreinforced responses. Interval and ratio may, of course, be either fixed or variable in pattern.

During the past 10 years there has been a growing interest in intermittent reinforcement with children, as shown by the publication of six investigations. Five studies have approached the problem by keeping number of training trials constant and varying number of reinforcements. Three of these experiments (3, 9, 12) had training patterns on variable ratios; two (6, 7) on fixed ratios. Although there were differences in the ages of the subjects, intelligence levels, types of reinforcers, number of trials and number of

reinforcements, all but one (6) found that intermittent reinforcement procedures showed more resistance to extinction.

The other study (15) treated the problem by holding the number of reinforcements constant and varying the number of trials. Using trinkets for rewards, Pumroy gave three reinforcers under each of four conditions of training according to percentage of trials reinforced; i.e., 3 trinkets for 3 responses (100%); 3 trinkets for 6 responses (50%); 3 trinkets for 9 responses (33⅓%); and 3 trinkets for 18 responses (16⅔%). The four schedules were given in a single session with order of presentation varied on a random basis. Furthermore, the schedules were interspersed with two-minute intervals of nonreinforcement to obtain measures of resistance to extinction. Under these conditions, number of responses during extinction increased with percentage of reinforcement, and the 100% schedule showed more resistance to extinction than the 16⅔% schedule.

PROBLEM

Our objective was to study further intermittent reinforcement with reinforcements held constant using a larger number of reinforcers and observing behavior under two types of schedules given to subjects in equated groups.

The specific problem may be stated as a question: For a given number of reinforcements, is there a difference in the extinctive behavior of two groups of preschool children when the training of one group is on a continuous reinforcement pattern, and the training of the other group is on a variable intermittent schedule with reinforcement following 20 per cent of the responses?

Information bearing on this question was derived from two experiments. Experiment I was a preliminary investigation.

EXPERIMENT I

SUBJECTS

Eighteen preschool children from the Nursery School of the Institute of Child Development, University of Washington, served as subjects. The school is conducted on a three-hour day, five-days-a-week basis. There were 8 boys and 10 girls ranging in age from 39 to 60 months. They came from families with fathers classifiable in the upper three occupational groups according to the Minnesota Scale for Occupational Rating (8, 19). The percentages are as follows: I, Professional, 65.6; II, Semiprofessional and managerial, 18.7; III, Clerical, skilled trades and retail business, 15.7.

Socioeconomic status of the children's families was also estimated by the Barr Scale Rating of Occupational Status (19). The mean rating for fathers' occupations was 15.17, which is 6.29 scale points above the mean for adult males in the general population.

Although not all the subjects had been given intelligence tests, the mean IQ of the group was estimated from Stanford-Binet scores of children attending the nursery school during the past three years. On this basis the mean IQ of the subjects is estimated to be about 116.

APPARATUS

The situation designed to produce and record the essential behavior has been described in detail (1). Salient features of the apparatus consist of: (a) a response arrangement in the form of a wooden box with two holes, one above the other—the lower one to present a small rubber ball to the child and the upper one to receive it in making a response; (b) a device for delaying the return of the ball; (c) a motor-driven machine to dispense plastic trinkets; [2] (d) a clear plastic box for catching the trinkets; and (e) an ink-writing marker for recording responses and reinforcements.

PROCEDURE

The 18 children were divided into two groups matched for age and previous experience in experimental situations. The mean age for Group A_1 (those to receive continuous reinforcement training) was 49.4 months, while the mean age for Group B_1 (those to have 20 per cent intermittent reinforcement training) was 48.4 months.

Prior to participating in the experiment, each child was "prepared" in a standardized manner. First, the experimenter, a young woman wearing an attractively colored smock, makes herself known to the children by watching them at play in the school yards and rooms. After a few days the children begin to regard her as a member of the teaching staff. Second, when a child is selected to serve as subject, the "teacher" invites him to come and "play with some toys." On entering the laboratory, she suggests that he sit in front of a table upon which are a plastic dog and small tin dog house. The experimenter then demonstrates how the toy works. She puts the dog in the house and shows that tapping on the table

---

[2] Trinkets were purchased from the Viking Company, 530 Golden Gate Avenue, San Francisco 2, California.

will cause the dog to shoot out. She demonstrates also that the dog pops out when called loudly by his name, "Sparky." The child is then encouraged "to make the dog come out." Once he takes charge of the toy, play is permitted until he has made the dog come out at least four times. A delay of 15 seconds between insertion and pop-out is the criterion for termination. Third, immediately after the termination of warm-up activity, the experimenter invites him to come to another table upon which the apparatus stands. When he is settled in the chair before the apparatus, a plywood screen is raised and the experimenter proceeds with the in-

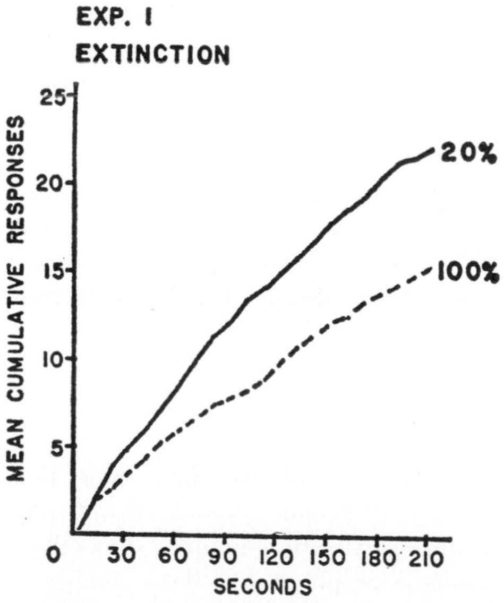

EXP. I
EXTINCTION

Figure 1. Mean cumulative responses during the three-and-a-half minute extinction period for the two groups in Experiment 1.

structions. She shows a handful of trinkets and says: "You can get some of these to keep, to take home with you." She hands the child the ball and says: "When you put the ball in there (pointing to the upper opening) some of these toys will

come down here (pointing to the covered plastic box). The ball will come out here again. You can put it back into the top hole as many times as you like. We will leave all the toys that come down in the box until we are finished, and are ready to go." The experimenter takes a seat six feet to the rear of the subject and offers no further suggestions or instructions.

Comments and questions directed to the experimenter are reacted to in a pleasant nondirective fashion, e.g., "You think the thing is broken." "You think no more will come out." When the session is over, and the receiving box is opened, the trinkets are given to the child, and he is returned to his group.

Children in Group A_1 were given six trinket reinforcements in consecutive order followed immediately by a period of three-and-a-half minutes of no reinforcement. On the other hand, those in Group B_1 were given six reinforcements distributed over 30 responses with trinkets delivered on trials 1, 6, 13, 17, 23, and 30. The apparatus was adjusted so that (a) the minimum time between responses during training and extinction was 3.3 seconds, and (b) each response during training, whether reinforced or not, was followed by a one-second motor hum from the trinket dispenser.

RESULTS

Results, in terms of the number of responses emitted during the three-and-a-half minute extinction period, are shown in Figure 1. The mean number of responses for the 20 per cent group is 22.0; the mean for the 100 per cent group is 15.3. The difference of 6.7 responses is statistically significant between the 5 and 10 per cent levels of confidence.

EXPERIMENT II

SUBJECTS

In this experiment, the subjects were 21 preschool children, 13 boys and 8 girls, from the Nursery School of the Institute of Child Development, none of whom had participated in Experiment I. They ranged in age from 32 to 55 months and like the children in the previous groups, had fathers in the upper categories of occupations. Also, it is highly probable that the mean IQ of this group was about the same—116.

APPARATUS

The apparatus was the one used in Experiment I, with one significant alteration. The trinket dispenser motor sound was *accentuated by a buzzer*. Duration of the buzzer sound was exactly the same as the motor hum in Experiment I.

PROCEDURE

The 21 children were divided into two groups. Group A_2 (continuous reinforcement training) consisted of 9 boys and 4 girls having a mean age of 44.1 months. Group B_2 (intermittent reinforcement training) had 4 boys and 4 girls with a mean age of 45.6 months. All had had a limited and equivalent amount of experience in previous experimental situations.

The preparation procedure was identical to that in Experiment I. Training and extinction procedures were similar, except that five rather than six trinkets were used as rewards. Children in Group A_2 received five consecutive trinket reinforcements while those in Group B_2 received five distributed over 25 responses in the following pattern: 1, 6, 13, 17, and 25. The buzzer sound followed each response during training whether reinforced or not.

RESULTS

Analyses of the data show that Group B_2 gave more responses than Group A_2 during extinction. Figure 2 shows these results in graphic form. Mean number of responses for Group B_2 is 26.2 and for Group A_2 is 13.0. The difference of 13.2 is statistically reliable at the 1.5 per cent level of confidence.

DISCUSSION

Findings from both studies indicate that under the experimental conditions described, for a given number of rein-

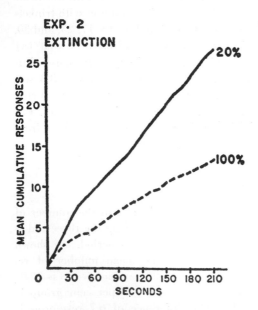

Figure 2. Mean cumulative responses during three-and-a-half minute extinction period for the two groups in Experiment 2.

forcements a variable ratio intermittent distribution is associated with more resistance to extinction than a continuous schedule. The fact that the difference in Experiment II is reliable at a higher level of confidence than that in Experiment I suggests that the increased distinctiveness of the auditory stimulus served as a stronger conditioned reinforcer.

Our results are consistent with findings from many studies with infrahuman subjects in which reinforcements are held constant, and they are similar to the results of most child studies in which a number of trials are controlled. They are in contrast to the findings of Pumroy (15) which were briefly described in the early part of this paper. Since the two studies had markedly different experimental designs, it is difficult to determine which conditions were influential in producing a reversed relationship. One aspect of Pumroy's study suggesting further analysis is the consequences of dispersing, in a single session, blocks of intermittent reinforcement with short periods of extinction. It would seem that large blocks of training might produce different results than short blocks, and that intervals between training blocks might be more influential in the earlier versus the later phases of training.

The present study provides information that should make it profitable to go on to investigate with groups of children intermittent schedules and their interrelationships. Investigators working with animals have offered some provocative leads. Their suggestions include an analysis of the definition of the response unit (13), the properties of the nonreinforced trials during training (5, 6), and the role of emotional behavior generated by the nonreinforced trials (2, 18). There is a great deal of potential material here for an experimental analysis of child behavior and development.

Even when information on intermittent reinforcement was based primarily on infrahuman subjects, writers could see possible applications to child growth and behavior. Thus Keller and Schoenfeld say:

With the facts of P-R (periodic reconditioning) in hand, you should be able to make some critical deductions about educational procedure which strive to control behavior. You should, for example, see how one would go about teaching a child to be persistent in the face of failure. One would make sure, in training for skill, for confidence at work, or for willingness to persist in social activities, that the child is guaranteed some measure of success and approval regularly at first, but later only occasionally, so that he will not give up in the face of setbacks (11, p. 101).

Perhaps the time is not too long before generalizations about the effects of adult-child interactions may be derived from laboratory studies with children.

SUMMARY

The problem for investigation is whether variable ratio intermittent reinforcement training results in more resistance to extinction than continuous reinforcement training when the number of reinforcements is held constant. Two experiments involving operant or instrumental conditioning techniques were performed with 39 preschool children. Six reinforcements (plastic trinkets) were used in the first experiment, five in the second. Intermittent training patterns consisting of reinforcements on 20 per cent of the responses were employed in both investigations. Results are in agreement with those from studies using subhuman subjects in that the intermittent reinforcement showed more resistance to extinction than the continuous reinforcement. The findings are discussed in relation to other investigations with children.

REFERENCES

1. Bijou, S. W.   A systematic approach to an experimental analysis of young children. *Child Develpm.*, 1955, *26*, 161–168.
2. Boyle, R. E.   The effects of two schedules of primary reinforcement on the potency of secondarily reinforcing cues. Unpublished doctor's dissertation, Univer. of Washington, 1955.
3. Caditz, S. B.   A study of partial reinforcement of a lever pressing response in young children. Unpublished master's thesis, Univer. of Washington, 1953.
4. Deese, J.   *The psychology of learning*. New York: McGraw-Hill, 1952.
5. Denny, M. R.   The role of secondary reinforcement in a partial reinforcement learning situation. *J. exp. Psychol.*, 1946, *36*, 373–389.
6. Fattu, N., Auble, D., & Mech, E. V.   Partial reinforcement in a bar-pressing situation with preschool children. *J. genet. Psychol.*, 1955, *87*, 251–255.
7. Fattu, N. A., Mech, E. V., & Auble, D.   Partial reinforcement related to "free" responding in extinction with preschool children. *J. exp. Educ.*, 1955, *23*, 365–368.
8. Goodenough, Florence L., & An-
derson, J. E.   *Experimental child study*. New York: Century, 1931.
9. Grosslight, J. H., & Child, I. L.   Persistence as a function of previous experience of failure followed by success. *Amer. J. Psychol.*, 1947, *60*, 378–387.
10. Jenkins, W. O., & Stanley, J. C., Jr.   Partial reinforcement: a review and critique. *Psychol. Bull.*, 1950, *47*, 193–234.
11. Keller, F. S., & Schoenfeld, W. N.   *Principles of psychology*. New York: Appleton-Century-Crofts, 1950.
12. Lasko, A. A.   A theoretical study of partial reinforcement within the framework of Rotter's social learning theory of personality. Unpublished master's thesis, Ohio State Univer., 1950.
13. Mowrer, O. H., & Jones, Helen M.   Habit strength as a function of the pattern of reinforcement. *J. exp. Psychol.*, 1945, *35*, 293–311.
14. Osgood, C. E.   *Methods and theory in experimental psychology*. New York: Oxford, 1953.
15. Pumroy, D. K.   The effects of intermittent reinforcement on resistance to extinction and emotional behavior in preschool children. Unpublished doctor's dissertation, Univer. of Washington, 1954.
16. Sheffield, Virginia F.   Extinction as a function of partial reinforcement and distribution of practice. *J. exp. Psychol.*, 1949, *39*, 511–526.
17. Skinner, B. F.   *The behavior of organisms*. New York: Appleton-Century-Crofts, 1938.
18. Skinner, B. F.   *Science and human behavior*. New York: Macmillan, 1953.

19. TERMAN, L. M. *Genetic studies of genius.* Vol. 1. Palo Alto, Calif.: Stanford Univer. Press, 1925.

20. TERMAN, L. M., & MERRILL, MAUD A. *Measuring intelligence.* Boston: Houghton Mifflin, 1937.

SOCIAL CONDITIONING OF VOCALIZATIONS IN THE INFANT

HARRIET L. RHEINGOLD
JACOB L. GEWIRTZ
HELEN W. ROSS

BY THREE MONTHS of age the infant gives a well-defined social response to the appearance of adults. He looks at them intently, smiles, becomes active, and vocalizes. This behavior is repeated again and again in sequence. Adults often respond to these acts of the infant; they may only look at the child, but they may also smile to him, touch or caress him, or vocalize in return. Frequently one observes "answering" social and, in particular, vocal play between mother and child. The adults' responses may therefore play an important part in maintaining and developing social responsiveness in the child (Rheingold, 1956). The principles of operant conditioning (Skinner, 1953) suggest that some of these adult responses, functioning as reinforcers, may affect the development of the child's social

Reprinted by permission from *Journal of Comparative and Physiological Psychology*, 1959, 52, 68–73.

behavior (Gewirtz, 1956). Thus, smiling in the infant has been shown to respond to conditioning (Brackbill, 1958).

The present study was an attempt to condition vocalizations in infants. Vocalizations were selected for study because they seem to provide an index of the whole social response (Rheingold, 1956). The reinforcing stimulus was a complex of social acts which resembled those an attentive adult might naturally make when a child vocalizes. If temporal contiguity between the infant's vocalization and the reinforcing stimulus, which follows it, brings about an increase in the vocalizations, conditioning may be said to have occurred. The possibility that the reinforcing stimulus may also have functioned as an arouser of vocalizations will be considered. In any case, the results of the study should provide further understanding about the development of social responsiveness, as well as of speech.

METHOD

Two parallel experiments were carried out in sequence. In the first, 11 babies (Ss) were studied, with one experimenter (E) and one observer-recorder (O), both women. In the second, 10 other Ss and one S from Experiment I were studied with the E and O of the first experiment exchanging roles. An experiment was composed of three successive units in each of which three or four Ss were studied at one time.

SUBJECTS

The Ss were 21 infants, all residents almost from birth in the same institution. (We are grateful to Sister Thecla and the staff of St. Ann's Infant Asylum, Washington, D.C., for their generous cooperation.) Their median age was 3.0 months; three-quarters of them were no more than three days older or younger than the median. In each experiment six Ss were male, five were female. Age was the main criterion for selection. Four possible Ss were rejected: one seemed immature, two had a very high rate of vocalizing during the first baseline measure, and one was markedly fussy.

The institution offers excellent care and, as is characteristic of institutions, there are multiple caretakers. In general, the Ss were well developed, healthy, alert, and socially responsive. The Es asked for no modifications in the usual caretaking routines. The caretakers knew that the Es were observing the development of social behavior, but they did not know the details of the experiment. The caretakers' usual behavior toward the Ss appeared not to be modified by the conditions of the experiment.

EXPERIMENTAL CONDITIONS

Baseline. In experimental Days 1 and 2 (first and second Baseline days) E leaned over the crib with her face about 15 in. above S's and looked at him with an expressionless face, while O tallied vocalizations, out of S's sight. The E moved her head as necessary to remain in S's line of vision, a condition which obtained throughout the experiments.

Conditioning. During experimental Days 3 and 4 (first and second Conditioning days), E again leaned over the crib with an expressionless face except that when S vocalized, E made an immediate response and then resumed the expressionless face until the next vocalization. The response, or *reinforcing stimulus*, consisted of three acts executed by E simultaneously, quickly, and smoothly. They were a broad smile, three "tsk" sounds, and a light touch applied to the infant's abdomen with thumb and fingers of the hand opposed. No more than a second of time was required to administer the reinforcer.

At the beginning of the conditioning periods each vocalization was reinforced. Sometimes, as the rate of vocalizing increased, only every second, and later, every third, vocalization was reinforced. In Experiment I, 72% of the reinforcers occurred after *each* vocalization; in Experiment II, 94%. Less frequent reinforcing seemed to depress the rate, at least initially, and, because of the rather severe time restrictions, was abandoned altogether by the end of the study.

Extinction. Experimental Days 5 and 6 (first and second Extinction days) were the same as Days 1 and 2; E leaned over the crib with an expressionless face and made no response to S's vocalizations.

THE VOCAL RESPONSE

Every discrete, voiced sound produced by S was counted as a *vocalization*. A number of other sounds characteristically made by very young infants, e.g., straining sounds and coughs, and the whistles, squeaks, and snorts of noisy breathing, were not counted as vocalizations. Sounds falling under the categories of protests, fusses, and cries (see Emotional Behavior below) were recorded separately. No attempt was made to record the phonetic characteristics of any of the sounds or their duration.

Observer agreement. Agreement between two Os on the number of vocalizations produced by Ss in 3-min. periods was high. Counts for 27 periods, using 13 different Ss, yielded a median percentage agreement of 96 (range, 67 to 100). About half of these reliability measures were obtained at the Ss' cribs, and the rest from tape recordings made during the experiment. These two techniques yielded similar percentages of observer agreement.

The unit of measurement. The unit for statistical analysis was the number of vocalizations an S gave in a 3-min. period. The counts were recorded by half-minutes and these were summed to give the score for the 3-min. period. After a rest period of 2 min., in which both E and O walked away from the baby's crib, another 3-min. count was made. After a second rest period a third count was made.

In each day nine such 3-min. counts were planned, distributed thus: one block of three in the first part of the morning, the second block of three in the late morning, and the third block of three after the midday meal. The minimum amount of time between blocks was 10 min., although usually an hour or more elapsed.

Actually, nine periods of observations were obtained during only 80% of the 132 subject-days (22 Ss $\times$ 6 experimental days). Since three or four Ss were studied at a time, it was not always possible to find nine periods in a day when each was awake, alert, and content. Further, because the experiments were carried out in the nursery which the Ss shared with 12 other infants, the presence and activities of these other babies, and of the caretakers in carrying out their routines, sometimes made it impossible to obtain the desired number of periods.

EMOTIONAL BEHAVIOR

A number of responses which seemed to be "emotional" were recorded during the observation periods. These were: "protests," discrete sounds of a whining nature; "fusses," a series of sounds separated by a catch in the voice, whimpering; "cries" continuous loud, wailing sounds; "persistent looking away from E," rolling of the head from side to side or staring to one side or the other of E; and "marked hand activity," hand play, finger sucking, or face or head rubbing. The last two activities seemed to be attempts to avoid E. Measures of observer-agreement in the recording of these responses were not made.

Each of these responses was given a credit of one for each half-minute in which it occurred. From the sum for each S a mean score was obtained for each experimental day.

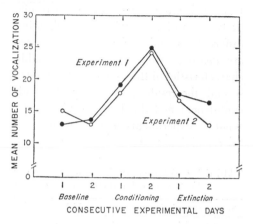

Figure 1. Mean number of vocalizations on consecutive experimental days.

RESULTS

SIMILARITY BETWEEN EXPERIMENTS

Figure 1 presents the means of both experiments for the six experimental days. Each point represents the mean of 11 individual means. It was expected that the effect of the experimental conditions would be similar from experiment to experiment, but the extent to which the slopes of the curves would be congruent was not predicted.

The amount of similarity between the two experiments was estimated by an analysis of variance (Table 1), using Lindquist's Type VI design (1953). The analysis reveals no evidence of a difference between Experiments. Further, no source of variation involving Experiments is significant. (The difference between the two experiments in second Extinction day means is not significant; it suggests, however, that the less frequent reinforcement in Experiment I may have made the behavior more resistant to extinction.)

Three conclusions may be drawn from such close agreement in the results of two parallel experiments, each using different Ss and different Es: first, we are dealing with some relatively stable characteristics of three-month-old infants; second, the results may be accepted with confidence; and third, the results of the separate experiments may be pooled for all remaining analyses.

TABLE 1 · ANALYSIS OF VARIANCE OF EFFECT OF CONSECUTIVE EXPERIMENTAL DAYS

Source of variation	df	MS	F
Between subjects	21		
Experiments			
(1 vs. 2)	1	1218	0.03
Error	20	45322	
Within subjects	110		
Conditions (baseline vs. conditioning vs. extinction)	2	71243 (1)[a]	10.63*
Days within conditions (1 vs. 2)	1	4205 (2)[a]	1.88
Conditions × days	2	22917 (3)[a]	9.24*
Days × experiments	1	1738 (2)[a]	0.78
Conditions × experiments	2	2031 (1)[a]	0.30
Conditions × days × experiments	2	866 (3)[a]	0.35
Error 1	40	6703	
Error 2	20	2233	
Error 3	40	2481	

[a] Number in parentheses refers to the error term used. The terms were not pooled because of statistically significant differences among them.
* Significant at .001 level.

EFFECT OF EXPERIMENTAL CONDITIONS

Table 1 shows that there was a difference in the effect of the three two-day experimental conditions ($p < .001$), and, also, in the effect of successive days within conditions ($p < .001$). These effects were assessed by t tests (for paired data) on the amount of change from one day to another in the mean number of vocalizations given by individual Ss. The error term was derived only from the scores for the two days being compared. The tests on the pooled sample (21 df) show that:

1. There was no statistically significant difference in the mean number of vocalizations given in a 3-min. period from the first to the second Baseline day ($t = 0.87$, $p > .30$).

2. The mean number of vocalizations increased from the second Baseline day to the first Conditioning day ($t = 2.69$, $p < .01$).

3. A further increase occurred from the first to the second Conditioning day ($t = 3.61$, $p < .001$).

4. On the first Extinction day, vocalizations decreased ($t = 3.19$, $p < .0025$).

5. The mean number of vocalizations on the second Extinction day was smaller than on the first Extinction day, but the difference was not reliable ($t = 1.35$, $p < .10$).

6. There was no statistically significant difference between the mean number of vocalizations given on the second Extinction day and on the second Baseline day ($t = 1.20$, $p > .20$).

The tests between Baseline days and between Baseline and Extinction days were two-sided tests; the others were one-sided.

If final days within conditions are compared, the differences are more marked: the mean for the second Conditioning day is higher than that of the second Baseline day at $p < .0005$ ($t = 4.80$), and the second Extinction day mean is lower than the second Conditioning day mean at $p < .0005$ ($t = 4.08$). Similar differences occur between the means of experimental conditions, obtained by averaging the first- and second-day results for each condition.

AMOUNT OF CHANGE IN NUMBER OF VOCALIZATIONS

The treatment effects have been found reliable. It seems in order, therefore, to present the means of vocalizations for each day and to calculate the amount of change produced by the experimental conditions. Under baseline conditions the three-month-old infants gave about 13 to 14 vocalizations in a 3-min. period. Individual differences were wide and ranged from 3 to 37 vocalizations. Using the social reinforcer for one day raised the rate to 18 vocalizations, an increase of 39%. A second day of conditioning elevated the rate to 25, a further increase of 34%. In all, conditioning brought about an increase of 86%. Removing the reinforcer depressed the rate to 17 during the first and to 15 during the second day, the latter approaching very closely the level of baseline performance.

EMOTIONAL BEHAVIOR

Emotional behavior, while striking when it occurred, was observed infrequently. The largest mean for any day in both experiments was 3.0, the smallest was 1.9. The order of the means by experimental days was identical in the two experiments. It was: first Extinction day, second Extinction day, second Baseline day, second Conditioning day, first Conditioning day, and first Baseline day. The greater number of emotional responses during Extinction agrees with the findings of others (e.g., Brackbill, 1958; Skinner, 1953; Verplanck, 1955). Because the responses labeled emotional occurred so infrequently and because observer-agreement measures were not made, no further statistical analysis seemed warranted.

ADDITIONAL FINDINGS

Performance of successive groups. It will be recalled that in any one experimental week the Ss were studied in groups of three or four. Inspection of the results suggests that in each successive group of each experiment an increasing number of Ss conformed to expectation, showing an increase in vocalizations during Conditioning and a decrease during Extinction. The Es apparently became more adept in executing the reinforcer as each experiment progressed.

Performance of individual subjects. Although differences between experimental conditions have been demonstrated for the Ss as a group, the performance of individual Ss is of interest. Of the 22 Ss, 19 showed an increase in vocalizations under Conditioning. For 14 of these 19 the increase was significant at the .05 level, according to the Mann-Whitney Test (1947). Under Extinction, 16 of the 22 Ss showed some decrease, and for 10 of these 16 the decrease was significant at the .05 level.

Three Ss departed widely from the group pattern. For two, not only did Conditioning depress the rate of vocalizing, but Extinction restored it to its Baseline rate. The first chewed her thumb more during Conditioning than before or after. The second strained (in an apparent effort to defecate) during Conditioning whenever anyone, E or the nurse, leaned over his crib. Both activities precluded vocalizing. Both babies were very active, and it is possible, therefore, that in the very first Conditioning period E may have inadvertently reinforced these activities. For the third S, in Experiment I the experimental conditions appeared not to affect the frequency of vocalizations. Developmental immaturity seemed the most likely reason, for two weeks later he was studied again in Experiment II (the only S to be used in both experiments) with satisfactory results.

Effect of Baseline performance upon Conditioning. The Ss tended to maintain their relative positions under Baseline and Conditioning. The rank-order coefficient of correlation (R) was .66, $p < .0005$. Further, the amount of gain under Conditioning was not correlated with original position $(R = .24, p > .05)$.

Sex differences. The 12 male Ss gave slightly more vocalizations during Baseline and gained more under Conditioning than the 10 female Ss, but the differences were not reliable.

DISCUSSION

The results of these experiments suggest that:

1. Infants' vocal behavior in a social situation can be brought under experimental control; that is, it appears to be conditionable.

2. A social event composed of an everyday complex of acts, performed by an adult who is not a caretaker, can function as a reinforcing stimulus.

3. The incidence of such behavior can be very quickly modified in as young an organism as the three-month-old infant.

ALTERNATIVE EXPLANATION

The question raised in the introduction may now be considered. Did the reinforcing stimulus function as an arouser of vocalizations? Would infants have vocalized more often because of the stimulation it provided, even if it had *not* been made contingent upon the infant's behavior? Or, did some part of the reinforcing stimulus (say, the smile) act as a social "releaser"? The findings appear to be compatible with the conclusion that conditioning occurred: The rate of vocalizing continued to rise on the second day of Conditioning; the rate did not fall to the Baseline level on the first day of Extinction; it continued to fall on the second day of Extinction; and Ss with low Baseline rates of vocalizing gained under Conditioning, although for them there was often a relatively long time interval (30 sec. or more) between the reinforcing stimulus and the occurrence of the next vocalization. Still, the decisive answer to the question must await an experiment in which the reinforcing stimulus is administered with equal frequency, but never directly after the infant vocalizes.

NATURE OF THE REINFORCER

The results seem to show that some everyday behavior of adults can function as a reinforcing stimulus for an infant. One would like to know from what sources its reinforcing properties arise. In the simplest case, the smiles, sounds, and caresses of adults may be reinforcing only because they provide a change in stimulation. Further information on this matter could be obtained by working with the separate parts of the reinforcing stimulus, one by one; by substituting for them lights or sounds dispensed by a machine; or by using a reinforcer of a less "affectionate" nature than the one used here appears to be. On the other hand, even for the three-month-old infant the smiles, sounds, and caresses of the adults may function as conditioned reinforcers because of their past association with caretaking acts.

It is possible that the Ss of this study, living in an institution, may have had a less rich experience with adults. Institutional babies were used as Ss only because they were more readily available, because more of them could be studied at one time, and because the complicating variable of differences in maternal care could be bypassed. They did not appear however to be "starved" for attention or affection. Indeed, the attendants were often observed responding to babies when they vocalized. While it is possible that mothers would respond more often, in the absence of a comparative study we believe that infants in general would respond as these infants did.

RELATION OF RESULTS TO THEORIES OF SPEECH

Since this study was limited to the vocalizing of infants in a social situation, attempts to reconcile the results with theories which account for all classes of prelinguistic utterances (babbling is the class frequently mentioned) cannot be complete. Thus, nothing in the findings of this study is incompatible with, for example, Holt's theory (1931) that the sound which the child hears himself make has reinforcing properties; with Lewis' theory (1951) that the adult's speech

calls forth the infant's speech (a kind of imitation); or with Piaget's theory (1952) that vocalizing is perpetuated for its own sake by the processes of assimilation and accommodation. These may be labeled circular theories, for they do not postulate the necessity for any class of events prior to the moment when the infant responds to his own or another's vocalization. The theories of Miller and Dollard (1941) and of Mowrer (1950), on the other hand, are based upon the infant's associating the gratification of his needs and the accompanying vocalizations of the caretaker. Again, the results do not contradict this possibility.

The present study, however, does demonstrate the operation of still another principle: that the speech of the infant, if only in a social situation, can be modified by a response from the environment which is contingent upon his vocalizing. Hence, what happens *after* the infant vocalizes has been shown to be important.

SIGNIFICANCE OF RESULTS

On the basis of the results of these experiments it is seen that responses of adults which do not involve caretaking can affect the vocalizing of the young in a social setting. If the results can be extended to life situations, then mothers might be able to increase or decrease the vocal output of their children by the responses they make when the children vocalize. Other kinds of social behavior in addition to vocalizing behavior should respond similarly to conditioning. Brackbill (1958) has shown that smiling in the four-month-old infant may be increased when followed by a social response from an adult. It is likely that still other kinds of social behavior in babies, such as showing an interest in people, reaching out to them or turning away, perhaps even fear of the stranger, may also be affected by the responses adults make to them.

SUMMARY

Infants often vocalize as part of the response they give to the appearance of an adult. The central question of this study is: Can the frequency of vocalizing be increased if the adult makes a social response contingent upon it?

The Ss were 21 normal infants, three months of age, living in an institution. Eleven of them were studied in Experiment I with one E; 10 different Ss and one S from Experiment I were studied in Experiment II with a different E.

During the first and second Baseline days E leaned over S with an expressionless face, and the number of vocalizations was tallied. During the next two days, the first and second Conditioning days, E reinforced vocalizations by simultaneously smiling, clucking, and touching S's abdomen. During the last two days, the first and second Extinction days, E returned to Baseline conditions.

The results indicated that: (a) there was no difference between Experiments, (b) Conditioning raised the rate of vocalizing above the Baseline level, (c) while Extinction lowered it until it approached the Baseline level.

The results suggest that the social vocalizing of infants and, more generally, their social responsiveness may be modified by the responses adults make to them.

REFERENCES

BRACKBILL, Y.   Extinction of the smiling responses in infants as a function of reinforcement schedule. *Child Develpm.*, 1958, *29*, 115–124.

GEWIRTZ, J. L.   A program of research on the dimensions and antecedents of emotional dependence. *Child Develpm.*, 1956, *27*, 205–221.

HOLT, E. B.   *Animal drive.* London: Williams & Norgate, 1931.

LEWIS, M. M.   *Infant speech: A study of the beginnings of language.* (2nd ed.) New York: Humanities Press, 1951.

LINDQUIST, E. F.   *Design and analysis of experiments in psychology and education.* Boston: Houghton Mifflin, 1953.

MANN, H. B., & WHITNEY, D. R.   On a test of whether one of two random variables is stochastically larger than the other. *Ann. Math. Statist.*, 1947, *18*, 50–60.

MILLER, N. E., & DOLLARD, J.   *Social learning and imitation.* New Haven: Yale Univer. Press, 1941.

MOWRER, O. H.   *Learning theory and personality dynamics.* New York: Ronald, 1950.

PIAGET, J.   *The origins of intelligence in children.* New York: Int. Univer. Press, 1952.

RHEINGOLD, H. L.   The modification of social responsiveness in institutional babies. *Monogr. Soc. Res. Child Develpm.*, 1956, *21*, No. 63 (No. 2).

SKINNER, B. F.   *Science and human behavior.* New York: Macmillan, 1953.

VERPLANCK, W. S.   The control of the content of conversation: Reinforcement of statements of opinion. *J. abnorm. soc. Psychol.*, 1955, *51*, 668–676.

THE REINFORCEMENT OF COOPERATION

BETWEEN CHILDREN

NATHAN H. AZRIN
OGDEN R. LINDSLEY

MOST METHODS for the development and experimental analysis of cooperation between humans require specific instructions concerning the cooperative relationship between the individual responses. Peters and Murphree have developed one of the most recent of these methods (1). Skinner has suggested (2), and shown with lower organisms (3), that cooperation between individuals can be developed, maintained, and eliminated solely by manipulating the contingency between reinforcing stimuli and the cooperative response.

The advantages of eliminating instructions concerning cooperation are that (a) the initial acquisition of cooperation can be studied, (b) subjects (Ss) that learn by demonstration and instruction with difficulty (i.e., infants, certain classes of psychotics, and lower organisms) can be studied, and (c) no problems involving the effects of instructions upon the behavior of the Ss are involved.

Some more general advantages of operant conditioning techniques are (a) a more continuous record of the cooperative process is obtained, (b) extraneous environmental variables are minimized, and (c) relatively long periods of experimental observation are possible.

Reprinted by permission from *Journal of Abnormal and Social Psychology*, 1956, 52, 100–102.

PROBLEM

Can cooperation between children be developed, maintained, and eliminated solely by the presentation or nonpresentation of a single reinforcing stimulus, available to each member of the cooperative team, following each cooperative response?

COOPERATIVE TEAMS

Twenty children, seven to twelve years of age, were formed into ten cooperative teams of two children. The children in each team were matched as to age and sex. Seven teams were boys and three were girls.[1] Selection was made via the request, "Who wants to play a game?" The first two volunteers of the same age and sex were chosen for each team. The age given by the children was verified against available community center records. No information concerning the game was given during the selection. No teams were rejected.

COOPERATIVE RESPONSE

Cooperation was assured by designing an apparatus that (a) could not be operated by one individual alone (assuring group behavior), and (b) demanded that one individual respond to the behavior of the other individual in order to produce reinforcement (assuring cooperation).

[1] We wish to thank the Harriet Tubman House and the South Bay Union of Boston, Mass., for providing the subjects and the use of their facilities.

PROCEDURE

The two children of each cooperative team were placed at opposite sides of a table with three holes and a stylus in front of each child (see Fig. 1). A wire screen down the center of the table prevented each child from manipulating the other child's stylus, which was on the other side of the table.

The following instructions were given: "This is a game. You can play the game any way you want to or do anything else that you want to do. This is how the game works: Put both sticks (styli) into all three of the holes." (This sentence was repeated until both styli had been placed in the three available holes.) "While you are in this room some of these" (the experimenter (E) held out several jelly beans) "will drop into this cup. You can eat them here if you want to or you can take them home with you." The instructions were then repeated without reply to any questions, after which E said: "I am leaving the room now; you can play any game that you want to while I am gone." Then E left the room until the end of the experimental session.

If the styli were placed in opposite holes within 0.04 seconds of each other (a cooperative response), a red light flashed on the table (conditioned reinforcing stimulus) and a single jelly bean (reinforcing stimulus) fell into the cup that was accessible to both children.[2] Cooperative responses were recorded on counters and a cumulative response recorder in an adjoining room.

EXPERIMENTAL DESIGN

Each team was studied for one continuous experimental session divided into the following three consecutive periods without experimental interruption:

1. *First reinforcement period.* Every cooperative response was reinforced for over 15 min. If the rate of response was not steady at this time, the reinforcement was continued until five minutes passed with no noticeable change in the rate of cooperation.

2. *Extinction period.* The cooperative responses were not reinforced for a period of at least 15 minutes and until a steady rate of response for at least five minutes was observed.

3. *Second reinforcement period.* The cooperative responses were again reinforced until at least three minutes of a stable rate occurred. This was done to determine whether a reduction in rate during the extinction period was due to extinction, satiation, or fatigue.

Figure 1. Apparatus used for the reinforcement of cooperation between children.

RESULTS

All teams learned to cooperate without specific instructions in the first 10 min. of experimentation. Observation through a one-way vision screen disclosed that leader-follower relationships were developed and maintained in most cases. Almost immediately eight teams divided the candy in some manner. With two teams, one member at first took all the candy until the other member refused to cooperate. When verbal agreement was reached in these two teams, the members then cooperated and divided the candy. Most vocalization occurred during the initial acquisition period and throughout the extinction period. This vocalization was correlated with a higher variability in rate during these periods. (See below.)

[2] Skinner (3) presented two reinforcing stimuli (one to each pigeon) following each cooperative response.

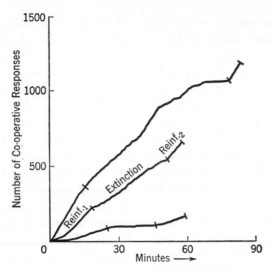

Figure 2. Cumulative response records for the teams with the highest, median, and lowest rates of cooperation.

Figure 2 contains cumulative records of the cooperative responses of the three teams with the highest, the median, and the lowest number of cooperative responses for the experimental session. These curves show a large difference in the rate of acquisition of cooperation. One team took almost 10 minutes to acquire a high cooperative response rate. Stable rates of cooperation can be observed during the latter parts of the first reinforcement period. The gradual, rather than immediate, decline in cooperation during extinction suggests an orderly extinction of cooperative behavior as is found with individual extinction curves. In all cases the variability of rate was greater during extinction than during reinforcement. Skinner has found this increased variability in rate during extinction with lower organisms and has described it as emotional behavior (2, p. 69). The high rate of response following the first reinforcement of the second reinforcement period shows that reacquisition is almost immediate.

Table 1 contains a quantification of the records for statistical analysis. The median and range of the number of cooperative responses per minute for all 10 teams during the critical periods of the experiment are given. The number of cooperative responses per minute for the first three minutes of the first reinforcement period was significantly lower than the rate during the last three minutes of the first reinforcement period ($p < .02$).[3]

TABLE 1 · THE MEDIAN AND RANGE OF THE NUMBER OF COOPERATIVE RESPONSES PER MINUTE FOR THE CRITICAL EXPERIMENTAL PERIODS

N 10	NUMBER OF COOPERATIVE RESPONSES PER MINUTE			
	First three mins. of first reinf. period	*Last three mins. of first reinf. period*	*Last three mins. of extinction period*	*Last three mins. of second reinf. period*
Median	5.5	17.5	1.5	17.5
Range	1–26	6–26	0–7	6–27

[3] Wilcoxon's nonparametric T for paired associates was used in all statistical treatments (4).

This shows that the rate of cooperation was significantly lower during initial acquisition than during maintenance of cooperation. The number of cooperative responses per minute during the last three minutes of extinction was significantly lower than the rate during the last three minutes of the first reinforcement period ($p < .001$). This shows that the removal of reinforcement during extinction significantly lowered the rate of cooperation between these children.

The number of cooperative responses per minute during the last three minutes of the second reinforcement period was significantly above the rate during the last three minutes of the extinction period ($p < .001$). This shows that the rate of cooperation was significantly increased during the second reinforcement period and that the drop in rate during extinction was due to the absence of the reinforcing stimulus rather than satiation or fatigue. The rates of cooperation during the second reinforcement period and the last three minutes of the first reinforcement period were not significantly different and show that the rate was almost immediately restored to its pre-extinction value upon the presentation of reinforcement for the second time. The rate of cooperative responding during the first three minutes of the second reinforcement period was significantly higher than during the first three minutes of the first reinforcement period ($p < .02$). This again shows that the reacquisition of cooperation was not gradual, as was initial acquisition, but occurred almost immediately.

CONCLUSIONS

Operant conditioning techniques can be used to develop, maintain, and eliminate cooperation between children without the use of specific instructions concerning cooperation. The rate of a cooperative response changes in much the same way as a function of single reinforcements as does an individual response. In the reinforcement of cooperative responses, a reinforcing stimulus need not be delivered to each member of the cooperative team following each cooperative response. The presentation of a single reinforcing stimulus, available to each member of the cooperative team, is sufficient to increase the rate of cooperation. The cooperative response gradually increases in frequency when reinforced and gradually decreases in frequency when no longer reinforced (extinction). Cooperative responses are maintained at a stable rate during reinforcement but occur in sporadic bursts during extinction. Reinforcement following extinction results in an almost immediate restoration of the rate of cooperation to its pre-extinction value.

REFERENCES

1. PETERS, H. N., & MURPHREE, O. D. A cooperative multiple-choice apparatus. *Science,* 1954, *119,* 189–191.
2. SKINNER, B. F. *Science and human behavior.* New York: Macmillan, 1953.
3. SKINNER, B. F. Classroom demonstration. Personal communication, 1952.
4. WILCOXON, F. *Some rapid approximate statistical procedures.* New York: American Cyanamid Co., 1949.

PROBABILITY LEARNING IN CHILDREN [1,2]

HAROLD W. STEVENSON
EDWARD F. ZIGLER

THERE HAS BEEN a great deal of interest during recent years in the investigation of probability learning in human Ss. In a large number of studies (1, 4, 5, 10, 11, 12, 14) it has been found that Ss tend to match the stimulus probabilities with their guesses. At the same time, it has been found that under certain conditions Ss tend to maximize their frequency of choosing the more frequently reinforced stimulus. Among these are the presentation of a gambling task or a game of skill rather than a problem-solving task (7, 9), an increased number of training trials (3, 6), the presence of a distracting stimulus (18, 19), and the lack of information concerning the appropriateness of some responses (2, 3, 14).

These studies have been done primarily with college students as Ss. It would be of interest to determine whether behavior similar to that of these Ss might be found with other populations of Ss, and to explore other conditions which might influence the tendency of Ss to choose the more frequently reinforcing stimulus. The present study, therefore, is concerned with testing normal and institutionalized feebleminded children in a situation similar to that which has been presented to adult Ss, and with determining whether the behavior of normal children in a probability learning task can be influenced by pretraining experience with different probabilities of reinforcement. Three experiments are presented and the hypotheses tested in each are discussed in later sections.

EXPERIMENT I

The purpose of this experiment is to determine whether the responses of normal children in a probability learning task are similar to those of adult Ss. A three-choice, contingent procedure was used in which the response to only one stimulus was reinforced. In this situation, adult Ss have been found (14) to show a rapid increase in frequency of choice of the reinforced stimulus and to reach an asymptotic level of response slightly above that corresponding to the frequency of reinforcement.

METHOD

Subjects. The Ss consisted of 45 children attending nursery schools in Austin, Texas. The Ss were selected at random from among children of the appropriate CA enrolled in the schools. The average CA was 5.5 yr.

Apparatus. The apparatus consisted of a yellow vertical panel 22 in. long and 16 in.

[1] The writers wish to express their appreciation to Morton Weir for testing the Ss and for suggestions concerning the conduct of the study. They also wish to thank Raymond Vowell, Superintendent, and Barbara Nellis, Chief Psychologist, of the Austin State School, and the Directors of the Tarrytown Methodist, Jack and Jill, Donnelly, and St. Austin Nursery Schools.
[2] This study was supported by a grant from the National Science Foundation (Grant 3280) to the senior author.

Reprinted by permission from *Journal of Experimental Psychology*, 1958, 56, 185–192.

high on which was centered a row of three identical black knobs. The knobs, 1¾ in. in diameter, projected 1 in. from the panel and were 2 in. apart. A red signal light was mounted on the midline, 2 in. from the top of the panel, and a hole through which marbles were delivered was centered 7 in. from the bottom of the panel. The marbles fell from the hole into a small enclosed box. The box had a clear plastic top and front which enabled S to see the marbles but not to handle them.

A mechanism behind the panel provided for the dispensing of the marbles and for the measurement of latency of response. The switch by which E turned on the signal light also turned on an electric timer. When S pushed one of the knobs, the light was automatically turned off and the timer stopped. In addition, the knob dislodged a marble which fell down a chute into the box.

Procedure. The S was seated in front of the apparatus and was told that he was to play a game. The E demonstrated the apparatus and said, "When the light comes on, you push one of the knobs. If you push the correct knob a marble comes out here like this. Now every time the light comes on you push the knob that you think will get you the marble. Remember, just push one knob each time the light comes on." The S was told that he was to get as many marbles as he could and when the game was over he could choose two toys from a selection of toys including balloons, plastic figures, etc., which E showed him. The E took a position behind the apparatus and did not interact further with S during the experiment. A second E seated in a distant part of the room behind S recorded the responses and their latencies.

Three conditions which differed in the percentage of reinforcement of correct response were used. For each S, one of the three knobs (either L, M, or R) was designated as the correct knob. The particular knob that was correct yielded reinforcement; choices of the other two knobs were never reinforced. In the three conditions the correct knob yielded 100%, 66%, and 33% reinforcement, respectively. In the 66% and 33% conditions the trials on which a choice of the correct knob was reinforced were

determined by a prearranged random schedule. The schedule was utilized in such a fashion that it insured S would receive the desired percentage of reinforcement of correct responses. Fifteen Ss were assigned at random to each of the three conditions. The Ss were given 80 trials and at the completion of the experiment S was allowed to select his prizes.

RESULTS

The three groups differed consistently throughout the 80 trials in the incidence of correct response, as may be seen in Fig. 1. An analysis of variance revealed that the differences among the groups were significant at beyond the .01 level ($F = 7.39$).

The general tendency seen in Fig. 1 is for the frequency of correct response to increase for a short period and then to level off. The 33% group did not show a significant improvement in performance between the first 20 and last 20 trials ($t = 1.66, P > .05$). The change in performance from the first 20 to the last 20 trials was significant for both the 66% ($t = 4.00, P < .01$) and the 100% group ($t = 2.97, P < .01$).[3]

The values of the asymptotic level of response, as estimated from performance on the last 20 trials, were .97, .79, and .53 for the 100%, 66%, and 33% groups, respectively. The values are quite similar to those obtained by Neimark (14), who tested adult Ss under similar conditions with 100% and 66% reinforce-

---

[3] Forty extinction trials were given to these Ss immediately after the training trials. During the extinction trials no response was reinforced. The difference in the frequency of choice of the stimulus correct during training between the last 10 acquisition trials and the last 10 extinction trials was significant for the 66% group ($t = 2.38, P < .05$) and in the 100% group ($t = 2.51, P < .05$), but not for the 33% group ($t = 1.46, P > .05$).

ment. The asymptotic levels of response obtained by Neimark for the last 20 of 100 training trials were .99 for the 100% group and .83 for the 66% group.

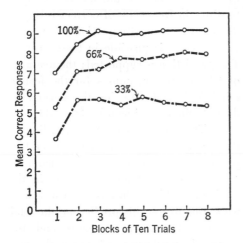

Figure 1. Mean number of correct responses by normal children for blocks of 10 trials.

There was a tendency for the average latencies of response in the 100% and 66% groups to decrease during the course of the 80 trials in the manner expected in learning problems of different difficulty. The changes for the 33% group were more erratic and appeared to represent a different process from that of the other two groups. An analysis of variance of the latency scores of the three groups during acquisition is not significant ($F < 1$).

EXPERIMENT II

Goodnow (7), in an analysis of the determinants of choice behavior, has suggested that one of the conditions influencing whether or not S will maximize his guesses of the more frequently reinforced stimulus is the level of success S will accept in the task. Goodnow suggests that maximizing behavior will be found when S will accept less than 100% success as a good final outcome, while other distributions of choices will be found when S has an interest in 100% success or in a level of success which is greater than that allowed in the situation.

On the basis of this analysis, it may be hypothesized that different types of behavior will be obtained with Ss who differ in the degree of success that they have learned to expect. Normal Ss, such as those of Exp. I and of most previous studies, may be assumed to have learned, on the basis of their everyday experience, to expect a high degree of success. Maximizing behavior would not be predicted for these Ss. Institutionalized feebleminded children, however, may be assumed to have learned to expect and to settle for lower degrees of success. These Ss, therefore, would be predicted to maximize their choices of the reinforced stimulus to a greater degree than would normal Ss. It is the purpose of this experiment (a) to determine whether institutionalized feebleminded Ss do tend to maximize their choices in such a manner, and (b) to determine whether their choices of the reinforced stimulus differ significantly from those found for the normal Ss in Exp. I.

METHOD

Subjects. The Ss consisted of 30 feebleminded children chosen at random from among individuals of appropriate MA and CA residing at the Austin State School. The individuals were all of the familial type of mental deficiency and no individuals with gross motor or sensory disturbances were used. The Ss were selected so that their average MA would be comparable to that of the normal Ss in Exp. I. Previous testing with the Stanford-Binet of more than 80 Ss from the population from which Ss in Exp. I were selected revealed an average IQ of 119. On the basis of this it was assumed that the Ss in Exp. I had an average MA of approximately 6.5 yr. The average MA of the feebleminded Ss was 6.1 yr. and their average CA was 12.8 yr.

Apparatus and procedure. The same apparatus and procedure employed in Exp. I were used. Ten feebleminded Ss were tested in each of the three conditions.

RESULTS

The frequencies of correct response made by the three groups of Ss are presented in Fig. 2. An analysis of variance of these data indicated that the three groups did not differ significantly in frequency of correct response ($F = 2.91$, $P > .05$). This is in marked contrast with the results for the normal Ss, where a highly significant difference among groups was found.

All three groups showed significant increases in frequency of correct response between the first 20 and last 20 trials. The difference is significant at less than the .05 level for the 100% ($t = 2.77$)

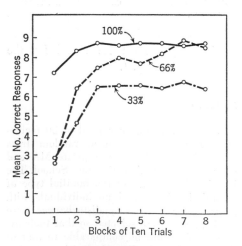

Figure 2. Mean number of correct responses by feebleminded children for blocks of 10 trials.

and 33% groups ($t = 2.48$), and at less than the .01 level for the 66% group ($t = 6.69$).

The normal and feebleminded Ss in the 100% groups would not be expected to differ in frequency of correct response during the acquisition trials, for complete success is possible in these groups. The prediction is supported; the averages of 67.5 correct responses for the feebleminded Ss and 70.1 for the normal Ss do not differ significantly ($t = .33$).

The feebleminded Ss, according to the hypothesis presented earlier, would be predicted to show a higher frequency of correct response than normal Ss in the 33% and 66% conditions. Two measures were used to test this prediction, the total number of correct responses and the change in performance between the first and last quarters of the acquisition series. An analysis of variance of total number of correct responses for the four groups resulted in an F of 2.41, which is not significant at the .05 level. The difference between the numbers of correct responses made during the first and last quarters of acquisition by the four groups of Ss were highly significant ($F = 5.35$, $P < .01$). The difference associated with type of S was highly significant ($F = 12.74$, $P < .01$). Neither the difference associated with conditions of reinforcement ($F = 3.22$, $P > .05$) nor the interaction between type of S and condition of reinforcement was significant ($F < 1.00$). The feebleminded Ss had a greater change in performance between the first and last quarters of acquisition than the normal Ss in both the 66% ($t = 3.52$, $P < .01$) and, with a one-tailed test, in the 33% group ($t = 1.81$, $P < .05$).

The differences among the average latency scores for the three feebleminded groups are not significant $(F = 1.82, P > .05)$. An analysis of variance of the latency scores for the normal and feeble-minded Ss indicated no significant differences among the six groups $(F < 1.00)$. The latency curves of the feebleminded Ss have the same trends as those of the normal Ss.

EXPERIMENT III

The purpose of Exp. III was to determine whether the behavior of normal Ss in the task can be influenced by pretraining with games involving different frequencies of reinforcement. It is assumed, in the manner outlined in Exp. II, that there will be less of a tendency for maximizing behavior to occur with Ss who have learned to expect high degrees of success than with those who have learned to expect lower degrees of success. It is predicted, therefore, that Ss with pretraining on other tasks with high frequencies of reinforcement will show a significantly lower frequency of choice of the reinforcing stimulus than will Ss who have pretraining with lower frequencies of reinforcement.

METHOD

Subjects. The Ss consisted of 30 preschool children attending the same nursery schools as Ss in Exp. I. The Ss were selected at random from among the children who had not performed in Exp. I. The mean CA was 5.9 yr.

Apparatus. Four tasks were used—the learning task used in Exp. I and II and three experimental games. The apparatus for the learning task was modified so that a small open box from which S could remove the marbles replaced the enclosed box. A marble board, with 50 holes into which S could place the marbles, was also used.

The games were the Card Game, the Picture Game, and the Nursery School Game. The *Card Game* apparatus consisted of two sets of cards. The cards were constructed of 2×3-in. cardboard on which were mounted small rectangles of black or red paper. One set contained 12 red cards and the other contained 8 black and 4 red cards. The *Picture Game* apparatus consisted of (a) 12 cards similar to those in the Card Game, each bearing a rectangle of a different color; (b) a panel containing a 7-in. square milk-glass screen; (c) a slide projector; and (d) 12 slides depicting different animals. The *Nursery School Game* apparatus consisted of (a) two green panels 17 in. square, each containing six hooks; and (b) 12 pictures of young children mounted in plastic covers with a wire loop at the top of each picture.

Two additional marble boards were also used, one containing 36 holes, and one containing 12 holes.

Procedure. The Ss were presented with the three games followed by the learning problem. The Ss were divided at random into two groups of 15 Ss each. Group 1 received 100% reinforcement and Group 2 received 33% reinforcement during the games. All Ss received 66% reinforcement during the learning problem. The games were dissimilar to each other and to the learning task. Since the games did not involve learning, the different percentages of reinforcement could be given regardless of the specific responses Ss made.

The S was seated at a small table and was told, "We're going to play several different kinds of games today and you can win some nice prizes." The E displayed prizes of the same types used in Exp. I and II, and proceeded with the instructions for the first game. During these instructions S was told that he would receive marbles for correct responses and was shown a marble board which he was to fill. The marble boards for the two groups differed; the 36-hole marble board was given to Ss in Group 1 and the 12-hole marble board to Ss in Group 2. The number of holes in the marble board corresponded to the number of times that S would be reinforced during the period in which S played the three games. The S was further told that when he filled the marble board he would be given another marble board which he could fill and could exchange for his choice of prizes. The use of different marble boards during this period was introduced to insure that the two groups of Ss, although receiving different numbers of reinforcements, would have attained the same degree of accomplishment towards their goal. The S was then allowed to proceed with the three games. The order in which the three games were played was randomized among Ss.

The instructions and procedures for the three games are described below:

In the *Card Game,* one of the decks of cards was placed in front of S. He was instructed to draw one card at a time from the top of the deck. He was told that every time he drew a red card he would be given a marble for his marble board. The S was allowed to draw 12 cards. The decks were prearranged so that for Group 1 the top 12 cards were red, and for Group 2 the top 12 cards contained 4 red cards and 8 black cards randomly mixed.

In the *Picture Game,* S was shown the apparatus and was told that as pictures appeared on the screen he was to select the card that went with the picture. There was no principle by which S could select an appropriate card, and reinforcement was given arbitrarily, depending upon the group in which S was placed. For Group 1, all of S's responses were reinforced by E's telling S that he was correct and giving S a marble. For Group 2, 33% of S's responses were reinforced. The four responses reinforced were determined by a prearranged random sequence.

In the *Nursery School Game,* S was told that the panels represented nursery schools and that half of the children in the pictures went to one nursery school and half to the other. The S was instructed to place each child in the nursery school which S thought the child attended. There was no principle by which the pictures could be separated and again reinforcement was given arbitrarily, depending upon the group in which S was placed. All of S's responses in Group 1 were reinforced and 33% of S's responses in Group 2. The responses reinforced in

Group 2 again followed a prearranged random sequence.

After completing the games S was asked to give the filled marble board to E and was given the marble board containing 50 holes. The S was told that when this marble board was filled he could select his prizes. The E then introduced the learning task. The instructions for this task were identical to those described in Exp. I and II, except that S was told to remove the marbles from the box after each reinforced trial and to place them in the marble board. The procedure did not differ for Groups 1 and 2; all Ss were tested under the 66% reinforcement schedule described in the previous experiments. The Ss were give 80 trials and were then given their prizes.

RESULTS

The results of the study are presented in Fig. 3. Following the initial 10

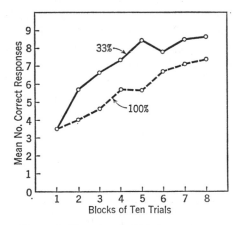

Figure 3. Mean number of correct responses in blocks of 10 trials.

trials the groups differed consistently. The Ss receiving 100% reinforcement on the games preceding the learning problem (Group 1) chose the correct knob less frequently than Ss who had received 33% reinforcement (Group 2). The correct knob was chosen an average of 44.7

times in Group 1 and 56.6 times in Group 2. The difference is significant at beyond the .025 level with a one-tailed test $(t = 2.11)$.

DISCUSSION

In this study it was assumed that children learn to expect certain frequencies of reinforcement on the basis of their everyday experience, and that children living in a normal, responsive environment develop a higher expectancy of reinforcement than do children living in an institution. It was also assumed that the expectancies that children develop may be modified by manipulating the frequency of reinforcement that the child receives in an experimental setting. It was hypothesized that different types of behavior would be obtained with Ss who differ in the degree of success that they have learned to expect, and it was predicted that Ss with low expectancies would show a greater frequency of choice of the reinforcing stimulus than would Ss with higher expectancies. This would result from the attempt by Ss with higher expectancies to seek, through variable behavior, a means by which they could obtain a frequency of reinforcement corresponding to the frequency which they expect.

The total number of correct responses made by three groups of normal children receiving different percentages of reinforcement differed significantly, but the number of correct responses made by three groups of feebleminded children tested under the same procedure as the normal Ss did not. The two types of Ss differed significantly in rate of learning under both 66% and 33% reinforcement,

but did not differ significantly under 100% reinforcement. In learning a response which yielded 66% reinforcement, normal Ss receiving 100% reinforcement on pretraining games showed significantly poorer learning than did Ss receiving 33% reinforcement on the pretraining games.

In Exp. I it was found that the mean response levels of normal children were similar to those for groups of adult Ss given 66% and 100% reinforcement in a similar situation (14). The results are also similar to those of Messick and Solley (13), who found that children tend to approach an asymptotic level of response in a probability learning situation.

In the 33% and 66% groups of Exp. I, a tendency was found for Ss to follow one of two modes of response; they either adopted the correct response relatively quickly or persisted in variable behavior throughout all of the trials. Individual differences in responses on a two-choice task have also been reported by Anderson and Grant (1). It is of interest that even Ss who persisted in responding in a variable fashion were able to tell E at the end of the experiment which knob had yielded reinforcement. The fact that Ss knew the correct response but did not make it supports the view that Ss with a high expectancy are unwilling to accept a solution which yields low frequencies of reinforcement.

There are several alternative interpretations of the differences in behavior of the normal and feebleminded children which differ from the one previously presented. One that seems quite reasonable is that institutionalized children may have less experience in playing games than normal children, hence are less likely to know the nature of such games. If this were the case, their behavior might be similar to that of adult *S*s, who, when tested in an obscure task, tend to depart from the probability matching behavior found in less obscure tasks (*19*). A second alternative interpretation is that feebleminded children may tend to choose the reinforced stimulus more frequently than do normal *S*s because they are more rigid and tend to perseverate more than do normal *S*s. This interpretation does not, however, appear to be tenable in light of the results of several recent studies in discrimination learning which show that normal and feebleminded *S*s of the same MA do not differ in rigidity of response or in learning speed (*16, 17*).

The results of Exp. III also provide support for the hypothesis that behavior in probability learning tasks is dependent upon *S*s' expectations concerning level of reinforcement. The fact that pretraining with different frequencies of reinforcement affects behavior in a probability learning task is in accord with the results of experiments with adult *S*s where the probability of reinforcement is shifted during the course of training. In these studies (*5, 8, 15*), differences in behavior have been found as a function of the shift in probabilities of reinforcement.

The form of the curves for the two groups in Exp. III tends to differ from that of the group in Exp. I which also received 66% reinforcement. The differences in the curves may be related to the differences in procedures used in the two experiments. In Exp. III, *S*s were given a more defined goal than were *S*s in Exp. I. The use of a more defined goal may lead to a greater tendency for *S*s to maximize their choices of the reinforcing stimulus.

SUMMARY

Three experiments are reported which investigate the performance of children in a probability learning task. In Exp. I and II, normal and feebleminded children were tested on a problem where the correct response resulted in either 100%, 66%, or 33% reinforcement. In Exp. III normal children were given pretraining on three nonlearning games with 100% or 33% reinforcement, and were then trained on the discrimination problem with 66% reinforcement of the correct response. Predictions were made from an hypothesis relating performance to *S*s' expected frequency of reinforcement. Feebleminded *S*s performed at a higher level in the 33% and 66% conditions than normal *S*s and at a comparable level in the 100% condition. The *S*s in Exp. III receiving 100% reinforcement during pretraining made significantly fewer correct responses in the learning problem than did *S*s receiving 33% reinforcement during pretraining.

REFERENCES

1. ANDERSON, N. H., & GRANT, D. A. A test of a statistical learning theory model for two-choice behavior with double stimulus events. *J. exp. Psychol.*, 1957, *54*, 305–317.
2. BRAND, H., SAKODA, J. M., & WOODS, P. J. Contingent partial reinforcement and the anticipation of correct alternatives. *J. exp. Psychol.*, 1957, *53*, 417–424.
3. DETAMBEL, M. H. A test of a model for multiple-choice behavior. *J. exp. Psychol.*, 1955, *49*, 97–104.
4. ESTES, W. K. Individual behavior in uncertain situations: An interpretation in terms of statistical association theory. In R. M. Thrall, C. H. Coombs, and R. L. Davis (Eds.), *Decision processes.* New York: Wiley, 1954.

5. Estes, W. K., & Straughn, J. H. Analysis of a verbal conditioning situation in terms of statistical learning theory. *J. exp. Psychol.*, 1954, 47, 225–234.

6. Gardner, R. A. Probability learning with two and three choices. *Amer. J. Psychol.*, 1957, 70, 174–185.

7. Goodnow, J. J. Determinants of choice distribution in two-choice situations. *Amer. J. Psychol.*, 1955, 68, 106–116.

8. Goodnow, J. J., & Pettigrew, T. F. Effect of prior patterns of experience upon strategies and learning situations. *J. exp. Psychol.*, 1955, 49, 381–389.

9. Goodnow, J. J., & Postman, L. Probability learning in a problem-solving situation. *J. exp. Psychol.*, 1955, 49, 16–22.

10. Grant, D. A., Hake, H. W., & Hornseth, J. P. Acquisition and extinction of a verbal conditioned response with differing percentages of reinforcement. *J. exp. Psychol.*, 1951, 42, 1–5.

11. Humphreys, L. G. Acquisition and extinction of verbal expectations in a situation analogous to conditioning. *J. exp. Psychol.*, 1939, 25, 294–301.

12. Jarvik, M. E. Probability learning and a negative recency effect in the serial anticipation of alternatives. *J. exp. Psychol.*, 1951, 41, 291–297.

13. Messick, S. J., & Solley, C. M. Probability learning in children: Some exploratory studies. *J. genet. Psychol.*, 1957, 90, 23–32.

14. Neimark, E. Effects of type of non-reinforcement and number of alternative responses in two verbal conditioning situations. *J. exp. Psychol.*, 1956, 52, 209–220.

15. Parducci, A. Alternative measures for the discrimination of shift in reinforcement-ratio. *Amer. J. Psychol.*, 1957, 70, 194–202.

16. Plenderlith, M. Discrimination learning and discrimination reversal learning in normal and feebleminded children. *J. genet. Psychol.*, 1956, 88, 107–112.

17. Stevenson, H. W., & Zigler, E. F. Discrimination learning and rigidity in normal and feebleminded individuals. *J. Pers.*, 1957, 25, 699–711.

18. Straughn, J. H. Human escape learning in relation to reinforcement variables in intertrial conditions. *J. exp. Psychol.*, 1956, 52, 1–8.

19. Wyckoff, L. B., & Sidowski, J. B. Probability discrimination in a motor task. *J. exp. Psychol.*, 1955, 50, 225–231.

DISCRIMINATION LEARNING PROCESSES IN CHILDREN | 8

THE EFFECT of discrimination learning processes is apparent in our everyday behavior. An automobile driver steps on the brake in response to a red light, and steps on the accelerator when he sees a green light. Men enter rooms that say "Gentlemen" on them, and women enter rooms marked "Ladies." Discrimination learning is that process whereby a subject acquires differential responses to two or more stimuli.

Learned discriminative responding should not be confused with discrimination *per se,* which is typically assessed by standard psychophysical techniques and is concerned primarily with the perceptual attributes of the organism. There is little doubt, for instance, that an adult can discriminate between the physical stimuli "Gentlemen" and "Ladies," but one has to learn to respond differently and appropriately to these two stimuli to indicate discriminative behavior.

It should be obvious that perception is related to discrimination learning, in that an organism could never learn to respond differentially and appropriately to nondiscriminable stimuli. Indeed, much of the interest that has centered on discrimination learning has actually been instigated by psychologists' concern with the development of techniques for psychophysical assessments in inarticulate organisms. It is impossible to ask a monkey or a six-month-old child to report verbally whether he sees a difference between two stimuli in front of him, one of them red and the other pink. One can, however, reward the subject for picking up only the red stimulus and not for picking up the pink one. To the extent that the subject increases his responding to red and decreases his responding to pink, it may be said that he has learned to respond differentially. We can also say now that he can discriminate (perceptually) these two hues. Discrimination learning procedures, then, permit assessment of the visual or other perceptual capacities in otherwise noncommunicating organisms.

Interest in discrimination learning processes, however, has not been limited to its usefulness as a perceptual assessment technique. It has been discovered that the learning process itself may be influenced by many psychological variables. Much of the discrimination learning literature has dealt with those variables that seem to influence the rapidity of acquiring differential responses to different stimuli. Indeed some rather elaborate theories (for example, Spence, 1960; Harlow, 1950) have been offered in an attempt to account for the various complexities of the discrimination learning process.

It is sometimes useful to use S–R tables to describe what is involved in a discrimination procedure. Take the case of a simple discrimination problem involving the presentation of two different colors to a subject. One of these colors we will call S_1, the other S_2. We will indicate that the subject has to respond to (approach, enter, lift) S_1 and not S_2, and he must respond to S_1 regardless of which position it is in, left or right. We will indicate with a plus sign that S_1 is the positive stimulus and with a negative sign that S_2 is the negative stimulus. By "positive" we mean that response to the stimulus will be rewarded. The S–R table for this problem would then appear as follows, taking into consideration the two possible stimulus settings:

$$(1) \; S_1+ \quad S_2-$$
$$(2) \; S_2- \quad S_1+$$

At the beginning of learning, presumably, the subject would not respond differentially; he would not go any more frequently to S_1 than he would to S_2. After he has been rewarded for responding to S_1 and not to S_2 for a number of trials, he would learn to go consistently and "correctly" to S_1 and he has learned the discrimination problem.

Now note that the same two stimuli, S_1 and S_2, can be presented in another fashion. Whereas the two different stimuli were presented simultaneously above, these stimuli may be presented successively. We might diagram such presentation as follows:

$$(1) \; S_1+ \quad S_1$$
$$(2) \; S_2 \quad S_2+$$

Here the subject must learn that when the S_1 stimulus is present, he must make one response, and when the other stimulus, S_2, is present, he must make another.

Most discrimination learning problems can be analyzed in the fashion above. In the first case, they are called simultaneous discrimination learning problems and in the second case, successive. It is interesting to observe that from the perceptual standpoint, an organism can learn the S_1–S_2 discrimination problem in either way, and we have the same information, that apparently the two stimuli are perceptually discriminable. But comparisons of the simultaneous and successive methods of stimulus presentation have suggested that the *process* occurs somewhat differently—or at least at different rates—in the two cases. In fact, it has been demonstrated that sometimes simultaneous presentation results in faster learning than successive, but sometimes the opposite occurs. The conditions that result in the superiority of one stimulus presentation procedure over the other have been the object of investigations reported in the first selection, by Lipsitt. When the children in this experiment responded directly to the stimulus source, windows in which the lights shone, the simultaneous procedure resulted in better learning. But when the children were required to respond to a locus removed from the stimulus source, the successive procedure tended to result in faster learning. Another study that demonstrates the importance of spatial factors associated with the stimulus, the reward, and the response is that of Murphy and Miller (1959).

It is a well-documented phenomenon that discrimination learning tends to proceed faster when the stimuli involved are physically distinctive. The more similar the stimuli, the slower does learning to respond differentially proceed. This effect is demonstrated in the second study, by Spiker, and it is presumed to be a result of stimulus generalization.

Another factor which has been shown to influence the acquisition of differential responses to different stimuli is that of stimulus pretraining. If a child has previously been required to respond differentially to stimuli, in a subsequent discrimination situation involving the same stimuli his perform-ance will tend to be facilitated. This effect is particularly evident in situations where the subject has previously been required to learn distinctive names for the stimuli to be discriminated, and the third selection, by Cantor, is pertinent to this set of findings.

It is a well-known phenomenon with infrahuman organisms, largely as a result of the work of Harlow and his colleagues, that with increased ex-perience in discrimination learning problems, subjects solve a series of dis-crimination tasks more and more quickly. It appears that with increased experience in similar situations, the subject learns to inhibit inappropriate re-sponses, to make responses more skillfully, and to seek and observe crucial aspects of the stimuli in appropriate places. This phenomenon has been at-tributed to "learning set," which has been variously interpreted as a transfer of training or a generalization phenomenon. The Shepard study provides an example of the learning set phenomenon as it occurs in children.

One of the important features of the discrimination learning situation is that it enables study of the relative effectiveness of different rewarding and punishing conditions. The Brackbill selection is an example of this type of study. One may investigate, in addition, the effects of delay and magnitude of reward, and the influence of different reinforcement schedules, on the acquisition of a discrimination learning task. Some of these other uses of discrimination tasks are dealt with in later sections of this book.

The psychological variables that may be studied with children in dis-crimination situations are numerous. Studies of discrimination learning are contributing substantially to the refinement of general behavior theory. Dis-crimination learning theory in turn has been most productive of hypotheses that can be adequately tested with children—indeed, some child psychologists think that many learning theory hypotheses are *best* tested with children.

REFERENCES

HARLOW, H. F.   Analysis of discrimination learning by monkeys. *J. exp. Psychol.*, 1950, *40*, 26–39.

MURPHY, J. V. and MILLER, R. E.   Spatial contiguity of cue, reward, and response in discrimination learning by children. *J. exp. Psychol.*, 1959, *58*, 485–489.

SPENCE, K. W.   *Behavior theory and learning.* Englewood Cliffs, N. J.: Prentice-Hall. 1960. Pp. 269–307, 359–367.

SIMULTANEOUS AND SUCCESSIVE DISCRIMINATION LEARNING IN CHILDREN [1,2]

LEWIS P. LIPSITT

IN DISCRIMINATION LEARNING with infrahuman organisms, two procedures for the presentation of the stimuli to be discriminated are available. In a discrimination problem to be learned in a T-maze or a Lashley jumping apparatus and involving a black and a white stimulus, for example, the "simultaneous" procedure involves the presentation of a black and a white stimulus on each trial with position counterbalanced. The "successive" procedure entails presentation of only one of the discriminative stimuli on each trial. The reinforced responses in the simultaneous situation might be going left to black in a black-left, white-right arrangement and going right to black in a white-left, black-right arrangement. Approach to black, therefore, would consistently result in reinforcement. The reinforced responses in the successive situation might be going right to a black presentation and left to a white presentation.

Spence (7) has described simultaneous discrimination learning as resulting

[1] Portions of this paper were presented in the symposium, "Recent Developments in Experimental Methods with Children," at the meetings of the Amer. Psychol. Ass., Washington, D. C., 1958.

[2] This research was supported initially by a Grant-in-Aid from the Sigma Xi-RESA Research Fund and subsequently by a National Science Foundation grant. The writer is indebted to Mr. Albert F. Ehnes, Superintendent of the Seekonk, Massachusetts, Public Schools, and to Mr. Edward Fitzgerald, Superintendent of the Bristol, Rhode Island, Public Schools for their cooperation and to the principals and teachers who helped make these studies possible.

Reprinted by permission from *Child Development*, 1961, *32*, 337–347.

from the strengthening of response to the reinforced component of the stimulus complex until it attains sufficiently greater strength than competing incorrect response tendencies to result in consistently correct choices. Spence (8) has also said that the successive problem can be solved as a patterned discrimination, i.e., by *S*'s approaching certain patterns or combinations of reinforced stimulus components, while response to other patterns is not reinforced. He suggested that on this basis the successive problem should be more difficult than a simultaneous learning problem involving the same stimuli, because the stimulus compounds to be discriminated on each trial are more similar than in the simultaneous problem, and he presented evidence for this proposition from rat studies.

Not all infrahuman studies have supported the contention that simultaneous stimulus presentation produces faster learning than successive presentation. Several studies have suggested that at least under some experimental circumstances successive provides better performance than simultaneous stimulus presentation (1, 2, 9). In general, however, those experimental instances in which successive proved easier than simultaneous learning have involved a different kind of response than those characteristic of the T-maze or typical Lashley jumping situation. When the animal is required to "orient towards and approach the stimulus complex (path, door, alley, window) containing the positive stimulus cue (white, form, etc.) . . ." (8, p. 89), simultaneous stimulus presentation tends to result in better discrimination learning than successive. When the animal is required, however, to make a response to a locus removed from the stimulus source (1, 2,

9), it is not unusual for successive to prove either equal to or easier than the simultaneous problem. Furthermore, the relative difficulty of the simultaneous and successive problems has been reported to be influenced greatly by the similarity of the stimuli to be discriminated (1, 3, 4, 8).

The studies reported here investigate the relative discrimination learning performances of children under the simultaneous and successive stimulus presentation procedures, varying the nature of the response required and stimulus similarity.

EXPERIMENT I [3]

Experiment 1 involves a learning situation for children in which the to-be-learned responses are to loci (buttons) removed from the stimulus sources (the windows or apertures).

METHOD

Apparatus.[4] The apparatus was a black plywood box, 12 in. high by $12\frac{1}{2}$ in. deep. The front panels were $25\frac{1}{4}$ in. wide. There were three stimulus apertures each faced with a milk glass window on the upper panel and three response buttons on the lower panel. Distance from the three stimulus apertures to their respective response buttons was $6\frac{1}{2}$ in. Behind each of the windows were five different colored bulbs (GE C-6 Series type) set in a metal reflecting unit. Three selector switches, one for each window,

[3] This experiment was reported at the meetings of Eastern Psychol. Ass., Philadelphia, April, 1958.

[4] The apparatus, financed by the Ruth Holton Memorial Fund, was constructed while the writer was at the Iowa Child Welfare Research Station. Thanks are due Mr. John Peterson, who aided in its construction.

were situated at the back of the apparatus where E could preselect which color would appear in each window. Another selector switch enabled E to preselect which of the three buttons would be correct on each trial. A jeweled reflector light, located just above the middle button, would be activated when S pushed the correct button. A toggle switch activated the entire circuit so that (a) the preselected lights came on in the three windows and (b) response to the appropriate button would turn out the stimulus lights and activate the signal light, while wrong responses would merely turn out the stimulus lights. Thus, correction on the part of the S was not possible. The buttons were attached to $\frac{1}{16}$ in. metal rods which passed through small holes in the response panel, each rod meeting a microswitch inside.

Subjects and Design. The Ss were 40 fourth grade children obtained from the Bristol, Rhode Island, Public Schools and randomly assigned to one of four groups. Half of the total number of Ss were administered a simultaneous discrimination learning problem, and half a successive discrimination problem. Half of the Ss in each of these groups were run in a "similar-stimulus" condition, and half in a "distinctive-stimulus" condition. For the similar stimulus group, the colors were red, pink, and blue. For the distinctive stimulus group, the colors were red, green, and blue. On the assumption that red and pink are more similar physically than red and green, it was presumed that a greater amount of generalization would occur for the similar stimulus group, thus retarding learning involving these stimuli.

Procedure. A three-stimulus, three-response procedure was employed for all Ss. Half of the Ss were administered the simultaneous procedure, and half the successive stimulus procedure. The manner of stimulus presentation for the simultaneous and successive conditions closely follows procedures used in infrahuman investigations of two-stimulus problems. An S under the simultaneous condition was presented with the three stimuli exposed together, one in each aperture. Response to the button under one of these colors was consistently followed by the onset of the reward light, while response to either of the other buttons on that trial was not.

The order of stimulus presentation was the same for all Ss under the simultaneous condition, and the successive order was the same for all Ss in those groups. There were three stimulus arrangements (A: 1, 2, 3; B: 2, 3, 1; C: 3, 1, 2) possible for the simultaneous groups, and three (A: 1, 1, 1; B: 2, 2, 2; C: 3, 3, 3) for the successive groups. Each of these arrangements occurred in each block of three trials. These three arrangements may be ordered in six different ways (ABC, BAC, BCA, CBA, CAB, ACB). The order in which these six combinations were administered was determined randomly (with the restriction that identical stimulus presentations should not occur on successive trials) to provide a total of 18 trials. The 18-trial block was repeated to produce two cycles or a total of 36 trials, the maximum number administered.

Thus, for both kinds of discrimination, each response button is correct once within each three-trial block, and no position response is ever correct two trials in a row. Furthermore, since the correct-response order is the same for both, neither group is provided mnemonic cues for possible response-sequence learning that is not provided for the other.

All Ss performed individually in a room away from the classroom. The same instructions were given all Ss, regardless of the condition of stimulus presentation to which they were assigned. When seated at the apparatus, they were informed that they would be shown some lights and that when the lights came on they were to press one of the buttons that they thought correct. In the beginning they would not know which buttons were correct, but after a while they would learn which buttons to push and then would not make so many mistakes. They were told that the green signal light would go on when they were correct, but that that light would not go on when wrong.

Ss were trained until they reached a criterion of nine consecutively correct responses or for a total of 36 trials. A trial is here defined in the conventional manner as the sequence proceeding with the onset of stimuli followed by the execution of one response, offset of the stimuli, and where appropriate onset of the reward light.

RESULTS

The response measure here is the number of correct responses in 36 trials with correct responses assumed for those trials for any S beyond nine consecutively correct. Figure 1 compares the number of correct responses made over 36 trials by the simultaneous and successive groups, disregarding similarity of stimuli. While the two groups perform about equally and at chance level during the first block of six trials, the successive

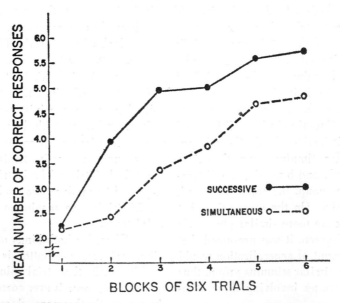

Figure 1. Learning curves for the simultaneous and successive groups of experiment 1, involving response to a locus removed from the stimulus source.

group overtakes the simultaneous and maintains its superiority through the remaining five blocks. Table 1 presents the over-all means and standard deviations for each of the four groups. An analysis of variance over the number-correct data, including analysis of trials effects, revealed that the superiority of successive over simultaneous training was reliable at the .01 level ($F = 7.39$, $df = 1$, 36). The main effect of stimulus similarity was not different from chance, but the trials by similarity interaction was reliable at the .05 level ($F = 4.04$, $df = 5$, 180), based on a tendency for the learning rate of the distinctive stimulus condition to be greater than that for the similar stimulus condition. Other than a trials effect significant at the .001 level, the only other reliable effect was the triple interaction ($F = 6.59$, $df = 5$, 180, $p = .001$) based on a tendency for there to be no differences in learning rate for the two successive groups, but a greater learning rate for the simultaneous-distinctive than the simultaneous-similar condition.

The major finding of this experiment is that under a procedure involving response to buttons removed from the stimulus source, successive stimulus presentation provided reliably better discrimination learning than simultaneous presentation.

TABLE 1 · MEANS AND STANDARD DEVIATIONS FOR THE FOUR GROUPS OF EXPERIMENT 1

| | TYPE OF STIMULUS PRESENTATION | | | | |
| | Simultaneous | | Successive | | Total |
	M	SD	M	SD	M
Similar (red, pink, blue)	21.2	7.7	27.3	6.1	24.3
Distinctive (red, green, blue)	21.3	7.8	27.5	4.8	24.4
Total	21.3		27.4		

EXPERIMENT 2

This experiment was designed to determine the importance of the button-pushing response involved in experiment 1. In the present experiment, all conditions were the same as in the first experiment except that now Ss were required only to point toward and touch the correct window on each trial.

METHOD

Apparatus. The apparatus was the same as that of experiment 1. The buttons, which were removable, were taken from the response panel leaving in their place very small ($\frac{1}{16}$ in. diameter) holes through which the button rods leading to the microswitches passed.

Subjects and Design. The Ss were 20 fourth grade children from the Pleasant Street School in Seekonk, Massachusetts. These Ss had not been subjects in previous experiments and had never seen the apparatus with the buttons attached. All Ss were administered the red-pink-blue discrimination. Half of the Ss were administered the stimuli under the simultaneous presentation procedure, and half under the successive procedure.

Procedure. The procedure of discrimination learning was exactly the same as that of experiment 1, except that response buttons were not available to Ss. Instead, the Ss were instructed that they would be shown some lights and that each time the lights were shown they were to point toward and touch the window that they thought correct. If they touched the correct window, they would be told that that was correct, while if they touched the wrong window the E would indicate that this was incorrect. Manner of stimulus administration and stimulus order followed exactly the same plan as that of experiment 1. *E* said "Yes" or "Wrong" after each trial.

RESULTS

The learning curves for the simultaneous and successive discrimination learning groups are seen in Figure 2. Here it may be seen that the simultaneous stimulus procedure is clearly superior to that of the successive group throughout training. The simultaneous group started at chance level within the first three trials of the experiment and by the third block of six trials was performing 100 per cent correctly. The successive presentation group, on the other hand, did not as a group depart from chance performance through the 36 training trials, and only one subject of 10 solved the successive

problem by the end of training. A median test of the over-all difference in performance between the groups resulted in a chi square with Yates' correction of 9.8 (*df* = 1), which is reliable beyond the .01 level of significance.

It seems quite clear from experiment 2 that, when the children are required to respond directly to the stimulus source, the simultaneous stimulus presentation results in better learning, in contrast to the finding of experiment 1 where *Ss* responded to a locus some distance removed from the stimulus source.

EXPERIMENT 3

The next experiment returns to the light-button procedure and investigates the relative ease of discrimination learning under the simultaneous and successive stimulus presentation procedures under

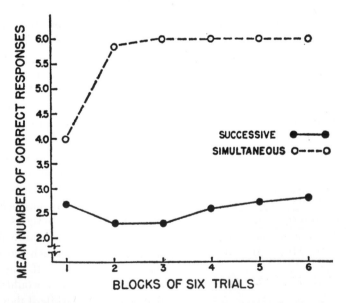

Figure 2. Learning curves for the simultaneous and successive groups of experiment 2, involving response directly to the stimulus source.

two levels of stimulus similarity. The purpose of the present experiment was to test the limit of the successive superiority over simultaneous of experiment 1 by using a condition of extremely high stimulus similarity. It was thought that, at some high level of stimulus similarity, the simultaneous condition must produce better discrimination than the successive even under the light-button procedure, on the assumption that the psychophysical difference thresholds must be smaller for paired comparisons procedures than for methods of single stimuli. Thus, if the stimuli are made highly similar, the problem should be more soluble for simultaneous Ss than for successive Ss.

METHOD

Apparatus. The apparatus was the same as that of experiments 1 and 2, with the buttons replaced.

Subjects and Design. The Ss were 40 fourth grade children from the Newman Avenue and North Schools in Seekonk, Massachusetts, who had not previously participated in discrimination learning experiments. They were assigned randomly to one of the four conditions: simultaneous-similar, simultaneous-distinctive, successive-similar, successive-distinctive. The colors for the similar stimulus conditions were red, pink, and orange (more similar than any set in the previous two studies), and for the distinctive stimulus condition red, green, and blue.

Procedure. The conditions of learning were essentially the same as those of experiment 1, with Ss being instructed that on each trial they were to push the button that they thought correct after looking at the lights. Particular caution

was used in insuring identical instructions for both the simultaneous and successive presentation groups. All Ss were trained for a total of 36 trials.

RESULTS

Figure 3 shows the mean number of correct responses made in 36 trials by the four experimental groups, and Table 2 contains the means and standard deviations on which a factorial analysis of variance was performed. Comparison of the distinctive with the similar stimulus conditions indicates that stimulus similarity has an over-all effect on performance significant at the .001 level ($F = 18.82$, $df = 1$, 36). It may be noted that the mean performance of the distinctive-successive group is somewhat superior to that of the distinctive-simultaneous group (as in experiment 1), but for the highly similar stimuli simultaneous presentation provides clearly superior performance to successive. This interaction between type of discrimination and level of stimulus similarity fell just short of significance at the .05 level ($F = 3.92$, $df = 1$, 36), and the difference between simultaneous and successive means under the similar-stimulus condition yielded a t of 2.33 ($df = 18$, $p = .05$).

While this experiment did not re-

TABLE 2 · MEANS AND STANDARD DEVIATIONS FOR THE FOUR GROUPS OF EXPERIMENT 3

	TYPE OF STIMULUS PRESENTATION				
	Simultaneous		*Successive*		*Total*
	M	SD	M	SD	M
Similar (red, pink, orange)	22.9	7.6	15.9	4.9	19.4
Distinctive (red, green, blue)	27.9	7.2	29.3	5.3	28.6
Total	25.4		22.6		

liably reproduce the successive over si-multaneous superiority of experiment 1, the direction of the difference is the same, and the expected inversion of the simul-taneous and successive means with a great increase in stimulus similarity is found. Thus, it appears that for children both stimulus similarity and the nature of the response required are pertinent parame-ters in the determination of the relative ease of learning simultaneous and succes-sive discrimination problems.

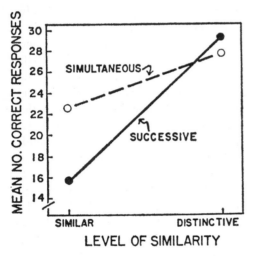

Figure 3. Comparisons of mean number of total correct responses from experiment 3 for the simultaneous and successive groups under two levels of stimulus similarity.

DISCUSSION

The three studies reported above considered together support the propo-sitions that in children (a) simultaneous stimulus presentation tends to provide better visual discrimination learning than successive when the response required is to the source of stimulation, but that, (b) if the response required is to a locus re-moved from the stimulus source, either no

differences occur or an inversion results with successive presentation yielding the better discrimination performance; fur-thermore, (c) this relationship is affected by degree of stimulus similarity, such that under conditions of high similarity, simultaneous presentation provides better learning than successive while with highly distinctive stimuli this difference may disappear or result in an inversion with successive superior to simultaneous. Thus, conditions which would tend to maximize simultaneous superiority over successive would involve high stimulus similarity and response to the stimulus source, with the obverse conditions tending to yield successive superiority over simultaneous.

Several studies with infrahuman organisms (1, 2, 4, 8, 9) have found some of the above phenomena, but few studies have investigated the problem of simul-taneous and successive stimulus presenta-tion in humans and fewer still have in-vestigated the interactions of parameters likely to lead to differential learning of the simultaneous and successive problems. Loess and Duncan (3) have shown that, under a highly similar stimulus condition or difficult discrimination, simultaneous proved better than successive learning, but when the stimuli were less difficult to discriminate there was no statistical dif-ference between the two procedures and in fact there tended to be superiority of the successive method. Perkins, Banks, and Calvin (6) investigated the effect of delay on learning in children. Their situation in-volved touching and picking up the dis-criminative stimuli, and simultaneous presentation tended to provide better learning than successive, with no effect whatever resulting from delay (a combi-nation of delayed reaction and delayed reward).

Recently, Murphy and Miller (5) have reported on a study with children using an experimental procedure designed to study the generality of a finding previously obtained with infrahuman primates. Their stimulus presentation procedures involved only the simultaneous method. They found that it is much easier for a child to learn a discrimination problem when he is responding directly to the stimulus source and that the problem becomes very difficult if the task is changed so that the child must now respond to a locus removed from the stimulus source, even if the child has had previous training on the same discrimination problem under the approach-to-stimulus procedure. The results of the present studies would suggest that such results would be most likely in simultaneous discrimination problems and that this phenomenon may not prevail so strikingly under a successive stimulus presentation procedure.

The present experiments suggest that the stimulus similarity continuum warrants more definitive study as it affects simultaneous and successive discrimination in children. They further suggest that other parameters (such as distance from the stimulus source of the response locus) could possibly produce similar behavioral effects and be superimposed upon the stimulus similarity dimension. It is possible also that other experimental manipulations which tend to depress discrimination learning generally such as increasing delay of reward, decreasing age, and large spatial or temporal separation of the stimuli, might have similar effects on performance in the simultaneous and successive problems. Stimulus generalization may be the pertinent mechanism producing the inversion effects

of the present studies and could result in similar findings when produced through other procedures.

SUMMARY AND CONCLUSIONS

The results of three discrimination learning studies of normal fourth grade children are reported. Comparisons of the methods of simultaneous and successive stimulus presentation are made under different levels of stimulus similarity and two types of response, either directly to the stimulus source or to a locus (buttons) removed from the stimulus source. The results of the three studies agree very well with the following propositions:

1. When response is directly to the stimulus source, simultaneous stimulus presentation tends to result in better learning than successive.

2. When the response is to a locus removed from the stimulus source, successive stimulus presentation may result in performance equal to or better than simultaneous.

3. The nature of the response involved in discrimination learning interacts with stimulus similarity, such that in procedures involving response to a locus removed from the stimulus source simultaneous may produce better learning than successive if the stimuli are very highly similar.

It is concluded that the relative ease of simultaneous and successive discrimination learning in children is a joint function of stimulus similarity and the type of response required. It is suggested further that other manipulable conditions undoubtedly interact with the two dealt with here and that possibly stimulus generalization is the mechanism underlying the effects of each.

REFERENCES

1. BITTERMAN, M. E., TYLER, D. W., & ELAM, C. B. Simultaneous and successive discrimination under identical stimulation conditions. *Amer. J. Psychol.*, 1955, *68*, 237–248.
2. BITTERMAN, M. E., & WODINSKY, J. Simultaneous and successive discrimination. *Psychol. Rev.*, 1953, *60*, 371–376.
3. LOESS, H. B., & DUNCAN, C. P. Human discrimination learning with simultaneous and successive presentation of stimuli. *J. exp. Psychol.*, 1952, *44*, 215–221.
4. MacCASLIN, E. F. Successive and simultaneous discrimination as a function of stimulus similarity. *Amer. J. Psychol.*, 1954, *67*, 308–314.
5. MURPHY, J. V., & MILLER, R. E. Spatial contiguity of cue, reward, and response in discrimination learning by children. *J. exp. Psychol.*, 1959, *58*, 485–489.
6. PERKINS, M. J., BANKS, H. P., & CALVIN, A. D. The effect of delay on simultaneous and successive discrimination in children. *J. exp. Psychol.*, 1954, *48*, 416–418.
7. SPENCE, K. W. The nature of discrimination learning in animals. *Psychol. Rev.*, 1936, *43*, 427–449.
8. SPENCE, K. W. The nature of the response in discrimination learning. *Psychol. Rev.*, 1952, *59*, 89–93.
9. WEISE, P., & BITTERMAN, M. E. Response selection in discrimination learning. *Psychol. Rev.*, 1951, *58*, 185–195.

EFFECTS OF STIMULUS SIMILARITY ON DISCRIMINATION LEARNING

CHARLES C. SPIKER [1]

INCREASE IN THE DIFFICULTY of a discrimination task, produced by increase in the similarity of the discriminal stimuli, has been explained in terms of increased generalization of incorrect approach and inhibitory tendencies (*1, 3, 4*). Observations of children in discrimination problems have led this investigator to consider the possibility that increase in stimulus similarity increases task

[1] The writer is indebted to Dr. Irma R. Gerjuoy who participated in the preliminary experiments upon which this experiment is based. He also wishes to thank his research assistant, Miss Ruth B. Holton, for her aid in collecting the data.
Reprinted by permission from *Journal of Experimental Psychology*, 1956, *51*, 393–395.

difficulty through the introduction of factors in addition to stimulus generalization. The present experiment is designed to test for the presence of such additional factors and to attempt to provide a measure of stimulus generalization that is not contaminated by them.

A successive discrimination task in which one or more of the available responses is always incorrect offers a means of isolating task difficulty contributed by stimulus generalization and that contributed by other factors. Increase in stimulus generalization would be expected to increase generalized (intralist) errors, but it would not be expected to increase the frequency of occurrence of responses that are never correct (extralist errors). On the other hand, if increase in stimulus similarity increases the potency of inattention, disinterest, frustration due to failure, etc., one would expect an increase in the frequency of both intralist and extralist errors.

METHOD

Apparatus. The apparatus was a black box, $18 \times 24 \times 16$ in. Six inches above a 3-button response panel was a 3-in. diameter aperture of flashed opal glass. White geometric figures (square, circle, or triangle) were painted around each of the buttons, each of which was approximately 7 in. from the other two. Two 75-w. projection lamps were mounted 6 in. behind the aperture, each enclosed in a light-proof reflecting container on the front of which a 2×2-in. glass color filter could be inserted. The E could turn on either one of the lamps and predetermine which of the three buttons would break its circuit. For each S, one button did not turn out either lamp. If S pushed the correct button, the lamp was turned out and a marble automatically delivered to S. Incorrect responses resulted in the disconnection of all buttons, thereby preventing more than one response per trial.

Experimental design. Three experimental groups differed only in the discriminal stimuli presented. The stimuli were obtained by diffusing light through glass color filters (Corning Glass Works) onto the aperture. Group HS was presented with a yellow-green (No. 4015) and a green (No. 4308 superimposed on No. 3484). Group S was presented with the yellow-green and a blue-green (No. 3385 superimposed on No. 4303). Group D received the yellow-green and a deep blue (No. 5330). The stimuli in each pair are readily discriminated by adults with normal color vision. Within these groups, the position of the disconnected button, which was never correct, was controlled by randomly assigning Ss to three subgroups.

Subjects. Sixty-five preschool Ss from the Iowa Child Welfare Research Station laboratories were randomly assigned to the experimental groups—25 to Group HS, 22 to Group S, and 18 to Group D. The Ss ranged in age from 4 yr., 2 mo. to 5 yr., 8 mo. Some Ss had previous experience with simultaneous and successive discrimination learning problems, but none had previous experience with the present apparatus.

Procedure. A familiar E brought S to the experimental room and allowed him to select one of a number of dime-store toys which he would attempt to win. The E then demonstrated the two stimulus lights one at a time, instructing S that marbles could be obtained by turning out the lights, and that the marbles could be used to buy the selected toy. The appropriate stimuli were presented in a prearranged order that was the same for all Ss. Each light appeared three times in successive blocks of six presentations, long series of alternations were avoided, and neither light appeared more than three times in succession. Button (position) preferences were verbally discouraged by E. All Ss received at least 30 stimulus presentations (trials); Ss who failed to attain 9 correct choices in 10 consecutive trials by Trial 30 were given additional trials until this criterion was attained or until 96 trials had been given. Eleven of the 65 Ss failed to reach this criterion in 96 trials.

RESULTS

Analysis of the total error scores for the subgroups, which differed only in terms of the position of the disconnected button, revealed no consistent or significant differences among them. Accordingly, the data for these subgroups have been combined within each experimental group. The scores used in subsequent analyses are the number of errors involving the button that was connected (intralist errors) and the number of errors involving the button that was disconnected (extralist errors).

Table 1 shows the means of the two

TABLE 1 · MEANS OF THE TWO TYPES OF ERROR

Groups	N	Intralist errors	Extralist errors	Total errors
HS	25	21.48	7.44	28.92
|S	22	17.64	6.95	24.59
D	18	6.44	3.28	9.72
Combined	65	16.02	6.12	

types of error for each of the three experimental groups. From inspection, it is apparent that both error types tend to increase in frequency with increase in stimulus similarity, and that the magnitude of the difference between the means of the two error types also increases with increasing stimulus similarity. For each group, the mean frequency of intralist errors is greater than that of extralist errors.

The statistical significance of these trends was tested by a Lindquist Type I analysis (2) and by further tests of the simple effects. The results of the Type I analysis are presented in Table 2. Here it is apparent that the experimental groups differ significantly in terms of mean total errors, and that frequency of intralist

TABLE 2 · ANALYSIS OF VARIANCE OF NUMBER OF ERRORS TO CRITERION

Source	df	Mean square	F	P
Ss:	64			
Stimuli (S)	2	1014.28	6.09	.005
Error (b)	62	166.47		
Within-Ss:	65			
Error type (E)	1	3180.38	32.34	.001
E × S	2	314.50	3.20	.05
Error (w)	62	98.34		
Total	129			

errors is significantly greater than the frequency of extralist errors for the combined experimental groups. Furthermore, there is an interaction ($P < .05$) between the stimulus groups and the type of error. The interaction indicates that, with increasing stimulus similarity, there is an increase in the magnitude of the difference between the mean frequencies of the two types of error.

The data were analyzed as two simple randomized designs to determine the stimulus effects on the two types of error separately. For the intralist errors, the stimulus effects were significant at the 1% level ($F = 5.54$; $df = 2, 62$). For extralist errors, the stimulus effects were significant at the 2.5% level ($F = 4.25$; $df = 2, 62$). Using the t test, comparisons were made of pairs of groups. For the intralist errors, the mean of Group D differs significantly from that of Group HS ($P < .01$) and from that of Group S ($P < .02$). The means for Groups HS and S do not differ significantly. For the extralist errors, also, the Group D mean is significantly lower than the Group HS mean ($P < .01$) and the Group S mean ($P < .02$), but the means for Groups HS and S are not significantly different. Clearly, an increase in stimulus similarity resulted in an increase of errors of both types.

Finally, t tests were made of the significance of the differences between means for intralist and extralist errors for the three experimental groups separately. Significantly more intralist errors than extralist errors were made by Groups HS and S ($P < .001$), but the difference for Group D was not statistically significant ($P > .05$).

DISCUSSION

The greater frequency of intralist than of extralist errors presumably reflects the operation of stimulus generalization, which, in the present experiment, is expected to increase intralist errors without directly increasing the number of extralist errors. The interaction between stimulus similarity and type of error is interpreted as the result of an increase in stimulus generalization with increasing stimulus similarity. This interaction is somewhat more statistically reliable ($P < .01$) when only the extreme groups are considered. It would seem that the interaction provides an index of the amount of generalization that is not affected by other factors that may be associated with increased stimulus similarity.

The increase in frequency of extralist errors with increasing stimulus similarity is only indirectly due to increased stimulus generalization. A task made difficult by high generalization is made even more difficult through loss of interest due to increased number of failures; elicitation of inappropriate responses (orienting away from stimuli, asking to leave the situation, hitting buttons indiscriminately, etc.); and the development of fatigue due to longer experimental sessions. Qualitative observations suggest that such factors were more frequent among Ss given highly similar stimuli than among those given distinctive stimuli.

The evidence indicates that errors on a discrimination learning task may provide an overestimate of the direct effects of stimulus generalization. Children's performance, at least, appears to be affected by stimulus similarity in a manner that can only partly be attributed directly to stimulus generalization.

SUMMARY

Three groups of preschool children were given a successive discrimination learning task in which generalized (intralist) or nongeneralized (extralist) errors could be made. The conditions for the three groups differed only in the similarity of the discriminal stimuli. The results indicated that increased stimulus similarity resulted in greater numbers of both types of error and an increased difference between the means of the two types of error. These results were interpreted as reflecting increased stimulus generalization as a function of increased stimulus similarity. The increase in extralist errors with increased stimulus similarity was interpreted as reflecting the operation of factors in addition to stimulus generalization, e.g., decrease in interest, motivation, or attention, and increase in fatigue.

REFERENCES

1. HULL, C. L. *A behavior system.* New Haven: Yale Univ. Press, 1952.
2. LINDQUIST, E. F. *Design and analysis of experiments in psychology and education.* Boston: Houghton Mifflin, 1953.
3. SPENCE, K. W. The nature of discrimination learning in animals. *Psychol. Rev.*, 1936, *43*, 427–449.
4. SPENCE, K. W. The differential response in animals to stimuli varying within a single dimension. *Psychol. Rev.*, 1937, *44*, 430–444.

Effects of Three Types of Pretraining on Discrimination Learning in Preschool Children [1]

GORDON N. CANTOR

THE PREDICTION that the possession of names for the stimuli in a learning task will enhance performance on that task has been tested in several studies. The enhancement phenomenon has been referred to as the "acquired distinctiveness of cues" (9, 10) and "stimulus predifferentiation" (2, 3, 5). In general, the experimental paradigm has involved a transfer task situation in which Ss are required to respond to certain discriminable stimuli. This task is preceded by a pretraining situation in which some of the Ss are taught names for these same stimuli, the names themselves having no connotations with respect to the nature of the responses in the transfer task. This type of pretraining has been termed "relevant-S." The more recent studies have utilized "irrelevant" pretraining groups, as well as or in place of "no-pretraining" groups, in order to control for warm-up and learning-to-learn effects (2, 3, 6, 8). The need for such controls has been demonstrated (4). Performances of relevant-S groups on various types of transfer tasks have been shown to be superior to those of irrelevant groups (2, 3, 6).[2]

The present experiment is concerned with the relative performances on a transfer task of three groups of children. Two of these involve the conventional relevant-S and irrelevant varieties of pretraining. The third—to be called hereafter the "attention" group—is made to attend to the relevant transfer task stimuli during a pretraining session, but is not given any verbal learning.

It is predicted that the relevant-S group will surpass the irrelevant and attention groups in performance on the transfer task. No prediction is made with respect to the relative performances of the irrelevant and attention groups.

METHOD

Subjects. The Ss were 60 children from the State University of Iowa Preschools and the Iowa City Parents' Preschool. There were 10 3-yr.-olds, 38 4-yr.-olds and 12 5-yr.-olds. An upper and a lower age group were constituted and Ss from within each age level were randomly assigned to the three treatment groups.

Procedure. The materials used in the verbal pretraining consisted of photographs

---

[1] This paper is based on a dissertation submitted to the Graduate College of the State University of Iowa in partial fulfillment of the requirements for the degree of Doctor of Philosophy. The writer is indebted to Dr. Charles C. Spiker for his generous guidance.

Reprinted by permission from *Journal of Experimental Psychology*, 1955, 49, 339–342.

[2] The terms "relevant-S" and "irrelevant" ε e McAllister's (8). The latter term refers to pretraining in which the stimuli are different from those occurring in the transfer task.

of pen and ink sketches of the following: (a) a pair of human adult female faces; and (b) a pair of human juvenile male faces.

The Ss in the relevant-S group received relevant-S pretraining in which they learned to associate the names "Jean" and "Peg" with the female faces (Pair A); learning was continued until a criterion of 15 consecutive pairs of correct responses was met. The Ss in the irrelevant group were given irrelevant pretraining, involving the male faces (Pair B) and the names "Jack" and "Pete," to the same criterion. The stimuli in these verbal learning situations were presented side by side to S. The right-left relationships of the pictures were varied in a prearranged and nonalternating fashion. An imitation coin reward was presented to S for each correct pair of responses. The S was corrected when erroneous responses were given. When the criterion was met, each S was allowed to cash in the accumulated coins for one-half of a toy set.

The attention pretraining did not involve verbal learning; rather, the Ss in the attention group were made to point to various parts of the relevant stimuli (Pair A). The stimuli were presented in a manner comparable to that involved in the relevant-S and irrelevant pretraining. Thirty trials were given to each attention group S, however, and a coin reward was given each time S pointed to the designated parts of the pictures in what E judged to be a "careful" manner. If S appeared lax in his pointing responses, the coin reward was withheld and S was urged to exercise more care.

All Ss were treated identically in the transfer task, which was administered immediately following pretraining. The apparatus and procedures of a recently reported study (1) on discrimination learning in preschool children were utilized, with slight modifications, in the transfer task. The stimuli were two wooden cars, identical in appearance except that each had a different one of the two faces from Pair A mounted on its side. The S's task involved choosing one of the two cars and rolling it down a track. The S was led to believe that the car's striking a dummy switch at the end of the track caused a marble dispenser to be activated. Actually, E controlled the operation of the dispenser by means of a hidden button. For each S, one of the two cars was arbitrarily designated by E as the "correct" stimulus. When this car was chosen by S and run down the track, a marble reward was dispensed; when the "incorrect" car was selected, no marble reward was delivered. The choice by S of one of the stimuli, followed by the car's run down the track and the subsequent reinforcement or nonreinforcement, constituted a trial. Thirty transfer task trials were given, S being instructed to obtain as many marbles as possible. Following Trial 30, S was allowed to exchange the accumulated marbles for the remainder of the toy set and the experiment was terminated. The response measure was the number of correct choices made in the transfer task.

RESULTS AND DISCUSSION

A treatments-by-levels analysis (7) of the pretraining data revealed that the relevant-S and irrelevant groups did not differ significantly from each other in mean number of trials required to meet the criterion. Table 1 shows the means and SD's for the subgroups. Table 2 presents the over-all means and SD's for the transfer task data.

TABLE 1 · PRETRAINING RESULTS—NUMBER OF TRIALS TO CRITERION

	RELEVANT-S		IRRELEVANT	
Age	Mean	SD	Mean	SD
L	26.0	10.80	27.3	10.24
U	28.8	14.32	21.8	6.79

TABLE 2 · NUMBER OF CORRECT RESPONSES IN 30 TRANSFER TRIALS

	RELEVANT-S		IRRELEVANT		ATTENTION	
Age	Mean	SD	Mean	SD	Mean	SD
L	23.6	5.97	16.5	5.50	18.0	5.44
U	20.9	7.16	17.2	5.44	17.4	3.98

In order to allow for a treatments × ages × trials analysis, the 30 trials were divided into six blocks of five trials each. A Type III analysis (7) was applied to these data, the results of which are summarized in Table 3.

TABLE 3 · SUMMARY OF ANALYSIS APPLIED TO TREATMENTS × AGES × TRIALS DATA †

Source	df	MS	F
Between Ss	59		
Treatments	2	28.10	4.74*
Ages	1	1.88	<1.00
Error (b)	54	5.93‡	
Within Ss	300		
Trials	5	4.25	4.01**
Treatments × trials	10	2.47	2.33*
Error (w)	270	1.06‡	
Total	359		

  * p < .05.
 ** p < .01.
 † All interactions involving age were nonsignificant.
 ‡ On the assumption of homogeneity of variance in the cells, the error terms obtained in this analysis, together with their respective df, were utilized in the analyses to be reported subsequently.

As indicated in Table 3, the treatments effect was significant at the .05 level of confidence, as was the treatments × trials interaction. Since no interaction involving age was significant, it was possible to compare the three treatment groups, taken two at a time, disregarding age levels. This was accomplished by the use of three Type I designs (7), the results of which are summarized in Table 4.

These analyses indicate that the relevant-S group surpassed both the irrelevant and attention groups in mean number of correct choices. The former comparison yielded a difference significant at the .01 level, whereas the latter difference was significant at the .05 level. The irrelevant and attention groups did not differ significantly from each other in terms of the treatment effects.

The treatments × trials interaction was significant at the .01 level for the relevant-S vs. irrelevant data and at the .05 level for the irrelevant vs. attention data, indicating that the learning curves differed from each other for the treatment groups involved.

TABLE 4 • SUMMARY OF ANALYSES APPLIED TO THE DATA COMPARING THE TREATMENTS TWO AT A TIME, DISREGARDING AGE LEVELS

Source	df	MEAN SQUARES		
		Relevant-S vs. irrelevant	Relevant-S vs. attention	Irrelevant vs. attention
Between Ss				
Treatments	1	48.60**	34.51*	1.21
Error (b)	54	5.93	5.93	5.93
Within Ss				
Trials	5	4.53**	4.43**	2.01
Treatments × trials	5	3.65**	.81	2.95*
Error (w)	270	1.06	1.06	1.06

  * p < .05.
 ** p < .01.

The results indicate that the experience of learning names for a pair of stimuli evidently did facilitate later performance on a task involving those stimuli, as predicted. By the use made of the irrelevant and attention groups, it was shown that the enhancement in performance attributable to the possession of names was greater than that which could be attributed either to the transfer of nonspecific reactions or to mere exposure to the relevant stimuli during pretraining.

SUMMARY

Three groups, each consisting of 20 3-to-5-yr.-old children, were given identical treatment in a transfer task situation after having experienced different types of pretraining. The relevant-S group learned during pretraining to associate names with each of the two pictures of faces that subsequently served as stimuli in the transfer task. The irrelevant group was given a comparable amount of paired-associate learning, but with stimuli unrelated to the transfer task. The attention group was not given a verbal learning experience, but rather was merely exposed to the relevant stimuli during pretraining. The transfer task involved a simple discrimination learning situation, the response measure being the number of correct choices made in 30 presentations of the relevant stimuli.

Analyses of the transfer task data revealed that the relevant-S group performed significantly better than did the irrelevant and attention groups. Significant treatments $\times$ trials interactions indicated that the learning curves of the relevant-S and irrelevant groups differed, as did the curves for the irrelevant and attention groups.

It was concluded that the results were in agreement with the prediction that the possession of names for the stimuli in a learning task would enhance performance on that task.

REFERENCES

1. CANTOR, G. N., & SPIKER, C. C. Effects of nonreinforced trials on discrimination learning in preschool children. *J. exp. Psychol.*, 1954, 47, 256–258.

2. CANTOR, J. H. Amount of pretraining as a factor in stimulus pre-differentiation. Unpublished doctor's dissertation, State Univ. of Iowa, 1954.

3. DYSINGER, D. W. An investigation of stimulus pre-differentiation in a choice discrimination problem. Unpublished doctor's dissertation, State Univ. of Iowa, 1951.

4. FARBER, I. E., & MURFIN, F.L. Performance set as a factor in transfer of training. Paper read at Midwest. Psychol. Ass., Chicago, April, 1951.

5. GAGNÉ, R. M., & BAKER, K. E. Stimulus pre-differentiation as a factor in transfer of training. *J. exp. Psychol.*, 1950, 40, 439–451.

6. GERJUOY, I. R. Discrimination learning as a function of the similarity of the stimulus names. Unpublished doctor's dissertation, State Univ. of Iowa, 1953.

7. LINDQUIST, E. F. *Design and analysis of experiments in psychology and education.* Boston: Houghton Mifflin, 1953.

8. McALLISTER, D. E. The effects of various kinds of relevant verbal pretraining on subsequent motor performance. *J. exp. Psychol.*, 1953, 46, 329–336.

9. MILLER, N. E. Theory and experiment relating psychoanalytic displacement to stimulus-response generalization. *J. abnorm. soc. Psychol.*, 1948, 43, 155–178.

10. ROSSMAN, I. L., & GOSS, A. E. The acquired distinctiveness of cues: the role of discriminative verbal responses in facilitating the acquisition of discriminative motor responses. *J. exp. Psychol.*, 1951, 42, 173–182.

LEARNING SET IN PRESCHOOL CHILDREN

WINIFRED O. SHEPARD

THERE IS AMPLE EVIDENCE from the work of Harlow (2, 3, 4), North (6, 7), and Riopelle (8, 9, 10) that the learning-set phenomenon is a genuine one in animal discrimination learning behavior. There are, however, to the author's knowledge, only two recorded instances of this phenomenon with human beings. One is Kuenne's study with preschool children mentioned by Harlow (2). The other is Adams' study with adult males (1). Furthermore, all but the last-mentioned study dealt with simple simultaneous discrimination tasks. Adams dealt with a fairly complex discrimination task in which Ss had to learn to associate each of four buttons with a different spatial arrangement of stimuli. The present study was designed to add to our knowledge of the learning set phenomenon by using conditional space discrimination tasks with preschool children.

METHOD

SUBJECTS

Twenty-six children between the ages of four and six from the Iowa Preschool Laboratories participated in the experiment. Six of these were dropped for failure to learn the first task.

STIMULI

The stimuli were 12 upper- and lower-case Greek letters randomly arranged in 6 pairs. Each symbol was cut from black con-

Reprinted by permission from *Journal of Comparative and Physiological Psychology*, 1957, 50, 15–17.

struction paper and mounted on a white 4- by 4-in. cardboard square. These six pairs constituted the stimuli for six learning tasks.

APPARATUS

The apparatus consisted of a black wooden baseboard which measured 17½ by 5½in. It had three 4½-in.–square shallow depressions in it. A red board 19½ by 9½ in. was hinged to this baseboard in such a manner that, between trials, it stood at right angles to the base, permitting E to manipulate the stimuli without being seen by S. During trials, it could be swung back, revealing the stimuli. There were also four black 4¼-in.–square boxes, each with one open end. The boxes could be fitted, three at a time, into the depressions in the baseboard. Two boxes were always kept in place in the outside depressions. The E slipped a chip under one of them on each trial. The other two boxes were fitted with grooves on one face. A stimulus card could be slipped into these grooves. On each trial one of the stimulus presentation boxes was presented in the middle depression.

PROCEDURE

The Ss were randomly divided into two groups, one group getting pair 1 first and pair 6 last, and the other group getting pair 6 first and pair 1 last. On each task Ss had to learn to pick the left-hand box when presented with one stimulus and the right when presented with the other. Correct responses were set up in order A, RLRRRLLR, and order B, its reverse. During the first task orders A and B were alternated until S reached criterion or was eliminated. The second task consisted of one run through order A (eight trials) ; the third, one run through order B, and so on through the sixth task.

Each child was brought into the experimental room and seated at a low table in front of the apparatus. The E sat opposite him behind the apparatus. The S was first told that he had to win a large quantity of poker chips in order to be able to select a prize. He was then told that every time E pulled back the red board he would see three boxes and that the middle one would have a picture on it. It was explained that he must look at the picture carefully each time and then tip back one of the other boxes to see if he could find a chip. Whenever S did tip back the right box, he was allowed to take the chip and place it in a box he kept next to him. Whenever he tipped back the wrong box, he was merely told to look at the picture again, but was not allowed to correct his response. The Ss were run on the first task to a criterion of ten successive correct responses. The Ss who made an incorrect response on trial 40 were eliminated, and Ss who made a correct response on trial 40 were continued until they either made an error or reached criterion. If an S showed no signs of learning the first task by trial 10, verbal encouragement was given. He was reminded frequently to look at the pictures carefully, because the picture would tell each time which box to pick. The Ss who showed strong position preferences were told that the chip was not always on the same side. All Ss who were not eliminated on the first task received eight trials on each of the remaining five tasks. No further verbal help was given. The entire experiment was run in one session with a 5-min. rest period after the third task.

RESULTS AND DISCUSSION

As mentioned earlier, 6 Ss were eliminated from the experiment for failure to learn the first task. The trials to criterion for the remaining 20 Ss (excluding criterional trials) ranged from 0 to 32 with a mean of 16.2.

Figure 1 shows the mean number of correct responses on trials 2 to 8 made by the 20 Ss on each task. Trial 1 data were not considered since it was always

a purely chance affair. As can be seen from the figure, the major facilitative effect took place from the first to the second task. The fact that the curve dips down after the second task can probably be explained in terms of boredom and consequent wandering of attention—phenomena quite often observed in the members of this particular population after they have, effectively, solved a learning problem.

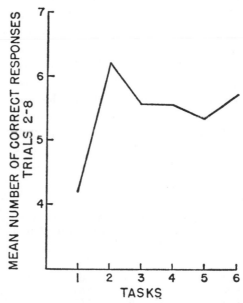

Figure 1. Mean number of correct responses in trials 2 to 8 on each task.

The data on which this figure was based were subjected to a treatments by subjects (5) analysis of variance which is summarized in Table 1. It can be seen from this table that the task effect was significant at less than the .001 level. When the simple effects of task were tested, it was found that performance on the first task differed from each of the others at less than the .01 level, but that none of the other intertask differences approached significance at this level, indicating that these Ss had "learned to learn" after successful completion of the first task.

Since half the Ss received the pairs in the order 1 to 6 and half in the order 6 to 1, it was possible to compare performance on each of these pairs when administered first and last. On pair 1 the mean number of correct responses on trials 2 to 8 for these ten Ss who received it first was 3.6 and for the ten who received it last 5.7 The probability of occurrence of this difference is less than .01. The mean number of correct responses on trials 2 to 8 for the ten Ss who received pair 6 first was 4.8. For those who received it last it was 5.7. This difference, while in the right direction, has a probability of occurrence between .1 and .2. It seems likely that both these differences were deflated by the boredom factor mentioned before.

TABLE 1 · SUMMARY OF ANALYSIS OF VARIANCE OF CORRECT RESPONSES IN TRIALS 2 TO 8 FOR SIX TASKS

Source	df	MS	F
Tasks	5	8.85	5.36**
Subjects	19	2.85	1.73
Tasks × subjects	95	1.65	

**p < .001.

Finally, a word should be said about the difference in results reported here and those found by Kuenne (2), who found it took a much longer series of tasks to demonstrate learning set in preschool children. Several factors probably account for this discrepancy. The Ss in the present study were older than hers, were not experimentally naive, and were given verbal encouragement. Furthermore, in this study, due to the press of time, Ss who

failed to learn the first task in a specified time were eliminated. In Kuenne's study, all problems were presented for six trials regardless of S's performance, and each S continued in the series of problems until he met a series criterion.

SUMMARY

Twenty preschool children were presented, on one day, with six conditional space discrimination problems. There was a marked improvement in performance from the first to the second task and then a slight decline, probably attributable to boredom.

REFERENCES

1. ADAMS, J. A. Multiple versus single problem training in human problem solving. J. exp. Psychol., 1954, 48, 15–18.

2. HARLOW, H. F. The formation of learning sets. Psychol. Rev., 1949, 56, 51–65.

3. HARLOW, H. F. Analysis of discrimination learning by monkeys. J. exp. Psychol., 1950, 40, 26–39.

4. HARLOW, H. F., & WARREN, J. M. Formation and transfer of discrimination learning sets. J. comp. physiol. Psychol., 1952, 45, 482–489.

5. LINDQUIST, E. F. Design and analysis of experiments in psychology and education. New York: Houghton Mifflin, 1953.

6. NORTH, A. J. Improvement in successive discrimination reversals. J. comp. physiol. Psychol., 1950, 43, 442–460.

7. NORTH, A. J. Performance during

an extended series of discrimination reversals. *J. comp. physiol. Psychol.*, 1950, *43*, 461–470.

8. RIOPELLE, A. J. Transfer suppression and learning sets. *J. comp. physiol. Psychol.*, 1953, *46*, 108–114.

9. RIOPELLE, A. J., & COPELAN, E. L. Discrimination reversal to a sign. *J. exp. Psychol.*, 1954, *48*, 143–145.

10. RIOPELLE, A. J. Learning sets from minimum stimuli. *J. exp. Psychol.*, 1955, *49*, 28–32.

THE RELATIVE EFFECTIVENESS OF REWARD AND PUNISHMENT FOR DISCRIMINATION LEARNING IN CHILDREN [1]

YVONNE BRACKBILL
JOHN O'HARA

THE PURPOSE of the present study was to compare the relative effectiveness of reward and punishment for discrimination learning in children. A similar problem was investigated in an early animal study by Warden and Aylesworth (6). They found that rats rewarded for correct responses and punished for errors learned a discrimination twice as fast as a punished-only group of animals and nine times as fast as rats run under a reward-only condition.

The hypothesis of the present study was that children would learn a discrimination problem faster under a combined reward-punishment condition than under a condition of reward only. The logically indicated third group, punishment-only, was not included because of the possibility that there would be complaints from Ss run under this condition which would reflect upon the school administration and ultimately endanger the continuance of the experiment.

[1] This research was done at San Jose State College. The authors wish to express their thanks and gratitude for the cooperation and assistance of Elizabeth Backlund, School Psychologist, Alum Rock School District; Clyde Hewitt, Principal, Linda Vista School; and Calvin Thomson, San Jose State College.

Reprinted by permission from *Journal of Comparative and Physiological Psychology*, 1958, *51*, 747–751.

EXPERIMENT I

METHOD

Subjects. Ss were 43 male kindergarten children from a single elementary school. Mean age was 70.3 months, $\sigma = 3.6$. The sample was relatively homogeneous in terms of race and socioeconomic status (white, middle class).

Procedure. The Ss were alternately assigned to the two experimental conditions. Both groups learned the same discrimination problem to a criterion. Group R ($N = 21$) was rewarded for correct responses but received no reinforcement for errors. Group R-P ($N = 22$) was rewarded for correct responses and punished for errors.

The discriminative stimuli were three cardboard boxes differing in color and size. Box 1 measured $4\frac{1}{4}$ by $3\frac{1}{2}$ by $1\frac{1}{8}$ in. and was painted with a mixture of two parts red dope to one part white dope. Box 2 had the same dimensions as Box 1, and was painted with a mixture of one part red dope to two parts white dope. Box 3 measured $3\frac{1}{8}$ by $2\frac{1}{4}$ by $1\frac{3}{8}$ in., and was painted with orange dope. Color and size, however, were irrelevant cues, as was also the presence of the third box, since the correct response was a simple position-alternation sequence of the reinforcement between the first and second boxes. The boxes were placed on a large piece of brown felt in order to minimize auditory cues. They were presented open side down, and were approximately 4 in. distant from each other. The end boxes were equidistant from S, and the position of the boxes was constant for all trials.

The S was seated opposite E at a small table on which lay the discriminative stimuli. On a second table, to S's right, lay a small pillow on which S rested his head between trials. This served two purposes: (*a*) it eliminated the necessity of placing a screen in front of S while E reloaded the boxes, and (*b*) it reduced sound localization in the event of any auditory cues during reloading.

As soon as S entered the experimental room, E gave the following instructions:

(Both groups) "Do you know what these are?" E paused and indicated an open box of M & M candies. "They're candy, they're chocolate."

(Group R-P) "I'm going to give you some of the candies for your very own" (E deposited 15 candies on a small piece of felt near S), "and I'll keep the rest over here. Now, I have something very special for you to do, and if you can do it, you can have

some more of the candy. I'm going to put one candy at a time under one of these boxes. And every time you pick up the *wrong* box, you'll have to *give back* one of your candies." E pointed to S's pile. "Understand? Now! *There is a way to find the right box every single time. See if you can find the way.*"

(Group R) "Now, I have something very special for you to do, and if you can do it, you can have some of the candy. I'm going to put one candy at a time under one of these boxes. And every time you pick up the box that has the candy under it, you can keep the candy. Understand? Now! *There is a way to find the right box every single time. See if you can find the way.*"

(Both groups) "Put your head down on that pillow and wait until I say 'ready'. . . . Ready. Pick up the box that you think has the candy under it." Following first correct choice, E said, "Now every time you get a candy, pick it up and put it down there, and all the candies that you put there will be for you to keep." For Group R-P, following first incorrect choice, E said: "That was the wrong box, so you'll have to give back one of your candies."

After the last trial, the following statement was repeated until S indicated agreement. The purpose of the statement was to "jam" inter-S communication. "Well, you found the way, didn't you? You found out that the candy was always under the *red* box." (E indicated simultaneously all boxes.) "Yes, the candy was always under the *red* box."

For the R-P group a contingency procedure was established to prevent the child from losing his initial stake of 15 candies in the first few trials during which success was largely a function of chance. If and when S's pile of candies first decreased in number to 9, E added one candy. Likewise, 1 more candy was added the first time S's candies decreased in number to 7. Five candies was established as the size minimum, and S's pile was not allowed to fall below this number. These additions were made only once, and only when candy pile size was decreasing, not when it was increasing. They were made between trials, as S rested his head on the pillow, facing away from E, and the added candy was always of the same color as the predominant color of S's own candies. Possibly because of these precautions there was no indication that any of the four Ss with whom the procedure was necessary was aware of the surreptitious additions.

The E recorded the outcome of each trial, S's verbatim verbalizations, and all nonverbal, task-irrelevant responses. Two learning criteria were used. The first one was the number of trials taken before S ceased to choose the irrelevant or never-reinforced Box 3 (in other words, the number of the last trial on which S chose this box). The second criterion was the number of trials taken to a run of 10 consecutive correct choices. An experimental session ended either when S reached the second criterion or after Trial 150. In the latter case, the score assignment was 150. Session length ranged from 10 to 25 min. per S, depending upon time taken to reach the second criterion.

RESULTS

Table 1 shows the means and standard deviations for both groups on both learning criteria. As predicted, acquisition of the discrimination proceeded more rapidly for Group R-P. The mean difference between groups was significant at the .002 level for the first criterion and at the .008 level for the second criterion. In regard to the significance level of the second criterion, it should be pointed out that the true mean difference was underestimated by assigning to nonlearners the limiting score of 150. This restriction worked against the hypothesis by virtue of the disproportionately larger number of nonlearners in Group R than in Group R-P (eight as compared with two).

The correlation between CA and number of trials to the second criterion was .02. The insignificance of this cor-

relation may reflect restriction of age range.

Inspection of individual protocols revealed some interesting within-group differences, particularly for the R-P group. First, 5 of the 22 Ss of this group were markedly deviant in speed of acquisition. Mean number of trials to the second criterion for these 5 Ss was 142, or 1.7σ above the total R-P group mean, whereas the next slowest learner was less than $.5\sigma$ above the group mean. To express this deviance in another way, without these five scores, the total R-P group mean would have been reduced from 64.3 to 41.4, and σ would have decreased from 46.3 to 20.3.

Subsequently noted were within-group differences in frequency of verbalization. The same five Ss of Group R-P made more separately recorded remarks than any other identifiable subgroup, including the eight nonlearners of Group R for whom experimental sessions were just as long and who therefore had equal opportunity to verbalize. The median number of separately recorded verbalizations for these two subgroups was 5.0 and 0.5, respectively. Since the experimental task in no way required S to talk, all verbalizations may be justifiably regarded as irrelevant responses.

Finally, examination of the recorded nonverbal, task-irrelevant responses showed a tendency, on the part of the same five slow learners of Group R-P, to emit responses of an irreal or "magical" nature, e.g., attempts to adjust eyes mechanically, "superstitious" sniffing of discriminative stimuli prior to choice, and ritualistic arranging of candies in geometrical forms.

In view of the current evidence indicating that both slow learning in complex tasks and a high frequency of ir-relevant responses are characteristic of anxious Ss (4, 5), it seemed possible that in the present study as well, high anxiety level might have accounted in part for the deviant performance of the five Ss of Group R-P. Since this study's principal interest was in the reward-punishment condition, a subsidiary experiment was conducted to test the validity of the above interpretation.

TABLE 1 · NUMBER OF TRIALS TO DISCRIMINA-TION LEARNING CRITERIA FOR THE TWO EXPERI-MENTAL GROUPS

			SECOND CRITERION:	
	FIRST CRITERION: NUMBER OF TRIALS TO ELIMINATE NEVER-REINFORCED BOX		NUMBER OF TRIALS TO AND INCLUDING 10 CONSECUTIVE CORRECT CHOICES	
	Group		Group	
Meas-ure	R-P (N=22)	R (N=21)	R-P	R
M	32.91	70.48	64.32	98.33
σ	36.27	48.88	46.26	46.27
CR	2.85		2.41	
p	.002[a]		.008[a]	

[a] One-tailed test.

EXPERIMENT II

The GSR was used as the independ-ent measure of anxiety for the following reasons: First, although the status of skin conductance as a psychological measure is not entirely clear, it is conventionally accepted as an index of anxiety. Further-more, there is a conspicuous lack of any other direct measures of anxiety that are appropriate to the five-year age level. Last, by using the GSR, a procedure could be employed in which the reinforcing con-ditions of the main experiment were ap-proximated even though a qualitatively different type of data was obtained. Whereas, in the main experiment Ss re-ceived material reward and punishment, in the present supplementary experiment they received verbal reward and punish-ment.

METHOD

The Ss were eight kindergarteners from the original sample. These Ss were the five slowest and three fastest learners from Group R-P of the main experiment. The ex-periment was conducted in a school room other than the one used for the learning ex-periment by a new E who was not acquainted with the Ss, their original group placement, or their original learning scores. The equip-ment operator was seated at a table facing the machine, a Stoelting Psychogalvano-scope, No. 24207. The E and S were seated at the opposite side of the table. The S was told that E was going to read a story, and that it could be heard better if E and S wore magic rings. The operator then attached false electrodes to E's forefinger, and, sub-sequently, real electrodes to S's forefinger.

E read to S from an advanced statistics text during an adaptation period, terminated by three consecutive minutes of stable resist-ance. The experimental phase began with the following instructions to S: "That's all for the story. *Now I'm going to give you a test to see how smart you are—how fast you can learn.*" Five questions were subsequently administered, at 1-min. intervals. A 1-min. interval was, in all cases, sufficient for re-laxation and return to base level (3). Maxi-mum needle deflection was recorded for each minute interval. Questions a, b, and d were easily answered items. These questions were: (a) "What is this?" (E pointed to ear); (b) "What is this?" (E pointed to nose); and (d) "What is an orange?" E rewarded all answers with the statement, "That's right."

Questions c and e were insoluble. These questions were: (c) "What is (does) tra-duce (mean)?" and (e) "What is (does) flout (mean)?". E followed S's admission of inability to answer these questions with verbal punishment: "Sure you know what _____ means. *All* the kids in this school know what _____ means. All the *smart* kids in your class know what _____ means. Don't you know what _____ is?"

Following the last item, *E* "discovered" that *S* had been given the "wrong" test. Thereupon, *E* administered the "right" test, a series of easy vocabulary items, for which all answers were rewarded with candy and praise.

Maximum needle deflection, as calibrated in reaction units, was recorded for each of the five 1-min. intervals of the experimental phase. Maximum needle deflection over all five intervals for each *S* was used as the basic score (3). This score may be regarded as an index of GSR reactivity.

RESULTS

The two groups, fast vs. slow learners, were compared in terms of GSR reactivity; results are shown in Table 2. From this table it is apparent that for the fast learners, GSR remained relatively stable during the experimental treatment. That is, neither failure nor success noticeably affected the GSR of these *S*s. The opposite results, high reactivity, characterized the group of slow learners.

TABLE 2 · COMPARISON OF FAST AND SLOW LEARNERS ON GSR AND INTELLIGENCE MEASURES

Measure	Fast learners (N = 3)	Slow learners (N = 5)
Trials to discriminate		
M	16.67	142.40
σ	0.94	3.68
GSR deflection range		
M	10.30	39.50
σ	6.85	4.96
t	5.36	
p	< .01	
WISC, full scale		
M	92.7	97.3
σ	2.1	8.0

Table 2 also shows a comparison of the two groups in terms of intelligence test scores.[2] The insignificant difference between groups suggests that their divergent acquisition rates in the discrimination task is not attributable to differences in intelligence although the groups are too small and differences in variability too large to draw definite conclusions.

DISCUSSION

The results of the primary experiment indicate that when a child learns a new problem, he will learn it more effectively, i.e., faster, if every response he makes is appropriately reinforced, rather than if only his correct responses are reinforced. Of course, the degree to which this conclusion may be generalized is a function, aside from the usual sampling limitations of age and sex, of the degree to which the particular learning task used is representative of children's learning situations in general, and also of the degree to which the particular parameters of reinforcement used are representative of the reinforcing conditions generally attendant upon children's behavior. Concerning this point, it might be noted that after the present experiment was completed, two studies (1, 2) were published reporting results similar to those of the present experiment even though sampling, learning task, and type of reinforcement were considerably different from those of the present research.

Why is a combination of reward and punishment superior to reward alone in speeding acquisition? Both theory and incidental observations suggest that the effect of a reward-punishment procedure

[2] These data were gathered by an independent investigator shortly after the termination of the present experiment. The authors are grateful to Don Farrer for his contribution in this respect.

is attributable to increased level of motivation. In other words, to say that learning is accelerated by a reward-punishment procedure seems equivalent to saying that learning is accelerated more under a high drive condition than under a low drive condition—or that punishment acts as an additional source of drive.

This interpretation may be extended to account for the fact that some Ss under the R-P procedure did not learn at all. The performance of these Ss appeared to be not only a function of high drive, but also a function of a relatively strong tendency to emit responses bearing no functional or facilitating relation to the criterional response. If it is true that an increase in drive—represented by the addition of punishment and by the GSR index of anxiety—will increase the strength of the strongest responses more than that of the weaker responses (5), then it was to be expected that those Ss of Group R-P who initially showed the greatest tendency to irrelevant responses would take a disproportionately large number of trials to reach criterion.

SUMMARY

Forty-three male kindergarten Ss were run on a three-choice discrimination task. Twenty-one Ss (Group R) were rewarded with candy for correct responses and were not rewarded for incorrect responses. The remaining Ss (Group R-P) were rewarded for correct and punished for incorrect responses (forfeiture of candy). Learning was significantly faster for the latter group. A supplementary study, using eight Ss of Group R-P, linked GSR reactivity to speed of original discrimination learning. Both sets of results are discussed in terms of effect on learning of level of motivation.

REFERENCES

1. Buss, A. H., Braden, W., Orgel, A., & Buss, E. H.   Acquisition and extinction with different verbal reinforcement combinations. *J. exp. Psychol.*, 1956, 52, 288–295.
2. Buss, A. H., & Buss, E. H.   The effect of verbal reinforcement combinations on conceptual learning. *J. exp. Psychol.*, 1956, *52*, 283–287.
3. Lacey, J. I.   The evaluation of autonomic responses: Toward a general solution. *Ann. N. Y. Acad. Sci.*, 1956, *67*, 123–164.
4. Palermo, D. S., Castaneda, A., & McCandless, B. R.   The relationship of anxiety in children to performance in a complex learning task. *Child Develpm.*, 1956, *27*, 333–337.
5. Spence, K. W.   *Behavior theory and conditioning.* New Haven: Yale Univer. Press, 1956.
6. Warden, C. J., & Aylesworth, M.   The relative value of reward and punishment in the formation of a visual discrimination habit in the white rat. *J. comp. Psychol.*, 1927, 7, 117–127.

GENERALIZATION AND TRANSPOSITION PHENOMENA | 9

FREQUENTLY IT IS OBSERVED that a child will make a response, previously learned to some other stimulus, to a new stimulus. In such cases the behavior of the child is labeled as generalization. The first three studies in this section provide data indicating that while a response is being learned in the presence of a particular stimulus or set of stimuli, to a lesser degree learning of that response to other similar stimuli, is also occurring. A child told to call a particular hue "red" is learning at the same time to call other similar hues "red." The child does not, however, make the same response to the hue green. There is a limit to generalization that is a function of the similarity of the stimuli. The studies presented here provide evidence of a gradient of stimulus generalization. The more similar a stimulus is to the training stimulus, the more likely it will be that the response learned to the training stimulus will be made to the new stimulus. Stated differently, the tendency to generalize decreases with the discriminability of the training and test stimuli.

The first three studies provide demonstrations of generalization along dimensions of light intensity, hue, and shape. The last of these studies is of particular interest for its illustration of the modification of the generalization gradient when negative as opposed to positive reinforcement is used.

Despite the clarity of these results in demonstrating generalization phenomena, it should be pointed out that with respect to these—and to most other studies of generalization—there is a methodological problem involved in their design which tempers the interpretation. In each case, the generalization gradients presented are based upon more than one test trial. When multiple test trials are used to establish the gradient of generalization, it is necessary either to reinforce or to withhold reinforcement when a response is made to the test stimuli. If the response is reinforced, then the tendency to make the response to that stimulus and to all other similar stimuli is increased for future trials. If reinforcement is withheld upon making a generalized response, the tendency to repeat that response is reduced for that stimulus and other similar stimuli. Therefore, any data representing the generalization gradient based upon more than one test trial per subject are contaminated by the effects of reinforcement or nonreinforcement upon all responses made after the initial generalization trial. These effects were minimized in the studies reported here by randomizing or by counterbalancing the order of presentation of the stimuli so that each test stimulus was equally affected by the reinforcement effects.

Nevertheless, a pure study of generalization unaffected by other variables has not been provided.

The last two experiments in this section deal with transposition behavior that involves the effects of two or more generalization gradients. When a child is reinforced for responding to one stimulus and nonreinforced for responding to another, similar stimulus, he is learning a discrimination problem. As a function of this training, however, he is also acquiring a tendency to generalize both the response of approaching the first stimulus to all other similar stimuli and the response of avoiding the second stimulus to all other similar stimuli. If the two training stimuli are similar, the generalization gradients of approach and of avoidance will overlap. It is under such conditions that transposition may occur. For example, training might consist of reinforcement for making an approach response to a light of 100 apparent foot candles and nonreinforcement for an approach response to a light of 75 apparent foot candles. The test for transposition would follow training and might present two lights, one of 100 and one of 125 apparent foot candles. If the subject transposes, he will respond by approaching the brighter light, never before seen, despite the fact that reinforcement had been provided during training for approaching the other stimulus. The theoretical basis for these predictions may be found in the fourth paper of this section. More detailed analyses of the problem may be found in a number of the references cited in that paper.

The problem of transposition is of particular consequence for child psychologists because of the marked effects that language acquisition has on transposition behavior. Spence's theory, which stimulated most of these studies, was developed to account for the behavior of lower organisms and, as the data of Kuenne illustrate, it may be extended to young children. It is equally clear from Kuenne's data that older children, presumably because of their ability to label both the stimuli and the relationships among stimuli, behave quite differently under the same circumstances. Thus, transposition for young children decreases from near to far test stimuli, as would be predicted from Spence's theory, but does not decrease in the case of the older children. It is apparent that those working with the human subject must take care in extending theoretical systems devised to account for the behavior of lower animals to human behavior. This does not, of course, mean that theoretical systems developed on the basis of behavior of other organisms should be ignored. Quite to the contrary, they may be valuable beginnings to the understanding of the principles underlying behavior of any organism, but the human organism is distinguished by its communicative skills, which lead to major behavioral differences. Additional evidence for the effects of language on learning of various kinds may be found in Section XI, "The Effects of Language on Learning."

The last study in this group indicates that modifications of the tendency to transpose may be brought about by factors other than language. In this case, the typical transposition gradient found in the other two studies of preverbal children is found when training involves a single discrimination, but different test behavior occurs when the subject is trained to transpose, or respond to the relational properties of the stimuli. This was accomplished by presenting two discrimination problems, both of which required a response to the larger stimulus. Although the children did not verbalize the relationship in the training task, they behaved in a fashion similar to older children of other studies who verbalized the relationship with only one pair of training stimuli. While these data do not involve a test of the theory since the study introduces new variables, it would seem clear that an extension of the theory is necessary to take them into account. It would appear that the subjects of this study are forming a concept "larger is correct," but the mechanisms which underlie this kind of generalization phenomenon have not been dealt with in the paper.

THE STIMULUS GENERALIZATION GRADIENT AS A FUNCTION OF THE INTENSITY OF STIMULUS LIGHTS

CHARLES C. SPIKER [1]

THE EXPERIMENT REPORTED HERE is the second in a series designed to develop procedures and apparatus appropriate for the study of the generalization behavior of children. In the first experiment (10), the amount of generalization was shown to be an increasing function of the number of reinforcements given on the train-

[1] The writer is indebted to Miss Kathryn Norcross and Mr. Lewis P. Lipsitt for aid in collecting the data and for valuable suggestions regarding procedural matters.

Reprinted by permission from *Child Development*, 1956, 27, 85–98.

ing stimulus. The present experiment is concerned with the hypothesis that the shape of the generalization gradient, for stimulus intensity dimensions, is dependent upon the absolute values of the stimuli selected as well as upon the degree to which the stimuli are separated on the stimulus dimension.

Several investigators have found that if the subject (S) is conditioned to an intense stimulus and is then tested on stimuli of lesser intensity, the generalization gradient is steeper than if the S is conditioned to a weak stimulus and tested on more intense stimuli. Hovland (3) reported this finding with the GSR for human Ss using auditory stimuli; Brown (1) and Perkins (8) obtained similar findings for an instrumental approach response of rats to lights differing in brightness; and Grice and Saltz (2) demonstrated the phenomenon in rats' approach responses to stimuli differing in size. Hull (4) attempted to explain some of these results in terms of his principle of stimulus dynamism. Although the details of his explanation are not given here, it involves the assumption that the intensity of a stimulus contributes to the general motivational level of S, and that the motivational factors multiply with the generalized habits. Thus, given two stimuli (S_1 and S_2) that are equally separated from the conditioned stimulus, S_1 being more intense and S_2 less intense than the conditioned stimulus, S_1 will have a greater reaction potential than will S_2. The deductive consequence of these assumptions, and others in the system, is that the generalization gradient will be steeper when the test is made with less intense stimuli than when made with more intense stimuli.

In this experiment, the tendency to respond to the conditioned stimulus was established by giving differential reinforcement during training, in which S was reinforced for responding to the conditioned stimulus and was nonreinforced for responding to another stimulus that was different from the conditioned stimulus in terms of one characteristic (hue), but the same with respect to the dimension being investigated (brightness). Subsequently, S's tendency to respond to other stimuli, differing from the training stimulus only in brightness, was determined in a generalization test. Two levels of reinforcement during training were also used in an attempt to confirm the findings of the previous experiment (10).

METHOD

SUBJECTS AND EXPERIMENTAL DESIGN

The Ss were 60 children from the Iowa Child Welfare Research Station preschool laboratories. They ranged in age from 3 years, 9 months, to 5 years, 8 months. Most Ss had been used in a previous study of generalization (10) in which the present apparatus was used, but in which the stimuli differed in hue rather than in brightness.

The experimental design was such that one-half the Ss were randomly assigned to a group that was trained to respond to a bright light and then tested on dimmer lights. The other half were assigned to a group trained to respond to a dim light and tested on brighter lights. One-half of each of these groups was randomly assigned to a group that received 12 presentations of the positive (white) light and 12 presentations of the negative (blue) light during reinforcement training. The other halves of the two groups received 24 presentations of each of the positive and negative stimuli. For convenience, these four subgroups will be referred to as B-12 (bright light, 12 presentations of each stimulus); B-24 (bright, 24 presentations); D-12 (dim, 12 presentations); and D-24 (dim, 24 presentations).

APPARATUS

The experiment was conducted in a semi-darkened experimental room with an adjoining observation room. The apparatus, which has been described elsewhere in detail (10), was placed in the window between the two rooms. S operated the apparatus from the experimental room; the experimenter (E) operated the controls and recorded S's responses from the observation booth. S faced a gray metal panel, 20 in. wide and 12 in. high; 3 in. from the top was centered an aperture, 2 in. in diameter, covered with flashed opal glass. Below and to the left of the aperture was a transparent container into which marbles were ejected. A metal rod with a hand grip extended from the panel below and to the right of the aperture. Directly below the apparatus was a wooden stand, 2 ft. square and 8 in. high, on which S stood during the experiment.

The apparatus was enclosed in a metal cabinet, 12 in. high, 20 in. wide, and 12 in. deep. Approximately 7 in. behind the aperture were six 75-watt projection lamps, arranged so that their beams focused on the aperture. Each lamp was enclosed in a reflecting container on the front of which 2 in. square wooden diaphragms or glass color filters could be mounted. A stepping relay controlled the current to the lamps and the relay was in turn controlled by two interval timers. One of the timers controlled the presentation interval and the other controlled the interval between presentations. A multi-contact selector switch was used to determine which stimuli would be presented and the order of their presentation.

If a stimulus lamp was on at the time the response occurred, the response was recorded on one of six electrical impulse counters. Each counter was associated with one stimulus, so that the responses to each stimulus were separately recorded. Approximately 8 pounds of pressure were required to move the lever the ¾ in. necessary to activate the counters and the marble ejector. The marble ejector was activated by a response only on those trials during which the reinforced stimulus was presented.

STIMULI

The stimuli were lights, different brightnesses being obtained by placing wooden diaphragms between the lamps and the stimulus aperture. The brightnesses of four stimuli, measured at the aperture with a McBeth Illuminometer, were approximately 2.5, 25, 80, and 250 ft.-candles. The difference between the common logarithms of 2.5 and 25, and of 25 and 250 is 1.0. The 80 ft.-candle stimulus is one-half a logarithm unit between the 25 and 250 ft.-candle stimuli. One-half the Ss were trained with the 250 stimulus, while the other half were trained with the 2.5 stimulus. Two additional stimuli were constructed by placing a blue glass color filter over the diaphragms for the 2.5 and 250 ft.-candle stimuli. This produced two pairs of stimuli, the members of each pair approximately equal in brightness but differing in hue. The blue stimuli were used as the nonreinforced (negative) stimuli in the training sessions.

PRELIMINARY TRAINING

S was brought to the experimental room, shown a variety of dime-store toys that were spread out on a small table, and was allowed to choose the toy that he wished to have. E informed him that he must buy the toy with marbles and that E would show him how to get the necessary marbles. The apparatus was turned on and set to present the training stimulus series. This series consisted of an equal number of separate presentations of the white (positive) and of the blue (negative) stimuli. Groups B-12 and B-24 were presented with a white and blue light of approximately 250 ft.-candles; Groups D-12 and D-24 received a white and a blue light of approximately 2.5 ft.-candles. Throughout the experiment, the presentation period was 3 seconds and the inter-presentation interval was 2½ seconds.

E first demonstrated the apparatus by pulling the lever several times while the training light was on and pointing to the container into which the marbles were being ejected. When the blue light came on, E pulled the lever a few times to demonstrate that no marbles were being ejected. S was then allowed to pull the lever to obtain marbles. The preliminary training was continued until S learned to pull more than once when the training light was on and failed to pull the lever between stimulus presentations. As soon as S had met these criteria, E stopped the apparatus and returned the stimulus presentation device to the starting position in preparation for the reinforcement training.

REINFORCEMENT TRAINING

E returned S to his position before the apparatus, and informed him that E was going into the next room to start the apparatus again and that S would be informed when he had obtained enough marbles to buy the toy. E went into the observation booth and started the apparatus. The reinforcement stimulus series was the same one given during the preliminary training. In each successive block of six presentations, there were three each of the positive and negative stimuli. Neither stimulus was presented more than twice in succession. Groups B-12 and D-12 were given 12 presentations of each the white and the blue lights and Groups B-24 and D-24 were given 24 presentations of each. E recorded on prepared sheets the number of responses S made to each stimulus presentation.

GENERALIZATION TEST

Following the last trial on the reinforcement training, E turned the selector switch so that the generalization stimulus series was presented. The time between the last reinforcement training trial and the first generalization test trial was eight seconds. The generalization series was introduced with no other changes in the procedure.

The series consisted of two cycles, each cycle having seven presentations of the positive stimulus with each response being reinforced, and five nonreinforced presentations of the test stimuli. The test stimuli were presented on trials 2, 4, 7, 9, and 12 of the cycle. The test stimuli included the positive stimulus, the negative stimulus, and each of the other three stimuli differing from the positive stimulus in brightness. The test stimuli were presented in counterbalanced order so that within each group each test stimulus appeared in each position an equal number of times. For each S, the second cycle was the same as his first.

RESULTS

RESPONSES TO THE REINFORCED STIMULUS DURING THE GENERALIZATION SERIES

An analysis was first made of the number of responses to the reinforced training stimulus during the generalization test. This analysis should reveal the differential effects on learning, if any, of the different conditions that prevailed during the acquisition stages. A Lindquist Type III analysis (6, p. 281) was conducted, in which the main effects were the number of reinforced trials during training, the brightness of the conditioned stimulus, and successive three-trial blocks for the first 12 of the 14 reinforced trials of the generalization test. The results of the analysis need not be presented in detail, since only the trial-block effect proved significant at less than the 5 per cent level. This significant effect reflects the fact that the number of responses to the reinforced conditioned stimulus tended to decrease with an increase in the number of previous test trials. This decrease is probably due to the generalized effects of nonreinforcement of the test stimuli.

This analysis makes tenable the hypothesis that the four groups did not differ significantly in performance to the conditioned stimulus as a function of the different conditions that obtained during training. This appears to be true both for the brightness of the conditioned stimulus and for the number of reinforcements received during training.

RESPONSES TO THE TEST STIMULI FOR THE COMPLETE GENERALIZATION TEST

Table 1 gives the mean number of responses made to each test stimulus for the first and second cycles of the generalization test series. An examination of this table reveals (a) a somewhat greater mean number of responses for the Groups B-24 and D-24 than for D-12 and B-12; (b) a greater mean number of responses for all groups combined during the first

cycle than during the second cycle; (c) a slightly greater mean number of responses to the test stimuli for Groups D-24 and D-12 than for Groups B-24 and B-12; (d)

TABLE 1 · MEAN NUMBER OF RESPONSES TO EACH TEST STIMULUS

	First cycle			Second cycle		
	Training reinforcements			Training reinforcements		
Test stimulus	12	24	Mean	12	24	Mean
	Bright-trained groups					
250	2.40	3.33	2.87	2.00	2.40	2.20
80	1.13	1.60	1.37	1.13	0.93	1.03
25	0.80	1.13	0.97	1.00	0.67	0.83
2.5	0.80	0.53	0.67	0.33	0.53	0.43
Mean	1.28	1.65	1.47	1.12	1.13	1.12
	Dim-trained groups					
2.5	2.33	1.80	2.07	1.93	2.27	2.10
25	1.40	1.87	1.63	1.60	1.07	1.33
80	1.40	1.27	1.33	0.87	1.13	1.00
250	1.07	1.47	1.27	0.67	1.00	0.83
Mean	1.55	1.60	1.58	1.27	1.37	1.32

a decrease, for all groups combined, in the number of responses to the test stimuli as the difference between training and test stimuli increases; and (e) a relatively greater decrease in these responses for Groups B-12 and B-24 than for Groups D-12 and D-24. The appropriate analysis for testing the statistical significance of these observations is an extension of Lindquist's Type VI design (6, p. 292). The main factors in the analysis are the number of reinforcements during training, the brightness of the training stimulus, the different test stimuli, and the cycles of the generalization test.

In order to analyze the data, the stimulus dimension was reversed for Ss trained to the dim stimulus. That is, the responses made by these Ss to the 2.5 ft.-candle stimulus, their training stimulus, were compared with the responses made by the bright-trained Ss to their 250 ft.-

TABLE 2 · Summary of Analysis of Variance of the Number of Responses to Each Test Stimulus Presentation

Source	df	Mean square	F	p
Subjects	59			
Reinforcement (R)	1	1.88		
Training stimulus (T)	1	4.01		
R × T	1	0.40		
error (b)	56	4.14		
Within subjects	300			
Test stimuli (S)	2	73.51	41.53	<.001
Cycles (C)	1	7.51	11.73	<.005
S × C	2	0.12		
S × T	2	9.88	5.58	<.005
S × R	2	0.68		
C × T	1	0.28		
C × R	1	0.54		
error (w)	280			
error₁ (w)	56	0.64		
error₂ (w)	112	1.77		
error₃ (w)	112	1.06		
Total	359			

Note. Higher order interactions have been omitted, since none was significant at less than the 10 per cent level. The stimulus dimension was reversed for Ss trained to the dim stimulus, and responses of all Ss to the 80 ft.-candle stimulus have been omitted.

candle training stimulus. Responses made by the dim-trained group to the 25 ft.-candle stimulus were compared with those made by the bright-trained group to the same stimulus; and responses made by the dim-trained group to the 250 ft.-candle stimulus were compared with those made by the bright-trained group to the 2.5 ft.-candle stimulus. By omitting the responses of both groups to the 80 ft.-candle stimulus, there are equal logarithmic steps between the training and test stimuli for both groups.

A summary of the analysis of variance is presented in Table 2. The triple and quadruple interactions have been omitted from the table since none was significant at less than the 10 per cent

level. As the table indicates, neither the reinforcement factor (R) nor the brightness of the training stimulus (T) proved to be significant. The significant cycle effect indicates the reduction in the number of responses made to the test stimuli from the first to the second cycle. The significant test stimulus effect indicates that the generalization gradient for the combined groups cannot be attributed to chance. The significant S × T interaction reflects the fact that the generalization gradient for Ss trained to the bright stimulus is significantly steeper than the gradient for Ss trained to the dim stimulus. This latter finding is illustrated in Figure 1, where the means of the numbers of responses per test stimulus presentation, for the pooled bright-trained and pooled dim-trained groups, are plotted against the difference between the com-

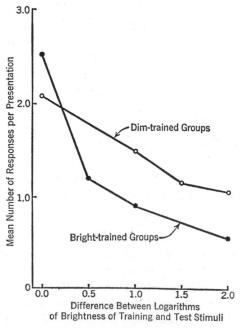

Figure 1. Mean number of responses per test stimulus for complete generalization series.

mon logarithms of the training and test stimuli. The mean number of responses to the 80 ft.-candle stimulus is also included for each group. It is apparent from Figure 1 that the gradient for the bright-trained Ss is steeper than that for the dim-trained.

In order to establish the existence of a generalization gradient for the bright-trained and the dim-trained groups, Lindquist's Type I analysis (6, p. 267) was made separately for these two groups. In this analysis, responses to the 80 ft.-candle stimulus were included. The response measure was the mean number of responses to each test stimulus for the entire generalization test series (disregarding cycles) and the level of reinforcement during training was ignored. Table 3 presents a

TABLE 3 · SUMMARY OF ANALYSIS OF VARIANCE OF THE NUMBER OF RESPONSES TO THE TEST STIMULI FOR THE BRIGHT-TRAINED AND THE DIM-TRAINED GROUPS SEPARATELY

Source	df	Mean square	F	p
Bright-trained groups				
Test Stimuli (S)	3	98.48	40.53	<.001
Subjects (I)	29	9.46		
S × I	87	2.43		
Dim-trained groups				
Test Stimuli (S)	3	25.69	7.56	<.001
Subjects (I)	29	12.02		
S × I	87	3.40		

Note. This analysis includes the responses to the 80 ft.-candle stimulus.

summary of these analyses. The effect of primary interest here is that for test stimuli, since a significant test stimulus effect indicates a significant generalization gradient. For both groups, the generalization gradient proves to be highly significant ($p < .001$). Table 4 gives the probabilities resulting from t tests of the

significance of the differences between the means for pairs of stimuli for the two groups separately. It appears that the significance of the gradient is primarily due to differences between responses to the training stimulus (under test conditions) and the other test stimuli. For the bright-trained group, however, there is a significant difference ($p < .005$) between the means for the 80 ft.-candle and the 2.5 ft.-candle stimuli.

TABLE 4 · PROBABILITIES OBTAINED FROM t TESTS COMPARING THE MEANS FOR PAIRS OF TEST STIMULI FOR THE BRIGHT-TRAINED AND DIM-TRAINED GROUPS SEPARATELY

Bright-trained group		Dim-trained group	
Stimulus pairs	p	Stimulus pairs	p
250 vs. 80	<.001	2.5 vs. 25	<.02
250 vs. 25	<.001	2.5 vs. 80	<.001
250 vs. 2.5	<.001	2.5 vs. 250	<.001
80 vs. 25	<.20	25 vs. 80	<.20
80 vs. 2.5	<.005	25 vs. 250	<.10
25 vs. 2.5	<.10	80 vs. 250	<.70

RESPONSES TO THE INITIAL TEST STIMULUS PRESENTATION

The failure to find a significant effect for reinforcement during training, contrary to the results of other studies, suggested that the additional reinforcements given during the generalization test may have obliterated any differences that existed initially between the two reinforcement groups. Accordingly, the number of responses made to the first test stimulus presented was obtained for each S. There were three Ss in each of the four main groups that received the same test stimulus on the first presentation. Since one of these subgroups received the negative stimulus first and another received the 80 ft.-candle stimulus, neither of which are of concern here, there remained 36 Ss, nine in each group, who could be used in this analysis. The means of these cases, each cell based on three Ss, are presented in Table 5. Trends corresponding to those in Table 1 may be observed here. A Lindquist Type III analysis (6, p. 281) was made of these data and the summary is presented in Table 6. The test stimulus variable is again highly significant. The data show a significant ($p < .025$) reinforcement effect, and a significant ($p < .05$) interaction between reinforcements and test stimuli. The interaction between brightness of the training stimulus and the test stimuli is not as pronounced as in the first analysis, although the pattern of the corresponding means is the same. In Figure 2, the means for Ss receiving 12 reinforcements and the means for those receiving 24 reinforcements are plotted as a function of the test stimuli. It is apparent that the reinforcement effect is due to the greater number of generalized responses by the 24 reinforcement Ss and that the interaction is due to the steeper slope of the gradient for these Ss. A t test of the simple effects shows that the group receiving 24 reinforcements made significantly more responses to the first and second test stimuli ($p < .05$). This analysis thus indicates that the greater number of reinforcements during the training resulted in significantly greater generalization to the stimuli near to the training stimulus, at least during the early stages of the generalization test.

DISCUSSION

Analysis of the number of responses made to the test stimuli during the generalization test reveals a highly significant stimulus generalization gradient for all

TABLE 5 · MEAN NUMBER OF RESPONSES TO FIRST TEST STIMULUS PRESENTED THE SUBJECTS

Training stimulus	Test stimulus	Reinforcements during training		
		12	24	Mean
250	250	1.33	3.00	2.17
	25	0.33	1.33	0.83
	2.5	0.67	0.33	0.53
	Mean	0.78	1.56	1.17
2.5	2.5	1.67	2.33	2.00
	25	1.33	2.33	1.83
	250	0.67	0.33	0.50
	Mean	1.22	1.67	1.44

TABLE 6 · ANALYSIS OF VARIANCE OF THE MEAN NUMBER OF RESPONSES TO FIRST TEST STIMULUS PRESENTED TO SUBJECTS

Source	df	Mean square	F	p
Training Stimulus (T)	1	0.70		
Reinforcements (R)	1	3.36	5.89	<.025
Test Stimuli (S)	2	7.53	13.21	<.001
T × R	1	0.25		
T × S	2	1.19	2.09	<.20
R × S	2	2.02	3.54	<.05
T × R × S	2	0.25		
Within Cells	24	0.57		
Total	35			

Note. The stimulus dimension has been reversed for Ss trained to the dim stimulus, and Ss given the 80 ft.-candle stimulus first have been omitted.

Ss combined. That this "group gradient" is not merely an artifact of combining individual step-wise gradients is demonstrated by the fact that 80 per cent of all Ss responded fewer times to the most distant test stimulus than to the nonreinforced training stimulus and 60 per cent responded fewer times to the most distant test stimulus than they did to the test stimulus nearest the training stimulus.

Analysis also indicated that the gradient for Ss trained to the bright stimulus is significantly steeper than that for Ss trained to the dim stimulus. This finding is in agreement with that of Grice and Saltz (2) for the size dimension, with that

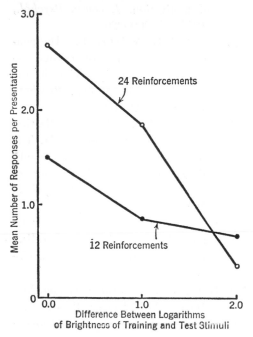

Figure 2. Mean number of responses to first test stimulus presentation.

of Brown (1) and Perkins (8) for the brightness dimension, and with Hovland's (3) for loudness. It is also in general agreement with the prediction made by Hull (4) on the basis of the principle of stimulus dynamism. Further analysis revealed that the generalization gradient for the dim-trained Ss is statistically significant, indicating that a generalization gradient can be demonstrated even when stimulus intensity operates in the opposite direction.

The significant effect of cycles—representing repeated presentations of nonreinforced test stimuli—is also one of the generalization phenomena frequently observed. This principle is one of the main axioms in stimulus-response theories that are designed to account for the various phenomena in discrimination learning (5, 9).

Although the effects of the number of reinforcements during training failed to achieve significance in the above described analysis, a significant reinforcement effect was obtained when only the responses to the first stimulus presentation were analyzed. In addition, a significant interaction between test stimuli and number of reinforcements was found, indicating a steeper gradient for the Ss receiving 24 reinforcements than for the group receiving only 12. This result may also be derived from Hull's formulations, and has been empirically demonstrated for the instrumental approach response of rats (7).

The results of this experiment indicate that the apparatus and procedures used offer a fruitful and practical means of investigating generalization phenomena with child Ss. The method has been tested on hypotheses derived from the results obtained with more conventional methods and subjects. The hypotheses that were verified deal with the establishment of a gradient of stimulus generalization; the effects of reinforcement on the amount and shape of this gradient; the effects of repeated nonreinforced stimulus presentations on the magnitude of generalization; and the effect of stimulus intensity on the shape of the gradient. It now appears that the method warrants use in the study of some of the generalization phenomena which may best be studied with children; e.g., the effect on the shape of the gradient of prior name-learning experience with the stimuli; the effects on generalization behavior of previous training to generalize or to discriminate; and the relationship between level of maturity (i.e., chronological or mental age) and the magnitude, range, and steepness of the generalization gradient.

SUMMARY

This experiment is primarily concerned with the study of the effects on generalization of the number of reinforcements with the conditioned stimulus and with the effects of the absolute brightness of the stimuli on the magnitude and shape of the generalization gradient. Sixty preschool Ss were given differential reinforcement to a white (positive) and a blue (negative) light. For one-half the Ss, the positive stimulus was the brightest of four stimuli differing from each other in brightness; for the other half, it was the dimmest. One-half of each these groups was given 12 presentations and the other half was given 24 presentations of each the positive and negative stimuli. The response was the repeated pulling of a lever for marbles during a 3-second presentation of the conditioned stimulus, and the response measure was the number of such responses that occurred during the 3-second periods. Immediately following training, the Ss were tested, without reinforcement, on each of the four stimuli differing in brightness. The main findings were (a) a statistically significant generalization gradient for all groups combined; (b) a steeper gradient for the bright-trained than for the dim-trained Ss, and (c) a greater number of generalized responses for Ss given 24 reinforced training trials than for Ss given only 12, and a steeper gradient for the former than for the latter.

REFERENCES

1. BROWN, J. S.   The generalization of approach responses as a function of stimulus intensity and strength of motivation. *J. comp. Psychol.*, 1942, *33*, 209–226.

2. GRICE, R. G., & SALTZ, E.   The generalization of an instrumental response to stimuli varying in the size dimension. *J. exp. Psychol.*, 1950, *40*, 702–708.

3. HOVLAND, C. I.   The generalization of conditioned responses: II. The sensory generalization of conditioned responses with varying intensity of tone. *J. genet. Psychol.*, 1937, *51*, 279–291.

4. HULL, C. L.   Stimulus intensity dynamism (V) and stimulus generalization. *Psychol. Rev.*, 1949, *56*, 67–76.

5. HULL, C. L.   *A behavior system.* New Haven: Yale Univer. Press, 1952.

6. LINDQUIST, E. F.   *Design and analysis of experiments in psychology and education.* Boston: Houghton-Mifflin, 1953.

7. MARGOLIUS, G.   Stimulus generalization of an instrumental response as a function of the number of reinforced trials. *J. exp. Psychol.*, 1955, *49*, 105–111.

8. PERKINS, C. C., JR.   The relationship between conditioned stimulus intensity and response strength. *J. exp. Psychol.*, 1953, *46*, 225–231.

9. SPENCE, K. W.   The differential response in animals to stimuli varying within a single dimension. *Psychol. Rev.*, 1937, *44*, 430–444.

10. SPIKER, C. C.   The effects of number of reinforcements on the strength of a generalized instrumental response. *Child Develpm.*, 1956, *27*, 37–44.

GENERALIZATION OF AN INSTRUMENTAL RESPONSE WITH VARIATION IN TWO ATTRIBUTES OF THE CS [1]

SHELDON H. WHITE

THE STIMULI INVOLVED in a discrimination usually differ on one physical dimension but have common values on others. If the difference between the distinguishing components of the stimuli is made larger, the discrimination is learned more easily. This can be explained by the principle of stimulus generalization, as used in discrimination learning theories (3, 6).

To date, studies of generalization have always involved the gradual alteration of one component of a CS while holding the others constant. Theory, however, has recognized the possibility that more than one component may be so varied and, by postulating summative rules for generalized reaction tendencies, can predict that discrimination learning will be superior with multiple, as opposed to single, dimensions of variation between discriminanda. This has been confirmed in several studies (1, 2, 8).

This experiment was an attempt to demonstrate that novel stimuli differing from a training stimulus along two physical dimensions will elicit fewer generalized responses than will novel stimuli which differ only on one of those dimensions.

METHOD

Apparatus. The apparatus was a modification of one developed by Spiker (7) to study generalization with children. It allows S to respond by repeated pulls of a handle during a trial.

The stimuli were presented by an experimental model of the Hunter Cardmaster, a device for the timed presentation of cards. This is a gray metal box, $14 \times 14 \times 14$ in., with a stimulus aperture 6 in. wide and 3 in. high. Within, a conveyor system slides a $6\frac{1}{4} \times 3\frac{1}{2}$-in. card from the bottom of a stack and presses it against the aperture. Black cloth curtains part to either side to reveal the card to S. When the curtains close, the card is returned to the top of the stack and a new one brought up. Each stimulus exposure lasted 3.8 sec., an interval which preliminary testing indicated would allow a sufficiently high rate of response for gradations in generalization to manifest themselves. Each intertrial interval lasted 3.5 sec.

The opening of the curtains closed a switch in the circuits of an impulse counter and a marble delivery device; these circuits were then completed when S pulled the response handle $\frac{3}{4}$ in. towards himself. (A 3-lb. pull would close the microswitch.) Thus, when the curtains were open, each pull would register on the impulse counter and cause a marble to be delivered. When they closed, the counting and marble delivery stopped. A hidden button enabled E to lock out marble delivery during any given trial.

[1] A portion of a dissertation submitted to the State University of Iowa in partial fulfillment of the requirements for the Ph.D. degree. The writer wishes to express his gratitude to Charles C. Spiker, who directed this research, and to Don Lewis, for valuable suggestions. John Peterson gave considerable aid in construction and maintenance of the apparatus.

Reprinted by permission from *Journal of Experimental Psychology*, 1958, 56, 339–343.

The handle protruded from the lower right-hand corner of a black wooden box on which the Cardmaster rested, and varied from waist to chest height for different Ss. Tubing, housed in a black box to the left, held a reserve of about 300 marbles. These were delivered into a plastic pail at S's left.

Stimuli. The stimuli were 3 × 5-in. sheets of Munsell colored paper, covered with li-

brary tape and mounted on white plastic cards. In Table 1, the colors are schematized in the Munsell notation (5), which is of the form: Hue Value/Chroma. The colors were illuminated by a 100-w. bulb about 2 in. above, shielded to prevent glare. The blinds of the various schoolrooms used were drawn, to make this the principal source of illumination of the stimuli.

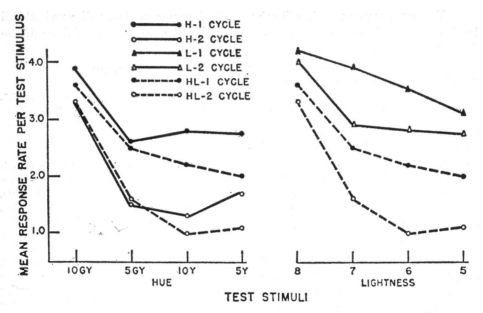

Figure 1. Mean response rates per test stimulus in Groups H, L, and HL, as a function of variation in hue and lightness.

Procedure and Ss. The children were told they were to play a game, and that the way to win it was to fill a pail with marbles. The E pulled the handle to two exposures of the training stimulus, and S was encouraged while pulling to six more. Occasionally, when S had not given three or more responses on each of two consecutive trials, he was given up to four more. Marbles were delivered on all pretraining trials.

All Ss were then given 16 reinforced trials with the training stimulus and, without pause, a sequence of 8 nonreinforced test trials distributed among 12 reinforced presentations of the training stimulus. Either 1, 2, or 3 reinforcements separated one test trial from the next.

TABLE 1 · MUNSELL VALUES OF COLORS USED AS STIMULI VALUE (LIGHTNESS)

Hue	8/	7/	6/	5/
10GY	10GY 8/6	10GY 7/6	10GY 6/6	10GY 5/6
5GY	5GY 8/6	5GY 7/6		
10Y	10Y 8/6		10Y 6/6	
5Y	5Y 8/6			5Y 5/6

Note. Group L's test stimuli along row, HL's along diagonal, H's in column. The training stimulus was 10GY 8/6.

The transition to testing produced a change in incidental stimulation. The color used in training, being always the same, was presented by opening and closing the curtains on one card. During the last training trial, *E* closed a switch causing the Card-master thereafter to change cards at the end of each trial. Card changing produced a sound noticeable to *S*. The first trial of the testing sequence was, therefore, a reinforced presentation of the training stimulus, in an attempt to counteract any change in behavior which might be produced by the new sound.

There were three testing groups. Group H had four test stimuli: the training color and three others differing in hue, but of the same lightness. Group L had test stimuli varying in lightness, but of the same hue. The novel stimuli for Group HL differed from the training color in both hue and lightness. Each HL color contained a Group H hue and a Group L lightness (Table 1).

The *S*s were kindergarten children in the Cedar Rapids public schools [2] who met a criterion of not more than one error on

[2] The writer wishes to thank Hale C. Reid, Director of Curriculum and Instruction for permission to use as *S*s children of the public schools of Cedar Rapids, Iowa. Ruth Phillips, principal of the Grant Wood School, and Florence Gritzner, principal of the Lincoln School, provided facilities for, and made pleasant, the running of *S*s.

Plates I–VI of the ISCC Pseudoisochromatic Colorblindness Test, administered before an experimental session. The data for 24 children were not used. Fourteen *S*s—four from H, four from L, and six from HL—were interrupted by mechanical failure of the apparatus. Three HL *S*s were dropped because of procedural errors, and three other HL *S*s because an extremely rapid rate of response overfilled their marble container. One *S* from H, and another from L, were eliminated because of distractions within the school. Two children failed to meet the color-blindness criterion. There remained a total of 72 *S*s, 24 in each group.

RESULTS

During training, Groups H, L, and HL averaged, respectively, 6.4, 6.5, and 6.6 pulls per trial. Analysis of variance did not reveal a significant difference between the groups.

The left half of Fig. 1 shows the mean number of pulls per test stimulus, cycles given separately, for Groups H and

TABLE 2 · Analyses of Variance Comparing Groups H vs. HL, and L vs. HL, on Number of Responses to Their Four Test Stimuli

Source	df	H vs. HL		L vs. HL	
		MS	F	MS	F
Between *S*s	47				
Groups (G)	1	9.69	<1	150.00	9.12**
Error (b)	46	11.04		16.44	
Within *S*s	336				
Stimuli (S)	3	64.34	30.21***	47.04	23.76***
Cycles (C)	1	83.44	71.93***	45.37	18.52***
G × S	3	2.40	1.13	3.81	1.92
G × C	1	1.63	1.41	1.26	<1
S × C	3	3.11	2.80*	2.57	2.40
G × S × C	3	0.03	<1	0.64	<1
Error (w)	322				
Error₁ (w)	138	2.13		1.98	
Error₂ (w)	46	1.16		2.45	
Error₃ (w)	138	1.11		1.07	
Total	383				

* $P < .05$.
** $P < .01$.
*** $P < .001$.

HL. There is little difference between them on their first two test values, but Group H gives more responses than Group HL on the two furthest points. For both groups, responses to the 10GY (training) value in test trials were markedly greater than to the three novel test stimuli, which did not differ greatly in numbers of responses elicited. There is a decrease in response rate from the first to the second cycle of test trials. These effects, except for the difference between groups, were found to be significant in an analysis of variance (4) (Table 2).

An analysis of variance with the factors shown in Table 2, but using only the data of the three novel test stimuli, was performed. In this analysis, only the cycles effect was significant, at the .001 level.

From the right half of Fig. 1, it is seen that (a) Group L gave more generalized responses to all four of its test stimuli than did Group HL to its corresponding stimuli; (b) a gradient of generalized responses sloping away from the training value is indicated; (c) there is a decrease in responses from the first to the second cycle. Analysis of variance indicated these effects to be significant (Table 2).

A repetition of this analysis using only the data of the three novel test stimuli of each group again showed these three effects, and no others, to be significant.

DISCUSSION

The fact that more Ss were eliminated from Group HL than from the H and L groups together raises the possibility that some sampling bias was inadvertently introduced. The most serious contamination would be in the selection of slower responders into Group HL, since evidence of this and other (8) studies tends to show low positive correlations between rates of response during acquisition and test trials. However, the acquisition data shows that all three groups gave about the same rate of response during training, and suggests that the groups' differences in generalization were probably not produced by selection of Ss.

The hypothesis of the present study can be predicted by considering each attribute of the training stimulus to be a separately conditionable component, with its habit strength summating with that of other attributes to produce the habit strength for the compound CS. Hull's laws of primary stimulus generalization and habit summation (3) would then predict that: (a) the three groups should respond identically on test trials to the training color; (b) the HL generalization gradient should be below those of the other two groups; and (c) the HL gradient should be steepest.

For Prediction a, we may note that the H, L, and HL groups averaged, respectively, 3.6, 4.1, and 3.5 responses over their two test trials to the training color, with nonsignificant differences. For Prediction b, we note that Group L was significantly above, and Group H tended to be above, Group HL in numbers of responses on their generalization test trials. With regard to Prediction c, it is evident in Fig. 1 that the differences between Groups H or L and HL are greater at the furthest test point than at the training point, as would be expected. However, the Groups × Stimuli effect fails to approach significance in either analysis of Table 2.

The above discussion of theory and

test has disregarded the extinction effects which resulted from a counterbalanced testing procedure, and which affect the generalization curves. The comparison of test stimuli within Ss was based, as it usually is, upon a consideration of the great economy of Ss which the method provided. In terms of theory, at least, the predicted effects should usually manifest themselves despite distortions produced by this method. The prediction which is most vulnerable to distorting effects of extinction is c, that of differing slope for the HL, as compared to the H or L gradients.

SUMMARY

Three groups of 24 kindergarten children were given 16 trials of training to pull a response handle freely during 3.8-sec. presentations of a colored stimulus. Two cycles of generalization test trials were then interspersed among reinforced presentations of the training stimulus. Group H was tested on the training stimulus and three novel stimuli of the same lightness, but having graded differences in hue. The novel stimuli of Group L were like the training stimulus in hue but differed in lightness, while those of Group HL differed in both hue and lightness.

The three groups did not differ in their rates of response during training. Group HL gave fewer generalized responses to its test stimuli than did Groups H or L to theirs, but only the comparison between L and HL was significant.

REFERENCES

1. ENINGER, M. U. Habit summation in a selective learning problem. *J. comp. physiol. Psychol.*, 1952, *45*, 604–608.

2. ERIKSEN, C. W., & HAKE, H. W. Multidimensional stimulus differences and accuracy of discrimination. *J. exp. Psychol.*, 1955, *50*, 153–160.

3. HULL, C. L. *A behavior system.* New Haven: Yale Univer. Press, 1952.

4. LINDQUIST, E. F. *Design and analysis of experiments in psychology and education.* Boston: Houghton Mifflin, 1953.

5. MUNSELL, A. H. *A color notation.* (8th ed., edited and rearranged.) Baltimore: Munsell Color Co., 1936.

6. SPENCE, K. W. The differential response in animals to stimuli varying within a single dimension. *Psychol. Rev.*, 1937, *44*, 430-444.

7. SPIKER, C. C. The stimulus generalization gradient as a function of the intensity of stimulus lights. *Child Develpm.*, 1956, *27*, 85–98.

8. TAYLOR, J. E. The effects of differential positive-negative cue differences on the changing strength of response tendency. Unpublished doctor's dissertation, State Univer. of Iowa, 1953.

GENERALIZATION OF CHILDREN'S PREFERENCES AS A FUNCTION OF REINFORCEMENT AND TASK SIMILARITY [1]

HAVA BONNE GEWIRTZ

THIS STUDY deals with the effects of certain social reinforcement conditions on the stimulus generalization gradients they produce in children. There have been several recent attempts to apply the concepts of generalization and reinforcement to complex human behavior. Among these, Miller's (7, 8) theoretical models for conflict and displacement phenomena are central. Yet the experiments upon which they are based most often involved infrahuman organisms, physiological reinforcement conditions, and a single dimension of stimulus similarity. And while some studies (4, 12) dealing with complex personality variables have incorporated Miller's conflict theory, generalization in these typically was inferred from assumptions about similarity between objects or situations which could not in themselves be tested because of situational or temporal distance.

In this study, an attempt is made to apply the concepts of generalization and reinforcement to a relatively complex human situation in which the reinforcement conditions are manipulated experimentally. An experiment was designed to investigate children's preferences for a series of problem-solving tasks, as a function of success and failure experiences (positive and negative reinforcers) associated with a training task, and as related to the tasks' degree of similarity to the training task. It was expected that if positive reinforcement followed the solution response to the training task, the differential preference values assigned to the tasks—ordered along the similarity dimension—would represent an approach gradient of preference (i.e., preference for the tasks would increase with their increasing similarity to the training task); and that negative reinforcement applied to the training task would produce an avoidance gradient (i.e., preference would increase with increasing dissimilarity to the training task). In addition, it was intended to compare the slopes of the two resultant gradients, for a fundamental assumption of Miller's conflict model is that avoidance gradients are steeper in slope than are approach gradients.

Studies of preferences and similar responses (3, 5) have suggested that such behaviors could be acquired according to the laws of conditioning and reinforcement. But it has been demonstrated also (2, 10) that complex social reinforcement

[1] This paper is based on a portion of a doctoral dissertation submitted to the Department of Psychology of the University of Chicago. The writer wishes to express her appreciation and gratitude to Helen L. Koch and to Lyle V. Jones for their guidance in the course of this study.

Reprinted by permission from *Journal of Abnormal and Social Psychology*, 1959, 58, 111–118.

experiences such as success and failure may have different implications for subjects with different reinforcement histories relevant to the treatment variable, and that these differences may be reflected in the effectiveness of experimental treatment conditions. This consideration has been taken into account in the design and interpretation of this study.

METHOD

SUBJECTS

One hundred children in the first and second grades of a university laboratory school served as subjects (Ss). They ranged in age from 6-1 to 8-0 years, and their median IQ score was 130.[2] Children who were considered behavior problems by their teachers and those who were unwilling to participate were excluded.

MATERIALS

A puzzle-solving situation was employed. The material consisted of five Masonite formboard-type puzzles. While all five puzzle

[2] IQ scores, most of which were based on the Revised Stanford-Binet, were obtained from the school records. A few scores based on different tests were well above or below the median value, so that it is unlikely that the median would have been altered had all Ss been given the Binet.

frames with their respective covers were of equal size ($11 \times 8\frac{1}{2}$ inches), the diamond-shaped depression within each frame (which constituted the puzzle proper) represented different points along a dimension of shape similarity (Fig. 1). The puzzles at the extremes of the dimension (1 and 5) were used as training puzzles. Each was equipped with two sets of seven triangular plywood pieces to be fitted into the puzzle depression: one was the *easy* set designed to insure successful solution, the other was the *difficult* set designed to produce failure. While both sets were similar in general appearance, the asymmetry of the pieces in the difficult set made solution practically impossible for Ss of the ages employed. The frames and covers of all five puzzles were painted a uniform gray, while the depression in each puzzle as well as all the pieces in the four sets were painted a bright red. In addition, the outline of each puzzle depression was reproduced in red on top of the puzzle's cover. In this way, Ss could observe the shape similarity dimension when the puzzles were covered, without the opportunity to discover clues about the correct placement of the puzzle pieces inside.

EXPERIMENTAL CONDITIONS

Three major conditions were employed: positive reinforcement, negative reinforcement, and control (no reinforcement). The reinforcement conditions represented a combination of three elements. *Positive rein-*

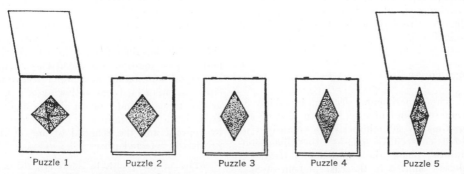

Figure 1. Puzzle Similarity Dimension. (Puzzles 1 and 5 [the training puzzles] are open and show the "difficult" sets of pieces as placed correctly inside. Puzzles 2, 3, and 4 are closed and their outlines are shown on top of the covers.)

forcement consisted of (*a*) objective success in the puzzle-solution attempt, (*b*) the experimenter's (*E*'s) approval (e.g., "Good," "That was fine!"), and (*c*) *S*'s winning a material reward or prize (a small plastic trinket of the kind found in gumball vending machines). *Negative reinforcement* consisted of (*a*) objective failure in the solution attempt, (*b*) *E*'s reproof (e.g., "That wasn't too good," "Uh-uh"), and (*c*) the withholding of the material prize. The three elements under each condition were combined in order to maximize the effects of the experimental treatment as well as to minimize individual differences among *S*s in their susceptibility to the different kinds of reinforcers involved.

The sample was divided into five groups of 20 *S*s each. With the exception of stratification according to sex and grade,[3] the assignment of *S*s to the five groups was made at random. These groups did not differ significantly in age or intelligence test scores. Of the five groups, two received positive reinforcement, two received negative reinforcement, and one served as the control. Of each two groups receiving the same reinforcement condition, one was trained on Puzzle 1 and the other on Puzzle 5. The two training puzzles were employed under each reinforcement condition as a crude control for the possibility that puzzles might be differentially attractive due to specific shape characteristics rather than to the effects of the experimental treatment. Thus, in addition to the control group, there were four treatment groups representing the four combinations of reinforcement condition and training puzzle: Positive 1, Negative 1, Positive 5, and Negative 5.

PROCEDURE

The experimental session, in which *S*s were seen individually for a period of approximately 20 minutes, was comprised of three consecutive phases: the dimension-training phase, the experimental treatment phase (omitted in the case of control *S*s),

and the paired-comparison testing phase. The *dimension-training* phase served to familiarize *S*s with the puzzle similarity dimension. *S* was shown the five puzzles, all covered and arranged in a row in a random order. He was asked to rearrange them in terms of their similarity to each other and to verbalize the relevant dimension characteristics. While no *S* failed to rearrange the puzzles correctly, some were unable to verbalize the basis for their arrangement. In such cases, *E* provided the relevant information (e.g., "See, they become longer and longer"). This procedure was adopted to insure that *S*s were equally aware of the shape similarity dimension.

The *experimental treatment* phase followed when *S* was led to a separate table and presented with the appropriate training puzzle (either 1 or 5). He was urged to try to solve the puzzle and was told he would win a little prize for each successful solution. At this point *S* was presented with a box containing about 20 prizes and was permitted to select and put aside his three favorites. To convince skeptical *S*s that solution was possible, *E* preceded the treatment by a brief demonstration, employing the set of pieces on which *S* was to be trained. This was carried out so rapidly that there seemed little danger that *S* would learn the difficult pattern or lose interest in the simple one. Actual treatment began only after this demonstration, and consisted of *three* trials of puzzle solution. Under the positive reinforcement condition, *S* was provided with the easy set of pieces. After each of the three successful trials he was praised by *E* and allowed to keep one of the three prizes. Under negative reinforcement *S* was provided with the difficult set of pieces. A trial under this condition was defined as an unsuccessful solution attempt, when *S* gave up either spontaneously or following *E*'s suggestion to end it and "start it all over again." Each of the three failures was accompanied by reproof and the removal of one of the previously selected prizes.[4]

[3] This stratification is ignored in the presentations which follow, because neither age nor sex was found to be related to the experimental results.

[4] Five of the positively reinforced *S*s were noticed to have considerable difficulty in solving the easy puzzle; and three of the negatively reinforced *S*s almost succeeded in solving the difficult one. These few cases, however, did not change the results and hence are not discussed further.

The *paired-comparison* testing phase followed the last training trial, when S was asked whether he would like to play some more, but this time with a puzzle of his own choice. The suggestion was welcomed by every S. E then presented to S, successively, the 10 different possible pairs of the five puzzles. During the presentation of each pair, S was asked to point to the puzzle with which he would *prefer* to play. The sequence of pair-presentation was random except that each puzzle appeared an equal number of times in the right and left position in the

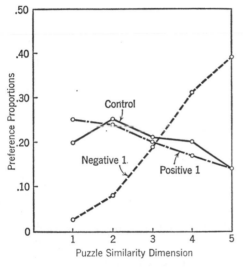

FIGURE 2. PREFERENCE GRADIENTS OF CONTROL, POSITIVE 1 AND NEGATIVE 1 GROUPS ($N = 20$ per group).

pair. When the presentation of all 10 pairs was completed, S was asked to give the reason for his preference choice ("Why did you pick those?"). Control Ss, who were not subjected to the treatment procedure, were presented with the paired-comparison test immediately following the dimension-training phase.[5]

_____

[5] Although the experimental session was concluded at this point, Ss in the control and negative groups were now permitted to play with the puzzle of their choice, to solve it successfully, and to win the three prizes. This was done in order to temper somewhat the experiences of all Ss before their return to their classrooms, and thus to prevent harmful rumors about failure or loss of prizes from reaching children who had not yet had their turn as Ss.

RESULTS

APPROACH AND AVOIDANCE GENERALIZATION GRADIENTS

The data were analyzed first by means of the rank analysis method (*1, 11*), which enabled testing two null hypotheses: (*a*) puzzle preference *equality* (i.e., that in each of the five groups there were no significant differences among the preference rankings assigned to the five

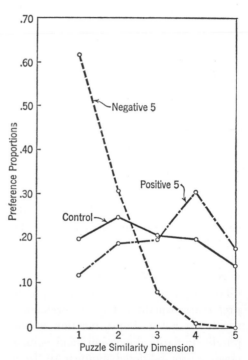

Figure 3. PREFERENCE GRADIENTS OF CONTROL, POSITIVE 5 AND NEGATIVE 5 GROUPS ($N = 20$ per group).

puzzles); and (*b*) *agreement* between groups (i.e., that there were no differences between each experimental group and the control group in terms of their respective preference patterns).

Figures 2 and 3 show the composite preference gradients (based on preference proportions derived from the rankings)

TABLE 1 · CHI SQUARE VALUES FOR THE RANK ANALYSIS TESTS: PUZZLE PREFERENCE EQUALITY WITHIN EACH GROUP AND AGREEMENT IN PREFERENCE PATTERN BETWEEN EACH TREATMENT GROUP AND THE CONTROL GROUP

Group	Puzzle preference equality	Agreement with control
Control	4.24	—
Positive 1	5.30	1.06
Negative 1	90.31**	59.87**
Positive 5	12.87*	8.75
Negative 5	171.99**	93.41**

Note. Large x^2 values (4 df) indicate *departure* from equality and *dis*agreement.

* $p < .02$.
** $p < .001$.

obtained from the groups trained on Puzzle 1 and Puzzle 5, respectively. The control group curve is the same in both figures. Table 1 presents the results of the tests of equality and agreement. As shown, the expectations advanced were fully confirmed only in the case of the two negative groups: each exhibited a reliable avoidance gradient which differed significantly from the preference pattern of the control group. In contrast, the results obtained from the two positive groups were less conclusive: only Positive 5 exhibited significant departure from puzzle preference equality, yet its preference trend was not a simple function of the puzzle similarity dimension; and neither positive group differed significantly from the control group. In addition, response pattern variability within the positive groups was considerably greater than it was within the negative groups, suggesting that a considerable number of Ss were unaffected by the positive treatment condition. This variability was unrelated either to age or sex of Ss, and appeared to be a function of randomly distributed individual differences.

To examine the nature of these differences, it was necessary to determine the number and type of preference response patterns given by *individual* Ss. Since this information could not be provided by the rank analysis method, another analysis was undertaken. It was based on frequency distributions of Ss classified into two major categories: those exhibiting "gradient" patterns, and those exhibiting "nongradient" patterns. S was said to exhibit a gradient pattern when the sum of his preference ranks represented the values 4, 5, 6, 7, 8 (or 8, 7, 6, 5, 4), respectively, for the five puzzles arranged in terms of the similarity dimension.[6] While this particular pattern represented the "perfect" individual gradient possible within the paired-comparison scoring method, slight deviations from this perfect order were included also in the gradient pattern category (e.g., a single reversal in adjacent puzzles; one or two ties on adjacent puzzles provided the order of preference was still maintained in relation to the similarity dimension). All Ss whose sums of ranks did not satisfy these criteria were classified in the nongradient category.

Table 2 presents the frequency distribution of Ss falling within the gradient and nongradient categories, including also classification by gradient *direction* (i.e., approach or avoidance relative to the training puzzle). Because the different training puzzles did not produce different

---

[6] These values are based on the paired-comparison scores, where the preferred member in the pair received the rank of 1 and the rejected member received the rank of 2. Each of the five puzzles appeared a total of four times in the ten-pair presentations. Hence, for a single S, the puzzle always preferred would receive the minimal total rank of 4, and the puzzle never preferred would receive the maximal total rank of 8.

TABLE 2 · Number of Ss Exhibiting Individual Gradient Patterns in Each Group, and Difference Between Treatment and Control Group Frequencies

Group	Gradient pattern			Non-gradient pattern	Difference from control[a]
	Ap-proach	Avoidance	Total		
Control	3	2	5	15	—
Positive	18	8	26	14	7.02*
Negative	0	30	30	10	11.73*

[a] x^2 corrected for discontinuity, two-tailed test (1 df).
* $p < .01$.

response gradients in Ss, in this table and in all subsequent ones the data are presented for the combined positive and the combined negative groups, with 40 Ss in each. As shown, the proportion of positively and of negatively reinforced Ss who exhibited gradient patterns was significantly greater, in each case, than that proportion among the control Ss. While it is seen that the treatments produced generalization gradients, this analysis reveals also that the positive reinforcement condition produced *two* kinds of gradients: approach and avoidance. This finding could explain the over-all similarity between the control and the positive groups shown in the rank analysis, since the individual gradients, opposite in direction, appear to have cancelled each other in the composite group scores.

FACTORS UNDERLYING THE EFFECTS
OF POSITIVE REINFORCEMENT

The question that still remained, however, was: why did some of the positively reinforced Ss exhibit avoidance gradients, which had been expected only under negative reinforcement? Since the experiment consisted of a goal-attainment situation, it was assumed that the variations found in Ss' response patterns reflected individual differences in the intensity of their involvement in success, i.e., in their *achievement* motivation. Two classes of information were available in this study for the purpose of testing this assumption: (*a*) the *reasons* given by Ss for their preference choices, and (*b*) their *IQ level*. These two variables were taken, each to be a plausible indicator of Ss' strength of achievement motivation (for reasons to be noted subsequently).

Of the various types of reasons given by Ss, two indicated involvement in achievement: preference for easy tasks (e.g., "Because it looks easier", "The others are too hard for me"); and preference for difficult tasks (e.g., "I think it is harder, I like to try it", "Harder is more fun"). These two types of reasons, *Ease* and *Difficulty*, were given by more than 50% of all experimentally reinforced Ss, but only by 10% of control Ss. For IQ level, Ss were divided into two groups: the "High" IQ group consisted of Ss whose scores were above the over-all sample median of 130, and the "Low" IQ group consisted of those with scores below and including that median. It was postulated that the avoidance gradients generated by the positive reinforcement condition were an outcome of strong achievement motivation, and as such would be exhibited more frequently by the more highly achievement-motivated Ss, who were expected to be in the High IQ group and to give Difficulty as their reason. Table 3 presents the frequency distribution of the 40 *positively reinforced* Ss in terms of these three variables. When the relationships were tested by means of exact one-tailed tests for fourfold tables (6), the following results were obtained, all at $p < .01$: (*a*) Ss who

TABLE 3 · Number of Ss in the Positive Group Classified in Terms of Gradient Direction, IQ Level, and Type of Reason

	GRADIENT PATTERN AND DIRECTION					
	Approach gradient		*Avoidance gradient*		*Non-gradient*	
Reason	L	H	L	H	L	H
Ease	10	1	0	3	0	1
Difficulty	0	0	1	4	0	1
Other	5	2	0	0	6	6
Total	15	3	1	7	6	8

Note. "L" and "H" refer to Low and High IQ groups, respectively.

exhibited avoidance gradients tended to give Difficulty as their reason (5/8), while Ss who exhibited approach gradients tended to give Ease as their reason (11/18); (b) Ss who exhibited avoidance gradients were predominantly in the High IQ group (7/8), while Ss who exhibited approach gradients were mostly in the Low IQ group (15/18); (c) when IQ level and type of reason were employed as a joint criterion, it was found that *all* 10 Ss who were simultaneously in the Low IQ and Ease categories exhibited approach gradients, while *all* four Ss who were simultaneously in the High IQ and Difficulty categories exhibited avoidance gradients. Thus, the postulated relationships between gradient direction, IQ level, and type of reason appear to be supported; and positive reinforcement was shown to generate quite different gradient patterns depending on Ss' strength of achievement motivation.

RELATIVE STEEPNESS OF SLOPE

The examination of the relative steepness of slope of the generalization gradients produced by positive and negative reinforcement involved classification of individual gradient patterns in terms of

their degree of *steepness*. The steepest gradient possible under the method employed was the "perfect" gradient, described earlier. All other gradient patterns were classified as "imperfect." Table 4

TABLE 4 · Number of Ss in the Two Reinforcement Groups Exhibiting Perfect and Imperfect Approach and Avoidance Gradients

Group	APPROACH GRADIENT		AVOIDANCE GRADIENT		TOTAL GRADIENT	
	Perfect	*Imperfect*	*Perfect*	*Imperfect*	*Perfect*	*Imperfect*
Negative	0	0	22	8	22	8
Positive	8	10	2	6	10	16

presents the distribution of Ss in the two reinforcement groups in terms of this steepness criterion, and also according to gradient direction. Two-tailed tests (χ^2 corrected for discontinuity, 1 df) were used. The first question addressed itself to the effects of each treatment condition on steepness, ignoring gradient direction. It was found that the proportion of steep gradients that were obtained after negative reinforcement (22/30) was significantly greater ($p < .02$) than the proportion obtained after positive reinforcement (10/26). When gradient direction was taken into account, however, it was found that *perfect* avoidance gradients were produced more frequently ($p < .01$) in the negative group (22/30) than in the positive group (2/8); but that no differences existed in the positive group between the proportion of its perfect avoidance gradients (2/8) and the proportion of its perfect approach gradients (8/18). These results indicate that, regardless of gradient direction, negative reinforcement produced more and steeper individual gradients than did the positive reinforcement condition.

DISCUSSION

ACHIEVEMENT MOTIVATION AND PREFERENCE GRADIENTS

It has been suggested (e.g., 2) that children's preferences for difficult goals are a function of strong achievement emphasis during socialization. Similarly, when, following success, S verbalized preference for a difficult task in the present study, it was taken to indicate that he was more motivated to demonstrate outstanding achievement than was another S who verbalized preference for the easy task on which success had already been experienced. The use of IQ level as the second index of achievement motivation was based on the notion that ability is a significant determinant of the *outcome* of past encounters with difficult tasks. Highly intelligent children are likely to be rewarded for attempts to excel on such tasks, either because of actual success, due to superior ability, or because parental approval is often contingent upon their accomplishing more than "just doing what everybody else can do." Hence, the highly able child should be more likely to acquire strong achievement motivation than the less able child. Another possible approach could be based on the notion that high IQ scores are, in part, an outcome of strong achievement motivation. The child who persists in his problem-solving efforts and refuses to give up easily is more likely to attain a higher score than one who is indifferent or gives up at first sight of difficulty.

These assumed relationships, regardless of their causal direction, appear to be supported by the present experimental results. Mastery of the difficult task appeared to have a stronger reinforcing value to the highly achievement-motivated S than repeated success on the easy one. Hence, it would seem more correct to conclude that rather than generating approach and avoidance gradients, the positive reinforcement condition produced *two kinds of approach gradients:* one by the less achievement-motivated Ss, directed towards the goal of easy and safe success (the approach gradient) ; and the other by the highly achievement-motivated Ss directed towards the goal of outstanding achievement in terms of solving the most difficult appearing task (the avoidance-like gradient). This conclusion seems supported also by the finding that these two kinds of gradients resembled each other in terms of the steepness criterion, regardless of direction.

NEGATIVE REINFORCEMENT GENERATES THE STEEPER GRADIENT

The limitations inherent in the paired-comparison method [7] restrict somewhat statements about the specific shape of the generalization gradients obtained. Nevertheless, the marked differences between the effects of the two treatment conditions suggest certain speculative interpretations. While the distinction between primary and acquired drives, as suggested by Miller and Murray (9), does not fit the case of the present study, an analogous differentiation between "internal" and "external' sources of motivation for the response might be applied here. The fact that no individual differences could be detected in the uniform response pattern exhibited by the negative group suggests

---

[7] Because the lack of independent response measures for each of the compared items, the effects of reinforcement on the response to each of the five puzzles is confounded with its effects on the discrimination of the training puzzle from all others.

that such differences—though theoretically present—were overshadowed by the powerful and unambiguous negative treatment condition. The avoidance response appears to have been contingent predominantly upon the external stimulus situation which, when changed, was readily discriminated and produced a decrease in response strength resulting in a steep generalization gradient. On the other hand, the variability in the positive group's response pattern indicated that this treatment condition was responded to by Ss primarily according to their individual aspirations and achievement needs. The "need to succeed" (being different perhaps for each S) was relatively more constant and more independent of the external stimulus situation. Hence, changes in that situation did not bring about a marked, or at least uniform, reduction in response strength, making for flatter generalization gradients than those produced under the negative reinforcement condition.

SUMMARY

An experiment was designed to study children's preferences for a series of problem-solving tasks as a function of the particular reinforcement condition associated with a training task, and the degree of similarity of each task to the training task. One hundred first- and second-graders served as Ss. Five formboard-type puzzles were constructed such that their shapes constituted a similarity dimension. The two puzzles at the extremes of this dimension served as training puzzles, each for one-half of a group receiving the same reinforcement. Forty Ss received positive reinforcement, consisting of successful puzzle solution, praise, and a material reward; 40 Ss received negative reinforcement, consisting of failure, reproof, and withdrawal of the reward; and 20 Ss were not reinforced, serving as a control group. Ss' differential preferences for the five puzzles were obtained through subsequent paired-comparison presentations.

The results were: 1. Following reinforcement, the differential preference rankings for the puzzles (arranged in terms of the similarity dimension) represented generalization gradients of preference. But while negative reinforcement uniformly generated avoidance gradients, positive reinforcement produced in some Ss approach gradients and in others avoidance gradients. 2. Those positively reinforced Ss who exhibited avoidance gradients tended to have superior IQ, and to verbalize preference for difficult tasks. It was postulated that these Ss were more achievement-motivated than those who exhibited approach gradients, and that their response pattern actually represented approach towards a more challenging task. 3. When the slopes of the gradients were compared, it was found that negative reinforcement generated a larger proportion of steeper individual gradients than did positive reinforcement. It was suggested that this finding could be related to the distinction between external and internal factors which determined the response.

REFERENCES

1. Bradley, R. A., & Terry, M. E. Rank analysis of incomplete block designs I: The method of paired comparisons. *Biometrika*, 1952, *39*, 324–345.
2. Child, I. L. Children's preferences for goals easy or difficult to attain.

Psychol. Monogr., 1946, *60,* No. 4 (Whole No. 280).

3. GEBHARDT, MILDRED E. The effect of success and failure upon the attractiveness of activities as a function of experience, expectation and need. *J. exp. Psychol.*, 1948, *38,* 371–388.

4. HOLLENBERG, ELEANOR, & SPERRY, MARGARET. Some antecedents of aggression and effects of frustration on doll play. *Personality,* 1951, *1,* 32–43.

5. HUNT, D. E. Change in goal-object preferences as a function of expectancy for social reinforcement. *J. abnorm. soc. Psychol.*, 1955, *50,* 372–377.

6. LATCHA, R. Tests of significance in a 2 x 2 contingency table: Extension of Finney's table. *Biometrika,* 1953, *40,* 74–88.

7. MILLER, N. E. Experimental studies of conflict. In J. McV. Hunt (Ed.), *Personality and the behavior dis-*orders. New York: Ronald, 1944. Pp. 431–465.

8. MILLER, N. E. Theory and experiment relating psychoanalytic displacement to stimulus-response generalization. *J. abnorm. soc. Psychol.*, 1948, *43,* 155–178.

9. MILLER, N. E., & MURRAY, E. J. Displacement and conflict: Learnable drives as a basis for the steeper gradient of avoidance than of approach. *J. exp. Psychol.*, 1952, *43,* 227–231.

10. SEARS, PAULINE S. Level of aspiration in academically successful and unsuccessful children. *J. soc. Psychol.*, 1940, *35,* 498–536.

11. TERRY, M. E., BRADLEY, R. A., & DAVIS, L. L. New designs and techniques for organoleptic testing. *Food Tech.*, 1952, *7,* 250–254.

12. WHITING, J. W. M., & CHILD, I. L. *Child training and personality: A cross-cultural study.* New Haven: Yale Univer. Press, 1953.

EXPERIMENTAL INVESTIGATION

OF THE RELATION OF LANGUAGE

TO TRANSPOSITION BEHAVIOR

IN YOUNG CHILDREN [1]

MARGARET R. KUENNE

INTRODUCTION

THE PHENOMENON of transposition in the discrimination behavior of animals and young children has received a considerable amount of attention from psychological theorists. The Gestalt psychologists, in particular, have made much of this ability of Ss to transfer a learned differential response, e.g., a response to the larger of two stimuli, to a new combination of stimulus objects differing in the same property (e.g., size), and they have cited it as conclusive evidence that the response was to the relative properties of the stimulus situation.

Relational theories of transposition, as has been pointed out by others (5, 27), fall into two groups. According to one type (1, 13, 15, 20, 22) the organism perceives the relationship between the training stimuli and employs this 'relational-perception' in responding differentially to the transposed stimulus situation. Thus, Kinnaman, the earliest investigator of this problem, wrote re-

garding the results in his brightness experiment with monkeys: "It would appear then that if the monkey managed to choose with measurable correctness, he very likely had a general notion of a low order which might be represented by *food-always-in-the-lighter*" (15, p. 143).

The second type of relational theory conceives of the organism as responding differentially to the training stimuli as a stimulus whole. The formulations of Köhler (17, 18), and Gulliksen and Wolfle (5) fall into this category. Thus, Köhler, in explaining his brightness experiments, stresses the 'togetherness' of the stimuli, recognizing that this togetherness may occur independently either as *color-wholes* or as *perceived color-relations*. He regards the two processes as distinct but their functions as similar, and so he chooses to ignore the differences. In either case, the colors (brightnesses) are assumed to attain an 'inner union' in which their role "depends not upon their absolute qualities, but upon their places in the system they compose. If their places with respect to each other are held constant, but a variation is made in their absolute quality, the Gestalt and the perceived relationship will be transposed" (17, p. 221). The occurrence of transposition is then regarded as evidence of such a configural response.

[1] This article is based on a dissertation submitted in partial fulfillment of the requirements for the degree of Doctor of Philosophy, in the Iowa Child Welfare Research Station, in the Graduate College of the State University of Iowa. The writer is deeply indebted to Professor Kenneth W. Spence for his advice and assistance throughout the course of the study.

Reprinted by permission from *Journal of Experimental Psychology*, 1946, 36, 471–490.

Köhler has made no further attempt to elaborate his theory so as to explain the occurrences of failure of transposition which have been found under a number of experimental conditions. A configuration theory more adequate in this respect is the recent one of Gulliksen and Wolfle (5). They conceive of the animal in the discrimination situation as responding directionally to the total stimulus configuration consisting of the stimuli varying in a single dimension and presented simultaneously in a given spatial order. Thus, in the two-choice size discrimination situation, the animal learns to respond differentially (left or right) to the two configurations, small on left and large on right, small on right and large on left. They assume, further, the operation of the law of effect and generalization of the effects of the learning on the training-stimulus configuration to similar configurations. On the basis of this theoretical schema, these writers were able to deduce a number of implications which are in agreement with existing experimental data. An outstanding exception is the failure of the theory to deduce one of the most well established experimental findings concerning transposition—the tendency for it to decrease as the distance between the training and test stimuli is increased.

Contrasting sharply with these two types of relational theories of transposition phenomena is the stimulus-response theory suggested by Spence (23, 24, 25, 26). Based on principles derived from experimental studies of conditioning, his theory represents an extension of an earlier theoretical treatment of the nature of discrimination learning in animals. According to this latter formulation, discrimination learning is a cumulative proc-ess in which reinforcement strengthens the excitatory tendency or association of the positive stimulus cue to the response of approaching it as compared with the response of approaching the negative stimulus cue which receives only nonreinforcement, hence developing an opposing inhibitory tendency. When the difference between the excitatory strengths of the two cue aspects is sufficiently large, so as always to be greater than any differences in the excitatory strengths of other stimulus aspects that may happen to be allied in their response-evoking action with one or another of the cue stimuli on a particular trial, the S will consistently respond to the positive stimulus; in other words, he will have learned.

In extending the theory to the problem of transposition, Spence assumes that the excitatory tendency to respond to the positive cue aspect generalizes to other members of the stimulus dimension according to the exponential function $E = Ae^{-c X^d}$, where X is the distance in logarithmic units between the positive stimulus and that stimulus point under consideration on the dimension. Similarly, the inhibitory tendency to respond to the negative cue aspect is assumed to generalize to other members of the stimulus dimension according to the function $I = Be^{-k X^d}$, X being the distance in logarithmic units between the negative stimulus and that stimulus point under consideration on the dimension. The excitatory and inhibitory tendencies to respond to a stimulus cue at any point on the dimension are assumed further to summate algebraically, yielding the effective excitatory strength at that point. Which of a pair of any stimulus members of a dimension will be chosen by an organism after training on a

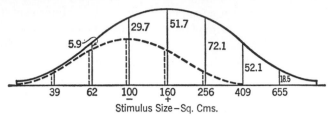

Figure 1. Diagrammatic representation of the relations between the hypothetical generalization curves, positive and negative, after training on the stimulus combination 160 (+) and 100 (—).

particular pair will depend upon the magnitude of the difference in the effective excitatory strengths of the competing stimulus cues as calculated from the values of the generalization curves.

The accompanying diagram, Fig. 1, taken from one of Spence's (27) recent papers, illustrates the workings of the theory. The S is assumed to have been trained to choose a square of 160 sq. cm., in preference to one of 100 sq. cm. The stimulus members indicated on the base line are placed at equal intervals on a logarithmic scale, and for each of these there is calculated the effective excitatory strength, determined by summing algebraically the excitatory and inhibitory generalization values for the given member. Comparing these hypothetical effective strengths for pairs of stimuli on the dimension, one would be led to predict that transposition will occur on pairs 256 vs. 160 and 100 vs. 62, but that transposition should fail to occur in the case of stimulus pairs farther removed from the training pair.

While insufficient knowledge as to the nature of the variation of generalization curves from individual to individual precludes the possibility of making specific deductions as to the exact results to be expected from individual Ss at each point on the stimulus dimension, nevertheless the theory does lead to certain

more general implications which are experimentally testable. One of these, that the amount of transfer will be less the farther removed the test pair from the original training pair, is of particular importance for the present investigation.

STATEMENT OF THE PROBLEM

The present study takes its point of departure from the theoretical formulation of transposition phenomena proposed by Spence. This theory was developed in relation to the behavior of nonarticulate organisms and is assumed to represent the underlying mechanisms (variables and laws) operating in infrahuman subjects and possibly in human Ss prior to the advent of verbal processes. In the case of an organism possessing verbal responses, however, behavior in discrimination situations presumably becomes cued to some extent to such words as 'bigger,' 'longer,' 'brighter,' etc. Observation and phenomenological reports suggest that verbal processes dominate such behavior in the case of the human adult. The relational theories originally proposed by the early American experimenters provide excellent examples of the recognition of the role of verbal processes in the human S. In line with the existing tendency to anthropomorphize, these writers projected their own processes into their animal Ss, although they usually acknowledged that such abstractions could function only as 'more general notions,' whatever that might mean.

As a basis for an attempt to extend our understanding of discrimination behavior and the phenomenon of transposition in human Ss, *the working hypothesis is here adopted that the mechanisms assumed by Spence to underlie this behavior in animals are also operative in the young child, and that with the development in older children of the capacity to employ verbal responses in such behavior situations, a shift occurs to the verbal type of control.*

According to this assumption, the child who has not yet learned the terms 'bigger' or 'smaller,' or who has not yet learned to control his overt behavior by means of such verbal responses or their implicit equivalents in a size discrimination problem, would learn the discrimination in much the same way as the animal S. Transfer of the learned response to another set of stimuli differing from the training set only with respect to size, would depend upon the generalization of excitation and inhibition from the positive and negative members of the training pair, respectively, to these other members of the size dimension. With increasing distance on the continuum of the test stimuli from the training pair, the differential effects of generalization would be expected to decrease until a point is eventually reached at which the difference would be too small to produce a differential response to the test stimuli. Non-cue factors would then be decisive and should produce a response which, except in the case of an original size preference, would be unrelated to the size aspect of the stimuli. A group of nonverbal Ss would, in such a case, be expected to respond in a manner consistent with original training only a chance number of times.[2]

The child whose discrimination behavior is controlled by verbalization of the cue aspect of the stimulus situation should, on the other hand, generalize equally well to all other pairs of test stimuli differing from the training stimuli in the same dimension. For example, if he learns to respond to the 'smaller' of a stimulus pair during training and is then tested on a new stimulus pair also maintaining the relationship 'smaller-larger,' it is expected that he will abstract the relationship in the new pair and respond on the basis of it to the smaller stimulus of the pair, whatever the distance of the test stimuli from the training stimuli. His choice behavior, in other words, will be controlled by some such verbal response as 'always in the smaller.'

Studies of transposition of response in children thus far reported in the literature consistently show that transposition occurs in a large proportion of cases, but they have employed only test stimuli near to the original training pair. Transposition would be expected under this condition whether the child used verbal responses effectively or not: in the first instance through generalization on a verbal basis; in the second, through generalization on a simple conditioning basis. Thus, the findings are not critical so far as the present hypothesis is concerned. Evidence for or against it can be obtained only on transposition tests with stimuli that are

---

[2] The size dimension has been used for illustrative purposes, but any other stimulus continuum such as brightness, weight, etc., would be equally applicable.

at a considerable distance from the training pair. This investigation attempts to provide such evidence.

In the absence of a measure of the extent to which the child employs the type of verbal concepts demanded by the theory, mental age has been taken as a rough indicator of the degree to which verbal or symbolic responses control behavior. *The implications of our working hypothesis are, then, that (mentally) very young children trained in a discrimination situation and in whom, presumably, verbal mechanisms are not highly developed, will respond on the distant transposition test in a chance manner, not in a manner consistent with training, while (mentally) older children, in whom the verbal-type mechanism is presumably well established, will exhibit transposition, that is, will respond in the distant test situation in a manner consistent with the original training.* It is probable that intermediate age groups will, as groups, fall somewhere between these two extremes, for some individuals will still be in the nonverbal stage, some will have progressed to the verbal level, while still others might possibly be in a stage of transition.

REVIEW OF PREVIOUS STUDIES

Comparatively few transposition experiments have employed child Ss, and none has treated the variables under consideration in the present study, namely: 1, the relation of the choice to the distance of the two test stimuli from the training pair on the stimulus dimension, and 2, the relation of choice to verbal development. Köhler (18), Frank (3), Klüver (16) and Jackson et al. (12) have demonstrated the predominance in children of relative choices on critical tests with stimuli one step [3] distant from the training pair on a size, brightness, or weight dimension, even under the condition of over-training. Other transposition experiments with children (7, 8, 9, 10, 11) have employed conditions irrelevant to the present problem.

In the animal field, a number of investigators have studied the relation of transposition to the distance of the test stimuli from the training stimuli on a single dimension. Gulliksen (4) and Flory (2) working with white rats, and Klüver (16) and Spence (25) working with chimpanzees, have consistently found that, in the size dimension, as the distance between the training and test stimuli increases from one to five steps, the frequency of relative choices decreases from a significantly high toward a chance level. Kendler (14), employing hooded rats, conducted a similar experiment in the brightness dimension through four step intervals. She found a progressive decrease in the relative choice through the first three steps, but a rise or leveling off thereafter, depending on whether training was to the brighter or duller stimulus. Thus, the findings with respect to the distance variable in transposition experiments with animals tend to be in line with the theory based on conditioning principles.

---

[3] 'Step,' a term introduced by Kendler (14), refers to the distance on the stimulus dimension of the test stimuli from the training stimuli, such that the members of the test set have the same relation to the corresponding members of the training set, as the members of the training set have to each other. One step interval is represented by the distance between a training pair 10 vs. 5, for example, and a test pair 20 vs. 10.

EXPERIMENT

A. SUBJECTS

Thirty-eight children from the preschools of the University of Iowa and 18 children from the kindergarten of the Horace Mann Public School in Iowa City were Ss in this experiment. They were selected on the basis of mental age scores within the range three to six years, and intelligence quotients of average or higher. In all, 12 who had from 140 to 630 training trials left school before they reached the learning criterion. Those who completed the study ranged in CA at the start of the experiment from 30 to 70 months, in MA from 36 to 83 months, and in IQ from 89 to 151.

Mental age and intelligence scores were obtained for all Ss on the New Revised Stanford-Binet Tests of Intelligence, Form L, within six months preceding the first day of training. With two exceptions, the investigator administered the tests. On the basis of the scores the children within each of the mental age levels 3, 4, 5 and 6 years, were divided into pairs matched for MA and IQ,

and for sex whenever possible. One member of each pair was randomly assigned to one test group and the other automatically fell into the alternate group.

B. APPARATUS

The apparatus, shown in Fig. 2, consisted of a stand 22 in. in height, on which rested a panel inclined at a 60-degree angle. Two 10-in. square openings were cut 10 in. apart in the panel, and covered with hinged lids. Behind these openings boxes were constructed. A thin strip of metal 3/8 in. wide was attached to the lower edge of the lid of each box to hold the stimuli in place. The metal extended over the inner edge of the lids and was bent slightly to form tabs for opening the boxes. Locks invisible to the S and manipulated from behind the apparatus were arranged so that the lid under the negative stimulus was always locked. Notched blocks of wood attached to the front legs of the table held a pressed wood screen in place between trials. A large variety of colorful toys, one of which was hidden each

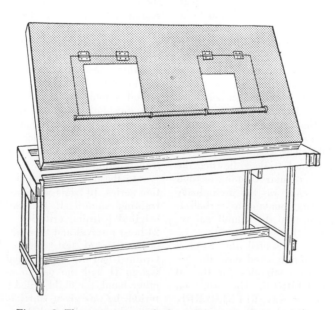

Figure 2. The apparatus with the training stimuli in position.

trial in the box on which the positive stimulus lay, served to motivate the child. The entire apparatus was painted flat black.

Stimuli were white-enameled ¼-in. pressed wood squares with the areas 2.0, 3.6, 21.0, 37.8 and 68.0 sq. in. These will be referred to by the numbers 1, 2, 5, 6 and 7, respectively. Numbers 3 and 4 are omitted to emphasize the links needed to complete the stimulus series whose successive members have areas maintaining the ratio 1.8:1 between them. A duplicate of stimulus 6, the postive training stimulus, was used for transposition tests as a control over responses on the near test to some specific characteristic (other than size) of the original training stimulus.

C. EXPERIMENTAL PROCEDURE

Training series. The procedure was identical for both experimental groups. Ss were trained to choose the box with the smaller of the two stimuli, 6 and 7. Fig. 2 shows these stimuli in position. In the event of a correct response, the box opened and a toy was found inside, while in the event of an incorrect response, the box was found to be locked. The S was never permitted to try both boxes. Toys were collected in a cardboard box which the child held on his lap.

Training began on the first day with a preliminary set of two trials during which E demonstrated the response. Instructions, uniform for all Ss, included no mention of the stimuli. On the first trial, the positive stimulus appeared on the left box, the negative on the right. The positions were reversed on the second trial. Following the demonstration the regular training session was begun. In no case was the preliminary series repeated. Any spontaneous verbalization of the cue aspect of the stimuli was recorded throughout the experiment.

Ten trials were presented the S each school day. On odd-numbered days the position of the positive stimulus for the 10 trials was LRLLRLRRLR. The order on even-numbered days was RLLRLRLRRL. Training was continued until the S chose the positive stimulus on at least the last nine of the 10 trials. In instances in which a child

responded nine consecutive times on the basis of position, E, on the ninth trial, indicated the correct box, saying, "Look! This box opens!" Trials were then given with the positive stimulus on the nonpreferred side until the child chose correctly once.

If, after 450 standard training trials, the S showed no indication of approaching the learning criterion, he was given at the start of the next session, five to 10 trials in which no stimuli were present, followed immediately by the regular training trials. Five trials without stimuli were given after 470 and 490 trials if learning still had not occurred. After 500 trials, the daily session opened with 10 trials in which the positive stimulus was presented alone. This series was followed immediately by 10 regular trials. Single stimulus presentation was continued on alternate days until there was evidence of learning.

Test series. Twenty-four hours after reaching the learning criterion the S was given a transposition test of 10 trials, during which all choices were rewarded. Group I was tested on the stimulus pair 5 vs. 6, while Group II was tested on the pair 1 vs. 2. If the child was not in school on the day after reaching the criterion, he was given training trials on his first day back. If he was able to choose the correct stimulus on five trials in five, he was given a 24-hour interval and then tested for transposition. If he failed on one of the five training trials, he was presented a total of 10 regular training trials that day and every day thereafter until he again reached the original criterion of nine consecutive correct choices in 10 trials. He was then given a 24-hour interval before the transposition series.

On the day following the first transposition series, 10 trials were presented with the training stimuli. If the child reached the original learning criterion, he was given a 24-hour interval and then presented with the other pair of test stimuli. For this test, Group I had the stimulus pair 1 vs. 2, while Group II had the pair 5 vs. 6. If, on the other hand, the child failed to reach the criterion, he was given 10 trials each day until he could reach it. As before, a transposition test was given after a 24-hour interval.

Elicitation of verbalization. Following the

final transposition test trial on the last day of the experiment, the screen was placed in position and the child was asked how he knew which box to open. If there was no response, the training blocks were placed in position, the screen was removed, and the S was asked how he knew which block to choose. If there was still no response he was asked how the blocks differed.

It was recognized, of course, that failure of the child to verbalize the size aspect aloud does not indicate that he also failed to verbalize internally; nor does failure to state a generalization in response to questioning indicate a similar failure during the course of the experiment. Furthermore, verbalizing at the conclusion of the experiment gives no cue as to the time the child actually formulated his generalization. On the other hand, the occurrence of spontaneous verbalization aloud is evidence of the presence of a verbal mechanism at least at that time. Verbalization in response to questioning indicates capacity for such a process and the possibility that it did occur during the learning period.

D. RESULTS

The various data obtained on the 44 Ss divided into four mental age levels are presented in Tables 1 to 4. The first column of each table identifies the S by

TABLE 1 · LEARNING AND TEST DATA FOR SUBJECTS AT THE THREE-YEAR LEVEL

Subjects	CA mos.	MA mos.	IQ	No. trials	No. 'smaller' responses in 10 trials	
					Near test	Far test
Group I (Ss given near test first)						
1	34	36	107	590	9	6
2	43	38	89	320	9	4
3	40	42	105	190	16	6
4	30	44	148	40	10	4
Group II (Ss given far test first)						
5	37	37	100	540	7	5
6	40	42	105	170	10	5
7	39	46	119	500	10	5
Means	37.6	40.7	110.4	335.7	9.3	5.0
Medians	39	42	105	320	9.5	5.0

number, and the next three contain data on CA, MA, and IQ, respectively, for each individual. The fifth column gives the total number of standard trials required to attain the criterion of learning in the discrimination situation. Finally, the last two columns show the number of responses consistent with the original training made in the 10 trials on the near test and the 10 trials on the far test. Each of the tables has been divided into an upper and lower part. The former includes those Ss (Group I) who were given the near test first; the latter, those Ss (Group II) who had the far test first. At the bottom of each table appear the means and medians of these various measures for each mental age group.

Learning. An examination of the data showing the number of trials to reach the learning criterion of nine consecutive correct choices in 10 reveals that the individual Ss ranged from 10 to 590 trials. There is evident a marked tendency for the low scores (fast learning) to be concentrated at the older age levels and the high scores (slow learning) to be found at the younger age levels. Both measures of central tendency for the four age groups reveal a decrease in the number of trials with increasing age, the means show-ing a consistent downward trend and the medians a single inversion between ages four and five. Further support for this relation between speed of learning and mental age is provided by the product-

TABLE 2 · LEARNING AND TEST DATA FOR SUBJECTS AT THE FOUR-YEAR LEVEL

Subjects	CA mos.	MA mos.	IQ	No. trials	No. 'smaller' responses in 10 trials	
					Near test	Far test
Group I (Ss given near test first)						
8	43	48	112	360	9	7
9	41	53	129	40	10	5
10	59	58	98	90	1	5
11	41	58	142	400	10	10
12	45	59	131	230	10	4
13	44	59	133	170	10	10
Group II (Ss given far test first)						
14	52	54	104	90	10	3
15	42	56	134	190	10	6
16	37	56	151	380	0	10
17	39	58	149	176*	1	6
18	46	59	128	380	10	6
Means	44.5	56.2	128.3	227.8	7.4	6.5
Medians	43	58	131	190	10	6

* On one training day, only six trials were given for reasons beyond E's control.

TABLE 3 · LEARNING AND TEST DATA FOR SUBJECTS AT THE FIVE-YEAR LEVEL

Subjects	CA mos.	MA mos.	IQ	No. trials	No. 'smaller' responses in 10 trials	
					Near test	Far test
Group I (Ss given near test first)						
19	61	60	98	290	10	10
20	64	65	102	270	10	7
21	65	65	100	50	10	8
22	68	66	97	160	10	4
23	66	70	106	110	10	2
24	62	70	113	200	10	10
Group II (Ss given far test first)						
25	63	65	103	200	10	7
26	64	65	102	210	10	9
27	62	66	107	30	10	10
28	67	67	100	250	10	10
29	65	70	108	310	10	8
30	63	71	113	220	10	9
Means	64.2	66.7	104.1	191.7	10	7.8
Medians	64	66	102.5	205	10	8

TABLE 4 · Learning and Test Data for Subjects at the Six-Year Level

Subjects	CA mos.	MA mos.	IQ	No. trials	No. 'smaller' responses in 10 trials	
					Near test	Far test
Group I (Ss given near test first)						
31	60	72	120	50	10	10
32	67	74	111	130	10	9
33	70	75	107	130	10	10
34	61	77	126	100	10	10
35	61	78	128	190	10	10
36	67	81	121	10	10	10
37	64	83	130	50	10	10
Group II (Ss given far test first)						
38	63	72	115	40	10	10
39	66	73	111	60	10	10
40	68	74	109	20	10	10
41	65	75	116	10	10	10
42	67	78	117	80	10	10
43	68	80	118	10	10	10
44	63	80	127	120	10	10
Means	65.0	76.6	118.3	71.4	10	9.9
Medians	65.5	76.0	117.5	55	10	10

moment coefficient of correlation of — .62 found between these variables. For a significant relationship at the one-tenth of one percent level with this number of cases, a coefficient of only .47 is needed. Speed of learning is also highly correlated with chronological age as shown by the r of — .55 between these two measures.

In addition to the regular training trials, special trials ranging in number from 2 to 199 were given to eight three- and four-year-old Ss and one five-year-old in an attempt to modify position habits. In line with the plan described in Section C, three three-year-old Ss—Nos. 1, 5, and 7—were given 5 to 20 trials without the stimuli present, and Ss 1 and 5 also received single-stimulus trials numbering 15 and 10, respectively. These data serve to add to the evidence that the problem was relatively much more difficult for the young Ss than for the older ones.

The majority of Ss, 28 in all, spontaneously commented on the size of the stimuli at some time during learning. Of these, nine mentioned the size aspect for the first time on the day they reached the criterion, or the day just preceding it, and 12 others verbalized the concept on one of these two days in addition to some earlier day or days. A number of other children talked about the 'big block' or 'little block' but never reached the learning criterion.

Relearning. Only three Ss of the 44 required more than the minimum of 10 trials to reach the learning criterion the second time.[4] Two of these three, Ss 8 and 22, met the criterion after 20 trials. Both, it is interesting to note, were among the three Ss who at no time during the experiment verbalized the size aspect of the stimuli. S 30 took 40 trials to relearn

―――――――――
[4] The relearning series, it will be recalled, came at least 24 hours after the first transposition test.

the discrimination, but the conditions in this case were exceptional in that a period of over three weeks elapsed between the first transposition test and the start of the relearning. With no other *S* was the interval greater than four days.

Transposition tests. The results of the near transposition test show that with very few exceptions the children tended to respond in a manner consistent with the original training, that is, to choose the smaller stimulus. Thus, if we select a score of 9 or more such responses in 10 as a significant one (a score of 9 would be expected on a chance basis only 10 times in 1024), it will be seen that there were only four *S*s in all who did not choose the smaller sitmulus a statistically significant number of times, that is, did not demonstrate transposition. One of these, *S* 5, was in the three-year-old group, while the other three, *S*s 10, 16, and 17, were in the four-year-old group. The results for these latter three *S*s on the near transposition test were quite different from those of the other children, their responses being predominantly (beyond chance) to the absolute stimulus cue.[5]

The findings of the far transposition tests present a somewhat different picture from those of the near test, particularly in the case of the younger *S*s. Thus, none of the *S*s at the three-year-level behaved

on this test in a manner consistent with original training. Rather, all seven responded to the two stimuli in more or less chance fashion, as may be seen from the data in the last column of Table 1. The percent of *S*s responding a statistically significant number of times (nine or more) to the smaller stimulus on this far test increased at each of the subsequent age levels. Thus, 27.3 percent (three *S*s) of the four-year-old group, 50 percent (six *S*s) of the five-year-old group, and 100 percent (14 *S*s) of the six-year-old group chose in accord with their original training in nine or more of the 10 far test trials.

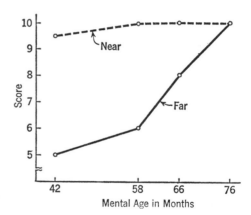

Figure 3. Graphic representation of the relation between mental age and median scores on near and far transposition tests.

The differences in the results for the two transposition tests are also revealed by the measures of central tendency included at the bottom of Tables 1 to 4. Fig. 3 brings together in graphic form the median near and far transposition scores made by *S*s at various age levels. The number of transposition responses in 10 trials appears on the ordinate, while the median mental age in months for each of the four groups is plotted on the ab-

---

[5] The results for these individuals are discussed in some detail in the original thesis, deposited in the library of the State University of Iowa. The behavior of *S*s 10 and 16 are not necessarily contrary to the proposed theory. Both appear to have learned the discrimination on a nonverbal basis. Their responses on the near test could possibly be explained as resulting from very narrow generalization curves. Such an assumption would require that the responses on the far test be random, which is in line with the experimental results. The absolute choice of *S* 17 on the near test, after transposing on the far test, is contrary to the theoretical expectation.

scissa. Inspection of the almost horizontal near test curve reveals that all four age groups showed transposition to a very high degree. The far curve, on the other hand, begins at chance (5) for the youngest group and rises to 10 for the oldest group, with the intermediate age groups falling at 6 and 8.

We turn now to the consideration of the relation of these experimental facts to the theoretical formulation elaborated at the beginning of this paper. It will be recalled that the implications of this theory were that the far transposition test would reveal significant differences between children of different age levels, whereas the near transposition test would not. In the first instance the theoretical expectation was that at some point in the age range, presumably at a very young level, the responses of the Ss on the far transposition test would approximate a chance result. At an older age, on the other hand, presumably when the stage of verbal abstraction and control of behavior is attained, the response of the child on this far test would be highly consistent with the direction of original training.

That the results of the experiment were in agreement with these theoretical expectations is readily apparent. The children of different age levels showed little, if any, difference in the near transposition test. In the far transposition test, however, the three-year-olds responded in a purely chance manner, while the six-year-olds showed practically 100 percent transposition. There now remains the task of ascertaining the degree of confidence we may have that these differences did not arise purely by accident.

Because of the nature of the data, for example, the skewed character of the distributions of the transposition scores

and the inequality of the variances at different age levels, it was not possible to apply analysis of variance, or to apply in most instances, the usual t-test of significance between means. The main theoretical implications may, nevertheless, be tested for significance in the following manner. If we set up the null hypothesis with respect to differences on the two tests, near and far, for both the three- and six-year mental age groups, then our theory would require that the experimental results for the three-year-old group would lead to the rejection of the null hypothesis of no difference between the two tests at this age, while the results for the six-year mental age group would lead to acceptance of that hypothesis.

In the case of the three-year-old group, we can apply the t-test for differences in the means of related measures (21). The resulting t is 8.25, which far exceeds the value of 5.96 required for a significant difference at the one-tenth of one percent level. From this we would be led, as our theory demands, to reject the hypothesis that there is no difference in the results on the two tests for this age group.

Unfortunately, a similar statistical test of the differences between the near and far transposition scores for the six-year-old group cannot be made because of the almost complete lack of variability in these test scores. The nature of the results is such, however, that one can readily accept the null hypothesis that no difference exists. All Ss but one responded 10 times on both tests to the smaller stimulus and, in the case of the single exception, the transposition scores were 10 on the near test and 9 on the far. Thus, there are 13 cases of zero difference and a single case of a difference of 1. The probability that one would obtain on the basis of chance 13 instances of zero in 14 is extremely remote.

As was true at the six-year level, the distributions of transposition scores at the intermediate ages four and five do not justify the assumptions of normality and homogeneous variability that are necessarily made in applying the t-test for differences between means. There are too few Ss to permit a chi-square test of independence on these two groups alone, but by combining the three- with the four-year group and the five- with the six-year one, the application of that test is made possible. We are interested in testing the hypothesis that there is no relationship between mental age and the occurrence of transposition (score of 9 or 10 in 10 trials) in the far test situation. The resulting chi-square, corrected for continuity by Yates' method, is 13.1, which, for one degree of freedom, exceeds the value required for significance at the one-tenth of one percent level. The hypothesis can, therefore, be rejected even if some reservation is made for the relatively small number of Ss. Further evidence against the hypothesis of no relation between mental age and far transposition scores is furnished by the product-moment correlation of .66 obtained between these variables for the 44 Ss. This coefficient is far in excess of the value .47 required for significance at the one-tenth of one percent level.

A chi-square test of independence could not be applied to the near transposition measures to test their relationship to mental age, because the data fail to satisfy the requirement that there be a theoretical (expected) frequency of at least five in each of the cells of the contingency table. The correlational approach is likewise not applicable to these results, for the transposition scores show almost no variability. Examination of the data, however, should make one extremely hesitant about rejecting the null hypothesis of the relation between mental age and near transposition.[6]

Verbalization. An analysis of the recorded verbalizations of the stimulus cue suggested the classification of the Ss into four mutually exclusive categories— A, B, C and D. A includes those Ss who at no time, either spontaneously or in response to questioning, verbalized the size aspect. In category B are those who did spontaneously mention the size variable at least once at any time during the experiment, but who failed to state the relation of size to the success or failure of choice behavior. Typical verbalizations of Ss in this group are: "This one is big and this one is little." "What a nice little block!" "This time I'll take the big one." Ss in the third class, *C,* verbalized the general principle of solution, but only in response to questioning at the conclusion of the experiment. Many of these individuals also mentioned the size of the stimuli during the training or transposition trials, but in no instance did they express generalizations at that time. Examples of replies judged as adequate generalizations

---

[6] Analysis of transposition scores based on only the first test trial gave results which corroborate those for 10 test trials. No significant differences were found between the different mental age groups on the near transposition test, whereas the percent of Ss who transposed on the far test increased from 14.3 percent for the three-year-old group to 100 percent for the six-year-olds. The four- and five-year-old groups fell in between these values, with 72.7 of the former and 86.7 percent of the latter showing transposition. Application of the chi-square test of independence permits one to reject, at a confidence level between two and five percent, the hypothesis of no difference in the percent of transposition for the four groups.

are: "It's (toy) always in the little one," or "The big one doesn't open." Category D includes those children who verbally generalized with respect to the size aspect of the stimuli at some time prior to the routine questioning at the conclusion of the experiment. All except three of these

*S*s repeated the principle in reply to the experimenter's questions following the last 10 trials.

The number and percent of *S*s at each age level who fall in the four verbalization categories are shown in Table 5. It is apparent that the three- and four-

TABLE 5 · NUMBER AND PERCENT OF SUBJECTS AT EACH AGE LEVEL IN THE FOUR VERBALIZATION CATEGORIES

| Category | MENTAL AGE | | | | | | | |
| | 3 | | 4 | | 5 | | 6 | |
	N	%	*N*	%	*N*	%	*N*	%
A	0	0	2	18.2	1	8.3	0	0
B	7	100.0	2	18.2	1	8.3	0	0
C	0	0	4	36.4	5	41.7	5	35.7
D	0	0	3	27.3	5	41.7	9	64.3

year-old children tend to be in the non-generalizing groups (A and B) while the five- and six-year-old children are predominantly in the generalizing ones. A chi-square test of the null hypothesis of no relationship between mental age and classification in the combined A-B or combined C-D categories yields a corrected chi-square of 12.22, permitting the rejection of the hypothesis at the one-tenth of one percent level of confidence. This result lends support to our proposed use of mental age as an indicator of the ability to make verbal generalizations in such situations.

Table 6 indicates the median transposition scores in 10 trials for *S*s in the four verbalization categories, and the median number of trials to learn the discrimination originally. It is evident that *S*s who failed to verbalize the size aspect of the stimuli explicitly, or who merely noted the size without stating the relationship of the size aspect to the solution of the problem, behaved differently on the far transposition test from *S*s who did

TABLE 6 · MEDIAN TRANSPOSITION SCORES FOR SUBJECTS IN THE FOUR VERBALIZATION CATEGORIES

| Category | *N* | Median trials | Median transposition responses (10 trials) | |
			Near test	Far test
A	3	176.0	9.0	6.0
B	10	250.0	10.0	5.0
C	14	100.0	10.0	10.0
D	17	130.0	10.0	10.0

formulate and state the relationship. On the near test, responses were similar from group to group.

It is possible to test the significance of the apparent relationship by using the chi-square test of independence. The obtained corrected chi-square of 18.37 permits us to reject at the one-tenth of one percent level the hypothesis of no relationship between the occurrence of transposition (a score of 9 or 10 in 10 trials) in the far test and the tendency to verbalize the solution of the discrimination problem. As in previous applications of this test, a chi-square of only 10.83 is needed for significance at this level for one degree of freedom. The chi-square test is not applicable to the near transposition data for the reason before discussed, of too small theoretical frequencies in the non-transposing categories. There seems to be no occasion for doubting, however, that the null hypothesis is tenable for the relation between near transposition and tendency to verbalize the principle.

Analysis of individual data with respect to the relation of verbalization to the phenomenon of transposition suggests the possibility that there are several verbal stages. There appears to be one stage in which the child verbally identifies the stimuli as 'little' and 'big,' but he fails to verbalize the relation of size to the success or failure of his choice responses. This occurred predominantly in the younger Ss and was associated in every case with chance performance on the far transposition test series. There is another stage—presumably a later one because of its much greater incidence in older Ss—in which the child states aloud or to himself that the little stimulus always leads to success and the big one to failure. The occurrence out loud of such verbal behavior in the learning or transposition series invariably was followed by transposition on the far test, regardless of the mental age of the child. In contrast, 43 percent of those who made such verbalizations only upon questioning at the conclusion of the experiment transposed on the far series with this consistency. In the case of three Ss who had failed to transpose in the far test and a few seconds later, upon questioning, verbalized the principle, there seemed to be no apparent recognition of the discrepancy between

this verbal formulation of the solution and their failure to act in a manner consistent with it in the immediately preceding test trials.

While the data on verbalization are not sufficiently clear-cut to permit any definite conclusions, there is, however, the suggestion that there are at least two developmental stages so far as the relation of verbal responses to overt choice behavior is concerned. In the first, the child is able to make differential verbal responses to appropriate aspects of the situation, but this verbalization does not control or influence his overt choice behavior. Later, such verbalizations gain control and dominate choice behavior.

SUMMARY AND CONCLUSIONS

Taking its point of departure from a theoretical formulation of discrimination learning based on the findings of conditioning experiments, this study hypothesizes that the simple mechanisms mediating transposition of response in infrahuman organisms are identical with those responsible for similar behavior in children in the preverbal stage of development. With the acquisition of verbal processes, however, and the transition to behavior dominated by such processes, it is hypothesized that the child's responses in the discrimination-learning situation become keyed to words relating to the cue aspect of the stimuli. Implications of this theory are that the preverbal child, like the animal S, will transpose consistently on test stimuli near on the dimension to the training pair, but will show only chance response on transposition tests with distant stimuli. The verbal child, on the other hand, would be expected to show transposition on both far and near stimulus tests.

As an empirical test of the proposed hypothesis, an experiment was conducted in which mental age was used as a rough indicator of verbal level. Ss were 44 Iowa City preschool and kindergarten children distributed over the mental age range three to six years and divided into two matched groups at each year level. Both groups were trained to select the smaller of a pair of squares whose areas were 37.8 and 68.0 sq. in. They were tested in counter-balanced order after learning, with two pairs of still smaller stimuli (21.0 vs. 37.8 sq. in., and 2.0 vs. 3.6 sq. in.). All spontaneous verbalizations of the size aspect of the stimuli were recorded throughout the experiment, and attempts were made at the conclusion, through questioning, to elicit verbalization of the general principle of solution.

Analysis of the results revealed a highly significant relationship between mental age and the occurrence of far transposition, and a low relationship between mental age and near transposition. The median number of responses on the far transposition test increased with age from 50 percent at mental age three years to 100 percent at six years. The corresponding value for the near transposition test was 90 percent or above at all four age levels.

With regard to verbalization, Ss tended to fall into four categories: 1, failure to verbalize the size aspect of the problem; 2, verbal identification of the size difference between the stimuli without explicit association of size with the success or failure of choice behavior; 3, verbalization of the principle of solution in response to questioning at the con-clusion of the experiment; and 4, verbalization of the principle spontaneously during training or transposition trials. Ss in the first two categories were significantly younger in mental age than those in the last two. No S in the first two categories transposed on the far test, while 73 percent of the individuals in the last two categories transposed. Analysis of the individual data suggests the possibility of two developmental stages so far as the relation of verbal responses to overt choice behavior is concerned.

On the whole, the experimental results were found to be in close accord with the proposed hypothesis.

REFERENCES

1. BINGHAM, H. C. Visual perception in the chick. *Behav. Monogr.*, 1922, *4*, No. 20, 1–104.
2. FLORY, R. M. A study of the factors determining discrimination of size by the white rat. Unpublished Master's thesis, Univ. Va., 1938.
3. FRANK, HELENE. Untersuchung über Sehgrössenkonstanz bei Kindern. *Psychol. Forsch.*, 1926, 7, 137–145.
4. GULLIKSEN, H. Studies of transfer of response: I. Relative versus absolute factors in the discrimination of size by the white rat. *J. genet. Psychol.*, 1932, *40*, 37–51.
5. GULLIKSEN, H., & WOLFLE, D. L. A theory of learning and transfer. *Psychometrika*, 1938, *3*, 127–149, 225–251.
6. GULLIKSEN, H., & WOLFLE, D. L. Correction of an error in 'A theory of learning and transfer.' *Psychometrika*, 1939, *4*, 178.

7. Jackson, T. A.   Studies in the transposition of learning by children. III. Transpositional response as a function of the number of transposed dimensions. *J. exp. Psychol.*, 1939, *25*, 116–124.

8. Jackson, T. A., & Dominguez, K. Studies in the transposition of learning by children. II. Relative vs. absolute choice with multi-dimensional stimuli. *J. exp. Psychol.*, 1939, *24*, 630–639.

9. Jackson, T. A., & Eckhardt, M. E. Studies in the transposition of learning by children. V. The number of stimuli in the training series as a factor in generalization. *J. exp. Psychol.*, 1940, 27, 303–312.

10. Jackson, T. A., & Jerome, E. A. Studies in the transposition of learning by children. IV. A preliminary study of patternedness in discrimination learning. *J. exp. Psychol.*, 1940, *26*, 432–439.

11. Jackson, T. A., & Jerome, E. A. Studies in the transposition of learning by children. VI. Simultaneous vs. successive presentation of the stimuli to bright and dull children. *J. exp. Psychol.*, 1943, *33*, 431–439.

12. Jackson, T. A., Stonex, E., Lane, E., & Dominguez, K. Studies in the transposition of learning by children. I. Relative vs. absolute response as a function of amount of training. *J. exp. Psychol.*, 1938, *23*, 578–600.

13. Johnson, H. M. Visual pattern discrimination in the vertebrates. *J. Anim. Behav.*, 1914, *4*, 319–339, 340–361; 1916, *6*, 169–188.

14. Kendler, Sylvia T. S. Experimental investigation of the effect of difference between training and test stimuli on the amount of transposition. Unpublished Doctor's dissertation, State Univ. Ia., 1943.

15. Kinnaman, A. J. Mental life of two *Macacus rhesus* monkeys in captivity. *Amer. J. Psychol.*, 1902, *13*, 98–148, 173–218.

16. Klüver, H. *Behavior mechanisms in monkeys.* Chicago: Univ. of Chicago Press, 1933.

17. Köhler, W. *Gestalt psychology.* New York: Horace Liveright, 1929.

18. Köhler, W. Simple structural functions in the chimpanzee and in the chicken. In: W. D. Ellis, *A source book of Gestalt psychology.* New York: Harcourt, Brace and Co., 1938. Pp. 217–227.

19. Koffka, K. *The growth of the mind.* (2nd ed., rev.) New York: Harcourt, Brace and Co., 1928.

20. Lashley, K. S. The mechanism of vision. XV. Preliminary studies of the rat's capacity for detail vision. *J. gen. Psychol.*, 1938, *18*, 123–193.

21. Lindquist, E. F. *Statistical analysis in educational research.* New York: Houghton Mifflin Co., 1940.

22. Perkins, F. T., & Wheeler, R. H. Configural learning in the goldfish. *Comp. Psychol. Monogr.*, 1930. 7, No. 31, 1–50.

23. Spence, K. W. The nature of discrimination learning in animals. *Psychol. Rev.*, 1936, *43*, 427–449.

24. Spence, K. W. Analysis of formation of visual discrimination habits in chimpanzee. *J. comp. Psychol.*, 1937, *23*, 77–100.

25. Spence, K. W. The differential response in animals to stimuli vary-

ing within a single dimension. *Psychol. Rev.*, 1937, *44*, 430–444.

26. SPENCE, K. W. Failure of transposition in size-discrimination of chimpanzees. *Amer. J. Psychol.*, 1941, *54*, 223–229.

27. SPENCE, K. W. The basis of solution by chimpanzees of the intermediate size problem. *J. exp. Psychol.*, 1942, *31*, 257–271.

28. WARDEN, C. J., & ROWLEY, JEAN B. The discrimination of absolute versus relative brightness in the ring dove, *Turtur risorius. J. comp. Psychol.*, 1929, *9*, 317–337.

RELATIONAL LEARNING
IN YOUNG CHILDREN

RONALD C. JOHNSON
RONALD C. ZARA

NUMEROUS EXPERIMENTERS have investigated transposition, since this is one area where cognitive and S-R theories make differential predictions. Typical transposition experiments first involve training an organism to make a discrimination between two stimuli that vary in some attribute, usually size. If an organism is trained on Stimuli 1 (small) and 2 (large) and is rewarded for responding to Stimulus 2, the organism will ultimately learn to respond to Stimulus 2 when forced to make a discrimination. Then the organism is presented with Stimuli 2 (large) and 3 (larger still), with either of the stimuli being rewarded. In this transposition test the organism usually responds to Stimulus 3—the stimulus that has never been previously rewarded. From the time of the original experiments by Köhler, cognitive theorists used this finding to attack S-R theories. They claimed that one would predict from S-R theory (in particular, Pavlovian conditioning theory) that Stimulus 2, having been rewarded in the training trials, would be responded to in the transposition trials. Instead of responding to the absolute stimulus size, the organism makes a relational response to the "bigger than" of the two stimuli, indicating the operation of some sort of cognitive process.

A telling blow to this cognitive interpretation of transposition came from Spence (1936, 1937, 1942). It had been found by Spence and by others (cited by Spence, 1942) that as the distance along

Reprinted by permission from *Journal of Comparative and Physiological Psychology*, 1960, 53, 594–597.

the stimulus dimension between training and test stimuli was increased, the proportion of relational responses to the transposed pair decreased. If trained on Stimuli 1 and 2, organisms nearly uniformly make relational responses if tested on Stimuli 2 and 3 ("near" transposition) but tend to respond randomly if tested for transposition on Stimuli 3 and 4 ("far" transposition). Spence explained these results in this way: A generalization curve of excitation is built up around Stimulus 2, the rewarded stimulus. A generalization curve of inhibition is built up around Stimulus 1, the nonrewarded stimulus. In the transposition test, the organism responds to the stimulus with the greater effective excitatory potential which is the algebraic summation of excitatory and inhibitory potentials. His illustration of these curves of inhibition and excitation (1942) shows that, within his S-R framework, one would expect transposition to occur in near, but not in far, transposition—exactly the results that are generally obtained. Spence's curves are hypothetical ones and are not claimed to represent reality. However, they must be of a certain shape such that: (1) The highest amount of inhibition is produced by the nonrewarded stimulus (No. 1) in the training series, (2) the highest amount of excitation is produced by the rewarded stimulus (No. 2) in the training series, (3) the effective excitatory potential of Stimulus 3 (the "larger than" of the "near" transposition pair) is greater than that of Stimulus 2; and (4) there can be no great difference in the effective excitatory potentials of Stimuli 3 and 4 (the "far" transposition pair) since neither is chosen significantly more often than the other.

While the preceding is true for non-verbal organisms, Kuenne (1946) found that far transposition did occur in children's responses when they were able to verbalize the concept "bigger than," though generally not before this time. The verbal concept was believed by Kuenne to be central in producing far transposition. Presence of the verbal concept has been shown by other researchers (Spiker & Terrell, 1955) to facilitate transposition, but it has not been proven that a verbal concept is essential for far transposition—in fact, the reverse has been demonstrated (Lawrence & DeRivera, 1954; Riley, 1958). The present study was designed in order to establish a training situation in which the relational aspects of the problem were emphasized. In typical transposition experiments one could easily argue that either the absolute or the relational response in the transposition series is in some way "better" than the other, since each is correct—one absolutely, the other relationally. We wished to point up the relational aspects of the training series in order to determine whether, when this was done, the organism developed a set to respond to the relational properties of the transposition pair regardless of how far one moved out on the size dimension. This approach would seem to us to bear on the problem of concept formation and on problems involving the formation of learning sets as well as having to do with the specific experimental procedures and theoretical questions of transposition.

METHOD

APPARATUS

The apparatus consisted of a large, medium-gray backboard, 4 ft. by 8 ft., containing two equally spaced sunken boxes within one of which the reward was placed. Seven removable, medium-gray doors, each 3 ft. by 3 ft., were prepared. On each door was painted a black square. The successive squares increased in linear dimensions by a ratio of 1:1.6. Stimulus sizes were 1.60, 2.56, 4.09, 6.55, 10.49, 16.78, and 26.85 in. square. On each door, and on the backboard, fixtures were attached so that the doors could be hung over the two boxes. Knobs were attached so *S* could lift the door easily when searching for a reward. Both reward-holding boxes were padded to prevent *S* from hearing the reward drop into the box from behind the backboard.

SUBJECTS

Subjects were obtained from community-supported day nursery schools. Forty-one *S*s were tested on the training series of the transposition experiment. The rewarded stimulus was the "bigger than." Any *S* who, spontaneously or after questioning, stated that he knew that the bigger stimulus was always rewarded was discarded. This was done since Kuenne has shown considerable difference between the transpositional responses of *S*s who could and *S*s who could not verbalize the concept involved in obtaining rewards in the training series of her experiment. Eleven *S*s did verbalize the concept in some way and were discarded. This left 30 *S*s ranging in age from 39 to 60 months. These *S*s were from lower socioeconomic groups so that it is unlikely that their mental ages were generally much higher than chronological age.

PROCEDURE

The *S*s were divided into two groups. The age range of Group I was from 40 to 60 months, Group II from 39 to 60 months. The *S*s were matched, between groups, so that no *S* in Group I differed more than one month in age from an agematched *S* in Group II. Group I was presented with the typical transposition training problem. The training series consisted of Stimuli 4.09 and 6.55. The training-series stimulus doors were presented to the *S*s in Group II in two sets of

pairs: 1.60 and 2.56 constituted one pair; 4.09 and 6.55 constituted the other pair (these figures being the size of the black-squares on the stimulus doors). The order of presentation of the pairs and the left-right position of each door were assigned from a table of random numbers. The larger square of the pair was always rewarded. The reward used was an M & M candy every fifth trial and raisins on the other four. The criterion for discrimination learning was set at 14 correct responses in a series of 15 presentations. The only difference between the two groups in the training series was this: Group I had a single discrimination to learn, while Group II had a double discrimination. Both discriminations in the double-discrimination group were soluble according to the same principle—responding to the larger of either stimulus pair. It seems likely that this training procedure would emphasize the relational elements involved in problem solution.

Trials took place in a closed-off room. The *S*s were given 100 trials a day on successive days unless they were successful in 8 of the last 10 trials in any day. In this case training continued until criterion was reached or else until 5 in any 10 successive trials were failed. The *S*, tested individually, sat in a chair facing the apparatus and about 8 ft. away. After establishing rapport, the *S* was told that there was a reward behind one of the doors. The instructions were: "Go to the door you think the reward is in and lift it up by the knob. Whatever you find is yours." Following the trial the *S* returned to his seat and remained seated until told to try again. The stimulus doors were removed from the backboard and placed on a table after every trial. They were then picked up again (in the double-discrimination group, the proper pair selected) and placed in the assigned position for the next trial. The removal and replacement of stimulus doors was not screened from the *S*'s view. Once the doors were back in place, *E* went to the back of the apparatus. A reward was deposited through a hole in the rear of the reward box behind the stimulus door containing the larger of the two squares. While this was being done, *E* stood equidistant between the two reward boxes, with one hand behind each of them so that cues could not be gained from the *E*'s body orientation.

As soon as *S* reached a criterion of 14 of 15 correct in the training series, he was presented with the transposition problem. Five *S*s in Group I (mean age 48.8 mo.) and in Group II (mean age 48.0 mo.) were presented with stimuli 6.55 vs. 10.49 on the transposition series. Five *S*s in Group I (mean age 52.2 mo.) and in Group II (mean age 52.6 mo.) were presented with stimuli 10.49 and 16.78 in the transposition series. Five *S*s in Group I (mean age 49.6 mo.) and five *S*s in Group II (mean age 50.6 mo.) were presented with stimuli 16.78 and 26.85 in the transposition series. This allowed for a test of both training groups on "near," "far," and "farther still" transposition problems. In the transposition series of 10 trials, either discrimination response was rewarded.

RESULTS AND DISCUSSION

TRAINING SERIES

The individual *S*s in Group I reached the learning criterion in their single discrimination training problem in 232, 261, 169, 206, 230, 165, 237, 129, 229, 184, 140, 132, 183, 225, and 178 trials. The *S*s in Group II, in learning the double discrimination, took 104, 147, 94, 41, 186, 196, 136, 133, 234, 134, 138, 136, 189, 176, and 117 trials, respectively, to reach the same training criterion. A Wilcoxon (1949) signed-ranks test shows the double-discrimination group to have learned the training discriminations significantly ($p = < .02$) more rapidly than the single-discrimination group. In this experiment the double discrimination would seem likely to make *S*s attend more to size differences (since sizes differed both within *and* between stimulus pairs) and less to position, more to relative size and less to absolute size. It is now well established (Harlow, 1949) that primates, presented with successive discrimination

problems, all soluble according to the same principle, generally solve each succeeding problem more efficiently or rapidly than the one before it—"they learn to learn." It appears, from these results, that the *simultaneous* presentation of several discrimination problems, soluble through responses based on the same principle, produces more rapid learning, at least in young humans, than the presentation of a single problem or of several successive problems.

TRANSPOSITION TEST

The 15 *S*s in each of the two groups were divided into subgroups of five for transposition tests (6.55 vs. 10.49—near transposition; 10.49 vs. 16.78—far transposition; and 16.78 vs. 26.85—farther still). The mean number of times, on the transposition trials, that *S*s in each group transposed to each of the transposition pairs is shown in Figure 1.

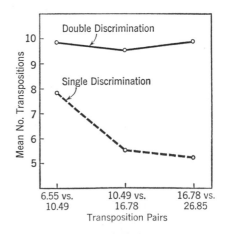

Figure 1. Mean number of transpositions for single- and double-discrimination training groups.

Those *S*s trained in the double-discrimination series transposed, no matter how far removed the transposition pair was on the size dimension. Those trained on a single discrimination generally transposed in near transposition but did not transpose in far transposition. It would appear that Spence's explanation of transposition is a valid one, so long as training is to a single discrimination. Even though Spence's curves are hypothetical ones, they do have to fit the requirements mentioned in the Introduction. It is difficult to determine how one could explain the transpositional responses of the double-discrimination group in terms of curves of inhibition and excitation.

SUMMARY

Fifteen Ss were trained to respond to the larger stimulus of a single stimulus pair during training preceding a test of transposition. Fifteen Ss, closely matched in age to Ss in the first group, were presented with a double-discrimination problem in the training series, with the larger of each stimulus pair being rewarded. None of these 30 Ss could verbalize the concept leading to successful discriminations in the training series. Upon reaching a criterion of 14 out of 15 correct responses, Ss were presented with the test of transposition. Five Ss in each group were tested on near transposition, 5 on far transposition, and 5 on "farther still" transposition. All responses in the transposition series were rewarded. Those Ss who learned a double discrimination in the training series reached criterion significantly more rapidly than the group that learned a single discrimination. Those Ss who learned a double discrimination in the training series transposed all along the size dimension while those Ss who learned a single discrimination transposed only in near transposition.

REFERENCES

HARLOW, H. F.   The formation of learning sets. *Psychol. Rev.*, 1949, 56, 51–65.

KUENNE, M. R.   Experimental investigation of the relation of language to transposition behavior in young children. *J. exp. Psychol.*, 1946, 36, 479–489.

LAWRENCE, D. H., & DeRIVERA, J.   Evidence for relational transposition. *J. comp. physiol. Psychol.*, 1954, 47, 465–471.

RILEY, D. A.   The nature of the effective stimulus in animal discrimination learning: Transposition reconsidered. *Psychol. Rev.*, 1958, 65, 1–7.

SPENCE, K. W.   The nature of discrimination learning in animals. *Psychol. Rev.*, 1936, 43, 427–449.

SPENCE, K. W.   The differential response in animals to stimuli varying within a single dimension. *Psychol. Rev.*, 1937, 44, 430–444.

SPENCE, K. W.   The basis of solution by chimpanzees of the intermediate size problem. *J. exp. Psychol.*, 1942, 31, 257–271.

SPIKER, C. C., & TERRELL, G.   Factors associated with transpositional behavior of preschool children. *J. genet. Psychol.*, 1955, 86, 143–158.

WILCOXON, F.   *Some rapid statistical procedures.* Stamford, Conn.: American Cyanamid Co., 1949.

LANGUAGE | 10

THE MOST OBVIOUS BASIS for distinguishing between man and other animals is in terms of language behavior. Since the human child begins as an inarticulate organism, not unlike any other kind of animal in its ability to communicate, and over a period of time becomes a very articulate, communicative individual, it would appear that one of the most fruitful research areas for child psychologists would relate to language behavior and the variables which affect its development. Although this proposition is quite obvious, there is a dearth of experimental literature in this area in comparison to many other areas that form sections of this book.

For some time linguists have attempted to comprehend the structure of language and some psychologists have attempted to examine aspects of the adult language system. Only recently, however, have the two disciplines become much aware of each other. There is now a growing group of researchers, becoming known as psycholinguists, who are making use of the knowledge and techniques of each discipline to make some approaches to the understanding of the development, structure, and function of language. Fortunately, some of these psycholinguists have directed their attention to child language (Berko and Brown, 1960).

Prior to this recent movement, however, child psychologists had not ignored the area of language development. There is a wide variety of normative information about the language development of children. There is, for example, a large number of studies related to the phonetic analysis of infant prelinguistic utterances, emergence of the first words of children, growth of vocabulary, sentence length and structure, and correlational studies of the relationships between these measures and broad classes of environmental variables (see McCarthy [1954] for a comprehensive review of this literature). Thus, we have a good deal of knowledge about what a child may exhibit in terms of language behaviors, but we know little about the specific variables that affect these behaviors. We know, for example, that there is a positive relationship between socioeconomic status of the family and the child's language development, but we know little about the factors associated with high socioeconomic status which lead to the more rapid language development of these children. We are sure that amount of money per se is not the important factor, but more likely some of the special educational advantages for example, which happen to be correlated with affluence.

The combination of these facts about children's language and the linguist's data relative to phonology, morphology, and syntax sets the stage for the experimental investigation of the variables that affect the acquisition of speech sounds, the associations between arbitrary sounds or symbols and referents, the development of speech categories, referent categories, and the ordering or grammar of the language system. Since we would not assume that laws related to language behavior differ from laws involving other kinds of behavior, it is expected that variables which affect other behavior will have similar affects on language behavior. For example, Rheingold, Gewirtz, and Ross report, in a study included in an earlier section of this book, that frequency of vocalization increases in three-month-old infants as a function of reward. Similarly, it would be anticipated that reward and nonreward would lead to the greater incidence of a child's emitting some sounds and not others, as in any other discrimination learning task. We might expect generalization of word responses from a specific referent to other physically similar referents. An analysis of the child's development of the "phrase structure grammar" used by adults (Chomsky, 1957) may reveal that the mechanisms of mediated stimulus and response equivalence and chaining play important roles.

The first two papers in this section illustrate the merger of descriptive linguistics and psychology in attempting to determine the variables affecting the development of referents for the linguistic utterances of children. When an adult wishes to know the referent or meaning of a word, he looks it up in the dictionary. The way in which a child discovers the meaning of a word seems considerably more complicated. It is clear from the first paper that children—who, by the age of twelve, presumably have a good grasp of how to use the language—do not acquire the meaning of words in a simple fashion. By the clever device of teaching the meaning of a nonsense word through the various contexts in which it is placed, the authors of the first paper indicate the complexity of the acquisition of meaning, which adults take for granted. Analysis of the errors the children made in this situation provides clear evidence of the difficulty the child has in determining what the relevant aspects of the statements are before the appropriate meanings can be determined. Additional quantitative and qualitative analyses of these data may be found in a later report by Werner and Kaplan (1950).

The study by Ervin makes use of words which appear in the natural language and demonstrates that words which have different meanings for adults may be confused by children because they appear together frequently in the language. Despite the fact that the children have had considerable experience with the words, it is clear that subtle distinctions which adults make among words are not so apparent to young children. Evidently it takes great use of words in various contexts before the meaning approaches the dictionary or lexical meaning assumed by adults. This seems to be a discrimination learning problem in which the correct responses are not clearly evident to the young learner.

The last paper in this section deals with a problem related to syntax. The study examines the associative characteristics of words and demonstrates how these characteristics differ in relation to the grammatical class or part of speech. When an adult is asked to give an association to a high frequency word he is more likely to give a word in the same grammatical class as the stimulus word. If the adult, however, is asked to give an association to a rare or low frequency word he more frequently gives a word in another grammatical class. It is clear from the data in this study that children respond in the same form class to high frequency words and shift classes in response to words of lower frequency just as adults do. The parallel findings of the word association test and the usage test indicates that word association tests for children may be sensitive indicators of the learning of syntax.

REFERENCES

BERKO, JEAN and BROWN, R.   Psycholinguistic research methods. In P. Mussen (Ed.), *Handbook of Research Methods in Child Psychology*. New York: Wiley, 1960.

CHOMSKY, N.   *Syntactic structures*. Gravenhage: Mouton & Co., N. Y., 1957.

McCARTHY, DOROTHEA.   Language development in children. In L. Carmichael (Ed.), *Manual of child psychology*. (2nd ed.) New York: Wiley, 1954.

WERNER, H. and KAPLAN, EDITH.   The acquisition of word meanings: a developmental study. *Child Develpm. Monogr.*, 1950, *15*, No. 51 (Whole No. 1).

DEVELOPMENT OF WORD MEANING THROUGH VERBAL CONTEXT: AN EXPERIMENTAL STUDY [1]

HEINZ WERNER
EDITH KAPLAN

A. THE TEST

IN THE MAIN, a child learns the meaning of a word in two ways. One way is direct and explicit, i.e., the adult names a thing or defines a word for the child. The other way is indirect and implicit, through experience with concrete and/or verbal contexts.

This study is concerned with the acquisition of word meanings through verbal contexts. The children participating in this investigation ranged from 8½ to 13½ years of age and were divided into five age groups with 25 children at each age level. The interquartile IQ range was from 101 to 111.

The test was as follows: The child's task was to find the meaning of an artificial word, which appeared in six different verbal contexts. In all, there were 12 sets of six sentences each. The 12 artificial words denoted either an object or an action. For example, the artificial word in the first set of six sentences was COR-PLUM, for which the correct translation was "stick" or "piece of wood." The contexts for CORPLUM were as follows:

1. A CORPLUM MAY BE USED FOR SUPPORT.

2. CORPLUMS MAY BE USED TO CLOSE OFF AN OPEN PLACE.
3. A CORPLUM MAY BE LONG OR SHORT, THICK OR THIN, STRONG OR WEAK.
4. A WET CORPLUM DOES NOT BURN.
5. YOU CAN MAKE A CORPLUM SMOOTH WITH SANDPAPER.
6. THE PAINTER USED A CORPLUM TO MIX HIS PAINTS.

B. PROCEDURE

The experimental procedure was as follows: After the child was made thoroughly familiar with the task, he was presented with a card on which Sentence 1 of Series I was printed. After the child responded to the first sentence, he was asked how and why the meaning he gave for the word fit into the sentence. He then was presented with the second sentence while the first context was still in view. After having given his interpretation of the word as it appeared in the second sentence (which may or may not have differed from his first response) the child was again asked how and why it fit and also whether it could be applied to the preceding sentence. This procedure was carried out until all six contexts had been presented to the child. The child's responses were carefully recorded.

[1] This study has been carried out under a grant from the Social Science Research Council; a comprehensive report will be published at a later date.

Reprinted by permission from *Journal of Psychology*, 1950, *29*, 251–257.

C. ANALYSIS AND RESULTS

Although correctness was not the major aspect of the study, it may be briefly mentioned that correctness of responses increased significantly from age level to age level.

Our main concern was with the ways children gave signification to the artificial words; we were especially interested in the development of the signification process. For the purpose of analysis, three judges derived 60 criteria from a preliminary inspection of the protocols. These criteria, pertaining to linguistic as well as semantic characteristics, were then employed by the three judges in the final analysis.

Studying the protocols one is impressed with the great variety of processes by which children acquired and generalized word meanings from verbal contexts. Many responses of the younger children indicate *a lack in the differentiation between the meaning of the word and the given verbal context*. Instead of conceiving the word as referring to a circumscribed meaning, many of the younger children regarded the artificial word as carrying the meaning of the whole or part of the context in which it appeared. We may call this type of conception a *sentence-core concept*. For instance, one sentence, containing the artificial word, BORDICK, (faults) was the following: PEOPLE TALK ABOUT THE BORDICKS OF OTHERS AND DON'T LIKE TO TALK ABOUT THEIR OWN. One child, dealing with this sentence, remarked: "Well, BORDICK means 'people talk about others and don't talk about themselves,' that's what BORDICK means." That this child seriously thought that BORDICK meant the whole sentence became clear when he tried to fit this meaning into the context: PEOPLE WITH BORDICKS ARE OFTEN UNHAPPY. The child fitted his sentence-core concept into this context as follows: "People talk about others and don't talk about themselves—they are often unhappy." To the question: "How does this meaning fit?", the child had this answer: "Say this lady hears that another lady is talking about her, so she'll get mad at her and that lady will be very unhappy."

A frequent method of fitting a sentence-core concept, formed for one sentence, into another context was by a process we have termed *assimilation*. The child interprets the context of a new sentence as the same or similar to the context of the previous sentence. Through such assimilation, the concept for the previous sentence now fits into the new sentence. To illustrate, in one series the artificial word is HUDRAY (for which such concepts as "increase," "enlarge" or "grow" are adequate). Sentence 6 of this series read: YOU MUST HAVE ENOUGH SPACE IN THE BOOKCASE TO HUDRAY YOUR LIBRARY. One child said: "Hudray means 'to have enough space.'" He took a part of the context as the referent for HUDRAY. Returning to the previous sentences, he said that the concept, "to have enough space," fit all six sentences. For example, it fit Sentence 1 (IF YOU EAT WELL AND SLEEP WELL YOU WILL HUDRAY): "If you eat well, that is, if you do not overeat, you will have enough room in your stomach and won't get too chubby; if you sleep well, but not too much, you don't get overlazy; so you leave some room for more sleep—so you leave space—like."

Not infrequently, the child derived two independent sentence-core concepts pertaining to two successive sentences. In attempting to apply the second solution to the first sentence, he often combined the two solutions. For instance, for the two sentences:

JANE HAD TO HUDRAY THE CLOTH SO THE DRESS WOULD FIT MARY. YOU HUDRAY WHAT YOU KNOW BY READING AND STUDYING.

One child gave as respective solutions: "Jane had to 'let out the hem' of the cloth" and "You 'learn by books' what you know." Coming back from the second to the first sentence the child said, " 'Learn by books' fits here. Jane had to 'learn by books' how to 'let out the hem' in the cloth. Jane used an encyclopedia of sewing." For this girl, the first solution "let out the hem" was so completely embedded in the sentence context that it became a part of the sentence and no longer a substitute for HUDRAY. The child could now introduce the subsequent solution ("learn by books") above and beyond the first, original solution. At times, we obtained as many as three independent solutions combined in one sentence.

Another indication that word and sentence were not clearly differentiated at the earlier levels was the frequent manifestation of what we have called *holophrastic gradient*. Here, the concept was not limited to the unknown word, but spread to neighboring parts, thus carrying pieces of the sentence with it; e.g., for the word, LIDBER (collect, gather), one child stated for the sentence: JIMMY LIDBERED STAMPS FROM ALL COUNTRIES, "Jimmy 'collected' stamps from all countries." The concept was extended from "collect" to "collect stamps." Thus the concept, "collect stamps" was applied to another sentence: THE POLICE DID NOT ALLOW THE PEO-PLE TO LIDBER ON THE STREET, in the following manner: "Police did not permit people to 'collect stamps' on the street."

Thus far, we have considered only those forms of signification of a word which are based on an intimate fusion of word and sentence (or sentence-parts). In our analysis, we found other forms of signification, in which the concepts, though they did not display sentence-word fusion, were still lacking the circumscribed, stable character of the more mature concepts. We called such products *simple contextual or simple holophrastic concepts*. Here the word meaning was definitely set apart from the context of the sentence; nevertheless, it differed from conventional word meanings in that it bore a wide situational connotation rather than a circumscribed, stable one. The artificial word did not refer, for the child, to a single object or action, but to a more inclusive context. Sometimes the broad situational connotation of the word was explicitly stated by the child, i.e., he employed a whole phrase to express the meaning of the word. In other cases, the child used a single word, seemingly delimited in its meaning, which on probing was found to be far more inclusive than it appeared on the surface. The following may serve as examples of explicitly stated holophrastic concepts.

The artificial word, ASHDER (obstacle), appears in the sentence, THE WAY IS CLEAR IF THERE ARE NO ASHDERS. One child responded: "The way is clear if there are no 'parts of a radio that don't fit in right' (together)." In the mind of this child, the word, ASHDER, referred to a radio-repair situation.

In the case of the sentence: THE POLICE DID NOT ALLOW THE PEO-

PLE TO LIDBER ON THE STREET, one child's translation of LIDBER was "throw paper around" (i.e., cluttering up the street by throwing paper around).

An illustration of implicit holophrastic concepts is the following, involving the word ONTRAVE (hope): ONTRAVE SOMETIMES KEEPS US FROM BEING UNHAPPY. A child substituted for ONTRAVE the seemingly circumscribed word "want." However, on probing, it became apparent that "want" referred to a broad contextual situation: "If you 'want a bow and arrow set and you get it,' that keeps you from being unhappy."

For this same sentence, another child came to the solution, "mother." "'Mother' keeps you from being unhappy." However, "mother" actually meant "mother when she gives you things you want."

One may note an important characteristic attached to such situational word meanings; the word has not only a broad situational content, but this content is fluid and lacks closure: i.e., the concept may change in range from sentence to sentence, elements being added or subtracted etc. This can be seen from the way children quite typically expanded a concept in order to fit it into another sentence. This process of expansion, denoting fluidity of conceptualization, we have termed *contextual* or *holophrastic expansion*. An example of this holophrastic expansion is the following: One child had developed the concept "books to study" for HUDRAY. "Books" became expanded to "throwing books" when the child attempted to fit the concept into the sentence: MRS. SMITH WANTED TO HUDRAY HER FAMILY. The child stated:

"Mrs. Smith wanted to 'throw books,' at her family."

Another child, who had arrived at the concept "long" for one sentence, expanded it to "get long hair" in another: THE OLDER YOU GET THE SOONER YOU WILL BEGIN TO SOLDEVE, ". . . the sooner you will begin to 'get long hair.'"

On occasion the contextual expansion was more systematically employed. The child formed a conceptual nucleus, which remained constant throughout the six contexts; and added to this nucleus elements varying with each sentence. We have termed this procedure *pluralization*. For example, one child formed a nucleus for all the sentences of one series containing the artificial word, LIDBER. This nucleus was "collect." In one sentence LIDBER meant "collect ribbons" (ALL THE CHILDREN WILL "collect ribbons" AT MARY'S PARTY); in another sentence, it was "collect autographs" (THE PEOPLE "collected autographs" from THE SPEAKER WHEN HE FINISHED HIS TALK); in a third sentence, it meant "collect information" (PEOPLE "collect information" QUICKLY WHEN THERE IS AN ACCIDENT), and so on.

We should like to mention two other forms of signification of a word, that were essentially based on contextual or holophrastic conceptualization. One we have termed *generalization by juxtaposition;* the other *generalization by chain*.

In the case of juxtaposition, a concept of an object A obtained in one sentence is applicable to a second sentence through the mediation of a concept of an object B that is spatially contiguous to the object A. For instance, a child gave the solution "plaster" for CONTAVISH in the sentence: BEFORE THE HOUSE

IS FINISHED, THE WALLS MUST HAVE CONTAVISHES. "Plaster" also fit into the sentence, A BOTTLE HAS ONLY ONE CONTAVISH. Here the child used "label" for CONTAVISH, saying, "A bottle has only one 'label.'" Nevertheless "plaster" was retained as the solution because "plaster," as the child explained, "is used to put on the 'label.'" In other words, the concept of an object such as "plaster" could be used as an over-all solution because the juxtaposed object ("label") fit into the sentence. Most likely, the concept was contextual: not just "plaster" but "plaster+."

A similar mechanism seemed to be operative in generalization by chain. This type of generalization probably differs from juxtaposition only insofar as the two objects in question are conceived of as temporally rather than spatially connected (e.g., cause and effect). As an example, "honor" was substituted for SACKOY in one sentence: WE ALL ADMIRE PEOPLE WHO HAVE MUCH SACKOY. In the next sentence, "guts" was the meaning attributed to SACKOY. "You need 'guts' to fight with a boy bigger than you." But "honor" still fit because, as the child explained, "If you have 'guts,' you are 'honored' aren't you?"

Finally, the two main groups of immature signification discussed in this paper may be briefly compared statistically. As will be recalled, in the first group, the word carries with it the whole or parts of the sentence context; in the second group, the word is clearly differentiated from the sentence context, though it still possesses a broad contextual meaning. Table 1 summarizes the occurrence of these two types of contextual word meanings at the various age levels.

TABLE 1

Age	8½-9½	9½-10½	10½-11½	11½-12½	12½-13½
I Sentence-contextual	11.9	9.2	1.8	0.2	0.5
II Non-sentence-contextual	11.7	10.8	7.9	4.6	3.3

The figures represent the mean occurrence per child at each age group. Both forms of word meanings decreased as age increased; however, there is a clearcut difference between the two developmental curves. Signification based on sentence-word fusion (Type I) decreased most sharply between the second and third age levels (around 10-11 years), with practically no occurrence after the third age level. The other type of contextual signification (in which there is no fusion of word meaning and sentence) showed an entirely different developmental trend: it gradually decreased, and even at the 13 year-level there were as many as 3.3 such solutions per child.

The abrupt decrease of Type I, the most immature form of signification, around the 10- to 11-year level suggests a rather fundamental shift in language attitude, toward a task, which, as in our test, is on a relatively abstract verbal plane. This points to important implications which will be treated at greater length in a future paper.

In closing, we should like to mention briefly that there are aspects of language development other than semantic, discussed in this paper, which showed similar abrupt changes at the same age levels. This is particularly true with respect to grammatical structure. The data indicate that there is a growing comprehension of the test sentence as a stable, grammatical structure. Younger children manipulated the sentence as a fluid medium, lacking closure; that is, in the case of giving meaning to the artificial word they frequently altered the grammatical structure of the test sentence. The frequency of such manipulation showed an abrupt drop at the end of the second age level with practically no occurrence at the fourth and fifth levels.

One of the most significant and little explored problems of language development concerns the relationship between the semantic and grammatical aspects of language. The close correspondence of the developmental curves, indicated by our data, between two seemingly independent aspects of language lends support to those theories that assume a genetic interdependence of meaning and structure.

THE DEVELOPMENT OF MEANING
IN CHILDREN'S DESCRIPTIVE TERMS [1]

SUSAN M. ERVIN
GARRETT FOSTER

CHILDREN FREQUENTLY CONFUSE the names for physical dimensions. If two objects differ in size, they may say one is STRONGER than the other. If they differ in weight, one may be called BIGGER than the other. This is, of course, just what one would expect in the early stages of learning if size, weight, and strength are empirically correlated.

Osgood, Suci, and Tannenbaum (1957) have found correlations of a similar sort in examining the structure of meanings measured by semantic differ-

ential scales. Three factors have been found repeatedly—Evaluation, Potency, and Activity. Little attention has been given to the development or origin of these factors. Inspection of the scales defining each factor suggests that two conditions would create correlations. One is verbal conjunction; if whatever is said to be GOOD is also said to be FAIR the scales will be correlated through verbal associations. Secondly, "ecological covariation" (Brunswik, 1947) exists for certain sensory dimensions. We would thus expect BIG, HEAVY, and STRONG to be correlated for all cultural groups.

It is clear that adults can discriminate the sensory dimensions that children confuse verbally. On the semantic differential, however, they are normally

[1] The authors acknowledge with gratitude the cooperation of Matt Griffeath, Principal, and the teachers of the Durant School in Oakland, California, in providing facilities and Ss.

Reprinted by permission from *Journal of Abnormal and Social Psychology*, 1960, *61*, 271–275.

asked to extend terms metaphorically, as in judging the size and weight of FREE PRESS or EDUCATION. Even on the semantic differential, the correlation of size and weight scales can be destroyed by inclusion of items like DIAMOND and MIST where a check with sense experience is possible and the usual trait correlation is reversed. To the extent that the semantic differential reflects covariation in experience of traits that are logically independent, we would expect that there would be an increase with age in denotative discrimination of the terms that are correlated on the differential. In the following study, age changes in children's verbal confusions are examined.

The more highly correlated two attributes are, the less probable are encounters with discrepant instances. It is useful to note three different variants on this situation. One category may constitute a subclass of a larger category. Thus, if 98% of a child's encounters with men, in which there is direct address or verbal reference to a man, involve his father, we would expect that the child might at first call all adult males DADDY. Discrepant instances would at first be too few for a differentiation to take place. If there were two adult males in the family such an extension would be unlikely. Thus Leopold (1939) noted that while his daughter called all men PAPA, women had individual names and there was no word for FRAU.

The subclass of a hierarchy of classes is actually an extreme instance of the second variant of correlation, a partial overlap of two classes. The degree of correlation or overlap should predict the probability of two terms being confused. Thus, communism and atheism might be confused by those unaware of discrepancies

such as religious communist settlements. From a matrix showing the probability of being right in applying the term COMMUNIST to an atheist, we can see that the higher the correlation of the two terms, the greater the probability of being right, and the greater the likelihood that the two ideologies are called by one term. There are other features that enter into the failure to differentiate terms. One is the relative size of the two categories. If there are more atheists than communists, one is more likely to be wrong in calling an atheist a COMMUNIST than calling a communist an ATHEIST. The extreme case would be that in which the whole size of the class of communists is equal to the overlapping class. That is, for example, all communists are atheists but the reverse is not true. This case is identical with the one cited earlier of hierarchical classes. Other relevant factors are the perceptibility of an attribute or class, the consequences of correct and incorrect class discrimination (which may not be the same for the classes involved), the frequency of the terms in usage, and degree of logical independence.

If the dimensions of reference are continuous attributes rather than classes, then the relation may be described by a scatterplot rather than a matrix of frequencies. The same observations apply; the probability of being correct in saying that a bigger object is HEAVIER is a function of the attribute correlations.

In adult speakers of English, the differentiation of the attributes weight, size, and strength is such that if speakers can make appropriate tests, they are unlikely to say that the heavier of two like-sized objects is BIGGER. There are, however, situations in which the attribute extension in this simple physical case is appropriate. One is in the situation of prediction, where a value on one attribute only is known. Then it becomes useful to be able to predict the probable value on the other attribute. The second situation is one in which metaphor is exploited in verbal or pictorial communication, and one attribute may be used to suggest another.

Thus, we would expect that correlated attributes would appear in experienced speakers' usage, in situations of prediction and metaphorical extension, but not in denotation where the evidence for attribute discrimination is available.

In new learners, however, one term may apply to both attributes, which are not in fact discriminated, or both terms may appear as interchangeable synonyms for the two undiscriminated attributes.

In the following study two semantic differential factors, Evaluation and Potency, are presented as far as possible in conditions requiring denotative discrimination of three attribute expressions of each. A reduction with age is predicted with respect to the use of the wrong terms when a difference in only one attribute of the correlated set is present.

METHOD

Subjects. There were two groups of Ss, a group of 16 male and 17 female first grade children, and a group of 18 male and 18 female sixth graders. Both groups were from the same school in a lower socioeconomic Negro district. To reduce variability, the extremely bright and extremely dull children were excluded, the criterion being the teacher's rating in the first grade, and deviations of 20 points from the norm on available IQ tests in the sixth grade.

Materials. In Part I of the experiment, materials were selected to vary successively three of the dimensions on Osgood's potency

factor. These three dimensions—weight, strength, and size—had been found to have loadings of .62 with the rotated factor analysis, involving concepts rated against scales, and coordinates of 1.68, 1.81, and 1.76, respectively, on another analysis of scales judged against scales. These were the largest components of the factor in each case.

The objects used were: (*a*) opaque salt shakers identical but for weight, (*b*) opaque jars identical but for weight, (*c*) cork balls differing in size, (*d*) sterofoam balls differing in size, (*e*) a pair of insulated wires with the wire removed from the middle third of one, leaving it flexible, and (*f*) a dry sponge and a damp one matched in size.

In Part II drawings of a girl's face were used to represent three of four dimensions representing Osgood's evaluative factor. The pictured dimensions were CLEAN-DIRTY, HAPPY-SAD, and PRETTY-UGLY. A fourth was included in the questioning: GOOD-BAD. These had loadings, respectively, of .82, .76, .86 (BEAUTIFUL-UGLY), and .88, and coordinates of 2.38, 2.09, 2.40, 2.29 on the first factor.

Procedure. All of the Ss were individually tested with the following questions:

I would like to ask you some questions and you can give me the correct answers. . . . OK? [For first graders:] It's kind of a game and lots of fun. First I'm going to ask about these objects. [2 objects contrasting in weight put in subject's hands.] Is one of these heavier and one lighter or are they both the same weight? [If says different] Which is heavier? Is one black and one white or are they both the same color? Is one bigger and one smaller or are they both the same size? [If says different] Which is bigger? Is one stronger and one weaker or are they both the same strength? [If says different] Which is stronger?

If the child failed to indicate the item that was heavier on the first question, he was eliminated from the rest of Part I. The second question, to which the answer was "the same" was to control set. A similar series of questions was asked about all the items, starting with the actual contrast as a screening question. One of the six possible key questions was omitted, concerning perception of weight in objects differing in size. If weight in the objects were controlled, the smaller object might be called heavier on the grounds of its scale weight. Because of the ambiguity of the term HEAVY applied to objects differing in size, the question was omitted.

In the analysis the percentages were computed over the whole set of responses, which included two for each question for each child because of the double set of materials. The Ns used in the significance tests were for the actual number of children tested.

In Part II a similar procedure was followed, with the control question "Does one picture have red hair and one black hair or are they both the same?" The questions and pictures were rotated, with every fourth question a control question.

RESULTS

In Table 1 it can be seen that between 39 and 66% of the first-grade children offered contaminated responses for the various dimensions of the physical materials. In the sixth grade the proportion was reduced to a range between 20 and 44%. While none of the individual changes in percentage was significant, there was a reduction for every comparison, including the subgroups by sex. A sign test is significant at the .01 level. The dimension that changes the least is the response that the heavier object is STRONGER; this is also the statement of highest frequency at both ages for both sexes. Since strength is less evident than weight, it is possible that this particular inference would continue in adult Ss. The inference that a bigger object is STRONGER is next in probability, supporting the notion that it is the inferred character of strength that is involved. Size is least often presented as a contaminated response, and it is also the most obvious.

It might be thought that the reduc-

tion in the sixth grade is due to a tendency to be more careful about differentiating at all, and thus to an increase in *same* responses. This was not the case. While the percentage of reversals was relatively low, it increased in the sixth grade. This increase occurred in stating that the heavier was SMALLER, that the stronger was SMALLER and LIGHTER. In the latter case these frequencies probably arise because a wet sponge is usually larger, and contains water. Only boys gave the last reversal, 22% of the boys in the sixth grade saying the stronger was LIGHTER, and no girls. Nine percent of the boys and 28% of the girls said the stronger was SMALLER. In the last case this was a larger proportion than those saying it was larger. It might be argued, then, that the reduction in the last two cases was due to sophistication with respect to one of the objects used.

On the study of the evaluative dimension using faces, almost no reversals occurred at either age. The age differences on Table 2 are striking. It may be noted that they do not occur markedly on three cases. Two of these refer to CLEAN. The frequency of children saying one child was CLEANER than the other for the other attributes was small at both ages. Clean may be said to be the most visible of the attributes. In fact it could be argued that it is the only one with a clear-cut physical criterion.

The third instance of lack of marked change was one in which the proportions were very high at both ages. The smiling face was said to be PRETTIER.

With the CLEANER dimension excluded, the range in the first grade is between 42 and 97% offering a contaminated response. The highest are those offering the smiling face as more GOOD and

TABLE 1 · Proportion Ascribing Correlated Attribute Differences to Objects

Stimulus differences	Response	FIRST GRADE			SIXTH GRADE			Differ- ences
		Boys	Girls	Total	Boys	Girls	Total	
Heavy	BIG	40.6	36.0[a]	38.6[a]	16.7	25.0	20.8	17.8
Strong	BIG	31.2	52.0	39.7	30.6	25.0	27.8	11.9
Strong	HEAVY	37.5	46.2	41.4	33.3	33.3	33.3	8.0
Big	STRONG	50.0	53.8	51.7	36.1	38.9	37.5	14.2
Heavy	STRONG	56.2	76.9	65.5	41.7	47.2	44.4	21.1
	N[b]	16	13	28	18	18	36	

[a] The number of cases in this cell is reduced by one due to loss of data.

[b] The Ss reported were those who correctly differentiated the stimulus attribute for all three attributes on all materials.

the cleaner face as PRETTIER. All of the first grade boys gave these responses. In the sixth grade the range is between 14 and 75% with the highest now being the smiling face which is seen as PRETTIER about as often as it was in the first grade. Thus, there is a shift in responses as with the physical attributes, but it is markedly different for the different attributes.

DISCUSSION

The slight rate of change with respect to discrimination of physical dimensions suggests the kind of learning to be expected where the criteria are most obvious.

With the personal attributes the findings are both more extreme and more uneven. It is clear that the only term of those used which designates a simple visible trait—CLEAN—is the one seldom offered to describe any other attribute. This finding agrees with the fact that BIG, the most obvious physical attribute, was less often used with the physical materials to describe other differences.

The other evaluative dimensions refer to more complex traits that are not entirely logically independent. PRETTY

TABLE 2 · Proportion Ascribing Correlated Attribute Differences to Faces

Stimulus differences	Response	FIRST GRADE			SIXTH GRADE			Differ- ences
		Boys	Girls	Total	Boys	Girls	Total	
Happy	CLEAN	12.5	5.9	9.1	0.0	11.1	5.6	3.5
Pretty	CLEAN	28.6	7.7	18.5	5.6	5.6	5.6	12.9
Clean	HAPPY	37.5	47.0	42.4	5.6	22.2	13.9	28.5*
Pretty	HAPPY	85.7	91.7	88.5	67.1	38.9	50.0	38.5*
Clean	PRETTY	100.0	82.4	90.9	50.0	50.0	50.0	40.9*
Happy	PRETTY	81.2	82.4	81.8	83.3	66.7	75.0	6.8
Clean	GOOD	50.0	70.6	60.6	27.8	33.3	30.6	30.0*
Happy	GOOD	100.0	94.1	97.0	77.8	55.6	66.7	30.3*
Pretty	GOOD	78.6	50.0	65.4	44.4	22.2	33.3	32.0*
	N[a]	16	17	33	18	18	36	

[a] Changes in N due to failure to name stimulus difference correctly: first-grade boys for PRETTY stimulus 14, girls 12; sixth-grade boys, 17, and girls, 16.

* Significant at the .01 level.

may also be said to designate a physical characteristic, but one that adults use both as a constant and a temporary trait, so that a clean smiling face might be deemed prettier than a dirty or frowning one. Thus, while the traits are discriminable they are not independent in the sense that the physical traits are.

HAPPY was used to designate a smiling face, but as children learn the use of the term they may find that it refers to a state of feeling only partially correlated with external evidence. Thus even the smiling–nonsmiling distinction might bear only an imperfect relation to the term HAPPY. One of the largest changes was in the use of HAPPY in describing the prettier girl, and the drop was most extreme in girls—a drop of 53%. The children were from the start, especially the boys, only moderately likely to describe the cleaner girl as HAPPIER.

One possible reason for a drop in the ascription of terms to a correlated difference is a change in metaphorical treatment of pictures. Occasionally children would refuse to say that both children were the same in hair color, but said that one had red and one black hair. The hair in the drawing was white, that is, not filled in in the black-and-white outline picture. Younger children, used to storybook imagination, may be less literal about what is on the page. While this might account for the increase in *same* responses with age, it does not predict the direction of the ascription, by the first graders, which was in no case in the opposite direction from that predicted.

Does the failure to differentiate on this test imply that the children use the terms as virtual synonyms for an undifferentiated referent? With respect to the physical dimensions, only one child was so extreme as to use the same terms interchangeably for all three attributes on all the materials. But if we examine the faces test and omit CLEAN which seems to fall out of the pattern, it appears that 62% of the children used HAPPY-GOOD-PRETTY synonymously, in the first grade.

We would like to argue that the factors that appear as clusters of correlated terms in the semantic differential studies of adults derive from empirical correlations of attributes. They could, of course, be linked purely by verbal associations, as in "He's a good clean player." If this were the case, differentiation of reference might still be accompanied by semantic differential correlations, since many of the terms on the semantic differential can be applied to the "concept" only metaphorically. DEMOCRACY is clean, fragrant, and sweet only in the poetic sense.

While verbal associations may be one source of such dimensions, we are proposing that the history of concept development in the child provides another source. What remains as a connotative, metaphorical relationship in adults may in many cases start as denotative nondifferentiation. In a sense, the child might be said to acquire first a concept, for instance, of "big-strong-heavy . . ." in other words, a potency referent. The terms he applies to this referent may variously be BIG, STRONG, HEAVY. He may prefer one of these terms for people, another for boats, another for baseballs. Presumably he will only come to differentiate the terms and apply them appropriately to different stimulus dimensions when uncorrelated instances occur and he is corrected, or hears others differentiate the terms. By chance, the sample he selects may have a 100% correlation and he may not encounter errors immediately.

SUMMARY

The physical dimensions of size, weight, and strength are empirically correlated. If the correlation delays discrimination of these attributes as referents for descriptive terms, then younger children should more often use incorrect terms to describe differences between objects. The terms GOOD, PRETTY, CLEAN, and HAPPY should also be used as synonyms prior to differentiation.

A set of materials was prepared in which size, weight, and strength were independently varied in pairs of objects. First-grade children more often than sixth graders said that the pairs of objects differed on other dimensions in addition to the attribute actually contrasted. In a set of pictures of faces, over half of the youngest children treated GOOD, PRETTY, and HAPPY as interchangeable synonyms.

The proportion dropped markedly with age. The more easily identified traits, such as the referents of BIG and CLEAN, were least often confused with other attributes.

The results are interpreted as showing that attributes which have metaphorical and connotative links in adult usage, may be denotatively confused at first. The factors found by Osgood on the semantic differential studies of verbal meaning may actually be the referents for several terms used as synonyms, prior to differentiation of finer distinctions between attributes.

REFERENCES

BRUNSWIK, E. *Systematic and representative design of psychological experiments.* Berkeley: Univer. California Press, 1947.

LEOPOLD, W. F. *The speech development of a bilingual child.* Evanston, Ill.: Northwestern Univer. Press, 1939–50.

OSGOOD, C. E., SUCI, G. J., & TANNENBAUM, P. H. *The measurement of meaning.* Urbana: Univer. Illinois Press, 1957.

WORD ASSOCIATION AND THE ACQUISITION OF GRAMMAR

ROGER BROWN
JEAN BERKO [1]

EVERY NATURAL LANGUAGE is a system. From knowledge of one part it is possible to anticipate correctly many other parts. The linguistic scientist studies some finite set of utterances (his linguistic "corpus") in search of the recurrent elementary units and patterns of combination that will generate the infinite set of utterances belonging to the language. Every child, in learning his first language, does much the same thing with the difference that he does not explicitly formulate most of the rules that govern his language behavior. A child is not, in his first few years, exposed to all possible utterances belonging to the community language but only to that small sample brought to him by his family, his friends, and television. Exposure to this sample, however, teaches him to understand and to produce utterances not actually experienced but implied by what has been experienced. The child may begin as a parrot imitating what others say, but he will end as a poet able to say things that have not been said before but which will be grammatical and meaningful in his community. This is the

terminal achievement which a theory of language acquisition must explain.

The linguistic scientist describes language systems at several levels: the *phonological* level of distinctive sound elements and their permissible combinations; the *morphological* level of elementary meaningful forms (*morphemes*) and their combination to make words; the *syntactic* level of sentence creation from words. We have described elsewhere (2) these three levels and have reported two studies (1, 3) concerning the acquisition by children of morphology and syntax. The present study is concerned with syntax and, more particularly, with the child's utilization of the English parts-of-speech.

The linguistic scientist defines the parts-of-speech in purely syntactic or formal terms. He has shown that the English teacher's semantic definitions (e.g., "a noun is the name of a person, place, or thing") are imprecise approximations to the underlying but less obvious syntactic facts. The noun, in descriptive linguistics, is a class of words having similar "privileges of occurrence." Nouns are words that can follow articles and can occur in subject and object positions and, in this respect, are distinct from such other classes of words as the verb, adjective, and adverb. The fact that the words of any language fall into classes of approximate syntactic equivalents is of great interest to the student of language acquisition be-

[1] This research was done while Dr. Berko held Public Health Service Postdoctoral Research Fellowship MF 9261 from the Division of Research Grants of the National Institutes of Health, and the research was facilitated by a Supply Grant accompanying that fellowship. Grateful acknowledgment is made of this support and also of the generous cooperation of the staff and students of the Michael Driscoll School in Brookline, Massachusetts.

Reprinted by permission from *Child Development*, 1960, *31*, 1–14.

cause it suggests one of the ways in which the lawful flexibility of speech is developed. A new word is ordinarily introduced to a child in a sentence, and this sentence will often serve to identify the part-of-speech to which the new word belongs. If the parts-of-speech have been internalized, this would mean that one vast array of sentence positions is available for the new word and other arrays are not. From the fact that X is a noun one can anticipate all of the grammatically acceptable uses of X and set aside all of the unacceptable uses. Is there evidence that children learn to operate with the parts-of-speech? We suspect that such evidence is to be found in certain well-established facts concerning word association.

Since the experiment of Woodrow and Lowell (7), it has been known that the word associations of children show consistent differences from the associations of adults. Woodworth (8) offers as examples of these differences the words appearing in Table 1. Woodrow and Lowell and others after them have conceptualized these differences in terms that are primarily semantic. Children are said to give more "contiguity" responses and more "whole-part" responses while adults are said to give more "coordinate," "contrast," and "similarity" responses. In several cases Woodrow and Lowell desert their semantic concepts and speak of "adjective-noun" associations and "verb-object" associations (both of which are more common in children's than in adult's responses). These classifications by parts-of-speech suggest a very general formal principle which contrasts the word associations of children and adults, a principle which so far as we know was first suggested by Ervin (4). The associative responses of adults belong to the same

part-of-speech as the stimulus word more often than do the associative responses of children. We shall speak of the adult type of association as homogeneous-by-part-of-speech (abbreviated Hmg.) and the child's type as heterogeneous-by-part-of-speech (Htg.).

Looking again at the examples of Table 1, we see that the response favored

TABLE 1 · WORD ASSOCIATIONS FROM ADULTS AND CHILDREN

Stimulus	Response	1000 Children	1000 Men and women
Table	{ Eat	358	63
	{ Chair	24	274
Dark	{ Night	421	221
	{ Light	38	427
Man	{ Work	168	17
	{ Woman	8	394
Deep	{ Hole	257	32
	{ Shallow	6	180
Soft	{ Pillow	138	53
	{ Hard	27	365
Mountain	{ High	390	246
	{ Hill	91	184

by adults is almost invariably Hmg. while that favored by children is Htg. Many of the largest differences found in the Woodrow and Lowell study conform to this syntactic principle though they were not so classified by the authors. In addition to these data from the past there are recent findings of Ervin (4) who used a list of common words belonging to various parts-of-speech with groups of children in kindergarten and the first, third, and sixth grades. She found large increases with age in Hmg. responses to nouns, verbs, prepositions, adjectives, and adverbs. What is the significance of this apparently reliable developmental trend in word association?

There are, of course, many kinds of

association that can link one word with another; similarity or contrast of referents, spatio-temporal contiguity of referents, and high transition probabilities between words are obvious possibilities. Similarity and contrast and contiguity between referents would sometimes lead to Hmg. responses (e.g., *table-chair*) and sometimes to Htg. responses (e.g., *table-eat*). Immediate transitions of high probability will very seldom exist between two words of the same part-of-speech, and so such pairs as *dark-night, deep-hole,* and *soft-pillow* are Htg. Elaborating a suggestion of Ervin's (2), we propose that the word associations of very young children are governed by such principles as we have cited but that, with increasing age, another principle of association begins to operate which has the effect of increasing the number of Hmg. responses.

From the time that a child begins to use phrases his speech repertoire will manifest the morphological structure that is a universal characteristic of adult speech in any language. The same meaningful forms (morphemes and words) occur in a variety of contexts; not all forms can occur in all contexts but some forms can occur in some of the same contexts. From these morphological universals it follows that words resemble one another in the degree to which they have similar privileges of occurrence. This syntactic similarity is always objectively present in speech involving phrases but probably it takes considerable time and maturity to analyze out syntactic similarity. The appreciation of syntactic similarity is, however, prerequisite to the ability to form meaningful and grammatical sentences that are not imitated from someone else. Suppose a child has learned that such words as *house, barn, table,* and *fence* can all occur in such positions as: "See the ——"; "I own a ——"; "The —— is new"; and "This —— is mine." If now he hears for the first time such a sentence as "See the *car*" in which *car* is a new word, he can be prepared to say "I own a *car*"; "The *car* is new"; and "This *car* is mine." Of course, the particular sentence uttered on a given occasion depends on semantic and motivational factors but the universe of sentences from which the particular can be drawn is established by the syntactic kinship linking *car* with *house, barn, table,* and *fence.*

Modern methods of teaching second or foreign languages begin, as does first language learning, with the repetition of phrases which recombine a limited set of meaningful elements. In second language learning, as in first, there comes a time when the student "creates" a phrase by realizing the syntactic implications of the material practiced. This is often accomplished nowadays by implicit induction without any explicit tuition in syntactic rules, and that is exactly the way it is accomplished by all children who become full participants in a first language.

Syntactic similarity is a matter of degree. The parts-of-speech are simply very large and very useful classes of approximate combinational equivalents. Animate nouns are more closely equivalent than nouns in general, and transitive verbs are more closely equivalent than verbs in general. Such popular adult word associations as *bright-dark* are not only semantic antonyms; they are also adjectives having highly similar privileges of occurrence. *Bright* has more sentence contexts in common with *dark* than with such another adjective as *virtuous*. It is our general hypothesis that, as utilization of syntax develops in children, syntactic similarity in words becomes an increasingly important determinant of word association and that the developmental trend from Htg. responses toward Hmg. responses is a manifestation of this great step forward into syntactic operations. We have undertaken to test this hypothesis by relating the child's tendency to give Hmg. word associations to his ability to make correct grammatical use of new words after hearing them in a couple of sentences.

METHOD

We worked with four groups of 20 subjects each. In each group there were equal numbers of male and female subjects. Groups I, II, and III were students from, respectively, the first, second, and third grades of the Michael Driscoll School in Brookline, Massachusetts. The Driscoll School is a public school in a middle-income residence area. Children in a given group were all taken from the same classroom and simply drawn in the order of the seating arrangement until 20 had served. The fourth group (Group Ad.) consisted of 20 adults, students or staff at M.I.T., who responded to an advertisement asking for subjects.

WORD ASSOCIATION TEST

This test consisted of 36 stimulus words such that there were six words representing each of six parts-of-speech. The words were selected because all have high frequency in the speech of American elementary-school children (6) and because in earlier studies they yielded large differences between the associations of children and adults. The words were presented in a constant order to all subjects.

Verbs in English may be subdivided into transitive and intransitives. Intransitive verbs can appear without an object (e.g., "We *laugh*") while transitives almost occur with some sort of object (e.g., "We *sent* something"). For the present experiment the transitives and intransitives were treated as two parts-of-speech, and there were six words representing each of them.

Nouns in English can be separated into "count nouns" and "mass nouns." The names are suggested from a distinction of reference; count nouns usually name bounded objects (e.g., *table, house*) while mass nouns name extended substances (e.g., *milk, sand*). However, there is also a clear syntactic distinction; count nouns in the singular can be preceded by *a* while mass nouns cannot (e.g., *a table* but not *a sand*) and, in addition, count nouns, when preceded by *some*, appear in the plural whereas mass nouns appear in the singular (e.g., *some tables* but *some milk*). On the present list of stimulus words there were six mass nouns and six count nouns.

In addition to the two varieties of noun and two varieties of verb, there were six adjectives and six adverbs on the list. The complete list is as follows:

Count Nouns (C.N.): table, house, foot, needle, apple, doctor.

Mass Nouns (M.N.): milk, water, sand, sugar, air, cheese.

Adjectives (Adj.): dark, soft, cold, white, sweet, hard.

Transitive Verbs (T.V.): to send, to bring, to find, to take, to hit, to invite.

Intransitive Verbs (I.V.): to skate, to come, to live, to laugh, to stand, to walk.

Adverbs (Adv.) : quickly, slowly, sadly, now, softly, gently.

Many English words belong to more than one part-of-speech. It is possible in English to *table* a motion and to *foot* a bill but *table* and *foot*, in the vast majority of their occurrences, function as nouns and, when presented in isolation as stimulus words, are apprehended as nouns by most English-speaking adults. The words on the present list belong primarily to one part-of-speech though they may have secondary membership in others. The verbs were presented as infinitives with preceding *to* so that their verbal character would be clear.

USAGE TEST

The general plan of this test was to introduce to *S* a new word (actually a pronounceable nonsense syllable) by using it in two sentences. The two sentences were adequate to place the word in one of six parts-of-speech: the count noun, mass noun, transitive verb, intransitive verb, adjective, or adverb. After this introduction to the word, *S* was asked to use it in sentences of his own creation, and these were scored as correct if the new word was used as it ought to be in view of the part-of-speech implied by the introductory sentences.

As "new words" 12 nonsense syllables were used: *wug, boff, latt, roog, stog, huft, nass, sib, bik, rik, nare,* and *pilk.* There were 12 problems in all with two syllables assigned to each of the six parts-of-speech. The syllables were rotated through all 12 problems so that there was no regular association between any syllable and any particular problem. The syllable *wug* will be used here to indicate the general character of the presentations.

For each problem, *S* was shown a colorful picture of either a girl, a boy, a man, a woman, a cat, or a dog, and *E* read text of the following kind: "Do you know what a *wug* is? This is a picture of a little girl thinking about a *wug*. Can you make up what that might mean?" This was the presentation identifying *wug* as a count noun. Where *wug* was to be identified as an intransitive verb, *E* would say: "Do you know what it means to *wug?* This is a picture of a little boy who wants to *wug*." With *wug* as mass noun there would be such sentences as: "This is a cat thinking about some *wug*." With *wug* as transitive verb such a sentence as this was used: "This is a woman who wants to *wug* something." Where *wug* was to be identified as an adverb, *E* spoke of a dog thinking of doing something *wuggily*.

There were two problems for each part-of-speech and a different syllable for each problem. There were two identifying sentences for each problem and, in the case of the adjectives and adverbs, the appended suffixes -*y* and -*ly*. The pictures gave no clue to the meaning of the new word and were only included to interest the child and keep his attention. The figures in the pictures were always simply thinking about the new word, not demonstrating its meaning.

PROCEDURE

E was introduced to the children in a class by the teacher, and the class was told that each member would have a chance to look at some pictures and play some games. The children were interviewed individually either in the corridor outside the classroom or in an unused classroom. The Word Association Test was presented first with the remarks: "This is a game called 'say a word.' Have you ever played 'say a word'? Well, this is the way it works. I'm going to say a word and I want you to listen to my word and then say another word, not my word but a different word. Any word is all right so long as it's the first word that comes into your head when you hear my word. Are you ready?"

When the word associations had been recorded, E brought out the picture cards and said: "Now we're going to play a making-up game. How are you at making things up? Pretty good? Well, let's see." The problems were presented so as to go through all parts-of-speech once before repeating any of them.

The procedure with adults was the same except that S knew he was participating in an experiment on language and E did not call either part a game. In explanation of the brightly colored pictures and rather childish text, the adults were told that the tests had been designed for use with children as well as with adults.

SCORING

Scoring on the Word Association Test involves assigning response words to a part-of-speech; scoring on the Usage Test involves determining from S's use of a new word the part-of-speech to which S has implicitly assigned the new word. Because English words can belong to more than one part-of-speech and because single sentences employing a new word do not always unequivocally indicate the part-of-speech membership of the new word, there were sometimes problems in scoring.

On the Free Association Test those response words that were marked with characteristic suffixes (adjectives and adverbs) or with the *to* of the verbal infinitive could be confidently classified. With most potentially doubtful responses membership in one part-of-speech is so much more common than membership in another that it was safe to assign the word this primary membership. Where there was some doubt, however, E asked S to use the response word in a sentence and, in doing so, S revealed the part-of-speech he had in mind. It was necessary for E mentally to score the responses as they were elicited so that he could resolve scoring problems where necessary.

On the Usage Test S sometimes translated the new word into a conventional English word. When told that a man was thinking about some *wug* and asked to "tell what that might mean," S sometimes provided a familiar word as a translation, saying for instance, "He is thinking about some *milk*." In such a case the part-of-speech membership of the familiar equivalent was scored and would be correct, in the present instance, as *milk* is a mass noun and that is the part-of-speech implied for *wug*. Where the translation word was not clearly of one part-of-speech, E encouraged S to "say some more about it."

In other cases S interpreted the Usage Test as calling for use of the new word in a sentence and so might provide: "The man has some *wugs* for breakfast every day." In such a case the part-of-speech was inferred from the sentence and, in the present instance, would be scored incorrect as *wug* has been used as a count noun. Not every sentence is unequivocal in this regard, and so it was sometimes necessary to urge S to say a little more.

RESULTS

There were 36 stimulus words on the Free Association Test, six words for each of six parts-of-speech. Each of the 36 response words (or phrases) was scored as Hmg. or Htg. with reference to its stimulus word, and so for every subject there was a possible maximal score of six Hmg. responses for each of six parts-of-speech. There were 12 new words on the Usage Test, two words for each of six parts-of-speech. Each of the new words was scored Hmg. or Htg. according to the agreement between the part-of-speech implied by the introductory sentences and the part-of-speech implied by S's use or translation of the new word. For each S, therefore, there was a possible maximal score of two Hmg. responses on each of six parts-of-speech. After the rules of scoring had been developed by one judge, another judge independently scored 10 complete protocols (360 response words on word association and 120 new words on usage) from the rules. The two scorings agreed perfectly except for three instances where more information should have been elicited, and so it appears that this is essentially an objective scoring problem with no difficulties in the reliability sphere. The mean Hmg. scores for each part-of-speech and each age group appear in Table 2.

TABLE 2 · MEAN HMG. SCORES ON FREE ASSOCIATION AND USAGE FOR EACH PART-OF-SPEECH AND EACH AGE GROUP

Group	C.N.	Adj.	I.V.	T.V.	Adv.	M.N.	Total
			FREE ASSOCIATION				
Ad.	5.10	5.00	4.80	4.45	4.95	2.35	4.44
3rd	4.65	3.65	3.40	2.95	1.95	2.40	3.17
2nd	4.55	3.90	2.75	2.40	2.25	1.90	2.96
1st	3.95	1.25	1.60	1.40	.80	1.20	1.70
Total	4.56	3.45	3.14	2.80	2.49	1.96	3.07

Group	C.N.	Adj.	I.V.	T.V.	M.N.	Adv.	Total
			USAGE				
Ad.	1.85	1.75	1.70	1.60	.95	1.20	1.51
3rd	1.45	1.65	1.65	1.75	.55	.55	1.27
2nd	1.55	1.50	1.20	1.10	.70	.45	1.08
1st	1.20	.75	.90	.90	.45	.10	.72
Total	1.51	1.41	1.36	1.34	.66	.58	1.15

A two-way analysis of variance with 20 cases in each cell was carried out for the Free Association means and another for the Usage means. The results are summarized in Tables 3 and 4. Both age and part-of-speech account for large amounts of variance. In addition, there is a significant interaction between the two variables, and it can be seen in both the Free Association and Usage means that the increase with age of Hmg. responses is far less for count nouns than for the other parts-of-speech.

We are not primarily interested in the effects of age and of part-of-speech and so will not compare the 24 individual means for each test. It is, however, worth noting the extraordinary uniformities in

TABLE 3 · ANALYSIS OF VARIANCE FOR FREE
ASSOCIATION MEANS

Source	Sum of squares	df	Variance estimate
Age (rows)	453.6167	3	151.2056
Parts-of-Speech (columns)	321.2167	5	64.2433
Interaction	84.6833	15	5.6456
Individual differences (within cells)	1345.3500	456	2.9503
Total	2204.8667	479	

Interaction $F = 1.91$; $p < .05$.
Age $F = 26.78$; $p < .001$.
Parts-of-Speech $F = 11.38$; $p < .001$.

TABLE 4 · ANALYSIS OF VARIANCE FOR USAGE
MEANS

Source	Sum of squares	df	Variance estimate
Age (rows)	40.0896	3	13.3632
Parts-of-Speech (columns)	67.2688	5	13.4538
Interaction	11.1673	15	.7445
Individual differences (within cells)	208.5556	456	.4574
Total	327.0813	479	

Interaction $F = 1.63$; p about .05.
Age $F = 17.95$; $p < .001$.
Parts-of-Speech $F = 18.07$; $p < .001$.

Table 2. The individual means have been
arranged in the order of the grand means
of the rows (age groups) and columns
(parts-of-speech). When this is done for
Free Association, there are only three
reversals of one position each in the age
order, only four reversals of one position,
and a single reversal of two positions in
the part-of speech data. The same sort of
ordering of the Usage means results in
only three reversals of one position each
in the age order, only one reversal of
three positions, and one reversal of two
positions in the part-of-speech order.
There is clear confirmation in this table

of the increase with age of Hmg. responses
found by Ervin (4) and also clear evidence that the count noun and adjective
function in child speech in advance of
other parts-of-speech. Finally, ordering
the Free Association and Usage cell means
in the order of their grand means results
in identical age and part-of-speech orders
(except for a reversal of the Adv. and
M.N. columns) in the two sets of data.
This is a good first indication of the
covariation in free association and usage
which is the effect predicted by our hypothesis. We proceed to a more detailed
presentation of the evidence for this effect.

It would have been possible to compute correlations between the individual
scores on usage and the individual scores
on free association for each part-of-speech
and each age group. We examined these
scores and saw that the correlations would
be very small, probably because the usage
scores can only range from zero to two
and because this small sample of usage
from each S is not a very reliable measure
of S's grammatical skills. We decided to
work instead with the means of Table 2
which yield a greater range of scores and
a more reliable estimate of grammatical
skill in a kind of S. The rank-order correlation between the 24 means from the
Free Association Test and the 24 means
from the Usage Test is .84, and this is
a relationship significant at far better
than the .001 level.

Contributing to the rank-order correlation of all 24 means is the tendency
for usage and free association scores to
increase with age as well as the tendency
for scores on the six parts-of-speech to
covary for usage and free association.
Insofar as the correlation is generated by
the former factor, it is possible that we
have nothing more here than a tendency

for all sorts of language performance scores to move together with increasing age towards adult values. We are interested in something more particular than this. We want to know whether the increasing tendency to give Hmg. responses in free association can be interpreted as evidence of the developing organization of vocabulary into parts-of-speech which define correct grammatical usage for new words. We shall have better ground for this interpretation if correlations exist with the age variation taken out. One way of accomplishing this effect is to correlate the grand means (across all age groups) for the six part-of-speech columns for free association and usage. This rank order *rho* is .94 and even with only six cases that value is significant at about .01. Another way of testing for this relationship is to correlate the six paired means for each of the four age groups. The results appear in Table 5 (together with the previously mentioned *rhos*); three are significant and one is not. The *p* values for these four samples can be combined to yield a single *p* value for the relationship of free association to usage. Mosteller and Bush (5) suggest transforming the individual *p* values into normal deviates, summing them, and dividing the sum by the square root of the number of observations. The resultant value is itself a normal deviate with a *p* of about .0002. It seems very certain, therefore, that Hmg. scores for free association are related to Hmg. scores for usage.

DISCUSSION

The change with age in both free association and usage is very striking when one examines individual protocols. For free association, consider the stimulus words *to send*. One first grade child responds *away*, another *letter*, another *a card*, another *mail*, etc. In response to this same word adults give: *to receive, to get, to deliver, to bring, to mail, to fetch*. Both the child responses and the adult responses are semantically related to the stimulus word, and the one set does not seem to be any more so than the other. The difference lies with the fact that the child responses are phrase completions (words that commonly follow the stimulus) while the adult words would almost never follow *to send* in an English sentence but are very closely matched with it in that they are transitive verbs. More specifically, the adult responses are transitive verbs, naming human actions which ordinarily have some small inanimate thing as object. This further similarity is semantic but, in addition, involves a closer syntactic match than would be true for transitive verbs in general.

Consider now the sort of thing that happens on the Usage Test with a nonsense syllable intended to be a transitive verb. One first grade child was told: "This is a cat who wants to *niss* something. Can you make up what that might mean?" The child replied: "The cat wants a fish. A *niss* is a fish." To this same problem an adult responded: "The cat wants to catch something. To *niss* is to catch." The child

TABLE 5 · RANK ORDER CORRELATIONS BETWEEN FREE ASSOCIATION AND USAGE HMG. SCORES

Rho for all paired means, N = 24	.84	*p* < .001
Rho for grand means of the parts-of-speech, N = 6	.94	*p* = .01
Rho for Adults, N = 6	.83	*p* = .05
Rho for 3rd grade, N = 6	.46	*p* = .40
Rho for 2nd grade, N = 6	.94	*p* = .01
Rho for 1st grade, N = 6	.83	*p* = .05
Combined *p* value for adults, 3rd grade, 2nd grade, 1st grade		*p* = .0002

seems to have put together knowledge about cats and the sound of *niss* to come up with a count noun—*fish*. He was not troubled by the fact that this translation violates the part-of-speech membership of *niss*. When *E* says "to *niss* something," that should exclude the possibility of saying "A *niss* is a fish," but, for this child, it does not. Apparently the first grade children paid little attention to the formal marks of the syntactic potentialities of *niss*. The adult, on the other hand, principally attended to these marks. In many cases the translations provided by adults seem to have been suggested by the sound of the new word even as *niss* suggested *fish* to the first grader. However, when this happened with adults, it was almost always within the limits of the class of words suggested by the syntactic cues. In general, then, both the free association results and the usage results seem to be manifestations of the developing organization of vocabulary into syntactic classes.

As the analyses of variance have demonstrated, both age and part-of-speech are highly significant determinants of the number of Hmg. responses on both the Free Association and Usage tests. These two variables may perhaps be conceptualized as a single determinant—the amount of experience with words belonging to a part-of-speech. Experience of words in all six parts-of-speech is bound to increase with age, and Hmg. responses on all parts-of-speech clearly do increase with age. In addition, however, we note in Table 2 that the count noun and the adjective produce more Hmg. responses across all age levels than do the other parts-of-speech. While we do not know of any exact tests of the frequency of occurrence in English of words belonging to the various parts-of-speech, it seems to

us that no test is needed to persuade the native speaker that count nouns and adjectives are more common than intransitive verbs or transitive verbs or adverbs or mass nouns. This is to say that at any given age a speaker of English is likely to have had more experience of count nouns and adjectives than of the other parts-of-speech we have studied.

The count noun has always the highest number of Hmg. responses and, indeed, does not change greatly in this respect from the first grade to adulthood because it is already at a near peak level in first graders. The count noun is, of course, the kind of word adults regularly undertake to teach children, for these are the names of denotable things: a *man*, a *dog*, a *car*, a *bike*. Surely speakers of English have greater experience of words in this class than of words in any other class.

The low number of Hmg. responses generally obtained for mass nouns requires a special comment. The Htg. responses given to mass nouns were usually count nouns, i.e., members of the same major part-of-speech. There is a good reason why these two varieties of noun were not usually distinguished even by adults. Mass nouns in English can always be used as count nouns. Ordinarily one says *some sand, some water, some marble* but one can say *some sands, some marbles,* and even *some waters*. The difference is that in the former cases a quantity of a uniform substance is suggested while in the latter case varieties or subspecies of some category of substances are suggested. This syntactic overlap seems to result in an overlap on the word association and usage tasks.

We have suggested that degree of experience of words in a part-of-speech is the basic determinant of the degree to which that part-of-speech functions in free association and usage. The significant sort of experience might be the number of words belonging to the part-of-speech or the variety of sentences for each word or the number of occurrences for each sentence. Probably all of these kinds of experience are close correlates in the natural situation. There are many different count nouns in English; there are many different sentences for most count nouns; and there are many sentences involving count nouns that occur very frequently. Without deliberate experimental manipulation of experience it probably will not be possible to determine the relative importance of these factors.

SUMMARY

It is a reliable finding that the response words provided by adults in a word association test usually belong to the same parts-of-speech as the respective stimulus words. There are fewer of these homogeneous-by-part-of-speech responses with young children; the tendency to associate words within a part-of-speech increases with age. The present paper suggests that this change in word associations is a consequence of the child's gradual organization of his vocabulary into the syntactic classes called parts-of-speech. To test the degree to which S has accomplished this latter grammatical task, a Usage Test was designed. In this test a new word was used in a couple of sentences which sufficed to indicate the part-of-speech to which the new word belonged. After hearing these sentences, S was asked to create some sentences of his own using the new word, and his performance was scored correct if it employed the word in ways permitted by its part-of-speech membership. Four groups of Ss (adults and first, second, and third grade children) were given a Word Association Test (consisting of stimulus words belonging to six different parts-of-speech) and also a Usage Test (consisting of new words assigned to the same six parts-of-speech). The Word Association Test was scored for homogeneous responses within each part-of-speech and the Usage Test for correct usage in accordance with each part-of-speech. It was found that scores on both tests regularly increased with age and that scores on the two tests were closely related to one another. It was concluded that the formal change in word association and the ability to make correct grammatical use of new words are two manifestations of the child's developing appreciation of English syntax.

REFERENCES

1. BERKO, JEAN. The child's learning of English morphology. *Word,* 1958, *14,* 150–177.
2. BERKO, JEAN, & BROWN, R. Psycholinguistic research methods. In P. Mussen (Ed.), *Handbook of research methods in child development.* New York: Wiley, 1960, Pp. 517–557.
3. BROWN, R. Linguistic determinism and the part of speech. *J. abnorm. soc. Psychol.,* 1957, *55,* 1–5.
4. ERVIN, SUSAN M. Grammar and classification. Paper read at Amer. Psychol. Ass., New York, September, 1957.
5. MOSTELLER; F., & BUSH, R. R. Selected quantitative techniques. In G. Lindzey (Ed.), *Handbook of social psychology.* Vol. I. Cambridge,

Mass.: Addison-Wesley, 1954. Pp. 289–334.

6. RINSLAND, H. D.   *A basic vocabulary of elementary school children.* New York: Macmillan, 1945.

7. WOODROW, H., & LOWELL, F.   Children's association frequency tables. *Psychol. Monogr.,* 1916, *22,* No. 97.

8. WOODWORTH, R. S.   *Experimental psychology.* New York: Holt, 1938.

THE EFFECTS OF LANGUAGE ON LEARNING | 11

IN CONTRAST to the paucity of studies of language per se, there has been a considerable interest recently in the effects that language may have upon essentially nonverbal learning tasks. The problem here revolves around the function of language. Can learning be facilitated by the use of language in conjunction with the usual learning procedures that might be employed with organisms unable to use language? Most of this research was stimulated by the hypothesis that verbal responses made during learning have stimulus or cue-producing properties—in other words, that verbal responses provide stimuli which add to those physical stimuli present in the learning task. Dollard and Miller (1950, p. 101) have suggested that, "Attaching the same cue-producing response to two distinctive stimulus objects gives them a certain *learned equivalence* increasing the extent to which instrumental . . . responses will generalize from one to the other." In addition, "attaching distinctive cue-producing responses to similar stimulus objects tends to increase their distinctiveness."

Thus, a response provides stimuli additional to those of the experimental stimulus situation. If you move your arm, for example, it is not necessary for someone to tell you that your arm moved to know that you have moved it. There are proprioceptive and visual stimuli associated with making that response which provide the information. Similarly, when you speak, there are stimuli associated with saying the words. It is assumed that the stimuli produced by such responses have the same properties as any other stimuli and, therefore, responses may be learned to the response-produced stimuli as well as to any other kind. According to the acquired-equivalence-of-cues hypothesis, if you learn to call the animal St. Bernard and the animal Chihuahua by the name "dog," distinctly different physical stimuli will come to acquire equivalence and you may learn to make the same responses to both of them, i.e., you will tend to generalize the responses learned to one of the animals to the other animal. According to the acquired-distinctiveness hypothesis, if you learn to call two quite similar stimuli, such as the weasel and mink, by their distinctly different names, the names will add distinctiveness and you may learn to avoid making the same responses to both of them.

In each of the studies included, it was assumed that a verbal response and its associated response-produced stimuli would have some effect upon the learning of the task presented to the child. It was anticipated, in each case, that the use of names by the subjects would provide additional stimuli for learning the task and that the responses required in the task would become associated with the stimuli produced by naming as well as with the physical stimuli presented by the experimenter.

The first study, a specific test of the hypothesis of acquired distinctiveness of cues, demonstrates that the particular words chosen to be learned to the similar stimuli make a difference in the degree to which they aid in subsequent learning of new responses to those stimuli. In this case, it was demonstrated that names which are themselves similar do not facilitate subsequent learning as much as do names which are more distinctive. Thus, the acquired-distinctiveness phenomenon depends upon the distinctiveness of the stimuli added to the situation by the response-produced stimuli associated with naming.

The second study shows, in another kind of learning situation, how the knowledge of a natural language name and the opportunity to use that name facilitates learning of a nonverbal response. Children who had the verbal label "middle sized" were able to learn a discrimination problem in which the middle sized stimulus was correct more easily than children who had not yet acquired this verbal label.

The third study deals with the possibility that verbal labels can modify the effects which the learning of one discrimination problem has on the learning of another. Initially the subjects were trained to approach one of two stimuli on one dimension, while two stimuli on another dimension were randomly associated with reward and nonreward. Subsequently the nonrewarded stimulus on the relevant dimension was designated correct (reversal) for half of the subjects and one of the stimuli on the irrelevant dimension was correct (nonreversal) for half of the subjects. Previous transfer studies of this kind had indicated that, relative to the reversal problem, rats learn the nonreversal problem more easily while college students learn the reversal problem relatively more easily. The results of this study indicate that kindergarten children require approximately the same mean number of trials to learn both types of problem. When the children were divided into groups of fast learners and slow learners, however, the slow learners, like the rats, had less relative difficulty with the nonreversal problem while the fast learners, like the college students, had less relative difficulty with the reversal problem. The authors interpret these results as indicating that a verbal mediator attached to the relevant stimulus dimension during the first task facilitates reversal learning. This may be a case in which verbal cues increase the distinctiveness of or attention to one stimulus dimension when another is present and irrelevant, rather than increasing the distinctiveness of one stimulus on a single dimension as in the first two studies.

The fourth study relates to the hypothesis of acquired equivalence of cues. The subjects were taught to give the same name to distinctive colors and then tested to determine the degree to which generalization occurred to the colors with the same name. The results indicate that while the children tended to generalize to some extent along the dimension of physical similarity, the gradient of generalization was heightened by the equivalence established through the learning of the same names for the different colors. In contrast to the first two studies, the acquisition of names reduced the effective difference between the different stimulus situations.

The last paper in this section is included to point out that verbalizations made by children in a learning task may under some conditions hinder rather than facilitate learning. In this case, the authors expected that verbal labels which the children had for the stimuli in the discrimination task would facilitate performance. In fact, the children required to name the stimuli before making a motor response did perform better than the children who were not required to name the stimuli. The children in the three- and five-year-old groups performed as expected, but the children in the seven- and nine-year-old groups did not perform as well as the five-year-olds. One of the hypotheses advanced by the authors for this surprising finding was that the seven- and nine-year-old children reasoned that this could not be such an easy task and as a result developed complex hypotheses about the responses required. This behavior resulted in poorer performance. The authors are suggesting that the older children verbalized to themselves about the solution of the task and this verbalization interfered with their performance.

REFERENCE

DOLLARD, J. and MILLER, N. E.   *Personality and psychotherapy*. New York: McGraw-Hill, 1950.

EFFECTS ON DISCRIMINATION PERFORMANCE OF SIMILARITY OF PREVIOUSLY ACQUIRED STIMULUS NAMES [1]

KATHRYN J. NORCROSS

If *S* learns discriminal verbal responses to a given set of similar stimuli in one task and is subsequently required to learn motor responses to these same stimuli presented in a transfer task, performance on that transfer task has been shown to be facilitated (6). It has been suggested that when verbal responses are learned to a set of environmental stimuli, the response-produced stimulation accompanying verbalization will contribute to each total stimulus complex. In conjunction with other principles in learning theory, facilitation in a transfer task may be predicted as an increasing function of the distinctiveness of the response-produced stimuli. On the assumption that the similarity of the responses is correlated with the similarity of the stimuli they produce, it would be predicted that Ss who learn similar names for the experimental stimuli will not do as well on the subsequent criterion task as Ss who learn distinctive names, since the effective stimulus complexes in the criterion task will be more distinctive the more dissimilar the responses learned in pretraining.

Pretraining experience involving one of two sets of stimulus names, either three nonsense syllables judged similar or three nonsense syllables judged dissimilar, was given by Gerjuoy (1). No advantage was indicated in the transfer task for the use of dissimilar names as compared to the use of similar names. The present experiments proposed to investigate further the effects of prior attachment of names of differing degrees of similarity to the stimuli to be discriminated in a transfer task. A within-Ss design was used in an attempt to control extraneous variables which are known to be factors in transfer, as well as to increase the precision of the experiments.

EXPERIMENT I

METHOD

Design. The experimental design is schematized in Table 1. Experimental stimuli were photographs of pen and ink line drawings of Indian children's faces—a pair of girls' faces and a pair of boys' faces. In pretraining, Ss learned highly similar nonsense names for one pair and dissimilar nonsense names for the other pair. Thirty kindergarten children [2] were randomly assigned to

[1] This research was the basis for a doctoral dissertation under the guidance and direction of Charles C. Spiker, who also contributed immeasurably to the paper in its present form.

Reprinted by permission from *Journal of Experimental Psychology*, 1958, *56*, 305–309.

[2] Appreciation is expressed to Hale C. Reid, Director of Curriculum and Instruction, for permission to obtain subjects in the Cedar Rapids Public School. Thanks are also due to John Manville, Principal, and to the staff of Hayes School for administrative assistance and cooperation in the collection of data for this study.

one of two subgroups used for purposes of counterbalancing. The transfer task, identical for all Ss, required S to push a different one of four buttons to each of the separately presented pictures. It was expected that the learning performance, in terms of correct responses, would be superior for the pair of stimuli with dissimilar names as compared to the pair with similar names.

TABLE 1 · Experimental Design

Pretraining		
Subgroup 1	Subgroup 2	Transfer task
Boy 1—zim	Boy 1—wug	Boy 1—button 1
Boy 2—zam	Boy 2—kos	Boy 2—button 2
Girl 1—wug	Girl 1—zim	Girl 1—button 3
Girl 2—kos	Girl 2—zam	Girl 2—button 4

Apparatus. The apparatus used in transfer was comprised of two main units. The stimulus unit, an engineering model of the Hunter Cardmaster, has been previously used and described by Norcross and Spiker (5). Briefly, this visual stimulus presentation device consists of a gray metal box $14 \times 14 \times 14$ in., with a 3×6-in. aperture in the front face. Plastic cards on which the stimulus pictures were mounted were presented before this aperture.

The response unit was below the stimulus aperture and in front of S. As seen by S, this consisted of a gray wooden box with the top panel sloping downward from the aperture. On this panel, four push-button switches were placed at what would be the corners of a 3-in. square. The two buttons appropriate for a given pair of pictures were diagonally located at the points of the square and were marked with colored tape—those for the Indian girls with yellow tape and those for the Indian boys with red tape. A small informational lamp was located immediately beside each button.

Procedure. The name learning was administered on Day 1. The E verbalized the names and indicated which name went with each picture, for the girls' and for the boys' pictures. Some practice was then given, without the pictures, in serial recitation of the two names appropriate for each pair. At E's discretion, the learning trials were begun in which a single picture was held up by E and S was asked for the name. When a name appropriate for a stimulus member of the other pair was given, E offered the names for the pair of which this picture was a member, and again asked for a response. If S did not give any name, E asked for a choice of the responses appropriate to the pair of which the picture was a member.

Following a correct response, the next picture was presented. If an incorrect name was given, S was first corrected and then shown the picture for which the name he had given was correct. The order was such that presentation of a boy's picture alternated regularly with presentation of a girl's picture. A trial refers to four successive presentations in which all pictures were shown. Pretraining on Day 1 was continued until a criterion was achieved of one trial in which S had correctly volunteered the names for all pictures. Pretraining was discontinued for any child who did not meet the criterion in 18 trials and his record was not considered.

On Day 2, one to three days later, the pictures were presented by means of the Cardmaster until the criterion of one errorless naming trial was again reached. Transfer learning was immediately begun. The S was asked to give the name and then push a button as each picture was presented. If a boy's picture was shown and either one of the boys' names was given, it was accepted. This was also true for the girls' pictures. If S gave a girl's name for a boy's picture, or vice versa, E reminded him of the appropriate pair of names.

Only one button response followed a picture presentation. After any pushing response, the informational light came on beside the button correct for that picture. A bell, located inside the response unit, was sounded if the correct button had been pushed. The E determined when a new picture was presented and which response would be appropriately rewarded or corrected on that presentation.

A block of four stimulus presentations in which all pictures were shown made up a trial. The order of presenting the stimuli was random with the restrictions that no one picture appear twice in succession and that the number of times three girls' pictures appeared in sequence equal the instances of a sequence of three boys' pictures. Fifteen transfer trials were administered, while all naming and pushing responses were recorded.

RESULTS

Verbal learning. An average of 7.37 trials, including criterial trials, was required to achieve criterion on Day 1. In those trials, the mean number of correct dissimilar-name responses was 8.67 and the mean number of correct similar-name responses was 7.40. The value of t obtained from a test of this difference was 1.09 ($P > .20$). Data of three Ss who did not meet criterion were not considered. An average of 3.17 relearning trials was given on Day 2. The mean difference between similar and dissimilar correct responses was .53 ($t = 1.70, P > .05$).

Motor learning. Preliminary analysis revealed that the subgroups used for

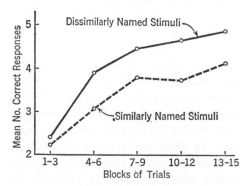

Figure 1. Mean number of correct motor responses in Exp. I.

counterbalancing did not differ in performance on the motor task and that they did not interact with experimental conditions. Therefore, the subgroup classifica-

tion was disregarded in further analyses. For all Ss combined, a mean of 20.20 correct motor responses followed presentation of those stimuli which possessed dissimilar names while a mean of 16.90 correct responses followed presentation of the stimuli with similar names. Figure 1 graphically shows the means of the number of correct responses in blocks of three trials for the two similarity conditions separately. A Treatment $\times$ Trials $\times$ Ss analysis (4) of correct responses is summarized in Table 2.

DISCUSSION

The results obtained confirmed the prediction that more correct responses would be made in the learning of discriminal motor responses to a pair of stimuli for which dissimilar names had been previously learned, as compared to a pair for which similar names had been learned. However, an examination of the verbal responses occurring in the motor task revealed that 103 incorrect dissimilar verbal responses were given while 341 incorrect similar responses were made. The mean difference of 8.27 is significant at the .001 level. The explanation could be offered that a greater number of motor

TABLE 2 · ANALYSIS OF VARIANCE OF CORRECT MOTOR RESPONSES, EXP. I

Source	df	MS	F
Treatments (T)	1	32.67	7.67*
Trials (t)	4	44.12	23.85**
Ss	29		
T $\times$ t	4	1.26	<1.00
t $\times$ Ss	116	1.85	
T $\times$ Ss	29	4.26	
T $\times$ t $\times$ Ss	116	1.50	
Total	299		

* $P < .01$.
** $P < .001$.

errors to the similarly named pair of stimuli occurred because the similar verbal cues were more inconsistently associated with their respective experimental stimuli than was true for the dissimilar verbal cues, and were therefore more irregularly reinforced with regard to the button responses. A second experiment was conducted which assured for each picture a consistent verbal response immediately prior to the motor response.

EXPERIMENT II

Experiment II differed from Exp. I only in that S was corrected for misnaming in the transfer task, and was required to verbalize the correct name prior to the button-pressing response. Twenty-six Ss were randomly assigned to one of the two subgroups.

RESULTS

Verbal learning. The mean number of trials on Day 1 was 7.54. An average of 3.31 relearning trials was required on Day 2. On neither day was there a significant difference between the number of correct similar and dissimilar responses

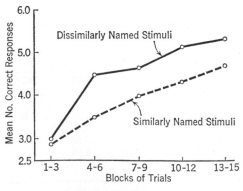

Figure 2. Mean number of correct motor responses in Exp. II.

$(P > .20)$. Data of three Ss who did not meet criterion were not considered.

Motor learning. A mean of 22.73 correct responses occurred to the pair with dissimilar names while a mean of 19.62 correct responses occurred to the pair with similar names. Table 3 summarizes a Treatment $\times$ Trials $\times$ Ss analysis of variance which again yielded both significant Treatment and Trials effects. Figure 2 depicts the results graphically.

DISCUSSION

Experiment II showed a significant difference in transfer performance for the two types of stimuli with names of differing degrees of similarity, a confirmation of Exp. I. These experiments were designed so that each S served in both experimental conditions. Thus, there should be no differential effects of warm-up and learning-to-learn, both known to be nonspecific factors in transfer of training (2, 7). Each S had the same amount of experience in learning to respond discriminally to the two pairs in pretraining. Therefore, any effects established by this experience, e.g., "observing responses" (3), should have transferred to the second task equally for both pairs of stimuli. It would not seem that any of these factors can be used to account for differences in performance for the two similarity conditions. In addition, Exp. II controlled verbalization so that S consistently gave the correct name immediately prior to the motor response. Thus it appears that it is the difference in similarity of the pairs of verbal responses which has differentially influenced performance on the criterion task.

It should be noted that the design of these experiments does not permit in-

TABLE 3 · Analysis of Variance of Correct Motor Responses, Exp. II

Source	df	MS	F
Treatments (T)	1	28.45	6.51*
Trials (t)	4	80.67	34.47**
Ss	25		
T × t	4	1.55	1.44
t × Ss	100	2.34	
T × Ss	25	4.37	
T × t × Ss	100	1.08	
Total	259		

* $P < .025$.
** $P < .001$.

ference as to whether the transfer was negative, positive, or both. In order to determine the direction of transfer in such an experiment a control condition is needed which involves criterion task stimuli for which the Ss have not previously learned names.

It has previously been shown that performance when learning motor responses to a set of stimuli will be affected if verbal responses have been learned to these same stimuli. This study suggests that, under certain conditions, the transfer effects depend at least in part upon the degree of generalization among the response-produced stimuli.

SUMMARY

This study measured the effects on discrimination performance in kindergarten Ss of the degree of similarity of previously acquired stimulus names. In Exp. I, Ss learned similar nonsense names to two stimuli and dissimilar nonsense names to two other stimuli. These same stimuli were then shown in a transfer task in which S was required to give a name and push a different one of four buttons in response to each stimulus singly presented. More incorrect names and fewer correct motor responses occurred to the similarly named pair as compared to the dissimilarly named pair.

Experiment II differed from Exp. I only

in that incorrect verbalizations were corrected prior to the occurrence of a motor response. Again, transfer performance with the dissimilarly named pictures was significantly superior to that for the pictures with similar names.

It was concluded that response-produced verbal cues may differentially affect a transfer task depending upon the degree of generalization among the verbal cue components.

REFERENCES

1. Gerjuoy, I. R.   Discrimination learning as a function of the similarity of the stimulus names. Unpublished doctor's dissertation, State Univer. of Iowa, 1953.

2. Hamilton, C. E.   The relationship between length of interval separating two learning tasks and performance on the second task. *J. exp. Psychol.*, 1950, 40, 613–621.

3. Kurtz, K. H.   Discrimination of complex stimuli: The relationships of training and test stimuli in transfer of discrimination. *J. exp. Psychol.*, 1955, 50, 283–292.

4. Lindquist, E. F.   *Design and analysis of experiments in psychology and education.* New York: Houghton Mifflin Co., 1953.

5. Norcross, K. J., & Spiker, C. C.   The effects of mediated associations on transfer in paired-associate learning. *J. exp. Psychol.*, 1958, 55, 129–134.

6. Spiker, C. C.   Experiments with children on the hypothesis of acquired distinctiveness and equivalence of cues. *Child Develpm.*, 1956, 27, 253–263.

7. Thune, L. E.   The effect of different types of preliminary activities on subsequent learning of paired-associate material. *J. exp. Psychol.*, 1950, 40, 423–438.

CHILDREN'S CONCEPT OF MIDDLE-SIZEDNESS AND PERFORMANCE ON THE INTERMEDIATE SIZE PROBLEM

CHARLES C. SPIKER,
IRMA R. GERJUOY,
WINIFRED O. SHEPARD

THERE HAS BEEN a recent increasing interest in the relationship between the degree to which verbal names for stimuli are available to S and his subsequent discrimination performance with these stimuli. Several experiments with adults (3, 5, 7, 10) and with children (2, 6, 11) have shown facilitation of discrimination learning following the learning of distinctive verbal responses to the discriminal stimuli. These experiments have involved nonrelational stimuli and verbal responses. The theoretical notions that have been utilized are "stimulus predifferentiation" as proposed by Gagné and Baker (5) and "acquired distinctiveness of cues" as elaborated by Dollard and Miller (4).

The present experiment attempts to determine the effect of the possession of a relational concept, middle-sizedness, upon the rate of learning to select the intermediate sized of three stimuli. Two groups of Ss were selected in terms of their performance on a test designed to determine whether or not the concept was understood. One-half of those Ss who under-

stood and one-half of those who did not understand the concept were given a discrimination problem requiring a relational solution—that is to say, a problem in which the absolute size of the intermediate stimulus varied from trial to trial. The other halves of each of these groups were given a similar problem in which the intermediate stimulus was of the same size from trial to trial. Assuming that the possession of the relational concept facilitates relational learning, it is expected that the difference between the concept and no-concept groups will be greater on the relational than on the nonrelational problem. Statistically stated, the hypothesis is that there will be a significant interaction between level of understanding the concept and the type of criterion task.

METHOD

SUBJECTS

The Ss were children from the preschool laboratories of the Iowa Child Welfare Research Station. They ranged in age from 40 to 67 months. The majority had had previous experience in experiments requiring discrimination learning with two-stimulus problems. So far as could be determined, none

Reprinted by permission from *Journal of Comparative and Physiological Psychology*, 1956, 49, 416–419.

had served in experiments requiring the selection of the middle-sized of three stimuli. The majority of Ss were therefore familiar with similar experimental procedures at the time the experiment was begun, and in addition, the Es spent several hours in the preschool groups becoming acquainted with the Ss prior to the experiment.

PRELIMINARY TEST

From one to two weeks prior to the main experiment, 84 Ss were given a pretest during which E attempted to elicit from them the verbal response, "middle-sized" or "medium-sized." A total of six cards was constructed for this purpose, each having three stimulus elements which were homogeneous in form but different in area in the ratio 1:2:4. Each of three different forms (triangles, trapezoids, and circles) was represented twice in the series of six cards. These cards included two (one with triangles and one with trapezoids) with elements having areas of 8, 4, and 2 sq. in.: two (circles and trapezoids), of 4, 2, and 1 sq. in.; and two (circles and triangles), of 2, 1, and $\frac{1}{2}$ sq. in.

The E first presented to S each of the six cards, saying each time, "This is the big one (pointing to the largest element), this is the little one (pointing to the smallest element), and this is the ———?" If S verbalized "middle-sized," "medium-sized," or "medium one," to each of the six cards, the pretest was discontinued. If S failed to verbalize one of these names to each card, the test was continued by instructing S to put a finger on the "middle-sized" one. When all six cards had been presented in this way, the pretest was discontinued regardless of S's performance.[1]

On the basis of their performance on the pretest, two groups of 30 Ss each were selected. In one group, the "concept" group, were placed those Ss who responded consistently with one of the conventional terms for middle-sizedness. Those Ss were put in the "no-concept" group who did not use the conventional terms at all, who were not able to point consistently to the middle-sized stimulus upon instruction, and who did not select consistently the large or small stimulus upon being instructed to select the middle-sized stimulus.[2]

STIMULI FOR THE MAIN EXPERIMENT

The stimuli were squares cut from black construction paper and pasted on white cardboard. The areas of the squares were $\frac{1}{4}$, $\frac{1}{2}$, 1, 2, 4, 8, and 16 sq. in. The squares were arranged on the backgrounds in five groups of three in such a way that the ratio of the areas, from the smallest to the largest, was always 1:2:4. The three squares in each of the five resulting sets (size-series) were placed in the six possible spatial orders, generating a total of 30 cards differing from each other in the absolute sizes of the squares and/or in the spatial positions of the large, small, and middle-sized squares.

These stimulus materials were so arranged that two tasks were formed. Each S given Task A (the nonrelational task) was presented with just one of the five size-series so that the correct (middle-sized) stimulus was of the same absolute size from trial to trial. The six cards in a given size-series were presented to S five times each, providing a total of 30 trials. Each S given Task B (the relational task) was given all five size-series, the 30 cards being presented in a random order, providing a total of 30 trials.

---

[1] Additional work suggests that it is advisable to use a third phase of the test for those Ss who respond consistently in the first phase with a name other than conventional terms for middle-sizedness, e.g., "mama one," "The kind of large one," etc. In the third phase, E instructs S to point to the "mama one," "the kind of large one," etc. Some such Ss are able to select consistently the middle-sized stimulus, and subsequently tend to learn the discrimination problems in much the same way as Ss who use the conventional names.

[2] This latter criterion was adopted after discovering that Ss who, in the second phase of the pretest, tended to respond consistently to the large or to the small stimuli subsequently learned the discrimination problem in much the same way as Ss who used the concept middle-sized correctly. Presumably, such Ss have had sufficient experience with the relational concepts "larger than" and "smaller than" that they are able to learn rather quickly to respond to the one that is not the larger and not the smaller of three stimuli.

Thus, Task A required the Ss to select the middle-sized stimulus on each trial, and this stimulus was always of the same absolute size from trial to trial. Task B required the Ss to select the middle-sized stimulus on each trial, but the correct stimulus varied in absolute size from trial to trial. Or, again, while each S given Task A was required to select, on each of 30 trials, a stimulus of a given size when it was presented with a larger and a smaller one, each S given Task B was in effect presented with five such problems and allowed only six trials on each.

EXPERIMENTAL DESIGN

The experiment was designed as a 2 $\times$ 2 factorial, with Tasks A and B constituting one factor, the two levels of understanding the concept "middle-sized" representing the second. Fifteen Ss from each concept level were assigned at random to each of the two tasks, thus yielding four groups. One group, C-A, consisted of Ss who knew the concept and were given Task A; a second group, C-B, who knew the concept and were given Task B; a third, NC-A, not knowing the concept, given Task A; and a fourth, NC-B, not knowing the concept and given Task B. Each fifth of the Ss in Groups C-A and NC-A was assigned just one of the five stimulus size-series. This procedure was adopted in order to control for the possibility that the five size-series differed in difficulty due to differential discriminability of the stimuli.

PROCEDURE

The S was brought into the experimental room and given the preliminary test. Following the test, he was shown the contents of a bag of dime-store toys and told that he would later play a game in which he would have a chance to win one of the toys. A few days later, he returned to the experimental room and was seated at a small table across from E. The S was instructed that he was going to play a game in which he would be able to win some money and that when he had won enough money, he would be able

to buy one of the toys. The stimulus cards were then presented one at a time. The S was instructed on each trial to put a finger on one of the squares. If the square selected by S was the middle-sized one, E gave S a toy coin. If the selected square was either the large or the small one, S was not given a coin and E pointed to the middle-sized one, informing S that it was the correct one. The term "middle-sized" was never used in E's instructions to S. The E recorded on prepared record sheets each of S's choices, in terms of both the spatial position of the choice and the relative size of the stimulus selected. The order of presenting the stimulus complexes was the same for all Ss receiving Task A, and for all Ss receiving Task B.

RESULTS

The number of correct responses in 30 trials was determined for each S. The means and standard deviations for the four groups are presented in Table 1. An analysis of variance was performed and the results are shown in Table 2. Task B was significantly more difficult than Task A ($p < .001$), and the "concept" groups performed significantly better than the "no-concept" groups ($p < .001$). The interaction between concept levels and tasks is significant at the .025 level, indicating that the difference between the concept

TABLE 1· Means and Standard Deviations of Number of Correct Responses in 30 Trials

| Learning task | Concept of middle-sizedness | | | |
| | Concept | | No-concept | |
	Mean	SD	Mean	SD
A	24.60	7.72	22.60	7.65
B	21.40	8.81	10.20	2.47

levels was significantly greater for Task B than for Task A.

As may be noted in Table 1, the standard deviation of Group NC-B is less than those for the other groups. This dif-

TABLE 2 · SUMMARY OF ANALYSIS OF VARIANCE OF NUMBER OF CORRECT RESPONSES IN 30 TRIALS

Source	df	Mean square	F	p
Tasks (T)	1	653.4	12.91	.001
Concepts (C)	1	912.6	18.04	.001
T × C	1	317.6	6.28	.025
Within cells	56	50.6		
Total	59			

TABLE 3 · NUMBER OF Ss IN EACH GROUP MEETING OR NOT MEETING CRITERION OF TEN CORRECT OF LAST TWELVE CHOICES

Group	Learners	Nonlearners	Total
C-A	12	3	15
NC-A	12	3	15
C-B	10	5	15
NC-B	0	15	15

ference proves significant at less than the .01 level. Thus, it seems desirable to supplement the analysis of variance with nonparametric tests to determine whether or not the differences exposed by the analysis of variance may be attributed entirely to differences in variabilities. A criterion of 10 correct responses in the last 12 trials was arbitrarily chosen to define learning. Table 3 presents the number of Ss who met and the number who did not meet this criterion within each group. The χ^2 obtained for the 2 × 4 table was 26.9, ($p < .001, df = 3$). When Group NC-B is eliminated from the table, the resulting χ^2 is 0.96 ($p > .50, df = 2$). When Group NC-B is compared with the other three groups combined, the χ^2 corrected for continuity is 22.9 ($p < .001, df = 1$).

The Mann-Whitney U test (9) was applied to compare Group NC-B with C-B and with NC-A, using the number of correct responses in 30 trials as the response measure. The obtained U in each case was significant at less than the .01 level. Groups C-A and NC-B, on the other

hand, were compared by the more sensitive t test. The resulting t value was .34 ($p > .70$).

The analyses indicate that Group NC-B performed at a significantly lower level than did the other three groups, whereas the hypothesis is tenable that the latter performed at about the same level.

DISCUSSION

The results of the experiment support the expectation that Ss who understand the verbal concept of middle-sizedness perform significantly better on the relational task than Ss who do not understand the concept, and that understanding the concept did not appreciably affect performance on a task that could be solved on a nonrelational basis. The question arises as to the plausibility of accounting for the difference between Groups C-B and NC-B in terms other than the possession of the concept. In any experiment in which the major variable is varied by subject selection rather than by experimental manipulation, an unequivocal answer to such a question cannot be given. In the present case, it is possible to eliminate one obvious possibility— chronological age. Although the concept groups averaged approximately 5½ months older than the no-concept groups, ($p < .01$), the correlation between chronological age and number of correct responses in 30 trials is .08 for the nonrelational task and −.05 for the relational task.

It seems worth while to point out the relationship between the present experiment and the ones conducted by Kuenne (8) and by Alberts and Ehrenfreund (1). These investigators were concerned with the study of transposition behavior of children in the two-stimulus size problem as a function of mental age and chronological age, on the assumption that these variables reflected concept ability. Task B in this experiment may be conceived as a three-stimulus transposition problem, in which transposition occurs or does not occur from one trial to the next. The concept levels are substituted for the MA or CA levels used by the earlier investigators. Thus, the results obtained support the contention of Kuenne (8) that if S has appropriate concepts available (e.g., possession of the concept of middle-sizedness), transposition will be more likely to occur.

SUMMARY

The experiment was designed to test the hypothesis that the learning of a discrimination problem involving selection of the intermediate sized of three stimuli, where the absolute size of the stimuli vary from trial to trial, is facilitated by Ss' possession of the verbal concept middle-sized. Sixty children were classified into two equal-size groups in terms of their levels of understanding of the concept middle-sizedness. One-half of each of these two groups was rewarded for selecting the middle-sized of three stimuli, where the absolute size of the stimuli varied from trial to trial. The other half of each of these groups was rewarded for selecting the middle-sized of three stimuli, where the absolute size of the stimuli remained constant from trial to trial. The results indicated that an understanding of the concept of middle-sizedness facilitated learning of the relational task more than it did the learning of the nonrelational task. These results were considered in relation to the findings of Kuenne (8) and Alberts and Ehrenfreund (1).

REFERENCES

1. ALBERTS, ELIZABETH, & EHRENFREUND, D. Transposition in children as a function of age. *J. exp. Psychol.*, 1951, *41*, 30–38.
2. CANTOR, G. N. The effects of three types of pretraining on discrimination learning in children. *J. exp. Psychol.*, 1955, *49*, 339–342.
3. CANTOR, JOAN H. Amount of pretraining as a factor in stimulus predifferentiation and performance set. *J. exp. Psychol.*, 1955, *50*, 180–184.
4. DOLLARD, J., & MILLER, N. E. *Personality and psychotherapy*. New York: McGraw-Hill, 1950.
5. GAGNÉ, R. M., & BAKER, KATHERINE E. Stimulus predifferentiation as as factor in transfer of training. *J. exp. Psychol.*, 1950, *40*, 439–451.
6. GERJUOY, IRMA R. Discrimination learning as a function of the similarity of the stimulus names. Unpublished doctor's dissertation, State Univer. of Iowa, 1953.
7. GOSS, A. E. Transfer as a function of type and amount of preliminary experience with task stimuli. *J. exp. Psychol.*, 1953, *46*, 419–428.
8. KUENNE, MARGARET R. Experimental investigation of the relation of language to transposition behavior in young children. *J. exp. Psychol.*, 1946, *36*, 471–490.
9. MANN, H. B., & WHITNEY, D. R. On a test of whether one of two random variables is stochastically larger than the other. *Ann. math. Statist.*, 1947, *18*, 50–60.
10. ROSSMAN, IRMA L., & GOSS, A. E. The acquired distinctiveness of

cues: the role of discriminative verbal responses in facilitating the acquisition of discriminative motor responses. *J. exp. Psychol.*, 1951, 42, 173–182.

11. SHEPARD, WINIFRED O. The effects of verbal pretraining on discrimination learning in preschool children. Unpublished doctor's dissertation, State Univer. of Iowa, 1954.

REVERSAL AND NONREVERSAL SHIFTS

IN KINDERGARTEN CHILDREN [1]

TRACY S. KENDLER
HOWARD H. KENDLER

THE PURPOSE of this study was to determine whether kindergarten children would respond to the experimental task in a manner consistent with a single unit or a mediational S–R theory of discrimination learning. The experimental task involved learning an initial discrimination between stimuli that differed on two dimensions. Only one dimension was relevant, i.e., rewarded. After the criterion was reached a second discrimination was presented. For reversal shift Ss the same dimension remained relevant but the reward patterns were reversed. For the nonreversal shift Ss a previously irrelevant dimension became relevant.

The single-unit S–R theory is a name applied to formulations that, like Spence's (1936) discrimination learning theory, assume a direct association be-tween physical stimuli and overt responses. This theory predicts that requiring an organism to make a response opposite to that which it has previously learned, as in a reversal shift, should result in slower learning than a nonreversal shift. Kelleher (1956), using albino rats as Ss, has corroborated this prediction.

Spence has been quite explicit about limiting his predictions to inarticulate organisms. Human beings learn to make verbal or symbolic responses, overt or covert, to physical stimuli. These responses produce stimuli that mediate between the external stimulus and the overt response. Kendler and D'Amato (1955) applied a mediational theory to predict the results of reversal and nonreversal shifts in a concept formation study on college students, using a card sorting technique. They reasoned that "a reversal shift should occur at a more rapid rate than a nonreversal shift because at the completion of the learning of the first con-

[1] This research was sponsored by a grant from the National Science Foundation.

Reprinted by permission from *Journal of Experimental Psychology*, 1959, 58, 56–60.

cept, the symbolic cues appropriate to the second concept were available to *Ss* in the reversal shift groups" (1955, p. 169). Their prediction was confirmed. Thus, if a card sorting situation can be compared with a discrimination learning situation, it appears that reversal shift results in positive transfer for human adults and negative transfer for rats.

In the present research Kelleher's experimental procedure and design have been adapted for use with children to determine whether it would be possible to identify a transitional process in the development of concept formation in children from behavior rendered accountable by a single-unit S–R theory to the more complex responses associated with the mediational-sequential S–R theories.

METHOD

Subjects. The *Ss* were 122 kindergarten children (age range from 58 to 78 mo.) from Willets Road Public School, Nassau County, New York. Firty-three of the children were girls and 69 were boys. Two of the girls were eliminated because of their failure to learn the first discrimination. All *Ss* were randomly distributed to the various groups without regard to age and sex.

Apparatus. The apparatus was an unpainted turntable made of a board 12 × 16 in., mounted on a swivel base and divided in half by a perpendicular plywood board 8 in. high and 15 in. wide. On one of the halves were two felt-padded depressions 1 in. sq. and 4 in. apart. The marble that served as the token reward was placed on one of the pads and covered by the opaque discriminanda. While these manipulations were in process the felt-padded half of the turntable was toward *E*. The perpendicular board served to screen *E*'s actions. When the stimuli were correctly arranged a swinging screen was brought down, concealing the discriminanda as they were swivelled into place in front of *S*.

The discriminanda for the initial training of the experimental groups and the test training for all groups were four metal tumblers 2½ in. in diameter that varied both in height and brightness. Two of the tumblers were 6¼ in. high (T). The other two were 4¾ in. high (S). One of each size was enamelled black (B) and the other white (W). The discriminanda for the initial training of the control group were four gray enamelled metal cookie cutters, two diamond and two circle shaped. One of each shape had two round, colored paper dots pasted on its upper surface.

The final items of apparatus were two marble boards, each with 50 holes capable of holding the marbles won by the child.

Procedure. Children were run individually in a room in which *E* and *S* were alone. The *E* sat facing *S* with the apparatus on a small table between them. When the child was comfortably seated *E* said, "This is the game we are going to play, (child's name). Before we start, listen carefully and I will tell you how the game is played. See, there are two things here. When we start the game you will choose one of them and pick it up. If you are right you will find a marble under it. If you are wrong then you won't find anything under it. Each time you may choose only one. Then I will close it, turn it around like this and then you will have another turn. But on each turn you may choose only one. The game is to see how soon you can get a marble every time you choose. If you get the marble you put it into one of these holes. When we finish the game you may choose one of the prizes over there." The *E* allowed time for *S* to survey the assortment of prizes, that consisted of two chocolate bars (one with almonds and one without), a bag of salted peanuts, a box of raisins, a box of animal crackers, and 10 gold charms. Then *E* said, "Remember, the game is to see how soon you can get a marble every time you choose." This sentence was repeated from time to time during the course of the experiment. All but eight *Ss* completed the experiment in one session. Of these eight *Ss* who required two sessions, four were nonreversal *Ss*, three were reversal *Ss*, and one was a control *S*.

For the training discrimination, Ss were randomly assigned to one of three groups. The 40 Ss of the control group were presented with the shape discrimination. For half, the diamond was positive, for the others the circle was positive. The presence or absence of the dots was an irrelevant cue. The experimental Ss were each presented with the tumblers paired as follows: SB-TW and TB-SW. Forty Ss learned to respond to brightness (B vs. W). For half, B was positive, for the other half W was positive. The remaining 40 Ss learned to respond to height, half to T and half to S.

The test discrimination was presented immediately after the criterion was reached, with no change in instructions or interruption in the procedure. Each of the experimental groups was divided equally into a reversal (R) and nonreversal (NR) group, equated for initial speed of learning. The same tumblers used in the initial discrimination were used as stimuli, but they were now paired so that on any one presentation they differed on only *one* stimulus dimension.[2] The R Ss whose initial training was on the brightness dimension and NR Ss whose initial training was on the height dimension were presented with TB-TW and SB-SW successively. For the R group, if W was previously correct B was now rewarded, and vice versa. For the NR group, half were rewarded for B and half for W choices.

Similarly, the R Ss for whom height was initially relevant and NR Ss for whom brightness was relevant were now presented with SW-TW and SB-TB. For the R group, if S was previously correct T was now rewarded, and vice versa. For the NR group half were rewarded for T and half for S choices. In short, the reversal Ss were required to respond to a stimulus feature which had been consistently nonreinforced. The nonreversal Ss were required to re-

[2] Buss (1953) has pointed out that if the stimuli in the second discrimination are paired as they were in the first, the nonreversal shift Ss are intermittently reinforced for the previously correct response. This change in the manner of presentation, which was adapted from Kelleher (1956), serves to minimize the retarding effect of such inadvertent reinforcement of a response that is no longer correct.

TABLE 1 · MEAN NUMBER OF TRIALS TO CRITERION ON TEST DISCRIMINATION FOR EACH DIMENSION

Group	Dimension		
	Size	Brightness	Combined
Reversal	13.5	16.8	15.2
Nonreversal	7.5	17.0	12.2
Control	6.2	7.9	7.1

spond to a stimulus feature that had received approximately the same number of reinforcements as nonreinforcements.

As for the control group, half was presented with TB-TW and SB-SW, with one-quarter rewarded for B and the other for S. The other half of the control group was presented with SW-TW and SB-TB, with one-quarter rewarded for T and the other for S.

Each cue appeared an equal number of times on the right and left. No combination of two cues appeared together on more than two consecutive trials. To reduce position effects during initial training, the position of the stimuli remained unchanged from trial to trial until a correct response was made. This practice was maintained only during the training and *not* during the test discrimination. The criterion of learning was 9 out of 10 successive correct responses.

RESULTS AND DISCUSSION

The response measure used was the number of trials required to reach the criterion. The means for the training discrimination for the R and NR groups were 18.77 and 17.77, respectively. This difference was not statistically significant.

Table 1 reports the data of the test discrimination. Five Ss, three in the R group and two in the NR group, did not meet the criterion. Their training was discontinued after 100 trials, and they were arbitrarily assigned a score of 100. Two of these Ss, one R and one NR, were among those who required two sessions.

Because the distributions were

skewed and the variances heterogeneous, a $\sqrt{X + .5}$ transformation was applied to the raw data to prepare them for a factorial analysis of variance. Neither of the main effects (the type of transfer or the dimensions transferred to), nor the interaction between them was statistically significant.

The theory that is based on the assumption of a direct connection between the physical stimulus and the overt response (the single-unit theory) predicts that reversal should be slower than nonreversal or control. The mediational theory predicts that reversal should be faster than nonreversal. Our results confirm neither prediction. One conclusion we can draw is that neither theory is applicable, but another more interesting possibility is that both apply. The failure to achieve results consistent with either those obtained from rats (Kelleher, 1956) or from college students (Kendler & D'Amato, 1955) may be due to the fact that these children are in a transitional stage of development, in which these tasks lead some to function on a single-unit S–R basis, while others are making relevant mediated responses. If these two groups were about evenly divided, they would yield total results such as we obtained.

No MA scores were available. But there was a measure of performance that was perhaps more relevant to the task in hand; namely, the number of trials to criterion in the training discrimination. The Ss were sorted into two groups on the basis of their initial performance on each dimension. Those scoring above the median, i.e., taking more trials to learn, were labelled slow learners. The Ss scoring below the median were labelled fast learners. The results of fast and slow learners were analyzed separately and are presented in Table 2.[3]

The difference between fast and slow learners could be accounted for along two possible lines. One of these is that the speed of initial learning reflects differences in general intelligence or ability to learn. If this were the case, it would be expected that results of the test discrimination for the fast and slow learners of the control group would show a difference that reflected the ability displayed in the initial discrimination. The obtained difference is both negligible and statistically unreliable, casting some doubt on the general learning ability explanation.

TABLE 2 · MEAN NUMBER OF TRIALS TO CRITERION ON TEST DISCRIMINATION FOR Ss SCORING ABOVE AND BELOW THE MEDIAN ON THE TRAINING DISCRIMINATION

| Group | PERFORMANCE ON TRAINING DISCRIMINATION | |
	Above median (slow learners)	Below median (fast learners)
Reversal	24.4	6.0
Nonreversal	9.0	15.5
Control	7.3	6.8
Combined	13.6	9.4

Another possibility is that fast learners approached the experimental task with verbal labels for the correct stimulus already strongly attached, due to prior experience with these stimuli. Liublinskaya (1957) demonstrated that attaching a verbal label to the distinguishing feature of the discrimination greatly facilitates learning. The slow learners in the present experiment may not have had appropriate

---

[3] The same analysis using errors instead of trials to criterion produced essentially the same result.

TABLE 3 · ANALYSIS OF VARIANCE OF TEST
DISCRIMINATION SCORES TRANSFORMED TO
$$\sqrt{X + .5}$$

Source	df	MS	F
Type of transfer (R, NR, C)	2	12.17	2.14
Initial learning (fast, slow)	1	10.00	1.76
Interaction	2	22.74	4.00*
Within cells	114	5.69	

* $P = <.05$.

verbal labels as strongly attached to the relevant stimulus as did the fast learners.

Regardless of whether the difference between fast and slow learners is based on general learning ability or the availability of relevant mediating responses (which may in the long run prove to be synonymous with learning ability), the expectation was that fast learners would, like the college students, perform according to the mediational S–R theory, and therefore reversal would be faster than nonreversal. Slow learners were expected to behave more like Kelleher's rats, in accordance with the single-unit S–R theory, and therefore reversal would be slower than nonreversal. Table 2 shows the confirmation of these expectations. The analysis of variance of the transformed scores,[4] as presented in Table 3, suggests that the predicted interaction is statistically reliable ($P < .05$). Statistical subdivision of the interaction term (Walker & Lev, 1953) revealed that the variation in this term arose almost exclusively from the shift in the relative efficiency of the reversal and nonreversal conditions for the fast and slow learners.

[4] A similar analysis of variance was performed on the raw scores to test for possible distortions due to the transformation. The raw scores yielded almost identical results.

On the basis of the results of the total groups and the analysis into fast and slow learners, it seems reasonable to conclude that these children, taken as a group, were in the process of developing mediating responses relevant to this task and that some were further along than others.

SUMMARY

The experiment compared the performance of kindergarten children in reversal and nonreversal shifts in a discrimination learning situation. The results obtained for the total group failed to support either a single-unit or mediational S–R theory, since there was no significant difference between reversal and nonreversal shifts. When the group was divided into fast and slow learners on the basis of their performance on the initial training series, suggestive differences were revealed. Fast initial learners responded in a manner consistent with a mediational S–R theory, i.e., reversal was faster than nonreversal. Slow initial learners responded in a manner consistent with a single-unit S–R theory, i.e., reversal was slower than nonreversal.

REFERENCES

BUSS, A. H. Rigidity as a function of reversal and nonreversal shifts in the learning of successive discriminations. *J. exp. Psychol.*, 1953, *45*, 75–81.

KELLEHER, R. T. Discrimination learning as a function of reversal and nonreversal shifts. *J. exp. Psychol.*, 1956, *51*, 379–384.

KENDLER, H. H., & D'AMATO, M. F. A comparison of reversal shifts and nonreversal shifts in human concept formation behavior. *J. exp. Psychol.*, 1955, *49*, 165–174.

LIUBLINSKAYA, A. A. Development of children's speech and thought. In B.

Simon (Ed.), *Psychology in the Soviet Union.* Stanford: Stanford Univer. Press, 1957. Pp. 197–204.

SPENCE, K .W.   The nature of discrimina-

tion learning in animals. *Psychol. Rev.,* 1936, *43,* 427–449.

WALKER, H. M., & LEV, J.   *Statistical inference.* New York: Holt, 1953.

THE EFFECT OF VERBAL TRAINING ON INITIAL GENERALIZATION TENDENCIES

WINIFRED O. SHEPARD

IT HAS OFTEN BEEN OBSERVED that Ss who learn a given response to a stimulus tend to generalize it to other stimuli which are physically similar to it. The amount of generalization decreases as the similarity between training and test stimuli decreases. This has been called primary generalization.

There are, however, other bases for generalization. Birge (*1*), Jeffrey (*4*), Murdock (*5*), Eisman (*3*) and Shipley (*6*) have all demonstrated that learning a common response for two or more stimuli increases the tendency to generalize other responses among them. This is known as mediated or secondary generalization.

In these studies, however, not much attention has been paid to the nature of the stimuli involved and so a question is raised as to whether or not there is a relationship between the similarity of the

Reprinted by permission from *Child Development*, 1956, *27*, 173–178.

stimuli and the effectiveness of a mediating response. Concretely one might ask, "When Ss are taught a common response to two highly dissimilar stimuli, is the tendency to generalize other responses between these stimuli raised to the same level as when Ss are taught a common response to two less dissimilar stimuli?"

The present study is a beginning attempt to answer this question. It is concerned with getting an indication as to whether or not a relationship exists between stimulus similarity and the effectiveness of a mediating response. To do this, a training stimulus and a series of test stimuli of increasing dissimilarity from it were used. An attempt was made to determine first the initial or primary generalization gradient and then to see how the gradient would be affected by teaching Ss a common name for the training stimulus and each of the test stimuli. It was predicted that such training would increase the amount of generalization at all test points, but no prediction was made as to the amount of increase that would be observed at each point.

SUBJECTS

Fifty-nine children from the Iowa Preschool laboratories and the Parent's Playschool in Iowa City were used as subjects. All were between the ages of $3\frac{1}{2}$ and 6 years at the time of participation.

APPARATUS

The apparatus was a rectangular black box $14\frac{1}{2}$ in. wide, $17\frac{1}{2}$ in. high and $10\frac{1}{2}$ in. deep. A circular flashed opal glass opening 4 in. in diameter was located in the upper center front of the box. Inside the box, behind the aperture, was a set of wooden compartments each containing a 75-watt projector lamp. It was possible to insert colored glass filters into grooves in front of these bulbs and thus project a colored light onto the glass in the aperture. A series of such lights could be presented manually by operating a push button or automatically through the activation of a stepping relay by two Hunter Timers.

There was also a small push button set in a wooden block which was placed on the table between S and the apparatus. Pressure on this button constituted the response measure.

STIMULI

Five 2 by 2 in. colored glass filters manufactured by the Corning Glass works were used as stimuli. They were a red, No. 2030, a reddish orange, No. 2418, an orange, No. 3480, a yellow, No. 3307 and a blue, No. 5030. Six staff members and graduate students at the Child Welfare Research Station judged that the stimuli as listed above constituted a series of decreasing similarity from the red.

PROCEDURE

The Ss were randomly divided into three experimental groups of 18 each and one control group of five. Each experimental group was tested twice for its tendency to generalize the button pushing response from the training stimulus to one of the test stimuli. The first test was given before S learned a common name for the training and test stimuli. The second test was given afterwards. The control group was also given two generalization tests, using the third test point, but members of this group had no intervening verbal training.

Each S was brought into a darkened experimental room and seated at a small table. Directly in front of him was the push button. About 18 in. behind that was the main apparatus with the aperture slightly above eye level.

Stage 1 for all Ss consisted of 24 random presentations of the red and blue stimuli. Ss were taught to push the button when the red light came on and not to push it when the blue light came on. E gave verbal reinforcement, "Right," or punishment, "Wrong," after each response throughout this stage.

Stage 2 for all Ss was an initial generalization test. Three presentations of the appropriate test stimulus for each group were randomly interspersed among the red and blue stimuli in a series of 12 presentations. No reinforcement for any response was given during this series. During both Stages 1 and 2 the lights were automatically presented with a 4-

second intra- and inter-presentation interval.

Stage 3 was given to all experimental groups, but omitted for the control group. Ss were given 24 presentations during which the red, blue and test stimuli were randomly interspersed. They were taught the name "Mo" for the red and the test stimuli and the name "Lee" for the blue stimulus. Then there was a rest period during which Ss were allowed to choose from among a group of dime store items the "prize" they wished to win when the session was over. After the rest, they were again given the three light series and asked for the name each time. Control Ss were merely given the rest period and allowed to choose their prizes.

Stage 4 for the experimental groups consisted of 10 random presentations of the red and blue lights. Ss were required to say the name of each light as soon as it came on and then to push the button for red and not to push for blue. As in Stage 1, verbal reinforcement was given throughout. Control group subjects were given these 10 presentations but were not, of course, required to say any names.

Stage 5, the final generalization test, was given to all subjects and duplicated Stage 2, except that experimental subjects were required to say the name of each light as it came on. During Stages

4 and 5 the lights were automatically presented. They were on for six seconds and off for four. The increase in the amount of time the lights were on was necessary to allow the experimental groups time to verbalize the names.

RESULTS AND DISCUSSION

The results are given in Table 1 and are graphically represented in Figure 1. Table 1 shows the proportion of pushing responses made to each stimulus on both the initial and final generalization tests. These figures represent the number of times the pushing response was made to each stimulus divided by the number of times that stimulus was presented. Figure 1 shows the mean number of generalized pushing responses made to each of the test points both before and after verbal training. It was necessary to use proportions in Table 1 since the number of times the red and blue stimuli were presented differed from the number of times the test stimuli were presented. Figure 1, however, deals only with the test points, each of which was presented an equal number of times; thus means are used in presenting the data. It is immediately apparent from both the table and the figure that, in terms of observed results, the prediction was confirmed. At

TABLE 1 · PROPORTION OF PUSHING RESPONSES MADE TO EACH STIMULUS BY ALL GROUPS ON INITIAL AND FINAL GENERALIZATION TESTS

	Red	Blue	Test Point 1	Test Point 2	Test Point 3
Initial test					
Experimental groups	.98	.01	.80	.24	.22
Control group	.96	.00	..	..	.33
Final test					
Experimental groups	.97	.03	.91	.44	.65
Control group	1.00	.00	..	..	.33

every test point there was more generalization after than before verbal training. The control group which received no verbal training showed no change at all.

In view of the extreme skewness of the data at each point, Dixon and Mood's nonparametric Sign Test (2) was used to test for statistical significance. For each experimental group the amount of generalization before and after verbal training was compared. Ss tested at point

1 showed no significant increase. Ss tested at points 2 and 3 did show significant increases with the respective probabilities of occurrence being 5 per cent and .05 per cent. It seems likely that the failure to find a significant increase at point 1 can be attributed to a ceiling effect. Ss tested at this point had such strong generalization tendencies initially that there was little opportunity to demonstrate an increase. In view of the small N in the con-

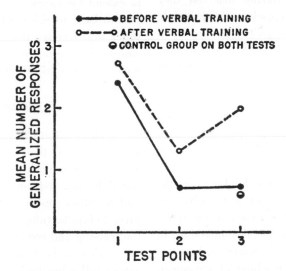

Figure 1. Mean number of generalized responses at each test point.

trol group, no test of significance was made. It is noteworthy, however, that not one of the Ss in this group changed at all from the first to the second test indicating that mere continued exposure to a set of stimuli will not, per se, result in increased generalization.

The notion of mediated generalization has been commonly used to explain generalization increases of the type found in this study. According to this view, the mediating response, in this case the name "Mo," itself produces a stimulus which

occurs in conjunction with each of the external stimuli to which it has been conditioned. The presence of this common response-produced cue in two (or more) stimulus complexes is said to make these complexes more similar to each other than are the external stimuli alone and hence there is more tendency to generalize among them. It follows then that the optimum situation for demonstrating mediated generalization is one in which Ss are forced to make the mediating response overtly during the generalization test, thus maximizing the probability that the response-produced cue will be present. These conditions were met in this study. Nevertheless, about half the Ss in each group showed no increase in generalization from initial to final test. A possible explanation for this lies in the operation of competing and incompatible response tendencies. Almost all the Ss who showed no increase were those who showed no generalization at all during the initial test. It appeared that during that test they formulated for themselves the principle that one should not pull to the test light. Many, in fact, verbalized this principle. Subsequent presentations of the test light during the final test elicited both the principle and the mediating response. Apparently the tendency to react to the principle was stronger than the tendency to react in accordance with the stimulation provided by the mediating response.

Viewed as a whole, however, the study provides at least a tentative answer to the question raised in the introduction and suggests the direction in which future research should go. Figure 1 indicates that the teaching of a common response, in this case the word "Mo," to the training stimulus and stimuli of decreasing similarity from it did raise generalization tendencies at all points. However, it is noteworthy that neither of the two furthest points was raised to the level of the nearest point indicating that there is a relationship between the similarity of two stimuli and the effectiveness of a mediating response. Unfortunately, with the present data it was impossible to make a precise statistical test of this observed interaction between training and test point. A future study using more tests at each point and instructions designed to

minimize the buildup of interfering response tendencies should yield data amenable to such analysis. Moreover, since these data do tentatively indicate the presence of the sought after relationship, it would now seem worthwhile to try to discover the precise nature of this relationship. Accordingly, future studies should use stimuli whose similarity to each other can be precisely indicated in j.n.d. units. Also, it would be worthwhile to extend the range of similarity beyond that utilized in this exploratory study in order to determine if a certain minimum amount of similarity is necessary before mediated generalization can be demonstrated.

SUMMARY

Three groups of preschool children were tested for their tendency to generalize a button pushing response from a red light to a reddish orange, an orange and a yellow respectively. One test was given before learning a common name for the training and test stimuli. One test was given afterwards. An increase in generalization following verbal training was observed at all points. The results were discussed in terms of the principle of mediated generalization.

REFERENCES

1. BIRGE, JANET. The role of verbal responses in transfer. Unpublished doctor's dissertation, Yale Univer., 1941.
2. DIXON, W. J., & MASSEY, F. J., JR. *Introduction to statistical analysis.* New York: McGraw-Hill, 1951.
3. EISMAN, BERNICE S. Attitude formation: The development of a color

preference response through mediated generalization. *J. abnorm. soc. Psychol.*, 1955, *50*, 321–326.

4. JEFFREY, W. E.   The effects of verbal and nonverbal responses in mediating an instrumental act. *J. exp. Psychol.*, 1953, *45*, 327–333.

5. MURDOCK, B. B., JR.   Effects of failure and retroactive inhibition on mediated generalization. *J. exp. Psychol.*, 1952, *44*, 156–164.

6. SHIPLEY, WALTER C.   An apparent transfer of conditioning. *J. gen. Psychol.*, 1933, *8*, 382–391.

THE EFFECT OF VERBALIZATION IN CHILDREN'S LEARNING AS A FUNCTION OF CHRONOLOGICAL AGE

MORTON W. WEIR [1]
HAROLD W. STEVENSON [2]

SEVERAL RECENT STUDIES have been concerned with the role of verbalization in children's learning. Children, as do adults (2), learn to discriminate among stimuli more rapidly if they are given pretraining experience in naming the stimuli (3, 4, 6, 9), or if they attach a verbal response to the stimuli during training (10, 11). Recall of stimuli has also been found to increase with prior naming of the stimuli (8). Significantly faster learning and a greater incidence of transposi-

tion have been found for verbal than for preverbal Ss (1, 7).

Although age differences in the effects of verbalization on learning have been noted (6, 9), possible changes in the effects of verbalization on discrimination learning with increasing CA have not been studied systematically. The purpose of this study is to investigate such effects with children of CAs 3 through 9 years.

One group of Ss at each age level is instructed to verbalize the name of the stimulus prior to each response, while another group is not instructed to verbalize in this manner. Several predictions about the performance of Ss are made. First, groups instructed to verbalize stimulus names should learn the discrimina-

[1] This study is adapted from a master's thesis submitted to the Department of Psychology of the University of Texas by this author (14).

[2] The study was supported by a grant from the National Science Foundation (Grant 3280) to this author.

Reprinted by permission from *Child Development*, 1959, *30*, 173–178.

tion more rapidly than Ss not given these instructions. This is in line with the assumption (12) that verbalization of stimulus names provides response-produced stimuli which increase the differences among the stimuli and aid learning by increasing the number of stimuli to which a discriminative response can become attached.

Second, in both verbal and nonverbal conditions learning rate should increase with increasing CA. Such an increase would be in accord with the assumption that learning ability improves with increasing age.

Finally, the difference in rate of learning between the verbal and nonverbal groups is predicted to decrease as CA increases. It is assumed (a) that as age increases Ss have stronger tendencies to verbalize implicitly the names of common stimuli, and (b) that such implicit verbalization provides response-produced stimuli similar to those occurring when Ss verbalize explicitly. Instructions to name the stimuli prior to responding should not be so helpful to S if S already has available the stimuli resulting from implicit verbalization. Older Ss, who are assumed to have stronger tendencies toward implicit verbalization than younger Ss, should be aided to a lesser degree than younger Ss by instructions to verbalize. As a consequence, the facilitative effects of instructions to verbalize should decrease with increasing CA.

METHOD

SUBJECTS

The Ss consisted of 128 preschool and elementary school children selected on the basis of CA. A group of 32 Ss was selected at each of the following CA levels: 3-0 to 3-11, 5-0 to 5-11, 7-0 to 7-11, and 9-0 to 9-11. All of the preschool Ss in attendance at the schools visited and of the appropriate ages were tested. The elementary school Ss were selected at random from the class roll.[3]

APPARATUS

The front of the apparatus was 17×37 in. and was painted gray. Protruding $\frac{1}{2}$ in. from the face of the apparatus were 10 $2\frac{1}{2} \times 3$ in. panels, with fronts of clear plastic bordered by $\frac{3}{4}$-in. red plastic tape. Behind each panel was a 2×2 in. slide depicting an animal. The slides were visible to S only when illuminated from behind by 110 v., 6 watt bulbs. The slides were photographic negatives; thus, the animals appeared as white line drawings. The apparatus was constructed so that any of the five vertical pairs of slides could be illuminated on a particular trial. The S's task on each trial was to choose the correct member of the illuminated pair. When S pressed the correct panel, the lights behind both members of the pair automatically turned off. If S pressed the incorrect panel, the lights did not go off.

A pretraining apparatus was constructed in the same manner as the apparatus described above, except that it contained only one vertical pair of panels. The front of the apparatus was 17×10 in.

Common animals, such as a monkey, cat, and elephant, were depicted in

[3] The writers wish to express their appreciation to the principals and the directors of the St. Louis School, Tarrytown Methodist Nursery School, All Saints Nursery School, Good Shepherd Nursery School, Austin High School Child Development Laboratory, and the University of Texas Nursery School for their cooperation in making Ss available for this study.

the training slides. The animals depicted in the pretraining slides were a bee and a pig. The rewards given at the end of the experiment consisted of a wide variety of balloons and small plastic toys.

PROCEDURE

The Ss were obtained individually from the classroom and brought to the experimental room by E. The room contained a low table upon which the apparatus was placed. To the right of the apparatus was a second table with the pretraining apparatus.

Pretraining procedure. The S was seated in a chair facing the pretraining apparatus. The training apparatus was out of S's view. The E stated that a new kind of game would be played and the pretraining apparatus was pointed out. The E said, "See these two boxes here. Well, you can push them like this." The E demonstrated how the panels could be pushed and then turned on the lights illuminating the pictures in both panels. The S was told, "Now you push on this one." (The E indicated the incorrect panel.) "See, nothing happens. Now try this one." (The E indicated the correct panel.) "See, the lights went out. Now that is what you are supposed to do. Every time two pictures come on you have to push on the one that you think will turn the pictures off. You always try to turn the pictures off on the very first push. Now let's try it again and see if you can turn the pictures off on the very first push." Pretraining was continued until S had made the correct response on three successive trials. The E concluded pretraining by saying, "It is always the same picture that turns the lights off. That's fine. Now this was just practice. Let's go

over here where you can win some prizes," and took S to the chair in front of the training apparatus.

During the pretraining period the upper panel was correct for half the Ss and the lower panel was correct for the other half. The panel which was correct was randomized among Ss.

The Ss at each CA level were randomly divided into two groups of equal size prior to the pretraining period. One of these groups was designated the non-verbal group and the other the verbal group. During the pretraining period the procedure outlined above was followed with the nonverbal group. During pretraining Ss in the verbal group were asked to name the animals depicted when the panels were first illuminated. Since all Ss knew the names of the animals, it was unnecessary for E to identify them. A second difference in the procedure introduced for verbal Ss was that E requested S to name the animal depicted in the panel which they were going to press. The E told the verbal Ss, "Now remember, before you push on any picture you have to tell me the name of the picture."

Training procedure. After S had been seated in the chair facing the training apparatus, E said, "See this. Well, it is just like the game we practiced on only there are more pictures. I can turn on these two, or maybe these two, or any two I want." (The E pointed out the pairs of panels at random.) "And just like when we practiced, whenever two pictures come on you have to push the one which you think turns both pictures off." The E informed S that if S learned to turn all the pictures off without making a mistake he could win any two prizes that he wanted. The *E* displayed the prizes that could be won. The *E* cautioned *S*s in the verbal group that they had to say the name of the picture before they pushed on it. As in pretraining, all *S*s were able to name the stimuli. The exact names were not required; for example, *S*s were allowed to substitute such words as "duck" for the goose. After every 25 trials *S* was told, "Remember, you have to turn the pictures off on the very first push."

A corrective procedure was employed. If *S* initially pressed the incorrect panel, he was allowed to make the correct choice. The criterion for learning was one run in which the correct panel in each of the five pairs was chosen first. If *S* did not reach this criterion in 100 trials, training was terminated.

The order of presentation of stim-

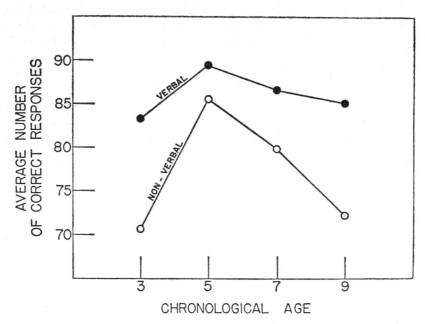

Figure 1. The average number of correct responses as a function of chronological age.

ulus pairs was randomized in blocks of five trials so that each pair was presented once in each block. No pair of stimuli was ever presented twice in succession. A prearranged schedule of 28 successive blocks of five trials was constructed and the training trials for each *S* began with a block selected randomly from this schedule. In order to control for possible position or stimulus biases, two proce-

dures were introduced. First, the panel in each pair which was to be correct was randomized separately for each *S* with the restriction that for an *S* no more than three upper or three lower panels were correct. Second, the slides were changed among the panels at random after every five *S*s had been tested. The *S*s at each age level were alternately assigned to the verbal and nonverbal conditions.

RESULTS

The average numbers of correct responses made in the verbal and nonverbal groups at each age level are presented in Figure 1. An analysis of variance reveals a significant difference in performance among the four age levels ($F = 2.96$, $df = 3, 120, p < .01$). The curves in Figure 1 do not, however, reveal a tendency for the average number of correct responses for either the verbal or nonverbal groups to increase consistently with increasing CA, as predicted. There is an increase in the average number of correct responses from CA 3 to 5 followed by a decrease from CA 5 through 9. An analysis taking into account the ordered character of the age variable (5) indicated a significant quadratic component in the over-all trend for the combined verbal and nonverbal groups ($F = 10.11$, $df = 1, 120, p < .01$). The linear and cubic components did not approach significance.

The verbal groups had on the average a greater number of correct responses than did the nonverbal groups. The analysis of variance indicates a significant difference between the verbal and nonverbal groups ($F = 14.37, df = 1, 120, p < .001$), which supports the hypothesis concerning the facilitative effects of verbalization on learning.

The prediction that the difference in average number of correct responses between the verbal and nonverbal groups would decrease with increasing CA was not supported by a significant interaction between verbalization and nonverbalization and CA ($F < 1$). A breakdown of the interaction term (5) does not reveal a significant linear, quadratic, or cubic component. As seen in Figure 1, such a tendency does emerge between CAs 3 and 5, but as CA increases to 7 and 9 the curves again diverge.

DISCUSSION

The prediction that instructions to verbalize would result in more rapid learning at all age levels was supported. This finding is in accord with the results of the studies cited earlier demonstrating that verbalization concerning the stimuli aids learning.

The prediction that rate of learning would increase with increasing CA was not supported. Although performance of the four age levels differed significantly, there was a decrease rather than an increase in rate of learning from CAs 5 to 9 in both verbal and nonverbal groups. Since these results are in contrast with a vast amount of evidence indicating that learning ability does improve with increasing CA, other variables must have been operating in this situation to provide the results that were obtained.

One possibility is that older Ss (CAs 7 and 9) came from a population different from that of the younger Ss. This does not seem likely, for the study was done at private schools attended by children of above-average ability. Children attending preschool are in general highly selected, and the results of group testing of the older Ss indicated they, too, were above average. The average IQ obtained for 28 of the 7-year Ss was 113.3 and for 28 of the 9-year Ss, 109.3. Thus, although the sampling of above-average children limits the generality of the results, the Ss at the various CA levels did represent increasing levels of mental ability. A second possible variable affecting the results is that the older Ss were not so highly motivated as the younger Ss. This also seems unlikely since no clear indications of motivational differences were observed. The possibility that seems most tenable is that older Ss developed complex hypotheses concerning the solution of the problem and that these hypotheses hindered their development of the more simple, correct solution. These Ss made such statements as, "I thought that it was going to be a pattern," and "I thought you were going to change them all around." The older Ss responded more slowly during pretraining than younger Ss, indicating that they may have been expecting a harder task and found it difficult to learn that the same response was always correct. A decrease in rate of learning with increasing CA found in a previous study of discrimination learning (13) has been interpreted in a similar manner.

The results do not support the prediction that verbalization would be of less value to the older than to the younger Ss. Although the difference in performance between the verbal and nonverbal groups was less at CA 5 than at CA 3, the difference increased again at CAs 7 and 9. The interaction between verbalization and CA was not, however, significant. The prediction was based on the assumption that the implicit verbalization of older Ss would be relevant to the solution of the problem. Since the older Ss in the nonverbal groups performed so poorly, it seems likely that, if implicit verbalization did occur, it hindered rather than aided the acquisition of the correct responses. The fact that explicit verbalization continued to aid Ss at the higher age levels in their performance indicates that verbalization of the names of the stimuli may have forced the older Ss to pay closer attention to the stimuli, thus increasing the relevance of the stimuli and decreasing the tendency of the older Ss to form complex hypotheses.

SUMMARY

Children at CAs 3, 5, 7, and 9 were trained to discriminate the correct member of five pairs of stimuli. Half of the Ss were instructed to name the stimulus prior to a response, while the other half learned the task without these instructions. Consistently better learning in the verbal groups and a curvilinear relationship between rate of learning and CA were obtained. The difference in rate of learning between the verbal and nonverbal groups was not found to vary significantly with CA.

REFERENCES

1. ALBERTS, E., & EHRENFREUND, D. Transposition in children as a function of age. *J. exp. Psychol.*, 1951, *41*, 30–38.

2. ARNOULT, M. Stimulus predifferentiation: some generalizations and hypotheses. *Psychol. Bull.*, 1957, *54*, 339–350.

3. CANTOR, G. N. Effects of three types of pretraining on discrimination learning in preschool children. *J. exp. Psychol.*, 1955, *49*, 339–342.

4. DIETZE, D. The facilitating effect of words on discrimination and generalization. *J. exp. Psychol.*, 1955, *50*, 255–260.

5. GRANT, D. A. Analysis of variance tests in the analysis and comparison of curves. *Psychol. Bull.*, 1956, *53*, 141–154.

6. JEFFREY, W. E. The effects of verbal and non-verbal responses in medi-

ating an instrumental act. *J. exp. Psychol.*, 1953, *45*, 327–333.

7. KUENNE, M. R. Experimental investigation of the relation of language to transposition behavior in young children. *J. exp. Psychol.*, 1946, *36*, 471–490.

8. KURTZ, K. H., & HOVLAND, C. I. The effect of verbalization during observation of stimulus objects upon accuracy of recognition and recall. *J. exp. Psychol.*, 1953, *45*, 157–164.

9. NORCROSS, K. J., & SPIKER, C. C. The effects of type of stimulus pretraining on discrimination performance in preschool children. *Child Develpm.*, 1957, *28*, 79–84.

10. PYLES, M. K. Verbalization as a factor in learning. *Child Develpm.*, 1932, *3*, 108 113.

11. SCHAEFFER, M. S., & GERJUOY, I. R. The effect of stimulus naming on the discrimination learning of kindergarten children. *Child Develpm.*, 1955, *26*, 231–240.

12. SPIKER, C. C. Experiments with children on the hypothesis of acquired distinctiveness and equivalence of cues. *Child Develpm.*, 1956, *27*, 253–263.

13. STEVENSON, H. W., ISCOE, I., & McCONNELL, C. A developmental study of transposition. *J. exp. Psychol.*, 1955, *49*, 278–280.

14. WEIR, M. W. The effect of verbalization on children's learning as a function of chronological age. Unpublished master's thesis, Univer. of Texas, 1958.

CONCEPT FORMATION | 12

STUDIES OF CONCEPT FORMATION usually involve a kind of discrimination learning in which a variety of stimuli are presented over a series of trials. The subject's task is to learn to make one response to several of the stimuli and another response to other groups of stimuli. The only way to respond correctly, since the stimuli may be different from trial to trial, is to learn to make the common response to a group or class of stimuli. If, for example, we presented on successive trials pictures of a dog and a tree, a cow and a cloud, a robin and a truck, and continued with other similar pairs, always reinforcing a response to the animal stimulus, eventually the child would learn to look for and respond to the animal stimulus, and ultimately he will be able to respond correctly on succeeding trials, even though the stimuli for those trials had never been seen before. If we now question the child we would probably find that he can tell us that responding to the animal stimulus always leads to reward.

Clearly language might play a very important part in such a discrimination. Once the verbal label for the concept has been acquired there should be little difficulty in making the correct response. Concept formation may, however, be achieved without language, as has been demonstrated with lower animals. Fields (1932) has shown that the rat can learn to respond consistently to triangles in a discrimination task when the size and orientation of the triangle is varied during training. Presumably, the animal learns the concept on the basis of primary stimulus generalization. Thus, if the animal is trained to respond to a large equilateral triangle he will generalize to smaller and larger triangles and to triangles that vary from the equilateral form. If the rat is also trained to respond to some triangles which are small and some which have varying length sides and varying angles, the generalization gradients will overlap to such an extent that the animal will respond to any stimulus which has the three-pointed characteristic of triangles. We may then attribute to the rat the concept of triangularity.

On the basis of research in the previous section it might be anticipated that the acquisition of language would facilitate the learning of such a problem. Once the child knows what a straight line, an angle and the number three refer to, it should be possible to teach him the label "triangle" for the appropriate physical stimuli. With this label, the variety of different stimuli that may be presented as triangles acquire equivalence and the same responses may be made to any stimulus member that falls in the concept category.

The papers in this section approach the problem of concept formation from two somewhat different, although not necessarily incompatible, orientations. The first two studies derive from a general S–R learning theory analysis of the problem quite similar to the papers in the preceding section. The latter two studies reflect the recent impact of Piaget's work and theory upon research on concept formation in this country.

In many respects the first study is similar to the study by Norcross in the preceding section. The difference lies in the fact that Dietze has used a variety of related stimuli for which a concept name was learned while Norcross used a single set of stimuli in a simple discrimination problem. In each case, the distinctiveness of the labels was demonstrated to be of importance in the acquisition of the appropriate motor responses in the discrimination task.

The second study goes beyond the simple discrimination task to demonstrate that complex stimuli can lead to many naming responses, most of which may be incorrect, and thus interfere with acquisition of the responses arbitrarily designated as correct by the experimenter. In this sense, the results of this study are related to the results of the experiment by Weir and Stevenson in the preceding section, in which it was hypothesized that the older children performed more poorly because they developed complex hypotheses about the responses which were incorrect for the task. In the present study, the children of high IQ apparently did the same in attempting to arrive at the solution of the object concept formation task. This behavior resulted in poorer performance in that task relative to the normal IQ group when they had, as anticipated, performed much better than the normal group in the less complex task.

Piaget has posited a number of stages through which a child progresses in the development of intellectual operations or concepts revealed in the child's behavior. He and his colleagues have examined the development, for example, of the concepts of numerical invariance, conservation of quantity, spatial relationships, speed-time-space, and chance and probabilities. The stages of development have been analyzed in terms of a logical model in an effort to identify the operations a child uses in solving problems involving these concepts (Piaget, 1950; Inhelder and Matalon, 1961).

The research upon which Piaget bases his theoretical notions is a combination of experimental situations and interview techniques. The effort is directed toward an assessment of what a child does when given concrete examples of concepts and the reasons he verbalizes for his behavior. This research approach has been criticized by many persons interested in Piaget's work because the methods are not standardized and little effort is made to evaluate statistically the behavioral differences obtained. Thus, the procedure may differ from subject to subject within an experiment and it is difficult to determine how much confidence one can place in the differences reported among groups of children.

The last two studies in this section deal with phenomena with which Piaget has worked, in an effort, in the first case, to determine whether the stages hypothesized by Piaget may be replicated under more rigorous conditions. Elkind has found in a series of studies, one of which is included here, that general support may be found for some of the developmental stages suggested by Piaget.

The second study is one of the more recent attempts to bring about a modification in the stages of development by instituting a training procedure designed to teach the child concepts reported by Piaget to be absent until a later age. As in the case of a number of other studies, the method used was not very successful in bringing about the modifications in the children's behavior that might have been anticipated. While these data support Piaget's contention that such modification is not easy, they do not, of course, prove that such modification is impossible. One can not prove the null hypothesis, and, of course, there are many teaching methods yet to be tried in such problems.

REFERENCES

INHELDER, BARBEL and MATALON, B.   The study of problem solving and thinking. In P. H. Mussen (Ed.), *Handbook of research methods in child development.* New York: Wiley, 1960. Pp. 421–455.

FIELDS, P. E.   Studies in concept formation: I. The development of the concept of triangularity by the white rat. *Comp. Psychol. Monogr.*, 1932, *9*, 1–70.

PIAGET, J.   *The psychology of intelligence.* London: Routledge, 1950.

THE FACILITATING EFFECT OF WORDS

ON DISCRIMINATION

AND GENERALIZATION [1]

DORIS DIETZE

FROM AN S–R POINT of view the formation of concepts involves two related processes—discrimination and generalization. When a person learns to respond selectively to similar stimulus situations, he is said to evidence discrimination; and when he learns to respond in the same way to different situations which serve equivalent functions, he is said to evidence generalization. (Generalization used in this sense refers to learned or "secondary generalization," as distinct from primary generalization, which occurs when stimuli evoke similar responses without previous learning.) The facili-

[1] Adapted from a thesis presented in partial fulfillment of the requirements for the M.S. Degree, Psychology Department, University of Washington, 1953. The writer is greatly indebted to Dr. Allan Katcher for his capable guidance.

Reprinted by permission from *Journal of Experimental Psychology*, 1955, *50*, 255–260.

tating effect of language in the establishment of these two processes may be formulated theoretically as follows: Stimuli produced by responding with highly distinctive names to different situations should tend to increase the difference between stimulus patterns, lessening primary generalization of responses from one of these situations to another. Increased differentiation based upon this process has been called "acquired distinctiveness of cues" (4). Stimuli produced by responding to different situations with the same verbal response should become a common element of the stimulus patterns, mediating increased amounts of generalization from one situation to another. This has been called "acquired equivalence of cues" or "secondary generalization" (4).

These theoretical statements imply

that correct attachment of distinctive names should be easier to learn than correct attachment of very similar sounding names, since there would be less primary generalization during the learning process. With fewer intrusions based on primary generalization, secondary generalization should proceed more rapidly.

In the usual experimental concept formation situation the two processes, discrimination and generalization, probably occur conjointly. However, many studies of concept formation (9, 10), by quantifying results in terms of the number of trials or the number of errors before achieving a final criterion, necessarily confound the two. Sometimes they are then inferred separately from introspective or spontaneous comments by the Ss. Some descriptions of human Ss' concept attainment give the impression that human learning differs in its basic processes from animal learning, by use of vague or poorly defined terms like "active search," "thing-like aspects," or "composite photograph" (9, 10).

Investigations of the attainment of concepts have been conducted largely at the adult level. However, in adults established problem-solving habits are applied to new learning situations, and what is observed may reflect not sc much the acquisition of new concepts as transfer from previous experiences. When Ss are young children, for whom language is a relatively new tool, the situation is likely to reveal more about the learning processes. Too often studies of concept development in children have been more concerned with their ability to conceptualize or with their repertory of concepts than with psychological processes. In several of these studies, however, superior performance was correlated with adequate verbalization during the acquisition process (2, 3, 5, 6, 7, 9). Additional evidence for the significance of language in discrimination was presented by Pyles (8), who found that children demonstrated superior performance in the discrimination of named, rather than of unnamed, nonsense figures.

For the present study a simple concept formation arrangement was designed to examine the part played by words in discrimination and generalization. Of particular interest was the effect of differences in the distinctiveness of names on three stages of learning to name objects: (a) initial discrimination, (b) subsequent discrimination of related objects, and (c) secondary generalization to related objects.

METHOD

Subjects. The Ss were 48 preschool children, ranging in age from 54 to 67 months (mean age: 60.6 months). The mean age difference between older and younger groups was 201 days; between boys and girls, 18 days; and between similar and different names groups, six days. These children were obtained on a volunteer basis from six day nurseries in Seattle, Washington.

Materials. Sixty nonsense figures, consisting of a circular core with numbers of projecting tips, were cut from masonite. The over-all size of these forms varied with the number of projections, but the core was a standard 1½ in. in diameter, while the projections were ⅜ in. wide and 1½ in. long. The figures were varied in four ways: (a) the numbers of projections ranged from 1 to 16, (b) the spatial arrangement or grouping of projections varied, (c) the tips of projections on each figure were all either rounded, pointed, or squared, and (d) the figures were painted three slightly different shades of red. Twenty sets of forms were prepared, each set consisting of three forms alike in number and spatial arrangement of projections, but differing in shape of tips and shade of red. The sets were arranged in series, with each set differing from previous sets in number and arrangement of projections, but containing one form with each shape of tips and shade of red. All forms with a particular shape of tips and shade of red were given the same name, regardless of number and spatial arrangement of projections; all forms alike in number and arrangement of tips had different names. Thus shade of red and shape of tips were cues upon which discrimination and secondary generalization were based. To prevent direct comparison of the common details, each set was kept in a separate numbered envelope at all times except when used.

Tiny trinkets of the type dispensed in chewing-gum vending machines were used to keep motivation at a high level.

Experimental design. A $2 \times 2 \times 2$ analysis of variance design was used. For half the *S*s, figures were called *jod, daf,* and *meep*, nonsense names chosen to have different initial and final consonants and different vowel sounds. For the other half the figures were called *beem, meem,* and *peem*, nonsense names chosen to be alike except for the aspiration of the initial consonants, which require practically the same lip formation to pronounce. Otherwise the two groups received identical treatment. Two control variables, age and sex, completed the balanced design. These were included because older children are verbally more experienced than younger and might be expected to show more skill in the type of task required by the experiment; and because several studies (9) have indicated that, in the age range considered here, girls show superior verbal ability compared to boys.

Procedure. The *S*s were chosen alternately for each condition from prepared lists upon which they had been assigned randomly to one or the other experimental condition. The selection was done in such a way that an equal number of boys and girls and older and younger children were tested at approximately the same time of day and during each third of the period of weeks during which testing was conducted. This precaution was taken to ensure balance among the groups of any effects dependent on regular nursery school schedule, fatigue, familiarity with *E*, changes in *E*'s attitude, etc. Since *S*s were tested from one day school at a time, this balance throughout the weeks of testing was also desirable to randomize effects of differences in intelligence, training or experience, and socioeconomic status that might exist from one school to another.

Testing was done with each *S* alone in a room separated from the regular playroom. The *E* demonstrated the first set of forms, saying, "These are the things we play with." The *E* pointed to each form, pronouncing its assigned name and asking *S* to repeat the names. The *S* was then asked to say the names alone. Care was taken to ensure that he could pronounce and remember all three names without aid from *E*, since, in order to use the names as an aid in discriminating the forms, he had to be able to discriminate the pronunciation of the names. When *S* had mastered the pronunciations, *E* rearranged the forms and said, "As soon as you can name these three blocks without my helping you, I will put one of these little toys (showing the trinkets) into this jar. Now, I have some more of these (indicating and naming the figures), and when you can name the first set we will go on and name the second set. Each time you can name them without my helping you, you can choose a toy, and at the end of the game, when you can tell me all the names without me ever telling you, I will take all the toys out of the jar and make you a bracelet. Do you understand how to play?" The usual response was an enthusiastic attempt to name the figures. The *E* then arranged the figures on the table and asked *S* to identify each form successively. Whenever *S* misnamed one, *E* renamed all three, rearranged them on the table, and again asked *S* to identify the figures, each time in a different succession. The form of the question was varied to maintain interest by such devices as, "Which one is nearest you?," "Put your thumb on the middle one —which one are you touching?" Questions in which *E* pronounced the name before *S*, like "Which one is *daf?*," "Put *jod* in your lap," were alternated with those requiring S to say the name first; but in every case S pronounced the name while indicating the appropriate figure. Effort was made to structure the situation so that each S had equal opportunity to verbalize during learning. Work with Set I continued until S correctly indicated all three forms without prompting on three successive trials. At this time he chose a trinket, Set I was put away, and Set II was placed before him. The E asked for the names as before, and the "game" continued. When S correctly anticipated the names on three consecutive sets, the final learning criterion was reached. This was accomplished in one session averaging about one-half hour. Interest and motivation appeared very high throughout.

Measures. Records were kept of the number of prompts necessary to learn to criterion each set of three similar but not identical forms. Also recorded was the number of sets (different from the first but related to it by common physical details associated with the same three names) which were required to complete the task. A prompt consisted of renaming all three forms each time an error was made on a single response. One correct trial included three consecutive correct responses, one to each form. The criterion of discrimination

learning of a particular set, three consecutive correct trials, consisted of nine consecutive successful responses. The largest number of prompts given on a particular set was 27 for the slowest S. The criterion of secondary generalization, correctly naming three sets three times each, involved 30 consecutive correct responses. The largest total number of prompts given was 73. Thus, the criteria of discrimination and generalization were sufficiently high to eliminate practically all possibility of chance success (*1*).

Four measures were considered in the analysis of the data: (*a*) number of prompts given during Set I was the measure of initial discrimination; (*b*) number of *prompts per set*, excluding Set I, was the measure of discrimination on sets after the initial discrimination; (*c*) *number of sets* completed after Set I and before reaching the criterion was the measure of secondary generalization; (*d*) *total* number of prompts was used as a general measure of efficiency of concept formation, involving both discrimination and generalization.

Because the ranges of scores were limited at the lower end, the distributions were highly skewed. To normalize them a square-root transformation was made, which produced the desired effect, with one exception on total prompts (see Table 1).

TABLE 1 · MEANS AND *SD*'s OF EACH SUBGROUP IN THE ANALYSES OF VARIANCE
(Each figure based on 6 cases)

Measure		SIMILAR NAMES					DIFFERENT NAMES				
		Boys		Girls			Boys		Girls		
		Older	Young-er	Older	Young-er	Total	Older	Young-er	Older	Young-er	Total
Set I	M	2.86	3.08	2.96	2.05	2.74	2.81	2.28	2.17	1.82	2.27
	SD	.39	1.15	.96	.52	.91	.88	.35	.54	.41	.68
Prompts	M	1.59	1.90	1.93	1.75	1.79	1.71	1.48	1.20	1.34	1.43
per set	SD	.23	.43	.52	.44	.44	.32	.42	.23	.36	.39
Number	M	2.50	2.50	3.04	2.77	2.71	1.89	1.44	1.58	1.86	1.69
of sets	SD	.64	.62	.63	.38	.62	.66	.52	.41	.60	.59
Total	M	3.60	4.02	5.17	4.21	4.25	2.42	1.94	1.68	2.28	2.08
prompts	SD	1.53	.70	1.33	1.45	1.42*	.56	.87	.43	.90	.78*

*Variances significantly different at the .01 level.

Four analyses of variance were performed, using data of each of the four measures of learning.

RESULTS

Table 1 shows the means and SD's of the eight subgroups on each of the four measures.

The largest difference between the similar- and different-names groups was on total prompts, the score which incorporated the other three measures. This F ratio was 43.05. (The magnitude of this ratio, however, may be questioned, since the variance of the similar-names group was significantly larger than that of the different-names group.) For prompts per set, the measure of subsequent discrimination, F was 8.89, and for number of sets, the measure of secondary generalization, F was 31.98. All three of these values exceed 7.31, the value of F required with 1 and 40 df for the .01 confidence point. The initial discrimination, Set I, yielded an F of 4.33, which is larger than the 4.08 required for the .05 confidence point. In each case the different-names group had the smaller mean.

Intercorrelations between measures, except for total prompts, were low: − .10 to .42. (For 22 df r's higher than ± .40 are different from zero at the .05 level.) The correlation between prompts per set and number of sets was − .10 for the similar-names group and .31 for the different-names group.

On Set I prompts there was a difference between boys and girls significant above the .05 point ($F = 5.15$) showing superior performance by girls. With this exception, the F ratios for the control variables and the interactions were not significant.

DISCUSSION

KIND OF NAMES

Discrimination. Results of the analyses of variance show clearly that the children learned to name similar appearing, nonconventional forms more easily when distinctive names were used than when similar names were used. Furthermore, they learned to apply these names to new forms more readily when the names were distinctive. Interpretation of these results, assuming the same principles that underlie simpler conditioning and discrimination problems, suggests two related phenomena—stimulus generalization and response generalization.

Before beginning the discrimination task, all Ss were familiarized with the nonsense names to be used to the point where they could recite all three without prompting. (The six words used in the study were considered equivalent in that each had a constant consonant-vowel-consonant construction. Although the different-names group actually had a larger number of sound combinations to learn, this initial phase was so brief for both groups that any differences in learning difficulty were assumed to be inconsequential.) In the discrimination situation the child was actually confronted with two different types of tasks: after receiving three similar appearing forms he had to (a) choose the correct form upon hearing each of the names, and, (b) say the correct one of the names as E pointed to each form.

In the first type of task both groups were required to make the same overt responses, such as pointing or putting the form in the lap. Only if these reponses were made to stimulus configurations which included more differentiating cues would the different-names group be expected to appropriately perform more readily. Since the same figures were used for each group, these differentiating cues must have existed in the names used.

In the second type of task, when E pointed to a specific form, S had three responses available. If he said the correct name, the combination of the visual stimulus of the form and the auditory and proprioceptive stimuli arising from pronouncing its name would be reinforced. Nonreinforcement of incorrect responses would tend to cause combinations of this visual form and response-produced cues from other names to lose relative strength. In the early stages of learning errors were frequent. In the different-names group, where available responses were (relatively) dissimilar, response generalization would be less likely than primary stimulus generalization among similar visual forms. In the similar-names group, however, both visual stimuli and available responses were similar; hence errors may be accounted for by response generalization. But in what sense are these responses similar? Similar stimuli, auditory and proprioceptive, are produced and received by pronouncing them. Thus again primary stimulus generalization can account for the less adequate performance of the similar-names group. In brief, stimuli produced by responding with the correct name became part of the visual-proprioceptive stimulus configuration, decreasing primary generalization among the stimulus patterns. This effect was more rapid when differentiating cues supplied by the names were distinctive.

In the very early stages of learning, conflicting responses (like "jaf" or "mod") somewhere between two of the prelearned responses, occasionally occurred in the different-names group. In the similar-names group, where such ex-

change of initial consonants would merely produce another of the available names, an occasional substitute, such as "leem" or "keem" was produced. This type of response may have appeared as evidence of close balance between the strength of available responses, and it may have appeared as response generalization.

Secondary generalization. A theoretical account of the results of the secondary generalization task poses quite a problem in the present framework. With fewer intrusions based upon primary generalization, secondary generalization should proceed more rapidly. However, nothing in the present data indicates that such intrusions were more frequent in the similar-names group. In fact, the absence of significant correlation between prompts per set and number of sets may be interpreted as evidence that performance in the secondary generalization task was not associated with discrimination. Additional research may provide an answer to this provocative situation.

CONTROL VARIABLES

Since previous studies have indicated age differences in verbal learning speed, age was included in the present design as a control variable. It is not surprising, however, that no significant differences attributable to age appeared. First, there was less than a year's difference between the older and younger groups. Second, when children are beginning to acquire language skills, development is so rapid that small age differences may be expected to produce large differences in relative verbal skill. However, Ss of this experiment were past the age period where verbal development is relatively most rapid.

The one significant sex difference,

on Set I (initial discrimination), conforms to the results of previous investigations which show that girls in this age range have a slight edge over boys in verbal learning. That this superiority was not maintained over the other measures suggests that girls may be superior in the initial rote-learning stage of acquisition, but that there is very little difference in generalizing ability once the names are learned.

SUMMARY

It was hypothesized that complex discriminations between similar appearing forms are easier if names applied to forms are distinctive than if names are very similar. The study used 48 four- and five-year-old children as Ss in learning a simple concept formation task. For the same objects one group learned similar sounding names and the other group learned different sounding names. Four measures of learning were employed to reveal initial discrimination, subsequent discrimination of related objects, secondary generalization to related objects, and general efficiency of concept formation.

Statistical results indicate that on each measure the different-names group learned faster than the similar-names group. For discrimination tasks these results were ascribed to primary stimulus generalization.

REFERENCES

1. GRANT, D. A.   Additional tables of the probability of "runs" of correct responses in learning and problem solving. *Psychol. Bull.*, 1947, *44*, 276–279.

2. KUENNE, M. R.   Experimental investigation of the relation of language to transposition behavior in young children. *J. exp. Psychol.*, 1946, *36*, 471–490.

3. LONG, L., & WELCH, L.   The influence of abstractness on reasoning ability. *J. Psychol.*, 1942, *13*, 41–59.

4. MILLER, N. E.   Theory and experiment relating psychoanalytic displacement to stimulus-response generalization. *J. abnorm. soc. Psychol.*, 1948, *43*, 173–176.

5. MUNN, N. L.   *Psychological development.* Boston: Houghton Mifflin, 1938.

6. MUNN, N. L.   Learning in children. In L. Carmichael (Ed.), *Manual of child psychology.* New York: Wiley, 1946.

7. OSGOOD, C. E.   *Method and theory in experimental psychology.* New York: Oxford Univ. Press, 1953.

8. PYLES, M. K.   Verbalization as a factor in learning. *Child Develpm.*, 1932, *3*, 108–113.

9. VINACKE, W. E.   *The psychology of thinking.* New York: McGraw-Hill, 1952.

10. WOODWORTH, R. S.   *Experimental psychology.* New York: Holt, 1938.

CONCEPT ATTAINMENT:

II. EFFECT OF STIMULUS COMPLEXITY

UPON CONCEPT ATTAINMENT

AT TWO LEVELS

OF INTELLIGENCE [1]

SONIA F. OSLER
GRACE E. TRAUTMAN

RECENT EXPERIMENTAL WORK has lent support to the notion that discrimination learning and concept attainment by children may be achieved either by mediational symbolic processes or simple S–R associations. The experimental evidence also points to an association between the specific learning process characteristic of S and his intelligence. In a study of discrimination learning Kendler and Kendler (1959) found that fast learners achieved a reversal shift more readily

[1] This investigation was supported by a grant from the National Institute of Mental Health, Psychopharmacology Service Center, made to Leon Eisenberg of Johns Hopkins University, and the senior author (Grant MY-2583).

The writers wish to express their gratitude to Mary A. Adams, Assistant Superintendent, Elementary Education, Lorne H. Woollatt, Former Director of Bureau of Research, Vernon S. Vavrina, Director, Junior and Senior High Schools, and to Arthur Lichtenstein, Director of Special Services for Pupils, Baltimore City Department of Education; and to B. Melvin Cole, Director, Elementary Education, Norris A. King, Director, Secondary Education, and Charles J. Leiman, Supervisor, Psychological Services, Baltimore County Department of Education; and to the principals and their staffs who cooperated in the conduct of the study.

They also wish to thank Nancy A. Freydberg, Sandra J. Weiss, and Frances Odette for testing Ss and for many suggestions concerning the conduct of the study.

Reprinted by permission from *Journal of Experimental Psychology*, 1961, 62, 9–13.

than a nonreversal shift, while the opposite was true of slow learners. From this result it was inferred that fast learners utilized mediators in the original discrimination, while the slow learners achieved the discrimination through an S–R association.

In a second study involving concept attainment by induction (Osler & Fivel, 1961) Ss were divided into gradual and sudden learners on the basis of the learning curves they generated. It was then found that in the group of superior intelligence there were more sudden learners than gradual learners, while the reverse was true in the group of normal intelligence. On the assumption that the gradual learners build up S–R associations and that sudden learners test successive hypotheses, it is concluded that the process mediating concept attainment is a function of intelligence.

The object of the present investigation was to provide an experimental means for testing the inferred relationship between intelligence and the specific learning mechanism involved in concept attainment. If hypothesis testing is more frequent among superior than normal Ss, it should be possible to influence the performance of the superior group by varying the number of irrelevant dimensions, on which hypotheses can be based, in the concept exemplars. For Ss of normal intelligence, who tend to achieve solution by the gradual building up of an S–R association, no systematic relation between the number of stimulus dimensions and speed of solution is anticipated.

The specific prediction, therefore, is that the performance measures in concept attainment will show a significant interaction between level of intelligence and the number of irrelevant dimensions in the concept exemplars.

METHOD

Stimuli. One concept was studied: the number *two* represented by two types of exemplars. The first method of representation consisted of two solid black circles, ¼ in. in diameter, placed in random fashion on a 5 × 5 grid on white cards 2¾ in. square. The complete set consisted of 150 different patterns; these were called the *formal two* (FT) stimuli. The negative stimuli in this set consisted of the same black circles in numbers varying from one to five, excluding two, placed in unduplicated random patterns.

The second method of representation was by means of two identical pictures of common objects pasted on cards identical to those used in the FT set. The pictures, which were in a variety of colors and sizes, were cut out from children's books and were different for each of the 150 cards. This set of stimuli was called the *object two* (OT). The negative stimuli for this set consisted of the same types of pictures in numbers other than two. An effort was made to have the negative stimuli match their positive mates in general area, brightness, and color combinations. Figure 1 contains examples of the two types of stimuli; but it should be remembered that the OT stimuli were actually multicolored. Altogether there were 600 different stimulus cards.

The reason for choosing naturalistic stimuli, rather than attempting to increase the complexity of the FT stimuli by introducing the variables of color or shape, was to create very large differences in the number of irrelevant dimensions in the concept exemplars without increasing their complexity to a point which gave the children of superior intelligence or older age an advantage in familiarity or in the availability of verbal labels. The use of common objects, pretested for familiarity, permitted the introduction of an exceedingly high number of attributes without the complications just enumerated. The weakness of this method of stimulus construction is that there is no control of the amount of irrelevant information; but for the purpose of this experiment this does not seem to be crucial, as long as it was reasonable to assume a *difference* in the amount of irrelevant information.

Prior to the actual investigation the stimulus material representing the object two was shown to 10 children in each age and intelligence group to be tested. These children were asked to identify the pictures and those which were not properly identified were discarded. The children used in this pretest did not serve as Ss in the experiment. The familiarity of the material was checked further by asking each S to identify 10 pairs of stimuli upon completion of the concept learning task. Different sets of 10 were used for each S. These data confirmed the fact that the pictures were entirely familiar to all Ss.

The rationale for the design of the stimuli was that the OT exemplars would suggest many more hypotheses than the FT exemplars because of the diversity in the shape, size, color, and content of the different objects represented. Preliminary work had shown that children gave three times as many different reasons for their choice of the OT as for the FT stimuli. For this reason it was anticipated that Ss of superior intelligence would find the OT stimuli more difficult than the FT stimuli, while this should not hold for Ss of normal intelligence.

Subjects. The Ss consisted of 120 school children attending elementary and junior high schools of Baltimore City and County, equally divided among 6, 10, and 14-yr.

Figure 1. Samples of the stimulus pairs used in the Formal Two (FT) and the Object Two (OT) concepts, respectively.

groups. Each S was within 6 months of the age specified. Half of the Ss within each age level had a WISC IQ of 90 to 109 (the mean IQ of the total normal intelligence group was 101.3, $SD = 5.73$) and half had an IQ of 110 or above (the mean IQ of the total high intelligence group was 119.7, $SD = 7.46$).

Apparatus and procedure. The apparatus and procedure have been completely described by Osler and Fivel (1961). Each S, who worked individually, was asked to choose the correct one of two stimuli. Reinforcement which followed the choice of the concept exemplar consisted of marbles to be exchanged at the end of the experiment for a prize of S's selection. The S worked until he gave 10 consecutive correct responses, which was the criterion of success. The maximum number of trials was 150 and any S

who did not achieve criterion performance at that point was considered to have failed. A second session, held within two weeks of the first, was devoted to the administration of the WISC.

Experimental design. A $3 \times 2 \times 2$ factorial design was used, with three ages constituting one variable, the two methods of concept representation the second variable, and the two intelligence levels the third variable. This resulted in 12 groups with 10 Ss in each group, consisting of approximately the same number of boys and girls.

RESULTS AND DISCUSSION

The results were analyzed in terms of two measures of performance: (*a*) the number of errors per group, and (*b*) the

TABLE 1 · MEAN NUMBER OF ERRORS PER GROUP FOR REACHING CRITERION OF 10 CONSECUTIVE CORRECT RESPONSES

Stimuli	6-YR. Ss				10-YR. Ss				14-YR. Ss				ALL AGES	
	Normal IQ		High IQ		Normal IQ		High IQ		Normal IQ		High IQ		Normal IQ	High IQ
	Mean	SD	Mean	SD	Mean	SD	Mean	SD	Mean	SD	Mean	SD	Mean	Mean
Object Two	48.6	29.5	55.1	25.3	42.1	23.4	49.1	27.2	18.2	20.2	19.3	26.3	36.3	41.2
Formal Two	48.0	28.9	36.6	16.1	47.6	24.0	23.6	29.0	15.5	19.3	9.7	12.7	37.0	23.3

Note. Each mean is based on 10 Ss, total $N = 120$.

number of Ss who attained the criterion of success. Table 1 shows the mean number of errors for each of the 12 experimental groups with the corresponding SDs. An analysis of variance of these data, shown in Table 2, indicates that, of the three independent variables, only age produced significant differences; neither intelligence nor mode of concept representation as main effects produced significant F ratios. However, as predicted, the interaction between intelligence and method of concept representation turned out to be significant at the 5% level. A breakdown of the actual data shows that the interaction is due to the fact that Ss of superior intelligence found the OT exemplars more difficult than the FT exemplars ($F = 7.739$, $df = 1/54$, $P < .01$); while Ss of normal intelligence found both types of stimuli of equal difficulty. In fact, with the OT stimuli the superior Ss lost all advantage of high intelligence,

an advantage which was evident with the FT stimuli and also in the previous concept studies by Osler and Fivel (1961), utilizing a similar procedure.

TABLE 2 · ANALYSIS OF VARIANCE OF ERRORS

Source	df	MS	F
Age (A)	2	10,994.28	17.09**
Intelligence (I)	1	589.63	
Stimuli (S)	1	2,201.63	3.42
A × I	2	124.06	
A × S	2	44.31	
S × I	1	2,594.70	4.03*
A × S × I	2	363.93	
Error (Within)	108	643.45	
Total	119		

* $P < .05$.
** $P < .001$.

The data on frequency of Ss who achieved the criterion of success are shown in Table 3. A Chi square analysis shows that age ($\chi^2 = 15.60$, $df = 2$, $P < .001$) and concept representation

TABLE 3 · NUMBER OF Ss PER GROUP WHO REACHED CRITERION PERFORMANCE

Stimuli	6-YR. Ss		10-YR. Ss		14-YR. Ss		ALL AGES	
	Normal IQ	High IQ	Normal IQ	High IQ	Normal IQ	High IQ	Normal IQ	High IQ
Object Two	4	3	6	4	9	7	19	14
Formal Two	5	8	6	8	9	10	20	26

$(\chi^2 = 6.26, df = 1, P < .02)$ produced significant differences, while intelligence $(\chi^2 = .036)$ did not. Because of the significant interaction in the error scores between intelligence and mode of concept representation, the frequency data were analyzed separately for each intelligence group. This analysis showed that for the normal Ss concept representation made no difference $(\chi^2 = .074)$, while for the superior Ss the OT stimuli were more difficult than the FT stimuli $(\chi^2 = 10.80, df = 1, P < .01)$. The results of the analysis of the frequency data are in complete agreement with those obtained from the error scores.

It has been demonstrated that the effect of increasing the number of irrelevant stimulus dimensions was to slow down Ss of superior intelligence without affecting those of normal intelligence. These findings are consistent with the interpretation that in concept attainment high intelligence is associated with hypothesis testing, while normal intelligence is characterized by associative learning.

In the experiment by Kendler and Kendler (1959) it was found that the use of mediating responses speeded up learning. Is the present finding of no difference between normal and superior Ss with the OT stimuli inconsistent with their finding? Any seeming inconsistency is easily dispelled by pointing out that where the number of irrelevant dimensions is small, as is the case with the FT stimuli, the present results are in complete accord with those reported by Kendler and Kendler, who also used simple stimuli. The more complex OT stimuli present a different problem, as is evident from the previous discussion.

Bourne and Restle (1959) recently suggested an inverse relationship between the number of irrelevant dimensions and the speed of concept identification, without restrictions as to S variables. They attempted a validation of this theoretical formulation with data from several studies, all of which used college students as Ss. Since these Ss are of superior intelligence, the findings are entirely consistent with those obtained in the present study for the high intelligence group.

But what about the group of normal intelligence for which the relationship proposed by Bourne and Restle did not hold? In casting about for a possible explanation one might ask whether the confounding of complexity with thematic quality of the stimuli used in the present investigation might not have altered the experimental situation. Theoretically it may have; but it is not immediately apparent why the effect of thematic stimuli should have been different for the two intelligence groups. Bruner, Goodnow, and Austin (1956, p. 108), who investigated selection strategies in concept attainment using abstract and thematic material, report that thematic material retarded the performance of their Ss by generating more incorrect hypotheses. Their Ss, who were Harvard undergraduates, are comparable to the superior group of the present study. Again, their results remain consistent with those reported here; but still this throws no additional light on the findings with the normals. It may be that either Bourne and Restle should not extrapolate from their data obtained with superior Ss to those of normal intelligence; or that there is an interaction effect with the age variable whereby additional dimensions produce effects upon adults but not upon children of normal intelligence.

SUMMARY

The aim of this investigation was to provide a means of testing a previous interpretation that Ss of superior intelligence attain concepts by testing hypotheses while Ss of normal intelligence attain concepts through S-R associative learning. One hundred and twenty Ss, 60 at each intelligence level, were tested on a concept attainment task. Half the Ss worked with simple stimuli and half with complex stimuli. In each case the concept to be attained was the same, that of the number two. Because the complex stimuli would generate more hypotheses than the simple ones, it was predicted that they would slow down the superior Ss, but not affect the normal Ss. On two measures of performance, number of errors to criterion and frequency of Ss attaining criterion, the prediction was confirmed.

REFERENCES

BOURNE, L. E., JR., & RESTLE, F.   Mathematical theory of concept identification. *Psychol. Rev.*, 1959, 66, 278–296.

BRUNER, J. S., GOODNOW, J. J., & AUSTIN, G. A.   *A study of thinking.* New York: Wiley, 1956.

KENDLER, T. S., & KENDLER, H. H.   Reversal and nonreversal shifts in kindergarten children. *J. exp. Psychol.*, 1959, 58, 56–60.

OSLER, S. F., & FIVEL, M. W.   Concept attainment: I. Effect of age and intelligence in concept attainment by induction. *J. exp. Psychol.*, 1961, 62, 1–8.

CHILDREN'S DISCOVERY OF THE CONSERVATION OF MASS, WEIGHT, AND VOLUME: PIAGET REPLICATION STUDY II

DAVID ELKIND [1]

A. INTRODUCTION

THIS STUDY is the second [2] in a series devoted to the systematic replication of experiments originally performed by the Swiss psychologist, Jean Piaget. For its starting point the present study takes one of Piaget's (1940) investigations dealing with the ages at which children discover the conservation of mass, weight, and volume. Piaget assumes that concepts develop and that the discovery of conservation earmarks the final stage of their development. By studying children's responses to demonstrations of the conservation of mass, weight, and volume Piaget sought to uncover the genetic stages in the formation of these concepts.

[1] This study was carried out while the writer was a Staff Psychologist at the Beth Israel Hospital in Boston. The writer is indebted to Dr. Greta Bibring, the head of Beth Israel's Dept. of Psychiatry, and to the members of the research committee for granting him the time to make the study.

[2] For a report of the first study cf. Elkind (1961).

Reprinted by permission from *Journal of Genetic Psychology*, 1961, 98, 219–227.

The present study differs from Piaget's investigation in its standardization of his procedures and in its use of statistical design.

In his investigation Piaget tested for the conservation of mass, weight, and volume by means of the "sausage" experiment. The purpose of this experiment was to determine whether the child could tell that a quantity remained the same (was conserved) after it was changed in appearance. For example, in testing for the conservation of mass Piaget showed the child two clay balls identical in size, shape, and weight. After the child agreed that both balls had equal clay, Piaget made one of the balls into a sausage. Then he asked the child to judge whether the ball and the sausage contained the same amount of clay. Piaget also asked the child to predict—while both pieces of clay were shaped as balls—if they would be the same were one made into a sausage and to explain his judgments and predictions.

Using the sausage experiment to test 5- 12-year-old children, Piaget found that discoveries of conservation followed a regular order that was related to age. The conservation of mass was discovered at ages 7-8; the conservation of weight was discovered at ages 9-10; and the conservation of volume was discovered at ages 11 and 12. These findings, together with his theoretical interpretations, Piaget reported with the aid of a great many illustrative examples but without statistics.

Starting from Piaget's procedures and results the present study was designed to test the hypotheses that, other things being equal, (a) the number of conservation responses does not vary significantly with the Type of Response (prediction, judgment, and explanation) required; (b) the number of conservation responses varies significantly with the Type of Quantity (mass, weight, and volume); (c) the number of conservation responses varies significantly with Age Level; (d) the number of conservation responses varies significantly with the joint effect of Type of Quantity and Age Level (the statistical test of Piaget's age-order of discovery finding). In addition children's explanations were categorized for comparison with the explanations given by Piaget's subjects.

B. METHOD

1. SUBJECTS

One hundred and seventy-five children attending the Claflin School [3] in Newton, Mass., were tested. Twenty-five children were randomly selected from each of the grades from kindergarten to sixth. The mean age and standard deviation for each grade were: Kindergarten, $M = 5:8$, $SD = 3.0$; Grade 1, $M = 6:8$, $SD = 3.9$; Grade 2, $M = 7:7$, $SD = 3.6$; Grade 3, $M = 8:6$, $SD = 3.8$; Grade 4, $M = 9:7$, $SD = 3.0$; Grade 5, $M = 10:7$, $SD = 2.5$; Grade 6, $M = 11:9$, $SD = 5.56$ months. Hereafter the grades will be referred to by their age level.

For 125 children at the five oldest age levels, Kuhlmann-Anderson Intelligence Test scores were available. The mean IQ for this group was 109 and the SD was 11.0 points. Most of the children came from middle to upper-middle class homes.

[3] The writer is grateful to the principal, Dr. Harry Anderson, and teachers of the Claflin School whose friendly cooperation made the study not only possible but enjoyable.

2. PROCEDURE

Each S was seen individually and questioned three times on each type of quantity. For each quantity S was asked first to predict, next judge, and then explain his conservation or non-conservation responses. The order of the questions and the order of presenting the quantities —mass, weight, volume—was the same for all Ss. A fixed order of presentation was used to provide a more rigorous test of Piaget's findings. Any practice effects resulting from the fixed order should have worked against the differences Piaget found. On the other hand if differences were developmentally determined, as Piaget assumes, then the minimal practice effect over a brief time span should have had little effect.

3. TESTS

In the test for the conservation of mass, two clay balls identical in size, shape, and weight were on the table. E, "Do both balls have the same amount of clay, is there as much clay in this ball as in this one?" S was encouraged to "make them the same," if he doubted the equality of the balls. When S agreed that the two balls were equal E asked, "Suppose I roll one of the balls out into a hot dog, will there be as much clay in the hot dog as in the ball, will they both have the same amount of clay?" (Prediction question.)

After S's prediction E actually made one of the balls into a hot dog while S looked on. E, "Is there as much clay in the ball as in the hot dog, do they both have the same amount of clay?" (Judgment question.) Then E asked "Why is that?" to S's response. (Explanation question.)

Exactly the same procedure was used to test for the conservation of weight and volume. To test for the conservation of weight E asked, "Do they both weigh the same, do they both have the same amount of weight?" etc. And to test for the conservation of volume E asked, "Do they both take up the same amount of space, do they both take up as much room?" etc. On each test the child was initially given the opportunity to handle the balls and to add or subtract clay as he liked to "make them the same."

4. SCORING

Each conservation response was scored 1 and all non-conservation responses were scored zero. For each S there was a total possible conservation score of 9 and for each Type of Quantity and Type of Response there was a total possible score of three.

5. STATISTICAL ANALYSES

To test for the effects of Type of Response an analysis of variance design described by Lindquist (1953, Ch. 6) was used. In this design chance differences between subjects were controlled by testing all subjects on all types of response.

To test for the separate and combined effects of Age Level and Type of Quantity a different analysis of variance design was used (Lindquist, 1953, pp. 267-273). In this design chance differences between subjects were controlled, for the Type of Quantity variable only, by testing all subjects on all types of quantity.

C. RESULTS

1. TYPE OF RESPONSE

In his investigations Piaget used children's predictions, judgments, and explanations interchangeably as signs of conservation or non-conservation. In the present study the F for Type of Response was NS and did not approach significance. This finding agreed with Piaget's use of these three types of response as equivalent signs of conservation.

2. TYPE OF QUANTITY

Piaget found that, other things being equal; the conservation of mass was easiest to discover, the conservation of weight was of intermediate difficulty, and the conservation of volume was the most difficult discovery of all. The F for Type of Quantity obtained in the present study was 255.55 and was significant beyond the .01 level. Individual t tests for the Type of Quantity means revealed that the mean for each type of quantity was significantly different than every other. For all subjects the average number of conservation responses given for mass was 2.08, the average number given for weight was 1.75, and the average number of conservation responses given for volume was 0.25. The order of difficulty obtained in the present study was the same as the order that Piaget observed.

3. AGE LEVEL

The Swiss children tested by Piaget showed that, other things being equal, their conservation responses increased with age. For the children in the present study the same held true. The F for Age Level was 14.38 and was significant beyond the .01 level. Individual t tests of Age Level means showed that the magnitude of the Age Level means increased significantly with age in agreement with Piaget's findings.

4. TYPE OF QUANTITY-AGE LEVEL INTERACTION

Piaget's illustrative examples indicated that age group differences varied with the type of quantity in question. For mass there was a marked difference between the 5-6 and the 7- 12-year-old groups; for weight there was a marked difference between the 5-8 and the 9- 12-year-old groups; and for volume there was a marked difference between the 5-10 and the 11- 12-year-old groups in their number of conservation responses.

In the present study the variations in the differences between age groups for each type of quantity appeared as the interaction effect of Type of Quantity and Age Level. This interaction F was 6.93 and was significant beyond the .01 level. Individual t tests for age group differences showed that: (a) For mass the 5-6 and the 7- 11-year-old groups differed significantly; (b) for weight the 5-8 and 9- 11-year-old groups differed significantly; and (c) for volume the 5-10 and the 11-year-old groups differed significantly from each other in number of conservation responses given. These findings agreed with expectations based on Piaget's results.

In Piaget's early studies (1951a) he assigned different tests to the age level at which the per cent passing was 75.[4] Although he gave no percentages for the

---

[4] For a test oriented approach to the replication of Piaget's work cf. Laurendeau & Pinard (1957).

TABLE 1 · Per Cent[a] of Conservation Responses for Mass, Weight, and Volume
at Successive Age Levels
(N = 25 at each Age Level)

Type of quantity	Age level						
	5	6	7	8	9	10	11
Mass	19	51	70	72	86	94	92
Weight	21	52	51	44	73	89	78
Volume	0	4	0	4	4	19	25

[a] Of 75 possible responses.

conservation experiments one can assume that he used the same criterion for assigning the conservation of mass to ages 7-8; the conservation of weight to ages 9-10; and the conservation of volume to ages 11-12. The results of the present study were converted into percentages for comparison with Piaget's criterion and these are presented in Table 1.

Table 1 shows that the 70 per cent point for mass was reached at the seven year level but that the 75 per cent point was not reached until age nine. For weight the 73 per cent was reached at age nine and the 75 per cent point by age 10. In this study the 75 per cent point for volume was not reached at the 11 year level.

The slight discrepancies between Piaget's results and those in Table 1 for weight and mass could easily be due to the small size of the samples used in the present study. The relatively low number of conservation responses at the 11 year level may be due to the fact that Piaget used a somewhat different procedure in his test for the conservation of volume. Piaget had his subjects say whether the ball and the sausage would displace the same amount of water. As a check the same procedure was used with some of the subjects of the present study (after the other testing was completed) and conservation seemed easier to discover by means of the displacement problem.

5. CHILDREN'S EXPLANATIONS

When Piaget interpreted the results of his investigation he made use of children's explanations without categorizing or quantifying them as he did in early studies (Piaget, 1951a). In the present study four types of explanation were distinguished. Two of these were explanations of non-conservation: (a) Romanc-

TABLE 2 · Per Cent for Each of Four Types of Explanation Given at
Successive Age Levels
(N = 25 at each Age Level)

Type of explanation	Age level						
	5	6	7	8	9	10	11
Romancing[a]	4	3	7	7	0	1	0
Perceptual[a]	85	64	53	57	36	32	33
Specific[b]	11	33	40	36	60	51	49
General[b]	0	0	0	0	4	16	18

[a] Explanation of non-conservation.
[b] Explanation of conservation.

ing (Piaget, 1951b, introd.), it's more because "My uncle said so"; (b) Perceptual, it's more because it's, "longer, thinner, thicker, wider, etc." The two types of explanation given for conservation were: (c) Specific, "You didn't add any or take any away," "You can roll it back into a ball and it will be the same," and "The hot dog is longer but thinner so the same"; (d) General, it's the same because "No matter what shape you make it into it won't change the amount." Table 2 shows the per cent for each type of explanation given at each age level.

Table 2 shows that Romancing and Perceptual explanations decrease with age while Specific explanations first increase and then level off with age. Piaget noted the same types and age trends in the explanations given by his subjects. The explanations are one type of evidence Piaget takes for his theory that as the child's thinking develops, it frees itself from its earlier domination by immediate perception. One step in this liberation is the interpretation of a perceptual effect as the result of a specific action which can be reversed (you can roll it back into a ball). A later step is to interpret a perception as but one of a great many possible instances (no matter what shape you make it into it will always be the same). The results in Table 2 agreed with the observations upon which Piaget builds his theory of the developmental changes in the relation between thought and perception.

D. DISCUSSION

The results of the present study agreed with Piaget's findings regarding the ages at which children discover the conservation of mass, weight, and volume. In both studies: the conservation of mass

did not usually appear before the ages 7-8; the conservation of weight did not usually appear before the ages 9-10; and the conservation of volume did not in most cases appear before the age of 11. The discussion will briefly summarize Piaget's interpretation of these results.

Piaget's theory [5] is that concepts of quantity develop in three stages with the final stage ear-marked by the discovery of conservation. Children at the first stage have only a general impression of quantity but are capable of judging crude weight, volume, and mass differences. In the sausage experiment they give non-conservation responses because to their general impression the sausage is different than the ball. When they are forced to break down this impression, by the explanation question, then they judge quantity by single dimensions which they are unable to coordinate one with the other.

Those children who are at the second stage have a differentiated impression of quantity and are unable to judge quantity differences two by two (long-wide, long-narrow, etc.) which Piaget calls *logical multiplication*. Children at this stage give non-conservation responses in the sausage experiment because to their differentiated impression the sausage is both more (in length) and less (in width) than the ball. They are unable to resolve the contradiction, as one child expressed it, "It's more and it's less, I'll take one of each." When these children are forced to explain their non-conservation answers they also judge quantity by single dimensions.

At the third stage children have an abstract quantity concept and judge quan-

---

[5] For more complete presentations of Piaget's theory cf. Piaget (1950; 1957; 1958).

tity in unit terms. In the sausage experiment they immediately predict and judge conservation. Their explanations indicate either that the perceived transformation can be cancelled (the sausage can be rolled back into a ball) or that the perceived differences can be equated (what the sausage gained in length it lost in width) and therefore the quantity is the same.

According to Piaget the *equation of differences* results in the formation of ratios and fixed units and underlies abstract quantity and number (Piaget, 1952) concept formation. On the perceptual plane the equation of differences enables the child to discover that an object which changes in appearance can still be the same in quantity. Piaget's theory is that once conservation is discovered it is immediately externalized and the subject has the impression that conservation is a perceptually given property of the object.

The initial appearance of the conservation of mass at ages 7-8 Piaget attributes to the development by that age of logical multiplication and equation of differences which he speaks of as *mental operations*. The time lag before the discovery of the conservation of weight at ages 9-10 and the even greater lag before the conservation of volume at ages 11-12 Piaget attributes to the quantities themselves. He argues that a quantity is difficult to conceptualize, and so to conserve, to the degree that it is associated with the subject's own action. Length, for example was more easily dissociated from the child's action than was weight. In Piaget's theory, therefore, the discovery of conservation is limited both by the maturational level of the subject and by the properties of the object and in this sense it is both a nature *and* a nurture theory.

E. SUMMARY

One hundred and seventy-five children were asked to predict, judge, and explain the conservation of mass, weight, and volume in a systematic replication of Piaget's investigation. Analysis of variance showed that the number of conservation responses varied significantly with: Age Level; Type of Quantity; Age Level-Type of Quantity Interaction; but not with Type of Response. Romancing and Perceptual non-conservation explanations decreased, while Specific and General conservation explanations increased, with age.

The results were in close agreement with Piaget's finding of a regular, age related order in the discoveries of the conservation of mass, weight, and volume. Briefly presented was Piaget's theory that quantity concepts develop through three stages with the final stage ear-marked by the discovery of their conservation.

REFERENCES

1. ELKIND, D. The development of quantitative thinking: A systematic replication of Piaget's studies. *J. Genet. Psychol.*, 1961, *98*, 37–46.
2. INHELDER, B., & PIAGET, J. The growth of logical thinking from childhood to adolescence. New York: Basic Books, 1958.
3. LAURENDEAU, M., & PINARD, A. Une methode rationelle de localization des testes dans echelles d'age. *Canad. J. Psychol.*, 1957, *11*, 33–47.
4. LINDQUIST, E. F. Design and Analysis of Experiments in Psychology and Education. Cambridge, Mass.: Riverside, 1953.

5. PIAGET, J., & INHELDER, B.   Le development   des   quantites   chez
l'enfant. Paris: Delachaux and
Niestle, 1940.
6. PIAGET, J.   The Psychology of Intelligence. London: Broadway, 1950.
7. PIAGET, J.   Judgment and Reasoning
in the Child. London: Routledge,
1951.

8. PIAGET, J.   The Child's Conception
of the World. London: Routledge,
1951.

9. PIAGET, J.   The Child's Conception
of Number. London: Routledge,
1952.

10. PIAGET, J.   Logic and Psychology.
New York: Basic Books, 1957.

EXPERIMENTAL ANALYSIS

OF THE DEVELOPMENT

OF THE CONSERVATION

OF NUMBER [1]

JOACHIM F. WOHLWILL
ROLAND C. LOWE

IN PIAGET'S THEORY of intellectual development (8), a central role is assigned to the child's conceptualization of the principle of "conservation," i.e., his realization of the principle that a particular dimension of an object may remain invariant under changes in other, irrelevant aspects of the situation. For instance, children who lack conservation will assert that the relative weight of two objects has changed when the shape of one

of them is altered or that numerical equality between two collections of objects no longer holds following a change in the length over which they extend. This phenomenon, which has been demonstrated for a variety of other dimensions, including those of volume, area and length, represents, according to Piaget, a manifestation of the immature level of functioning of the child's mental processes and of their failure to conform to the operational structures of logical thought.

Although Piaget has described some of the precursors of this notion of conservation in children who have not yet attained this level, little is known thus far

[1] This investigation was supported by a research grant to the senior author from the National Science Foundation (G-8608). Nelson Butters assisted in the collection of data.

Reprinted by permission from *Child Development*, 1962, *33*, 153–167.

about the specific ways in which the transition from lack of conservation to the presence of conservation takes place. It is apparent, however, that an adequate explanation of this problem ultimately requires a clearer understanding of the psychological processes at work in this transition phase.

One approach to this goal is to expose children presumed to be slightly below the age of onset of conservation to selected, systematically manipulated learning experiences, designed to call into play different factors believed to be important in the development of conservation. Any differential changes in the children's tendency to give conservation responses should then reflect the role played by the particular factors manipulated. At the same time, a more detailed examination of the interrelationship among different tasks involving conservation and closely related concepts should likewise extend our understanding of the nature of this problem.

The domain of number lends itself particularly well to the investigation of the development of conservation, for several reasons. First of all, recent empirical work (3, 4, 12) has given strong support to the notion that the attainment of the level of conservation marks a clearly defined stage in the formation of the number concept. Secondly, in this domain the problem of conservation can be readily related to development in other aspects of the number concept (e.g., counting, arithmetical skills, etc.), rather than constituting the somewhat isolated, *sui generis* problem which conservation appears to represent for such dimensions as weight or volume. Thirdly, and most important, the number dimension occupies a unique position in regard to the question of con-

servation, insofar as the number of elements contained in a particular collection is exactly identifiable by the corresponding integer; by the same token, the *fact* of conservation—i.e., that the number of a collection remains invariant under changes in the spatial arrangement of its elements—is readily verifiable, through the operation of counting. This feature creates an opportunity for assessing the role of symbolic, mediational processes, as well as of reinforcement, in the development of conservation.

This very uniqueness of the number dimension represents of course a potential limitation, as regards the applicability of the results to the problem of conservation in general. It is of considerable interest, therefore, that a rather similar investigation of the acquisition of the conservation of weight has simultaneously been carried out by Smedslund (10); its results will thus provide us with a valuable basis for comparison, as we will note in the discussion section.

THREE ALTERNATIVE THEORETICAL VIEWS OF NUMBER CONSERVATION

If one looks closely at the problem confronting the child in the conservation situation, several different interpretations of the acquisition of this principle suggest themselves. We may label these alternatives the reinforcement hypothesis, the differentiation hypothesis, and the inference hypothesis.

The *reinforcement* hypothesis would propose that, as a child obtains increasing experience in counting numerical collections of different types and in different arrangements, he gradually learns that alterations in the perceptual dimensions of a set do not change its number, i.e., that the same number is obtained from counting the set after as before such a change. Accordingly, systematic reinforced practice in counting rows of elements prior and subsequent to changes in the length of the rows should promote conservation.

The *differentiation* hypothesis would interpret lack of conservation in the young child as a response to an irrelevant but highly visible cue (length) which typically shows substantial correlation with that of number. The child thus has to learn to differentiate the dimension of number from this irrelevant cue. Repeated experience designed to neutralize the cue of length, and thus to weaken the association between it and the dimension of number in the child's thinking, should be expected, then, to facilitate conservation responses.

The *inference* hypothesis, finally, is based in part on Piaget's own analysis of the role of learning in the development of logical operations (9). Piaget maintains that experiential factors can only become effective, in this realm of development, to the extent that it builds on the child's previously developed structures of thought, as through the activation of a reasoning process prior to, but logically related to the one to be developed. In the case of conservation, one possible implication might be that by dint of cumulative exposure to the effects of adding an element to a collection, or subtracting one from it, the child may be led to *infer* conservation as the result of a change involving neither addition nor subtraction. This implication is supported, incidentally, by the explanations frequently voiced by children who admit conservation, e.g., "it's still the same, because you haven't taken any away."

Prior work by the senior author

also bears on this last alternative. First, in the course of a sequential analysis of the development of the number concept (12), it was found that success on tasks involving simple addition and subtraction not only regularly preceded success on a task embodying the principle of conservation, but appeared, in a certain number of subjects, to lead to the emergence of conservation responses. In a subsequent pilot study (11), it was found, furthermore, that subjects given a limited set of trials involving addition and subtraction subsequently made more conservation responses than subjects given equivalent training on conservation, though the difference did not reach significance.

The results of this pilot study suggested the possibility of a more extended investigation of the development of the conservation of number, by bringing to bear each of the above-mentioned theoretical interpretations in the context of a small-scale learning experiment and determining the effectiveness of the various conditions of learning in bringing about conservation, both in a limited and a generalized sense. This is the main aim of the study to be reported, a subsidiary purpose being to provide information regarding the cross-situational generality of number conservation and its relationship to other types of number skills.

METHOD

The experiment was conducted in two sessions over two successive days (except for two Ss, for whom the interval between sessions was two and six days, respectively). The general design called for (a) a predominantly verbal pretest, partly of a diagnostic character, to reveal S's ability to deal with number concepts,

TABLE 1 · DESIGN OF THE STUDY

Order	First day	Order	Second day
1.	Diagnostic questions	1.	Training series (trials 10 to 18)
2.	Verbal conservation pretest	2.	Nonverbal conservation posttest
3.	Pretraining in number matching	3.	Verbal conservation posttest
4.	Nonverbal conservation pretest		
5.	Training series (trials 1 to 9)		

and partly dealing specifically with conservation; (b) a "nonverbal" test of conservation given in the form of a series of multiple-choice trials; (c) a training series on tasks presumed to be related to number conservation; and finally (d) a repetition of both the nonverbal and verbal tests of conservation to provide a measure of learning or change with respect to the understanding of this notion. This design is summarized in Table 1.

PROCEDURE

Diagnostic Questions. 1. *Number Production.* S was shown a pile of red poker chips and was told, "Give me six of them."

2. *Number Equivalence.* E laid out a row of seven red chips. S was told, "Put down just as many of your chips over here (indicating an imaginary row paralleling E's row), as I have here."

3. *Number vs. Length.* E laid out a row of six blue chips extending beyond the limits of his own row of seven red chips (S's row being longer than E's). S was asked, "Who has more chips, you or I?" If he answered that he had more, but without having counted the chips, he was asked, "How do you know?"

These three questions concerned, respectively, the child's ability to (a) reproduce a particular cardinal number, (b) establish a relationship of numerical equivalence between two collections, and (c) respond to the dimension of number independent of irrelevant perceptual cues (e.g., length).

Verbal Conservation Pretest. 4. Two rows of seven chips each, one blue and the other red, were placed parallel to each other so that both rows were of the same length, and the chips in one row were directly opposite those in the other. S was asked, "Who has more chips, you or I?" This question, hereafter referred to as Q, was repeated for all the items in this part.

5a. E then extended the red row in both directions to a length about twice that of the blue row. (Q)

5b. The red row was subdivided into two rows of four and three chips placed parallel to S's blue row. (Q)

5c. The red chips were placed in a vertical pile in front of the blue row. (Q)

5d. The red chips were inserted into an opaque tube. (Q)

Question 4 served chiefly a preparatory function, i.e., to set up the following questions of conservation. Question 5a represented the main criterion of number conservation, while 5b to 5d indicate the generalizability of conservation. Accordingly, questions 5a to 5d were cumulative: if an S did not assert equality at any point, the remaining questions were omitted.

6. Questions 4 and 5a were repeated with 12 chips in each row instead of seven.

The suggestive nature of the questions (Q) used above ("Who has more chips, you or I?") requires comment. It should be noted that its initial use (in question 4) is in a situation where perceptual cues mitigate against the child's following the suggestion of inequality implicit in the question: the matched rows of chips afford a strong cue for direct perception of equivalence.[2] Second, the suggestion applied both in the pre- and the posttests and thus may be presumed to have played a constant role on both occasions.

Pretraining in Number Matching. The apparatus used here, shown in Figure 1, consisted of an upright panel containing three windows which had the numer-

---

[2] All but 14 of the Ss did in fact resist E's suggestion, usually through some such answer as "we both do" or "you and me." The 14 Ss who failed to do so were made to count the two rows, whereupon the question was again put to them. If S persisted in following the suggestion of inequality, E confronted them with the results of their counting and, if necessary, told him outright "So we both have the same, don't we?" This procedure was necessary in order to proceed to the following part, where S's prior knowledge of the equivalence of the two rows had to be presupposed.

als 6, 7, 8 inscribed on them from left to right. The Ss were told they were going to play a game, in which they would find a chip hidden behind one of the windows, and that the object of the game was to get as many chips as they could. For the pretraining phase, the procedure consisted in presenting singly a series of six 5 by 5 in. cards showing six, seven, or eight colored stars arranged in simple configurations. On each trial a colored chip was hidden behind the corresponding window. S was informed that the number of stars on the card would tell him behind which window the chip was hidden and urged to count the stars. When S opened the correct window, he was instructed to remove the chip and place it onto a board at his side. He was told to fill up the board with chips; if he found "a lot" of them, he would on the following day receive a toy. The purpose of this series was to create a set in the child to respond to number, as well as to familiarize Ss with the specific numbers shown. A correction procedure was used which involved having Ss correct any mistakes

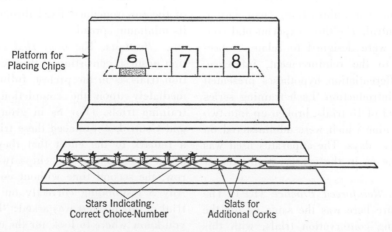

Figure 1. Apparatus for nonverbal conservation and training trials, showing device for presenting variable-length rows of sample numbers and display-board for choice numbers.

made in counting the stars and guiding S to the correct window when, as occasionally happened, a S counted correctly but made an incorrect choice.

Nonverbal Conservation Pretest. This series consisted of three two-phase trials. Ss were presented with a row of colored stars, either six, seven, or eight in number, mounted on a set of corks which rested on a series of connected scissors-like slats. This apparatus, depicted in Figure 1, permitted lengthening or shortening the row while preserving the straight-line arrangement. E told S that he was to count the stars in order to find the chip behind the correct window. Following S's initial response, he was made to return the chip to E, who replaced it behind the same window, and then, depending on the trial, either extended or shortened the row of stars. S was allowed to count only on the first phase; he thus had to find the correct window on the second phase on the basis of the knowledge gained in the first and in the face of the perceptual changes in the row of stars.

Training. There were four conditions of training: Reinforced Practice, Addition and Subtraction, Dissociation, and Control. The three experimental conditions were designed to relate, respectively, to the reinforcement, inference, and differentiation hypotheses presented in the introduction. Each training series consisted of 18 trials, broken up into two sets of nine which were administered on successive days. The apparatus used was the same as in the conservation pretetst trials.

a. *Reinforced Practice* (RP). The procedure here was the same as for the preceding conservation trials, with this modification: if S made an incorrect response on the second phase of the trial, he was told to count the stars, so as to find out which window he should have chosen. E then exposed the chip behind that window but did not allow S to remove the chip.

b. *Addition and Subtraction* (A&S). These trials were similar to the conservation trials, except that on two-thirds of the trials, following the S's initial response after counting, E either added or subtracted a star at the end of the row before changing its length. The remaining third of the series consisted of straight conservation trials which were interspersed with the A&S trials.

c. *Dissociation* (Diss.). Unlike the above, these were single-phase trials, with the length of the row varying from one trial to the next over a range of four times the smallest length. S was urged to count the stars and open the corresponding window; if correct, he received the chip. Over the series of trials each number of stars appeared equally often at each of the different settings of length.

d. *Control.* This series of trials consisted likewise of single-phase trials as in the Dissociation condition, but the length of the row remained fixed throughout at its minimum spread.

Posttests. The *nonverbal* conservation posttest, consisting of three conservation trials as in the pretest, followed immediately upon the completion of the training trials. (For Ss in groups Diss. and Control, E prefaced these trials with a remark to the effect that they would again have to find the chips twice in a row, the second time without counting.) Any S responding correctly on the last trial of this posttest was asked: "How did you know where to look for the chip that time?"

The *verbal* conservation posttest,

consisting of a repetition of questions 4 through 6 as given in the pretest, concluded the experimental session.

At the end of the second session, each child was shown a variety of dime-store toys from which he picked one to take back with him as his "prize." Altogether, each of the sessions lasted about 20 to 25 minutes per child. The children's level of attention and motivation appeared to have remained high throughout these sessions, the "game" aspect of the situation apparently having proved effective in capturing their interest. This was reflected in their universal eagerness to return to it when called for the second session.

SUBJECTS

Subjects for this study were 72 kindergarten children, 35 boys and 37 girls, with a mean CA of 5 years, 10 months. (This age level was selected as one at which most children would still show lack of number conservation, while yet being old enough to be able potentially to profit from the learning experience; in other words, an interaction between learning and developmental level is presumed.) There were 18 Ss in each condition of training, Ss being assigned to their group according to a predetermined order. The four subgroups were closely matched as to their mean CA. (The range of the means was one month.)

The children were enrolled in the kindergarten classes of three public schools in Worcester, Massachusetts, located in predominantly lower-middle-class neighborhoods. They thus had been and were being exposed to a variety of activities in the area of number skills, consisting mainly of counting, number-matching, and identifying simple numerals.[3]

RESULTS

The presentation of the results of the experiment is divided into three sections: the verbal pretest, including the diagnostic and verbal conservation questions; the learning of nonverbal conservation; and the transfer of training to the verbal posttest.

Verbal Pretest. Considering first the diagnostic questions, only one of the 72 Ss failed question 1, while four failed question 2. On question 3, however, only 20 Ss gave a correct response (i.e., based on counting the chips either before or in justification of their judgments). These results show that the Ss had adequate facility in counting and dealing with numbers symbolically in simple situations, such as producing a required number of elements and in matching two groups for number. Their success on these two tasks, however, contrasted sharply with their performance on question 3 where the task required the abstraction of number as independent from certain irrelevant perceptual cues. It should be noted that, since this question followed question 2 without a break, some Ss may have seen E take a chip from his row in setting up question 3. Thus, some of the correct responses may have been facilitated by this circumstance. In fact, nine Ss explicitly based their answers on this cue. (Control over

[3] The authors are greatly indebted to the principals and teachers of the Freeland, Columbus Park and Woodland Elementary Schools in Worcester, Massachusetts, for their splendid cooperation in providing subjects and facilities for this investigation. We also wish to acknowledge the assistance of the Worcester Country Day School in connection with a pilot study from which this investigation evolved.

this factor in a subsequent study did indeed result in lowering still further the number of Ss succeeding on this question, so as to equate it in difficulty with the conservation question, 5a.)

On the verbal conservation items, only nine of the 72 Ss answered correctly on question 5a. A breakdown of the incorrect responses shows that 41 Ss responded to the length of the rows, while 22 responded to the density of the elements. This tendency to regard the longer row as more numerous was also found on question 3 of the diagnostic questions.

As for the generality of the Ss' concept of number conservation, of the nine Ss who succeeded on question 5a, six extended their conservation to 5b, five to 5c, and four to 5d. On question 6, on the other hand, involving conservation for 12 elements, seven of these Ss showed conservation, in addition to one who had not responded correctly on question 5a. Thus, when conditions were qualitatively different, generalization was somewhat lower than it was when the new situation differed only in a quantitative way.

Nonverbal Conservation Learning. Table 2 summarizes the performance of each group on the verbal and nonverbal tests of conservation, before and after the learning series.

TABLE 2 · PERFORMANCE ON CONSERVATION BEFORE AND AFTER TRAINING

Condition of training	VERBAL CONSERVATION*			NONVERBAL CONSERVATION†		
	Pretest	Posttest	Net change	Pretest	Posttest	Net change
A&S	1	3	+2	1.05	1.77	+.72
RP	2	3	+1	1.22	1.50	+.28
Diss.	4	2	—2	1.05	1.16	+.11
Control	2	4	+2	1.44	1.96	+.52

* Number of Ss giving correct responses on question 5a.
† Mean correct responses out of three trials.

An analysis of variance revealed no significant differences among training groups with respect to learning of nonverbal conservation ($F = 1.73$; $p > .05$ for 3 and 68 df). However, the mean overall difference scores differed significantly from 0 ($t = 3.95$; $p < .01$), showing that for the total group as a whole conservation did increase from pre- to posttest.

A comparison between the responses of the A&S and RP groups on the conservation trials of their respective training series shows that the former Ss were correct on 48 per cent of their trials, while the latter were correct on 47 per cent. It will be recalled that only six conservation trials were given in the A&S series, while the RP series consisted wholly of 18 conservation trials for which, in addition, a correction procedure was used. Hence, direct training on conservation was no more effective than the more intermittent practice afforded on the A&S trials.

It was also found that the A&S group had greater success on the A&S trials than on the straight conservation trials: for the former, 59 per cent of the responses were correct, as compared to the 48 per cent for the conservation trials. This finding, which is consistent with the results of previous research (*12*), represents of course a prerequisite for the use of the A&S trials as a training experience.

The training trials under the control and dissociation condition, which involved only rote counting, were quite easy for these Ss: a near perfect performance was the norm.

Transfer of Training to Verbal Posttest. With respect to verbal conservation, there were very few changes in any group. The number of Ss showing conservation of number on the pretest was nine, while 12 Ss showed it on the posttest. Two Ss changed to conservation from the A&S group, two from the Control group, and one from the RP group. Two Ss, in the Diss. group, who had shown conservation on the pretest, failed to do so on the posttest (cf. Table 2).

It is interesting to note that, whereas on the pretest of verbal conservation only four of the nine Ss having conservation showed perfect extension of this concept on items 5b through 5d, on the posttest nine of the 12 Ss showing conservation did show this extension, the remaining three Ss belonging to the group of five who had not shown conservation on the pretest. This seems to indicate the unstable nature of the Ss' conservation, as acquired in this situation.

Of the 12 Ss showing conservation on question 5a of the posttest, 11 again showed conservation for 12 elements (question 6).

DISCUSSION

In this section we will consider some of the more specific implications of the results for the nonverbal conservation learning and for the transfer to the verbal test, leaving until a later section certain more general conclusions suggested by this investigation.

Nonverbal conservation learning. As regards the "learning" of conservation within the limited context of the training trials, a significant amount of improvement from pre- to posttest did take place for the group as a whole, but the lack of significant differential effects due to the conditions of training and the fact that the Control group gained more than either the Reinforced Practice or the Dissociation groups clearly prevents us from attributing beneficial effects to any specific learning condition.

The failure of the RP group to outperform the others nevertheless deserves comment. It had actually been anticipated that this group, which received essentially one continuous series of conservation trials, would as a result of this extended practice show the greatest amount of learning from pre- to posttest, although such learning might not necessarily transfer to the verbal posttest. The contrary results bear out the ineffectiveness of continued reinforced practice in bringing about conservation responses, even of a purely empirical sort (i.e., "pick the window where the chip was before"), which the above-mentioned pilot study (*11*) had already hinted at in a much shorter training series. Whether a still more extended series than that used in the present study might have yielded a greater amount of learning remains an open question, of course.

The greatest amount of improvement from the pre- to the posttest trials, on the other hand, took place in the A&S group, exposed to 12 addition and subtraction trials, set off against six conservation trials; these results are thus at least consistent with the possible role of a process of inference (i.e., conservation as the end-product of changes involving neither addition nor subtraction) to which the previous studies (*11, 12*) had pointed.[4]

Finally, as regards the virtual absence of learning in the Dissociation group, it might be suggested, in retrospect, that the very act of counting the stars interfered with directing the child's attention to the cue of length, which the condition was designed to neutralize. If so, no improvement on the conservation trials, based on explicit disregard of the biasing cue of length, would result.

Transfer to verbal conservation questions. Perhaps the major finding of the study is that none of the above procedures proved in any way effective in leading to an understanding of the principle of number conservation, such as the verbal posttest demanded. For instance, over the four training groups combined, a total of 10 *S*s shifted from zero or one conservation responses on the nonverbal pretest to three on the posttest, yet these shifts did not bring with them a single change to conservation on the verbal posttest.

In explanation for this failure of the nonverbal conservation learning to transfer to the verbal posttest, one might suggest that the nonverbal learning situation favored the development of an essentially empirical rule, i.e., "the correct number remains the same as before after *E* shortens or lenthens the row," or simply "look for the chip behind the window where the chip was just previously." If this were

the case, little if any transfer to the very different situation confronting the child in the verbal conservation questions would be expected. The verbalizations elicited from those *S*s who made a correct response on the last posttest conservation trial lend some support to this argument: many of the *S*s actually gave no meaningful explanation for their choice at all (e.g., "I just knew," or "I thought hard about the stars"), while most of the rest responded in such terms as "It was there before."

Interestingly enough, Smedslund (*10*), on the basis of his work on the learning of the conservation of weight, similarly argues for the very limited, nonconceptual nature of such learning. In his study, *S*s were exposed to an extended series of judgments of the relative weight of two masses of plasticine, before and after one of these was deformed in shape; each judgment was reinforced by weighing the two objects on a balance. While *S*s did learn to anticipate correctly the conservation of weight of the deformed object, the author feels that this learning was mainly that of an empirical fact, rather than of a logical principle, as shown both in the kind of explanations offered by the children, and in the lack of transfer of the learning to problems embodying logically equivalent principles (e.g., transitivity relationships).[5] Paren-

---

[4] It is worth noting that in a subsequent study, modeled closely after the present one, training with addition and subtraction again resulted in the greatest amount of improvement in (nonverbal) conservation, though the superiority over the control group still failed to be significant. In other respects, too, this study, in which the learning series was increased to 24 trials and the pre- and posttests of conservation to six trials each, yielded results which were closely comparable to those reported here.

[5] Perhaps more convincing evidence on this point comes from an ingenious "extinction" procedure which Smedslund (personal communication) has most recently utilized. This consisted in confronting *S*s with apparent nonconservation, the weight of the deformed object being altered by surreptitiously adding or removing a small amount of plasticine. Under these circumstances *S*s who had acquired conservation through their learning experience readily acceded to the lack of conservation which they seemed to be witnessing, i.e., abandoned their recently "learned" conservation. In contrast, *S*s who had developed conservation spontaneously

thetically, it is worth noting that in Smedslund's study a training procedure embodying addition and subtraction of matter, in a manner somewhat analogous to that of our A&S condition, yielded nearly as much learning as continued practice on conservation problems.

There remains, however, an alternative interpretation of our results. It is based on a major difference between the nonverbal and verbal tests of conservation, which might itself have accounted for the lack of transfer observed: while the nonverbal test involved a match between a given collection of elements and the corresponding, symbolically indicated number, the verbal test entailed rather the equivalence of the numerosity of two collections of elements. Thus, it is conceivable that the children did in fact learn, in their nonverbal training, that the *absolute* number of elements remained unchanged, without transfering this principle to the *relative* number of elements in two collections, in the verbal test. Implausible as this possibility may seem to a sophisticated adult, it is borne out by the total inefficacy of asking the children to count the two collections after a nonconservation response on the verbal posttest: of 23 Ss who were asked to do so, 19 persevered in their nonconservation responses when the question was repeated, immediately after ascertaining that there were seven chips in each row. Most recently, furthermore, Greco (5) has obtained clear evidence that children may

show conservation in the first or absolute sense, without showing it in the second or relative sense.

Finally, the use of nonverbal methods in the investigation of children's thinking deserves brief comment. While the ineffectiveness of the nonverbal training procedures in our study may seem to cast doubt on the fruitfulness of such methods, they have been used to good advantage in several other recent studies (2, 12); moreover, the pitfalls of the verbal interrogation approach, at least as used by Piaget, have been persuasively analyzed (1, pp. 536f; 2).[6] Perhaps the central point is that it is incumbent on those applying nonverbal methods to determine, by varied and appropriate transfer tests, the breadth and depth of the child's understanding of the principles or concepts in question—a point which appears of special relevance to the application of automatic teaching methods to instruction in this and similar areas.

CONCLUSIONS

Although the predominantly negative outcome of this investigation does not allow us to give any definitive answer to the question posed at the outset, concerning the mechanisms involved in the child's acquisition of the concept of the conservation of number, a few general conclusions regarding this problem may be permissible.

---

tended to invent explanations in order to reconcile this apparent contradiction, such as "we must have lost something on the floor."

Since the preparation of this paper portions of Smedslund's work (including the material of the personal communication referred to in the previous paragraph) have appeared in print (10). (Additional papers in this series, to be published in the same journal, are in press as of this writing.)

[6] Relevant in this connection is a study most recently reported by Yost, Siegel, and McMichael (13), demonstrating considerable positive transfer from a nonverbal presentation of a probability-relationship problem to the corresponding verbal version of this problem as used by Piaget. These authors likewise found that by their nonverbal procedures the problem could be dealt with successfully at a much earlier age than Piaget had found, thus confirming the similar findings of Braine (2).

First, the strong tendency of the children in this investigation to respond on the basis of differences in length in making numerical comparisons between two collections, even without the element of perceptual *change* introduced in the conservation situation (cf. question 3), lends some weight to the interpretation of lack of conservation as a failure to differentiate number from irrelevant perceptual cues, pointing to an aspect of the problem which appears to have received insufficient attention in Piaget's theoretical account of conservation.

Second, the consistent tendency across several studies for the A&S conditions to yield the most improvement in nonverbal conservation suggests that a process of inference may be operative in the development of number-conservation, even if this inference may be too limited in scope to lead to a generalized understanding of the principle. In view of the fact that children typically receive considerable experience in simple addition and subtraction in the very time period in which conservation generally appears (i.e., in late kindergarten and early first grade), this factor merits further attention.

Third, our investigation highlights the considerable gap separating the ability to *enumerate* collections by counting from a true understanding of the number concept, as it is reflected in the principle of conservation. In this respect the present results are entirely in agreement with those obtained in previous work on the development of the number concept (3, 12). Furthermore, even repeated identification of a collection with a particular number symbol, independent of length, appears to be relatively ineffective in

bringing about conservation, thus raising the question of the adequacy of a mediation-theory approach to this particular aspect of concept formation.

In a more positive vein, two suggestions for future attacks on this problem might be offered. The first is to construct a set of learning experiences which would not only be more extended but, more important, cover a wider variety of situations (i.e., stimulus materials, configurations, specific numbers involved, etc.). This would be in line with Harlow's (6) emphasis on *generalized* experience as a prerequisite for the learning of broad concepts and principles in primates as well as in man. It is plausible to suppose, in fact, that it is precisely such generalized experience—in the classroom, at play, and in other everyday activities of children of this age level—which represents the basis for the seemingly spontaneous appearance of conservation in the child.

The second suggestion is to undertake a thorough, intensive analysis of the ontogenesis of conservation in a selected number of children followed longitudinally. Special attention might be paid to the types of explanations given by the child at various stages, as well as to the stability and generalizability of conservation responses once they appear. Inhelder and Noelting, at the University of Geneva, have in fact already launched such a longitudinal project, with preliminary results that appear promising (cf. 7).

SUMMARY

This study represents an attempt to determine more specifically the nature of the processes at work in the development of the notion of the conservation of number (invariance of number under changes in length or configuration of a collection), as studied by Piaget. The investigation was in the form of a nonverbal matching-from-sample type learning experiment, preceded and followed by verbal questions to measure the child's understanding of the conservation principle. There were four conditions of training, involving respectively the role of reinforced practice on conservation, of dissociation of biasing perceptual cues, and of inferential mechanisms based on the recognition of the effects of addition and subtraction of elements; a control group was also included. Subjects were 72 kindergarten-age children.

The results indicate an over-all increase in nonverbal conservation responses from a pre- to a posttest, within the limited context of the learning task, but they show no significant differences attributable to the conditions of training. Transfer of conservation learning to the verbal posttest was negligible under all conditions, indicating that whatever learning may have taken place was of a rather restricted type, representing perhaps more the formation of an empirical rule than the understanding of a general principle.

These results, together with additional findings pertaining to the relationship of certain number skills to conservation, are discussed in terms of their implications for the problem of the development of conservation.

REFERENCES

1. Berko, J., & Brown, R. *Psycholinguistic research methods*. In P. H. Mussen (Ed.), *Handbook of research methods in child development*. Wiley, 1960. Pp. 517–557.

2. Braine, M. D. S. The ontogeny of certain logical operations: Piaget's formulation examined by nonverbal methods. *Psychol. Monogr.*, 1959, *73*, No. 4 (Whole No. 475).

3. Dodwell, P. C. Children's understanding of number and related concepts. *Canad. J. Psychol.*, 1960, *14*, 191–203.

4. Elkind, D. The development of quantitative thinking: a systematic replication of Piaget's studies. *J. genet. Psychol.*, 1961, *98*, 37–46.

5. Greco, P. Quotité et quantité. In J. Piaget (Ed.), *Structures numériques élémentaires*. Paris: Presses Univer. France, in press. (Etudes d'épistémologie génétique, XIII.)

6. Harlow, H. F. Thinking. In H. Helson (Ed.), *Theoretical foundations of psychology*. Van Nostrand, 1951. Pp. 452–505.

7. Inhelder, B., & Noelting, G. Le passage d'un stade au suivant dans le développement des fonctions cognitives. *Proc. 15th Int. Congr. Psychol.*, Brussels, 1957, 435–438.

8. Piaget, J. *The psychology of intelligence*. London: Routledge & Paul, 1950.

9. Piaget, J. Apprentissage et connaissance. In J. Piaget (Ed.), *La logique des apprentissages*. Paris: Presses Univer. France, 1959. Pp. 159–188. (Etudes d'épistémologie génétique, X.)

10. Smedslund, J. The acquisition of conservation of substance and weight in children. *J. Scan. Psychol.*, 1961, *2*, 71–87.

11. Wohlwill, J. F. Un essai d'apprentissage dans le domaine de la con-

servation du nombre. In J. Piaget (Ed.), *L'apprentissage des structures logiques*. Paris: Presses Univer. France, 1959. Pp. 125–135. (Etudes d'épistémologie génétique, IX.)

12. WOHLWILL, J. F. A study of the development of the number concept by scalogram analysis. *J. genet. Psychol.*, 1960, *97*, 345–377.

13. YOST, P. A., SIEGEL, A. E., & MC-MICHAEL, J. E. Nonverbal probability judgments by young children. Paper read at Soc. Res. Child Develpm., Univer. Park, Pa., March, 1961.

PAIRED-ASSOCIATE LEARNING AND MEDIATION | 13

SINCE THE BEGINNING of psychologists' interests in learning and memory, verbal materials have been used for research purposes. The classic work of Ebbinghaus, which dates back to 1885 (translated into English some years later: Ebbinghaus, 1913), stands as an outstanding contribution to the field in terms of method and results. It was Ebbinghaus who introduced the nonsense syllable, which consists of a vowel between two consonants and can not be found as a word in the dictionary. These syllables were introduced with the hope that the learning process could be examined independently of other variables which might affect the learning of real words. This hope turned out to be somewhat naive in light of the fact that even nonsense syllables may be shown to be associated with real words in such a way as to markedly affect the learning process. As a way of illustrating this relationship and measuring it, a number of researchers have scaled nonsense syllables in terms of their association value so that this important factor may be controlled and/or systematically varied in experiments of verbal learning (see Hilgard, 1951, pp. 539–559).

While nonsense syllables are highly useful for many kinds of experiments, real words were used by Ebbinghaus and continue to be used frequently in studies of verbal learning. As the nonsense syllable has been scaled for association value, efforts also have been made to determine the associations among words (Russell and Jenkins, 1954).

While a variety of methods have been used to study verbal learning, the two methods that have received the greatest amount of attention are those of serial and paired-associate learning. The serial-learning method involves the presentation of a series of words one after the other in a set order over and over until the subject is able to anticipate each word in the list when he sees or hears the preceding word. Children begin learning the number system in this way. They learn that one is followed by two, and two by three and so on.

If we analyze the serial method carefully, however, we find that it is rather complex. The first word in the list is a stimulus for the second word, the second word then becomes a stimulus for the third word and so on. Each word except the first and last acts as both a stimulus and a response in the learning of the list. Such an arrangement makes it difficult to separate, for theoretical purposes, the functions of stimulus and response in the learning process.

Although serial learning is particularly suited to some problems, in order to avoid some of the complications of analyzing serial learning psychologists have used the method of paired-associate presentation to study the learning process. This method presents the subject with a list of pairs of words. The first word in the pair is the stimulus and the second the response. The subject is required to learn for each stimulus the response that is paired with it. The list of pairs is presented in a different order on each trial to avoid serial learning and to force the subject to learn the list by pairs. Children probably learn their first words in this way. Mother is presented as a stimulus with the verbal response "mama" required. Interspersed with presentations of mother are presentations of other stimuli such as father, milk, doll, dog, and other familiar stimuli to which appropriate verbal responses are being learned. Learning a foreign language is frequently done by the paired-associate method, as when flash cards are used with the English word stimulus on one side of the card and the foreign word response on the other.

It is perhaps surprising, in light of the vast literature using these two methods, that so little has been done with children. Considering the complexity of the problem investigated with these methods, it might be appropriate to use children as subjects in order to reduce or eliminate the importance of some of the variables ordinarily affecting such learning. Two difficulties that immediately face the researcher interested in using children as subjects are the inability of the young child to read and the lack of any substantial body of methodological information equivalent to that available to the psychologist who works with adults. It is necessary to know the appropriate time intervals for presentation of stimuli and responses, intertrial intervals, length of lists, kinds of materials that may be presented, association strengths among words, and many other factors that may vary with the age of the child but are related to initiating research of this kind.

Some beginnings have been made, however, in solving these problems. An apparatus allowing the presentation of pictures as well as many other varieties of materials has been devised and is used by several of the investigators included here. Pictures have been used rather than words to avoid reading problems. The effects of various interpair intervals on learning rate have been investigated (McCullers, 1961). Association norms for 200 words have been collected over a wide age range (Palermo and Jenkins, in press).

The first study in this section reports on the word associations for a set of words that was obtained from children and that demonstrates the importance of knowing about this variable in designing a study of paired-associate learning. Lists of pairs with high associative strength are more rapidly learned than lists composed of pairs of low associative strength.

The second study provides a definitive set of data relative to the interfering effects of learning a new response to a stimulus to which another response has previously been learned, in comparison to learning a response to a stimulus to which no response has previously been learned. This study demonstrates that the relative difficulty of learning a new response varies as a function of the amount of training an old response has had in that situation and represents an important contribution to a historical problem.

The last three studies deal with a problem older than the pioneering research of Ebbinghaus. The British associationist psychologists were much concerned, in their reflections about the human mind, with the problem of how one thought or idea leads to others. They were concerned with trains of thought or the associations of the mind. The British associationists, however, did no laboratory research, and one hundred years later psychologists are just beginning to develop some methods for experimental investigation of the associations of the mind. The approach has come through the study of mediated associations, a part of the concern of the earlier psychologists.

In its simplest form, mediated associations refer to the linking of a chain of responses from A to B to C. In the third experiment in this section, using the traditional paired-associate method, the child is taught to respond to A with B and then is taught to respond to B with C, and finally he is presented with A again and is found to respond with C. The assumption, outlined in detail in the Norcross and Spiker paper, is that when A is presented in the third task B occurs implicitly (it does not occur explicitly because it is inappropriate to the task), and since C has previously been learned to B, C then occurs to A.

Each of the last three studies deals with the chaining of responses. In the first case, pictures are used as stimuli and words as responses, while in the second case, colors are used as stimuli and words and muscular movements are used as responses. In the third case, colored objects are used as stimuli and word choices as responses. Together the three studies give strong support to an analysis of the association of thoughts in terms of stimuli and responses.

REFERENCES

EBBINGHAUS, H. *Memory: a contribution to experimental psychology.* (Translated by H. A. Ruger and C. E. Bussenius.) New York: Teachers College, Columbia Univ., 1913.

HILGARD, E. R. Methods and procedures in the study of learning. In S. S. Stevens (Ed.), *Handbook of experimental psychology.* New York: Wiley, 1951.

McCULLERS, J. C. Effects of associative strength, grade level, and interpair interval in verbal paired-associate learning. *Child Develpm.*, 1961, *32*, 773–778.

PALERMO, D. S. and JENKINS, J. J. *Word association norms: Grade school through college.* Minneapolis: University of Minnesota Press. In press.

RUSSELL, W. A. and JENKINS, J. J. The complete Minnesota norms for responses to 100 words from the Kent-Rosanoff Test. Technical Report 11, University of Minnesota, 1954.

Associative Characteristics of Sixty-Three Adjectives and Their Relation to Verbal Paired-Associate Learning in Children [1]

ALFRED CASTANEDA
LEILA SNYDER FAHEL
RICHARD ODOM [2]

CONSIDERABLE INFORMATION regarding verbal learning phenomena has been derived from studies employing the paired-associate method of learning. Fruitful use of this method has been made in conjunction with adult (college age) populations in the empirical and theoretical analyses of such areas of investigation as learning, motivation, and personality. Although it would seem readily adaptable, and considering that only major requirement determining selection of subjects to be studied by this method is the ability to read, it is surprising that it has not received systematic attention in connection with younger (elementary school age) populations. Characteristically, work with this method has employed verbal material (word lists), e.g., adjectives, nonsense syllables, etc., whose associative characteristics have been assessed. Examples of word lists which have been standardized on adult populations and used extensively in paired-associate as well as serial learning experiments are those described by Hilgard (1). However, comparable lists which have been standardized on younger populations are not currently available.

The present report describes the associative characteristics for 63 common adjectives obtained from a population of fourth, fifth, and sixth grade children. The procedure that was used is an adaptation from one followed by Russell and Storms (2) in their development of norms of associative strength in a college age population. Basically, the procedure represents a variation of the word-association method. The frequencies with which given associations occurred to each adjective are described. In order to assess the utility of the present list for paired-associate learning in children, two lists consisting either of high or low association values between the word pairs were employed in a paired-associate experiment involving fifth and sixth grade children.

[1] This study was supported by grants from the Hogg Foundation, University of Texas, and the National Institute of Mental Health (M-4240).
[2] The writers wish to express their appreciation to Mr. T. Houston Foster, Principal, I. W. Popham School, Del Valle, Texas, and Sister Julia, Principal, St. Austin's School, Austin, Texas, for their assistance and cooperation.

Reprinted by permission from *Child Development*, 1961, *32*, 297–304.

METHOD

The experimental list was composed of a total of 69 common adjectives judged to be within the range of reading ability of fourth, fifth, and sixth grade children. However, six adjectives are omitted from the present report since approximately 13 to 22 per cent of the Ss in the present sample failed to read these words correctly.

The words were typed in upper case letters and exposed by means of a Hunter Card Master (Model 340). Each word was exposed for 8 sec. with 2 sec. between exposures and a 10-sec. interval between exposure of the 23rd and 24th words and between the 46th and 47th words. Three different orders of exposing the words were used, and Ss were randomly assigned to one of these conditions.

The S was required to call out any words that the adjective made him think of after first having read it aloud. Each S was given a practice list in order to insure that he comprehended what was to be required of him and to identify those Ss with marked reading disabilities. During the practice list S was prompted to give single words rather than phrases and encouraged to give as many word-associations as possible within the 8-sec. interval. The practice list consisted of 10 words exposed in the following order: CAT, BOY, RUN, DOG, GIRL, ONE, SPOT, BROWN, JUMP, MOTHER. All Ss met a criterion of nine or more words read correctly and one association given to each word on the practice list.

A total of 95 Ss participated. However, the data of 13 Ss from the total sample were excluded. These Ss either failed to read correctly approximately 50 per cent of the first 23 words on the experimental list or failed to give associations to approximately 50 per cent of the first 23 words.

RESULTS

The 63 adjectives are listed alphabetically. Following each adjective are the associations given to it in order of decreasing frequency. Frequency is given as the percentage (in parentheses) of the Ss from the final sample of 82 who gave the word as an association. In order to facilitate use of the present list, associations which also appear as stimulus items in the list are reproduced in capital letters. Also, an association which is asterisked indicates that it occurred as an association to one or more of the other stimulus items in the list. All associations which were either proper nouns or pronouns have been excluded. Finally, all associations which occurred with a frequency of one (1.2 per cent) are not reported. Since there were over 2,000 such associations they are omitted for reasons of space.[3]

_____

[3] Copies of these are available upon request.

Stimulus	_Response_
ABLE	do(12) can(11) unable(8) can't(2) good*(2) well(2)
AFRAID	scared*(61) frightened(16) brave(8) fear(4) unafraid(4) coward(2) ghost(2) good*(2) happy*(2) knife(2) nervous(2)
ANGRY	mad*(61) happy*(12) mean*(6) BAD*(5) SAD*(5) good*(4) NICE*(4) cruel(2) glad*(2) unhappy*(2)
BAD	good*(37) mean*(18) naughty(11) NICE*(6) ANGRY(4) WRONG(4) COLD*(2) mad*(2) terrible(2)

Stimulus	*Response*

BEAUTIFUL PRETTY*(62) ugly*(23) NICE*(10) lovely*(7) beauty*(6) wonderful*(6)
flower*(5) girl*(4) gorgeous*(4) awful*(2) butterfly(2) house*(2)
tall*(2)

BEST good*(46) worst(8) BAD*(7) NICE*(7) clothes*(4) awful*(2) BETTER(2)
FINE*(2) flower*(2) friend*(2) less*(2) like*(2) wonderful*(2)

BETTER good*(24) worse(13) BAD*(5) NICE*(5) awful*(4) well*(4) work(4)
BEST*(2) butter(2) FAIR*(2) FINE*(2) OLD*(2)

BIG LARGE*(37) LITTLE*(28) SMALL*(24) tall*(23) huge*(8) medium*(7)
FAT*(6) enormous*(5) giant*(5) round*(5) high*(4) gigantic*(2)
man*(2) STRONG(2)

BRIGHT LIGHT*(33) sun*(17) moon*(16) DARK*(15) shiny*(7) PRETTY*(6) sky*(6)
dull(5) star(5) day*(5) color*(4) dim*(4) night*(4) black*(2)
colorful(2) glaring(2) NEW*(2) smart(2) sunny*(2)

BROKEN fixed(12) cracked(8) glass*(7) leg(7) break(6) broke(6) arm*(5) HURT(5)
dish(4) unbroken(4) vase(4) car*(2) dropped(2) fell(2) half(2)
pieces(2) shatter(2) toys*(2)

CLEAN dirty*(43) filthy(5) CLEAR(4) clothes*(4) dirt(4) DRY*(4) bath*(2)
house*(2) mean*(2) NICE*(2) PRETTY*(2) room*(2) sanitary(2)
wash*(2) white*(2)

CLEAR glass*(10) water*(10) BRIGHT*(7) CLEAN*(7) DARK*(5) see(5) sky*(5)
cloudy(4) dirty*(4) NICE*(4) blue(2) clouds(2) COOL*(2) day*(2)
FAIR*(2) foggy(2) LIGHT*(2) sunny*(2) WARM*(2) wash*(2) white*(2)
window(2)

COLD HOT*(33) WARM*(28) freezing*(23) COOL*(21) snow(7) ice(6) winter*(6)
chilly(5) freeze(5) froze(4) weather*(4) rain*(2) shiver(2) water*(2)
WET*(2)

COOL COLD*(50) HOT*(37) WARM*(24) freezing*(7) NICE*(4) water*(4)
winter*(4) air(2) aircondition(2) boiling*(2) fresh(2) freezer(2)
spring*(2) weather*(2)

DARK night*(38) LIGHT*(37) black*(15) moon*(8) day*(6) BRIGHT*(5)
brown(2) CLEAN*(2) green(2) room*(2) scared*(2) stars*(2) sun*(2)
sunny*(2)

DEEP shallow(22) hole(18) water*(15) down*(7) LONG*(6) high*(5) ground(4)
BIG*(2) DARK*(2) far*(2) ocean*(2) sea(2) SHORT*(2) steep(2) up*(2)
WIDE*(2)

DIFFERENT SAME*(22) alike*(8) people*(5) STRANGE(5) something*(4) unusual*(4)
colors(2) girls(2) kind*(2) NEW*(2) other*(2) things*(2)

DRY WET*(44) damp*(7) clothes*(6) water*(6) CLEAN*(5) desert(4) HOT*(4)
WARM*(4) land(2) soak(2) sun*(2) sunny*(2) weather*(2)

ENOUGH much*(7) plenty*(7) lots*(6) all(5) MORE*(5) food*(4) FULL*(4)
books*(2) eggs(2) had(2) HUNGRY(2) less*(2) not(2) through(2)

EVEN straight*(13) uneven(7) crooked(6) numbers*(5) good*(4) LONG*(4)
SAME*(4) fine(2) LARGE*(2) level(2) odd*(2)

FAIR good*(10) carnival(8) weather*(7) circus(6) cheat(5) fun*(5) game(5)
right*(5) honest(4) NICE*(4) animal*(2) chair(2) fairy(2) mean*(2)
play*(2) unfair(2)

FAST SLOW(41) run*(38) running*(11) go*(6) jump(6) play*(5) speed(4)
stop*(4) hurry(2) skip(2) swift*(2) quickly(2)

FAT skinny*(34) BIG*(22) chubby(12) round*(12) medium*(10) LARGE*(7)
SMALL*(6) thin*(6) pig(5) LITTLE*(4) boy*(2) dogs(2) man*(2)
SHORT*(2)

Stimulus	*Response*
FEW	MANY*(21) lots*(16) LITTLE*(13) MORE*(8) less*(7) much*(4) several(4) three(4) hundred(2) least*(2) one*(2) SMALL*(2) things*(2)
FINE	good*(24) NICE*(7) well*(7) BAD*(5) PRETTY*(4) SOFT(4) BEST*(2) coarse(2) great(2) okay(2) mine(2) something*(2) thin*(2)
FREE	freedom(4) jail(4) SAFE(4) ABLE(2) caught(2) cost(2) happy*(2) money*(2) OLD*(2) pay(2)
FULL	empty*(20) ENOUGH*(8) eat*(4) fill(4) filled(4) plenty*(4) water*(4) basket(2) FAT*(2) glass*(2) happy*(2) lots*(2) milk(2) overflow(2) top(2) up*(2)
FUNNY	laugh(17) silly(16) clown(11) SAD*(7) laughing(6) fun*(5) happy*(5) giggle(4) people*(4) gay*(2) party(2) smile(2) unhappy*(2)
HOT	COLD*(32) WARM*(28) COOL*(17) sun*(10) boiling*(8) stove(6) burn(5) DRY*(5) fire*(5) burning(4) day*(4) steam(4) steaming(4) sunny*(4) heat*(2) heater(2) sweat(2) water*(2) WET*(2)
HUNGRY	starve(21) food*(17) starving(11) full*(6) thirsty(6) eat*(5) animal*(2) empty*(2) POOR*(2)
HURT	cut(12) injured(10) BROKEN(6) BAD*(5) sore(5) cry(4) skin(4) arm*(2) awful*(2) bleeding(2) crying*(2) feelings(2) good*(2) scratch(2) SICK*(2) unhurt(2)
LARGE	BIG*(56) SMALL*(26) tall*(13) huge*(8) enormous*(7) LITTLE*(7) medium*(7) gigantic*(5) giant*(4) high*(4) round*(4) building(2) FAT*(2)
LIGHT	DARK*(38) BRIGHT*(24) sun*(16) day*(10) moon*(10) night*(6) bulb(5) morning(4) darkness(2) dim*(2) HOT*(2) shiny*(2) stars*(2) white*(2) yellow(2)
LITTLE	SMALL*(60) BIG*(34) SHORT*(16) tiny*(12) tall*(10) LARGE*(8)baby*(7) medium*(6) FAT*(5) midget(2) people*(2) thin*(2) WIDE*(2)
LONG	SHORT*(37) tall*(16) BIG*(12) straight*(7) WIDE*(7) SMALL*(6) far*(5) LARGE*(5) mile(5) rope(5) skinny*(5) high*(4) thin*(4) FAT*(2) line(2) LOW(2) medium*(2) road*(2) slender(2) stick(2)
LOW	high*(37) SMALL*(20) BIG*(8) down*(7) LITTLE*(6) DEEP(5) SHORT*(5) medium*(4) tall*(4) LONG*(2) mountains(2) skinny*(2) under(2)
MANY	lots*(28) FEW*(18) much*(10) MORE*(6) things*(6) less*(5) people*(5) LITTLE*(4) LARGE*(2) money*(2) none*(2) numbers*(2) pencils(2) SMALL*(2) toys*(2)
MORE	lots*(16) less*(12) MANY*(10) ENOUGH*(5) LITTLE*(5) money*(5) plenty*(4) books*(2) candy*(2) empty*(2) FAST*(2) FEW*(2) for(2) people*(2) POOR*(2) want(2)
MOST	lots*(24) MORE*(16) MANY*(7) less*(10) LITTLE*(5) much*(5) FEW*(4) LEAST*(4) things*(4) almost(2) ENOUGH*(2) none*(2)
NEW	OLD*(41) PRETTY*(8) dress*(6) shoes(6) car*(4) shiny*(4) bought(2) boy*(2) BRIGHT*(2) girl*(2) good*(2) house*(2) NICE*(2) skirt(2)
NICE	good*(32) BAD*(16) kind*(13) SWEET*(10) mean*(8) PRETTY*(5) mice(4) polite(4) AWFUL*(2) dog*(2) happy*(2) helpful(2) lady*(2)
OLD	YOUNG(30) NEW*(20) grandfather(6) age*(4) grandmother(4) COLD*(2) elderly(2) feeble(2) gray(2) lady*(2) middleaged*(2) people*(2) torn(2) used(2)
POOR	RICH(48) money*(10) OLD*(5) wealthy*(4) house*(2) NICE*(2) sick*(2)
PRETTY	BEAUTIFUL*(43) ugly*(24) NICE*(13) handsome(5) beauty*(4) cute(4) gorgeous*(4) lovely*(4) color*(2) dress*(2) FUNNY*(2) girl*(2) hair*(2) look(2) SWEET*(2)

Stimulus	*Response*
QUIET	noisy(23) loud(10) STILL(10) library(4) people*(4) listening(2) peaceful(2) talk(2)
REAL	true(10) alive (8) fantastic(4) play*(4) book(2) cat*(2) dead(2) fables(2) fake(2) fiction(2) horse(2) live(2) money*(2) people*(2) right*(2) unbelievable(2)
RICH	POOR*(44) money*(23) gold(6) wealthy*(6) lots*(4) people*(4) happy*(2) house*(2) millionaire(2) plentiful(2) PRETTY*(2) silver(2)
SAD	happy*(33) unhappy*(23) glad*(13) good*(6) crying*(5) joyful(5) mad*(5) sorry(5) BAD*(4) gloomy(4) lonely(4) gay*(2)
SAFE	unsafe(7) money*(5) street(5) careful(4) danger(4) dangerous(4) policeman(4) safety(4) bank(2)
SAME	DIFFERENT*(12) alike*(11) like*(6) thing*(6) clothes*(5) dress*(2) one*(2) other*(2) person*(2) twins(2) unalike(2) unusual*(2)
SHORT	SMALL*(32) tall*(28) LITTLE*(22) LONG*(16) BIG*(11) FAT*(10) medium*(6) high*(4) skinny*(4) hair*(2) LARGE*(2)
SLOW	FAST*(50) car*(8) walk(7) go*(5) run*(5) medium*(4) pokey(4) stop*(4) down*(2) running*(2) swift*(2) turtle(2)
SMALL	LITTLE*(49) BIG*(23) tiny*(13) LARGE*(10) tall*(10) baby*(8) SHORT*(7) child*(4) children(2) doll(2) FAT*(2) size(2) skinny*(2) thin*(2)
SOFT	hard(32) fluffy(11) bed(10) pillow(8) smooth(6) feathers(5) cushion(4) kitten(4) rough(4) BEAUTIFUL*(2) furry(2) fuzzy(2) medium*(2) NICE*(2) ugly*(2)
STILL	QUIET(21) move(11) moving(11) BAD*(2) FAST*(2) read(2) sitting(2) stand(2) water*(2) wiggle(2) working(2)
STRANGE	DIFFERENT*(8) known(6) friend*(5) stranger (5) man*(4) NEW*(4) queer(4) thing*(4) unusual*(4) feeling(2) FUNNY*(2) mysterious(2) odd*(2) person*(2)
STRONG	weak(26) muscles(16) healthy(15) BIG*(11) man*(5) FAT*(4) heavy(4) powerful(4) good*(2) lift(2) LITTLE*(2) men(2) tough(2)
SWEET	NICE*(20) good*(17) sugar(13) sour(13) candy*(10) apple(7) bitter(5) orange(5) BAD*(4) PRETTY*(4) BEAUTIFUL*(2) flower*(2) gentle(2) kind*(2) mean*(2) salt(2) taste(2)
WARM	HOT*(57) COLD*(35) COOL*(12) sun*(7) heat*(5) boiling*(4) sunny*(4) blanket(2) coat(2) DRY*(2) fire*(2) spring*(2) summer(2) water*(2) weather*(2)
WET	DRY*(37) rain*(12) water*(12) damp*(11) rainy(7) COLD*(5) sopping(5) swimming(4) bath*(2) CLEAN*(2) dirty*(2) floor(2) lightning(2) ocean*(2) sick*(2) soaked(2) soaking(2) thunder(2)
WIDE	BIG*(26) LARGE*(13) LONG*(8) thin*(7) broad(6) FAT*(6) narrow(5) skinny*(5) tall*(5) LITTLE*(4) room*(4) round*(4) SMALL*(4) ocean*(2) open(2) road*(2) width(2)
WRONG	right*(51) BAD*(7) answer(4) good*(4) awful*(2) did(2) shouldn't(2) something*(2)
YOUNG	OLD*(49) LITTLE*(7) age*(5) baby*(5) boy*(5) NEW*(5) child*(4) girl*(4) middleaged*(4) BIG*(2) cat*(2) dog*(2) NICE*(2) people*(2) SMALL*(2) tall*(2) twelve(2)

RELATION TO PAIRED-ASSOCIATE LEARNING

Two sets of six word pairs (both of which contain common stimulus items) were constructed from the present list. One set consisted of word pairs of high association values, the other of low association values. These pairs are presented in Table 1 along with their association values in percentages.

The words were presented by means of the Hunter Card Master. A 3-sec. anticipation interval during which the stimulus item was exposed preceded a 3-sec. exposure of the response item. There was a 2-sec. interval between exposures of the pairs and 8 sec. between trials. A trial consisted of one exposure of each of the six pairs. In order to prevent the pairs from being learned serially, three different orders of exposing the pairs were employed. The Ss were carried to a criterion of one perfect (errorless) trial or to a maximum of 15 trials.

TABLE 1 · Word Pairs and Their Association Values (in Parentheses)

	Response	
Stimulus	Group I	Group II
Angry	mad (61)	kind (1)
Beautiful	ugly (23)	sorry (1)
Big	tall (23)	thin (1)
Dark	night (38)	far (1)
Fast	run (38)	high (1)
Rich	money (23)	good (1)

A total of 50 fifth and sixth grade Ss were randomly assigned to one of two groups. Group I consisted of 28 Ss and group II of 22. The list for group I consisted of word pairs of high association values and of low association values for group II.

A precautionary measure designed to identify those Ss unable to read the words comprising the experimental list was employed. The appropriate words were typed in alphabetical order on separate sheets, and the S was required to read these words immediately prior to the paired-associate task (see instructions). All Ss read the words without error.

The instructions to S were as follows: "This is a game to see how well you can remember. This is how it goes. Here on this side (E points to left aperture) a little window will open up, and you will see a word. A few seconds after this window opens, the window on this side (E points to right aperture) will open and you will see a second word. Your job is to guess what the second word is before its window opens. You say the word out loud so that I can hear you. (E hands S the words used in the experiment prepared in alphabetical order.) Here are the words that we will use. Would you read each one for me first. Fine, now we are ready to start. Remember, you are to say out loud the second word which is going to appear in the second window before the window opens. In the beginning you will make a lot of mistakes, but as you learn how it goes, you won't make so many mistakes."

RESULTS AND DISCUSSION

In terms of the mean number of trials to reach the criterion of one perfect recitation, the means for groups I and II were 3.4 and 11.0, respectively. The difference between the means was significant at the .001 level ($t = 10.76$). These results indicate that performance in paired-associate learning was better where the association values between the stimulus-response items were initially high.

These results suggest that one of the parameters found to be important in work with adults, i.e., associative strength, may be varied in paired-associate learning in children by use of the present list or other lists constructed by comparable methods. The present list, however, is limited in the number of adjectives, and additional research concerned with increasing the number of adjectives in the present list, as well as constructing other lists appropriate in reading level for children in the lower grades, would be desirable. Furthermore, the adaptations necessary for work with this method in child populations of different ages would require research on those variables more immediately connected with the paired-associate method, e.g., anticipation intervals, rates of presentation, presence of competing associations, instructions, length of list, etc. Knowledge of the variables would be useful to studies more directly concerned with other factors, e.g., motivational and personality factors. As indicated earlier, these latter factors have been studied in adult populations with the paired-associate method, and there appear to be no *a priori* reasons why they could not be studied in conjunction with this method in younger populations.

SUMMARY

The present report describes the word associations and the relative frequency with which they occurred in a sample of 82 fourth, fifth, and sixth grade children to a list of 63 common adjectives. Also, two lists composed either of high or low association values between the to-be-learned stimulus and response items were constructed from the standardization list and employed in a paired-associate learning experiment with fifth and sixth grade children. Learning by the anticipation method was found to be significantly better the higher the association values.

REFERENCES

1. HILGARD, E. R.   Methods and procedures in the study of learning. In S. S. Stevens (Ed.), *Handbook of experimental psychology*. Wiley, 1951. Pp. 517–567.
2. RUSSELL, W. A., & STORMS, L. H.   Implicit verbal chaining in paired-associate learning. *J. exp. Psychol.*, 1955, *49*, 237–293.

ASSOCIATIVE TRANSFER IN MOTOR PAIRED-ASSOCIATE LEARNING AS A FUNCTION OF AMOUNT OF FIRST–TASK PRACTICE

CHARLES C. SPIKER
RUTH B. HOLTON [1]

THE CLASSICAL DESIGN for associative interference in paired-associate learning is the A–B, A–C sequence. The S first learns one set of responses to a set of stimuli and then learns a new set of responses to these same stimuli. Studies of associative interference in verbal paired-associate learning have differed in the type of control condition against which the amount and direction of the associative transfer in the A–B, A–C series was assessed. One of the more common designs varies the amount of first-task practice given to different groups and compares the performance of these groups on the second task. Whether the amount of first-task practice is none versus some (7, 8, 10, 11) or is varied through several degrees (1, 12, 13), the results have consistently showed over-all positive transfer, with relatively small amounts of interference restricted to the early trials.

Associative transfer has also been studied with unrelated lists. It has been established that positive transfer occurs from initial to subsequent unrelated lists (4, 14, 15) and that the amount of positive transfer is a direct function of the amount of immediately prior practice (9) and an inverse function of the time between first and second tasks (5). Thus, if one wishes to study the second-task interference resulting from the necessity for unlearning the responses learned to the stimuli in the first task (associative interference), the total amount of prior practice must be either statistically or experimentally controlled. The statistical control may be obtained by providing, at each level of first-task practice, a control condition in which Ss have had equivalent amounts of practice on a first task in which the associations are unrelated to those of the second task. Thus, Gibson (3) found that Ss given the A–B, D–C series performed significantly better on their second task than Ss given the A–B, A–C sequence. Since Gibson was not primarily interested in associative transfer, however, she neither equated the A–C and D–C lists nor counterbalanced them for difficulty, with the consequence that her results, in this respect, cannot be unequivocally interpreted. A similar reservation

[1] From October, 1956, to May, 1957, the investigators collaborated in the design and conduct of a series of studies on associative transfer. The second investigator met her untimely death on May 9, 1957, in an automobile accident enroute to the school system in which the data were collected. The first investigator is responsible for the preparation of the manuscript. He is indebted to Don Lewis, I. E. Farber, and Boyd R. McCandless for helpful suggestions in its preparation.

Reprinted by permission from *Journal of Experimental Psychology*, 1958, 56, 123–132.

holds for the nonsignificant findings in the same direction by Bruce (2). Experimental control of prior practice may be obtained by giving all Ss the same amount of total practice prior to the transfer task, at the same time varying the proportion of total practice which is given on a task having the same stimulus items as those of the transfer task. The writers know of no experiments with associative interference in which amount of prior practice was experimentally controlled.

Four experiments were conducted to investigate associative interference in motor paired-associate learning. In Exp. I and II, amount of prior practice was statistically controlled; in Exp. III and IV, amount of prior practice was experimentally controlled. All experiments utilize intra-S comparisons in order to increase the precision of the experiments.

EXPERIMENT I

METHOD

Apparatus. The apparatus was designed to present motor paired-associate learning tasks in which S learns to associate a different push button with each of six stimulus lights differing in hue. It consists of four parts: a stimulus presentation unit, the response unit, a control box, and a timing unit. It permits the presentation of a stimulus for a set anticipation time interval, followed by a timed interval during which the stimulus is presented jointly with an informational light beside the correct button, followed in turn by a timed interstimulus interval. The S is instructed to respond by pushing the correct button prior to the onset of the informational light. A bell sounds immediately if his response is correct, and, whether or not it is correct, the informational lamp is automatically turned on at the end of the anticipation interval.

The *stimulus unit* is a black box 4 in.

high, 20 in. wide, and 12 in. deep. On the front face of the box is the stimulus aperture, 2 in. in diameter, covered with flashed opal glass. Inside the box, each of six 75-w. projection lamps is enclosed in a compartment on the front face of which is an opening over which a 2 × 2-in. glass color filter may be placed. Glass color filters obtained from the Corning Glass Co. were used. The stimuli were a red (No. 2404), a green (No. 4060), a yellow (No. 3387), a violet (No. 5113), an aqua (No. 4305), and a white (no filter). The stimulus box is mounted on 5-in. legs.

The *response unit* consists of a 12 × 20-in. black panel that slopes downward toward S. Arranged in a semicircle on the panel are nine push-button switches approximately 2½ in. apart. Beside each button, a small 6-v. pilot (informational) lamp is mounted with the glazed tip of the bulb projecting through the top surface of the panel. At the end of each anticipation interval, one of these lamps is energized to indicate which button S should have pushed. The buttons are numbered, starting at the left, from 1 to 9 with small white numerals painted on the panel beside the buttons. During the task, the response unit is placed directly in front of the stimulus unit so that the stimulus aperture is approximately 3 in. above the center button.

The *control unit* enables E to select the particular stimulus-response pairings appropriate for a given task and to determine which stimulus will be presented on a given trial. The *timing unit* consists of three Hunter decade interval timers to control the time between the onset of the stimulus and the onset of the informational lamp, the length of the joint presentation of the stimulus and the informational lamp, and the interstimulus interval. During the interstimulus interval, E turns a selector switch to that one of six positions which simultaneously determines for the next presentation the appropriate stimulus and the corresponding correct response button and informational lamp.

Subjects and design. The Ss were 18 Grade 4 and Grade 5 children from the Ottumwa Public Schools.[2] All *S*s were given three stimuli in Task I and were required to learn to associate a different one of the nine buttons with each stimulus. In Task II, they were given these same three stimuli and three stimuli they had not previously seen, and were required to learn to associate new buttons with each of the six stimuli. Thus, in Task II, half the light-button pairs represent an A-B, A-C paradigm and the other half, an A-B, D-C paradigm. Three *S*s were randomly assigned to each of six subgroups in order to control for the possible differential difficulty of the stimulus-response pairs. The complete design is schematized in Table 1. The numbers in the table designate the buttons (from left to right) which were correct for each of the six color stimuli for Task I and Task II within each of the six counterbalancing subgroups.

Procedure. The *S* was seated before the apparatus, shown the six stimulus lights one at a time, and asked to name them. He was then told that the experiment was concerned with a comparison of adults and children in their abilities to discriminate among and to remember colors. He was given instructions concerning the nature of the task and was urged to guess on the first trial. The need to respond prior to the onset of the informational lights was emphasized. Immediately following the instructions, the first stimulus was presented and *S* was asked to respond.

During Task I, the anticipation interval was set at 3 sec., the joint presentation interval was 2 sec., and the interpresentation interval was 3 sec. Task I training for each *S* was continued until he met a criterion of three successive errorless trials, although all *S*s received at least 12 trials, where a trial was defined as the presentation of all

[2] The investigators are indebted to R. O. Wright, Director of Curriculum, Ottumwa Public School System, Ottumwa, Iowa, for his generous permission to use the *S*s of these experiments. They are also indebted to M. E. Wilson, Principal, Agassiz Elementary School, and his teaching staff for their fine cooperation in providing facilities and for their assistance in many other ways during the conduct of Exp. I and II. Thanks are also due Albert Whittlesey, Principal, Wilson Elementary School, and his teaching staff for equally fine cooperation during the conduct of Exp. III and IV.

three stimuli in some order. In each successive block of six trials, all six possible orders of presenting the three stimuli were used.

When *S* reached the Task I criterion, *E* announced that he was going to make the task harder by including more lights. He then set up the light-button connections which were appropriate for that *S*'s Task II. This required, on the average, about 2 min.

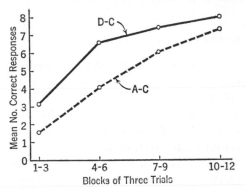

Figure 1. Mean number of correct responses in the transfer task of Exp. I for both conditions.

No instructions were given *S* concerning the change in the light-button pairings from Task I to Task II. Next, *E* immediately began to administer 12 trials on Task II, where each trial included one presentation of each of the six stimuli. Six different orders of presenting the stimuli within a trial were used in each successive block of six trials. All three time intervals were set at 2 sec. for Task II.

TABLE 1 · LIGHT-BUTTON CONNECTIONS IN TASKS I AND II FOR THE COUNTERBALANCING SUBGROUPS
(Exp. I and Exp. II)

Stimuli	SUBGROUPS											
	1		2		3		4		5		6	
	I	II	I	II	I	II	I	II	I	II	I	II
Red		5		4		6	2	9	3	8	1	7
Green		8		7		9	4	6	6	1	5	2
Yellow		1		2		3	7	3	9	5	8	4
Violet	2	9	3	8	1	7		5		4		6
White	4	6	6	1	5	2		8		7		9
Aqua	7	3	9	5	8	4		1		2		3

The E recorded, on prepared sheets, the first button to which S responded on each stimulus presentation. Responses made by S to correct initial errors were recorded, but were not counted as correct in the tabulation of the data. Responses occurring after the onset of the informational light were recorded with a notation of their tardiness, but such responses were always scored as omissions in the analysis of the data.

RESULTS

The mean number of trials required to reach the criterion of three consecutive errorless trials in Task I was 6.33 (SD = 3.50). Since all Ss were given a minimum of 12 trials, the majority of Ss received considerable overtraining.

The performance of Ss in Task II on the types of S–R connections is shown in Fig. 1. An analysis of variance of these data was conducted (6, Type VI, p. 292), with conditions (type of pair) and trial blocks as intra-S factors and the counterbalancing subgroups as an inter-S factor. A summary of this analysis is given in Table 2. Clear evidence is provided for the superiority of the D–C condition (P < .001) and a significant interaction (P < .025) was obtained between the Conditions and the Trial Blocks. The counterbalancing Subgroups effect was not statistically significant. The results of Exp. I thus permit the conclusion that the A–B, A–C series results in associative interference relative to the A–B, D–C.

EXPERIMENT II

Experiment II was conducted to determine whether or not the amount of interference in the A-B, A-C condition is a function of the amount of first-task practice. Fifty-four children from Grades 5 and 6 were randomly assigned in equal numbers to

TABLE 2 · ANALYSIS OF VARIANCE OF NUMBER OF CORRECT RESPONSES PER THREE-TRIAL BLOCKS FOR A-C AND D-C CONDITIONS (Exp. I)

Source	df	MS	F	P
Between Ss	17			
Subgroups (Sg)	5	11.58	1.21	
Error (b)	12	9.56		
Within Ss	126			
Trials (T)	3	196.80	102.50	.001
Conditions (C)	1	93.45	43.67	.001
T $\times$ Sg	15	2.35	1.22	
T $\times$ C	3	5.37	4.01	.025
Sg $\times$ C	5	3.78	1.77	
Sg $\times$ C $\times$ T	15	1.03	<1.00	
Error (w)	84			
Error$_1$ (w)[a]	36	1.92		
Error$_2$ (w)[b]	12	2.14		
Error$_3$ (w)[c]	36	1.34		

[a] Error term for T and T $\times$ Sg.
[b] Error term for C and C $\times$ Sg.
[c] Error term for T $\times$ C and T $\times$ C $\times$ Sg.

three experimental groups.[3] Groups 5, 10, and 20 were given 5, 10, and 20 trials, respectively, on Task I. All Ss were then given 12 trials on Task II. All other procedures were the same as those in Exp. I.

RESULTS

The means and SD's of total correct responses for the three groups in different phases of the experiment are shown in Table 3. Correct responses for the first five trials of Task I indicate that the three groups were initially rather well matched, a simple analysis of variance yielding an F ratio less than unity. A similar analysis of the number of correct responses in the last five trials for the three groups yielded a significant F ratio (P < .01). The mean of Group 5 differed significantly (P < .01) from those of Groups 10 and 20; the latter means did not differ significantly. The different amounts of first-task practice were thus adequate to bring

[3] See Footnote 2.

TABLE 3 · MEANS AND SD's OF TOTAL NUMBER OF CORRECT RESPONSES IN TASKS I AND II (Exp. II)

Task	GROUP 5		GROUP 10		GROUP 20	
	Mean	SD	Mean	SD	Mean	SD
Task I						
First 5 trials [a]	6.17	3.20	7.22	2.69	6.11	2.85
Last 5 trials	6.17	3.20	13.11	2.05	14.77	0.55
Task II						
(12 trials)						
A–C			14.33	6.84	17.78	5.81	15.61	7.18
D–C			17.28	5.87	22.28	5.93	23.22	4.82

[a] For Group 5, the first 5 trials were also the last 5 trials.

about different performances between Group 5 and the other two groups.

The mean numbers of correct responses per three-trial block are shown in Fig. 2. Here it may be observed that the difference between the A–C and D–C curves increases with increasing amounts of first-task practice. A preliminary analysis of these data indicated that the subgroups did not differ significantly from one another and that they did not interact significantly with other variables. Consequently, a simpler analysis (6, Type I, p. 267) was conducted and a summary is presented in Table 4. For this analysis, only Groups 5 and 20 were used, since these are the extreme groups and permit the most sensitive test for the trend predicted by the major hypothesis. As is apparent in Table 4, the difference between performance on the A–C and D–C conditions is significant at the .001 level. Furthermore, there is a significant interaction between the two conditions and the amount of training ($P < .05$). This interaction reflects the greater interference for Group 20 relative to Group 5.

Related t tests were used to compare the A–C and D–C means separately for each group. Performance on the D–C con-

dition was significantly superior to that on the A–C for each group (Group 5, $P < .05$; Group 10, $P < .025$; and Group 20, $P < .001$). Thus, even five trials on Task I were adequate to produce statistically significant interference on the A–C condition. A simple analysis of variance of the number of correct responses for the three groups on the D–C condition alone showed that performance on the D–C con-

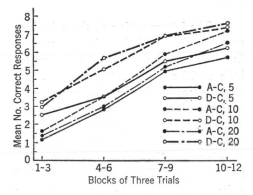

Figure 2. Mean number of correct responses in the transfer task of Exp. II for all three groups under each condition.

dition improved significantly ($P < .005$) with increasing first-task practice. On the other hand, the same analysis for the A–C condition showed no significant variation in A–C means with first-task practice ($P > .10$).

TABLE 4 · ANALYSIS OF VARIANCE OF CORRECT RESPONSES FOR GROUPS 5 AND 20 (Exp. II)

Source	df	MS	F
Between Ss	35		
Groups (G)	1	220.5	3.49
Error (b)	34	63.1	
Within Ss	36		
Conditions (C)	1	480.5	24.64**
C × G	1	88.9	4.56*
Error (w)	34	19.5	

* $P < .05$.
** $P < .001$.

TABLE 5 · Total Frequency of Different Types of Error on Task II (Exp. II)

Type of error	GROUP 5		GROUP 10		GROUP 20	
	A-C	D-C	A-C	D-C	A-C	D-C
Omissions	98	102	108	58	105	70
Intralist errors	169	168	148	137	175	116
Task I intrusions	123	67	72	51	87	48
Old habit errors	(41)		(39)		(51)	
Total errors	390	337	328	246	367	234

The interpretation of these findings assumes that variation in amount of first-task practice simultaneously varies both positive and negative transfer. The positive transfer is presumably the result of nonspecific factors such as warming-up (5, 9) and/or learning-to-learn (4, 14, 15). The negative transfer is the result of learning specific incompatible associations in Task I. Performance on the D–C pairs reflects only the positive transfer effects. Performance on the A–C pairs reflects both the positive and negative transfer effects. These opposing effects resulted in no significant net transfer for the A–C condition. The evidence for associative inteference is obtained by comparing Ss' performance under the A–C and D–C conditions, in which comparison the positive transfer is held constant.

It is informative to consider the frequency of different types of error during the learning of Task II. The total frequencies are shown in Table 5, where "omissions" are defined as failures to respond during the anticipation interval, an "intralist" error is the selection of a button that is correct for a stimulus other than the one presented, and "Task I intrusions" involve selections of buttons used in Task I. Task I intrusions involving response to a stimulus in Task II with the button that was correct in Task I were designated "Old habit errors" and are shown separately for the A–C conditions in Table 5.

The major trends in Table 5 may be summarized briefly. The frequencies of omissions, intralist errors, and Task I intrusions on the D–C pairs tend to decrease with increasing amounts of first-task practice. No consistent trends for these three types of error are apparent for the A–C pairs. The differences between the D–C and A–C totals for both omissions and intralist errors tend to increase with increasing first-task practice. The differences between D–C and A–C totals for Task I intrusions tend to decrease, if anything, with increasing first-task practice. No marked trend for the old habit errors is apparent. From these data, considered by themselves, it appears that either omissions or intralist errors constitute the most sensitive index of associative interference and that Task I intrusions are either inversely related or unrelated to associative interference.

EXPERIMENT III

The failure in Exp. II to show a decrease in the A–C correct anticipation means, with increase in first-task practice,

TABLE 6 · Light-Button Pairings for Task I and Task II (Exp. III and Exp. IV)

Pair	Stimuli	Correct buttons	
		Task I	Task II
A	Red	4	1
	White	7	3
B	Blue	2	5
	Yellow	10	6
C	Green	12	9
	Violet	8	11

is presumably due to the effect on A–C performance of such nonspecific factors as warm-up and learning-to-learn. An experiment that varied amount of first-task practice within Ss, by giving different amounts of practice on subsets of first-task pairs and then requiring Ss to learn a new response to each of these stimuli, should show steadily increasing interference as a function of amount of first-task practice. Such a design would assure that Ss have had equal amounts of total practice with the task for each of the different amounts of first-task practice. Experiment III is an attempt to demonstrate this hypothesis.

METHOD

Apparatus. The apparatus for Exp. III was the same as that for Exp. I and II except that the response unit consisted of 12 push-button switches instead of 9.

Subjects, design, and procedure. The Ss were 30 children from Grade 4 of the Ottumwa Public School System.[4] All Ss were given six stimuli in Task I and were required to associate a different one of 6 of the 12 buttons with each stimulus. In Task II, they were given these same six stimuli and were required to associate a different one of the other six buttons with each stimulus. The light-button pairs for the two tasks are shown in Table 6. The amount of Task I practice was varied within Ss by presenting,

[4] See Footnote 2.

in Task I, two stimuli 5 times, two others 10 times, and a third pair 20 times. Six subgroups of five Ss each were randomly formed in order to counterbalance for the intrinsic difficulty of the S-R pairs. All six ways of combining the three stimulus pairs (A, B, and C of Table 6) with the three levels of first-task training were thus represented.

The procedures for Exp. III were the same as those for Exp. I and II with the following exceptions. During Task I, a total of 70 stimulus presentations was administered. In each successive block of 14 presentations, the first pair of stimuli was presented once; the second pair, twice; and the third pair, four times. Within a block of 14 presentations, the order of presenting the stimuli was random with the restriction that no stimulus appear twice or more successively. For each of the 5 blocks of 14 presentations, a different order was used. During the interpresentation interval following the last stimulus presentation of Task I, E unobtrusively turned a selector switch to re-pair the lights and the buttons for Task II. Thus, S was started on Task II without warning. Twelve trials on Task II were administered, where each trial included one presentation of each of the six stimuli.

RESULTS

Task I. The first two columns of Table 7 give the means and SD's of the number of correct responses to the first five presentations for each of the three conditions of first-task training. It is apparent that there are fewer correct re-

TABLE 7 · MEANS AND SD's OF NUMBER OF CORRECT RESPONSES IN TASK I FOR DIFFERENT CONDITIONS OF TRAINING

Conditions of training	EXPERIMENT III				EXPERIMENT IV			
	First 5 presentations		Last 5 presentations		First 5 presentations		Last 5 presentations	
	Mean	SD	Mean	SD	Mean	SD	Mean	SD
5[a]	3.23	2.32	3.23	2.32	3.93	2.08	3.93	2.08
10	2.80	2.58	6.13	2.86	2.67	2.06	6.20	3.32
20	2.65	1.79	8.27	2.65	2.93	2.00	8.37	1.78

[a] For Cond. 5, the first five presentations were the same as the last five.

sponses to the first five presentations for the stimuli presented 20 times in Task I than for those presented five times. An analysis of variance of these scores yielded an F ratio significant at only the 10% level. The meaning of these differences will be discussed in connection with the results of Exp. IV.

The third and fourth columns of Table 7 present the means and SD's of the number of correct responses to the last five presentations for the three conditions of first-task practice. The final level of performance is seen to be an increasing function of the number of previous presentations. Analysis of variance, with amount of first-task practice and stimulus pairs as within-S factors (3, Type II, p. 273), indicates that these differences are highly significant ($P <$ .001).

Task II. The first three columns of table 8 give the means for Task II of the different types of error that were considered in Exp. II. As expected, the number of total errors increases with increasing number of first-task presentations. Analysis of variance (3, Type II, p. 273), however, showed the difference in these means to be nonsignificant ($P > .20$). Examination of the means for response omissions indicates that they increase with an increase in the number of Task I presenta-

tions. This trend was found to be significant at only the 10% level. Intralist errors, Task I intrusions, and old habit errors do not manifest a systematic change with variation in degree of prior learning, and in each case, the differences among means were nonsignificant ($P >$ .20).

EXPERIMENT IV

On the assumption that omissions best reflect interference in the A-B, A-C design, Exp. IV was conducted in an attempt to increase the number of omissions by reducing the length of the anticipation interval during Task II. Experiment I was replicated with another group of 30 fourth-grade children from the same school,[5] the sole procedural change involving a reduction in the anticipation interval in Task II from 2 sec. to 1½ sec.

RESULTS

Task I. The means and SD's of the correct responses to the first and to the last five presentations are given in the last four columns of Table 7. The Ss were again found to perform better to the first five presentations of the stimuli that were presented only five times than they did to the stimuli presented either ten or twenty times. Analysis of variance showed the

[5] See Footnote 2.

TABLE 8 · Means of Different Types of Error in Task II for Different Conditions of Training

Type of error	EXPERIMENT III			EXPERIMENT IV		
	Task I presentations			Task I presentations		
	5	10	20	5	10	20
Omissions	4.27	4.97	5.63	5.17	5.47	7.97
Intralist errors	5.07	5.43	5.17	5.03	6.10	4.60
Task I intrusions	3.27	2.60	3.00	5.20	4.57	5.07
Old habit errors	(0.93)	(0.60)	(0.80)	(1.43)	(0.97)	(1.20)
Total errors	12.60	13.00	13.80	15.40	16.13	17.63

differences among the three means to be significant $(P < .01)$. The number of correct responses to the last five presentations again was found to increase significantly $(P < .001)$ with an increase in the number of previous presentations.

Task II. The means of the different types of error in Task II are shown in the last three columns of Table 8. Total errors were again found to increase with increase in number of Task I presentations, and

TABLE 9 · ANALYSIS OF VARIANCE OF TOTAL ERRORS IN TASK II FOR EXP. IV

Source	df	MS	F
Between Ss	29		
T × P (b)	2	10.35	<1.00
Error (b)	27	41.83	
Within Ss	60		
Training conditions (T)	2	38.88	3.82*
Stimulus pairs (P)	2	64.68	6.35**
T × P (w)	2	2.32	<1.00
Error (w)	54	10.19	

  * $P < .05$.
 ** $P < .005$.

omissions again appear to reflect the increasing interference somewhat more sensitively than does any one of the other error measures.

The analysis of variance conducted on number of total errors is summarized in Table 9. Stimulus pairs were found to differ significantly $(P < .005)$ reflecting the greater ease in learning Pair A (Table 1) than in learning the other two. The means for the three conditions of training differed at the 5% level of confidence. Using the error term from this analysis, a *t* test was conducted for the means of the 5 and 20 conditions. The resultant *t* was 2.71, $P < .01$.

The same type of analysis was conducted over each of the other four types

of error. No significant differences among means were found for old habit errors, intralist errors, and Task I intrusions $(P > .10)$. The analysis of omissions, however, yielded a significant F ratio for the three conditions $(P < .001)$, and *t* tests showed that Cond. 5 and 10 each differed significantly from Cond. 20 $(P < .001)$, but did not differ significantly from each other $(P > .20)$.

DISCUSSION

The results of Exp. III and IV are consistent in showing amount of interference in Task II to be an increasing function of amount of first-task practice, when nonspecific transfer is experimentally controlled. In Exp. III, the results were not statistically reliable. In Exp. IV, the results were in the same direction, and, apparently due to the reduction in anticipation time, were more reliable.

The finding that Task I performance on the first five presentations differed for the three conditions of practice requires some consideration. The five presentations of the stimuli in Cond. 5 were spread throughout the 70 stimulus presentations of Task I, while the first five presentations of the stimuli in Cond. 20 were given in the first 18 presentations. Thus, in Cond. 5, Ss were receiving some of the presentations late in Task I, while in Cond. 20, they were receiving all the presentations early in the task. The finding, then, represents an instance of positive transfer within a single task, the positive transfer presumably due to amount of prior practice on the task. The fact that it is potent enough to be statistically significant in such a relatively crude test emphasizes the need to control such effects if one wishes to assess interference due to the prior learning of incompatible associations.

It is of interest that omissions in Task II appear to reflect the interference of Task I training more directly than any other type of error measure considered. The relative infrequency of Task I intrusions is consistent with the results of verbal paired-associate experiments. In the A–B, A–C paradigm, Ss apparently inhibit the old responses rather easily, but this inhibition is not always followed by the immediate selection of a new response. It frequently results in a temporary blocking of any overt response.

If this analysis is correct, one should expect the reaction time or latency, even of a correct response, to increase with increasing strength of incorrect competing responses. In Exp. III and IV, for example, if the latencies of all responses in Task II had been obtained, longer latencies of correct responses would be expected to those stimuli presented 20 times in Task I than to those presented only five times.

SUMMARY

Four experiments were conducted to study interference in the A-B, A-C design with motor paired-associate tasks. In Exp. I and II, an intra-S experimental design, with an A-B, D-C control condition, was devised in order to provide statistical control of warm-up and learning-to-learn. In Exp. I, 18 grammar school Ss were given preliminary training on a motor paired-associate task consisting of three S-R pairs. In the second (criterial) task, Ss were required to learn three new responses to these same stimuli, and three new responses to three additional stimuli. The results, in terms of number of correct responses in each condition, showed significant interference for the A-C condition. In Exp. II, 18 grammar school children were assigned to each of three experimental groups differing only in amount of Task I practice. It was found that the amount of interference on the A-C, relative to the D-C, condition was an increasing function of amount of Task I practice.

Experimental control of nonspecific transfer was obtained in Exp. III and IV. In Exp. III, 30 grammar school children were required to learn to push the appropriate one of 12 available response buttons to each of six different stimuli. In Task I, they were given 5 presentations of two of the S-R pairs, 10 of another two, and 20 of the third two. In Task II, they were required to learn to push the appropriate one of the six buttons not used in Task I to each of the same stimuli. Number of errors in Task II was found to increase with number of Task I presentations, although the differences were nonsignificant. An additional 30 Ss were used in Exp. IV which differed from Exp. III only in that a shorter anticipation interval was used. The findings of Exp. III were replicated in Exp. IV at a statistically significant level of confidence.

REFERENCES

1. ATWATER, S. K. Proactive inhibition and associative facilitation as affected by degree of prior learning. *J. exp. Psychol.*, 1953, *46*, 400–404.

2. BRUCE, R. W. Conditions of transfer of training. *J. exp. Psychol.*, 1933, *16*, 343–361.

3. GIBSON, E. J. Retroactive inhibition as a function of degree of generalization between tasks. *J. exp. Psychol.*, 1941, *28*, 93–115.

4. GREENBERG, R., & UNDERWOOD, B. J. Retention as a function of stage of practice. *J. exp. Psychol.*, 1950, *40*, 452–457.

5. HAMILTON, C. E. Length of interval betwen two tasks and performance

on the second task. *J. exp. Psychol.*, 1950, *40*, 613–621.

6. LINDQUIST, E. F. *Design and analysis of experiments in psychology and education.* Boston: Houghton Mifflin, 1953.

7. McGEOCH, J. A., & UNDERWOOD, B. J. Tests of the two-factor theory of retroactive inhibition. *J. exp. Psychol.*, 1943, *32*, 1–16.

8. MORGAN, R. L., & UNDERWOOD, B. J. Proactive inhibition as a function of response similarity. *J. exp. Psychol.*, 1950, *40*, 592–603.

9. THUNE, L. E. The effect of different types of preliminary activities on subsequent learning of paired-associate material. *J. exp. Psychol.*, 1950, *40*, 423–438.

10. UNDERWOOD, B. J. Retroactive and proactive inhibition after five and forty-eight hours. *J. exp. Psychol.*, 1948, *38*, 29–38.

11. UNDERWOOD, B. J. Spontaneous recovery of verbal associations. *J. exp. Psychol.*, 1948, *38*, 429–439.

12. UNDERWOOD, B, J. Proactive inhibition as a function of time and degree of prior learning. *J. exp. Psychol.*, 1949, *39*, 24–34.

13. UNDERWOOD, B. J. Associative transfer in verbal learning as a function of response similarity and degree of first-list learning. *J. exp. Psychol.*, 1951, *42*, 44–53.

14. UNDERWOOD, B. J. Studies of distributed practice: III. The influence of stage of practice in serial learning. 1951, *42*, 291–295.

15. WARD, L. B. Reminiscence and rote learning. *Psychol. Monogr.*, 1937, *49*, No. 4 (Whole No. 220).

EFFECTS OF MEDIATED ASSOCIATIONS ON TRANSFER IN PAIRED-ASSOCIATE LEARNING

KATHRYN J. NORCROSS
CHARLES C. SPIKER

SEVERAL EXPERIMENTERS have demonstrated that a given response (R_o) may be elicited by a stimulus (S_1) to which R_o has never been conditioned, even when S_1

Reprinted by permission from *Journal of Experimental Psychology*, 1958, *55*, 129–134.

is physically dissimilar to any stimulus to which R_o has been conditioned ($1, 3, 6, 8, 11$). These results have been explained in terms of the principle of secondary, or mediated, generalization (4). Briefly, the principle states that the conditioning of a response, R_a, to each of several dissimilar stimuli (S_1, S_2, etc.) assures that on subsequent presentations of these stimuli, the stimulation, s_a, produced by R_a, will be present. Any other response, R_o, subsequently conditioned to one of these stimuli (e.g., S_2) will also be conditioned to s_a. Thus, if any other of the stimuli (S_1, etc.) is presented, R_a will tend to occur, together with s_a, and s_a will tend to elicit R_o.

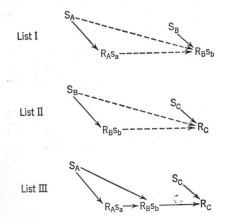

Figure 1. A schematic analysis of mediated association in paired-associate learning.

The principle of mediated generalization also appears applicable to the phenomenon of mediated associations in paired-associate verbal learning. The paradigm for mediated associations provides for two preliminary lists and a third test list administered in an A–B, B–C, A–C sequence. A schematization of the analysis of this situation is presented in Fig. 1. In List I, S is presented with visual stimulus A, to which he makes the (overt or covert) verbalization R_A with attendant stimulation, s_a. S_B is presented in close spatial and temporal relationship with S_A and elicits R_B, which in turn produces s_b. The experimental conditioning

that occurs is represented by the dotted lines in Fig. 1. As a result of List II experience, s_b comes to evoke R_C. The subsequent learning of R_C in response to S_A is facilitated through mediation by s_b.

An early series of experiments on mediated association with some positive findings was reported by Peters (9). Associative facilitation was investigated by Irwin (5) with a B–C, A–B, A–C sequence for an experimental group as compared to a D–C, A–B, A–C control sequence. A significant difference between the two groups in the learning of the A–C list was found, with the group given the B–C list superior. Bugelski and Scharlock (2) used an experimental design in which the third A–C list was constructed from previously associated nonsense syllables in such a way that experimental pairs were made up of an A syllable and a C syllable that had been associated with a common B syllable; control pairs were composed of the remaining A and C syllables paired at random so that none had a common specific B associate. A significant difference was obtained in the mean rank order of learning the two types of pairs. Russell and Storms (10) have recently demonstrated mediational effects with experimentally established learning and inferred pre-existing language habits.

The differences that obtained in the latter experiments (2, 10) may have resulted from a combination of positive transfer for the experimental condition and negative transfer in the control condition, since mediated but incorrect response tendencies presumably exist for the "control" items. The present experiments attempt to demonstrate both positive and negative transfer in learning the third list in the mediated association design.

EXPERIMENT I

METHOD

Apparatus. The apparatus used is an electrically operated visual stimulus presentation device.[1] It consists of a gray metal box 14 $\times$ 14 $\times$ 14 in. The front face of the apparatus contains a 3 $\times$ 6 in. aperture. A mechanical arrangement delivers to the aperture a 3½ $\times$ 6 in. plastic card from the bottom of a stack of cards. Mounted on each card was a pair of pictures taken from the *Golden Play Book of Picture Stamps for the Very Young.* Each picture was a colored representation of a single familiar object; e.g., a dog, horse, ice cream cone, etc. Black cloth curtains on the aperture serve as shutters to expose or conceal independently the left and right pictures on the stimulus cards. Following a presentation, the curtains close simultaneously and the card is released from the aperture and returned to the top of the stack by a conveyor belt. A system of electronic timers controls the rate of presenting the cards and the exposure times of the stimulus and response pictures.

TABLE 1 · Schematic Illustration of the Design for Exp. I

LIST I		LIST II		LIST III	
S	R	S	R	S	R
1	7	7	13	1	13*
2	8	8	14	2	14*
3	9	9	15	3	16**
4	10	10	16	4	15**
5	11	19	17	5	17†
6	12	20	18	6	18†

  * Pairs in List III for which facilitation is predicted.
  ** Pairs in List III for which interference is predicted.
  † Control pairs in List III.

Experimental design. Each S learned three lists of stimulus-response pairs. Each list consisted of six pairs of pictures. In or-

[1] The apparatus was especially constructed by the Hunter Mfg. Co., Iowa City, Iowa. The authors are indebted to Dr. Alfred Castaneda for aid in formulating the specifications for the apparatus.

der that S might more easily comprehend the task, List I was constructed of picture pairs which were highly associated; Lists II and III were not so constructed. Table I illustrates the design, which provides that each S serve under each of three experimental conditions. For two pairs in List III, the mediational chain is expected to facilitate learning. For two other pairs, the mediational chain is expected to elicit incorrect responses and thus interfere with learning. Two other pairs have no experimentally established mediating tendencies, since the response items paired with the stimuli in List I were not presented in List II.

Subjects. The Ss were 30 kindergarten children.[2] Ten Ss were randomly assigned to each of three groups. These three groups were designed to control for possible differential difficulty of the stimulus-response pairs in List III. All groups received the same form of Lists I and III. The groups differed with respect to which of three forms of List II they received. These three forms were constructed so that for a given List III pair, facilitation was predicted in one group, interference in another, and neither mediated facilitation nor interference for the third group.

Procedure. Each S was given three experimental sessions separated by from two to seven days. After the child had been brought by E from the classroom to the experimental room in order to play a "guessing game with pictures," he was seated facing the aperture in which the stimulus cards were presented. The E was seated immediately beside S in order to control the apparatus, give appropriate verbal instructions to establish understanding of the procedure, and to record responses made in the anticipation interval.

At the beginning of training, the right half of the aperture was opened and the six response members of List I were shown once

[2] The authors are indebted to Hale C. Reid, Director of Curriculum and Instructions, for permission to use subjects in the Cedar Rapids Public Schools. Special thanks are also due to Ray Churchill, Principal, and to the staff of Harrison School in Cedar Rapids, for administrative assistance and cooperation in the collection of the data of Exp. I.

each. The S was asked to name them. Any reasonable name given was accepted; if necessary, a name was supplied. The same procedure was followed as the stimulus members were presented in the left half of the aperture. A second naming trial was then given with the response members. During the first paired presentation, the stimulus side of the pair was exposed while E asked S each time what he thought was behind the curtain on the other side. The stimulus and response items were then simultaneously exposed while S gave the response name, either voluntarily or upon request. After the first trial, E instructed S to try to guess which picture was behind the curtain each time. Presentation was continued until a learning criterion of two consecutive correct trials had been reached.

Three varying orders of presentation were used for all lists in order to control for serial learning. A 6-sec. anticipation period was followed by a 5-sec. period of joint presentation of the stimulus and response items. The between pair interval was 2.2 sec. All verbal responses occurring in the anticipation interval were recorded verbatim throughout the experiment.

On the second experimental day, List II was administered in the same way as was List I, except that a simultaneous presentation of both the stimulus and response members was given rather than the second presentation of the response items alone.

On the third day, Lists I and II were each reviewed to criterion. A short rest period of approximately 2 min. followed. List III was then introduced in the same way as List I on the first day. Five trials on List III were given, terminating the experiment.

RESULTS AND DISCUSSIONS

The mean number of trials to criterion for all Ss on List I was 2.13. The means of the number of trials for the various forms of List II did not differ significantly; the overall mean was 3.47. The more rapid learning of List I than of List II is probably due to the higher associations within pairs for List I.

An analysis of variance of correct anticipations on List III is summarized in Table 2. In this analysis, the main effect of control groups appears as a between-S factor and the main effect of conditions as an intra-S factor (7, p. 267, Type I). This analysis revealed that the means for the groups designed as controls for possible differential difficulty of the picture pairs did not differ significantly. The means for the facilitation, control, and interference conditions differed at better than the .001 level of significance. For all 30 Ss combined, the mean numbers of correct responses in five trials were 7.40 for the facilitation, 4.83 for the control, and 4.40 for the interference conditions. Individual t tests showed that the mean differences for the facilitation and control comparison and for the facilitation and interference comparison were significant at better than the .001 level. The difference between control and interference means, although in the predicted direction, was not significant.

According to the mediation hypothesis, the learning of Lists I and II should

TABLE 2 · ANALYSIS OF VARIANCE OF CORRECT RESPONSES ON LIST III (EXP. I)

Source	df	MS	F
Between Ss	29		
Control groups (G)	2	2.98	<1.00
Error (b)	27	8.48	
Within Ss	60		
Conditions (C)	2	78.88	28.89*
G × C	4	2.48	<1.00
Error (w)	54	2.73	
Total	89		

* $P < .001$.

have set up a tendency for the stimulus member of each interference pair in List III to elicit the response that was correct for the other pair. Thus, the hypothesized interference effects may be further tested by comparing the number of these within-set errors for the two interference pairs with the number that occurred for the two control pairs, the latter reflecting the chance frequency of such reversals. The mean number of reversals per S for the interference condition was 1.50 and for the control condition, .20. A related t test indicated that the mean difference was significant at the .001 level.

Thus, the results of Exp. I indicate clear-cut positive transfer with a mediating facilitation sequence. Significant overall negative transfer was not shown, but the interference condition produced significantly more within-set errors than did the control condition. This latter finding is consistent with the hypothesis that specific incorrect responses are mediated under the interference condition.

EXPERIMENT II

Experiment II was conducted to investigate further the interference effects due to the mediational sequence. It was thought that by increasing the number of pairs in the interference and control conditions and by omitting the facilitation condition, a significant overall negative transfer might be obtained for the interference condition. The apparatus was the same as that used in Exp. I. The stimulus materials were of the same type as those in Exp. I.

METHOD

Experimental design. Each S learned three lists of stimulus-response pairs with six pairs of pictures per list, List I again being constructed of high association pairs. Table 3 illustrates the design. List III was composed of three control pairs and three

TABLE 3 · SCHEMATIC ILLUSTRATION OF THE DESIGN FOR EXP. II

LIST I		LIST II		LIST III	
S	R	S	R	S	R
1	7	7	13	1	14*
2	8	8	14	2	15*
3	9	9	15	3	13*
4	10	19	16	4	16**
5	11	20	17	5	17**
6	12	21	18	6	18**

* Pairs for which interference is predicted in List III.
** Control pairs in List III.

pairs for which mediated interference was predicted. Thus, each S served in both the interference and control conditions.

Subjects. The Ss were 24 first grade children.[3] Twelve Ss were randomly assigned to each of two groups. These groups were designed to control for possible differential difficulty of the stimulus-response pairs in List III. Both groups were given identical forms of Lists I and III; the groups differed only with respect to which of two forms of List II they received. These two forms were constructed so that any given pair in List III would be a control pair for one group and an interference pair for the other.

Procedure. The procedure for Exp. II was essentially the same as that for Exp. I. In order to adjust the difficulty of the tasks to the older first-grade Ss, the anticipation interval was reduced from 6 sec. to 4 sec., and the joint presentation interval was reduced from 5 sec. to 2 sec.

RESULTS AND DISCUSSION

The mean number of trials to criterion for all Ss on List I was 1.67. The means of the number of trials for the two forms of List II did not differ significantly; the combined mean was 2.38. As in Exp. I, it should be noted that the pairs

[3] Appreciation is expressed to Dr. Jerry Kuhn, Principal, University Elementary School, Iowa City, Iowa, for his permission to use the first grade class and for providing experimental facilities for Exp. II.

TABLE 4 · Analysis of Variance of Correct
Responses on List III (Exp. II)

Source	df	MS	F
Between Ss	23		
Control groups (G)	1	35.02	2.33
Error (b)	22	15.07	
Within Ss	24		
Conditions (C)	1	31.68	7.90*
G × C	1	2.53	<1.00
Error (w)	22	4.01	
Total	47		

    * P = .01.

in List I were of highly associated items.

Table 4 presents a summary of the analysis of variance of correct anticipations in five trials on List III. The stimulus control groups did not differ significantly. The mean number of correct anticipations for all 24 Ss was 7.83 for the control condition and 6.21 for the interference condition. The difference is significant at about the 1% level.

As in Exp. I, the within-set errors were tabulated for the interference and control pairs. There were 37 such errors for the interference condition and only 9 for the control. The mean difference of 1.17 yields a t of 3.19 (P < .01).

Experiment II thus provides statistically significant evidence that the conditions designed to produce the mediation of incorrect responses result in overall negative transfer in learning List III. When both experiments are considered, it appears that, under appropriate conditions, both positive and negative associative transfer is a consequence of mediated associations.

It is of interest to compare the results of the present experiments with those of Bugelski and Scharlock (2). Their experiment is like these in that the mediational tendencies were experiment-ally manipulated. Their experimental condition corresponds to the facilitation condition of Exp. I, while their control condition is analogous to the interference conditions of Exp. I and II. They found no significant differences in the mean or median number of trials to criterion for the two conditions; a significant difference was found in the mean rank order of learning the pairs in the two conditions. In the present investigation, the use of a control condition, in which no mediational tendencies existed that did not also exist for the other conditions, permitted the separation of the facilitation and interference effects.

SUMMARY

This investigation proposed to study the effects of mediated associations on the positive and negative associative transfer in the paired-associate learning of kindergarten and first-grade Ss.

In Exp. I, a different list of six stimulus-response picture pairs was learned by each of 30 Ss on each of three days. The learning sequence was such that mediation would be expected to have facilitating, interfering, and no effects for each S in the learning of different pairs of List III. A statistically significant difference was found between the mean number of correct anticipations for the control and facilitation conditions during List III learning. The difference between the means for the control and interference conditions, although in the predicted direction, was not statistically significant.

In Exp. II, each of 24 Ss learned a different list of six stimulus-response picture pairs on each of three days. The first two lists were arranged so that, in the learning of List III, interference effects were predicted for three pairs relative to the other three pairs. A statistically significant difference was found in the mean number of correct anticipations for the interference and control conditions.

It was concluded that, under the appropriate conditions, mediated associations can produce both positive and negative associative transfer.

REFERENCES

1. BIRGE, J. The role of verbal responses in transfer. Unpublished doctor's dissertation, Yale Univer., 1941.
2. BUGELSKI, B. R., & SCHARLOCK, D. P. An experimental demonstration of unconscious mediated association. *J. exp. Psychol.*, 1952, *44*, 334–338.
3. EISMAN, B. S. Attitude formation: the development of a color-preference response through mediated generalization. *J. abnorm. soc. Psychol.*, 1955, *50*, 321–326.
4. HULL, C. L. The problem of stimulus equivalence in behavior theory. *Psychol. Rev.*, 1939, *46*, 9–30.
5. IRWIN, IRL A. Associated facilitation as a function of the strength of the associative connection between first and second list response words. Uupublished doctor's dissertation, State Univer. Iowa, 1951.
6. JEFFREY, W. E. The effects of verbal and non-verbal responses in mediating an instrumental act. *J. exp. Psychol.*, 1953, *45*, 327–333.
7. LINDQUIST, E. F. *Design and analysis of experiments in psychology and education.* New York: Houghton Mifflin, 1953.
8. MURDOCK, B. B., JR. Effects of failure and retroactive inhibition in mediating an instrumental act. *J. exp. Psychol.*, 1952, *44*, 156–164.
9. PETERS, H. N. Mediate association. *J. exp. Psychol.*, 1935, *18*, 20–48.
10. RUSSELL, W. A., & STORMS, L. H. Implicit verbal chaining in paired-associate learning. *J. exp. Psychol.*, 1955, *49*, 287–293.
11. SHEPARD, W. O. Mediated generalization with high interstimulus similarity. Unpublished M.A. thesis, State Univer. Iowa, 1953.
12. SHIPLEY, W. C. Indirect conditioning. *J. gen. Psychol.*, 1935, *12*, 337–357.

THE EFFECTS OF VERBAL AND NONVERBAL RESPONSES IN MEDIATING AN INSTRUMENTAL ACT [1]

WENDELL E. JEFFREY

AN IMPORTANT ASPECT of human learning is the acquisition of language and the consequent effect of language on behavior. The clearest analysis of this has been made by Dollard and Miller who have stressed the importance of language in supplying human beings with cue-producing responses which function to produce a cue that is part of a stimulus pattern leading to another response. Thus they state that: "Attaching the same cue-producing response to two distinctive stimulus objects gives them a certain *learned equivalence* increasing the extent to which instrumental and emotional responses will generalize from one to the other. . . . Conversely, attaching distinctive cue-producing responses to similar stimulus objects tends to increase their distinctiveness" (*3*, p. 101).

Similarly, Hull in discussing secondary generalization concludes that, ". . . the common-sense notion of similarity and difference is based upon the presence or absence of primary generalization gradients, whereas so-called logical or abstract similarities and differences arise from secondary, learned, or medi-ated similarities and differences, particularly those mediated by verbal reactions" (*6*, p. 194).

If one assumes that the conditioning between an internal stimulus and an overt response can take place in the same way as conditioning involving external stimuli, it is possible that the conditioning of a verbal response to an external stimulus can take place independently of the conditioning of a motor response to the internal stimuli produced by a verbal response. Thus, an external stimulus which hitherto has not been associated with a particular motor response, may now elicit the response through the mediation of the label.

That discriminations can be learned more quickly when labels (verbal responses) are attached to the stimulus objects has been indicated by Pyles (*10*), Gagné and Baker (*5*), and Rossman and Goss (*11*). Kuenne (*7*) and Alberts and Ehrenfreund (*1*) have demonstrated that transposition of response on a size-discrimination problem is more likely to occur when the children have in their verbal repertoire a relational statement with respect to size, and a study by Birge (*2*) indicated that if two different objects are assigned the same name by *E*, these objects are more likely to be responded to in the same manner by *S* than if the objects are given different names.

Although investigations of the me-

[1] This paper is based on a dissertation submitted in partial fulfillment of the requirements for the Ph.D. degree in the Department of Child Welfare of the State University of Iowa. The writer is indebted to Professor Vincent Nowlis for advice and assistance throughout the investigation.

Reprinted by permission from *Journal of Experimental Psychology*, 1953, *45*, 327–333.

diational process have usually involved verbal responses, it is conceivable that any other response which produces sufficiently distinct proprioceptive stimulation might also serve in this manner. Most relevant to this hypothesis is the research of Shipley (12), and Lumsdaine (9), and the aforementioned study of Birge which demonstrated that a new stimulus object, to which reaching responses were reinforced, was more likely to be called by the name that was attached to the previous object to which reaching responses had been reinforced.

The present research was designed to further evaluate the mediational process in a situation where E could train the mediational responses and to a great extent control the subsequent use of the responses in a discrimination problem. Three groups of Ss were used, one provided with verbal mediational responses, and two, one of which was a control, provided with manipulative mediational responses. By mechanically obstructing the mediational response in the control group during the training and test series following its acquisition, it was possible to evaluate the importance of the training sequence associating the internal stimuli of the mediational response with the response to be mediated.[2] Comparison between the two experimental groups gave an estimate of the effectiveness of a manipulative response in a mediational capacity.

Children were employed as Ss in order to minimize the number of mediating responses, sets, or associations that might tend to operate in an experimental

situation to mediate, or otherwise cause transfer of response from one stimulus to another. Furthermore, it was assumed that of human Ss, young children would be capable of the least amount of spontaneous verbalization with respect to the mode of solution, or the relationship between the several tasks involved in the experimental procedure.

METHOD

Subjects. The Ss were 56 children from the State University of Iowa Preschool Laboratories. They ranged in chronological age from 3 yr. 3 mo. to 5 yr. 6 mo. and in mental age from 3 yr. 3 mo. to 7 yr. 10 mo. Eight of these 56 children were dropped from the experiment after the initial training session because of failure to learn and/or rejection of the experimental situation.

The 48 remaining Ss were arbitrarily divided into two MA groups of 24 each on the basis of an MA above or below 5 yr. 5½ mo. Within each MA group Ss were randomly assigned to the experimental and control groups as well as to the order in which they would be tested.

Apparatus. The stimuli consisted of three different shades of Hering gray papers, No. 3, 16, and 50. Number 3 was not quite white, No. 16 was gray, and No. 50 was black. The reflected light of these three stimuli as measured in apparent ft.-candles by a Macbeth illuminometer was 7.70, 2.47, and .35, respectively.

The stimulus exposure device was a Hull-type memory drum, the stimuli being affixed to the tape so that on each exposure a color patch of ⅞ by 1½ in. was displayed. Three stimulus series were used and were affixed to a single tape so that each series could be selected by moving the aperture across the front of the drum. The three series were as follows: (a) random presentation of black and white stimulus patches; (b) random presentation of black and white, with a gray stimulus patch interspersed as every fifth stimulus; (c) random presentation of white, gray, and black.

---

2 The possibility that covert muscular responses might still occur even though the gross movement was not permitted has not been overlooked. However, such responses were not thought to be as important a source of stimulation or as likely to occur as subvocal responses after verbal training.

The memory drum was in a circuit so wired that by pressing a push button switch the drum would operate through an open-close shutter cycle and stop. This allowed E to prepare S before each stimulus presentation.

The response mechanism consisted of a piece of iron rod ⅜ in. in diameter and 4 ft. long. One end of this was bent to form a handle which projected from the apparatus on the right side of the memory drum. This handle could be slid in and out with a total excursion of 12 in., and could be turned 45° to the left or right. It was possible to control the movement of the handle by placing differently grooved boards in the base of the support through which the rod slid. A smaller rod, projecting perpendicularly 1¼ in. from the handle rod, ran in these grooves and by changing the boards the handle could be pushed or pulled only, turned only, or set so that it had to be turned before being pushed or pulled.

A Standard Electric Timer was wired in the circuit so that the timer started when the shutter opened, and stopped, either when the handle was moved 1 in. forward or backward from the center position, or when the shutter closed.

The reward delivery mechanism was electrically operated but manually controlled by E. Marbles were used as secondary reinforcement and were delivered into a box to the left of the memory drum. The S took each marble and placed it in a board containing 38 circular recesses, each holding a single marble.

Procedure. The Ss served individually in two sessions of approximately 25 min. each which were run on consecutive days whenever possible. However, owing to the intervention of weekends and absences the between-test interval varied from one to five days. This variation would not be expected to make any difference in the results since there was a retraining session on the second day. Session 1 consisted of initial training and initial test; Session 2 consisted of mediational training, retraining, and retest.

For the *initial training* in Session 1 white and black patches were presented serially in random order, and the reinforced response was the pushing or pulling of the handle. Direction of movement was balanced, half of the Ss being reinforced for pulling the handle to the white stimulus, the other half being reinforced for pushing the handle to the white stimulus. The opposite response to the black stimulus was reinforced in each case. The S was seated in front of the memory drum with his right hand on the handle. After instructions, training proceeded to a criterion of 25 correct responses in 26 trials. Each correct response was reinforced immediately with a marble. When 38 marbles had been collected, they were cashed in for a cellophane-wrapped after-dinner mint. In case S earned more than 38 marbles before reaching the training criterion, he was given the piece of candy and asked to continue playing for another piece. In most cases, Ss met the criterion within 25 to 45 trials.

Initial test data were obtained after reaching the above criterion by shifting the stimulus exposure aperture to the second stimulus series of black and white patches with a gray stimulus interspersed every fifth trial. In this series there was a total of 30 trials, the second, third, and fifth stimulus in each block of five being arbitrarily designated test stimuli. This provided six test responses to each of the three different stimuli. By starting at two different places in the series the order in which the test stimuli occurred, and their relation to previous stimuli in the order was balanced. To eliminate the reinforcement or nonreinforcement of any particular response during the test series, the reinforcement procedure was changed. The Ss were now told that no more marbles would be delivered until they were through but that they were to keep on responding as they had before and the experimenter would keep account of the number of marbles they earned. After 30 trials enough marbles were dispensed to obtain the candy regardless of S's performance.

In Session 2 the stimuli for *mediational training* were white, black, and gray patches presented with equal frequency. The Ss within each MA group had been assigned at random to three treatment groups (I, II, and III), each further subdivided into two conditions (A and B). Group I was trained

TABLE 1 · Reinforced Responses During
Mediational Training for the Various
Groups and Subgroups

Stim-ulus	SUBGROUPS OF GROUP I		SUBGROUPS OF GROUPS II & III	
	A	B	A	B
White	"White"	"White"	Left turn	Left turn
Gray	"White"	"Black"	Left turn	Right turn
Black	"Black"	"Black"	Right turn	Right turn

to make the verbal mediational response
"black" or "white" and Groups II and III
learned the motor response of turning the
handle left or right. The two subgroups (A
and B) under each of the three treatments
differed with respect to the response made to
the gray stimulus. The Ss in Subgroup A
were reinforced for making the same response to gray as to white, while Ss in Subgroup B were reinforced for making the
same response to gray as to black (cf. Table 1). The direction of turning was counterbalanced in each of the motor groups.
Training proceded to a criterion of 25 correct responses in 26 trials.

During *retraining* the first stimulus series
of white and black patches was utilized
again in order to connect the stimuli of the
mediational response to the original push-
pull response while relearning the latter.
This time, Group I was required to make
the verbal mediational response prior to the
push-pull response and Group II the turning mediational response before the push-
pull response. Group III was used as a
control for the effects of combining the mediational and original responses and was not
permitted to make the turning response
while relearning the push-pull response. All
Ss were trained to a criterion of 15 correct
responses in 16 trials and were given a piece
of candy at the end of the series regardless
of the number of marbles earned. If any S
received 38 marbles before reaching the criterion, he was given the candy and asked to
continue playing for another piece.

In the *retest*, the Ss were tested on the
stimulus series of white and black patches
with gray on every fifth trial as in the original test. The effectiveness of retraining with
the mediational response was measured here

since Group I was instructed to continue
naming the stimuli before moving the handle and Group II had to make the turning
response before the push-pull response was
possible. Otherwise the Ss were told to keep
on responding as they had been and the individual trials were again not reinforced.

For all training series, *instructions* included (a) a demonstration by E of the response to be learned, and (b) direction and
correction by E of S's trial responses to each
stimulus in the series being used. It is to be
emphasized that neither the stimuli nor the
direction of movement were ever named except to say, "When it is this color, move the
handle this way, and when it is this color,
move the handle this way." This statement
was accompanied by the demonstration of
the appropriate movement of the handle.

Any verbalizations or questions by S
about the stimuli or direction of movement
were ignored or interrupted by giving the
ready signal for the next trial. In the few
cases where S did not appear to be learning, another demonstration was given ac-
centuating the relationship between the
stimuli and the direction of movement.

Response measures. The latency, frequency, and direction of response were obtained on 6 trials to the white stimuli, 6
trials to the gray stimuli, and 6 trials to the
black stimuli in both the test and retest
series each of which consisted of 30 trials.

Because of difficulties presented by un-
limited latencies, and the fact that the retest
latencies were inflated by the inclusion of
the mediational response with the push-pull
response, the latency measures were not
analyzed. The frequency measures, however,
were converted to a difference score reflecting the change in response to the gray stimuli from the test to retest trials. This score
was obtained by arbitrarily assigning the
value $+1$ to correct responses, i.e., responses
which were in the same direction as mediational training for that S, and -1 to responses in the opposite direction. If no response was elicited within approximately 3
sec. after the shutter opened, a zero score
was given. The sum of the values for the six
trials was then obtained for the test and retest sessions separately and a difference

score was computed by subtracting the test score from the retest score. In the initial test series only three Ss responded in a consistent direction to the six presentations of the gray stimuli. Thirteen Ss made no responses and the rest varied in making from one to five responses. In the retest series three Ss in Groups I and II made a single response in the opposite direction to that predicted and the rest of the Ss responded in the direction of mediational training if they responded at all.

RESULTS

The mean frequency of response in the direction of white or black for each stimulus in the test and retest series is indicated in Table 2, for all groups. The

difference scores were subjected to an analysis of variance with results as shown in Table 3. It may be noted that none of the interaction variances was significantly larger than the within-groups variance, thus permitting the use of the within-groups variance as the estimate of error (8). Bartlett's (4, pp. 195–197) test was used to test the hypothesis of homogeneity of variance and the resultant chi square was not significant.

The difference in difference scores for the A and B groups was not significant indicating that the magnitude of change was approximately the same irrespective of the direction of change.

TABLE 2 · MEAN RESPONSE TO GRAY IN TEST AND RETEST SERIES AND THE
DIFFERENCE SCORES
(Four Ss in each group)

Groups	MA I			MA II		
	Test	Retest	Difference: retest-test	Test	Retest	Difference: retest-test
I$_A$	.25	5.50	5.25	—2.50	5.75	8.25
I$_B$	.25	5.75	5.50	— .75	5.50	6.25
II$_A$	— .50	2.50	3.00	—1.50	4.50	6.00
II$_B$	1.00	4.00	3.00	— .25	4.75	5.00
III$_A$	—1.00	3.00	4.00	—1.00	.50	1.50
III$_B$	— .75	—1.75	—1.00	— .75	2.25	3.00

TABLE 3 · ANALYSIS OF VARIANCE OF DIF-
FERENCE SCORES

Source of variation	df	Mean square	F
Conditions (Groups A & B)	1	13.02	1.65
Treatments (Groups I, II, III)	2	78.90	9.98**
Levels (MA I & II)	1	35.02	4.43*
C × T	2	1.64	—
C × L	1	3.52	—
T × L	2	3.14	—
C × T × L	2	22.40	2.83
Within groups	36	7.90	
Total	47	116.59	

* Significant at the .05 level.
** Significant at the .01 level.

The mean differences between the test and retest scores for the treatments were 6.31 for Group I, 4.25 for Group II, and 1.875 for Group III, when subgroups were combined. As shown, the F for these treatment differences was highly significant. A test of the differences between the means for Groups I and II, and Groups II and III, produced t's of 2.06 and 2.38 ($p < .05$), respectively. The within-groups variance was used as the error estimate, allowing 36 df. The hypothesis that the Group III scores did not differ significantly from chance was tested and a t of 2.67 ($p < .02$) was obtained.

The difference between the higher and lower MA groups was significant $(.05 > p > .01)$. On the assumption that some Ss in the higher MA group might formulate verbal statements with respect to the gray stimulus during mediational training, and assuming these verbal statements might occur in the retest situation to aid in mediating the appropriate response, it was predicted that there would be real interaction between the different treatments and mental age, the mentally older Ss demonstrating more mediated generalization in Groups II and III. Contrary to this prediction, however, the treatment by levels interaction variance was not significantly larger than the within-groups variance.

DISCUSSION

The results of the present study have clearly demonstrated that response mediation can occur in young children and that motor responses as well as verbal responses are effective in the mediational role.

That the verbal group (Group I) would perform significantly better than the motor group (Group II) was expected on the assumption that auditory stimulation provided by verbal responses increases the number of internal stimuli as well as provides more distinctive cues. If one accepts this assumption, it would be presumed that the mediational stimuli provided by the verbal responses were nearly optimal in terms of distinctiveness. If this is the case, the relative performance of the motor group is especially striking, since the stimuli resulting from the simple turning of the hand 45° to the left or right would not be expected to produce particularly distinct stimulation and therefore other more discrete motor responses such as the movement of the left and right hands, or one hand and one foot, when used in a mediational role, might more closely approach the results obtained with the verbal responses.

If one further assumes that response mediation depends on a stimulus-response connection between the response-produced stimuli and the instrumental response, then one is obliged to propose some explanation for the results obtained from Group III (Control) since this group was not provided with the opportunity to build up this S–R connection. Although the performance of this group was relatively poor, the mean difference score was significantly larger than one would expect from chance. It had been predicted that spontaneous verbalization might occur during the mediational training which could later serve in a mediational capacity. It this were the case, it was expected that since verbal behavior is related to mental age, spontaneous verbalizations would be more likely to occur in the higher mental age groups. On the assumption that the performance of the higher MA Ss in Groups II and III would be increased relatively more than Group I which was given the appropriate mediational cues, one would expect relatively less difference in performance between the treatment groups in the higher MA level than between the treatment groups in the lower MA level. This effect then would show up in the treatment by levels interaction. However, since this interaction was not significant one may assume that either verbalization was occurring equally in both MA levels, or that the mediation was resulting from the continuation by S of a slight turning response which provided differential pressure on the fingers, or slight muscular tension which produced sufficient stimulation to serve in a mediational capacity.

The significance of the difference between the two MA levels appears to reflect a general superiority in performance on the part of the older Ss. It was noted in the experimental situation that the younger Ss often became concerned with such things as the number of marbles they had obtained or irrelevant aspects of the situation. Such behavior tended both to lower the number of responses and increase the number of errors, thus causing a decrease in the general performance level of the younger Ss.

In general the present investigation has also demonstrated that young children are capable of performing fairly complex tasks when instructions are given to point out the relation of the stimuli to the response and when sufficient motivation is provided. This fact, along with the knowledge that motor responses can serve in a mediational capacity, is particularly helpful. If, from further research of this sort, we can conclude that such responses parallel verbal responses in their general effects, then our interpretation of verbal behavior may be simplified. The motor response then offers an excellent opportunity to study the effects of mediational responses on behavior without incurring many of the complications involved in the use of verbal responses.

SUMMARY

Forty-eight preschool children were trained to respond differentially to white and black stimuli. After meeting a criterion the generalization of the responses to gray was tested and found to be practically absent. Following this, Groups I and II acquired verbal and motor mediational responses, respectively, with subgroups which learned the same response for either black and gray or white and gray and these responses were then incorporated with the response previously learned. Group III learned the same motor mediational response as Group II but was not permitted to use this response during the retraining of the original response. Again the generalization to gray was measured and the data analyzed as difference scores between the first and second series. The verbal mediational response was found to produce significantly greater generalization than the motor response, but the motor response in turn produced relatively good generalization. That is, consistent responses were made to the gray stimuli in the retest session

as the result of the inclusion of a mediational response with the original response learned to black and white.

Since Group III was a control group, the mediational response was not continued after the mediational training and consequently this group demonstrated very poor mediation. The difference scores, however, differed significantly from chance. This was explained by assuming that either spontaneous but subvocal verbalizations or covert turning responses were serving to mediate the generalization of the initial response.

The mediational process was assumed to depend on a stimulus-response connection between the stimuli produced by the mediational response and the instrumental response. Thus, when the mediational response which was trained to gray was the same as that trained to white, and when the mediational response to white was made prior to the pushing response to white for a number of trials, it was assumed that a stimulus-response connection was built up which later elicited the pushing response when this mediational response was made to the gray stimulus.

REFERENCES

1. ALBERTS, E., & EHRENFREUND, D. Transposition in children as a function of age. *J. exp. Psychol.*, 1951, *41*, 30–38.
2. BIRGE, J. S. The role of verbal response in transfer. Unpublished Ph.D. thesis, Yale Univer., 1941.
3. DOLLARD, J., & MILLER, N. E. *Personality and psychotherapy*. New York: McGraw-Hill, 1950.
4. EDWARDS, A. L. *Experimental design in psychological research*. New York: Rinehart, 1950.

5. GAGNÉ, R. M., & BAKER, K. E.   Stimulus predifferentiation as a factor in transfer of training. *J. exp. Psychol.*, 1950, *40*, 439–451.

6. HULL, C. L.   *Principles of behavior.* New York: D. Appleton-Century, 1943.

7. KUENNE, M. R.   Experimental investigation of the relation of language to transposition behavior in young children. *J. exp. Psychol.*, 1946, *36*, 471–490.

8. LINDQUIST, E. F.   *Design and analysis of experiments in psychology and education.* (Mimeographed preliminary copy prepared at the State Univer. of Iowa, 1950.)

9. LUMSDAINE, A. A.   Conditioned eyelid responses as mediating generalized conditioned finger reactions. *Psychol. Bull.*, 1939, *36*, 650. (Abstract.)

10. PYLES, M. K.   Verbalization as a factor in learning. *Child Develpm.*, 1932, *3*, 108–113.

11. ROSSMAN, I. L., & GOSS, A. E.   The acquired distinctiveness of cues: the role of discriminative verbal responses facilitating the acquisition of discriminative motor responses. *J. exp. Psychol.*, 1951, *42*, 173–182.

12. SHIPLEY, W. C.   Indirect conditioning. *J. gen. Psychol.*, 1935, *12*, 337–357.

ATTITUDE FORMATION: THE DEVELOPMENT OF A COLOR-PREFERENCE RESPONSE THROUGH MEDIATED GENERALIZATION [1]

BERNICE S. EISMAN LOTT

THE PRESENT INVESTIGATION of attitude development has had as its major

[1] This paper is based on a portion of a dissertation, prepared under the guidance of Professor F. Fearing, and submitted in partial fulfillment of the requirements for the Ph.D. degree, U.C.L.A., 1953. The author also wishes to thank Professors Gilhousen, Maltzman, Centers, Seagoe, and Turner for their critical suggestions, and Miss C. Seeds, Principal of the University Elementary School, for her cooperation in supplying the subjects for the reported experiment.

Reprinted by permission from *Journal of Abnormal and Social Psychology*, 1955, *50*, 321–326.

stimulus Doob's 1947 discussion (7) and reinterpretation of the concept. His placement of attitude within the framework of behavior theory and his emphasis on attitude as a learned response to definable stimuli appears to be a more research oriented and potentially fruitful approach to the problem than has been taken in the past. An equally important source of stimulation for this study has come from the work on mediated and semantic generalization, particularly from the work of

Birge (2), Cofer and Foley and associates (3, 4, 5, 8, 9), Keller (11), Razran (13, 14), and Reiss (15, 16).

An attitude is here defined, as suggested by Doob, as a learned implicit anticipatory response having both cue and drive properties. An anticipatory response is one which originally came after a rewarded response but as a result of being most closely associated with the reward moves forward in the behavior sequence. This results in its "anticipatory" occurrence directly to the external stimulus before its original time in the response series. As a response with stimulus properties, an attitude falls into the class of "pure stimulus acts" defined by Hull (10) as responses whose major function is to serve as stimuli for other acts. It follows, therefore, that once such an implicit response-produced stimulus (r-s) has been established, it can be conditioned to evoke overt behavior. In this way an attitude acts as a mediator of responses. It is these responses, mediated by an attitude, which are measured by attitude questionnaires in attitude experiments, etc.

The property of drive value ascribed to an attitude is derived from the fact that an attitudinal response is assumed to produce strong stimulation. Any strong, persistent stimulus is considered by Miller and Dollard (6, p. 30) to constitute a drive. Reduction of the strong stimulus is drive reducing and therefore reinforcing. It is expected, therefore, that any overt response which leads to a significant reduction of the strong stimulus will be learned. Ascribing drive value to attitudes distinguishes them from other implicit, anticipatory response-produced stimuli and is in line with traditional views. Attitudes, wrote Allport (1), "both motivate

and guide; they supply both drive and direction." Sherif and Cantril (17, p. 300) offer, as one criterion of an attitude, its affective property. Krech, too, speaks of attitudes as motivational, thus distinguishing them from beliefs (12, p. 152).

STATEMENT OF THE PROBLEM

The purpose of the present study has been to demonstrate experimentally that attitude formation is amenable to laboratory observation and control, and can be adequately conceptualized and explained by reinforcement learning theory. The general hypothesis of this study can be formally stated as follows: A positive preference or attitude toward an object with which an individual has had only neutral experience can be developed through mediated generalization. In more operational terms, it is predicted that if individuals are taught to attach the same label to two stimuli which differ from one another in all other relevant ways, and if these individuals subsequently have rewarding experience with one of these stimuli, then a positive preference for the other stimulus, as well as for stimuli resembling the latter, will be demonstrable. This type of learning experience follows the general paradigm for mediated generalization. In this study the subjects develop a positive response for a color after being subjected to such a series of learning experiences.

To test this general hypothesis four different test situations, in which a color preference could be demonstrated, were employed. These situations, differing in context, complexity, and social significance, will be described in detail below.

METHOD

APPARATUS AND SUBJECTS

A wooden stage, 20.5 in. high, 30 in. wide, and 19 in. deep, with a raised, slanted platform, at an angle of about 35 degrees from the horizontal, was constructed and used for the presentation of various stimulus objects to the subjects. An unbleached muslin curtain could be pulled in front or away from the platform in order to hide or expose objects on it. Three small depressions about 8 in. apart were drilled into the platform to serve as receptables for marbles which were used as rewards during certain portions of the training.

The following stimulus objects were used: (a) three wooden *geometrical blocks*, each painted white and .75 in. thick, triangular, circular, and square, respectively; (b) three *thin rectangular blocks*, each 2.5 in. by 6 in. and .75 in. thick, painted green, yellow, and black, respectively; (c) three metal *jar tops*, 2.5 in. in diameter, also painted green, yellow, and black, respectively; (d) three *glasses*, 3.5 in. high, painted green, yellow, and black, respectively; (e) three *thick rectangular blocks*, 1.5 in. by 1.5 in. by 4.5 in., painted green, yellow, and black, respectively; (f) three white wooden *"nonsense" blocks*, .75 in. thick, and of three different nonsense shapes.

Eighty-one subjects (Ss) were used, 41 boys and 40 girls, ranging in age from 5 years, 10 months to 8 years, 10 months. All Ss were attending an elementary school operated by the Department of Education of U.C.L.A. All members of each of the classes used in this study were utilized by the experimenter (E), i.e., there was no arbitrary selection of Ss from within any class. The Ss were told that E had a new game she wanted to try out and that she would play with each of the children in a class, one at a time. Owing to the nature of the school, all children in it were accustomed to observation by strangers and many of them were also accustomed to leaving their classes for some time for testing or other "play"-research purposes.

PROCEDURE

The 81 Ss were randomly divided into four groups with 9 Ss in Group I, 18 Ss in Group II, and 27 Ss each in Groups III and IV. One third of the Ss in each group was randomly selected to be trained positively for each of the three colors, yellow, green, and black. The E worked with one S at a time. Since the name of each S had been assigned to an experimental group prior to the start of the experiment, the order in which Ss came to E was not fixed, and either the teacher or the last S chose the next S.

Part 1. Name learning for the geometrical blocks. Each S sat facing E and the front of the stage. The Ss in all four groups were treated alike during this portion of the training. The three geometrical blocks were placed on the stage by E, and S was told that all three had names which S had to discover, the names being "egg" (for the triangle), "car" (for the circle), and "shoe" (for the square). Each S was shown one block at a time in a predetermined random order which was the same for all Ss. When a block was presented, S guessed at its name and E told S if he was right or wrong. The S was given as many trials as was necessary in order for him successfully to identify each of the three blocks five times in succession. Each S was told that learning the names of the blocks was necessary in order to proceed to the next part of the game during which he could win some marbles.

Part 2. Reward series. Here, too, Ss in all four groups were treated alike. The geometrical blocks were again placed on the platform and S was told that E would hide a marble under one of them when the curtains were closed and then ask S to guess where the marble was. The S was instructed to point to the block under which he thought the marble was hidden and to call the block by its *name*, the name learned in Part 1. When placing a marble under the proper block, E was careful to make extraneous noise so that sound would not serve as a reliable cue with respect to the hiding place of the marble.

A marble was always hidden under the

same block for any given S. For those who were to be trained to prefer green, the marble was always placed under the triangle ("egg"); for those to be trained for yellow, the marble was placed under the circle ("car"); and for those to be trained for black, the marble was always placed under the square ("shoe"). The relative positions of the blocks were shifted per trial according to a random, predetermined order which was constant for all Ss.

Each time a marble was hidden S was permitted only one guess as to its location. If S guessed correctly, he kept the marble; if he guessed incorrectly, E closed the curtains and hid the marble again, under the same block but in a new position with respect to the other two. The reward series ended when S had made six consecutive correct guesses. If the criterion was not reached by the fourteenth trial, a correction procedure was instituted, i.e., when S guessed incorrectly, E lifted the correct block and showed S where the marble was.

The purpose of this part of the training was to provide differential reinforcement for one of the three names ("egg," "car," or "shoe") which S had learned in Part 1. This is the only portion of the training in which such differential reinforcement could be obtained.

Part 3. Name learning for the thin rectangular blocks. Immediately after the reward series, E presented the three colored rectangular blocks, instructing S that one was called "egg" (the green block), one was called "car" (the yellow block), and one was called "shoe" (the black block). The S was again asked to discover which block had what name. The procedure followed here was identical to that followed in Part 1 and again Ss in all four groups were treated alike.

Part 4. Review series. Groups I and II. Immediately following Part 3, Ss in both of these groups were tested for recall of the names of the geometrical blocks and of the colored rectangles and for recall of the marble game (reward series).

Groups III and IV. For Ss in these groups a longer and more elaborate review was given in order to introduce more reward and color-naming experience. This was done because the results of a preliminary investigation had led to the conclusion that owing to the nature of the test situations (to be described below) given Ss in Groups III and IV, additional reward and naming experience would be necessary for mediated generalization to be demonstrable.

The E presented three new stimuli, the colored jar tops, and asked S to guess what their names were. The S received a marble each time he correctly named all three stimuli. When S reached the criterion of three correct identifications, the colored glasses were presented and the same procedure was followed. The E next presented the three thick rectangles and asked S to guess their names. Correct identifications were calling the green objects "egg," the yellow ones "car," and the black ones "shoe."

The Ss were then reviewed on the marble game (reward series). Then one jar top, one glass, and one rectangle, each of a different color, were presented. All three of the possible combinations were presented successively and S was asked to name the objects. No marble rewards were given.

Part 5. Test for mediated generalization and color preference. Here the major differential treatment for the four experimental groups was introduced. The tests were given immediately after the review.

Group I. The Ss in this group were presented with the three thin rectangular blocks used in Part 3 and told, "Now we'll play the marble game with these. You tell me where you think the marble is. Don't forget to tell me the name of the block you think the marble is under." With the curtains hiding the platform, E placed a marble under each block. Only one trial was given, and after S made his choice he was told that there would be no more games. A right choice was picking that colored rectangle which had the same name as the geometrical block under which S had consistently found marbles in Part 2.

Group II. The Ss in this group were also told that they were going to play the marble game again. The curtains were drawn, but instead of placing the three thin rectangles on the platform, as was done with Group I,

E substituted three new stimuli, the colored jar tops, with which Ss in Group II had had no prior experimental experience. A marble was placed under each jar top. When the curtains were opened, S was told to choose that jar top under which he thought a marble was hidden and to give its name ("egg," "car," "shoe"). The E did not tell Ss that these were the names of the new objects, and Ss had had no experience in so naming them. Only one choice trial was given. A correct choice was picking that jar top which was the same color as the rectangle which S, in Part 3, had learned had the same name as the geometrical block under which marbles had consistently been found in Part 2.

Group III. The Ss in this group were presented with three new stimuli, the white "nonsense" blocks, and instructed that one was called "green," one "black," and one "yellow." The S was told that he had to discover which block had what name. The same name-learning procedure as was used in Parts 1 and 3 was utilized here, and again a criterion of five successive correct identifications of each block was employed. After S reached the criterion, he was asked, "If you could take one of these blocks home, which would you pick?"

The color name learned for each of the three "nonsense" blocks was varied from S to S in order to correct for possible preference for one of the blocks because of its shape. Thus, for example, of three subjects, all trained to prefer black ("shoe") by having been given differential reinforcement for the square block ("shoe") in Part 2, each learned to call a different "nonsense" block "black" in this test situation. Each of the three Ss was expected to choose that block which he had learned to call "black."

Group IV. The E told Ss in this group a story about a pair of twins who had just moved into a new neighborhood. During the course of the story the twins meet three groups of children, a green, a yellow, and a black group. The play activities described for the three groups are almost identical. The climax of the story is reached when the twins decide to have a birthday party and their parents insist that they can invite only *one* of the groups of their new friends. The

twins must choose only one of the groups for their party. Each S was asked by E to choose the group he would invite. A correct choice was picking that group having the same color as the rectangular block which S had learned, in Part 3, had the same name as the geometrical block under which he had consistently found marbles in Part 2.

RESULTS

Table 1 summarizes the generalization results obtained from Ss' responses in their respective test situations. The numbers in parentheses represent expected frequencies. It was expected that since each S had to choose among three colors or three colored objects in the test situation, one third of the group could choose the correct (i.e., trained for) color and two thirds of the group could choose the incorrect color by chance alone. A significant deviation from these proportions in the direction of more than one third *Yeses* and less than two thirds *Noes* refutes the null hypothesis and lends support to the experimental hypothesis.

TABLE 1 · Generalization Results: Responses of Subjects in All Groups in Their Respective Test Situations

Group	N	No. of Ss making correct choice	No. of Ss making incorrect choice	χ^2	p^*
I	9	8 (3)	1 (6)	—	<.002**
II	18	14 (6)	4 (12)	16.00	<.001
III	27	16 (9)	11 (18)	8.17	<.01
IV	27	17 (9)	10 (18)	10.67	<.01

* Probability that the difference between obtained and expected frequencies could have occurred by chance alone.

** Since the theoretical frequencies and total N of Group I are too low for the reliable use of χ^2, the probability figure shown was obtained by evaluating the data by means of the binomial expansion (both tails of the distribution considered).

It can be seen from Table 1 that the performance of all groups verified the experimental hypothesis. The null hypothesis of no significant difference between obtained and theoretical frequencies can be safely rejected, and the training given each group is thus shown to be adequate for the generalization of a positive choice response from one stimulus to a previously neutral one.

A chi-square test of independence was also run on the data shown in Table 1 to see if there were any significant differences among the four groups in the success-failure ratio. No such differences were found ($\chi^2 = 3.0$; $p > .30$). A test between Groups I and II combined and Groups III and IV combined also yielded significant results, although there is an indication that the more difficult task required of Ss in these latter two groups served to lower the number of correct responses ($\chi^2 = 3.37$; $p > .05$).[2]

GENERAL DISCUSSION AND CONCLUSIONS

The results of this experiment have shown that conditions which allow for mediated generalization, and which, in certain cases, offer Ss additional opportunities for reward and "labeling" experience, are sufficient to produce a positive response toward a previously neutral color with which Ss had had no differential reward experience. From this positive response, a favorable "attitude" to-

wards this color is inferred. In addition, this favorable attitude has been demonstrated in more than one type of situation.

Space limitations do not permit a full presentation of the analysis of the results of this study in terms of learning theory concepts and principles. One illustration of the kind of analysis performed will have to suffice.

Figure 1 represents the conditions for and results of training for Ss in Group IV. Stage A represents Parts 1 and 3 of the experimental training, i.e., the name-learning sessions; stage B represents Part 2, the reward session; and stage C represents Part 5, the test situation. Stage A might have been better represented by three diagrams—one for each geometrical block and colored rectangle pair to which S learned to give the same name. For convenience, only one diagram, however, is used to represent all three. In stage B only one S_g is referred to, depending upon which geometrical block a particular S was consistently rewarded for choosing.

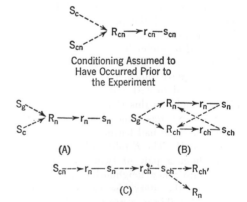

Conditioning Assumed to Have Occurred Prior to the Experiment

(A)   (B)

(C)

Figure 1. CONDITIONS FOR AND RESULTS OF TRAINING FOR Ss IN GROUP IV. S stands for stimulus of either geometric blocks (g) or colors (c); R stands for overt responses of either naming (n) or choosing (ch); r stands for implicit responses and s stands for stimuli produced by these implicit responses.

---

[2] The influence of age and sex on generalization in this experimental situation was tested by means of chi square. No significant differences were found to exist between Ss above and below the median age of their respective groups with respect to success and failure on the generalization tests. Similarly, no significant difference in the success-failure ratio was found to hold between the sexes.

In stage C, the test situation, color names of three groups of children in a story were presented as oral stimuli to the Ss by E. S_{cn} represents these color-name stimuli. Each of the color-name stimuli can evoke a specific $r_n\text{-}s_n$ because of the relationship shown in Fig. 1 under the heading "conditioning assumed to have occurred prior to the experiment." It is assumed that the Ss, outside the experimental situation, have learned to make this same response to both S_c (a visual color stimulus) and S_{cn} (an auditory color stimulus, i.e., a color name). This same response is R_{cn} (naming the color, for example, "yellow"). If we now invoke the principle of mediated generalization we can say that any response subsequently conditioned to S_c will also be evocable by S_{cn}. In stage A such a new response was conditioned to S_c, namely the "egg," "car," or "shoe" response, R_n. As a result, when S_{cn} is presented in stage C, it can evoke the implicit and anticipatory component of R_n, namely $r_n\text{-}s_n$.

Once we have thus accounted for the evocation of $r_n\text{-}s_n$, we can see how this can evoke the anticipatory component of R_{ch}, namely $r_{ch}\text{-}s_{ch}$, the "attitude." This stems from the conditioning which took place in stage B and from the anticipatory nature of $r_{ch}\text{-}s_{ch}$. In this situation we see that $r_{ch}\text{-}s_{ch}$ evokes, not the old R_{ch} of stage B, but a slightly different choice response ($R_{ch'}$). Both choice responses can be understood as being part of a habit family associated with the same stimulus, $r_{ch}\text{-}s_{ch}$, the "attitude." The evocation of the correct choice response, $R_{ch'}$, cannot be fully explained without assuming, as we have done, its evocation by its implicit component, the attitudinal response-produced stimulus $r_{ch}\text{-}s_{ch}$.

There is one part of our diagram which has thus far been ignored. We have said that in stage B $r_n\text{-}s_n$ becomes conditioned to R_{ch} and that similarly $r_{ch}\text{-}s_{ch}$ becomes conditioned to R_n. That this is indeed the case was demonstrated by the fact that many Ss, when choosing the colored group of their choice also used an "egg," "car," or "shoe" name to refer to it. Stage C, therefore, has been diagrammed to include the evocation of R_n by $r_{ch}\text{-}s_{ch}$.

Analyses of the conditions and results of training for Ss in Groups I, II, and III involve the application of similar principles.

It is hoped that the present study represents a step in the direction of experimentally validating certain principles of learning theory on a human level in more or less uniquely human situations. The author has shown that at least one of these principles (mediated generalization) can be used to predict a certain type of human behavior, preference for a class of stimuli with which individuals have had only neutral experience. This type of behavior is common and shows itself most dramatically in the exhibition of attitudes toward social or ethnic groups with which individuals have had little or no direct experience. That such attitudes may be directly taught by parents or other "teachers" and maintained by group reinforcement is one possibility. That they may also be formed in the indirect manner experimentally demonstrated by this study is another. It is not too big a step to assume that if children can learn to prefer the color yellow, for example, over the colors green and black as a result of the type of training given them in this investigation, they can also, as a result of similar training, learn to prefer people called Englishmen over those called Poles and Italians, even though they have had no differential reward or punishment experience with any of those three national groups. The essential requirement for this learning is that individuals should learn to attach the same labels to the word "Englishman" as to stimuli with which they have rewarding experience, and to attach the same labels to the words "Pole" or "Italian" as to stimuli with which they have had neutral or punishing experience.

SUMMARY

Eighty-one elementary school children of grades 1, 2, and 3 were trained to label a white triangular block and a green rectangular block "egg," to label a white square block and a black rectangular block "shoe," and to label a white circular block and a yellow rectangular block "car." In a subsequent situation all Ss were rewarded for choosing one particular geometrical white block. The Ss in Group I were then tested for mediated generalization by being asked to choose which of the colored rectangles they thought would bring a reward. The Ss in Group II were presented with three new, i.e., previously unexperienced, color stimuli and asked to guess which one would bring a reward. The Ss in Group III learned to label three different white "nonsense" blocks "yellow," "black," and "green," respectively, and then were asked to choose the block they would like to take home. The Ss in Group IV were told a story about three groups of children, a yellow, a black, and a green group, and then asked which group they would invite to a hypothetical birthday party.

For each group it was predicted that Ss would choose that stimulus in the test having the same actual color or color name as the colored rectangle which they had learned had the same "egg," "car," or "shoe" name as the geometrical block for the choice of which they had previously been rewarded. These predictions were verified. Significantly more Ss in each group made the correct choices in the test than would have been expected by chance.

The investigation was designed to test the general hypothesis that a color-preference response (positive attitude) could be developed through mediated generalization, and that this preference could be demonstrated in four situations differing in context, complexity, and social significance. An analysis, in terms of reinforcement learning theory principles and concepts, of the experimental conditions and results for Group IV was presented as illustrative of the type of analysis necessary for a full explanation of the behavior of Ss of all four groups in their respective test situations.

REFERENCES

1. ALLPORT, G. W. Attitudes. In C. Murchison (Ed.), *A handbook of social psychology*. Worcester, Mass.: Clark Univer. Press, 1935. Pp. 798–844.

2. BIRGE, JANE S. The role of verbal responses in transfer. Unpublished doctor's dissertation, Yale Univer., 1941.

3. COFER, C. N., & FOLEY, J. P., JR. Mediated generalization and the interpretation of verbal behavior: I. Prolegomena. *Psychol. Rev.*, 1942, *49*, 513–540.

4. COFER, C. N., & FOLEY, J. P., JR. Mediated generalization and the in-

terpretation of verbal behavior: II. Experimental study of certain homophone and synonym gradients. *J. exp. Psychol.*, 1943, *32*, 168–175.

5. COFER, C. N., JANIS, MARJORIE G., & ROWELL, MARY M. Mediated generalization and the interpretation of verbal behavior: III. Experimental study of antonym gradients. *J. exp. Psychol.*, 1943, *32*, 266–269.

6. DOLLARD, J., & MILLER, N. E. *Personality and psychotherapy.* New York: McGraw-Hill, 1950.

7. DOOB, L. W. The behavior of attitudes. *Psychol. Rev.*, 1947, *54*, 135–156.

8. FOLEY, J. P., JR., & MATHEWS, M. A. Mediated generalization and the interpretation of verbal behavior: IV. Experimental study of the development of interlinguistic synonym gradients. *J. exp. Psychol.*, 1943, *33*, 188–200.

9. FOLEY, J. P., JR., & MACMILLAN, Z. L. Mediated generalization and the interpretation of verbal behavior: V. Free association as related to differences in professional training. *J. exp. Psychol.*, 1943, *33*, 299–310.

10. HULL, C. L. Knowledge and purpose as habit mechanisms. *Psychol. Rev.*, 1930, *6*, 511–525.

11. KELLER, MARGARET. Mediated generalization: the generalization of a conditioned GSR established to a pictured object. *Amer. J. Psychol.*, 1943, *56*, 438–448.

12. KRECH, D., & CRUTCHFIELD, R. S. *Theories and problems of social psychology.* New York: McGraw-Hill, 1948.

13. RAZRAN, G. H. S. Salivating and thinking in different languages. *J. Psychol.*, 1935–36, *1*, 145–151.

14. RAZRAN, G. H. S. A quantitative study of meaning by a conditioned salivary technique (semantic conditioning). *Science*, 1939, *90*, 89–90.

15. REISS, B. F. Semantic conditioning involving the GSR. *J. exp. Psychol.*, 1940, *26*, 238–240.

16. REISS, B. F. Genetic changes in semantic conditioning. *J. exp. Psychol.*, 1946, *36*, 143–152.

17. SHERIF, M., & CANTRIL, H. The psychology of attitudes. *Psychol. Rev.*, 1945, *52*, 293–319.

MOTIVATIONAL FACTORS
IN LEARNING | 14

THE DEVELOPMENT of the concept of motivation, or drive, and the variables which are subsumed under it suggests that this is an area to which experiments with children can make unique and valuable contributions. While the definition of motivation is not agreed upon by all persons in the field, there is general agreement that motivation has the property of energizing behavior. Other things being equal, an increase in motivation will lead to an increase in response rate and amplitude, and a decrease in response latency. Frequently it is assumed that reduction in motivation is rewarding and that responses associated with a reduction in motivation will tend to be learned.

There is also general agreement that there are two kinds of motivation which may be distinguished, those labeled primary motives and those labeled secondary motives. Primary motives are assumed to be present when a state of need, relative to the survival of the organism, exists with respect to the organism. Such needs include those for food, water, air, avoidance of tissue injury, and other biological necessities. Secondary motives, on the other hand, are acquired or learned. These motives are presumed to be learned when neutral stimuli are repeatedly associated with the evocation of a primary or previously learned secondary motive and with the reduction of that motive. The neutral stimuli, through such associative pairing, acquire motivational properties. Secondary motives would include fear, anxiety, stress, need for achievement, need for avoidance of social isolation, and any other motive that may be learned in the manner indicated above.

It is the secondary drives that are of particular importance to the child psychologist. It is impossible to conceive of undertaking an extensive program of research on the primary drives with children. Practical problems and humane considerations rule out the experimental manipulation of a wide range of need states, which are the basis of the primary drives of the human organism. While some studies using human subjects have involved manipulation of the primary drives of hunger, thirst, fatigue, body temperature, and (particularly) pain, they have been necessarily limited to relatively low levels of motivation with respect to the total amount that can be tolerated by the human organism. As a result, the study of motivation at the human level has focused upon the secondary motives, which are more feasibly manipulated. Although the work with children in this area has been relatively limited until recently, it would seem that the child is an excellent subject for such research.

If it is assumed that the newborn infant has not had the opportunity to learn any secondary drives and that the adult has a wide variety of them, it is clear that the secondary motives are learned during the child's development. Investigations of the circumstances that bring about the learning of secondary drives would certainly be a major contribution to the understanding of human behavior.

One of the few systematic experimental attempts to determine the effects of motivation upon the behavior of human adults has centered around the development of the Taylor manifest anxiety scale (1953). This test was originally developed as a measure of drive, on the assumption that variations in manifest anxiety, as judged by the clinician, reflect variations in drive level. The selection of subjects obtaining extreme scores on the test allowed the study of the effects of high and low motivation on performances in various tasks. Numerous studies have verified the usefulness of this procedure in testing hypotheses (Spence, 1958; Taylor, 1956).

The first article in this section is one of a number of studies that demonstrate the usefulness of a children's form of the manifest anxiety scale. In this case, as with the studies of college students, it was found that extreme scores on the test could be assumed to reflect differences in motivation and thus allow the prediction of children's behavior in a learning task.

Although studies using the anxiety scales have proven fruitful in advancing our knowledge of the functions of motivation, the use of tests for this purpose has two major drawbacks. First, the selection of subjects who obtain extreme scores on a test is very wasteful. It is necessary to administer the test to a large number of subjects and then use only those subjects in the larger pool who score at the low or high ends of the scale. The rest of the subjects are seldom used for the experiment itself. Second, the type of problem that can be studied using subjects selected in this way is limited. It is not possible, for example, to design an experiment that has more than one stage, as in the learning of two successive tasks. The reason for this is that it would be expected, in most tasks, that subjects with high motivation would reach a different level of performance on the first task than subjects with low motivation. Therefore, the interpretation of the results of the second task would not only be a function of the level of motivation of the subjects, but also of the different levels of performance on the first task.

A more satisfactory method for studying motivation, which avoids the problem of using tests, relies upon the experimental manipulation of motivation by use of instructions or other variations of the environment. The other studies in this section vary motivation by experimental manipulation. The second study uses a pacing method of increasing motivation. The children are allowed to work at their own pace on a task or are instructed that they have only a very short time in which to make their response. The stress placed upon the children to respond quickly is used to raise the motivation level of the child. Perhaps the most interesting aspect of this study is the demonstration that the effects of increasing motivation are not necessarily to increase performance. It is often said that children will do better if they are more highly motivated. This study indicates that an increase in motivation will raise the level of performance under some circumstances but lower it under other circumstances. The results substantiate the useful derivations made by Spence (1956) from Hull's theory (1943) about the effects of increased motivation on performance.

The next two studies make use of another technique for the manipulation of motivation, which stems directly from the methods used in manipulating the primary drives in animal experimentation. Studies of motivation in animals frequently use deprivation conditions to vary motivation, for example, the animals may be deprived of food for specified periods of time. The children in the studies included here are deprived of other persons for specified periods of time. Both of these studies demonstrate that social deprivation does act to increase motivation level, resulting in predictable behavioral consequences.

The last two studies in this section deal with motivation based upon still other antecedent conditions. Both studies are concerned with frustration, but different methods are used in each study to induce frustration and thus increase motivation. The study by Davitz provides evidence about the effects of frustration upon the behavior of children in a situation similar to the well-known research of Barker, Dembo, and Lewin (1943). More importantly, it indicates the variability of behavior under conditions of frustration as a function of prior learning. An increase in motivation energizes behavior, but the particular behavior that occurs is a function of the responses that have been acquired in the past.

The last study manipulates frustration by withholding reinforcement for a previously reinforced response. The results indicate the effects of number of prefrustration reinforcements upon the amount of frustration induced. In addition, the study has implications for the broader problem of why partial reinforcement results in greater resistance to extinction, as was reported, for example, in the study by Bijou in a previous section.

REFERENCES

BARKER, R. G., DEMBO, T. and LEWIN, K. In Roger Barker, Jacob Kounin, and Herbert Wright, *Child development and behavior*. New York: McGraw-Hill, 1943. Pp. 441–458.

HULL, C. L. *Principles of behavior*. New York: Appleton, 1943.

SPENCE, K. W. A theory of emotionally based drive (D) and its relation to performance in simple learning situations. *Amer. Psychologist*, 1958, *13*, 131–141.

SPENCE, K. W. *Behavior theory and conditioning*. New Haven: Yale University Press, 1956.

TAYLOR, J. A.   A personality scale of manifest anxiety. *J. abnorm. soc. Psychol.*, 1953, *48*, 285–290.

TAYLOR, J. A.   Drive theory and manifest anxiety. *Psychol. Bull.*, 1956, *53*, 303–320.

COMPLEX LEARNING AND PERFORMANCE

AS A FUNCTION OF ANXIETY

IN CHILDREN AND TASK DIFFICULTY

ALFRED CASTANEDA
DAVID S. PALERMO
BOYD R. McCANDLESS

WITHIN THE LAST FEW YEARS a number of experiments by Spence (7, 8), Farber (3), Taylor (9, 11) and Montague (5) have attempted to compare the performance of adult anxious and nonanxious Ss in classical conditioning as well as in more complex forms of learning situations. The presence of anxiety in these Ss had been defined in terms of their responses on a personality inventory of manifest anxiety developed by Taylor (10). Ss receiving high scores on this test characteristically exhibit a higher level of performance in the conditioning situation than those receiving low scores. These results have been interpreted to support the assumption that these scores are an index of S's readiness to respond or excitability, which in turn is assumed to reflect their

Reprinted by permission from *Child Development*, 1956, 27, 327–332.

general drive level. Reasoning on the basis of Hull's (4) theoretical formulation relating response strength to drive, i.e., that all habit tendencies aroused by the stimulus situation are multiplied by the total effective drive level then operating, two opposing, though not contradictory, expectations have been derived by Spence and his associates (6) regarding the role of anxiety as a determinant of performance. If, as in classical conditioning, there tends to be but a single or highly dominant response tendency, an increase in the strength of drive should enhance the strength of that response thereby benefiting performance (3, 7, 8, 9). In situations where there is greater likelihood that more than one response tendency is aroused by the stimulus situation, as in complex learning tasks, whether or not an increase in the drive level will aid or impede performance depends on whether or not the criterion (correct) response tendency is stronger (dominant) in relation to other competing tendencies aroused by the stimulus situation. If the correct response tendency is the stronger, performance should be aided by an increase in the drive level. However, should the incorrect response tendency be stronger, the effects of heightened drive should be deleterious to performance. Empirical support for these expectations has also been found in studies dealing with more complex forms of learning in which the Taylor scale has been used as the empirical variable assumed to reflect differences in drive level (*3, 5, 11*).

The present study is concerned with the performance of fifth grade children on a complex learning task as a function of the relative difficulty of the various components comprising the task and of their scores on a scale of manifest anxiety adapted for children from Taylor's adult form.

METHOD

SUBJECTS

The 37 Ss in the present study were from among those who participated in the standardization of the children's form of the anxiety scale (*1*) and who, in addition, participated in a complex learning experiment (*2*) a year previously. The present study, then, reports the relationship between the anxiety scale scores of these Ss and their performance in the experiment of the previous year. Although the conventional practice with the adult form is to select Ss whose scores fall within the upper or lower 20th percentiles

of the distribution, the small number of Ss available in the present study precluded such a procedure. The anxiety scores of the present Ss ranged from a low of three to a high of 33; hence a score of 18 or above was arbitrarily designated as falling in the high anxious category and a score of 17 or below in the low anxious category. The high anxious group, then, consisted of 21 Ss, 9 boys and 12 girls, and the low anxious group was composed of 16 Ss, 6 boys and 10 girls. In addition, the L scale, i.e., that part of the present form of the test assumed to provide an index of S's tendency to falsify his responses to the anxiety items, was not employed. Preliminary analyses based on the L scale indicated that its use would not have appreciably affected the results. In addition, the loss in the number of subjects resulting from designating a criterion of a score of three or less on the L scale would have resulted in a loss of approximately 30 per cent of the subjects from the present sample.

APPARATUS

Since a more detailed description of the apparatus may be found in (*2*), only a brief description of it will be presented here. In essence, it consisted of a rectangular shaped box approximately 9 by 18 by 9 in., painted flat black. A response panel containing five linearly arranged push buttons projected from the box. Centered 3 in. above the response panel was a 1 in. diameter aperture of flashed opal glass. Behind the aperture were five pilot lamps colored either dark red, green, amber, blue or light red. All controls used by E were situated at the back of the apparatus. By a simple switching arrangement,

E could actuate any single light and set any single push button so that depressing it turned off the light. Depression of any other of the four remaining buttons did not affect the light.

PROCEDURE

All *S*s had to learn the same five light button combinations. These five combinations had been previously determined on a random basis. Each single light was presented five times and randomly interspersed within the total 25 presentations. All *S*s were allowed to continue responding until the correct button had been depressed, at which time the next light was presented. *S*s were merely instructed that the task required learning which buttons were associated with which colored lights and in case of an error to select another button until the correct one had been depressed. The particular buttons depressed and the order in which they were depressed for each presentation were recorded for each *S*.

RESULTS AND DISCUSSION

Studies with the adult form of the anxiety scale have indicated that the differential performance of high and low anxious *S*s can differ depending on the particular characteristics of the task. For example, the tendency for the high anxious *S*s to perform more poorly in comparison to low anxious *S*s increases as the difficulty of the task increases (3, 11). Conversely, if the difficulty of the task can be sufficiently decreased, differences in anxiety level may result to the benefit of the high anxious *S*s (5). Hence, these studies indicate that the difficulty existing

either among several different tasks (5) or among the various components comprising a given task (3, 11) should be assessed, preferably on some basis independent of the performance of the high and low anxious groups which are being studied. Therefore, in order to determine the possibility that the five light button combinations in the present task may not have been equal with respect to the ease with which they could be learned, 20 *S*s from among those who had participated in the previous experiment, and for whom anxiety scores were not available, were drawn at random and their performance on each of the five combinations was determined. The index of the difficulty of learning a given combination was the number of times, out of five, the first response to the light was the correct one, or more simply, the number of errorless trials.

Table 1 presents the results of this comparison. The combinations are numbered from I to V in order of increasing difficulty, i.e., in order of the decreasing number of errorless trials. For the present purposes it was decided to compare the performance of the high and low anxious *S*s on the two easiest (I and II) and the two most difficult (IV and V) combinations.

TABLE 1 · MEAN NUMBER OF ERRORLESS TRIALS MADE BY THE RANDOM SAMPLE OF 20 SUBJECTS ON THE FIVE SEPARATE LIGHT-BUTTON COMBINATIONS

	Combination number				
	I	II	III	IV	V
M	3.40	3.05	2.45	2.40	2.00
SD	1.48	1.02	1.02	1.62	1.10

Table 2 presents the number of errorless trials for the high and low anxious groups for the easy and difficult combinations separately. It is apparent, on the basis of these data, that the high anxious children performed better, in comparison with the low anxious children, on the easy combinations, but more poorly on the difficult combinations. It can be noted that the performance of the high anxious children appeared to be more affected by the differences in the difficulty of the two sets of combinations than that of the low anxious children.

Table 3 presents a summary of an analysis of variance based on the data presented in Table 2. This indicates that the main effect of anxiety was not significant while the effects of task difficulty were significant at only the .10 level. Of greater interest, however, is the significant interaction between anxiety and task difficulty. This interaction may be interpreted to indicate that the effects of anxiety are dependent on the degree of difficulty involved in the task. This is in accord with the data presented in Table 2, showing

TABLE 2 · MEAN NUMBER OF ERRORLESS TRIALS ON THE EASY AND DIFFICULT COMBINATIONS FOR THE HIGH AND LOW ANXIOUS GROUPS SEPARATELY

| | Difficulty level | | | |
| | Easy | | Hard | |
Group	M	SD	M	SD
High anxious	5.00	2.41	3.33	1.29
Low anxious	4.38	2.13	4.81	2.66

TABLE 3 · SUMMARY OF ANALYSIS OF VARIANCE BASED ON NUMBER OF ERRORLESS TRIALS

Source	df	MS	F	p
Anxiety	1	3.31	..	
Error (b)	35	6.23		
Difficulty	1	10.59	2.99	<.10
Anxiety × Difficulty	1	20.10	5.68	<.025
Error (w)	35	3.54		

that the position of superiority of the high anxious children on the easy combinations, in comparison with the low anxious children, is completely reversed on the more difficult combinations. Tests of the simple effects indicated that only the difference between the low and high anxious children on the difficult combinations was significant at beyond the .05 level ($F = 4.99$, $df = 1, 35$).

The present results are in general agreement with those found with the adult form of the anxiety scale in similar learning situations. In view of the fact that a difference in a scale score of only one was used as the basis for differentiating the low from the high anxious children in lieu of the more conventional procedure of selecting Ss from the extreme ends of the distribution, and that there was approximately a one-year interval between participation in the experiment and the time the anxiety scores were obtained, these results offer some encouragement to any future use of the scale with children.

Assuming that the index of the difficulty of the two sets of combinations reflected the presence of competing response tendencies of increasing strength, the present results indicated that the effects of anxiety varied as a function of this index. Consistent with the theoretical formulations outlined earlier, it could be assumed that on the easy combinations the correct response was stronger in relation to other competing responses which may have been aroused by the stimulus elements of these combinations. Under such conditions the effects of high anxiety should be expected to be beneficial to performance. In the case of the difficult combinations it could be assumed that other competing response tendencies were stronger in relation to the correct one; hence the effects of high anxiety, according to the theory, should be expected to be deleterious to performance.

In general these results suggest that the presence of anxiety in children can serve to determine performance in much the same way as with adults. Of more general importance, perhaps, the present results support the notion that the effects of anxiety can be more profitably studied if the characteristics of the task can be specified with regard to the number and relative strength of the competing response tendencies that may be aroused, as well as to whether or not the correct response is dominant. This appears to be in accord with clinical and casual observation that the consequences of a heightened level of anxiety may vary with the particular stimulating circumstances and the particular responses the individual has learned to make in such situations on the basis of previous experience.

SUMMARY

The present study was concerned with the performance of fifth grade children in a complex learning task as a function of their scores on a scale of manifest anxiety adapted from Taylor's adult form for use with children and the relative difficulty of the various components comprising the task.

The high anxious group was composed of 21 children and the low anxious group of 16. The relative difficulty existing among the five components comprising the task was determined on the basis of performance of an independent sample of Ss. A statistically significant interaction was found between anxiety and task difficulty. This interaction was based on the tendency for the performance of the high anxious children to be inferior, in comparison with the low anxious children, on the difficult components of the task but with a tendency for their performance to be superior on the less difficult components.

REFERENCES

1. CASTANEDA, A., McCANDLESS, B. R., & PALERMO, D. S. The children's form of the manifest anxiety scale. *Child Develpm.*, 1956, 27, 317–326.
2. CASTANEDA, A., & PALERMO, D. S. Psychomotor performance as a function of amount of training and stress. *J. exp. Psychol.*, 1955, 50, 175–179.
3. FARBER, I. E., & SPENCE, K. W. Complex learning and conditioning as a function of anxiety. *J. exp. Psychol.*, 1953, 45, 120–125.
4. HULL, C. L. *Principles of behavior.* New York: Appleton-Century, 1943.
5. MONTAGUE, E. K. The role of anxiety in serial rote learning. *J. exp. Psychol.*, 1953, 45, 91–96.
6. SPENCE, K. W. *Symposium on relationships among learning theory, personality theory, and clinical clinical research.* New York: Wiley, 1953.
7. SPENCE, K. W., & FARBER, I. E. Conditioning and extinction as a function of anxiety. *J. exp. Psychol.*, 1953, 45, 116–119.
8. SPENCE, K. W., & TAYLOR, J. A. Anxiety and the strength of the

UCS as determiners of the amount of eyelid conditioning. *J. exp. Psychol.*, 1951, *42*, 183–188.

9. TAYLOR, J. A. The relationship of anxiety to the conditioned eyelid response. *J. exp. Psychol.*, 1951, *41*, 81–92.

10. TAYLOR, J. A. A personality scale of manifest anxiety. *J. abnorm. soc. Psychol.*, 1953, *48*, 285–290.

11. TAYLOR, J. A., & SPENCE, K. W. The relationship of anxiety level to performance in serial learning. *J. exp. Psychol.*, 1952, *44*, 61–64.

PROACTIVE INTERFERENCE

AND FACILITATION

AS A FUNCTION OF AMOUNT

OF TRAINING AND STRESS [1]

DAVID S. PALERMO

IN A RECENT STUDY, Castaneda (2) found a significant interaction between stress and type of S-R pair learned in a second task. One type of S-R pair was identical to those learned in a previous task, and the other type involved re-pairing of stimuli and responses learned in the first task, a procedure suggested by Duncan (4) and Porter and Duncan (6). The interaction was based on a tendency for performance of the stress group to be poorer than that of the nonstress group where re-pairing was required, but better where it was not. Assuming that the incorrect response tendency was dominant where re-pairing was required, while the correct response was dominant where it was not, and that the pacing condition (stress) served to increase the drive level, these results were interpreted as consistent with Spence's derivations (7) from Hull (5). Using a similar procedure, Castaneda and Palermo (3) obtained results suggesting that the magnitude of impairment or facilitation of performance as a result of an increase in drive varies as a positive function of the strength of the dominant habit.

The present experiment employed a modification of the procedure reported elsewhere by Castaneda (1) to investi-

[1] The present paper is a portion of a dissertation submitted to the Graduate College of the State University of Iowa in partial fulfillment of the requirements for the Ph.D. degree in the Iowa Child Welfare Research Station. The writer is indebted to Dr. Alfred Castaneda who directed the dissertation.

Reprinted by permission from *Journal of Experimental Psychology*, 1957, 53, 293–296.

gate the effects of stress on performance of a task in which the dominant habit associated with a given stimulus was either a correct habit which was either relatively weak or strong, or an incorrect habit which was either relatively weak or strong.

METHOD

Subjects and design. A total of 78 fourth-grade Ss participated in the present experiment.[2] However, following the procedure reported by Castaneda (2), 27 of these Ss were eliminated from the analysis because of failure to attain a criterion of 16 correct responses in the first task. Of the remaining 51 Ss, 25 were assigned to the paced (stress) group and 26 to the nonpaced (nonstress) group.

Apparatus and procedure. The apparatus, identical to that reported by Castaneda (2), consisted of a box with a response panel on which was located two push buttons and a green jeweled reflector. Above the panel the four colored stimulus lights were presented through an aperture. If the correct button was selected, the stimulus light went off and the green light went on. Incorrect responses affected neither the stimulus light nor the light on the response panel.

The procedure was the same as reported by Castaneda (2) except that in the first task 20 trials were given such that two of the lights appeared eight times apiece, two appeared twice apiece, and no single light appeared twice in succession. Each light remained on until the correct response was made. Thus, each S received two reinforced presentations to two lights and eight to the other two. In the second task each light was presented 10 times, and again, no single light appeared twice in succession. However, only one response was permitted to each light.

In both tasks two of the lights were turned out by one button and two were

[2] Gratitude is expressed to Mr. David K. Stewart, Elementary School Curriculum Coordinator, Iowa City, Iowa, for his assistance and cooperation in arranging for facilities and subjects.

turned out by the other button. Of the four lights used in the first task, one which had appeared eight times and one which appeared twice were selected for re-pairing in the second task.

The instructions for the first task were designed to indicate to S that he was to learn which button turned off each light and that if an error was made, correction would be allowed. The second task followed immediately, and neither group was given any information regarding the fact that two of the pairs required re-pairing. The nonpaced group was told to continue but that now correction would not be allowed when an error was made. The paced group was given the same instructions, and in addition, instructions designed to indicate that speed of response was highly important. The E demonstrated that the light would be on for 1 sec. and told S that a response had to be made before the light went off or it would be counted as an error. However, during the task the interval timer was set to give a 2-sec. exposure of the light rather than the 1-sec. exposure demonstrated. If a response was not made during this interval, the same

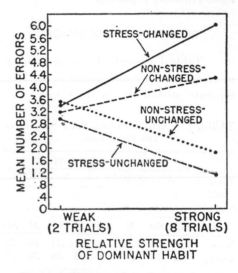

Figure 1. Mean number of errors for stress and nonstress groups on the stimuli which received different amounts of training and were re-paired or not re-paired.

light was represented until a response could be recorded for that trial. Errors due to failure to respond within the interval were not included in the data. No S had to have any single light represented more than once. Failure to respond within the interval occurred among 14 Ss for a total of not more than three trials for any one S. Of the total number, 9 responses were to the lights requiring no re-pairing, and 13 were to the lights requiring re-pairing.

RESULTS AND DISCUSSION

Table 1 presents the mean number of errors made by each group to the four separate stimuli in the first task. The

TABLE 1 · ERRORS TO THE FOUR STIMULI IN THE FIRST TASK

Level of habit strength	PAIRING IN SECOND TASK							
	Not re-paired				Re-paired			
	Non-paced		Paced		Non-paced		Paced	
	M	SD	M	SD	M	SD	M	SD
Weak	.73	.53	1.12	.59	.73	.71	.80	.75
Strong	.12	.33	.40	.57	.38	.56	.40	.49

group which was paced in the second task made more errors on all four stimuli; however, the differences are significant ($P < .01$) on only those stimuli which were not re-paired in the second task. Since it was predicted that the stress group would make fewer errors than the nonstress group on these two stimuli in the second task, these results would appear to work against the hypothesis.

Figure 1 shows the mean number of errors made in the second task to the various stimuli by the stress and the nonstress groups. It can be noted that, for both groups, more errors occurred on the two stimuli for which the response learned in the first task was no longer correct than to the two stimuli for which the

previously learned response was correct. The effectiveness of the amount of training is revealed in the tendency for errors to be greater on the stimulus which had been presented eight times in the first task and for which the previously learned response was no longer correct, and less on the stimulus which had been presented eight times but for which the previously learned response was still correct. Also, the effects of stress appear to depend on the type of stimulus involved, i.e., the stress group, in comparison to the nonstress group, made more errors on those stimuli for which the previously learned response was no longer correct, but fewer errors on the stimuli for which the same response was correct. Only in the case of the stimuli for which the previously learned response was no longer correct, however, does this latter effect appear to depend on the amount of training.

A summary of an analysis of variance based on these data, presented in Table 2, indicates that the main effects of stress and amount of training are not significant, while the effects of type of stimulus are highly significant. The interaction of stress and type of stimulus is significant, as well as the interaction of type of stimulus and training level. The triple

TABLE 2 · SUMMARY OF ANALYSIS OF VARIANCE OF ERRORS MADE IN THE SECOND TASK

Source	df	MS	F	P
Stress (S)	1	1.44		
Error (b)	49	7.55		
Stimuli (St)	1	176.96	31.10	<.001
Training (T)	1	.08		
St × T	1	165.96	62.39	<.001
St × S	1	31.17	5.48	<.025
T × S	1	5.69	2.14	<.20
St × S × T	1	8.49	3.19	<.10
Error₁ (w)	49	5.69		
Error₂ (w)	49	2.66		
Error₃ (w)	49	2.66		

interaction, indicating that the magnitude of the effects of stress and type of stimulus varied with amount of training, was significant at only the .10 level.

Support for the assumptions that the four stimuli in the second task had associated with them either a correct habit which was relatively weak or strong or an incorrect habit which was relatively weak or strong, is evident in the significant main effects of stimuli and the significant interaction between stimuli and training. Considering the stimuli which required learning of two responses successively, the present findings are in line with those reported by Porter and Duncan (6) and Castaneda (1) that the amount of interference, under such conditions, varies as a positive function of the associative strength of the first learned response. Considering the stimuli for which the same response was correct in both tasks, the present results indicate that the amount of facilitation in the second task varied as a positive function of the associative strength, i.e., the amount of training in the first task. The significant interaction between stress and stimuli is consistent with the two previous studies (2, 3) and in accord with expectations from the assumptions upon which the present study was based. It should be noted here that despite the fact that the stress group made significantly more errors on the unchanged stimuli than the nonstress group in the first task, the effects of stress tended to facilitate performance in the second task on these stimuli.

The expectation that the effects of stress would be a positive function of habit strength, based on the assumption that habit and drive combine multiplicatively, was substantiated in the triple interaction at only the .10 level. On the basis of Fig. 1, the effect appeared more pronounced on the re-paired stimuli than on the stimuli which were not re-paired. It may be noted, however, that a mean of less than 2.0 errors was made by both groups on the one stimulus presented eight times in the first task and not re-paired, hence leaving little room for further improvement.

SUMMARY

The present experiment was concerned with the relation of drive strength to performance in a complex learning situation. The specific theoretical implication investigated was that the performance of stress (high drive) Ss would be poorer than that of nonstress (low drive) Ss in a task which involved stimuli for which a response previously learned was no longer correct, but that the performance of the stress Ss would be better on the same task involving stimuli for which a response previously learned was still correct. Further, the study investigated the implication that the greater the magnitude of the difference between the strength of the correct and the incorrect habit the greater would be the differences between the performance of the high and the low drive groups.

All 51 Ss were given 20 trials on the first task in which four S-R pairings had to be learned. Two of the stimuli were presented more times than the other two. In the second task, 25 Ss worked under a stress condition and 26 Ss worked under the same conditions as in the first task. One of the stimuli which received a greater amount of practice and one of the stimuli which received a lesser amount of practice were re-paired in the second task, and the other two stimuli were not re-paired.

The results were in agreement with the theoretical expectation that the stress Ss would make more errors than the nonstress Ss on the re-paired stimuli and fewer errors on the stimuli which were not re-paired. A triple interaction, significant at only the .10 level, was obtained indicating that the magnitude of the effects of stress and type of stimulus vary with the strength of training of the stimulus.

REFERENCES

1. CASTANEDA, A.   Proactive interference as a function of amount of original training. *Proceed. Iowa Aca. Sci.*, 1955, 62, 411–414.
2. CASTANEDA, A.   Effects of stress on complex learning and performance. *J. exp. Psychol.*, 1956, 52, 9–12.
3. CASTANEDA, A., & PALERMO, D. S. Psychomotor performance as a function of amount of training and stress. *J. exp. Psychol.*, 1955, 50, 175–179.
4. DUNCAN, C. P.   Transfer in motor learning as a function of degree of first-task learning and inter-task similarity. *J. exp. Psychol.*, 1953, 45, 1–11.
5. HULL, C. L.   *Principles of behavior.* New York: D. Appleton-Century, 1943.
6. PORTER, L. W., & DUNCAN, C. P. Negative transfer in verbal learning. *J. exp. Psychol.*, 1953, 46, 61–64.
7. SPENCE, K. W.   Current interpretations of learning data and some recent developments in stimulus-response theory. In *Kentucky Symposium: Learning Theory, Personality Theory and Clinical Research.* New York: Wiley, 1954.

DEPRIVATION AND SATIATION

OF SOCIAL REINFORCERS

AS DRIVE CONDITIONS

JACOB L. GEWIRTZ [1]
DONALD M. BAER [2]

IN AN EARLIER STUDY (6) we received what appeared to be an affirmative an-

swer to the question: Are there social drives that respond to reinforcer deprivation as do the primary appetitive drives? In this investigation we extend the question, asking in addition if the behaviors maintained by social reinforcers are responsive also to a condition of relative

[1] This study was carried out when the senior author was on the faculty of the University of Chicago, and was facilitated by a grant given to him by the Social Science Research Committee of that institution. The writers acknowledge with gratitude the discriminating assistance of Chaya H. Roth.

Reprinted by permission from *Journal of Abnormal and Social Psychology*, 1958, 57, 165–172.

[2] At the time of this study, the junior author was a Public Health Service Predoctoral Research Fellow of the National Institute of Mental Health at the University of Chicago.

satiation for such reinforcers. Children are again employed as subjects (Ss).

In the earlier study it was found that when an adult made words and phrases like "Good!" and "Hm-hmm" contingent upon an arbitrarily chosen response in nursery school children, that response was reinforced (i.e., conditioned). This effect was similar to that found in several other studies using verbal stimuli appealing to the concept of *approval* as reinforcers (e.g., *2, 9, 12, 16*). It was found, in addition, that this reinforcing effect of approval could be increased when the children experienced a preceding 20-minute period of social isolation, relative to its effectiveness for the same children when they had not been isolated. While this result held primarily for boys tested by a female (rather than male) experimenter, other aspects of the data clearly supported the equating of isolation to the deprivation of social reinforcers: *social isolation increased reliably the reinforcing power of adult approval for children as a positive function of the degree to which they typically sought such approval in other settings.* Approval was taken to be representative of the reinforcers which control the purely social initiations made by children to adults.

Deprivation implies a period of unavailability of a given reinforcer, which results in an increase in behaviors for it; *satiation* implies a period of availability of a reinforcer, sufficient to effect a decrease in behaviors for it. Thus, deprivation and satiation represent two statements of a single concept, a dimension characterized by the relative supply of a reinforcer in the recent history of an organism which determines the incidence of behaviors for that reinforcer. The concept of deprivation-satiation has considerable precedent as a drive operation in general behavior theory (e.g., *11, 14*), where it has been employed to order contemporary conditions which account for variance in reinforcer effectiveness. As such, drive is generally defined as the functional relation between deprivation (or satiation) for a reinforcer and responding for that reinforcer. Further, concepts like deprivation have been somewhat loosely applied in a number of speculative formulations of the antecedents of certain social behaviors (e.g., *1, 8, 13, 15*). Hence, laws relating social deprivation as an empirically defined dimension to certain basic characteristics of social behaviors would have considerable integrative value (*5*). But first, the experimental operations of deprivation and its inverse, satiation, must be implemented effectively in social terms.

In the earlier study cited (*6*), a beginning attempt was made to implement social deprivation: brief social isolation of a child was equated to a condition of deprivation of all social reinforcers (including approval), and the differential effects of that condition and of a comparison nonisolation (nondeprivation) condition were reflected in the reinforcing effectiveness of an adult's approval. The present study represents an attempt to simplify (and replicate) the social deprivation operation of the earlier study, as well as a beginning in the direction of establishing an operation of social satiation. Satiation will be equated to a condition in which an abundance of approval and social contact is supplied to a child by an adult. Experimental operations implementing the conditions of deprivation and of satiation for a class of social reinforcers are both reflected against an intermediate or nondeprivation (nonsatiated) condition. The hypothesis is that these conditions should enhance the effectiveness of the reinforcer in the order: Deprivation > Nondeprivation > Satiation.

METHOD

SAMPLE

The Ss were 102 middle-class children selected from the classes of the first and second grades of a university laboratory school and randomly assigned to experimental conditions. Sixteen were Negro, the remainder white. Their mean age at the time of testing was seven years, six months, with a range from six and one-half to nine years. Their mean and median Stanford-Binet IQ score was 127 (the scores of only 3 Ss were below 100). One-half of the Ss under each condition were girls and one-half boys. The Ss were selected by their teachers according to the order in which their names appeared on alphabetical class lists. No S refused to participate.

INDEPENDENT VARIABLE

Deprivation. Seventeen boys and 17 girls were subjected to a condition of social isolation before playing the game. Each of these Ss was introduced to the experimenter (E) in the classroom by the teacher. The E was a young woman in her early twenties.[3] She walked with S a distance of several hundred feet through the school corridors to the experimental room. During this walk, E responded to S's questions and comments only when necessary, and maintained a somewhat distant but not unfriendly manner at all times. Upon reaching the experimental room, E showed S around the room, seated him and told him that someone else was using the game which he was to play and that she would have to fetch it but would be back in a little while. E then left the room and went (unobserved) to an adjacent observation booth from which S was observed during his isolation. She returned after 20 minutes

[3] This E served as one of the two Es in a companion study *(6)*.

with the toy. The game was then played in the usual fashion. The Ss, who occasionally accompanied adults in the school setting for tests, and who had experience in awaiting their turns, all accepted this condition without question.

Nondeprivation. Seventeen boys and 17 girls were subjected to a condition of nonisolation, i.e., they played the game immediately upon their arrival at the experimental room. (Since this condition represents both relative nondeprivation and relative nonsatiation for approval, it served as an intermediate control condition for the other two conditions.) Until they entered the experimental room, Ss in this group were treated identically as were Ss in the Deprivation group.

Satiation. Seventeen boys and 17 girls were subjected to a condition of relative satiation for approval from the adult before playing the game. Again, each of these Ss was introduced to E in the classroom by the teacher, but during the walk to the experimental room, E maintained a very pleasant and interested attitude toward S, responding to all details of his comments and questions, asking questions to draw out more of S's conversation, and generally approving of anything about S which might reasonably be praised or admired. Upon reaching the experimental room, E showed S around the room, seated him, told him that the game was in use elsewhere and that she would go fetch it in a little while when it would be free. She suggested that meanwhile S might like to draw pictures or cut out designs, and proffered the essential materials. Then, for 20 minutes S drew or cut out designs, while E maintained a stream of friendly conversation with him, inducing him to talk about himself if he did not do so naturally. The E alternated her praise and admiration of whatever S did with whatever he said about himself, all in an appropriate fashion, and attempted to dispense 30 such reinforcers during the 20-minute satiation period at an approximate rate of three every two minutes. In fact, E dispensed to the boys an average of 31.6 such reinforcers ($\sigma = 6.9$) and to the girls an average of 28.2 reinforcers ($\sigma = 8.1$).

THE GAME SETTING

Following the experimental treatment, the central task for S (which was the same for all three groups) was to place marbles into either of the two holes of the toy (shown in Fig. 1) while E, who sat beside him, looked on. (This procedure was identical to that employed in the earlier study (6) and is only summarized here.) The E observed S's play for a "baseline" period of four minutes, during which *no* reinforcers were dispensed. Meanwhile, E responded to any of S's comments and questions in a friendly but brief manner. Without pause, the baseline period was followed by a 10-minute test of reinforcer effectiveness. That is, E proceeded at this point to dispense the reinforcer, consisting of words like "Good," "Hm-hmm," and "Fine," according to a schedule incorporating several, successively higher, fixed ratios, whenever S dropped marbles into the *correct* hole, defined as that preferred *least* during the last (fourth) minute of the baseline period.

DEPENDENT VARIABLES

Reinforcer effectiveness score. The determination of the effectiveness of approval as a reinforcer was made from the "game" which followed immediately the treatment condition (i.e., the 20 minutes of Deprivation or of Satiation, or in the Nondeprivation condition, the arrival at the experimental room). The basic data were the numbers of marbles dropped in the correct and incorrect holes during each minute of play. These generated four pairs of frequency scores for the baseline period, and 10 such pairs of scores for the reinforcer effectiveness test period. For each minute of play, the *relative frequency* of a correct response was the ration of correct responses to total responses, i.e., # correct/(# correct + # incorrect). The score employed as dependent variable was taken as the difference, for each S, between the relative frequency of correct responses in the last (fourth) minute of the baseline period (when no reinforcers were dispensed) and the median relative frequency of correct responses of the 10 rein-

forcer test period minutes. This *reinforcer effectiveness score* represents the *gain* in relative frequency of the correct response attributable to the social reinforcer provided by the adult's approval.

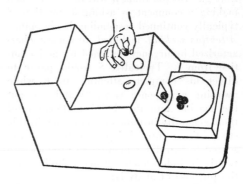

Figure 1. A schematic diagram of the experimental apparatus (The "game").

Spontaneous social initiations. In addition, the verbal and purely social initiations of the child to the adult were tallied, but *only during the baseline period of the game*, before she began to dispense approval. The E treated the game as S's central task and, while permissive, generally discouraged lengthy initiations on the part of S, suggesting, when necessary, that they could converse at length after the game. Where a reply to an initiation of S was required, E's response was always friendly, yet brief, leaving responsibility for continuing that interaction sequence in S's hands. All such responses by S were tallied by an observer in an observation booth. These responses took the form most frequently of Comments, less frequently of Questions, and least frequently of overt Attention-seeking.[4] They could be expected to represent behaviors by S for a variety of social reinforcers, in addition to

---

[4] These three observation categories are defined in detail in (3). High agreement between observers was found there on these behavior categories, and they entered into similar patterns of relationship with the independent variables. Moreover, they were found in (4) to have high loadings on a single factor and appeared to involve an active attempt to gain or to maintain the adult's attention, perhaps differing in the degree to which their initiations for attention were overt or direct.

approval. *Comments* were casual remarks which usually required no formal response from *E* (e.g., "We're going away for the holiday"). *Questions*, which were also casual, required only brief, token replies from *E* (e.g., "Do you think it will rain?"). When making a comment or asking a question, *S* typically continued responding in the game. *Attention-seeking* included responses characterized by urgency designed for active notice from *E*. Typically, *S* would pause to direct his complete attention to *E* while awaiting a response (e.g., "Watch me put the marble into this hole!"). Because of their generally infrequent occurrence in this study, these three behavior categories are scored in two different ways to produce two relatively independent response indices for the purpose of analysis:

a. *The sum of the frequencies* in the three social response categories, Comments, Questions, and Attention-seeking, which weights those categories in proportion to their frequency of occurrence (i.e., Comments contributes most and Attention-seeking least to that index).

b. The score of a *cumulative Guttman-like scale (10)*, indexing what appears to be the intensity of social contact, formed similarly as in *(3)* when the frequency scores for each verbal response category were dichotomized for each *S* into gross response alternatives, zero or nonzero frequency of occurrence.[5] A scale score of 3 indicated that an *S* had exhibited some of all three behaviors; a score of 2 indicated that some

---

[5] Of all 102 *S*s in the four-minute baseline period, the proportion showing nonzero category frequencies was .71 for Comments, .53 for Questions, and .15 for Attention-seeking. When the response categories were arranged in the order of their decreasing popularities (the proportion of *S*s exhibiting nonzero frequencies), it was concluded that, for present purposes, a satisfactory three-item Guttman-like scale was produced: only .03 of the 306 responses produced scale errors, the few scale errors found appeared random, and every observation category contained far less error than nonerror. Of the 68 *S*s in the Deprivation and Nondeprivation groups, five each produced one scale error in his response pattern. Such response patterns were assigned scale scores corresponding to the higher pattern which would have been attained had there been no scale error.

Comments and Questions were exhibited, but no Attention-seeking; a score of 1 indicated that only Comments were exhibited; and a score of zero indicated that no social response of any type was exhibited. Hence, the scale scores are weighted in favor of the less frequently occurring behavior categories, Questions and Attention-seeking.

RESULTS

The hypothesis advanced is that the mean reinforcer effectiveness scores for the treatment groups would rank in the order Deprivation > Nondeprivation > Satiation. To test this, two relatively independent statistical procedures are followed: the first is sensitive to the rank-order of the treatment means but does not take account of the degree of overlap between the distributions upon which the means are based; and the second, which takes such information into account and allows parametric statements about the means, is somewhat less sensitive to the rank-order hypothesis.

REINFORCER EFFECTIVENESS SCORE

Rank-order of the means. In Table 1, it is seen that the rank-order predicted for the three means is found separately for Boys and for Girls. The sex variable may be taken as an independent replication of the experiment. The theoretical probability of obtaining a predicted rank-order of three independent means is $1/6$, and with one independent replication the probability of obtaining two such orders is $1/6 \times 1/6$ or $1/36$. On this basis, we can conclude that the null hypothesis, that all six rank-orders of the three means are equally likely, is rejected at $p < .03$. Hence, the alternative hypothesis, that the predicted rank-order of the three means prevails, is accepted.

Regression analysis. For the purposes of the regression analysis (and for theoretical reasons as well), the three treatment conditions are considered as points along a single continuous dimension representing the degree of social deprivation. The analysis then proceeds from three working assumptions: (*a*) the units separating the treatments along this deprivation dimension are roughly equal in size, (*b*) their relationship to the reinforcer effectiveness means is linear, and (*c*) it is the *pattern* of the three means that is relevant to the rank-order hypothesis advanced, not the contrasts between mean pairs representing adjacent points on the postulated treatment dimension. On this basis, it appears most efficient to carry out the analysis of variance according to a regression model: in essence, to analyze the regression of the reinforcer effectiveness score means on the treatment dimension.

TABLE 1 · TABLE OF MEANS

Sex	Depri-vation (D)	Satia-tion (S)	½ (D + S)	Non-depri-vation
Boys	.36*	.18*	.27**	.21*
Girls	.33*	.07*	.20**	.23*
Combined	.34**	.13**	.23***	.22**

   * 17 cases; S.E. of a mean difference is .068.
   ** 34 cases; S.E. of a mean difference is .048.
   *** 68 cases.

The reinforcer effectiveness scores of the Ss were classified in the six cells of a 3 × 2 factorial, there being three treatments and two sexes of Ss. After a Bartlett test indicated that the variances were homogeneous and an examination of

TABLE 2 · SUMMARY OF THE ANALYSIS OF VARIANCE OF THE REINFORCER EFFECTIVENESS SCORE

Source of variation	df	Mean square	F
Boys vs. Girls (Sex)	1	.0412	.524
Treatments			
Total	(2)	(.4032)	(5.123*)
Deprivation (D) vs. Satiation (S) [a]	1	.8031	10.200**
Nondeprivation (N) vs. ½ (D + S) [b]	1	.0034	.043
Sex × Treatment interaction			
Total	(2)	(.0356)	(.452)
Sex × D vs. S	1	.0268	.341
Sex × N vs. ½ (D + S)	1	.0444	.564
Error (within groups)	96	.0787	—

  [a] Due to regression.
  [b] Due to the deviation of the *N* mean from the regression line.
   * $p < .01$.
  ** $p < .005$.

the data suggested that the other assumptions underlying the analysis appeared to hold, the data were subjected to an analysis of variance. Table 2 indicates that there is no over-all sex difference, and that the treatment conditions do not affect the sex groups differentially. From Fig. 2, it is seen that the group means corresponding to the three levels of the experimental variable rank-order according to the hypothesis. It is seen in Table 2 that the Deprivation vs. Satiation comparison is reliable and in the order predicted. In the case of three means, this comparison represents the regression of those means on the treatment dimension. A Nondeprivation vs. ½ (Deprivation + Satiation) comparison, which represents the deviation of the Nondeprivation mean from the regression line, indicates that that mean falls remarkably close to the regression line. Hence, the regression predicted was found. (This result provides presumptive evidence only for the effectiveness of either of the extreme treatments, Deprivation or Satiation, relative to the intermediate Nondeprivation treatment.)

Approval as a Reinforcer. A question of interest is whether the reinforcer dispensed was effective as such under Nondeprivation, which would be comparable to the usual experimental case under

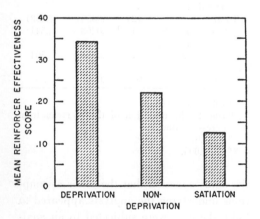

Figure 2. A pictorial representation of the means for the three levels of the experimental variable (34 Ss per condition).

which the effectiveness of the reinforcer would be examined, as well as following Satiation, when the reinforcer was relatively least effective in this experiment. The hypothesis is tested that the mean reinforcer effectiveness score under Nondeprivation is zero, employing an error term based only upon those 34 scores and a one-tail t test. That mean score (.22) is found to be reliably greater than zero at $p < .0005$. A similar test indicates that the Satiation condition of this study did not reduce the reinforcing effectiveness of approval to a zero level; the mean reinforcer effectiveness score following

Satiation (.13) was reliably greater than zero at $p < .01$. Hence, it may be concluded that approval was effective as a reinforcer under all conditions, and that satiation was not complete but only relative.

SPONTANEOUS SOCIAL INITIATIONS

An examination of Ss' spontaneous verbal initiations to E during *only* the four-minute baseline period of the game can reinforce the conclusions drawn from the reinforcer effectiveness score (which reflects only the susceptibility of Ss to approval as a reinforcer). These initiations could be expected to represent behaviors by S for a variety of social reinforcers from E and, hence, might be sensitive as well to the treatments. It should be noted that E did not dispense approval during the baseline period, but merely looked on as S put marbles into the toy. (Because the Satiation treatment consisted of a period of intensive social contact between E and S, which could encourage S to continue to make social initiations during the game, only a comparison of the verbal social response scores between the Deprivation and Nondeprivation groups would be meaningful.)

The *total frequency of verbal initiation* scores was classified in a 2×2 factorial (Deprivation vs. Nondeprivation and Boys vs. Girls) and subjected to an analysis of variance. The mean number of verbal responses (Comments, Questions, and Attention-seeking) after Deprivation (4.4) was found to be reliably greater than that after Nondeprivation (2.3) at $p < .05$ ($F = 3.70$, 1 and 64 df, one-tail test). At the same time, the Treatment $\times$ Sex interaction effect was not reliable, indicating that the two treatments did not affect the sexes differentially.

The scale scores represent what appears to be the *intensity of social contact*, or the degree to which certain social reinforcers apart from approval (e.g., attention) are sought from the adult, and could take any one of the four values from zero to three. They were classified in a fourfold table, with *low* scores of zero and one taken to represent less intense social contact, and *high* scores of two and three taken to represent more intense social contact. It was found that 20 out of the 34 Ss exhibited high scale scores after Deprivation, while only 12 of the 34 Ss exhibited such high scale scores after Nondeprivation, indicating that $p < .05$ (chi square corrected for discontinuity = 2.89, 1 *df*, one-tail test) that a greater proportion of Ss exhibited more intense social contact scores after Deprivation than after Nondeprivation.

Hence, the two relatively independent indices derived from the three categories of spontaneous verbal initiations to E *both* reinforce the conclusions derived from the measure of the reinforcing effectiveness of E's approval.

DISCUSSION

In the earlier study cited (as in this study), the experimental operation of brief social isolation of the child was equated to a condition of deprivation[6] of all social reinforcers (including approval). Hence, it became important to demonstrate that this condition increases the incidence of behaviors for approval relative to an empirically defined level of satiation for that reinforcer. The results

[6] An analysis of some possible Deprivation condition artifacts is made in *(6)*.

suggest that this has been accomplished. And since under the Nondeprivation condition Ss had just come from class, with no further experimental treatment, it seemed reasonable that it would represent some point intermediate between the other conditions. The rank-order of the mean reinforcer effectiveness scores for these three conditions followed this logic precisely and was uncomplicated by an interaction involving sex of Ss. Hence, the results replicate the finding of the earlier study concerning the greater effectiveness of approval after Deprivation, relative to Nondeprivation. While the mean difference between reinforcer effectiveness scores for Deprivation and Nondeprivation for the Ss in this study (ranging in age from 6-6 to 9-0) appears to be of the same order as that for the Ss in the earlier study (who ranged in age from 3-10 to 5-3), the absolute level of the means appears to be higher.

The two indices drawn from the three spontaneous verbal social initiation categories reinforced the conclusions based on the index of the reinforcing effectiveness of E's approval for the Deprivation and Nondeprivation conditions (where a difference test was meaningful). It seems likely then, if the game-set were dispensed with and the natural or spontaneous social initiations to E were employed as the sole dependent variable, that similar conclusions would be drawn from the results. However, if the present establishing operation for satiation were to be employed in such a study, it would still be almost impossible to separate the social effects of satiation from the artifactual effects of Ss' greater familiarity with E.

The essence of the parallel between our use of the term drive for social reinforcers and the traditional use of the term for the deprivation of food and water reinforcers, as in hunger and thirst, lies in the definition of a drive as the functional relation between deprivation for a reinforcer and responding for that reinforcer. In that special sense, then, it would appear that there exist for children social drives that respond to social reinforcer deprivation similarly as do many primary appetitive drives. Yet it should not be supposed that the results of this study validate decisively the conclusion that a social reinforcer follows a deprivation-satiation logic. The responsiveness of a reinforcer to relative values of both deprivation and satiation represents only one requirement under this logic. Social reinforcers may be supplied and deprived in a variety of ways, and it is important to discover their responsiveness to many of these ways. It would be especially important, for example, to implement the deprivation of a *single* social reinforcer, rather than of all social reinforcers. Further, it is essential to have some assurance that the social reinforcers are more or less homogeneous in this regard, for verbal approval may not be representative of the reinforcers controlling the purely social initiations made by children to adults. Replications of these effects with other social reinforcers (e.g., attention) would strengthen the conclusions, as would parametric studies of the deprivation-satiation dimension. Another assumption is that approval had acquired reinforcing value for children through a history of conditioning. A stronger case would result if approval were demonstrated to be a more effective reinforcer than, say, a comparable nonsocial noise produced by a machine; or if that noise were shown to be less affected than ap-

proval by deprivation-satiation conditions like those employed here. Even so, the earlier finding (6) that isolation enhanced the reinforcing power of adult approval for Ss as a positive function of the degree to which they sought adult approval in other settings would indicate against both these possibilities. And the difference in spontaneous social initiations following Deprivation and Nondeprivation supports the more general conclusions drawn here; those behaviors were very likely employed for social reinforcers other than approval.

While the results of this study can stand in their own right, several additional experimental conditions could help elucidate the processes at issue. Thus, it would be useful to separate the effects of some of the three components of the satiation condition employed, namely, (*a*) *E*'s physical presence, (*b*) the social interaction between *E* and *S*, and (*c*) the approval reinforcers dispensed by *E* to *S*. To do this, it would be necessary to employ such conditions as, for example, one in which *E* sits with *S* for 20 minutes but says nothing, or one in which approval is dispensed without *E*, possibly out of "thin air." While some such conditions might be difficult to implement, the attempt to establish conditions like these would be worth while in the context of this experiment. Even so, the results of an experiment (3) on related behavior (for attention) suggest that a condition in which *E* sits near *S* but interacts minimally with him (only upon request) functions more as a condition of social deprivation than as one of satiation (7).

Apart from these considerations, the standard primary-conditioned reinforcer issue in the study of animal drives cannot be involved as such in this case. We have assumed that some sort of conditioned reinforcer is at issue, but haven't separated out conclusively the effects of the several stimulus components of that conditioned reinforcer. At the very worst, then, it isn't clear that the social reinforcer dispensed is independent of E. We have already noted the possibility that noise, rather than social noise, might constitute the reinforcing stimulus. Apart from this, however, it does not seem significant to consider social reinforcers as separate from the person dispensing them: they are eminently social noises in our logic; and their social character refers not only to their presumed history but also to the method of their delivery.

Additional considerations. In the earlier study, two Es were employed to dispense the social reinforcer, one male and one female. An interaction effect was found which indicated, among other things, that the increase in the effectiveness of approval as a reinforcer, brought on by Deprivation relative to Nondeprivation, was greatest for boys with the female E. This change was not reliable for the other three Sex of S × Sex of E groups. In this experiment, in which both boys and girls were tested by a female E, no Treatment × Sex interaction was found (although the Satiation mean of girls may not have differed from zero). Hence, to that extent, the previous results are not replicated, but the conclusions can be drawn more generally. (This finding could be referred to the postulate that Ss of this study are "latent" [in the Freudian sense], while those in the earlier study were "Oedipal." However, there exist other possibilities, including slight changes in method, to explain the discordant results of the two studies on this issue.)

Only one reinforcer-dispensing E was employed, and she was not unaware of the expected direction of the results. Her behavior was scored by objective and easily discriminated criteria and judged satisfactory. Still, there remains some reason for caution; for the findings of this experiment cannot be conclusive until they are widely replicated with similar and improved procedures. Nevertheless, the reliability of the results is supported by the difference between the Deprivation and Nondeprivation groups on the spontaneous social initiations made to E before she began to dispense the reinforcer: there, where it was even less likely that E could influence the outcome, the finding paralleled precisely that derived from the reinforcer effectiveness index.

SUMMARY

On the assumption that approval is representative of the reinforcers controlling the purely social initiations of children to adults, the verbal approval of a female E was made contingent upon one response in a two-response game for 102 first- and second-grade children (Ss) of a university laboratory school. The change in relative response frequency from a baseline level following introduction of the reinforcer indicated the degree to which approval was reinforcing for an S.

Before playing the game, Ss were subjected to one of three experimental conditions: 34 Ss were subjected to a 20-minute period of isolation (conceived to be social *Deprivation*); 34 Ss played the game immediately upon coming from class (conceived to be an intermediate condition between deprivation and satiation, and called *Nondeprivation*); and 34 Ss devoted 20 minutes to drawing and cutting out designs, while E maintained a stream of friendly conversation with each of them and approved and admired their art efforts and statements in an appropriate fashion (conceived to be *Satiation* for approval and social contact). There were 17 boys and 17 girls in each experimental group.

Employing two independent tests (one on the order of the means, the other on the regression of the means on the treatment dimension), it was found that the rank-order hypothesis advanced was reliably supported (at $p < .03$ and $p < .005$ respectively). The reinforcing effectiveness of approval was relatively greatest after Deprivation, intermediate after Nondeprivation, and least after Satiation. Approval functioned as a reinforcer after all conditions, even Satiation ($p < .01$). Boys and girls were affected similarly on this measure by the experimental conditions.

The spontaneous social initiations made by Ss to E, before she had begun to dispense approval in the game, supported the results based on the index of the effectiveness of approval as a reinforcer. Following the Deprivation condition, there resulted a greater mean frequency of social initiations ($p < .05$), and a larger proportion of Ss exhibiting apparently intense social interaction ($p < .05$), than there did following the Nondeprivation condition. (The nature of the establishing operation for the Satiation condition precluded a meaningful comparison of the other conditions with it on these social behaviors.)

Thus, a reinforcer appearing to be typical of those involved in children's social drives appears responsive to deprivation and satiation operations of a similar order as those controlling the effectiveness of reinforcers of a number of the primary appetitive drives.

REFERENCES

1. Bowlby, J. Maternal care and mental health. *Bull. World Hlth. Org. Monogr.*, 1951, *3*, 355–533.
2. Chase, Lucille. Motivation of young children: An experimental study of the influences of certain types of external incentives upon the performance of a task. *Univer. Iowa Stud. Child Welf.*, 1932, *5*, No. 3. Pp. 119.
3. Gewirtz, J. L. Three determinants of attention-seeking in young children. *Monogr. Soc. Res. Child Develpm.*, 1954, *19*, No. 2 (Serial No. 59).
4. Gewirtz, J. L. A factor analysis of some attention-seeking behaviors of young children. *Child Develpm.*, 1956, *27*, 17–36.
5. Gewirtz, J. L. A program of research on the dimensions and antecedents of emotional dependence. *Child Develpm.*, 1956, *27*, 205–221.
6. Gewirtz, J. L., & Baer, D. M. The effect of brief social deprivation on behaviors for a social reinforcer. *J. abnorm. soc. Psychol.*, 1958, *56*, 49–56.
7. Gewirtz, J. L., Baer, D. M., & Roth, Chaya H. A note on the similar effects of low social availability of an adult and brief social deprivation on young children's behavior. *Child Develpm.*, 1958, *29*, 149–152.
8. Goldfarb, W. Psychological privation in infancy and subsequent adjustment. *Amer. J. Orthopsychiat.*, 1945, *15*, 247–255.
9. Greenspoon, J. The reinforcing effects of two spoken words on the frequency of two responses. *Amer. J. Psychol.*, 1955, *68*, 409–416.

10. GUTTMAN, L. The basis of scalo-
    gram analysis. In S. A. Stouffer
    et al. Measurement and prediction.
    Princeton, N.J.: Princeton Univer.
    Press, 1950. Pp. 60–90.
11. HULL, C. L. *A behavior system.* New
    Haven: Yale Univer. Press, 1952.
12. HURLOCK, ELIZABETH B. The value
    of praise and reproof as incentives
    for children. *Arch. Psychol., N.Y.,*
    1924, *11,* No. 71, 5–78.
13. RIBBLE, MARGARET. Infantile expe-
    rience in relation to personality de-
    velopment. In J. McV. Hunt (Ed.),
    *Personality and the behavior dis-
    orders.* New York: Ronald, 1944.
    Pp. 621–651.

14. SKINNER, B. F. *Science and human
    behavior.* New York: Macmillan,
    1953.
15. SPITZ, R. A. Hospitalism: An in-
    quiry into the genesis of psychiatric
    conditions in early childhood. In
    Anna Freud *et al.* (Eds.), *The psy-
    choanalytic study of the child.* Vol.
    1. New York: Int. Universities
    Press, 1945. Pp. 53–74.
16. WOLF, THETA H. The effect of
    praise and competition on the per-
    sistent behavior of kindergarten
    children. *Univer. Minn. Child Welf.
    Monogr. Series,* 1938, No. 15. Pp.
    138.

SOCIAL ISOLATION vs. INTERACTION WITH ADULTS IN RELATION TO AGGRESSION IN PRESCHOOL CHILDREN

WILLARD W. HARTUP
YAYOI HIMENO

SEVERAL RECENT STUDIES have been concerned with the effects of nonpunitive social isolation and inconsistent adult nurturance on the behavior of young children. Isolation has been studied chiefly by Gewirtz and his associates. These in-

Reprinted by permission from *Journal of Abnormal and Social Psychology,* 1959, 59, 17–22.

vestigators hypothesized that one result of isolating a child from an adult would be to increase the child's behavior to obtain social reinforcers (e.g., verbal approval or attention). Preschool and primary-grade subjects in two studies by Gewirtz and Baer (1958a, 1958b) made more correct marble-dropping responses when given approval after being isolated for 20 minutes than after a period of interacting with the experimenters. Gewirtz (1954) reports elsewhere that children seek attention more frequently when the adult is not immediately available to the child than when the adult is nearby. These results were interpreted as suggesting that *deprivation* of social reinforcers increases the child's behavior "for" these reinforcers.

Hartup (1958) and Rosenblith (1957) employed inconsistent nurturance rather than isolation as an experimental condition. They have suggested that the adult's withdrawal from the child frustrates the child's dependency behavior (in addition to depriving him of social reinforcers) and that the emotion resulting from frustration is related to the changes in behavior observed in the child. They predicted, much as did Gewirtz and Baer, that inconsistent nurturance would be associated with more efficient performance than consistent nurturance on tasks leading to reassurance for the child. In confirmation they found that children mastered a concept-formation problem more readily and performed better on the Porteus mazes after experiencing inconsistent nurturance than after interacting with the experimenter.

It thus appears that disruption of adult-child interaction, whether by isolation or inconsistent nurturance, quite clearly increases a child's dependence. There remains the question as to whether this change is solely a function of deprivation of social reinforcers or whether frustration is also involved. Further study of children's dependence does not offer the best possibility for differentiating deprivation-produced effects from frustration-produced effects of isolation (or inconsistent nurturance) on children's behavior. Presumably *either* deprivation or frustration should increase the frequency of dependency responses or responses "for social reinforcers." The present study is intended to clarify the effects of nonpunitive social isolation on the child by studying children's aggression, a type of child behavior to which a frustration hypothesis is relevant, but to which a deprivation hypothesis is not.

Children's aggressive behavior following a period of social isolation was compared with their aggressive behavior following interaction with an adult. It was assumed (a) that frustration is a component of isolation for the child even when the isolation is nonpunitive and (b) that frustration is a stimulus commonly eliciting aggression (among other responses) in American children. If these assumptions are tenable, children should be more aggressive following isolation than following interaction. Positive results, of course, would not rule out the occurrence of deprivation effects as a result of nonpunitive isolation; they would suggest only that other motivational changes (frustration) occur.

A second area of interest in the present study has been the relationship between the sex of the interacting adult (especially as it relates to the sex of the child) and the occurrence of aggressive behavior in the child. Sex of experimenter and sex of child have figured in most of the experimental studies on isolation and inconsistent nurturance cited above. Gewirtz and Baer (1958a) and Gewirtz (1954) found that children behaved more frequently "for" the social reinforcers of opposite-sexed experimenters than "for" like-sexed experimenters following isolation or low availability; this was most marked for boys. Hartup (1958), who used only female experimenters, reported larger differences in performance on learning tasks between consistent and inconsistent nurturance groups of girls than between similar groups of boys. Rosenblith's results (1957) showed boys performing better at maze-copying when the male experimenter *withdrew* attention than when the female withdrew attention or when attention was *given* to boys by either experimenter. No differences were found in this study for girls. Sex of the child in relation to sex of the adult has not, then, produced consistent behavior changes in children subjected to isolation or inconsistent nurturance.

METHOD

SUBJECTS

The Ss for this experiment were 24 boys and 24 girls in attendance at the Preschool Laboratories of the Iowa Child Welfare Research Station. At the time of the investigation, the children ranged in age from 4-0 to 5-8; the mean age of the group was 4-10.

Ss from the preschool population of children over four years of age were randomly assigned to two sequence-of-session groups. The children in each of these sequence groups were then assigned on a random basis to four experimenters, two males and two females.[1] Boys and girls were assigned to subgroups separately so as to place an equal number of both sexes in each group.

Each child participated in two experimental sessions. One involved nonpunitive isolation from the adult experimenter, the other a period of interaction with the experimenter. After each session the child participated in modified doll play. Each child therefore served as his own control in the

---

[1] The authors wish to acknowledge the assistance of Jean Eddy, Frances Horowitz, and Morton Rieber in collecting the data for this investigation.

experiment. Since other studies (Hollenberg & Sperry, 1951; Pintler, Phillips, & Sears, 1946; Sears, 1951) have shown that amount of aggressive behavior typically increases from the first to the second doll play session, sequence of sessions was counter-balanced: the 24 Ss in Sequence I experienced the isolation condition during their first session, and the interaction condition during their second session. The Ss in Sequence II were treated in the reverse order: interaction with the experimenter in the first session and isolation from the experimenter in the second session.

EXPERIMENTERS

The two men and two women Es were between 20 and 30 years of age and were either staff or graduate students of the Iowa Child Welfare Research Station. An analysis of variance indicated that individual experimenter effects on the children's aggressive behavior were not significant. Each S had the same E for both experimental sessions. Sessions were separated by an interval of from five to eight days; one exception of 20 days occurred because of illness.

PROCEDURE

Isolation Condition. E approached the child in his nursery school group in a warm, friendly manner and asked if the child "would like to see some new toys." When the child's consent was given [2] they left the group; E talked to the child during the trip to the experimental room—a period of two to five minutes. When E and the child came into the room E asked the child to wait for a "few" minutes because he had "something to do first." Then E left the room and closed the door. Four toys (two books, a puzzle, a rubber-band game) were within reach if the child wanted to examine them.

E remained in a room across a narrow hall and occasionally made noises so that the child could tell that E really was "doing something." At the end of 10 minutes, E re-

---

[2] Three out of 58 children refused to leave the group when approached in this manner.

entered the room with a collection of doll play materials. The isolation condition used is thus essentially parallel to that used by Gewirtz (1958a, 1958b), except that it lasted for 10 instead of 20 minutes.

Only one child of 55 pretest and experimental Ss refused to stay alone in the room during this condition, although a number of children indicated concern in the situation (e.g., restless wandering about the room, coming to the door and looking out, nervous oral or manipulatory habits, etc.).

Interaction Condition. When E and the child arrived in the laboratory room, E continued in conversation with the child and suggested playing with the toys. E interacted verbally with the child during a 10-minute period. The Es were instructed to show interest and involvement in what the child was doing, to smile or laugh when appropriate, to give help and praise, to answer the child's questions, etc. After 10 minutes, E told the child that there were more toys. E then went to an adjoining room and returned immediately with the doll play materials.

One child of 55 pretest and experimental Ss wanted to return to preschool during the interaction condition.

Doll Play. The play materials used were as follows:

> Plasticine male figure, 7½″ high, ¾″ thick
> Plasticine female figure, 7″ high, ¾″ thick
> Plasticine child figure of indeterminate sex, 4″ high, ½″ thick
> Doll furniture: double bed, circular dining table, kitchen table, kitchen chair, occasional chair
> Child's hammer and four 1″ wire nails
> 8″ wooden mallet
> 6″ wooden smasher
> 6″ wooden roller
> Tongue depressor
> Standard size knife and fork
> Doll nursing bottle

The dolls were stylized figures, firm but malleable. They were standardized by being molded to a cardboard outline. The materials were displayed on a 20″ x 18″ plywood board. Two spare sets of dolls were kept out of sight until needed in the play session.

At the beginning of the doll play E handed the dolls to the child as follows: male, female, child. After the child had identified each doll, E said, "You can play with them in any way you like." Timing of the session then began and continued for 10 minutes. During the session, E's interaction with the child followed the pattern of experimenters in other permissive doll play experiments (Caron & Gewirtz, 1951; Hollenberg & Sperry, 1951; Levin & Turgeon, 1957; Pintler et al., 1946; Sears, 1951; Yarrow, 1948). Care was taken that all reassurances to the child were of a general nature; approval given for specific acts was avoided. Whenever a particular doll lost head and limbs or was completley mashed out of shape, the remnants of the figure were removed and a new doll supplied.

A record of each S's aggressive behavior during the doll play was kept by an observer who watched from a booth equipped with one-way screening. Behavior was considered as aggression which involved injury, destruction or chastisement, physical or verbal or both, expressed by the child or through the medium of the dolls (Sears, 1951). Some examples of the children's aggression in this type of doll play are: (*a*) hammering, smashing, cutting, gouging, twisting, tearing apart of the plasticine figures; (*b*) scolding, threatening, (*c*) having a doll become sick or dead, and other of the types of aggression found in standard doll play. The large majority of aggressive behaviors observed in this study were of the type listed in (*a*) above.

Total frequency of aggressive behavior over 10 minutes was recorded for each S. The children's aggression varied widely in intensity, but this aspect of behavior was not rated. Single units of aggression were distinguished from one another by (*a*) changes in the object of aggression, (*b*) changes in the agent of aggression, (*c*) changes in materials used to express aggression, (*d*) changes in the type of aggression (e.g., change from striking to gouging, both with the hammer). When one act continued repetitively, an additional unit of aggression was recorded every 15 seconds. Information recorded for each unit of aggression included (*a*) object, (*b*) type, (*c*) time of occurrence.

A single observer was used to record the children's behavior in the 96 sessions. To obtain an estimate of observer reliability a second observer (naive with respect to which experimental condition preceded the doll play) also recorded the sessions of 12 *S*s. In computing reliability it was possible to identify specific units of aggression in the protocols of both observers. The time of occurence, materials used, and object of the aggression were all noted by the observer. A unit of agreement required like records on these three characteristics from both observers. Per cent agreement between the two observers based on agreements plus disagreements ranged from 68% to 91%. Agreement for the 12 *S*s combined was 82%, based on 466 agreements and disagreements.

A less stringent estimate of observer reliability, without regard to the categories mentioned above, but based on total scores, was 93%.

A square-root transformation acted successfully to reduce the skewness and heterogeneity of variance in the distributions of raw frequency scores employed in the major analysis of the data.

RESULTS AND DISCUSSION

The effects of isolation vs. interaction, order of session, sex of *E* and sex of *S* on the aggressive behavior of the *S*s were studied by means of an extension of Lindquist's Type IV analysis of variance (Lindquist, 1953). The summary of

TABLE 1 · SUMMARY OF ANALYSIS OF VARIANCE OF AGGRESSIVE BEHAVIOR IN DOLL PLAY WITH FOUR FACTORS: ISOLATION EXPERIENCE VS. INTERACTION EXPERIENCE PRECEDING THE DOLL PLAY, SESSION I VS. SESSION II, SEX OF EXPERIMENTER, AND SEX OF CHILD

($N = 48$)

Source	df	MS	F
Between *S*s	47		
Sex of experimenter	1	2.278	—
Sex of child	1	26.783	4.95**
Sex of experimenter × sex of child	1	18.217	3.37*
Isolation vs. interaction × session	1	11.943	2.21
Isolation vs. interaction × session × sex of experimenter	1	4.195	—
Isolation vs. interaction × session × sex of child	1	.171	—
Isolation vs. interaction × session × sex of experimenter × sex of child	1	18.878	3.49*
Error (b)	40	5.412	
Within *S*s	48		
Isolation vs. interaction	1	10.451	10.51***
Session	1	.955	—
Isolation vs. interaction × sex of experimenter	1	1.764	1.78
Isolation vs. interaction × sex of child	1	.139	—
Session × sex of experimenter	1	.978	—
Session × sex of child	1	.513	—
Isolation vs. interaction × sex of experimenter × sex of child	1	.054	—
Session × sex of experimenter × sex of child	1	3.470	3.49*
Error (w)	40	.994	
Total	88		

* $p < .10$.
** $p < .05$.
*** $p < .005$.

this analysis is presented in Table 1 in which the F ratio for isolation vs. interaction is highly significant. The means shown in Table 2 indicate that the frequency of aggressive behavior in the doll play situation was greater after isolation experience than after interaction experience. The data thus bear out the prediction.

TABLE 2 ·MEAN FREQUENCY OF AGGRESSIVE BEHAVIOR ($\sqrt{X}$) FOR BOYS AND GIRLS UNDER MALE AND FEMALE EXPERIMENTERS FOLLOWING ISOLATION EXPERIENCE AND INTERACTION EXPERIENCE IN FIRST AND SECOND DOLL PLAY SESSIONS

($N = 48$, 24 boys, 24 girls)

	ISOLATION		INTERACTION[a]	
	Session I	Session II	Session I	Session II
Boys				
Male E	5.83	6.15	5.08	5.10
Female E	3.69	5.30	4.51	3.94
Girls				
Male E	2.73	5.46	3.86	2.40
Female E	4.95	3.91	3.93	3.91

[a] The reader should note that treatments was a within-groups effect in this experiment and that the order of sessions was counterbalanced. Thus Ss who experienced isolation in their first session experienced interaction in their second session; those who experienced interaction in the first session had isolation in the second session.

It should be noted at this point that a control session involving neither isolation nor interaction was not included in this study.[3] Therefore, it is not known whether the findings resulted from increased aggression due to isolation experience, decreases in aggression resulting from warm interaction with E, or a combi-

nation of both processes. Children's aggression tends to increase in the presence of permissive adults in experimental doll play, however (Hollenberg & Sperry, 1951; Sears, 1951). It therefore seems unlikely that interaction with E prior to doll play reduced aggressiveness in the present experiment. Extrapolation from other doll play experiments is not entirely appropriate, however, since interaction with E came before doll play as well as during it in the present case.

The findings show that the consequences of social isolation extend to the behavioral area of children's aggression as well as to dependency; nonpunitive isolation appears to produce complex motivational changes in young children. It may be that increases in aggression are related to frustrating aspects of the isolation situation; there is also the possibility that disruption of the adult-child interaction aroused anxiety or uncertainty in the preschool Ss. The exact nature of the motivational changes resulting from isolation are not clear from the present experiment; isolation would appear, however, to affect young children in some way other than by sheer deprivation of social reinforcers.

A statistically significant sex difference in aggressive behavior is shown by the analysis of variance summarized in Table 1. The means in Table 2 show a greater frequency of aggressive behavior in this situation for boys than for girls, a finding that replicates many other doll play studies (e.g., Caron & Gewirtz, 1951; Pintler et al., 1946; Sears, 1951; Yarrow, 1948), and thus affords some validation of the doll play technique used here.

Of borderline significance in the analysis of variance are the following interactions: (a) Sex of E × Sex of S, $p <$

[3] It may be that a "true" control session or control group cannot be achieved for a study such as this. Neither beginning doll play immediately nor placing child and adult together (but not interacting) are adequate in this regard.

.10; (b) Sex of E × Sex of S × Session, p < .10; (c) Isolation vs. Interaction × Session × Sex of E × Sex of S, p < .10. Tentative interpretation of these effects may suggest hypotheses for further study.

The means reported in Table 2 show that boys were somewhat more aggressive with male Es than with female Es. Thus the male adult presumably had greater capacity to incite aggression (or less capacity to inhibit it) than did the female adult. The female adult tended to incite more frequent aggression in girls than did the male adult, but this pattern appears less consistently in the data for girls than in the data for boys.

The borderline triple interaction involving Session, Sex of E and Sex of S may be interpreted as follows: boys were more aggressive with male Es than with female Es in both Session I and Session II. Girls, on the other hand, were more aggressive with female Es than male Es, but only in Session I. In Session II there was no difference in mean frequency of aggression for girls with female as opposed to male experimenters.

This interaction effect appears to vary from treatment condition to treatment condition. The quadruple interaction effect also approaches significance in the analysis of variance. Examination of the means in Table 2 leads to the following interpretation of this interaction: boys were more aggressive with male Es than with female Es in both Session I and Session II under both isolation and interaction. These differences, however, were largest when Session I involved isolation and Session II involved interaction. Girls were more aggressive with female Es than with male Es in Session I, this difference being largest when Session I involved isolation. In Session II girls were more ag-

gressive with female Es only when the session involved interaction; when Session II involved isolation, girls showed more aggression with male than female Es.

There is some indication in these borderline findings that the conditions of the experiment modified the effects of sex membership on the child's aggressiveness. The tendency for children to be more aggressive with like-sex Es than opposite-sex Es was very apparent only for the 24 children who were isolated in the first session. These Ss had little opportunity to establish rapport, learn to expect reinforcement for dependency behavior from E, etc. When they reached the doll play part of the session it is possible that these Ss responded to the adult who was present in terms of habits learned outside the experimental situation, perhaps at home; i.e., if the like-sex parent is more threatening and frustrating to many children than the opposite-sex parent at these ages (as is suggested by Freud's description of the Oedipus complex) and the child generalizes responses to frustration from home to laboratory situation, results like those obtained for these Ss would occur.

The other 24 Ss began their sessions by interacting with the adult. Perhaps the warm interaction of the first session established expectations of social reinforcement from E regardless of E's sex and regardless of expectations for this kind of reinforcement that the child had learned at home. If such were the case, the differential capacity of male and female Es to frustrate the child would be reduced. Reduced sex-of-experimenter differences would then be noted in the children's doll play; such was the case for this group of Ss in the experiment.

The tendency for aggression to increase from first to second doll play session that has been reported in other doll play studies was not observed. Several recent studies (Hollenberg & Sperry, 1951; Levin & Turgeon, 1957; Siegel, 1957) have shown that the particular nature of the experimental conditions can reduce session-to-session changes in amount of aggression; the present results indicate that nonpunitive isolation and interaction before doll play also affect such session changes.

Changes over time in the amount of aggression in the two treatment groups was studied by a treatment × Ss analysis of variance (Lindquist, 1953). Table 3

TABLE 3 · SUMMARY OF ANALYSIS OF VARIANCE OF AGGRESSIVE BEHAVIOR IN DOLL PLAY BASED ON EXPERIENCES OF ISOLATION VS. INTERACTION, TIME INTERVALS, AND SUBJECTS
(N = 48)

Source	df	MS	F
Isolation vs. Interaction	1	12.48	9.27*
Time Intervals	3	2.74	4.44**
Subjects	47	7.12	
Isolation vs. Interaction × Time Intervals	3	.38	
Isolation vs. Interaction × Subjects	47	1.35	
Time Intervals × Subjects	141	.62	
Isolation vs. Interaction × Time Intervals × Subjects	141	.68	

* $p < .005$; tested against Isolation vs. Interaction × Subjects.
** $p < .005$; tested against Time Intervals × Subjects.

TABLE 4 · MEAN FREQUENCY OF AGGRESSIVE BEHAVIOR ($\sqrt{X}$) IN 4 TIME INTERVALS OF TEN-MINUTE DOLL PLAY
(N = 48)

Time interval		Isolation	Interaction
First	2.5 minutes	2.03	1.70
Second	2.5 minutes	2.30	2.09
Third	2.5 minutes	2.21	1.73
Fourth	2.5 minutes	2.42	2.00

shows the results of this analysis. The effects of the experimental conditions are significant, duplicating the previous analysis. Table 4 shows that the mean frequency of the Ss' aggressive behavior is greater in each 2½-minute interval following isolation than in the corresponding interval following interaction. Thus, a single burst of aggression at the beginning of doll play did not restore "emotional equilibrium" to the children in the experiment. On the other hand, conflict did not delay the occurrence of the isolation-produced increases in aggression. This finding suggests that the motivational changes resulting from nonpunitive isolation have a considerable duration.

Amount of aggression did vary, however, in the different portions of a given session. The effects of time interval are highly significant in the analysis reported in Table 3. Table 4 shows that the greatest change in aggression over time was that between Block 1 and Block 2. Aggression increased between these two blocks. The means show some decrease in frequency of aggression for both groups from Block 2 to Block 3 and a second increase from Block 3 to Block 4. Appropriate t tests showed that the differences between Block 1 and Blocks 2 and 4 were the only ones significant at acceptable levels of significance ($t_{1,2} = 2.85, p < .01$; $t_{1,4} = 3.00, p < .01$).

SUMMARY

In an attempt to clarify the effects of social isolation on the motivations of the child, the aggressive behavior of 48 children in a 10-minute modified doll play situation was studied in relation to other experimental conditions of isolation and interaction with adult experimenters, order of conditions, sex of child, and sex of experimenter.

The major findings were: (a) the children showed a significantly greater frequency of aggressive behavior in doll play preceded by isolation than in doll play preceded by interaction experience; (b) boys were more aggressive than girls; (c) there were no differences in frequency of aggression from first to second session; (d) frequency of aggression was greater in each 2½-minute interval following isolation than in the corresponding interval following interaction.

The most important implications of these results are (a) that frustration effects (as well as deprivation effects) occur in consequence of a child's being isolated in a nonpunitive fashion by an adult; (b) sex of child is a significant variable in experimental studies of children's aggression.

REFERENCES

CARON, A. J., & GEWIRTZ, J. L. An investigation of the effects of sex category of the interacting adult, chronological age and sex of child on aggressive behavior in doll play. *Amer. Psychologist,* 1951, *6,* 307. (Abstract)

DOLLARD, J., DOOB, L. W., MILLER, N. E., MOWRER, O. H., SEARS, R. R., FORD, C. S., HOVLAND, C. I., & SOLLENBERGER, R. T. *Frustration and aggression.* New Haven: Yale Univer. Press, 1939.

GEWIRTZ, J. L. Three determinants of attention-seeking in young children. *Child Develpm. Monogr.,* 1954, *19,* No. 2, 1–48.

GEWIRTZ, J. L., & BAER, D. M. The effect of brief social deprivation on behaviors for a social reinforcer. *J. abnorm. soc. Psychol.,* 1958, *56,* 49–56. (a)

GEWIRTZ, J. L., & BAER, D. M. The effects of deprivation and satiation on behaviors for social reinforcers. *J. abnorm. soc. Psychol.,* 1958, *57,* 165–172. (b)

HARTUP, W. Nurturance and nurturance-withdrawal in relation to the dependency behavior of preschool children. *Child Develpm.,* 1958, *29,* 191–201.

HOLLENBERG, ELEANOR, & SPERRY, MARGARET. Some antecedents of aggression and effects of frustration in doll play. *Personality,* 1951, *1,* 32–43.

LEVIN, H., & TURGEON, VALERIE. The influence of the mother's presence on children's doll play aggression. *J. abnorm. soc. Psychol.,* 1957, *55,* 304–308.

LINDQUIST, E. F. *Design and analysis of experiments in psychology and education.* New York: Houghton Mifflin, 1953.

PINTLER, MARGARET H., PHILLIPS, R., & SEARS, R. R. Sex differences in the projective doll play of preschool children. *J. Psychol.,* 1946, *21,* 73–80.

ROSENBLITH, JUDY F. Attention-withdrawal in relation to the effects of children's learning by imitation. Unpublished doctoral dissertation, Harvard Univer., 1957.

SEARS, PAULINE. Doll play aggression in normal young children: Influence of sex, age, sibling status, father's absence. *Psychol. Monogr.,* 1951, *65,* No. 6 (Whole No. 323).

SIEGEL, ALBERTA E. Aggressive behavior of young children in the absence of an adult. *Child Develpm.,* 1957, *28,* 371–378.

YARROW, L. J. The effects of antecedent frustration on projective play. *Psychol. Monogr.,* 1948, *82,* No. 6 (Whole No. 293).

THE EFFECTS OF PREVIOUS TRAINING
ON POSTFRUSTRATION BEHAVIOR [1]

JOEL R. DAVITZ

IN RECENT YEARS the concept of frustration has been central in both mental hygiene and social psychology. Psychologists and other social scientists have shown their interest in frustration and its effects by developing several theories, by performing a number of experiments and by using the concept of frustration to account for the deviant behavior of persons and of social groups. In spite of this extensive interest, many issues relating to the effects of frustration remain unresolved and the current theories remain incompletely tested.

The research reported here deals with the influence of one variable upon reactions to frustration. The principal hypothesis is that a person's response to frustration will be affected by his previous experience in situations similar to that in which frustration is encountered. Specifically, the experiment studies the differential effects of *aggressive training* and of *constructive training* on the responses to frustration made by children seven to nine years of age.

In order to develop the theoretical rationale for the present study, three major theories of frustration presented in the recent literature will be critically reviewed. The frustration-aggression hypothesis, which assumes a high degree of correlation between frustration and an "instigation to aggression," interprets postfrustration behavior in terms of direct aggression, displaced aggression, or substitute activity (3, 4). That direct or indirect aggression is not a universal response to frustration has been widely discussed in the literature of frustration-aggression criticism. Thus, the category of "substitute activity" necessarily covers an extremely wide range of behavior. The interpretation of this wide range of non-aggressive behavior as substitute activity, "substitute" only from the perspective of a theoretician anticipating aggression, requires the manipulation of unverified inferred variables, and does not provide an adequate general theoretical framework within which to analyze, predict, and understand this behavior.

The frustration-regression theory suggests that the change of behavior which occurs after frustration is predominantly in the direction of regression (1). While there is little question that regression may occur as a result of frustration, a change of behavior in this direction is certainly not the only possible change in direction. There are instances in the classroom every day in which the change of behavior after frustration is in the direction of growth rather than regression. There would seem to be no general factor in frustration per se which determines the direction of behavioral change, and the a

[1] The writer wishes to express his appreciation to Professors Irving Lorge, Laurance F. Shaffer, Edward J. Shoben, Jr., and Lincoln Moses of Teachers College, Columbia University, for their invaluable assistance in the present study.

Reprinted by permission from *Journal of Abnormal and Social Psychology*, 1952, 47, 309–315.

priori assumption that the change is always in one direction is not consistent with everyday observations. Therefore, because it predicts a change of behavior after frustration in only one direction, viz. regression, the frustration-regression theory does not provide a general theory of frustration.

Maier has suggested that postfrustration behavior is nonmotivated behavior without a goal (6). This challenge of the postulate that all behavior is motivated rests on Maier's experiments with animals forced to respond in insoluble problem situations. Maier observed that these animals developed consistent patterns of behavior, yet there was no apparent goal, and he concludes that postfrustration behavior is qualitatively different from motivated behavior because it is behavior without a goal. Maier's theoretical position restricts the definition of motivation to goal-seeking, neglecting the widely recognized definition of motivation in terms of antecedent conditions. The chief criticism of Maier's position is that his basic experimental data, upon which he bases his fundamental postulate of motivated and nonmotivated behavior, can be adequately interpreted and predicted in terms of avoidance behavior, utilizing the concepts of learning theory and without invoking a new theoretical sphere of nonmotivated behavior.

Having briefly examined these theories of frustration, it is suggested that a general theory of frustration cannot be restricted to the prediction of a particular mode of response or to a particular directional change of behavior after frustration. This critical examination also suggests that frustration theory may be most fruitfully treated in terms of a more gen-eral theory of adjustment, rather than in terms specific to frustration alone.

It is suggested that postfrustration behavior tends toward adjustment, and that the process of adjustment may be analyzed in terms of learning theory as suggested by Shaffer (10) and Miller and Dollard (7). For purposes of this study, frustration is defined as the blocking of drive-evoked behavior. When this behavior is blocked and the drive continues, the cumulative intensification of the drive evokes an emotional response. The particular pattern of behavior evidenced by the organism is a function of the organism's hierarchy of responses related to the emotional stimulation and the particular situation in which frustration is encountered. While it is suggested that this hierarchy of responses is a significant determinant of the organism's postfrustration behavior, it is recognized that this is not the only determining factor. The intensity of the original frustrated drive and the resultant emotional response, the degree to which the original drive-evoking situation continues to impinge upon the organism, and the degree of active punishment involved in the frustrating circumstances may be several other factors involved in this complex process.

Frustration theory is treated as merely one case of a general adjustment theory employing the concepts of learning theory. No specific behavioral responses are predicted as general results of frustration nor is the direction of behavioral change, either in terms of regression or growth, suggested as a general rule. As in all cases of behavior, the analysis of postfrustration behavior involves the interaction of a particular organism and a particular situation, and the theoretical framework suggests general relationships among the various factors involved in this interaction.

The principal focus of the present research was the development of differential response tendencies, prior to subjecting the subjects (Ss) to frustration. One group of Ss was trained aggressively before frustration, and another group was trained to act constructively. All Ss were trained in the same physical setting as that in which the effects of the frustration were observed. It was assumed that the training received would develop in the individuals of each group a specific behavioral tendency related to that physical situation, and it was hypothesized that their learned behavioral tendencies would differentially affect the behavior of each of the groups following frustration.

The two major hypotheses of the study were:

1. Subjects trained aggressively will behave more aggressively after frustration than will subjects trained constructively.

2. Subjects trained constructively will behave more constructively after frustration than will subjects trained aggressively.

PROCEDURE

The experimental procedure may be divided into four major sections: (a) free play; (b) training; (c) frustration; and (d) free play. In the first experimental session each of the ten groups was allowed free play with any of the materials in the experimental playroom. This was followed by a series of training sessions in which five groups were trained aggressively and five groups were trained constructively. The final sequence of the experiment consisted of a frustrating situation followed by a second period of free play.

The experimental population consisted of 40 subjects, 24 girls and 16 boys between the ages of seven and nine, selected from a group of children in residence at a summer camp. The mean age of the subjects was 100 months and the standard deviation of age was nine months. The total population was divided into five pairs of experimental groups (10 groups), each pair matched on the basis of age and sex. There were four Ss in each group, and the particular type of training, aggressive or constructive, assigned to each group was determined in a random manner.

The playroom was twelve feet long and nine feet wide, and it was bounded on one end by a black wire screen which permitted cameras, placed at a small opening in a wall fourteen feet from the screen, to record the behavior during the pre- and postfrustration play sessions. The play materials, which were arranged in an identical fashion before each free play session, consisted of clay, three dolls, building logs, dump truck, large plastic punching doll, hammer, saw, nails, and wood. Each group received seven thirty-minute training sessions.

Aggressive training is defined as that which encourages and rewards behavior the goal of which is injury to some object or person. The aggressive training was a series of games designated as: Cover the Spot, Scalp, and Break the Ball. These games are briefly outlined below.

Cover the Spot: At the center of a mat placed on the floor was a small x marked in black chalk. Each S was instructed to cover the spot with some part of his body, and that person covering the spot at the end of the game was the winner. Only one person could cover the spot at one time, and it was emphasized to the Ss that there were no rules limiting their aggressive behavior during the game.

Scalp: A piece of cloth was tied around the arm of each subject and he was informed that this was his scalp. The object of the game was to tear the scalps from the other S's arm while protecting one's own scalp.

Break the Ball: Each S was provided with a ping pong ball which was placed on the floor and could not be touched by hand. The object of the game was to break everyone else's ping pong ball while protecting one's own ball.

The several games described above were played for a period of ten minutes and repeated during the seven training sessions. During these training sessions a chart for each group was kept on the wall, and the winner of each game was awarded a star on this chart. Throughout these sessions aggressive behavior was praised and encouraged by the experimenter (E), and, in general, there was a high degree of aggressive behavior evidenced.

Constructive training is defined as that which encourages and rewards behavior involving the use of materials for the construction of designated objects. The constructive training consisted of drawing murals and completing jigsaw puzzles. Dur-

TABLE 1 · EXPERIMENTAL PROCEDURE

Section	Session	Procedure	Time
I.	1.	Prefrustration free play	18'
II.	2.	Training*	30'
	3.	Training	30'
	4.	Training	30'
	5.	Training	30'
	6.	Training	30'
	7.	Training	30'
	8.	Training	30'
III.	9.	Frustration	15'
IV.	10.	Postfrustration free play	18'

* During the training sessions (2–8), five groups of Ss were trained aggressively and five groups of Ss were trained constructively.

ing four sessions a long sheet of paper was placed on the wall and a box of crayons was placed on the floor. Instructions were given to draw a single picture on the entire sheet of paper, and E emphasized the constructiveness of each S as well as the cooperation of the group. During the remaining sessions, each group was presented with a jigsaw puzzle containing thirty pieces. The Ss were told that if the pieces were put together correctly, they would form a picture of American Indians or a familiar fictional character. When the group completed the first puzzle, a second puzzle was provided, and this was

continued until the end of each training period. Throughout the training periods all aggressive behavior was discouraged by E, while constructiveness, on the other hand, was praised and encouraged.

The final phase of the experiment consisted of the frustration and a second free play session. The Ss were seated on the floor next to a projector outside of the playroom and told that they were to see movies. Five reels of film, arranged next to the projector, were contained in boxes which displayed the titles of the film and a picture of the leading character. The first reel was shown completely. At the start of the second reel, each S was given a bar of candy, and at the climactic point of the film, E stepped in front of the seated Ss, removed the candy from their hands, and ushered them into the playroom. As E locked the screen door of the playroom, he made the following statement, "You cannot have any more candy or see any more films, but you can play with anything in the room." Although the Ss could see the projector, which continued to run, through the screen door, the movie screen was not visible. E did not answer any questions and made no comment on behavior. In no case was there any contact between groups during the final phase of the experiment.

The behavior evidenced in the pre- and postfrustration free play sessions was recorded on moving picture film for a period of eighteen minutes, starting in each case with the moment the Ss entered the playroom. Two eight-mm. cameras with automatic self-winding devices and wide angle lenses were used for this purpose. In order to analyze the data, the pre- and postfrustration behavior recorded on film was observed and written protocols of the behavior of each S were made. Pre- and postfrustration periods were not identified and the observations were made independently by two observers. During each viewing of the film the observers made a continuous record of a single S. These protocols were compared, differences between observers noted, and the procedure was repeated until agreement between observers was reached concerning the behavior of each S.

RESULTS

The data were analyzed in terms of the two major hypotheses, and the statistical analysis pertaining to each hypothesis will be presented separately.

AGGRESSIVENESS

It is hypothesized that Ss trained aggressively will evidence more aggressive behavior after frustration than will Ss trained constructively. The eighty protocols of behavior, including the records of pre- and postfrustration behavior of all forty Ss, were presented to four judges, who were asked to rank the protocols in order of aggressiveness. The playroom and materials were described to the judges; however, the pre- and postfrustration sessions and the individual Ss were not identified. The eighty protocols were presented in random order, and the protocols were ranked independently by each judge. The judges were doctoral students in psychology who had previous experience in ranking procedures.

The agreement among judges was determined by the coefficient of concordance as presented by Kendall (5, p. 61). All four judges agreed that twenty protocols evidenced no aggression and could not be ranked along the aggression continuum. Including these protocols in the evaluation of agreement among judges would result in a spuriously high coefficient of concordance, since the concordance of judges on protocols not on the continuum is +1. Therefore, in computing the coefficient of concordance these protocols were omitted. The value of the coefficient of concordance, corrected for ties, for the four rankings of sixty protocols

was found to be .903,[2] indicating an extremely high degree of agreement among judges.

In the following analysis of the data, the pre- and postfrustration ranks of each S were determined by summing the ranks assigned to each protocol by the four judges and arranging these summed ranks in order from the lowest to the highest sum. It should be noted that the form of the population of ranks cannot be specified; therefore, the analysis of the data is in terms of non-parametric inference.

In order to test the major hypothesis concerning aggressiveness, the pre- and postfrustration ranks of each S were compared, and a gain of rank was indicated by a +; a loss in rank, by a −. The null hypothesis which was tested may be stated as follows: The probability of gains after frustration of the aggressively trained group is less than, or equal to, the probability of gains of the constructively trained group. The null hypothesis would be rejected for a high number of gains in the aggressive group.

Only pairs of ranks (the pre- and postfrustration ranks of each individual) were considered. Therefore, these observations may be treated as independent,

---

[2] Since there were a number of ties within the rank order of each rater, the computation of W must correct for these ties.

$$W = \frac{S}{\frac{1}{12}(m)^2\left[(m^3-n)-m\sum_{T^1}T^1\right]},$$

where W is the coefficient of concordance; m is the number of raters; n is the number of ranked protocols; S is the sum of the squares of deviations from the mean rank;

$$\sum_{T^1}T^1 = \frac{1}{12}\sum_{t}(t^3-t),$$

where t is the number of ties in the rank order of each rater.

and the significance of the difference of gains and losses between the two groups may be tested by the ordinary method of chi-square. In computing chi-square, the ties for each group were split, half added to the number of gains and half to the number of losses in each group. This procedure increased the numerator of chi-square, thus providing the most conservative estimate of probability. The obtained chi-square corrected for continuity is 3.63. However, the hypothesis under consideration is a one-sided hypothesis and the chi-square values is in terms of a two-sided hypothesis. For moderate samples, if chi-square has one degree of freedom, the square root of chi-square has a distribution which is the right hand half of a normal distribution. Therefore, in order to test the present one-sided hypothesis,

the chi-square value must be converted into the equivalent value in terms of a unit normal deviate. This value is 1.90; therefore, the null hypothesis is rejected at the .05 level of significance. It is concluded that aggressively trained Ss behaved more aggressively after frustration than constructively trained Ss.

The equivalence of the location of prefrustration ranks of the two groups is evaluated by the *median test* as presented by Mood (8, p. 394). The hypothesis that the two population medians are equal is tested. The resulting value of chi-square is 1.6 and the hypothesis cannot be rejected even at the .10 level of significance. Therefore, we may conclude that in terms of the location in the rank order of aggressiveness before frustration, the aggressive and constructive groups were equivalent.

TABLE 2 · Rank Order of Aggressiveness, Pre- and Postfrustration

	Constructive				Aggressive		
Subject	Pre	Post	Difference*	Subject	Pre	Post	Difference*
1	40	48	—	21	70	55	+
2	38	70	—	22	70	50	+
3	59	70	—	23	70	52	+
4	70	70	0	24	42	70	—
5	8	7	+	25	5.5	10.5	—
6	31	35	—	26	4	1	+
7	9	5.5	+	27	15.5	10.5	+
8	34	47	—	28	12	2	+
9	19	70	—	29	58	54	+
10	20.5	39	—	30	56	70	—
11	23.5	70	—	31	70	70	0
12	22	51	—	32	45.5	57	—
13	26	15.5	+	33	49	53	—
14	20.5	43	—	34	60	23.5	+
15	29.5	13	+	35	27.5	18	+
16	32	25	+	36	70	44	+
17	70	70	0	37	33	17	+
18	70	70	0	38	45.5	14	+
19	70	29.5	+	39	36	3	+
20	41	70	—	40	37	27.5	+
	Gains:	6			Gains:	14	
	Losses:	11			Losses:	5	
	Ties:	3			Ties:	1	

* + indicates gain in rank; — indicates loss in rank; 0 indicates no change in rank.

CONSTRUCTIVENESS

It is hypothesized that the constructively trained Ss will behave more constructively after frustration than the aggressively trained subjects. The analysis of the data in terms of this hypothesis is essentially the same as the procedure discussed above in terms of aggressiveness. The eighty protocols were ranked from most to least constructive by five judges, and the agreement among judges was determined by the coefficient of concordance. The value of the coefficient of concordance was found to be .904,[3] indicating an extremely high degree of agreement among judges.

The pre- and postfrustration protocols were arranged in rank order of constructiveness by taking the sum of ranks assigned to each protocol by the five judges. Correcting for continuity, the resulting value of chi-square was 5.10. This value was converted to the corresponding value in terms of a unit normal deviate and the value 2.25 was obtained. Therefore, the null hypothesis, that the probability of gains of the constructively trained group is less than, or equal to, the probability of gains of the aggressively trained group, was rejected at the .02 level of significance. It may be concluded that the constructively trained Ss behaved more constructively after frustration than the aggressively trained Ss.

The equivalence of the location of prefrustration ranks of the two groups is evaluated by the *median test*. The hypoth-

---

[3] The coefficient of concordance, W, is obtained by the following formula: $W = \dfrac{12S}{m^2 (n^3 - n)}$, where W is the coefficient of concordance; m is the number of raters; n is the number of protocols ranked; S is the sum of the squares of deviations from the mean rank.

esis that the population medians are equal is tested. The resulting value of chi-square is 0.4, and the hypothesis cannot be rejected even at the .10 level of significance. Therefore, it may be concluded that in terms of location in the rank order of constructiveness before frustration, the constructive and aggressive groups were equivalent.

CONCLUSIONS

Both of the experimental hypotheses were supported by the experimental results. Therefore, it may be concluded that under the conditions specified in the present experiment previous training in situations similar to that in which frustration is encountered is a significant determinant of the organism's postfrustration behavior. These results are in contrast with past studies of frustration which have interpreted postfrustration behavior primarily in terms of the frustrating situation itself.

The experimental results do not seem to be consistent with the frustration-aggression hypothesis as a general theory of frustration. While fourteen of the Ss of the aggressively trained group behaved more aggressively after frustration, the postfrustration behavior of five subjects was ranked as less aggressive than their prefrustration behavior. The evidence countering the frustration-aggression hypothesis is even more striking when the constructively trained group is considered; 11 of the 20 Ss in this group behaved less aggressively after frustration, while only six behaved more aggressively. Furthermore, it does not seem reasonable to interpret the general decrease of aggressiveness evidenced by the constructive

TABLE 3 · Rank Order of Constructiveness, Pre- and Postfrustration

| CONSTRUCTIVELY TRAINED | | | | AGGRESSIVELY TRAINED | | | |
| | Rank | | Direction of | | Rank | | Direction of |
Subject	Pre	Post	difference*	Subject	Pre	Post	difference*
1	24	21	+	21	37	41	—
2	17	8	+	22	22	47	—
3	12	9.5	+	23	14	30.5	—
4	15	11	+	24	13	29	—
5	68.5	76	—	25	67.5	80	—
6	45	3	+	26	77	75	+
7	74	78	—	27	61	73	—
8	38	36	+	28	66.5	79	—
9	62	7	+	29	33	48.5	—
10	51	6	+	30	56.5	46	+
11	48.5	1	+	31	23	25	—
12	50	68.5	—	32	44	40	+
13	52	71	—	33	53	34	+
14	56.5	28	+	34	27	60	—
15	39	55	—	35	35	64.5	—
16	32	70	—	36	5	42	—
17	16	20	—	37	30.5	63	—
18	26	2	+	38	4	64.5	—
19	18	58.5	—	39	43	72	—
20	19	9.5	+	40	54	58.5	—
	Gains:	12			Gains:	4	
	Losses:	8			Losses:	16	

* + indicates gain in rank; — indicates loss in rank.

group and the increase of constructiveness evidenced by 12 members of this group as "substitute activity." It would seem to be more consistent with objective psychological theory to interpret these results in terms of a general theory of adjustment rather than in terms of a specific mode of response such as aggression.

The frustration-regression theory suggested by Barker, Dembo and Lewin (1), and Maier's (6) interpretation of postfrustration behavior as behavior without a goal, are not supported by the data. While growth and constructiveness as defined in this study are not synonymous, there is a close relationship between these two concepts. Therefore, to interpret the increase of constructiveness as evidenced by 16 of the 40 subjects in this experiment

in terms of regression or behavior without a goal does not seem to be a valid theoretical procedure. While 22 Ss did evidence less constructiveness after frustration, it is obvious that the change of behavior is not necessarily in the direction of regression. Previous training is at least one factor which determines this change of direction.

It should be noted that in the experiment presented here the two major hypotheses are interdependent. The data used for testing the two hypotheses were obtained from the same population and the behavior of each S was treated in terms of aggressiveness and constructiveness. All other things being equal, a high degree of constructiveness was associated with a low degree of aggressiveness, and vice versa, as indicated by a rank order correlation of −.83 between aggressive and constructive ranks of the 40 subjects.

The effects of prefrustration training in this experiment were not invariant. Six individuals within the constructively trained group behaved more aggressively after frustration and four Ss in the aggressively trained group behaved more constructively after frustration. This indicates that while the experimental training was a significant factor in terms of the behavior of the group, the total past history of the individual must be considered in predicting and understanding his behavior after frustration.

It has been demonstrated that postfrustration behavior cannot be treated only in terms of the stimulus conditions associated with the frustration. The external stimulus conditions of the frustrating situation were identical for the aggressive and constructive groups, while the previous training of the groups differed. Therefore, in this case the previous training was the significant factor which determined the differences of the change of behavior in the two groups after frustration. It is suggested that previous experience in situations similar to that in which frustration occurs is one factor which must be considered in the understanding of postfrustration behavior.

The results of this single experiment are presented neither as conclusive evidence of the inadequacy of present frustration theories nor as final evidence of the effects of previous experience on postfrustration behavior. For the writer, the most significant result is a realization of the need for further experimental study in this area.

REFERENCES

1. BARKER, R., DEMBO, T., & LEWIN, K. *Frustration and regression: an experiment with young children.* Univ. of Iowa Studies, Studies in Child Welfare, *18*, No. 1.

2. DIXON, W. J., & MASSEY, F. J. *Introduction to statistical analysis.* Eugene, Oregon: Univ. of Oregon Press, 1950.

3. DOLLARD, J., DOOB, L. W., *et al. Frustration and aggression.* New Haven: Yale Univ. Press, 1939.

4. DOLLARD, J., DOOB, L. W., *et al.* The frustration-aggression hypothesis. *Psychol. Rev.,* 1941, *48,* 337–342.

5. KENDALL, M. G. *Rank correlation methods.* London: Griffin, 1948.

6. MAIER, N. *Frustration: the study of behavior without a goal.* New York: McGraw-Hill, 1949.

7. MILLER, N. E., & DOLLARD, J. *Social learning and imitation.* New Haven: Yale Univ. Press, 1941.

8. MOOD, A. G. *Introduction to theory of statistics.* New York: McGraw-Hill, 1950.

9. SEARS, R. R. Non-aggressive reactions to frustration. *Psychol. Rev.,* 1941, *48,* 343–346.

10. SHAFFER, L. F. *The psychology of adjustment.* Boston: Houghton Mifflin, 1936.

THE EFFECTS OF NON-REINFORCEMENT
ON RESPONSE STRENGTH
AS A FUNCTION OF NUMBER
OF PREVIOUS REINFORCEMENTS [1]

RONALD K. PENNEY

THE OMISSION of a customary reward has been observed by many investigators to lead to an increase in the strength of a previously rewarded response (Miller, 1936; Rohrer, 1949; Sheffield, 1950, 1954). These investigators have all entertained some notion of the motivational effects of non-reward (the frustration hypothesis) in interpreting their observations. Although these studies support the frustration hypothesis, they are not crucial since alternative hypotheses of this increased vigor are readily available in terms of associative factors. Brown and Farber (1951) have reviewed a number of "non-motivational" interpretations of frustration. For example, the subject may have learned in the experimental situation, or in similar situations in his previous history, to make more effortful responses in the presence of non-reinforcement cues.

In an effort to restrict the number of alternative interpretations, Amsel and his associates (Amsel & Hancock, 1957;

Amsel & Roussel, 1952; Roussel, 1952) utilized a two-runway situation in which the criterion response was spatially different from the non-reinforced instrumental response. Amsel and Roussel trained rats to run down an alley into a goal box and then into a second alley to another goal box. Performance in the second alley, when reward was omitted from the first goal box, was superior to performance on test trials when reward was received at this goal box. The facilitative effect that this non-reinforcement had on the subsequent response was termed the frustration effect. Roussel (1952) also used the two-runway situation and studied the development of the frustration effect under conditions of partial reinforcement. Roussel found that the frustration effect was not immediate but only developed after a certain number of reinforced trials. Wagner (1959) followed up the Tulane studies and confirmed the developing nature of the frustration effect when the first runway response was partially reinforced.

Both the Roussel and Wagner studies imply that the frustration effect is a function of the number of reinforcements prior to non-reinforcement. Two studies (Holton, 1956; Marzocco, 1950) have systematically investigated the effect

[1] Part of a dissertation submitted to the Graduate College of the State University of Iowa in partial fulfilment of the requirements for the Ph.D. degree. The author is indebted to Alfred Castaneda for his advice and assistance throughout the course of the investigation.

Reprinted by permission from *Journal of Canadian Psychology*, 1960, *14*, 206–215.

of non-reinforcement when the number of continuous reinforcements was varied prior to non-reinforcement. Holton, using children, found the increased vigor of responding following non-reinforcement to be dependent on the number of previous reinforcements. Marzocco, using rats, did not find a relation between the vigor of responding following non-reinforcement and the number of prior reinforcements. Neither study utilized a criterion response that was spatially different from the non-reinforced instrumental response.

The present study was designed to determine whether the frustration effect is a function of the number of continuous reinforcements prior to non-reinforcement when children are used as subjects. A modification of Amsel's technique for studying the frustration effect was adopted for use with children.

METHOD

SUBJECTS

The Ss were 88 kindergarten children obtained from two elementary schools in Washington, Iowa. Twenty-two Ss were randomly assigned to each of the four treatment groups.

APPARATUS

Figure 1 is a schema of the apparatus. The face of the apparatus consists of two levers (R_1 and R_2 in Figure 1), two stimulus lights (S_1 and S_2) and a goal box (GB_2). In addition, a clear piece of plastic tubing was attached to the side of the apparatus and extended down past the base of the apparatus. The entire apparatus was painted flat black with the exception of the two levers, which were flat grey.

R_1 moved to the left of S through an excursion of 5 in. R_2 moved towards S through an excursion of 11 in. At the completion of R_2's excursion, a marble was released at GB_2. At the completion of R_1's excursion. a marble dropped into the clear plastic tubing on the rewarded trials. A door chime sounded at the same time as the marble was released into the plastic tube.

The two stimulus lights, S_1 and S_2, served to elicit responses to R_1 and R_2 respectively, and were turned off at the completion of these responses.

As shown in Figure 1, a hand pattern was located on the lower right corner of the face of the apparatus. The S was required to place his hand on this pattern after he had manipulated R_1. The onset of S_2 served as a signal for S to remove his hand from the hand pattern and pull down on R_2.

Additional material included assorted candy of the chocolate bar and gum drop variety. At the beginning of each experimental session, one chocolate bar and one gum drop were placed in the clear plastic container immediately above the plastic tubing.

PROCEDURE

The S was brought into the experimental room and the apparatus was introduced as a marble game. He was instructed that if he filled the clear plastic tube with marbles, he could have the two pieces of candy in the container immediately above the plastic tube.

The experimental period consisted of a training phase and a testing phase. There were three phases of training.

TRAINING PHASE I

Each S was given four training trials in Phase I. The details of procedure on an individual trial are as follows: (a) the first stimulus light (S_1) was illuminated; (b) S pushed R_1 and at the completion of R_1's excursion a marble dropped into the plastic tube; (c) S placed his hand on the hand pattern; (d) the second stimulus light (S_2) was illuminated at the end of 10 sec.; (e) S removed his hand from the hand pattern and pulled R_2 through its excursion; (f) a marble was released at the goal box (GB_2)

when R_2 completed its excursion; (g) S placed this marble in the plastic tube. All Ss received four reinforced trials to R_1 and four reinforced trials to R_2 in the sequence indicated above, during Phase I.

TRAINING PHASE II

During Phase II of training, differential treatment was administered in that the Ss were divided into two groups. The Hi-Habit Group received 10 trials on R_1 alone (i.e., not followed by trials on R_2). The Lo-Habit Group received one trial on R_1 and similarly did not receive any trials on R_2.

TRAINING PHASE III

In order to re-establish the R_1—R_2 sequence of responding, two trials were administered following the same details of procedure as outlined in Phase I.

TESTING PHASE

During the testing phase, the two groups were further divided into two additional groups—an experimental group and a control group. The experimental group received 18 trials, where a trial consisted of an R_1 response followed by an R_2 response, as in the

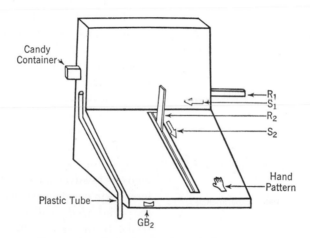

Figure 1. Schematic drawing of the apparatus.

first phase of training. For the experimental group the details of an individual trial were the same as those outlined in Phase I of training, except that on 12 of these trials, a marble did not drop into the plastic tube when S pushed R_1 through its excursion. The trials on which the marble failed to appear were designated the non-reinforced trials. Test trials, 1, 2, 3, 4, 6, 8, 9, 10, 12, 15, 16, and 18 represented the non-reinforced test trials. Thus the experimental groups of the Hi-Habit and Lo-Habit conditions received 12 non-reinforced trials and six reinforced trials on R_1 during the testing phase. On the other hand, the control groups of the Hi-Habit and Lo-Habit conditions were always reinforced for an R_1 response and an R_2 re-

sponse. The control groups, therefore, received 18 reinforced trials to both manipulanda.

When non-reinforcement was first introduced, the marbles in the plastic tube had accumulated to the same location in the tube. This was accomplished by affixing a piece of plastic tubing to the bottom of the plastic tube at the beginning of the experimental session for the Hi-Habit groups. This extension contained the nine additional marbles that the Hi-Habit groups received prior to the first non-reinforcement. After the first non-reinforcement, however, the control groups were closer to filling the plastic tube than were the experimental groups as the control groups received two marbles on every trial. The measurements of perform-ance were made in relation to R_2. A move-ment time measure involved the time it took S to pull R_2 through its excursion.

RESULTS

In analysing the R_2 movement time measure, the reciprocal of each measure multiplied by ten was obtained for each subject. These scores were referred to as movement speed. Figure 2 presents the movement speed curves for the Hi-Habit

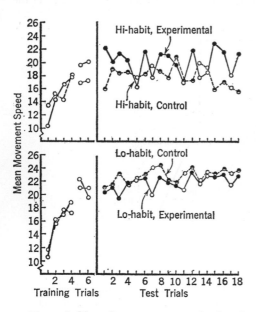

Figure 2. Mean R_2 movement speeds plotted over the reinforced (open circles), nonrein-forced (solid circles) and corresponding (semi-solid circles) trials for each condition.

experimental and control groups and the Lo-Habit experimental and control groups. Considering these curves, it is evident that the Hi-Habit experimental group shows no overlap between the re-inforced and non-reinforced test trials while all the other groups exhibit con-siderable overlap. Furthermore, greater

movement speed is associated with the non-reinforced trials rather than the rein-forced trials for the Hi-Habit experi-mental group. Table 1 presents the mean movement speeds over the last two train-ing trials, all the reinforced test trials and all the non-reinforced trials.

In order to determine whether the groups differed in movement speed prior to differential treatment, the first six train-ing trials were blocked in trials of one and an analysis of variance (Lindquist, 1953) was performed. None of the sources of variation was significant except the effect of trials. Similarly, an analysis of variance was performed over the mean of the last two training trials for all four groups and again no reliable difference was found.

To determine the effect of non-re-inforcement on movement speed during testing, an analysis of variance was con-ducted over the test trials for all four groups. For the experimental groups this analysis involved a comparison of the dif-ferences in mean movement speeds between the reinforced and non-reinforced test trials. In the case of the control groups, however, the analysis compared differ-ences in mean movement speeds between the reinforced test trials and the rein-forced test trials corresponding to the non-reinforced trials of the experimental group. Table 2 summarizes this analysis and, as indicated, a reliable triple inter-action was found suggesting that the non-reinforcement effect depended on the level of habit. Accordingly, the above compari-sons were repeated for each level of habit separately. Under the Lo-Habit condition, all Fs were less than one. However, under the Hi-Habit condition a reliable ($F = 20.57$, df $= 1,42$, $p < .001$) test trials by experimental versus control interaction

TABLE 1 · MEANS AND SD's OF MOVEMENT SPEEDS OVER THE LAST TWO TRAINING TRIALS, THE REINFORCED TEST TRIALS, AND THE NON-REINFORCED OR CORRESPONDING TEST TRIALS

Group	LAST TWO TRAINING TRIALS		REINFORCED TEST TRIALS		NON-REINFORCED OR CORRESPONDING TRIALS	
	M	SD	M	SD	M	SD
Hi-Habit experimental	19.92	7.01	17.59	6.57	21.34	7.68
Hi-Habit control	17.15	5.55	18.39	6.50	17.84	5.53
Lo-Habit experimental	20.94	6.41	21.53	6.54	21.69	6.37
Lo-Habit control	20.85	7.98	23.11	8.81	22.83	7.58

was found. This interaction indicated that the difference in mean movement speeds between the reinforced and the non-reinforced test trials was greater for the experimental group alone. Comparing the reinforced with the non-reinforced trials a reliable difference ($t = 7.08$, df = 21, $p < .001$) was found for the experimental group with the faster mean movement speed being associated with the non-reinforced test trials. A similar t-test was computed for the control group and no reliable difference in mean movement speeds was found between the test trials corresponding to the reinforced and the non-reinforced test trials of the experimental group.

Inspection of the Hi-Habit experimental and control group curves of Figure 2 suggested that the effect of non-reinforcement depended on the stage of testing. Accordingly, an analysis of variance was performed on mean movement speeds of the twelve non-reinforced test trials of the Hi-Habit experimental group and the corresponding trials of the Hi-Habit control group. The test trials by experimental versus control interaction was reliable ($F = 2.30$, df = 11, 462, $p < .01$) and suggested that the difference between the experimental and control groups was a function of the particular trial. A series of t-tests computed for each trial yielded reliable differences between the experimental and control groups on trials 1, 10, 11 and 12 of the non-reinforced test trials, that is, on the first and last three non-reinforced trials. In each case the experimental group's performance was superior to that of the control group. On the other

TABLE 2 · SUMMARY OF THE ANALYSIS OF VARIANCE OF MEAN MOVEMENT SPEEDS OVER ALL THE REINFORCED TEST TRIALS AND ALL THE NON-REINFORCED OR CORRESPONDING TEST TRIALS FOR ALL FOUR GROUPS

Source	df	ms	F	p
Between subjects	87			
Habit	1	547.07	5.52	
E vs. C	1	0.01	—	
Habit × E vs. C	1	78.31	—	
Error (b)	84	99.12		
Within subjects	88			
Test trials	1	27.23	6.90	<0.01
Test trials × habit	1	28.75	7.26	<0.01
Test trials × E vs. C	1	64.46	16.28	<0.001
Test trials × habit × E vs. C	1	39.13	9.88	<0.005
Error (w)	84	3.96		
Total	175			

hand, when the *reinforced* test trials were compared with the corresponding trials of the control group no reliable differences in mean movement speed were found.

DISCUSSION

The main finding of the study is that non-reinforcement of a response, R_1, increases the speed of a subsequent (10 sec. later) response, R_2, when both R_1 and R_2 have been reinforced by the same reward (marble). Further, the increment in speed of R_2 was found to be a function of the number of continuous reinforcements prior to the introduction of non-reinforcement. It should be noted, however, that the increment in R_2 speed was found to be reliable only on the first and the last three non-reinforced trials. Under the experimental conditions of the present study, the effect of non-reinforcement is not stable but relatively transient.

Amsel (1952) suggested that the non-reinforcement of a previously reinforced response (frustration) results in an increase in generalized drive strength. According to Hull (1943) an increment in generalized drive strength would increase the strength of some ongoing response provided the drive conditions did not lead to a response which was antagonistic to the ongoing response. Applying Amsel's motivational interpretation to the present study, the non-reinforcement of R_1 introduced frustration into the motivational complex and strengthened the subsequent response R_2. However, frustration appeared to be dependent on the number of reinforced R_1 trials prior to non-reinforcement. Some expectation or an anticipatory goal reaction may be a necessary condition for frustration and may be dependent on the number of re-

inforced trials prior to non-reinforcement.

The frustration interpretation meets some difficulties, although not insurmountable, in "explaining" a number of other aspects of the results. First, if a given number of reinforcements prior to non-reinforcement is essential to frustration, why does the Lo-Habit experimental group not show a frustration trend by the end of the test trials? This aspect is not inconsistent with a frustration interpretation if partial reinforcement does not lead to the same motivational increment as continuous reinforcement. That is, although the Lo-Habit experimental group has received thirteen reinforced R_1 trials by the end of testing, these reinforcements have been interspersed with ten non-reinforced R_1 trials. It is quite likely that for humans the partial condition produces less generalized drive strength than a series of continuous rewards prior to non-reward. This hypothesis is testable and would involve comparing a group that received 50 per cent R_1 reward from the beginning of training with a group that received 100 per cent R_1 reward prior to the first non-reward.

The second difficulty that the frustration hypothesis encounters concerns a possible sampling error. Evidence for sampling error may be found in the performance trend of the Hi-Habit experimental and control groups over the last two training trials. The Hi-Habit control group exhibited slower (not significantly) mean R_2 speeds relative to the Hi-Habit experimental groups. However, even assuming that the between-groups effect was due to sampling error, the within-groups effect (reinforced *versus* non-reinforced trials) must be accounted for and is consistent with a frustration interpretation. That is, the Hi-Habit experimental group exhibited faster R_2 speeds over the non-reinforced trials relative to the reinforced trials.

One other aspect of the data should be mentioned. Inspection of Figure 2 reveals that the R_2 speed of the Hi-Habit groups was slower than the R_2 speed of the Lo-Habit groups over the test trials. The depressed performance of the Hi-Habit groups may be due to fatigue resulting from the additional nine trials they received. One argument against such a factor is that according to this fatigue hypothesis the Lo-Habit groups should have shown a comparable depression approximately midway through the test trials. No such depression was found. However, in support of the fatigue hypothesis, it should be noted that almost twice as much pressure was required to push R_1 through its excursion as to push R_2. The Hi-Habit groups made ten R_1 responses in succession while the R_1 responses of the Lo-Habit groups were interspersed with R_2 responses and rest periods. Under these conditions it is conceivable that the fatigue factor may have been less for the Lo-Habit groups. At any rate, since the frustration effect involves a comparison between the experimental and control groups at each level of habit (a within-habit effect) this factor is not crucial to the frustration interpretation.

SUMMARY

The present investigation studied the effects of non-reinforcement on response speed as a function of the number of reinforcements prior to non-reinforcement. Eighty-eight kindergarten children were trained to manipulate a lever (R_1) and receive a marble and then manipulate a second lever (R_2) and receive another marble. Differential training on R_1 was interspersed amongst this R_1—R_2 reinforcement sequence. The Hi-Habit Group received nine more trials than did the Lo-Habit Group. During the test series, the Hi-Habit and the Lo-Habit groups were randomly divided into two groups—an experimental group and a control group and responded in an R_1—R_2 sequence. However, for the experimental groups a marble was omitted following an R_1 response on 12 of the 18 test trials. The control groups continued to receive a marble after each R_1 response. The time it took to begin to manipulate R_2 after a signal was presented (starting time) and the time it took to manipulate R_2 were recorded on each trial.

The Hi-Habit experimental group showed reliably faster mean movement speeds over the non-reinforced trials relative to the reinforced trials when the differences in mean movement speeds were compared for all groups. In addition, the mean movement speeds of the Hi-Habit experimental and control groups were compared over the non-reinforced trials and corresponding trials. The experimental group was found to perform significantly faster over the first and last three non-reinforced trials. The Lo-Habit groups did not show any non-reinforcement effect over the test series.

REFERENCES

AMSEL, A.   The role of frustrative non-reward in noncontinuous reward situations. *Psychol. Bull.*, 1958, 55, 102–119.

AMSEL, A., & HANCOCK, W.   Motivational properties of frustration: III. Relation of frustration effect to antedating goal factors. *J. exp. Psychol.*, 1957, 53, 126–131.

AMSEL, A., & ROUSSEL, J.   Motivational properties of frustration: I. Effect of a running response on the addition of frustration to the motivational complex. *J. exp. Psychol.*, 1952, 43, 363–368.

BROWN, J. S., & FARBER, I. E.   Emotions conceptualized as intervening variables —with suggestions toward a theory of frustration. *Psychol. Bull.*, 1951, *48*, 465–495.

HOLTON, R. B.   Variables affecting the change in instrumental response magnitude after reward cessation. Unpublished Ph.D. dissertation, State University of Iowa, 1956.

HULL, C. L.   *Principles of behavior.* New York: D. Appleton-Century, 1943.

LINDQUIST, E. F.   *Design and analysis of experiments in psychology and education.* Boston: Houghton Mifflin, 1953.

MARZOCCO, F. N.   Frustration effect as a function of drive-level, habit strength and distribution of trials during extinction. Unpublished Ph.D. dissertation, State University of Iowa, 1950.

MILLER, N. E., & STEVENSON, S. S.   Agitated behavior in rats using experimental extinction and a curve of spontaneous recovery. *J. comp. Psychol.*, 1936, *21*, 205–231.

ROHRER, J. H.   A motivational state resulting from nonreward. *J. comp. physiol. Psychol.*, 1949, *42*, 476–485.

ROUSSEL, J.   Frustration effect as a function of repeated nonreinforcements and as a function of consistency of reinforcement prior to the introduction of nonreinforcement. Unpublished master's thesis. Tulane University, 1952.

SHEFFIELD, V. F.   Resistance to extinction as a function of the spacing of extinction trials. *J. exp. Psychol.*, 1950, *40*, 305–313.

SHEFFIELD, F. D., & CAMPBELL, B. A.   The role of experience in the spontaneous activity of hungry rats. *J. comp. physiol. Psychol.*, 1954, *47*, 97–100.

WAGNER, A. R.   The role of reinforcement and nonreinforcement in an "apparent frustration effect." *J. exp. Psychol.*, 1959, *57*, 130–136.

15

PROBABLY NO PROPOSITION in modern psychology is better known than Thorndike's Law of Effect, which holds, in essence, that behavior which is followed by a satisfying state of affairs (is rewarding) tends to be selected and fixated (learned). Most psychological experiments dealing with the instrumental learning process, and particularly with discrimination learning, involve the administration of a "reward" to the subject for correct responses. Correctness of response is arbitrarily defined pre-experimentally as a push on a lever, the selection of a certain stimulus object rather than another, or simply traversing a runway to a goal-site. The Siegel and Foshee study (1953), found in Section VII, demonstrates, in fact, that the strength of a response, as measured by its resistance to extinction, is a direct function of the number of responses previously followed by reinforcement. Observation of the learning process in everyday settings and in the laboratory, moreover, suggest that some rewards produce faster responses or faster learning than others. This observation has led some researchers with children to obtain ratings or rankings of various reward objects that would be used subsequently in learning situations (Brackbill and Jack, 1958; Witryol and Fischer, 1960).

The reinforcing circumstance in a learning situation may be varied in different ways. For example, a reward may be administered to a subject immediately upon correct response, or the reward may be delayed for a set number of seconds or minutes following the response. Also, the magnitude of a single reward may be varied in such a way that a child might receive either one candy (or marble) after each correct response or he might receive three. Similarly, a child might be rewarded with one candy for approaching or responding to one stimulus but might receive three candies for approaching another stimulus. Another way in which the reinforcement circumstance following certain responses may be varied is in terms of the "schedule" of reinforcement (see the Bijou paper in Section VII). Thus, a child might be rewarded every time he engages in a given behavior or he might be rewarded only on every other response; or he might be rewarded on the average for every three responses he makes; or he might be rewarded no more frequently than once every minute regardless of the number of responses above one that he makes in that minute. All of these variations in the reinforcing circumstances probably have an effect on the child's behavior, and they are classified by some writers as incentive-motivational variables. They are distinguishable

519

from other kinds of motivational variables, such as hunger, thirst, curiosity, or need for achievement, in that they are characteristics of the external environment rather than attributes of the behaving organism.

The first selection, by Terrell and Kennedy, is a study of discrimination learning and transposition in children as a function of the nature of the reward. Studying a group of four five-year-old-children and another of eight nine-year-olds, they assigned the children to five groups, reinforced by praise, reproof, candy, or token, or without reinforcement. In this way they were able to establish in a simple learning task that candy reward proved the most effective, in that this group learned the task significantly more quickly than the others. In another study, by Terrell and Ware (1961), it was demonstrated that in both size and form discrimination learning tasks, immediate reward for correct responses resulted in faster acquisition than did a delay of seven seconds in reward. It would therefore appear that both qualitative and quantitative characteristics of the rewarding circumstance play a role in learning, and, with Thorndike, one might conclude that at least in these particular learning circumstances, candy and immediate reward produce more "satisfaction" than praise or a delay of seven seconds. It is important, however, to appreciate that any such conclusions about the relative effects of different reinforcing events must be qualified by a statement about the nature of the task in which the behavior occurs. For instance, Hockman and Lipsitt (1961) have demonstrated that increasing delays of reward have an increasingly deleterious effect upon relatively difficult discrimination learning tasks, but that if the learning task is a relatively simple one no such delay-of-reward gradient is obtained. As in most areas of psychological inquiry, it seems that the characteristics of the rewarding circumstance interact with other parameters to determine jointly the final effect on behavior. Much parametric work is needed that would involve the simultaneous variation of several such independent variables before a comprehensive understanding of any of them singly will be achieved (Meyer and Seidman, 1961; Screven and Nunis, 1954; Rieber, 1961).

The second selection in this series, by Baer, is a rare study of children's escape and avoidance behavior. Such behavior is, of course, instigated primarily by aversive or punishing stimulation, and for obvious reasons one wants to avoid the administration of strongly aversive circumstances to youngsters. However, one innocuous way of achieving avoidant behavior in children is to capitalize upon the aversive quality of positive-reinforcement withdrawal. In this case, the children were allowed to watch movies for a certain length of time but they could continue watching only by engaging in certain prescribed behaviors. That is, the movies were turned off if the child did not perform the required response. This ingenious study compares two different schedules of reinforcement on the maintenance of the required behavior.

Again, studies of the effects of the magnitude or size of reward on children's behavior are very scarce. The selection by Cantor and Hottel is one, and involves the manipulation of the amount of an edible reward on mental defectives' learning speed. It so happens that a reliable effect of reward magnitude did not obtain in this particular study, but it nevertheless serves as a good example both of how the amount-of-reward variable may be studied in children's learning and of how psychological researchers do not always get significant results from the parameters they manipulate.

Finally it may be stated that the area covered by this section is one in which much remains to be learned through systematic exploration. It happens to be the case that both the delay-of-reward and the amount-of-reward variables play a prominent role in modern behavior theories. It would appear that fruitful leads may be taken from these theories for the understanding of children's behavior under variations in these parameters and it is not improbable that studies with children will contribute to further refinements of the theories. Similarly, most of the instances in which different schedules of reinforcement have been similarly studied in animals and children suggest that the major characteristics of different species' performances are very similar. Thus, it seems likely that adaptations of techniques devised with animals will continue to be used in the study of child behavior.

REFERENCES

MEYER, W. J. and SEIDMAN, S. B.   Relative effectiveness of different reinforcement combinations on concept learning of children at two developmental levels. *Child Develpm.*, 1961, *32*, 117–127.

SCREVEN, C. G. and NUNIS, T. E.   Response strength as a function of reduction in rate of subgoal reinforcement. *J. comp. physiol. Psychol.*, 1954, *47*, 323–325.

WITRYOL, S. L., and FISCHER, W. F.   Scaling children's incentives by the method of paired comparisons. *Psychol. Rep.*, 1960, *7*, 471–474.

HOCKMAN, C. H. and LIPSITT, L. P.   Delay-of-reward gradients in discrimination learning with children for two levels of difficulty. *J. comp. physiol. Psychol.*, 1961, *54*, 24–27.

BRACKBILL, Y. and JACK, D.   Discrimination learning in children as a function of reinforcement value. *Child Develpm.*, 1958, *29*, 185–190.

TERRELL, G. and WARE, R.   Role of delay of reward in speed of size and form discrimination learning in childhood. *Child Develpm.*, 1961, *32*, 409–416.

RIEBER, M.   The effect of CS presence during delay of reward on the speed of an instrumental response. *J. exp. Psychol.*, 1961, *61*, 290–294.

DISCRIMINATION LEARNING

AND TRANSPOSITION IN CHILDREN

AS A FUNCTION

OF THE NATURE OF THE REWARD [1]

GLENN TERRELL, JR.
WALLACE A. KENNEDY

SEVERAL STUDIES have attempted to show the relative effects of different types of rewards in learning problems involving children as Ss. The problems presented to Ss in these experiments have been relatively complex. Hurlock (3) found that children solve an arithmetic problem more effectively when praised than when reproved, ignored, or treated in a "work as usual" manner. Abel (1) found that children trained on a maze problem under delayed-reward conditions made fewer errors than did those who were given praise, a penny, no reward at all, or a combination of these.

The effects of various rewards on children's learning of very simple responses need to be studied. This provides for a more rigorous control of extraneous variables which may be associated either with the experimental (reward) conditions, or the behavior to be learned. Siegel and Foshee (6) represent this point of view in their recent study of the law of primary reinforcement in children.

A matter of considerable practical importance concerns the difficulties other Es have encountered in selecting appropriate motivational devices when studying children under conditions similar to the present study. Using a small plastic toy as a reward, Kuenne (4) found that preschool children required a mean of 206 trials to respond consistently to the larger of two squares. Using a gumdrop as a reward, Alberts and Ehrenfreund (2), in what was in many respects a repetition of the Kuenne study, found that preschool children learned the same response in a mean of 47 trials.

All of the previous experiments in this area have employed as a dependent variable some acquisition criterion. It would appear significant to obtain some measure of transposition effect. The purpose of the present experiment was, therefore, to study the relative effects of verbal praise, reproof, candy, and token rewards on the acquisition and transposition of a simple discrimination problem by children. The response learned and transposed was a simple button-pushing response to the larger of two three-dimensional geometric objects.

METHOD

Subjects. The Ss were 160 children. There were 80 4- and 5-year-olds, and 80 8- and 9-year-olds. The 4- and 5-year-olds were from five different preschools. The 8- and

[1] This paper is based on the doctoral thesis of the junior author under the guidance of the senior author.

Reprinted by permission from *Journal of Experimental Psychology*, 1957, 53, 257–260.

9-year-olds were from four elementary schools. The Ss were randomly selected by schools from all available preschools and elementary schools of Tallahassee, Florida.

Materials. The stimuli for the problem were three pairs of three-dimensional geometric figures in the shape of cubes, cones, and cylinders (hereafter referred to as the training-stimulus sets). The basal surface area for the three types of geometric figures was the same for each size category. The small member of each stimulus set had a basal area of 4 sq. in., while the large member had a basal area of 8 sq. in. A third cube with a basal area of 16 sq. in. was used in a transfer test along with the large cube of the cube-training-stimulus set. This set is hereafter referred to as the test-stimulus set. The stimulus sets were presented to the Ss unmixed. That is, the large and small cubes were presented together, as were the cones and cylinders. The order of presenting the stimulus sets and the position of the positive stimulus (large) were randomized alike for each S.

Additional apparatus consisted of a background board and a panel board (Fig. 1). The background board was a 16 x 24 x ¾-in. piece of plywood with two jacks and two push-button mounts. The stimuli were placed into the jacks on each trial. The push buttons were on a line 5⅓ in. apart, 5⅓ in. from the sides, and 1 in. from the front edge of the background board. The jacks were in line with the push-button mounts and were 5⅓ in. from the front edge. The plywood background board was screwed to the top of a 16 x 24 x 4-in. box which contained the batteries and circuits necessary to operate a signal light. Locked onto the rear edge of the background board was a 10 x 16 x ¼-in. panel board which contained the signal light. This light was mounted in the center of the panel board, 6 in. from the top. The circuits were arranged so that a correct response, pushing the button at the base of the large stimulus, caused the light to go on.

Design. There were five experimental groups, all of which were rewarded by a light flash after each correct response. The differential reward condition for each group was as follows: The Ss of Group I, the praise

group, were told "That's fine—you are doing well" after each correct response. The Ss of Group II, the reproof group, were told "No, not that—you are wrong" after each incorrect response. The Ss of Group III, the candy group, were given a small piece of candy, which they immediately consumed, after each correct response. The Ss of Group IV, the token group, were allowed to transfer a dried bean from one jar to another after each correct response. The Ss were told that as soon as all of the beans were transferred to the second jar they could have

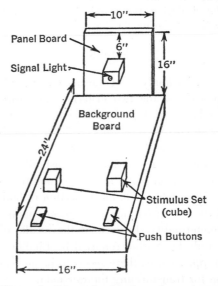

Figure 1. Schematic drawing of apparatus.

a small bag of candy. The candy was given to these Ss immediately upon reaching the acquisition criterion. The Ss of Group V, the control group, received no reward other than the light flash after each correct response. The experimental design consisted of two levels of chronological age in addition to the five treatment groups. The 4- and 5-yr. children constituted one level, while the 8- and 9-yr. children were the other level. Within each level, Ss were randomly assigned to the five treatments, making a total of 16 Ss in each treatment-level combination.

Procedure. The Ss were tested individually. Each S received the following instructions: "This is a game I want you to try.

Choose one of these (*E* points to both the large and small stimulus) and push the button in front of the one you choose. If you are right, that light will go on (*E* points to light on the panel board). If you are wrong, the light will not go on. Now remember, the game is to see how soon you can learn to make the light go on every time." The last sentence was repeated after every tenth trial. Immediately after reaching a criterion of 9 of 10 correct responses on the training-stimulus sets, each *S* was given a 4-trial transposition test on the test-stimulus set. The same differential incentive conditions employed during the acquisition trials were continued during the test trials.

RESULTS

An analysis of variance was made on each of the two criterion measures: number of trials to the criterion, and number of correct responses on the transposition test. The Bartlett test for homogeneity of variance resulted in a nonsignificant chi square on both the training and transposition data. Also, an inspection of both of these distributions revealed no marked non-normality. In view of the results of a study by Norton reported by Lindquist (5, pp. 78–86), there seems to be no reason for transforming the raw data.

TABLE 1 · MEANS AND *SD*'S OF TRIALS TO CRITERION IN TRAINING AND CORRECT RESPONSES IN TRANSPOSITION TESTS

(Each treatment group *N* = 32)

Group	TRAINING		TRANSPOSITION	
	Mean	SD	Mean	SD
Reward:				
Candy	14.66	4.80	3.91	.29
Praise	26.09	15.04	2.72	1.42
Token	26.53	13.28	3.03	1.44
Reproof	28.16	14.18	2.62	1.59
Control	35.47	17.83	2.78	1.32
Age level:				
4 and 5	28.75	18.15	3.06	1.33
8 and 9	23.61	11.09	2.96	1.44

TABLE 2 · ANALYSIS OF VARIANCE OF NUMBER OF TRIALS TO CRITERION

Source	df	Mean square	F
Rewards	4	1784.91	9.65**
Age levels	1	1055.75	5.70**
Interaction	4	335.60	1.91
Within cells	150	184.92	
Total	159		

** *P* < .01.

Table 1 contains both the training and transposition data. As can be seen from this table, the rank order of effectiveness of the five reward groups on the mean number of training trials to the criterion is as follows: candy, praise, token, reproof, and control. The summary of the analysis of variance of the training data appears in Table 2. The interaction is nonsignificant, while the main effects of the reward groups and age levels are significant well beyond the .01 level. The candy group learned the task significantly more quickly than did any of the other groups. No other differences were significant, although the difference between the group that was praised and the one that received only a light flash (control) approached significance in favor of the former (*P* = .06).

An inspection of Table 1 reveals the rank order of effectiveness of the five

TABLE 3 · ANALYSIS OF VARIANCE OF NUMBER OF TRANSPOSITION RESPONSES

Source	df	Mean square	F
Rewards	4	8.71	4.98**
Age levels	1	.29	
Interaction	4	2.74	1.57
Within cells	150	1.75	
Total	159		

** *P* < .01.

groups on the mean number of correct transposition responses to be as follows: candy, token, control, praise, reproof. The summary of the analysis of variance of the transposition data appears in Table 3. The interaction and age effects are non-significant, while again the differences between the treatment-group means reach significance well beyond the .01 level. The candy group transposed significantly more than the praise, reproof, and control groups. The remaining differences between the experimental treatments are nonsignificant, although the candy-token difference approaches significance in favor of the former $(P = .06)$.

DISCUSSION

As previously noted, the candy reward was the most effective in both acquisition and transposition, the only exception to this being the candy-token difference on the transposition test. Since there was no significant interaction present either in training or transfer, this finding applies to ages 8 and 9 as well as to ages 4 and 5. The marked effectiveness of candy as an incentive in this experiment supports a suggestion derived from the Kuenne (4) and the Alberts and Ehrenfreund (2) studies—where it will be remembered that the Ss of the latter study, rewarded with candy, learned the same response as the Ss of the former experiment, rewarded with a toy, in one-fourth the number of trials. Apparently Es concerned with the problem of selecting the most effective reward for children, an immensely important practical concern, might well consider the results of this experiment. This applies particularly to those who are interested in bringing all Ss to a training criterion as quickly as possible in order that they may study the effects of certain experimental manipulations on other learning criteria.

An observation of some importance arises from the fact that there were no differences between the older and younger Ss assigned to the token group either in speed of acquisition or in transposition consistency. For the children trained under this condition the mean number of trials required to reach the criterion were 26.06 and 27.00 for the younger and older Ss, respectively. The mean number of transposition responses for the younger and older age levels were 3.00 and 3.06, respectively. Though the writer knows of no research on this matter, supervisors and teachers of children frequently report on the ineffectiveness of delayed rewards with very young children. Apparently 4- and 5-yr. children can learn as effectively as 8- and 9-yr. children under delayed-reward conditions, provided they are clearly able to observe progress toward the ultimate goal. It is obvious that this hypothesis needs to be tested in experiments concerned with other types of learning problems and performed with Ss from the same and different age levels before much confidence may be placed in its accuracy.

SUMMARY

Subjects (80 4- and 5-yr. children and 80 8- and 9-yr. children) were randomly assigned to five reward conditions: praise, reproof, candy, token, and control (light flash). Training to the larger of two three-dimensional stimuli was continued until Ss had reached a criterion of 9 of the last 10 responses correct. A 4-trial transposition test was then given with stimuli one step removed from the training pair. The candy-reward group learned significantly more quickly than did any of the other groups;

while on the transposition test, the candy group was significantly superior to all groups except the token-reward group. The older children learned significantly more quickly than did the younger, but there was no age-level difference on the transposition test.

REFERENCES

1. ABEL, L. B.   The effects of shifts in motivation upon the learning of a sensorimotor task. *Arch. Psychol., N. Y.,* 1936, No. 205.

2. ALBERTS, E., & EHRENFREUND, D. Transposition in children as a function of age. *J. exp. Psychol.,* 1951, *41,* 30–38.

3. HURLOCK, E. B.   The value of praise and reproof as incentives for children. *Arch. Psychol., N. Y.,* 1924, No. 71.

4. KUENNE, M. R.   Experimental investigation of transposition behavior in young children. *J. exp. Psychol.,* 1946, *36,* 471–490.

5. LINDQUIST, E. F.   *Design and analysis of experiments in psychology and education.* Chicago: Houghton-Mifflin, 1953.

6. SIEGEL, P. S., & FOSHEE, J. G.   The law of primary reinforcement in children. *J. exp. Psychol.,* 1953, *45,* 12–14.

ESCAPE AND AVOIDANCE RESPONSE

OF PRE-SCHOOL CHILDREN

TO TWO SCHEDULES

OF REINFORCEMENT WITHDRAWAL

DONALD M. BAER [1]

RECENT DEMONSTRATIONS by Sidman (1953) and Brady (1958) show that aversive control can establish an operant response which is regular in rate, efficient in the avoidance of the aversive stimulus which controls it, and durable over long periods of time during which the aversive stimulus is perfectly avoided. These characteristics alone make avoidance schedules a logical tool to apply to the de-

[1] The research reported herein was supported in part by Public Health Service Grant M-2208, United States Department of Health, Education, and Welfare, and in part by a grant from the Research Fund of the Graduate School, University of Washington. The author is particularly indebted to Mrs. Susan Lagunoff and Mrs. Ann Pilisdorf, for their reliable and intelligent performances as *A;* and to Mrs. Josephine Reed,

Reprinted by permission from *Journal of Experimental Analysis of Behavior,* 1960, 3, 155–159.

Director of the Seattle Day Nursery Association schools, and Mrs. Katherine M. Radovich, Director of the Union Bay Nursery School, for their gracious cooperation.

velopment of social behaviors in humans. A primary problem in any such attempt is the demonstration of avoidance responding under aversive control in the laboratory, especially with children as subjects. The present study represents a beginning at implementing avoidance techniques for children, and an exploration of possibly significant variations in the way an aversive event may be programmed by a response. The aversive event used is the temporary withdrawal of positive reinforcement.

SUBJECTS AND APPARATUS

The subjects were pre-school children, ranging in age from 4 to 6 years, in attendance at day-care schools during the course of the study. They represent low-income and student families.

The study was conducted in a mobile laboratory built into a 19-foot house trailer (Bijou, 1958), which was parked close to the nursery school. The interior of the laboratory included a one-way observation room for the experimenter and a playroom for the child. The playroom contained a small chair, two tables holding toys or apparatus, a movie screen mounted on a wall, and a partitioned corner in which an accompanying adult (A) could sit, out of the child's sight but still present.

The child was seated beside one table, facing the movie screen, with a bar to press located at his right hand such that he could respond to the bar while watching movies projected onto the screen. The bar was housed in a red box approximately 1 foot on a side. The movie screen was a 9- by 11-inch rectangle of translucent plastic, located in the wall separating child and experimenter. The

movie projector, a Busch "Cinesalesman," operated from the experimenter's side. The projector contained as many as three cartoons on an "endless" reel of film, and could repeat these in an uninterrupted sequence for an indefinite number of cycles without rewinding or other adjustment. The cartoons were of the Castle Films' Woody Woodpecker series (Woody Plays Santa Claus, The Hollywood Matador, and The Dizzy Acrobats); each was in black and white, with sound, and lasted 7 minutes.

PROCEDURE

Ss were dealt with entirely by young female adult, A. Before the experiment started, A had been a constant member of the play group for several days and was thoroughly familiar to the Ss. In addition, she had told them that a trailer was coming, and that all the Ss would be allowed to enter and see cartoons. This created a good deal of enthusiasm. Two As were used in the course of the study, each seeing about half of the Ss of each experimental group. Any S was dealt with always by the same A.

The Ss were brought to the laboratory repeatedly by A, who told them on each occasion that it was "their turn to see the cartoons (again)." These occasions typically were spaced at 4- or 5-day intervals. When S entered with A, he was seated before the movie screen, the bar at his right hand, and A then retired to her corner (saying on S's first visit, "I'll be right back here"). The cartoons started immediately and played through without interruption. Some Ss saw two cartoons (14 minutes), and some saw three cartoons (21 minutes). The operant level of bar pressing was measured.

Procedure was similar for the second session, except that the cartoons played for only 1 minute before the first interruption. The cartoons were interrupted (i.e., positive reinforcement was withdrawn) by opening the voice coil of the projector's loud-speaker and flipping an opaque shield over the projector lens, operated by a small electric motor built into the projector. This procedure has been shown to constitute a punishing event in a previous study (Baer, 1960) with children of this age range. The cartoons stayed off (the projector running, nevertheless) until S responded to the bar. After this point, further withdrawals were programmed by S's response according to one of two schedules.

Under one of these schedules, a response had these consequences: any response automatically programmed the next withdrawal for n seconds later. But if another response was made before n seconds elapsed, the withdrawal was reprogrammed for n seconds after this last response. This is the avoidance schedule typical in Sidman's studies, except that the aversive event (the withdrawal of the cartoons) remains in effect until a response is made. It is precisely the schedule used by Hefferline (1959) to set up avoidance responding in adults, and will be referred to here as a Hefferline escape-avoidance schedule.

Under the other schedule, a response had somewhat different consequences: any response added n seconds to the interval between that response and the next programmed withdrawal of the cartoons. In effect, time could be "saved up." For example, if S, during an interruption, made one response, he received n seconds of cartoons, and then was interrupted again. If he had made 10 responses, how-

ever, then he would have been interrupted 10n seconds after his first response. If, before this programmed interruption, he again emitted 10 responses, the next interruption would be programmed another 10n seconds into the future, giving a total period of 20 n seconds of uninterrupted cartoons. Because of the very precise similarity of this procedure to attempting to walk up an escalator going down, Sidman (1959) has called a schedule very similar to this an "escalator" schedule. It was implemented in this case by a modified Guardian add-subtract stepper,[2] which was added one step towards a withdrawal every 3 seconds by a timer, and subtracted by S's responses. In the event of a response and a timer impulse being fed to the stepper within 0.1 second of each other, the effect of the response was lost. This was rare.

During each subsequent visit to the laboratory, Ss viewed the same cartoons under one of these schedules. At the conclusion of the last cartoon, the projector was turned off from the experimenter's room and A came out of her partitioned corner, telling the child, "That's all for today." She then took the child back to the play group.

A group of 16 children was observed under repeated applications of the Hefferline escape-avoidance schedule. Some children were seen as many as 12 consecutive times. Response-interruption intervals (n) of 3, 5, and 10 seconds were used, always the same interval for a given S. Another group of 17 children was observed under repeated applications of the "escalator" schedule. Some were seen as

---

[2] This stepper had a capacity of 40 steps, thus allowing S to put off the next interruption a maximum of 40n seconds. This limit was rarely reached.

many as eight consecutive times. The same intervals (3, 5, and 10 seconds) were used.

RESULTS AND DISCUSSION

Cumulative-response curves representative of developing response under the Hefferline escape-avoidance schedule are shown in Fig. 1. These represent Sessions 2 through 12 of a single S seeing the same two cartoons each session. The response-interruption interval (n) shown is 5 seconds. (Operant level is not shown, since it was a precise–and typical– zero.)

Each curve represents a single session. Interruptions are indicated by the usual vertical blip. The horizontal extent of the blip indicates the time S allowed the interruption to continue.

Clearly enough, response comes increasingly under control of the escape contingency of the schedule, and shows a decreasing (if any) sensitivity to the avoidance contingency also programmed. Performance during the final session is an extremely regular escape response, very closely discriminated to the interruption and much like S's initial performance on this schedule. Many Ss returned to this re-

Figure 1. Developing response under the Hefferline escape-avoidance schedule of reinforcement withdrawal.

sponse pattern somewhat earlier, and then maintained it consistently through out the tenure of the study.

Failure to evoke avoidance responding with this schedule hardly removes the schedule from consideration as a significant variable in child behavior. It must be emphasized that the interruption itself is a very mild event, the prospect of viewing the same three cartoons again not constituting an extremely powerful reinforcer for this population. (However, several Ss were observed under a schedule in which an interruption could not be escaped until 5 seconds has passed. Response was not essentially different from that shown in

Fig. 1.) And there is reason to assume that further hours of experience with this schedule eventually would produce avoidance responding.

Cumulative-response curves indicating a quickly developing avoidance response under the "escalator" schedule are shown in Fig. 2. These represent Sessions 2 through 6 of a single S seeing the same three cartoons each session. In this case, the response-interruption interval (n) is 3 seconds.[3] (Again, operant level is

[3] The response-interruption intervals used in this study did not prove to be a significant variable in predicting the development of avoidance responding.

not shown, being zero.) Each curve represents a single session.

Initial response is exclusively to the escape contingency of the schedule, as was the case of Ss under the escape-avoidance schedule (Fig. 1). And, as was the case for Ss under the escape-avoidance schedule, before the session ends, a burst of responses appears. But under this schedule, the consequence of such a burst is to give S a relatively long period of uninterrupted cartoons. Subsequent response develops then to be primarily of an avoidance character, rather than of an escape character: the response pattern is one in which rapid bursts of response alternate with plateaus which typically end in reinforcement withdrawals. As the sessions proceed, this pattern shifts such that pleateaus tend to end in renewed bursts of response just prior to the next scheduled reinforcement withdrawal. By the sixth session, response rate has fallen to the point where it is reasonably smooth, plateaus are rare and short, and the reinforcement is rarely withdrawn (although the withdrawal often is potentially only a few seconds away).

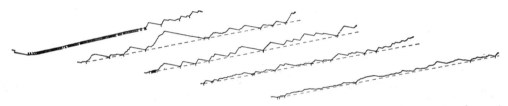

Figure 2. Developing response under the "escalator" schedule of reinforcement withdrawal.

Most Ss are slower to come to this pattern, but clearly are developing toward it in the course of eight sessions. In these cases, it is typical to find a relatively longer phase in which plateaus following response bursts end in reinforcement withdrawals, rather than renewed bursts of responding.

In Fig. 2, the dotted lines indicate a minimal rate for keeping just ahead of the next interruption (i.e., one response per 3 seconds). With this schedule and cumulative recording, the response curve will intersect this projected line exactly at the time of the next programmed interruption, as long as S responds almost instantaneously to any interruption (which is invariably the case).

The difference in avoidance behavior observed in response to these schedules may be a function of the discriminative stimuli each schedule allows the subject—if the avoidance response is viewed essentially as a temporally discriminated operant. Under the Hefferline escape-avoidance schedule, the essential S^D for avoidance responding may be simply time since the last response, independent of the rate or extent of recent responding. Under the "escalator" schedule, possible S^D's may include time since the last response, and the rate and extent of recent responding. However, to imply that the subject will discriminate his response to the latter two of these three variables will involve an assumption that a response is reinforced in proportion to the length of time it delays the next reinforcement withdrawal, or, alternatively, that it is punished in inverse proportion to the length of time it delays the next reinforcement withdrawal. Clearly, the present study does not contain data in direct support of these assumptions. It is probably best simply to point to the variables which program the next reinforcement withdrawal (time since last response, in the Hefferline escape-avoidance schedule; time since last response, rate and extent of responding, in the "escalator" schedule) as a target for explanatory research.

Conceivably, the "escalator" schedule of reinforcement withdrawal (or of other aversive events) is a typical and important schedule in the developing child's reinforcement history. It seems reasonable that when a human is absentmindedly programming punishment for "bad" behavior, he is likely to be placated longer by an intensive burst of "good" responses than by only one or two. At any rate, the "escalator" schedule seems to have certain advantages in promoting the rapid development of avoidance responding, and deserves attention.

REFERENCES

BAER, D. M. The effect of withdrawal of positive reinforcement on an extinguishing response in young children. *Child Develpm.*, 1961, *32*, 67–75.

BIJOU, S. W. A child study laboratory on wheels. *Child Develpm.*, 1958, *29*, 425–427.

BRADY, J. V., PORTER, R. W., CONRAD, D. G., and MASON, J. W. Avoidance behavior and the development of gastroduodenal ulcers. *J. exp. anal. Behav.*, 1958, *1*, 69–72.

HEFFERLINE, R. F., KEENAN, B., and HARFORD, R. A. Escape and avoidance conditioning in human subjects without their observation of the response. *Science*, 1959, *130*, 1338–39.

SIDMAN, M. Avoidance conditioning with brief shock and no exteroceptive warning signal. *Science*, 1953, *118*, 157–158.

SIDMAN, M. An adjustable avoidance schedule. Paper read at Eastern Psychol. Ass., Atlantic City, April, 1959.

DISCRIMINATION LEARNING IN MENTAL

DEFECTIVES AS A FUNCTION

OF MAGNITUDE OF FOOD REWARD

AND INTELLIGENCE LEVEL [1]

GORDON N. CANTOR
JOHN V. HOTTEL

IN THE 1951 REVISION of his postulate set, Hull (1) utilized the variable of magnitude of reward to define the so-called "incentive motivation" construct. This construct, together with other intervening variables, was assumed to multiply with "habit strength" to determine "reaction potential." Applying these concepts to a simple discrimination learning task and assuming all variables constant other than magnitude of reward, one would predict better performance, up to a certain point, the larger the food reward obtained after each correct discriminative response. One of the purposes of the present study was to test this prediction, utilizing mentally defective Ss and two amounts of food reward. It must be emphasized from the start that, since maintenance of a deprivation schedule was out of the question with these Ss, one very relevant variable (i.e., "drive") was not constant and so the test can be regarded only as a very rough one.

Tredgold (3), in discussing the "mental and nervous condition" of defectives, notes with respect to all levels of deficiency a lack of facility in discriminating

geometrical forms. A second purpose of the present study was to compare the abilities of high- and low-grade defectives in the learning of a simple geometrical form discrimination problem.

METHOD

Apparatus. Two cube-shaped boxes, measuring 3¾ in. on each edge, were utilized. The boxes were open on one side and were painted flat black. On one of the surfaces adjacent to the open end, a 3 x 3 in. white card was mounted. The card on one box contained a black equilateral triangle measuring ⅜ in. on a side; an identical figure in inverted position was on the card mounted on the second box.

Small peanuts of the Spanish variety were used for food reward. The nuts were placed in very small paper cups to facilitate handling.

Subjects. The Ss were 44 males from the Tennessee Clover Bottom Home, a residential institution for mental defectives. For each of the Ss there was available an IQ score obtained on the Stanford-Binet (Form L) or a Binet IQ equivalent based on the Wechsler. Twenty of these Ss had IQ's below 50, whereas 24 had IQ's above 50; these will be referred to, respectively, as the "low IQ" and "high IQ"

[1] This research was supported by grants from the National Institute of Mental Health and the Tennessee State Department of Mental Health. Reprinted by permission from *American Journal of Mental Deficiency*, 1955, *60*, 380–384.

groups.[2] Half of each IQ group was assigned at random to a "low reward" group, the other half constituting the "high reward" group. Table 1 summarizes the composition of the four treatment groups.

Procedure. Each S was run individually. The S and E were seated on opposite sides of a table which contained the two boxes placed side by side with the stimuli facing S and a supply of peanuts. The S was first shown the boxes, his attention being directed by E to the pictures on them. It was explained that E would hide peanuts under one of the pictures (i.e., boxes) and that the nuts would always be

TABLE 1 · EXPERIMENTAL DESIGN

| IQ groups | Reward groups | |
	low	high
Low	N = 10	N = 10
High	N = 12	N = 12

under the same picture. The left-right relationship of the boxes was then reversed and S was told that sometimes the boxes would be in one position, sometimes in the other, and that each time the boxes were presented, his task would be to try to find the peanuts by lifting one of the boxes.

Before each presentation, S's view of the boxes was blocked by a movable shield and the position of the boxes was changed several times. The boxes were presented 48 times, each presentation constituting a trial. When S made a correct choice, he was allowed to eat the food re-

2 Means and sigmas for the Binet IQ distributions of the two IQ groups were not computed, because: (1) six scores in the low group were reported simply as "below 30"; and (2) several of the measures used were transformed Wechsler scores. The low IQ group had a median measure of 36; the median for the high IQ group was 56.5.

ward; when an incorrect choice was made, S was not allowed to lift the correct box, thus being deprived of the reward. The position of the boxes was varied in a prearranged, non-alternating fashion. For half the Ss in each of the four sub-groups, the upright triangle was arbitrarily designated as the "correct" stimulus, while for the other half the inverted triangle was "correct." Each of the authors ran half the Ss in the various treatment groups.

In all other respects, every S was given the same treatment, with the exception of the amount of reward obtained. As a result of each correct response, Ss in the low reward group received one peanut, whereas Ss in the high reward group received four peanuts.

Since an attempt to control for time of food deprivation did not appear feasible, Ss in the various sub-groups were run in a quasi-random order, the assumption being made that there was no systematic difference among the groups in length of time between the previous meal and the testing session. The Ss were run during the morning and afternoon hours, with times of food deprivation ranging from about one to four hours.

Statistical Design and Predictions. The 48 trials were divided into eight blocks of six trials each. A four-dimensional analysis of variance design (2) was utilized, the criterion measure being the number of correct choices made by S in each trial block. The main effects involved in the design were as follows: (1) low vs. high reward; (2) low vs. high IQ; (3) trial blocks; and (4) experimenters. The latter two effects were taken into account in order to increase the precision of the analysis. A 5 per cent coefficient of risk was adopted for all statistical tests.

The following predictions were

made: (1) the high reward group would surpass the low reward group in performance; and (2) the performance of the high IQ group would exceed that of the low IQ group.

RESULTS

Table 2 presents the means and sigmas for the main effects involving magnitude of reward and IQ level.

It will be noted that, on the average, the low reward group slightly exceeded the high reward group in perform-

TABLE 2 · NUMBER OF CORRECT CHOICES IN 48 TRIALS—MEANS AND SIGMAS FOR THE REWARD AND IQ GROUPS

Measure	Reward		IQ	
	Low	High	Low	High
M	31.41	39.27	27.10	33.96
S.D.	9.75	8.68	8.28	18.01
N	22	22	20	24

ance, while the high IQ Ss surpassed the low IQ Ss.

Table 3 summarizes the pertinent results from the analysis of variance.

As indicated in Table 3, the IQ difference, which was in the expected direction, was significant at the .05 level.

The reward × experimenter interaction, significant at the .05 level, resulted from the fact that for one experimenter, the high reward group exceeded the low reward group in performance, whereas for the other experimenter, the reverse relationship held between the two reward groups. A comparable set of relationships existed with respect to the groups run by the two experimenters; that is, in the high reward group, Ss run by one experimenter exceeded Ss run by the second experimenter, whereas the reverse relationship held within the low reward group.

Cancelling effects stemming from these differences resulted in there being no significant main effect involving either amount of reward or experimenter.

The trial block effect was significant at the .01 level, reflecting the fact that, for

TABLE 3 · SUMMARY OF ANALYSIS OF VARIANCE APPLIED TO THE REWARD x IQ x EXPERIMENTER x TRIAL BLOCK DATA†

Source	df	MS	F
Between Ss	43		
Reward	1	1.78	<1.00
IQ	1	64.14	6.85*
Experimenter	1	9.89	1.06
Reward x experimenter	1	47.27	5.04*
Error (b)	36	9.37	
Within Ss	308		
Trial block	7	9.16	8.25**
Trial block x IQ	7	6.63	5.97**
Error (w)	252	1.11	
Total	351		

† The interaction effects not significant at the .05 level are omitted.
* Significant at the .05 level.
** Significant at the .01 level.

the 44 Ss as a group, performance changed from block to block. (The average performance increased with each successive block, with the exception of one very slight inversion between blocks 3 and 4.) The trial block × IQ interaction, significant at the .01 level, indicates that the performance curves of the two IQ groups differed in shape. The differential patterns of the IQ groups are shown graphically in Figure 1.

The quadruple interaction, the four triple interactions, and the remaining four double interactions were not significant.

DISCUSSION

The first prediction—that the high reward group would be superior to the low reward group—was not upheld. Since

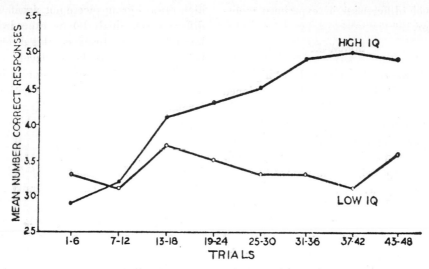

Figure 1. Performance curves for the two I.Q. groups.

the time of food deprivation was not constant for the various Ss and since no S was more than about four hours hungry, the present experiment cannot be considered a crucial test of the relevance of magnitude of food reward to simple discrimination learning in defectives. The possibility exists that with a constant and large degree of deprivation for each S, a significant difference in the predicted direction might have been obtained. One must also consider the possibility that the difference between one and four peanuts per correct choice would be of no import for this group of Ss, whatever the circumstances characterizing the learning situation.

The results confirmed the second prediction—that the high IQ group would exceed the low IQ group in performance. As the curves in Figure 1 indicate, the superiority of the high IQ Ss clearly prevailed from the third trial block throughout the remaining trials. It will be noted that, in the seventh block of trials, the low IQ Ss as a group were performing at a level barely exceeding chance. The lack of

learning in the low IQ group suggests the following questions: (1) how many trials in a task of this nature would be necessary before individuals with IQ's below 50 could succeed in performing at a level well above chance, and (2) what techniques could be utilized to speed up simple discrimination learning in such individuals? Further studies designed to attack these problems are now in progress.

As noted previously, the high reward group exceeded the low reward group in performance in the case of one experimenter, while the reverse was true for Ss run by the second experimenter. These relationships were responsible for the significant reward × experimenter interaction. Such an effect suggests the presence of inter- and/or intra-experimenter inconsistencies in the handling of the two reward groups. This finding is of some interest, since it illustrates the potency of the experimenter variable in discrimination learning studies, and also indicates that defective Ss are not insensitive to such differences in experimenter behavior.

SUMMARY

Twenty "low IQ" and 24 "high IQ" mental defectives were randomly assigned to a "low reward" and a "high reward" group. Each S was given 48 trials on a task requiring a discrimination between a triangle and an inverted triangle. The low reward Ss obtained one peanut for each correct response, whereas the high reward Ss received four peanuts. The authors each ran half the Ss in the various subgroups. A four-dimensional analysis of variance design was used to analyze the data, the criterion measure being number of correct choices made in each block of six trials.

The performances of the low and high reward groups were not significantly different. The high IQ Ss exceeded the low IQ Ss in performance, this difference being significant at the .05 level. An IQ $\times$ trial block interaction, significant at the .01 level, reflected the differential performance patterns of the two IQ groups.

REFERENCES

1. Hull, C. L. *Essentials of behavior.* New Haven: Yale University Press, 1951.
2. Lindquist, E. F. *Design and analysis of experiments in psychology and education.* Boston: Houghton Mifflin, 1953.
3. Tredgold, A. F. *Mental deficiency.* (7th Ed.) London: Bailliere, Tindall, & Cox, (reprinted) 1949.

MEMORY FACTORS IN PERFORMANCE | 16

In a sense, the study of all learning is the study of memory, for it would be impossible for a subject to respond with consistent correctness at the end of training were it not that the effects of previous training accrue over time or trials. It may be said that when a subject comes to perform correctly trial after trial, it is because he "remembers" the rewarding effects of having performed in certain ways in the past. When we speak of memory in this way, it becomes apparent that memory is a function of all of those experiential circumstances that tend to influence performance, such as number of previous trials, similarity of the stimuli to be "remembered," and level of motivation. But there is an operational difference between the kind of memory we speak of above and memory as dealt with in this section.

In the situations we have mentioned, all the stimuli necessary to make a correct discriminative response are present at the time the response is made; that is to say, the stimuli are present "out there" in the stimulus settings or the stimulus arrangements. For example, in a red-green simultaneous discrimination learning situation, the positive stimulus, say red, is always present on every trial. Red is a part of the experimentally controlled stimulus situation; the subject merely has to approach red to be rewarded. Similarly, in the successive discrimination learning situation, the red or the green is present on any given trial, and the subject must make one response to the red stimulus present and another to the green stimulus.

Contrast these circumstances with a situation in which there are two identical doors present on the far wall of a room. Suppose a child is sitting with two experimenters in this room. One experimenter gets up and walks out through one of the doors. The other holds the child in his seat for 5 minutes, after which time the child is free to follow the first experimenter out through the same door. If the child is rewarded for using the same door as the first observer and nonrewarded for using the other, his "delayed reaction" or memory-mediated behavior may be studied. If the child can learn to use the same door consistently, it may be said that he "remembers" for the delay period what he saw previously. In this general way, the "memory" of the subject may be studied. The difference between this type of situation and the discrimination situations described previously is that here the stimuli pertinent to making correct responses are not present *at the time the response is made.* That is to say, after the first experimenter walks through the door to the other side, the two doors look the same again. There are no differential cues. The stimuli necessary to making the correct discriminative response are no longer "out there"—they reside in the subject. We speak of these experiential residues of past experience as "stimulus traces" or "memories." In a sense they are discriminative stimuli "from within" the organism.

Walter S. Hunter, the author of the first section, pioneered the experimental study of such memorial processes in animals and children. He described the delayed reaction process as follows (Hunter, 1913, p. 73): "By applying the term 'ideas' to these cues, I mean that they are similar to the memory idea of human experience so far as *function* and *mechanism* are concerned. They are the residual effects of sensory stimuli which are retained and which may be subsequently reexcited. The revival, moreover, is selective and adaptive to the solution of a definite problem, and when aroused they function successfully as a necessary substitute for a definite component of the objective stimulus aspect of the problem."

It is of interest to note that Martin has recently (1960) asserted that child development and child psychology are only lately beginning to redis-cover the mind of the child, the mind having lain more or less dormant at the hands of the behavioristically inclined American psychology of the twenti-eth century. It is a tribute to Walter S. Hunter that in an important sense the mind of the child was never really lost. Hunter's work on memorial proc-esses and the antecedent conditions that influence these processes spanned the years from about 1912 to 1948. In his work, he was not content, however, to assert merely that the child had a mind, but rather wished to specify opera-tionally the meaning of the concept, and to discover the mediating behavioral processes ("functions and mechanisms") that the term represents.

The first selection in this section, that of Hunter on the delayed re-action procedure with children, indicates that Hunter was interested in memory processes from the standpoint of comparative psychology. He was curious to determine the memory limits of various species when tested under similar conditions. For that purpose, he used analogous experimental set-ups (1913) for different species, simply altering the size of the experimental apparatus to conform with the relative size of the organism studied. His emphasis, as may be seen in the selection included here, was on the perform-ance *limit* of the subject under delay conditions. It is of interest to note that Hunter was always alert to the mediating functions that helped his sub-jects bridge the gap between the stimulating circumstance (observation of the baiting of the box) and the execution of the response.

The second selection, by Spiker, elaborates upon one of those media-tional mechanisms by which subjects may "bridge the gap" or remember which of the discriminative stimuli has been baited. In this study, Spiker com-pared the learning progress of two groups of subjects, one of which had been given training involving the learning of distinctive names for the discrimi-native stimuli, prior to the delayed reaction procedure. The control group was simply provided with comparable discriminative pretraining, without learning such distinctive names. As was expected, the subjects given the verbal pretraining performed better in the subsequent delayed reaction condition than did the control group. Thus it may be concluded that the possession of distinctive mediational responses for the to-be-discriminated stimuli facilitates the subjects' endurance of the delay period without loss in correct perform-ance.

It should be noted here that Spiker's technique in the above study in-volves the combining of the traditional delayed-reaction "test" with modern discrimination learning procedures. That is, Spiker's second or transfer task is basically a discrimination learning procedure involving the simultaneous presentation of different stimuli to which differential responses must be learned. The introduction of delay into such a situation enables the study of effects of delay on discrimination learning. In most of Hunter's experiments, interest was in the limits of delay *once the discrimination had already been learned.* For example, he would first train an animal to go to whichever one of three windows was lit (lighted window the positive stimulus). Once the animal had learned this discrimination and was performing correctly, *then* delay was introduced into the task. It is quite clear, particularly when cross-species comparisons are made, that it is necessary that precisely the same experimental conditions be used in the testing of both species. It is conceivable that a given type of animal may be able to perform in delayed reaction situations, but only after the initial discrimination is learned, and that the same animal would not be able to respond correctly if delay is combined with a discrimination learning procedure.

The last selection in this section is concerned with double alternation learning in children. In this type of situation, the learning subject can perform correctly only by remembering to which stimulus he responded on the last or previous trial. It is like the delayed reaction procedure in that all of the stimuli necessary to making a correct response are not "out there." Some representation or vestige of the subject's last trial performance must be added to the external stimuli in order for a correct response to occur, for the double alternation procedure necessitates that the subject go twice to the left, then twice to the right, then twice to the left, and so on.

Mediational processes in general seem to function importantly in the articulate learning organism. Children are particularly suitable subjects for the study of mediational and memory processes. There is obviously a great deal more information to be learned in this area, information on the processes that probably distinguish man from animal more than any other differential set of characteristics.

REFERENCES

HUNTER, W. S.   The delayed reaction in animals and children. *Behav. Monogr.,* 1913, 2, No. 1, 1–86.

MARTIN, W. E.   Rediscovering the mind of the child: a significant trend in child development. *Merrill Palmer Quart.,* 1960, 6, 67–76.

THE DELAYED REACTION IN A CHILD

WALTER S. HUNTER

INTRODUCTION

THE PRESENT PAPER derives its chief significance from the fact that the child tested did not possess vocal language and probably not gesture language either.

In the work with the delayed reaction on children previously published,[1] five subjects were used: M., 8 years, Hd., L., and H., each 6 years, and F., 2½ years. All of these children possessed vocal language. M. received 38 trials on delays; Hd., 46 trials; H., 15 trials; L., 41 trials. All of them succeeded with delays as great as 25 minutes. There was some indication that the children first encountered particular difficulty in the intervals from 4–6 secs. The child F. received 507 trials on delays. Her maximal delay was 50 secs. The periods of greatest difficulty were at 5 secs., 7 secs., 10 secs., 15 secs., 30 secs., and 40 secs. Although F. was given 45 trials on the one-minute delay and failed, it is possible that more prolonged training would have enabled her to master the interval.

When the present tests were begun, the writer hoped to secure subjects who would fill in the great gap between the child F. and the older children. Success has not attended these efforts mainly because of a lack of convenient material. One three-year-old child was tested, but the data are of so little value that they will not be presented. The second and fundamental purpose of this study was, however, to study the delayed reaction in a child too young to possess vocal language. This is of particular importance because of Watson's insistence that the delayed reaction, if solved by internal factors other than orientation, must be solved by vocal language.

THE SUBJECT TESTED

The subject of these tests was the writer's daughter, Thayer, thirteen to sixteen months of age from first to last of the experimentation. She was a normal, healthy child physically—a little slow perhaps on the behavior side, due to the lack of the constant attention that many children receive. She learned to walk alone rather suddenly at about 15 months; and by 16 months, she could indicate with a little certainty her eyes, ears, nose and mouth. When 13 months old, she could 'throw a kiss' and wave 'bye-bye.' Even before this, as early as the tenth month, she swayed and waved her arms to music. These observations are presented as a sample of her best accomplishments. She had no vocal language. She made many sounds, some of which were in response to definite stimuli; but in no case did she use the sounds spontaneously and in no case did she use them as symbols. Her equipment was not large in the first place, and what there was was purely of a stimulus-response nature. During the period covered by the experimentation, the following vocal behavior was present:

[1] Hunter, Walter S., "The Delayed Reaction in Animals and Children," *Behav. Monogr.,* 1913, 2, No. 1, pp. 52–62.

Reprinted by permission from *Psychological Review*, 1917, *24,* 74–87.

'Dăddy' she said whenever a distant door was heard and I was away, or when she heard me coming up the steps. 'Whĭtte' came in response to the striking of the clock or the ringing of the door bell. She could say 'bōōb-bōōb' for the dog; 'dăy-dăy' for the duck; 'm-m-m' for the cow; a funny noise for the donkey; and 'y-gŏb, y-gŏb' for the turkey. These were in response to the specific questions, "What does the dog say?" etc. Some of these she got mixed up and later forgot all but the duck, the turkey, and the cow. In addition to these vocal responses there occurred only the more conventional baby noises.

One gesture might possibly be termed language, viz., raising her arms to be taken up. It is impossible to say, however, that this was not in response to present stimuli. It is also impossible to say with any certainty whether or not the child used a vocal cry specifically "to attract attention" to her needs. I have no evidence to indicate that such was the case. Experimentation was purposely stopped before the first signs of language (in the conventional sense) appeared.

APPARATUS AND METHOD

The apparatus used is shown in Fig. 1. It consists of three boxes placed upon a stand whose top is 6 inches above the floor. Each box is approximately 3 inches deep, 4 inches wide, and 5 inches long. Each is covered by a hinged top. The apparatus was wired for electric lights, but these were never used. Another type of apparatus more nearly approximating that used with children in the previous work was constructed. It, however, proved unsuited to Thayer and was used only with the three-year-old child.

The only features necessary to secure in devising an apparatus for the delayed reaction are these: (1) It must be adapted to the size of the subject and to its mode of response—walking, reaching, swimming or flying. (2) It must provide a means for presenting a stimulus in one of several places. (3) These stimulus positions must be equally accessible to the response. And (4), the stimulus and the method employed should be such as to present no differential cues to the subject during the intervals of delay. These requirements, although rigid, are simple and can be met for practically all organisms. I am therefore unable to agree with Professor Yerkes when he says [2] that the multiple choice method of studying ideational behavior is superior to all others in: (1) applicability to a wide range of conditions; (2) susceptibility to standardization; (3) quantitative nature of results; and (4) intelligibility of data acquired. Nor can I acquiesce in the claim that "It is already obvious that the method enables us to compare, as has never before been possible, the responses to certain standard situations, of human and infrahuman, normal and abnormal, mature and immature subjects." Both the multiple choice and the delayed reaction methods are valuable for the sutdy of human and animal behavior; but they are applicable, I think, to very different problems.

In the experiments reported in this paper, the following method was used. Thayer sat in front of the apparatus and the stimulus object was placed in her hand. A great variety of things were used for stimuli: dolls, keys, rattles, shoe-buttoners, small books, etc. Every effort was made to keep up the child's interest.

[2] Yerkes, Robt. M., "Methods of Studying Ideational Behavior in Man and Other Animals," Psychol. Bull., 1915, 12, 330-331.

Occasionally two different stimulus objects were used in the course of the day's work. Such methods are necessary if a child of this age is even to approximate to the vigor with which a hungry animal attacks its problem. The stimulus object was taken away from the child almost as soon as she received it and was placed in one of the boxes. The lid of the box was left open and Thayer was pushed over (or permitted to lean over) and made to look into the box. Often she tried to reach in and get the stimulus; but in every case, her hand was withdrawn and she was raised back to an upright position. The lid of the box was now closed. Save for a few instances to be mentioned in due time, the subject was distracted during the interval of delay. Distraction took either one of several forms: (1) I might place my hands over her eyes and rock her body back and forth from right to left. (2) She might be stood up, turned around with her back to the apparatus, kept there awhile and then put down. (3) I might cause her to turn her head by speaking to her. She would remain in this position and imitate animals for me (as described above under vocal habits) as long as any delays here used required. About 2 secs. before the end of the delay period, her body was straightened around and she sat facing the middle box, b, entirely free from contact with me. (She almost never looked back at me; and when she did, she paid no further attention to the problem. I never spoke to her during the delay. These facts together with the child's inability to reach delays of a minute or more, indicate that she was not deriving cues from the experimenter.) Thayer was now left to her own devices until she opened the box containing the stimulus object. In all but a few cases, she began to hunt for the stimulus as soon as she was straightened around. Time was taken with an ordinary watch and was counted from the moment the box lid was closed until the subject made some movement toward one of the boxes. In the records particular attention was given to the orientation at the time of response and to the behavior during the delay. A reaction was counted wrong if the child opened any box save that containing the stimulus.

EXPERIMENTAL RESULTS

In this experiment there was no period of learning the association between the stimulus object and the three boxes. Seeking for objects that had disappeared was already a part of the subject's behavior equipment. I noticed as early as her eleventh month that if I showed her a toy and then hid it behind something, she would immediately reach or creep toward the spot. I have no doubt, however, that this type of reaction occurred earlier. The present test was more complex than this in that the toy might be in either one of *three* different places.

I quote the following from my diary records indicating the results at the very beginning of the work. "Date, 10–23–15. Trial 1. Toys put in middle box and door shut. (All this done by Thayer on her own initiative.) I now put my hands over her eyes and shook her head and whole body playfully but thoroughly. No orientation of upper part of body retained. 13 secs. delay from time she straightened up after closing box until she reached toward b. She reacted correctly, straight to middle box."

"Trial 2. Toys put in right box, a. 12 secs. delay with distraction as above. Reacted correctly."

"Trial 3. Same as No. 2, 13 secs. delay. O. K."

"Trial 4. Thayer preferred right or middle box. I had her put toys in left one, c. Distractoin by standing her up and turning her to me. 17 secs. O. K."

"Trial 5. Middle box used. Baby tired of test. 14 secs. Distracted as in first trial. Reaction wrong."

In these tests made on the first day, Thayer missed one of five or 20 percent. The delays ranged from 12–17 secs. Distraction was always used. The same orientation at the moment of release was held for all, viz., orientation to b. These long delays were very startling and held out a promise of very rapid development through training. This was the last of October. A longer stage of delay was not successfully reached and consistently maintained until after Christmas. This fact is shown in Table 1.

TABLE 1

Delay in secs.	Correct trs.	Wrong trs.	Percent. correct
3	3	0	100
4	1	0	100
5	6	0	100
6	3	0	100
7	2	2	50
8	4	2	66
9	4	1	80
10	11	4	73
11	6	2	75
12	6	3	66
13	5	0	100
14	6	8	42
15	13	11	54
16	5	5	50
17	4	3	57
18	2	1	66
19	1	1	50
20	9	15	37
21	1	5	16
22	2	3	40
23	1	0	100
24	2	3	40
25	0	3	0
26	1	1	50
30	3	5	37
35	2	0	100

This table shows the size of the delays and the number of correct and incorrect reactions made. All trials given the subject through December 2 are included. The statement is not chronological. The reason the intervals of delay increase so gradually is that within a few seconds variation, Thayer herself determined when she would begin the reaction. All I could do was to place her facing the apparatus and await results. Table 2

TABLE 2

Delays	Percent correct
3–7 secs.	88
8–12 "	72
13–17 "	55
18–22 "	37
23–35 "	44

groups the delays into five classes which may be called the 5 sec., 10 sec., 15 sec., 20 sec., and 25 sec. intervals. The 10 sec. interval may be regarded as mastered, but no higher interval. (This is understated, as will be indicated below.) Table 3

TABLE 3

Delay in secs.	Right	Wrong	Percent right
5	4	0	77
6	0	1	
7	3	1	
8	2	0	
9	1	0	82
10	10	3	
12	2	0	
15	25	8	75
20	24	10	70
25	2	2	50

gives data gathered from January 2 through January 10. An interval of one month had elapsed during which no tests were made. A comparison of Tables 2 and 3 indicates a marked gain in ability to deal with the 15 sec. and 20 sec. intervals. In Table 3 the 15 sec. interval can be regarded as mastered and the 20 sec. interval as practically perfected.

The tables just given are valuable in showing just what the child actually did in the work *as a whole*. Her achievements are much obscured, however, by such a presentation, inasmuch as poor incentives and position factors frequently dragged her total percentages down. Here, *e.g.*, is the diary record for the ten tests made November 12. (Data included in Table 1.) The delays were all above 20 secs., and 7 trials of 10 were successful. Where the word 'distracted' is used, Thayer's eyes were covered and her body was shaken back and forth; or she was induced to look up at the ceiling and listen to me count while I waved her arms about. The letters in the last column indicate to which box the reactions were made. In every case the subject was oriented, body and face, to *b* at the moment of reaction. This day's record is better than any that preceded it. Two weeks previously, she had succeeded with intervals between 11 and 19 secs. But during those two weeks that followed, she was largely the victim of position habits. The day following the above diary record, she again fell back into posi-

TABLE 4

Box with toy	Delay		Behavior
a	20 secs.	distracted	a
a	22 "	"	bca
c	21 "	"	abc
c	20 "	"	c
b	35 "	"	b*
a	22 "	stood her up	a
c	26 "	distracted	c
b	20 "	"	b
c	22 "	"	c
c	24 "	stood her up	ac

* Very slow and 'careful.'

tion habits. I kept holding pretty well to 15 and 20 sec. delays with an occasional one at 30 secs. The task was too difficult, however, and she shifted from one position habit to another.

Work was discontinued for a month. By the end of this time, the following changes had occurred in the child: (1) old position habits were temporarily lost; (2) new interest was taken in the problem; (3) greatly increased control of her own body appeared—shown mostly in walking and balancing; and (4) a stronger aversion to being held during distractions had developed.

Table 3 above summarizes the results for this period. It also understates the subject's behavior. On January 5, she made the entire day—9 trials—at 15 secs. without error and with no correlation between orientation and direction of response. She now fell into a position habit, but recovered and made 20 secs. delay correctly 5 times in succession, again with no dependence upon orientation.

Thayer's best delays may be recorded as 20–24 secs. The child F. used in the earlier work reached a delay of 50 secs. F.'s record would probably have been higher had she been tested with a method similar to the one here employed, *i.e.*, a method where the satisfaction is derived from the stimulus object and not from an associated food supply. The gap between Thayer and F. would undoubtedly be bridged in a gradual manner by a continuous increase in periods of delay. Greatest interest now centers on children of less than one year of age. How early ontogenetically does this ability to react independently of orientation appear?

It remains to comment upon the position habits and errors that appeared. The frequency with which these stereotyped forms of response interfered with the work and *the fact that the child if permitted would watch the box containing the toy during the interval of delay*, indicate the great importance of kinaesthesis in the response. Position habits occurred with each of the three boxes so that during a particular position habit period Thayer always chose a particular box first. I made no tests where the choice lay between two boxes as opposed to three. Time is limited both by the speed with which a baby grows and even more by the necessity of staying within the limits of the child's interest and patience. Table 5

TABLE 5

Order of response				Total reactions made
Order of response	cba	cab	ca	cb	
No. made	17	13	8	28	66
Order of response	abc	acb	ac	ab	
No. made	6	3	2	11	22
Order of response	bac	bca	bc	ba	
No. made	7	3	7	9	26

analyses all incorrect responses and gives the relative number of times the subject followed the different possible orders. Thus when an error was made, 17 times Thayer first opened *c*, then *b* and then *a*. The table shows that three times more errors were made beginning with box *c* than with any of the others. When the subject opened *c* first, she opened *b* next 45 times out of 66, or 68 percent of the time. When she opened *a* first, she chose *b* next 15 times out of 20, or 75 percent of the time. When *b* was opened first, *a* was chosen next 16 times out of 26, or 61 percent of the time. In other words, when the

reaction began at the end of the apparatus the tendency was to take the boxes in order until the solution was reached. Only six times in all did the subject go to the same box twice in the same trial. These cases are distributed throughout the entire period of experimentation. The following is a record of the order of the boxes chosen:

> cccab
> bcba
> cacb
> cacb
> bcba
> cacacab.

Of the 114 errors recorded in Table 5, 32 (28 percent) occurred when the box containing the toy on the last previous trial was re-selected. Inasmuch, however, as such a mode of response often led to success the percentage is very low. This form of behavior as well as that of the six instances above given is apparently far less current in the present subject than in Hamilton's dog.[3] The later study made by Hamilton [4] reports the case of a child 26 months old. Out of 38 trials, 60.53 percent (34.21 plus 26.32) of the reactions involved the type of behavior given just above as occurring but 6 times during the present work, 264 trials. Since Thayer missed 120 trials (66 plus 22 plus 26 plus 6), her percentage is 5. This extreme difference in behavior is undoubtedly due to one or both of the following causes: (1) the guiding influence of the absent stimulus in the delayed reaction tests; and (2) the fact that only three boxes were

---

[3] Hamilton, G. V. T., "An Experimental Study of an Unusual Type of Reaction in a Dog," *J. of Comp. Neur. Psychol.*, 1907, *17*, 329–341.
[4] Hamilton, G. V. T., "A Study of Trial and Error Reactions in Mammals," *J. of Animal Behav.*, 1911, *1*, p. 51.

used here as opposed to Hamilton's four. It would be very interesting to determine whether a variation in the number of boxes would result in a corresponding variation in 'reaction tendencies.' If this were true, the possibility of phyletic correlations would be pushed still farther back than appears in Hamilton's work.

It will be valuable to put beside this work, similar data gathered on rats and raccoons in 1910–1912. The records here given are representative and include only tests made with three boxes on periods of delay. The following indicates the maximal delays attained by the animals whose records are used in this paper:

Rat No. 9, maximal delay 10 secs.
Rat No. 2,   "   "   1 "
Dog Blackie,   "   "   5 mins.
Raccoon Bob, "   "   30–35 secs.[5]

Table 6 summarizes the errors made by these four animals. It includes for comparative purposes the data for Thayer. The raccoon's records include delays from 1 sec. through 20 secs.; those for the dog, from 1 sec. through 7 secs.; those for rat No. 9, from the third stage of delay (turning light off just as animal was released) through 7 secs.; and those for rat No. 2, from the third stage of delay through 1 sec. I have included the data represented by 'percent of B to C' be-

cause Hamilton's percentages are based only on those reactions that included all the boxes of his apparatus. The column '3 place errors' includes the trials that involved a testing by the animal of each of the three boxes. By 'persistent errors,' I mean all errors that involve trying any one box more than once each trial. These were all 3 place errors. This column corresponds to reactions belonging to Hamilton's types D and E.

The only one of Hamilton's human subjects whose percentage in D plus E rose above 6.45 percent was a 26-months-old child whose grade was 60.53 percent. Of the animals below man, the lowest grade (best record) was 22.58 percent made by a dog. Hamilton's results and my own here presented indicate a marked difference between man and other animals in reactive tendencies, i.e., in forms of kinaesthetic habits. (There is, I think, no clear evidence as yet that the tendencies are instinctive.) Whether this is caused by phyletic factors, or by experimental and environmental conditions is a matter undecided. My infra-human animals are essentially on a par. And so I think are Hamilton's in that practically all of them made their highest percentages in what I here term 'persistent errors.' (His curves would be quite different, naturally, if D and E were combined and if B and C were combined.[6]) Much work is undoubtedly

[5] These data are taken from my "Delayed Reaction," pp. 35–38.

[6] Hamilton, op. cit., 1911, p. 54.

TABLE 6

Animal	No. of trs.	Total no. of errors A	3 Place errors B	Persistent errors C	Percent. of A to C	Percent. of B to C
Thayer	264	120	54	6	5	11
Raccoon, Bob	720	209	78	29	13	37
Dog, Blackie	570	127	75	25	19	33
Rat No. 9	575	144	42	13	9	30
Rat No. 2	345	152	69	47	32	60

needed to determine how minute a classification of reaction tendencies can be and still be significant for animal ability.

THEORETICAL CONSIDERATIONS

There is very little in the way of interpretative comments that I can add to what has already been said in other papers.[7] The delayed reaction problem can be solved at least in two ways:[8] (1) by the maintenance of bodily orientation in whole or in part during the interval of delay or by the chance recovery of the proper orientation just at the moment of release; and (2) by the use of some intra-organic factor which is *non*-observable by the experimenter. In the first method, the animal always responds in accordance with orientation; in the second, he does not. The cue used in the second method may or may not be retained in the focus of neural activity during the delay. It is highly improbable that such retention occurs under conditions of distraction. What

one has, then, is a system of processes or cues which 'stand for' certain differential responses as a result of association. These cues are susceptible to selective re-arousal and subsequent successful functioning in initiating responses. This is the condition which I have previously found in raccoons and in one child, F., 2½ years old. It is the condition here presented by Thayer, ages 13–16 months. This second method of solution which I am describing may be mediated by any type of intra-organic process which can be re-aroused without the presence of the external stimulus, toys as used in the present study. Inasmuch as kinaesthetic factors can be so aroused,[9] and inasmuch as they have been demonstrated to have great importance not only in animal reactions in general but in the delayed reaction in particular (position habits and maintenance of orientation), it is most probable that the intra-organic factors are kinaesthetic in nature. (The genetic relations of sensation, image and imageless thought are discussed in 'The Delayed Reaction,' pages cited.) In certain cases this type of process has its locus in the vocal organs with frequent resulting audible sounds. This we term vocal language as it occurs in normal human adults and in children of a certain development. In other cases the observance of the sounds and their accompanying behavior does not indicate that the organism uses either the sound or the parallel kinaesthetic as a substitute of the type above described. This is the situation in all animals that indulge in vocalization. But this intra-organic kinaesthetic factor may arise elsewhere than from the throat. Some part of the general bodily muscu-

---

[7] "Delayed Reaction," pp. 62–79 and Hunter, W. S., "A Reply to Some Criticisms of the Delayed Reaction," *J. of Phil. Psychol.*, & c., 1915, *12*, 38–41. See also Watson, J. B., "Behavior," 1914, pp. 224–227; and Ch. X.

[8] If there is a present determining external stimulus, the reaction is not delayed.

A. C. Walton, "The Influence of Diverting Stimuli during Delayed Reaction in Dogs," *J. Animal Behav.*, 1915, *5*, 259–291, has shown that dogs can react successfully to three boxes after delays of 30 secs. when they have been distracted during the intervals. This is better than I had been able to show. Before deciding that the dog belongs in a class with the raccoons— as perhaps he does— it will be necessary to have data on the animals' orientations at the moment of response. This Walton unfortunately does not give. The only facts that we have are that the animals did not maintain their orientations during the delays. If it should appear that the animal is able to recover the proper orientation in a large number of instances after a thorough distraction and can then react correctly, this fact will itself be of great significance and will require careful analysis.

[9] See the all too brief comments in my review of Calkins' "First Book in Psychology," *Psychol. Bull.*, 1915, *12*, 189–190.

lature may be the origin. Here, when the behavior is overt, we speak of gesture language. When it is not overt, the delayed reaction method has proved serviceable in detecting it. Language is ideational in function. So also are the cues which function in many responses of raccoons, of children and possibly of dogs (Walton). The resulting conception of these cues is that they are kinæsthetic sensory ideas. This line of reasoning leads one to conclude that a true language non-vocal in character appears phylogenetically and ontogenetically prior to vocal language. Such language, although undoubtedly of great service to the individual in controlling his reactions, is of little social significance.

STIMULUS PRETRAINING AND SUBSEQUENT PERFORMANCE IN THE DELAYED REACTION EXPERIMENT

CHARLES C. SPIKER [1]

SEVERAL INVESTIGATORS have reported studies of the delayed reaction in children (1, 2, 6, 10, 11, 12, 14), although much remains to be done in discovering the relevant experimental variables and in specifying the theoretical significance of the delayed reaction experiment itself. One of the factors that has been suggested by Hunter (10, 11) and by Skalet (14) as influencing the correct performance of children in the delayed reaction experiment, as well as in determining the length of delay that can be tolerated by Ss without interfering with the correctness of

the performance, is the presence of symbolic or linguistic responses to represent the relevant stimulus features. Skalet reported that her child Ss could tolerate longer delays with stimuli for which the Ss had names (familiar animal forms) than for stimuli for which the Ss did not have names (geometrical figures). She concluded that the children's abilities to represent the animal forms with symbolic responses in some way facilitated recall following delay.

Although the writer is unaware of published studies of the relationship between stimulus similarity and the correctness of the delayed reaction or the length of delay that can be tolerated by S, this variable is undoubtedly relevant. In the extreme case, if identical stimuli

[1] The writer wishes to thank his research assistant, Miss Ruth B. Holton, for suggestions concerning experimental procedures and for aid in collecting the data.

Reprinted by permission of *Journal of Experimental Psychology*, 1956, 52, 107–111.

were used, S would have no basis at all for a correct response following the delay. It is conceivable that the animal forms which Skalet used were less similar than the nonsense figures, and therefore that the better performance with the former is due to stimulus distinctiveness rather than to possession of names.

The present experiment is concerned with a more direct test than Skalet's of the hypothesis that the possession by children of names for the stimuli leads to more correct choices following a delay period. In the present design, half the Ss are taught different names for two similar stimuli in a pretraining session, while the other half are given discriminative experience with the same stimuli but without learning names for them. All Ss are then run in a delayed reaction situation involving these stimuli. Since older Ss, even without pretraining, are more likely than younger Ss to invent names or other descriptive phrases for the stimuli, the prior learning of names should be relatively more effective for younger Ss than for older Ss. Accordingly, each experimental group consisted of a younger and an older subgroup in order to study the interaction between age and type of pretraining.

METHOD

Apparatus. The primary apparatus consisted of a round wooden disc, 18 in. in diameter, mounted on the shaft of an electric motor. Fastened to the top surface of the disc, one opposite the other, were two identical wooden boxes, 4 in. on each side, with hinged covers. The hinges were placed on the outsides of the boxes on the sides toward the center of the disc. The tops of the boxes were covered with a transparent acetate, under which the stimuli could be placed, and a wad of white cotton was put in the bottom of each box to prevent the rattling of the

rewards placed in the boxes. A normally open push-button microswitch was wired into the circuit of the motor so that the motor could be started or stopped by pressing or releasing the switch. A section of rubber garden hose was mounted on the outer rim of the disc in order to protect S from the rotating disc and to provide E with a smooth area to grasp in stopping the disc. The entire apparatus was covered with a heavy coat of flat black paint.

There were two stimuli, each consisting of a set of black-lined concentric circles placed on white backgrounds 4 in. square. One of the stimuli (S-7) had 7 concentric circles, the other (S-5) had only 5. The inner circle in each stimulus was ¾ in. in diameter; the outer circle, 3 in. The remaining circles were spaced equidistant between the outer and inner circles. Thus, the two stimuli differed in the number and density of concentric circles. Two additional pairs of the stimuli, identical to those described above, were used in the pretraining session.

Experimental design. The experiment was conducted in four distinct phases, all given to each S on the same day. In the first phase, the pretraining stage, the stimuli were presented two at a time and Ss in one group (Group N) were required to call S-5 by the name "five" and S-7 by the name "seven." The second group (Group D) was required to discriminate the stimuli by saying "same" when both stimuli were S-5 or S-7, and "different" when one stimulus was S-5 and the other S-7. In the second phase, E familiarized Ss with the delayed reaction experiment by putting an orange stimulus on one box and a blue stimulus on the other, baiting one of the boxes with a toy coin, spinning the disc briefly, and then asking S to find the coin. In the third phase, the test problem, the concentric circles were used as stimuli on the boxes, one box was baited each time, the disc was rotated rapidly for 25 sec., and S was then asked to find the coin. Finally, in a check phase, concentric circles were removed from the boxes, one of the boxes was baited, the disc was briefly rotated, and S was asked to find the coin. This last step was taken in order to control for the use of extraneous cues by S.

Subjects. The Ss were 54 children from the Iowa Child Welfare Research Station preschool laboratories. They were divided into two age groups; the younger group of 26 Ss ranging from 3 yr., 9 mo. to 4 yr., 9 mo.; the older group of 28, from 4 yr., 10 mo. to 5 yr., 6 mo. One-half of each age group was randomly assigned to Group N, the other half to Group D. Seven additional Ss were eliminated from the experiment following failure to learn the pretraining task in the 72 trials allowed. Of these, 4 were in Group N and 3 were in Group D.

Most of the Ss had previous experience in name-learning experiments and about 12 had previous experience in a delayed re-action experiment. In neither case, however, were the stimuli and the names of the present experiment used.

Procedure. The S was brought into the experimental room by a familiar E. The E lay out two pairs of the concentric circle stimuli on a table before S. Group N Ss were told that the name for S-5 was "five" and that the name for S-7 was "seven." The stimuli were then presented two at a time and S was informed that he could tell the difference between "seven" and "five" by the number of circles. The Ss were not urged to count, although a few Ss in both groups did count. Four different stimulus settings were used: in one, both stimuli were S-5; in a second, both were S-7; in a third, S-5 was on the left, S-7 was on the right; and in the fourth, S-7 was on the left, S-5 on the right. The stimuli were presented in a prearranged order such that in each successive block of four trials, each of the four settings appeared once. A trial was counted correct only if S named both stimuli correctly. Group D Ss were treated like those of Group N except that they were not told the names of the stimuli and their task was structured for them as saying "same" when both stimuli were S-5 or S-7, and "different" when one stimulus was S-5 and the other S-7. The stimuli were presented in the same order for Group D as for Group N. The Ss in both groups were continued in the first phase until they made correct responses on 12 consecutive trials, or until 72 trials had been

given. In the latter case they were eliminated from the experiment.

In the familiarization phase, S was taken to the apparatus described above. A 4-in. square piece of orange construction paper was placed on top of one of the two boxes, and a similar piece of blue paper was placed on the other. While S watched, E dropped a toy coin onto the wad of cotton in the bottom of one of the boxes and closed the lid. The E then asked S which box contained the coin. If S responded correctly, E immediately spun the disc rapidly and stopped it. The time required to spin and stop the disc was ordinarily about 1 sec. When the disc was stopped, S was asked to find the coin. This procedure was repeated with the orange and blue stimuli, in an irregular alternation, until S had made three consecutive correct responses.

Before beginning the test problem, S was told that he would now have an opportunity to win more toy coins, and that when he had won enough he would be able to buy a toy with them. The orange and blue stimuli were replaced with the concentric circles. Six trials were given to each S with the coin being placed in one of the two boxes in the order: S-5, S-7, S-7, S-5, S-7, and S-5. The E would bait the appropriate box for that trial and would then ask S to point to the baited box in order to assure that he had observed the baiting. Group N Ss were also asked to name the baited box. When S had responded correctly, E immediately spun the disc and kept it spinning for 25 sec. at a speed that made it impossible for S to follow the baited box visually. At the end of the 25-sec. period, E immediately stopped the disc and asked S to find the coin. The between-trial interval averaged approximately 1 min.

The check problem was given in order to determine whether or not S's delayed reaction was based on extraneous cues. The discriminal stimuli were removed from the boxes and S was given 6 trials with a delay of about 1 sec. as in the second phase. The Ss' choices were recorded on prepared sheets throughout the delayed reaction phases of the experiment. The Ss' verbalizations regarding the stimuli were recorded through-out the experiment.

RESULTS

Pretraining. The number of trials to the criterion of 12 consecutive correct responses was determined for each S. The means and SDs of these are presented in Table 1. It is apparent that both the younger and older Ss of Group D reached the criterion in fewer trials than did those of Group N. Despite sizable differences in the means, a treatment by levels analysis of variance failed to show significant differences in the main effects for age or pretraining or in their interaction for either the raw data or a square-root transformation of the raw data $(P > .10)$. With some caution, it may be assumed that the two pretraining groups had approximately equal experience with the stimuli during the pretraining task. In any event, all Ss had demonstrated discrimination between the stimuli at the same high response criterion.[2]

Only nine incorrect responses were made during the familiarization phase,

[2] Correlations obtained between the number of pretraining trials to criterion and the number of correct responses on the test suggest that even if the difference were significant, it could be safely disregarded for present purposes. The Pearson correlation coefficients for the various groups were: D—O, — .05; N—O, — .05; D—Y, — .27; and N—Y, .03. The correlation for all Ss combined was — .17.

and no S made more than two incorrect choices prior to reaching the criterion of three consecutive correct responses.

Test for extraneous cues. The mean number of correct choices in the six-trial check for extraneous cues is presented in Table 1 for each group. A mean of 3.0 is expected on the basis of chance alone. It is apparent that none of the four groups differs markedly from the expected mean and this observation is borne out statistically in a treatment-by-levels analysis of variance. None of the main or simple effects is significant at less than the 10% level. Thus, it seems safe to assume that Ss were unable to respond correctly, even with short delay, without the use of the discriminal cues on which they had received pretraining.

Test phase. Table 1 gives the means and SDs of the number of correct responses for the four groups during the critical test phase of the experiment. From this table, it is apparent that Group N, on the average, performs better than Group D; that the older Ss perform better than the younger Ss; and that the younger Ss in Group D perform considerably worse than Ss in any other subgroup. A treatment-by-levels analysis of these data is summarized in Table 2. The significant interaction of age and pretraining suggests the need for an examination of the simple effects. The difference between

TABLE 1 · MEANS AND SDs IN THE PRETRAINING, THE TEST PHASE, AND THE CHECK FOR EXTRANEOUS CUES

Group	N	PRETRAINING PHASE: TRIALS TO CRITERION		TEST PHASE: CORRECT CHOICES		EXTRANEOUS CUE CHECK: CORRECT CHOICES	
		Mean	SD	Mean	SD	Mean	SD
D—Young	13	20.8	21.2	2.92	1.40	2.85	1.28
D—Old	14	14.8	16.7	5.00	0.96	3.36	1.34
N—Young	13	25.7	17.8	4.77	1.01	3.23	1.17
N—Old	14	25.8	20.1	5.14	1.10	2.79	1.26

means for Group N and D was evaluated by a *t* test separately for the older and younger groups. For the older Ss, $t = .20$ and $P > .20$. For the younger Ss, *t* was 3.96, $P < .001$. Thus, it appears that the effectiveness of the name-learning was restricted primarily to the younger Ss.

Additional evidence for the relevance of names to the performance in the delayed reaction situation is provided by an examination of the records of Ss in Group D. The *E* recorded verbalizations of 8 Ss in this group who used discriminal names to refer to the concentric circles (e.g., "bigger one," "shiny one," "darker one," "wider one," etc.). The mean number of correct responses on the test for these Ss was 5.38 and the mean for the remaining 19 was 3.42. The value of *t* obtained was 3.15 with $P < .005$.

TABLE 2 · ANALYSIS OF VARIANCE OF THE NUMBER OF CORRECT CHOICES IN SIX-TRIAL TEST SESSION

Source	df	MS	F	P
Pretraining (P)	1	12.52	8.35	<.01
Age (A)	1	20.24	13.49	<.001
P × A	1	9.78	6.52	<.025
Within cells	50	1.50		
Total	53			

DISCUSSION

The results indicate clearly that the pretraining requiring Ss to learn names for the discriminal stimuli resulted in a performance in the delayed reaction test that was superior to the performance of Ss who had pretraining that involved only discrimination of the stimuli. The superiority of Group N appears due primarily to the younger Ss, since the older Ss in the two pretraining groups did not differ markedly. This interaction of the pretraining with age levels may be attributed to the fact that older Ss of Group D were

more inclined to invent names for the stimuli than were the younger Ss. Six of the 8 Ss in Group *D* who spontaneously verbalized names for the stimuli were in the older age level. On the other hand, the experimentally introduced names provided the younger Ss of Group N with symbolic responses to the stimuli that they might not otherwise have attained.

There are two alternative, although not necessarily incompatible, explanations for these results. The first makes use of the hypothesis of acquired distinctiveness of cues (3, 8, 9, 13) which assumes that the learning of distinctive (verbal) responses to similar stimuli decreases the interstimulus generalization in subsequent learning of other discriminal responses. In the present experiment, the concentric circles were made functionally more dissimilar for Group N by virtue of the distinctive names that had been learned for them. According to this explanation, Skalet's (14) animal forms may have been more distinctive than the geometric figures *because* the children had names available.

Another explanation of the findings is offered by Skalet's suggestion that the symbolic responses of articulate organisms serve as substitutes for the absent crucial stimuli (e.g., "box 'seven' is baited"). During the delay period, S reproduces the name for the baited stimulus, and following the delay, the name serves to direct his choice. This hypothesis is rather well supported by the verbalizations of Ss in Group N during the test phase. Nine of the 27 Ss spontaneously verbalized the name of the baited box during delay periods, sometimes repeating the name several times during a single delay period. This verbalization was not observed for Ss in Group D. This hypothesis can also be used to account for the results of several experiments (*3, 4, 5, 7, 8, 9, 13*) in which was found that discrimination learning problems are learned more rapidly by *S*s who have had verbal pretraining with the relevant stimuli. In this case, the delay period that is presumed to be bridged by means of the names is the intertrial interval; that is to say, the names facilitate *S*'s recall of correct and incorrect stimulus-response sequences on previous trials.

SUMMARY

Fifty-four preschool *S*s were divided into two groups. One group was given training on a pair of stimuli that involved learning distinctive names for the stimuli. The other group was given discrimination training with the stimuli without being required to learn their names. Subsequently, *S*s were given a delayed reaction test involving the pretraining stimuli. The *S*s who had learned names made more correct choices of the baited stimuli following delay than did *S*s who had not learned names, although this difference was due primarily to the younger *S*s. The results were interpreted in terms of a hypothesis that the possession of verbal names for the stimuli permits *S* to produce a representation of the absent stimuli during the delay period.

REFERENCES

1. ALLEN, C. N.   Individual differences in delayed reaction of infants. *Arch. Psychol., N. Y.*, 1931, *19*, No. 127.

2. BUHLER, C.   *The first year of life.* New York: Day, 1930.

3. CANTOR, G. N.   The effects of three types of pretraining on discrimination learning in preschool children. *J. exp. Psychol.*, 1955, *49*, 339–342.

4. CANTOR, J. H.   Amount of pretraining as a factor in stimulus prediferentiation and performance set. *J. exp. Psychol.*, 1955, *50*, 180–184.

5. DYSINGER, D. W.   An investigation of stimulus pre-differentiation in a choice discrimination problem. Unpublished doctor's dissertation, State Univer. of Iowa, 1951.

6. EMERSON, L. L.   The effect of bodily orientation upon the young child's memory for position of objects. *Child Develpm.*, 1931, *2*, 125–142.

7. GAGNÉ, R. M., & BAKER, K. E.   Stimulus pre-differentiation as a factor in the transfer of training. *J. exp. Psychol.*, 1950, *40*, 430–451.

8. GERJUOY, I. R.   Discrimination learning as a function of the similarity of the stimulus names. Unpublished doctor's dissertation, State Univer. of Iowa, 1953.

9. GOSS, A. E.   Transfer as a function of the type and amount of preliminary experience with task stimuli. *J. exp. Psychol.*, 1953, *46*, 419–428.

10. HUNTER, W. S.   Delayed reaction in animals and children. *Behav. Monogr.*, 1913, *2*, No. 6. Pp. 86.

11. HUNTER, W. S.   Delayed reaction in a child. *Psychol. Rev.*, 1917, *24*, 75–87.

12. MILLER, N. E.   The perception of children: a genetic study employing the critical choice delayed reaction. *J. genet. Psychol.*, 1934, *44*, 321–339.

13. ROSSMAN, I. L., & GOSS, A. E.   The acquired distinctiveness of cues: the role of discriminative verbal responses in facilitating the acquisition of discriminative motor responses. *J. exp. Psychol.*, 1951, *42*, 173–182.

14. SKALET, M.   The significance of delayed reactions in young children. *Comp. psychol. Monogr.*, 1931, *7*. Pp. 82.

DOUBLE ALTERNATION BEHAVIOR

IN YOUNG CHILDREN

WALTER S. HUNTER

SUSAN CARSON BARTLETT

INTRODUCTION

SINCE HUNTER'S FIRST EXTENDED RE-PORT on the double alternation problem with rats (4), various additional studies have been made of the problem using rats, cats, dogs, raccoons, monkeys, and human Ss. Some of these investigations are listed in the references (2, 3, 4, 5, 6, 7, 8). For the purposes of the present paper, Geller-mann's investigation with children is the most important.

Gellermann (2) used a T-shaped temporal maze six feet high, with outside dimensions of 18 feet by 12 feet and with alleys three feet wide. The doors which were used to regulate the pathway in double alternation were operated from outside the maze where the experimenter stood behind a one-way screen. Thirty-eight children aged three to 13 years were tested with a minimum of verbal instructions about the task. After three preliminary trials in which the S was familiarized with the apparatus, massed training was begun using eight responses as a trial, *rrllrrll*, and with 15 sec. between trials. The criterion of mastery was three successive trials without error. The Ss learned the problem in an average of 15 trials, range 4–37, except that the one three-year-old S and the one four-year-old S failed to learn in 30 and 42 trials respectively. Gellermann presents evidence

Reprinted by permission of *Journal of Experimental Psychology*, 1948, *38*, 558–567.

indicating a strong probability that verbal (symbolic) responses control perfected double alternation in the temporal maze. After learning was completed, the Ss were tested on their ability to extend the series of double alternations beyond the customary eight responses. The two five-year-old Ss failed to extend the series. The three six-year-old Ss succeeded with some difficulty. Older Ss readily made such an extension.

The present experiment on the behavior of young children from two to seven years old seeks to determine, more nearly than did Gellermann, the age at which double alternation problems can be solved by the child. The temporal maze was not used, but rather a double alternation box apparatus similar in principle to the one used by Gellermann with monkeys (3).

APPARATUS, METHOD, AND SUBJECTS

The apparatus used in the present experiment, was similar to the alternation box-apparatus used by Gellermann (3) with monkeys. It was made of one-fourth in. plywood, painted light green. The two boxes, three in. apart, rest on the base of the apparatus. Perpendicular to the base is an upright board 24 by 18 in. from which the two boxes project. This board is attached to the base by hinges so that the apparatus can be easily collapsed into a compact unit. The upright board serves as a screen to hide the manipulations of the experimenter. As the boxes rest on the base, the floor of the boxes is continuous with it. The upright screen from which the boxes project is attached to the base eight in. from the front edge of the base. Rectangular openings are cut in the upright board at the places the boxes are attached so that stimulus-objects may be inserted by the E from behind the screen. The lids of the boxes project one-fourth in. beyond the box and are attached by light hinges allowing them to be opened easily by the children. Attached to each lid underneath and projecting back beyond the screen are brass strips. With these the E can open or close the lids. The strips serve also to indicate to the E behind the screen when the Ss have lifted the lids even a fraction of an inch.

The stimulus-objects used were small pieces of candy of uniform size. However, with the young children it was necessary to use other small pieces of food that they were known to like, such as raisins and bits of cracker or marshmallow.

Thirty-one children were tested. Their chronological ages ranged from six years, nine months, to two years exactly at the time of their final experimental sessions. Their mental ages ranged from eight years to two years, three months. Nineteen children were members of a private school in Providence and the others were from professional families with whom the E was acquainted.

Table 1 lists each S's chronological age and mental age at the time of his last experimental session. The mental ages were computed from scores on the 1937 Revision of the Stanford-Binet Intelligence Test. All Ss were given this test within two months of the time of the experimental sessions. All Ss but two were tested on Form L. The two youngest Ss were tested on Form M.

As in Gellermann's experiment with human Ss, verbal instructions were kept at a minimum. With Ss four years old or more, the procedure was as follows. The experiments were always conducted in a closed room with no third person present. The apparatus was set up on the floor with E sitting behind it. The stimulus-objects (candy) were kept in a box behind the apparatus. When the S entered for the first experimen-

tal session E asked, "Would you like to play this game?" Then for one min. the S was allowed to look at the apparatus, opening and closing the boxes. Then E said, "I'll put candy in the boxes," and then, "Shall we begin?" The two boxes were closed and E put one hand into each box leaving a piece of candy in the correct one. Although E was sitting behind the screen her head and top of shoulders could be seen. It was for this reason that the E always put a hand into each box so that there would be no differential cues from sound or from E's visible body movements.

The S opened one box or the other. If he opened the correct box, he could take out the candy and eat or keep it as he chose. If he opened the incorrect box, he found it empty. He either immediately afterward opened the correct box and got the candy or kept opening and closing the empty box until he changed to the correct one and was rewarded. At first, E tried to hold the lid of the incorrect box closed by means of the brass strip, but the Ss would keep trying to get it open and would start to cry or lose all interest. This procedure was therefore abandoned and neither box was ever held shut. The S was always rewarded upon opening the correct box by finding a piece of candy, whether he had made an incorrect response first or not. After eight responses, rrllrrll, during which time the S had received eight pieces of candy, E said, "Let's stop now," and after 15 sec. said, "Let's begin again." One session usually lasted for about 12 trials, i.e., 96 responses. It varied somewhat on either side of this, depending upon the S's attention. When the S volunteered that he wanted to stop or when he was paying poor attention, the session was brought to a close. Most of the Ss learned in one or two sessions. An attempt was made to have the sessions as near together as possible, separated by only one or two days.

With the Ss younger than three years old, the procedure could not be so rigid. Here, there were deviations in the length of experimental sessions; and during the first sessions with the two youngest Ss, their mothers held them on their laps during the experiment until the children became more at ease with E and with the apparatus. Furthermore, there was an important deviation in procedure. Instead of breaking up the trials into eight responses, the number of responses per trial varied greatly. The S was given a continuous series of double alternation responses to make and there was no fixed number of responses per trial. This procedure was necessary because any interference with the Ss after eight responses (if the S was still very actively opening and shutting the boxes) was met with crying, screams, or a complete lack of further co-operation. Also, some trials were shorter than eight responses when the S (voluntarily) crept away in the middle of a trial. Thus in order to secure the best attention and cooperation of the young Ss, the number of responses during one session had to vary greatly. However, in calculating the number of trials in the results, four responses, i.e., one complete double alternation is considered a trial for both older and younger Ss.

The criterion of learning for all Ss was three correct successive series of eight responses *rrllrrll, rrllrrll, rrllrrll.* Although in tabulating results a trial has been considered as four responses, eight responses were presented in a single run to the older Ss, and three such runs were used as the criterion of success. Following the attainment of the criterion, the series was extended to 12 responses in one trial, i.e., one more sequence of *rrll*. After this, if the S had not by this time volunteered information indicat-

TABLE 1 · Chronological Ages, Mental Ages, and Number of Trials to Learn the Problem

Subject	C. A.	M. A.	I. Q.	Trials to reach criterion (one trial equals 4 responses)
1	6–9	7–0	103	9
2	6–2	7–0	113	12
3	6–2	7–8	124	2
4	6–0	8–0	133	3
5	5–9	6–10	119	11
6	5–9	7–0	121	8
7	5–6	7–6	136	10
8	5–3	7–2	136	11
9	5–2	6–8	129	15
10	4–11	5–8	113	24
11	4–9	5–2	129	5
12	4–7	5–2	112	11
13	4–3	(?)		15
14	4–3	5–3	123	23
15	4–3	5–1	119	12
16	4–2	5–8	136	24
17	4–2	5–5	130	21
18	4–2	5–0	121	24
19	4–2	5–6	131	26
20	4–0	5–9	143	4
21	3–11	4–8	129	never in 52
22	3–9	4–7	122	12
23	3–9	4–6	129	never in 45
24	3–7	(?)		28
25	3–7	4–9	132	never in 49
26	3–4	4–7	137	never in 46
27	3–0	4–1	136	never in 43
28	3–0	(?)		never in 40
29	2–6	3–6	140	never in 106
30	2–1	3–1	148	never in 89
31	2–0	2–3	104	never in 74

ing that he had learned the correct sequence, he was asked, "How do you manage to open the right ones first?" If the answer did not state the general solution of the problem, he was then asked, "Well, how did you learn how to do it?"

Records were kept of every response each S made, of all conversation of the S in any way pertinent to the work, and of the answers to the E's questions.

RESULTS

Table 1 shows the chronological age, mental age, I.Q., and number of trials necessary for each S to learn the problem to the criterion of three errorless successive series of eight responses: *rrllrrll, rrllrrll, rrllrrll*. In this table and in others, where the number of trials is counted for both older and younger children, a trial is considered four responses, i.e., one complete double alternation, *rrll*. The data are compiled in this way in order to keep the results of these Ss comparable with Gellermann's results with children, where four responses were counted as one trial. The youngest child who learned the problem was three years and seven months old, with an undetermined mental age.

In Table 2 the results are averaged for each age level in order to compare

them with Gellermann's results. (The year six, for example, includes all Ss between six years and six years and eleven months.) Learning double alternation with the present box apparatus is evidently easier than learning the temporal maze. The average number of trials for Gellermann's six- and five-year-old Ss was 18.3 and 22.5 respectively as compared with 6.5 and 11 for the Ss in the present experiment. Also all of the present four-year-old Ss learned the problem in an average of 16.9 trials; and two three-year-old Ss, in an average of 20 trials. Although these group averages decrease as age increases, there is marked overlapping in the distributions.

The correlation (rank-difference) of C.A. and number of trials to learn is .86 ± .03, using all but Subjects 13, 24, and 28. For M.A. and trials to learn, rho is .81 ± .04. In these determinations, the eight youngest Ss (Subject 28 omitted) who never learned the problem were each assigned an average rank of 24.5 on the number of trials to learn. (If only one S who did not learn is included, the C.A. versus trials correlation is .54 ± .10 and M.A. versus trials is .59 ± .10.) There was no correlation between I.Q. and trials to learn. This is not unexpected in the

TABLE 2 · AVERAGE AND RANGE OF NUMBER OF TRIALS TAKEN BY Ss TO LEARN PROBLEM AT EACH YEAR LEVEL

| Age | SUBJECTS OF PRESENT EXPERIMENT | | | GELLERMAN'S SUBJECTS | | |
	Number of subjects	Average no. trials	Range	Number of subjects	Average no. trials	Range
6 yrs.	4	6.5	2–12	3	18.3	8–29
5	5	11.0	8–15	2	22.5	8–37
4	11	16.9	4–26	1	Not in 42 trials	
3	2	20.0	12–28			
3	6	Not in 40–52 trials		1	Not in 30 trials	
2	3	Not in 74–106 trials				

present group, since some of the highest I.Q.'s were possessed by children too young to learn, Gellermann found a correlation between C.A. and trials to learn of .28 ± .11. For adults his correlation with intelligence was .58 ± .09, using the Thurstone Psychological Examination for College Freshmen. Skalet (9), in a delayed reaction experiment with pre-school children, found a correlation of .66 ± .09 between performance and C.A. and one of .75 ± .08 with M.A. (It is to be recalled that the delayed reaction test is now used at year II in Form M of the 1937 revision of the Stanford-Binet intelligence test.)

The great change in ability to solve the double alternation problem under the conditions of the present experiment, is found in the three-year age-level. Of the eight three-year-old Ss, only two learned the problem. No two-year-old succeeded. It should be noted, however, that motivation was difficult to control in the youngest Ss. Every effort was made to give them rewards they were known to like, but with the older Ss another motivating factor seemed to be involved. The older children were more perturbed by making incorrect responses. They often made such remarks as, "I'm going to open all the right ones," or, "You're trying to fool me," when they had made an error. These comments appear to be evidence of a desire to learn the correct responses although the E never

indicated that there was a problem or system to be learned. The youngest Ss showed relatively little of this type of behavior. They appeared to be interested in eating the candy and getting as much of it as they could; but the opening of an empty box did not seem as disturbing to them as to the older Ss.

In the case of the children who did not learn the problem to the criterion of three correct consecutive sequences of eight responses, there were, however, some correct partial sequences of double alternation. Table 3 shows the number of trials before Subjects 27, 29, 30, and 31 performed the first correct double alternation series (*rrll*) and the total number of times a correct series of 4(*rrll*), 5(*rrllr*), 6(*rrllrr*), 7(*rrllrrl*), and 8(*rrllrrll*) responses were performed. Subject 30 made the largest proportional number of correct responses of these four children. Her I.Q. was 148, the highest of any S tested. Her M.A. was 3–1 at the time of the last experimental session when she was still younger chronologically than any S who learned the problem. No one of these Ss was able to maintain a steady high level of performance, but the occasional series of correct responses indicate that even the youngest Ss had some ability to perform double alternation. The youngest S made no correct sequences longer than five responses. He had not yet

TABLE 3 · CORRECT SEQUENCES OF RESPONSES (*rrll*) MADE BY SOME OF THE TWO- AND THREE-YEAR OLD Ss

Subject	C. A.	No. of trials before first correct response	No. of double alternation sequences of the following single response lengths:				
			4	5	6	7	8
27	3–0	5	6	1	0	1	0
29	2–6	3	6	2	2	1	1
30	2–1	7	12	4	4	1	1
31	2–0	1	3	2	0	0	0

TABLE 4 · CHILDREN'S PERFORMANCE ON THE DELAYED RESPONSE TEST
(DATA FROM MAUD A. MERRILL)

C. A.	1.5	2	2.5	3	3.5	4	4.5	5
N	101	104	102	100	103	105	101	112
% passing 2 successes	50	80	83	90	96	99	100	—
% passing 3 successes	15	46	50	73	93	97	98	99

learned to talk at the time of the last experimental session. All other Ss had some vocal language by the time of their last experimental sessions.

No one of the four Ss above referred to showed any regular decrease in percent of errors, no evidence of a learning curve. The correct runs occurred at random and were often followed by trials with a high percent of incorrect responses. It is impossible to say whether these Ss would have reached a consistently accurate level of performance after more trials. The delayed reaction problem seems to be a more practical test of the symbolic process at the two-year level than the double alternation problem. In delayed reaction the stimulus is presented and withdrawn, thus setting the problem for the S. In double alternation the S must discover the problem himself. However, the high correlation of the ability to perform double alternation with age indicates that, for all but the youngest Ss, it is a good indication of the development of an ability which, we believe, involves a symbolic process. Both Subjects 30 and 31 were given Form M of the Stanford-Binet test. They both passed the delayed reaction test. The other Ss were given Form L and so were not tested on delayed reaction.

Data from the use of the delayed reaction in the Stanford-Binet examination are of interest in the present connection. Merrill [1] reports tetrachoric correlations between the delayed reaction test, 10 sec. delay, as used in the Stanford-Binet test, and the various tests on Forms L and M at the two-year and the two-year-six-months levels. These correlations range from −.040 for motor coordination to .605 for identifying objects by name. Table 4 (data supplied by Merrill) shows the number of children passing the delayed reaction test at chronological ages from 1.5 to 5 years.[2] With respect to the behavior of the Ss, Merrill writes as follows: "My observation is that the child is usually intent upon the task in hand watching the examiner with laughing eagerness while the counting proceeds and ready to make his choice instantaneously when the shield is removed revealing the boxes. The children appear to regard the test as a very delightful game and want to continue hiding the kitty."

Let us now turn to a consideration of the verbal behavior of the children in the present experiment. Although many of the Ss said little during the experimental sessions, some Ss made remarks that throw light on the learning and on the administration of self-instructions.

[1] Personal communication from Dr. Maud A. Merrill, dated Jan. 19, 1943.

[2] Allen (1) reports for one-year-old Ss that 61 percent of responses at the 10 sec. delay were successful with 52 boys and 66 percent, with 48 girls.

Examples of this verbal behavior are as follows:

Subject 1. Several times said, "Oh darn it," when making an error. Just before reaching the criterion of learning she asked, "Have you put two in this one yet?"

Subject 5. Said, "Yes," after every correct response and, "No," after every incorrect response.

Subject 6. Said, "I know which to start with," preceding the fifth trial and made the first response correctly every time. After a correct response following hesitation said, "I almost opened the other."

Subject 7. Said, "Wrong one," several times after making an error.

Subject 8. Made the following remarks preceding various responses, "It'll be in here, won't it?" "I know which will be next."

Subject 9. Commented after every response. After the third response of the first trial indicated that he realized there was a problem to be learned by saying, "You're trying to fool me." Other frequent remarks were: "Right one," "Wrong one," "Got it," "I know what's next."

Subject 14. Just before learning, during a period of regular trials of *rlll*, remarked, "Two times." Later, after an error, "Let's start again. I'll get seven in six minutes."

Subject 16. "I can remember the right one sometimes." "It's hard to tell where the candy is." "Sometimes I forget which ones."

If the S had not volunteered the solution of the problem by the time he reached the criterion, he was asked, "How do you know which box to open?" They either spontaneously gave the solution, or responded after questioning, or said they did not know. Some examples of the three classes of responses are:

SPONTANEOUS SOLUTIONS:

"I know which to open—this (point to right) then this (R) then that (left) and then that (L) then that (R)."

"It's in there (R) two times and in there (L) two times."

"I know how now: two times and two times."

"I see how you do it; I count how many times you do it."

ANSWERS TO QUESTIONING:

"Just do—first in one box twice, then the other box twice."

"They go one and then in the same and then in the other."

"I get one (referring to the candy) in a different one after I get two in another; then I get another in the same one I've had right before the other two."

Ss WHO COULDN'T VERBALIZE THE SOLUTION:

"I don't know—I just figure them out. It's funny."

"I don't know how I know."

"I know how 'cause I do." (Silence after further questioning.)

The records indicate that the Ss who were five years or older could give the principle of double alternation verbally, in fact most of them did so spontaneously. The younger Ss, although able to perform the problem, were not able to verbalize the solution.

All of Gellermann's Ss who learned the problem, mostly older than the Ss in this experiment, expressed the principle of 'two, two' verbally. Gellermann stated that all of his Ss gave evidence that extension of the series was at least partially controlled by their verbal formulation of the problem. He concluded that the verbal formulation of the solution supplements non-differential external and interoceptive stimuli to call out the double alternation of responses, i.e., that language is the symbolic process enabling human Ss to learn the problem.

One of the interesting questions involved in double alternation behavior is whether or not the S who has mastered a given series, *rrll* or *rrllrrll*, will continue to respond in a double alternation manner if he is not removed from the apparatus. Will the factor or the symbol which has controlled the original habit be of such generality that it will continue to function beyond the customary series of responses? Rats show only a slight ability to extend a double alernation series (5, 6). Monkeys and human Ss, on the other hand, show a considerable facility in this respect (2, 3). Gellermann (2) found some ability of six-year-old children to extend the series, but five-year-old children failed. In the present experiment all Ss who learned the double alternation problem were able to extend the series of responses whether or not they were able to formulate verbally the principle of 'two, two.' This ability to extend the series is therefore present at least in some children as early as three years and seven months of age.

SUMMARY

1. Thirty-one children ranging in chronological age from two years to six years and nine months were trained on a double alternation box-apparatus. The youngest child to attain the criterion of three successive errorless trials of eight responses each was three years and seven months old. Younger children could perform double alternation, but at a lower criterial level.

2. There was a positive correlation between trials to learn and both C.A. and M.A.

3. Children five years old or older could state verbally the principle of double alternation by the time they had reached the criterion of learning. Younger children could not do so, even though they had mastered the problem.

4. Children at least as young as three years and seven months can extend their double alternation responses beyond the length of the series on which they have been trained.

5. The double alternation problem is not as well adapted to the behavior characteristics of the young child as is the delayed reaction test, although both appear to involve in their mastery a symbolic process. In the delayed reaction, the disappearance of the stimulus object sets the problem for the S, whereas in the double alternation problem the S must discover for himself the pattern of response required.

REFERENCES

1. ALLEN, C. N.   Individual differences in delayed reaction of infants. *Arch. Psychol.*, 1931, *19*, No. 127.

2. GELLERMANN, L. W.   The double alternation problem: II. The behavior of children and human adults in a double alternation temporal maze. *J. genet. Psychol.*, 1931, *39*, 197–226.

3. GELLERMANN, L. W.   The double alternation problem: III. The behavior of monkeys in a double alternation box-apparatus. *J. genet. Psychol.*, 1931, *39*, 359–392.

4. HUNTER, W. S.   The temporal maze and kinesthetic sensory processes in the white rat. *Psychobiol.*, 1920, *2*, 1–18.

5. HUNTER, W. S., & HALL, B. E.   Double alternation behavior of the white rat in a spatial maze. *J. comp. Psychol.*, 1941, *32*, 253–266.

6. HUNTER, W. S., & NAGGE, J. W.   The white rat and the double alternation temporal maze. *J. genet. Psychol.*, 1931, *39*, 303–319.

7. KELLER, F. S.   A new type of double alternation. *J. genet. Psychol.*, 1937, *51*, 454–459.

8. SCHLOSBERG, H., & KATZ, A. Double alternation lever-pressing in the white rat. *Amer. J. Psychol.*, 1943, *56,* 274–282.

9. SKALET, M. The significance of delayed reactions in young children. *Comp. Psychol. Monogr.,* 1931, 7, No. 4.

INDEX